C000178959

*S*urvival
*K*it

Eastern Europe

Travellers
Survival
Kit

Eastern Europe

EMILY HATCHWELL &
SIMON CALDER

Published by
VACATION WORK, 9 PARK END STREET, OXFORD

TRAVELLERS SURVIVAL KIT: EASTERN EUROPE

by Emily Hatchwell and Simon Calder

Copyright © Vacation Work 1994

ISBN 1 85458 113 9

Cover Design
Mel Calman
Miller Craig Cocking Design Partnership

Illustrations by William Swan

Publicity: Roger Musker

Maps by Andrea Pullen

Printed by **Unwin Bros,** Old Woking, Surrey, England

Contents

EASTERN EUROPE — PRACTICAL INFORMATION

THE COUNTRIES OF EASTERN EUROPE

The first part of each country chapter appears in the following order:

Climate — History — The People — Language — Getting There — Red Tape — Money — Communications — Getting Around — Accommodation — Eating and Drinking — Exploring — Entertainment — Sport — Shopping — Health and Hygiene — Crime and Safety — Help and Information

Sections on large cities are dealt with as follows:

City Layout — Arrival and Departure — City Transport — Accommodation — Eating and Drinking — Exploring — Entertainment — Shopping — Crime and Safety — Help and Information

MAPS

PREFACE

From the end of World War II until this decade, visiting Eastern Europe implied immersion in an alien political system. Travellers were obliged to adhere to an often bizarre tangle of bureaucracy and frequently fell foul of the oppressive regulations which sustained state socialism. The massive political changes of 1989 mean, however, that the region can now be enjoyed for what it is: a diverse and delightful slab of Europe, with a wealth of cultural traditions which have survived communism. Most rewarding of all to the traveller is the chance to meet interesting and interested peoples, who are coming to terms with the West's version of freedom.

The newly liberated nations fly ten different flags. They offer magnificent scenery and rich traditions. During communism, the region's art and architecture signalled the existence of an epic past, from the exquisite painted monasteries of Romania to the much-photographed rooftops of Prague. The tyrant Nicolae Ceausescu tried to destroy Romania's past, and now the tyranny of tourism is threatening to do the same to the Czech capital.

Visitors can avoid the crowds by heading for handsome cities such as Riga, Tallinn and Sofia, or for the barely trodden slopes of the Carpathian and High Tatra mountains. Skiers can take advantage of good runs and low prices in Romania, Bulgaria and the Slovak Republic. Sunseekers are able to capitalise on cheap, cheerful and reliably warm beaches on the Black Sea or Albania's Adriatic coast, or sample the more adventurous (and certainly chillier) Baltic resorts.

Eastern Europe is in a dreadful economic mess due to decades of existence in a commercial fiction. Factories relied upon raw materials at artificially low prices, and turned out shoddy goods for a captive market. Now that free enterprise has become the ideological order of the day, the process of economic transition is exacting a high social cost. As Eastern Europe struggles to catch up with the 20th century, hope is tempered with foreboding. For the visitor, there has never been a more enthralling time to visit.

Emily Hatchwell and Simon Calder
Oxford
January 1994

Acknowledgements

Many travellers and citizens of Eastern European countries have helped with the production of this book. We especially wish to thank the following: Louise Boddington, John Denham, Mike McCormick, Laura Mullin, Adam O'Neil and Jaap Terpstra. Guy Perry worked intensively on the chapter on Albania, and Lawrence Hourahane covered Poland. Susan Griffith provided the information on working in Eastern Europe.

NOTE: While every effort has been made to ensure that the information contained in this book was accurate at the time of going to press, some details are bound to change during the lifetime of this edition. If in the course of your travels you encounter errors or omissions, please write to Simon Calder at Vacation Work Publications, 9 Park End Street, Oxford OX1 1HJ. Those whose contributions are used will be sent a free copy of the next edition.

From 16 April 1995, British telephone numbers will change. The digit 1 will be inserted after the initial 0 in UK area codes. So, for example, the code for Oxford — 0865 — will become 01865. In addition, the code for dialling another country from the UK will change from 010 to 00.

EASTERN EUROPE — PRACTICAL INFORMATION

Planning a trip to Eastern Europe is no longer the battle with bureaucracy it once was, and exploring independently can be highly rewarding. Gradually, the region is adapting to the needs of travellers who prefer to plan as they go along. But the long-established infrastructure which offered organised tours (in the days when governments preferred regimentation) is still mostly in place. So you can, if you wish, hand the burden of organisation to somebody else. Suggestions of experienced companies are given in this section. It also contains options for getting to Eastern Europe, what money to take, insurance recommendations, health advice, etc., and outlines what you can expect in terms of accommodation, public transport and so on.

Getting There

AIR

The opening-up of Eastern Europe has spawned a whole new breed of air routes into the region. Competition means that flights to the most popular destinations such as Prague and Budapest are often cheaper than the equivalent train fare. Open-jaw flights (flying in to one city and returning from another) can offer good value. If you can't find a cheap flight direct to your chosen destination, it may be worth investigating a discount ticket to a neighbouring city, such as Vienna, which is within easy reach of Prague, Bratislava and Budapest. Germany is also a good gateway to Eastern Europe, and if you are flying in from outside Europe, you may well find yourself routed via Berlin or Frankfurt.

From Britain. Any travel agent should be able to book you a flight to Eastern Europe, but the best range of options and the cheapest fares are available through specialists. Agencies specialising in a particular country are listed in the relevant chapter, but the following cover a range of Eastern European countries. Most offer package deals in addition to flights:

Canterbury Travel (London) Ltd, 246 Streatfield Road, Kenton, Harrow, Middlesex HA3 9BY (tel 081-206 0411, fax 081-206 0427).
Fregata Travel, 100 Dean Street, London W1V 6AQ (tel 071-734 5101; fax 071-494 1567). Main USA office: 5324 Lawrence Avenue, Chicago IL 60630 (tel 312-282-1188).
Instone Travel, 19-20 Connaught Street, London W2 (071-247 3434).
Intourist Travel Ltd, Intourist House, 219 Marsh Wall, London E14 9FJ (071-538 5965).

Progressive Tours, 12 Porchester Place, Marble Arch, London W2 2BS
(tel 071-262 1676, fax 071-724 6941).
Regent Holidays, 15 John Street, Bristol BS1 1DE (tel 0272-211711,
fax 254866).
VIP Travel, 42 North Audley St, London W1Y 2DU (tel 071-499 4221).

It is also worth calling agencies specialising in discount travel, such as STA
Travel (86 Old Brompton Road, London SW7; 071-937 9921) and Campus
Travel (52 Grosvenor Gardens, London SW1; 071-730 3402). Both these
companies have networks of UK branches. Other agents advertise in the
weekend papers or magazines such as *Time Out* or *TNT* in London.

From North America. While there is a growing number of links between
North America and Eastern Europe (especially on the Delta network via
Frankfurt), flying to London first is often your best option. Not only is it
easy to get a cheap transatlantic ticket to the UK, onwards flights are
normally excellent value too. Even with a day or two spent in an overpriced
London hotel, you should still save money on the deal.

From Australasia. Similar advice applies to people arriving from Australia
and New Zealand: go via London to save money. One option which may be
worth checking out, however, is a flight on the Greek airline Olympic. It
serves Athens from Sydney and Melbourne, and you can travel on by land
from Greece to Albania, Bulgaria and beyond.

From Southern Africa. In 1993, Balkan Bulgarian Airways opened a link
between Sofia and Johannesburg. This is likely to prove the cheapest route
from South Africa to anywhere in Eastern Europe, since Balkan is one
of the more energetic discounters and has onward connections to many
destinations.

RAIL

Rail travel from Western to Eastern Europe is not necessarily cheap, though
young people are eligible for significant discounts. Train fares are cheaper
in Eastern Europe than in Western Europe, but you won't benefit much
from the price differential if you pay for your entire ticket at home. To save
money, purchase a ticket just to the Western/Eastern Europe border (or to
the first town across the frontier) and buy an onward ticket from there.

Young travellers who plan to travel along a fixed route within Europe can get a discount of 20-40% with a so-called BIJ ticket, valid for a particular routing for two months. Contact Eurotrain at 52 Grosvenor Gardens, London SW1 (071-730 3402) or Wasteels at 121 Wilton Road, London SW1 (071-834 7066). A Rail Europe Senior Card gives good discounts for those over 60.

Useful sources for planning travel by rail include *Thomas Cook's European Timetable* (which you can consult in a library) and the *Thomas Cook Rail Map of Europe.*

Rail Passes. Owing to the good value of rail travel within Eastern Europe, rail passes are rarely a worthwhile investment unless you plan to do a lot of travelling in a fairly short time. Passes are usually valid for 15 days or one month and allow unlimited second class travel on European railway networks. They don't cover compulsory seat reservations or supplements, so getting a rail pass doesn't mean you can avoid tedious queuing. Some countries have their own rail pass, but again you would need to travel fairly singlemindedly to make a 'profit' on one.

The InterRail and Eurail passes described below are valid in all Eastern Europe countries except Albania and the Baltics. For information in the UK, call the International Rail Centre at Victoria Station (071-834 2345); many large BR stations should be able to help too.

InterRail: there are two comprehensive InterRail passes for European residents (minimum six months residence). Anyone under the age of 26 can buy a pass which costs £249 for one month. It doesn't cover the buyer's home country nor cross-Channel ferries, but it does give a 30% discount on these. The InterRail 26+ pass covers the same area, but costs around £100 more — for only 15 days.

InterRail Zone Fares: travellers under 26 who intend to visit a smaller selection of countries or spend less than a month away can buy zone tickets which allow you to focus on one or more smaller areas of Europe for a (small) reduction in cost. For travellers to all the countries in this book except Albania and the Baltic republics — but with the addition of Croatia — a 15-day pass costs £179. Unfortunately this does not cover the cost of getting there. If you want to travel by rail, a three-zone pass for a month works out at £229 — not a huge saving on the original fare.

Eurail: available outside Europe, the Eurail pass gives unlimited travel on national railways in most of Western Europe. Presently, the only country in this book to be included in the scheme is Hungary, though this may change. Any youth/student travel agency should be able to advise you. The Eurail Youthpass, for those under 26, is reasonable value — about $500 for one month, $650 for two. The standard pass costs from $450 for 15 days.

BUS

The thought of spending a day or more in a bus may not appeal, but travelling by road is an increasingly efficient way to reach Eastern Europe. For those aged 26 or over, bus fares are at least 20% cheaper than the equivalent rail fare.

The number of buses travelling to Eastern Europe, as well as between countries within the region, has risen dramatically. One of the main operators from Western Europe is Eurolines (52 Grosvenor Gardens, London SW1; 071-730 8235), which is run by National Express and has representatives in most European capitals. Currently, Eurolines serves Budapest, Prague, Brno, Bratislava, Kraków, Gdańsk and Warsaw.

The fare to Warsaw, for example, is currently about £90 adult return or £85 youth return. Given that Warsaw is the main starting-point for buses and trains into the Baltics, taking a bus to Poland is seriously worth considering; see page 90 for the options.

It is also well worth checking the fares on the privately run companies. Several companies offer competitive services to Poland, while Kingscourt Express (081-673 6883) has a return fare of £85 to Prague — by any standards, excellent value.

SEA

There are various ferry routes to the Baltic Republics from Germany, Sweden or Finland. Travelling by ship is not usually a cheap option, but for motorists it can provide a relaxing short-cut to the northern corner of Eastern Europe. See the country chapters for further information.

TOURS

The appeal of a package tour may be its cheapness or the fact that the logistics of a trip are taken out of your hands. The travel agents listed above run tours, together with those listed below:

Explore Worldwide, 1 Frederick Street, Aldershot, Hants GU11 1LQ (0252-319448).
New Millennium Holidays, (021-711 4306). Coach holidays to Poland, Romania, the Czech Republic and Hungary for very low prices, from around £130 for ten days half board.
Travelscene, 11-15 St Anne's Road, Harrow HA1 1AS (081-427 8800). City break specialists.
Time Off, Chester Close, Chester Street, London SW1X 7BQ (071-235 8070). City break specialists.

DRIVING

Despite some recent improvements, road conditions in the former communist bloc are still far behind what most Western European drivers are used to. Some rural roads are positively Third World, and even some major through routes have surfaces fit to break your axles. Motorways, as we know them in Western Europe, are scarce, although a lot of main roads are colloquially called 'motorways', earning the title mainly by the volume of traffic they are forced to carry. However, some major roads have already benefitted from massive investment and are a joy to drive on. The opening up of modern service stations makes life for motorists a good deal more pleasant too.

The disadvantages of driving in Eastern Europe must, however, be weighed against the advantages: principally, the freedom it allows and the lack of traffic on most roads. And given that car rental can be expensive, it is well worth considering taking your own car. Information about documentation and so on is given below, but for general hints and information about driving conditions see *Getting Around.*

Membership of a motoring organisation is a good investment: they offer information about the documents required and other advice. The main organisations in the UK and elsewhere are as follows:

AA, Fanum House, Basingstoke, Hampshire RG21 2EA (0256-20123).
RAC, PO Box 100, 7 Brighton Road, Croydon CR2 6XW (081-686 0088).
AAA, 1000 AAA Drive, Heathrow, FL 32746, USA (407-444-7883/ 7000).
CAA, 60 Commerce Valley Drive East, Markham, Ontario L3T 7P9, Canada (416-771-3170).
AAA, 212 Northbourne Avenue, Canberra ACT 2601, Australia (61-6247-7311).

Documents. An International Driving Permit (IDP) is legally required in Albania and Bulgaria, but in other countries a national licence will do. Even so, you may find that an IDP will smooth your progress if you are stopped by the traffic police; unlike British licences, it shows your age and photograph.

Insurance is mandatory: you need either a green card or frontier insurance. Not all motor insurers issue green cards for travel to Eastern European countries, however, and some countries are not covered. Currently, for example, it is difficult to buy insurance in advance for travel in the Baltics. You are therefore compelled to purchase insurance at the border, where its cost and quality will be highly variable. See *Breakdowns,* below, for information on insurance policies available.

Maps. Good motoring maps are produced by GeoCenter International. Its Euro Atlas series (scale 1:300 000), already includes the Czech and Slovak Republics, Hungary, Romania and the Baltic States; the average price for each is £5.99.

Breakdowns. The best way to ensure against breakdowns is to make sure your car is in perfect working order before you set off. Have it thoroughly serviced and take a few spares, as they may be difficult to find abroad. The obvious ones are lights, fan belt, plugs, hoses, ignition coil, ignition key and fuses; also take your own pressure gauge.

Unless you're hyper-confident about the condition of your car, invest in AA Five-star Insurance or RAC Eurocover Motoring Assistance. Reciprocal agreements with sister organisations (these are of varying efficiency and usefulness in Eastern Europe) mean that you will be entitled to free roadside assistance should you break down, plus cover for expenses including repatriation, accommodation, car hire or emergency cash, as well as legal advice.

If you have a breakdown or accident which is so bad that you abandon your vehicle, ensure that you obtain an official confirmation of this from the police or insurance authorities; border officials might otherwise assume that you have sold it illegally, and fine or detain you accordingly.

Information on what to do in the event of an accident is given under *Getting Around*, but note that it is a legal requirement in most Eastern European countries to carry a red warning triangle and a first aid kit.

Fuel. Petrol quality has improved greatly compared with the acrid, poorly refined stuff available some years ago. The choice of grades has increased too, but there will still be occasions when the best available fuel is of a quality lower than what your own car is used to. Unleaded petrol is no longer the rarity that it was, but it is still available only in big cities or along international highways, where companies like BP and Q8 have opened up petrol stations. Being supplied by the West rather than the CIS, these service stations are the most reliable source of fuel. All the Eastern European countries — particularly Romania, Bulgaria, Poland and Hungary — have had problems negotiating oil supplies from the former Soviet Union, and the flow of petrol can be extremely erratic. It is a good rule to fill up whenever you can — also because petrol stations are few and far between in country areas. Be prepared to queue, as the supply rarely meets the demand of the region's new breed of private motorists.

The price of fuel is comparable to that in the rest of Europe, though usually a little cheaper.

MOTORCYCLING

The information and advice given above is clearly relevant also for motorcyclists. Bear in mind too that uneven road surfaces can play havoc with your motorbike's suspension, and nuts and bolts have a nasty habit of falling off after a severe jolt. Clearly, good brakes and tyres are essential.

Note that filtering through columns of traffic is not always legal. Although most traffic officials turn a blind eye, don't disregard the rule too blatantly. In some instances, however, motorcyclists may be singled out for a hard time. On one occasion, a traveller crossing at the northernmost German/Poland entry point was refused passage while all other vehicles were allowed through. No reason was given, but the only option was to divert to Szczecin.

CYCLING

There is terrain to suit every type of cyclist: swathes of flat country in the Baltics, Poland and Hungary, and unlimited hills and mountains in the Czech and Slovak Republics, Romania and Bulgaria. Hire facilities are limited, and keen cyclists should take their own bicycle: when you need a rest, you shouldn't have too much trouble loading your bike onto a train (though not an express as a rule) or bus. You may be asked to pay an extra 10% of the normal fare.

The Cyclists' Touring Club provides members (£25 per annum) with general information sheets on cycling abroad, as well as trip reports. For further details contact the club at 69 Meadrow, Godalming, Surrey GU7 3HS (tel 0483-417217, fax 426994). If you'd like someone else to take over the logistics (and carry your bags), you might consider a cycling holiday organised by Bike Tours (PO Box 75, Bath BA1 1BX; tel 0225-480310, fax 480132). A favourite tour runs from Krakow in Poland to Budapest. There may be as many as 100 people on one tour, but you travel at your own pace, covering an average of 60 miles a day.

What to Take. Owing to the state of minor roads (and to the cobblestones in old town centres), take a rugged bike with good chunky tyres, ideally a mountain bike; though anything which looks too flash is bound to attract unwanted attention.

Take your own supply of tools, and suggested spares include: brake pads; spokes (these can be taped to the frame of the bike and forgotten about); gear cable (long), which can double as break cable if necessary; inner tubes; a small selection of nuts and bolts; and of course, a puncture repair kit.

Transporting your Bike. Always check with the airline, bus or train company about bicycle carriage before you buy a ticket: different companies have different policies. Most airlines allow you to take a bike free of charge providing your total luggage weight (including bike) is less than the airline's baggage allowance (usually 20-25kg per person). This should suffice for a touring bike plus two panniers (including one for hand luggage). Charter flights tend to be less accommodating.

When packing up the bike for transportation, you should ideally tape cardboard around the whole thing or, failing that, just around the gear and brakes levers and the rear wheel gear assembly; remove the pedals and deflate the tyres to avoid explosions at high altitude, and turn the handlebars parallel to the frame: try this at home first.

Passports. A full ten-year passport is required for travel to all the countries covered in this book. Most countries require your passport to be valid for at least six months beyond your projected date of arrival.

If your passport is lost or stolen while travelling, contact first the police and then your nearest Embassy. Obtaining replacement travel documents is easier if you have a record of the passport number and its date and place of issue, ideally a photocopy of the relevant pages. In most parts of the world your Embassy can do the paperwork for you more or less immediately. In Eastern Europe, however, your wait could be several days. This is largely because the immigration officials of the country concerned need to supply you with an exit permit, and the bureaucracy involved can take a long time.

Visas. Regulations have been relaxed considerably since the fall of communism, but vary according to your nationality: British nationals, for example, currently require a visa only for Romania and Bulgaria. If you travel to Eastern Europe by land, check whether or not you require visas for the countries through which you will be in transit.

Where possible, you will do best to arrange any visas you require before you leave home, though this may depend on how long you plan to be away: most visas are valid for six months from the date of issue. The addresses of consulates in the UK and North America are given under *Red Tape* in each country section. You can also obtain a visa at the relevant consulate anywhere within Eastern Europe or, usually, at the airport or at land borders, but you may face a longer-than-average wait and higher-than-average fee. Visas must always be paid for in hard currency.

IMMIGRATION

Provided you have the necessary visa (if required), your passport should be stamped with alacrity: most countries in Eastern Europe permit an initial stay of one month (which can then be extended), though in some cases the immigration official will ask you how long you plan to stay: if you are unsure, always go for the maximum period allowed.

Customs officials tend to pay scanty attention to most travellers, though crossing into Romania can still involve draconian searches complete with sniffer dogs. Elaborate electronic equipment can still arouse special interest wherever you are.

The fall of communist regimes in Eastern Europe, and the universal adoption of free market policies, means that prices have risen substantially since 1989. This has affected local people far more than tourists, for whom the cost of living remains comparatively low. However, prices vary dramatically. So while you'll encounter almost Western prices in Prague or Budapest, life is considerably cheaper in rural areas.

Changing Money. Take your funds in cash and travellers cheques, with a credit card or two to fall back on.

Banks almost invariably offer the best exchange rates. Eastern Europe still has a long way to go before it catches up with the West in terms of personal finance. However, hole-in-the-wall cash dispensers are increasingly common and some city banks have automatic currency exchange machines. Normally, however, to change money out of banking hours, you'll have to rely either on bureaux de change or hotels. Both offer either a poor rate or slap on an outrageous commission. Changing currency at the border is usually a bad deal too. This is one reason to avoid having any surplus currency when you leave. If you want to change local money back into hard currency when leaving the country, you will usually be asked to show your original exchange receipts.

Travellers Cheques. The safest way to carry money is in travellers cheques, preferably as US dollars, German deutschmarks or pound sterling. In response to the number of stolen travellers cheques in circulation, some banks may ask to see the sales receipt: don't leave home without it.

Thomas Cook or American Express travellers cheques are equally acceptable in Eastern Europe, though you'll probably find it easier to obtain a refund for stolen cheques if you are an AmEx customer: there is an American Express office or representative in every Eastern Europe capital.

Cash. Travellers to Eastern Europe should take a higher proportion of cash than they would on a holiday elsewhere in Europe. This holds true for the Baltic Republics in particular, where travellers cheques are not widely accepted, even in the banks.

Many establishments are happy to accept either local or hard currency, whether you're buying souvenirs in a shop or paying for a private room. Some shops accept travellers cheques, but cash is always preferred. Take US dollars or deutschmarks (in low denominations to avoid the recurring problem of a shortage of change). Don't bother trying to pay the bill at an out-of-the-way restaurant in sterling or Irish punts.

In some cases, certain goods and services must still be paid for in hard currency, including international train tickets. In these situations, only cash may be acceptable.

Credit and Charge Cards. American Express, Diners Club, Access/Master-Card and Visa are welcomed by most airlines, leading hotels and smart restaurants and shops. Since some places occasionally run out of vouchers, it might be to your advantage to have a couple of credit cards. Note that most American Express offices will allow their cardmembers to draw cash against a personal cheque.

Withdrawing cash on a credit card is commonplace in Budapest and Prague, but don't think that you could live off plastic in Tirana or Bucharest. Articles that are difficult to pay for with plastic wherever you are include train tickets and petrol — though, like everything else, this may change.

Emergency Cash. The British Embassy will, with some reluctance, cash a cheque for up to £50 backed by a UK cheque guarantee card. This will not be enough to pay for a ticket out of the country, so if you're entirely destitute you'll have no option but to be repatriated and surrender your passport upon arrival back home; you won't get it back until you have repaid the Foreign Office. Repatriation is unlikely, however, until all other avenues, such as finding someone at home to pay for your journey, have been tried.

You can ask your bank to wire money to a named bank abroad, but this is often an unreliable business which can soak up four or five days of your holiday. Alternatively, ask someone to send money through American Express, Thomas Cook or Western Union. The last two have few outlets in Eastern Europe as yet, but tend to charge less commission than AmEx.

Black Market. A little black market dabbling used to be part of the thrill for many visitors to Eastern Europe, but the potential gains have virtually disappeared in most Eastern European countries. From Budapest to Bucharest you'll still find a few desperados trying to hatch deals with tourists, but all are unsavoury types, out to rip you off.

If you are tempted to trade, choose carefully with whom you deal. Rather than do business on the street, you may find it safer to deal with hotel or restaurant staff — though gone are the days when lift attendants stopped between floors to do a little covert trading. If you opt for the street, choose an individual and try to make sure he has no accomplices. Ideally there should be two of you. Firstly, agree how much you are going to exchange and the rate. The dealer should give your companion the money to count. He or she should check the notes, then move slightly away (out of grabbing range). You then hand over the dollars. Some rules should be observed to minimise the chances that you'll be conned.

1. Never try to change a huge amount of money; if you are going to be ripped off, better that it is just $10 or $20.
2. Keep the amount that you want to change in a separate pocket. It is foolish to reveal where all your funds are kept.
3. If, after agreeing to change money, you feel threatened, don't hesitate to pull out of the transaction.
4. Given the introduction of a range of new currencies in Eastern Europe, check that you're not being fobbed off with either obsolete or foreign notes.

With all the care in the world, you cannot always avoid being cheated. Favourite tricks include excessive haste, to make you panic and pass over the dollars before you've checked the money, and the old chestnut of shouting 'police' and running off leaving you with insufficient notes or perhaps none at all.

Tipping. The power of tips and gifts is not what it once was, but there are still occasions when services or goods will be 'unobtainable' until a hard currency tip (or a packet of cigarettes) is produced. More official tipping was not a common habit before 1989, but is spreading rapidly in areas frequented by tourists. A 10% tip on a meal in a smart restaurant tends to be accepted these days.

The best way there is to get to know Eastern Europe properly is to live and work there. Do not expect to make money though, unless you work for a Western company. A local firm will pay a local salary, which will just about cover living costs but nothing else. The vast majority of jobs available for foreigners are as teachers of English. But as the barriers between East and West crumble through the 1990s, it is clear that opportunities for working travellers will increase.

TEACHING

After the revolutions of 1989, English replaced Russian almost overnight as the first foreign language taught in schools. A knowledge of English is regarded as a crucial step towards economic regeneration, and there is a big demand for both qualified English teachers and native speakers. While it is harder now than it was a couple of years ago for someone without training and experience to get a job, anyone who looks for work on the spot still has a fair chance of being employed, particularly as many trained teachers simply aren't willing to accept the low salaries and working conditions offered in Eastern Europe. Anyone who is well qualified or experienced should be able to fix up a job without difficulty, whether you arrange it in advance or once in the region. Unqualified teachers will find it difficult to arrange a job from abroad.

The opportunities are greatest in the Czech Republic, Hungary and Poland, even though Prague, Budapest and Warsaw are positively saturated with English-speakers. Your chances of landing a job will be greatly enhanced if you head out of the big cities, particularly if you are unqualified. While simply being a native English-speaker will be enough for some places, most schools in the capital cities can afford to be more choosy.

Needless to say, experience and a teaching or TEFL qualification will get you the better-paid jobs. The RSA and Trinity Certificate Courses are the most sought after. Most schools express no preference for nationality, though Americans are probably in the ascendancy, particularly in Prague.

Jobs are available in state schools and universities as well as private language schools. Inexperienced teachers are used by state schools primarily for conversation classes. Teaching in state schools is usually most rewarding — you see more a slice of life than in private schools. Working for the state also guarantees a salary, the possibility of accommodation, access to state health insurance, and long-term contracts (which makes it easier to obtain a work permit). Jobs attached to universities usually offer stability and a light workload. At the university level you will normally require a degree. State schools and many other institutions have organized English lessons at the end of the working day, so anyone with initiative can create a job for him or herself with hours and a location to suit. Not always teaching just English. Teachers in private schools must expect to teach everything from grammar to conversation. Private schools offer less financial and job security though they usually pay slightly better.

English language materials vary, and are not necessarily better in a private than a state school. Some have ancient texts, others the latest books and satellite TV. Pupils are generally keen and no problem to teach. Some pupils may find modern teaching methods strange as they are used to a more teacher-centred approach, and more creative techniques may take some getting use to.

Pay can vary enormously, but teachers can usually expect to earn $100-150 per month. It is essential to find out whether your pay is net or gross: while in Poland you pay about 20% tax, in Hungary this can go up to almost 50%. Some language projects are funded from the West, so pay better. A full-time salary should be just about adequate to live on by local standards but will not allow you to save anything, unless you take on lots of private teaching. The pay for private lessons can be $7 an hour, as high as $15 per hour for businesses. Some people manage to get free accommodation in exchange for giving conversation lessons. Given the choice, most employers will give priority to candidates who already have somewhere to stay, but most will try to help fix you up with a room. The advantage of working in the state system, particularly at a university, is that accommodation is likely to be provided.

When the Eastern European countries first began rebuilding, teacher shortages were so dire that red tape for foreign teachers was kept to a minimum. But work permits are increasingly difficult to obtain. While those with qualifications and experience normally have nothing to worry about, people with only their native-speaker status may encounter problems. Short contracts make it more difficult to get a work permit, since the authorities are reluctant to undertake the paperwork. Note too, that in some countries you may find it hard to change status if you were admitted on a tourist visa.

Finding a Job. Many of the native speaker teachers working in Eastern Europe at present are under the auspices of a British or American agency, such as VSO and the Peace Corps. The Central Bureau for Educational Visits and Exchanges (Seymour Mews House, Seymour Mews, London W1H 9PE; 071-486 5101) selects students and teachers to work at various UNESCO-sponsored holiday language camps in Poland and Hungary. All you pay for is the flight. The organisations listed below, which recruit for more than one country in the region, will consider qualified teachers only.

Bell Educational Trust, Overseas Dept, The Lodge, Redcross Lane, Cambridge CB2 2QX.
British Council, 10 Spring Gardens, London SW1A 2BN (071-389 4931).
East European Partnership, 15 Princeton Court, 53-55 Felsham Road, London SW15 1AZ (081-780 2841).
International House, 106 Piccadilly, London W1 9FL (071-491 2598).
Soros Professional English Teaching Program, 888 Seventh Avenue, Suite 1901, New York, NY 10106 (tel 212-757-2323, fax 974-0367).
Soros English Language Programme, 79 Lee Road, London SE3 9EN (tel 081-852 5495, fax 081-297 8788). The UK branch of the above.

If you opt to look for work once in Eastern Europe, the British Council can be a good place to start. Every office abroad keeps a list of English language teaching centres, and the main British Council offices have large English teachers' resource centres from which you may be able to benefit. Most have lists of language schools. At the very least, you would be able to read notices on the notice boards and meet teachers. Look in local English-language newspapers, if they exist, or approach schools listed in the Yellow Pages.

Whether looking for work in advance or on the spot, *Teaching English Abroad* by Susan Griffith (Vacation Work, £9.95) is an excellent companion. It provides numerous addresses of state and private schools throughout the region as well as providing background information on red tape, pay, conditions of work and so on. Contacting private schools ahead of time is rarely productive (unless they recruit via a foreign agent), since most will want to interview you before making any commitment.

Teaching private lessons is the most lucrative but the most difficult to fix up. When looking for private teaching, a small notice placed on a prominent university notice board or in a daily newspaper would certainly produce results. Many executives need English for business, so you could even try approaching local companies.

VOLUNTARY WORK

While the decentralisation of power in the former communist bloc means that the old state-run voluntary organisations have either disintegrated or are losing their funding, there has been a dramatic increase in the number of contacts between voluntary groups in the East and West. The international workcamp organisations operating in Eastern Europe include the following:

International Voluntary Service, Old Hall, East Bergholt, Colchester, Essex CO7 6TQ.

Quaker International Social Projects, Friends House, Euston Road, London NW1 2BJ (071-387 3601).

Christian Movement for Peace (CMP), 186 St Paul's Rd, Balsall Heath, Birmingham B12 8LZ.

United Nations Association (Wales), International Youth Service, Temple of Peace, Cathays Park, Cardiff, South Glamorgan (0222-223088).

British Trust for Conservation Volunteers (BTCV), 36 St Mary's Street, Wallingford, Oxfordshire OX10 0EU (0491-39766).

Projects vary from excavating the ancient capital of Bulgaria to working in an orphanage. Some camps are agricultural since there is a severe shortage of labour in some rural areas. In many cases, the projects are a pretext for bringing together young people in an effort to dismantle prejudice on both sides. Often discussion sessions and excursions are a major part of the three- or four- week workcamps, with very little work expected. There is normally a registration fee of £25-£50; only travel expenses incurred once you have arrived in Eastern Europe will normally be met. Applications for workcamps should be sent through the partner organisation in the applicant's own country.

US and Canadian citizens should contact the CIEE (Council on International Educational Exchange at 205 East 42nd Street, New York NY 10017 (tel 212-661-1414), which runs study programmes and workcamps in Eastern Europe.

OTHER OPPORTUNITIES

The new democracies are all targeting tourism as a means of aiding their economies and are encouraging foreign tour operators to develop resorts; in time these may have large staff requirements.

If you are looking for some casual work, ask discreetly around the universities or among expatriates teaching English. Your services as anything from a disc jockey to a freelance copy editor may be in demand. There are many niches that keen foreigners willing to stay for a while can fill.

People based in the cities of Eastern Europe are taking advantage of the new entrepreneurial spirit to take up more conventional forms of employment. Prague and Budapest are popular for film-making — extras can get paid $50 a day. In these cities you could find work writing articles for one of the English-language papers, such as *Prognosis* in Prague. Though these capitals have ever-growing expat communities, and thus more competition.

Computer geeks are in demand. Many companies advertise in the English papers for programmers in all fields. There are busking possibilities. The competition is getting stiff, with Andeans in ponchos drawing the biggest crowds. Street tourist markets, like that on Charles Bridge in Prague, are easy places to set up shop: vendor laws are not enforced very stringently, but local traders will probably be more of a worry.

Communications

Telephone. The Eastern bloc used to be cursed with some of the world's most inefficient telecommunications organisations. Foreign companies are busy upgrading the networks and have already made notable improvements, but progress is slow. Since the emphasis seems to have been laid on improving international connections, you'll often find it easier to call home than a neighbouring town: domestic telephone lines, when you eventually get through, vary between tolerable and inaudible. Some countries have wonderful new cardphones, but the older variety of public telephones are still a nightmare. Where new payphones don't yet exist, the easiest and cheapest way to make a call is to go to a public telephone station, which you'll find in every town of any size. The operators rarely speak English, but this is not usually a problem since all you need to do is to write down the number and wait. If you make a call from your hotel, expect to be charged at an exorbitant rate.

Phoning Ahead. You can dial direct to all the countries included in this book. Dial the international access code (010 from the UK, 16 from the Irish Republic, 011 from the USA and Canada, and 0011 from Australia or New Zealand), followed by the country code:

Albania — 355	Latvia — 372
Bulgaria -— 359	Lithuania — 370
Czech Republic — 42	Poland — 48
Estonia — 372	Romania — 40
Hungary — 36	Slovak Republic — 42

Next dial the area/city code, without the initial zero, and then the subscriber's number. Eastern European nations are between one and three hours ahead of GMT.

Telegrams. These are a cheap and effective means of communication. Every post office can handle them, and they are often more reliable and less stressful than the phone.

Fax. Top hotels have fax facilities, but they are not nearly as widespread as the ubiquitous telex. Since fax transmissions use ordinary telephone lines, the service is not 100% reliable.

Mail. A letter posted abroad from an Eastern European capital should reach its destination in less than a week. Anything sent from the provinces, however, will probably take two or three times longer. The delivery of parcels is rather more haphazard, wherever they are posted. If you want to post goods of any value, use a courier service such as DHL, which has opened up offices all over the place.

Poste Restante: in theory, poste restante should be available in any town, but in practice you would do best to rely on the central post office in the capital city (addresses are given under *Help and Information* in the relevant city sections). Check under both your first and last name, since letters are not always filed correctly.

The delivery of incoming mail is patchy whatever the address, but the chances of letters arriving are enhanced slightly if you use American Express. Any AmEx customer can use their offices abroad for poste restante: addresses are given in the text, or call 071-930 4411 for a worldwide directory.

KEEPING IN TOUCH

Newspapers. Keeping up on international events is increasingly easy given the blossoming of homegrown English-language newspapers and the expanding circulation of the foreign press in Eastern Europe. There is already a choice of locally produced English-language weekly newspapers in Prague and Budapest, and *The Baltic Independent* circulates in Estonia, Latvia and Lithuania. The capital cities are where you're most likely to find foreign dailies, from the *Guardian* and the *Daily Mail* to the ubiquitous and worthy *Herald Tribune*. Street kiosks usually have a good choice, though in the more out-of-the-way capitals, such as Bucharest and Tirana, only top hotels stock foreign newspapers — and then probably only a three-day old *Herald Tribune*. In such places, your embassy will be a better source of reading matter.

Broadcasting. While there is the odd broadcast in the English language by some radio stations, the BBC World Service provides the best source of news. Ring the Broadcast Coverage Department on 071-257 2685 for information on World Service reception.

The influence of the West on the new democracies is perhaps most visible on television. Some new commercial TV channels have been set up with the aid of foreign money, but the most startling development has been the spread of satellite television. Sky TV is beamed into thousands of homes and hotels. Many top hotels have the 24-hour news networks CNN and BBC World Service TV.

LANGUAGE

It is wrong to assume that everyone in Eastern Europe speaks English. It is quite possible to spend a month in the region and have only a handful of protracted conversations with a local person.

While English is the preferred foreign language in Albania and Bulgaria, for example, in most other countries German is the most common second language. A lot of Eastern Europeans speak Russian too, though most would rather not for emotional/political reasons. In Romania a little Italian will go a long way, and many local people understand French. In Hungary, you're on your own.

A basic vocabulary is included for each of the countries covered in this book. Learning a little more, however, will add considerably to your enjoyment. If you are planning to visit several countries, learning some German can save you having to try to assimilate bits of a number of different languages. Since Germans aren't especially popular, however, it's as well to establish your nationality if you should opt to communicate in their language. Alternatively, buy the Lonely Planet *Eastern European Phrasebook* (£3.95), which covers all the countries in this book except the Baltic states.

Between them, buses and trains enable you to penetrate most corners of any country in Eastern Europe. Buses are almost invariably better for nipping about from day to day. Express trains are good for long journeys or when travelling between countries, but otherwise are slower and less frequent than buses. Even so, slow trains are full of bustle and interest, and for some people epitomise travel at its best. Furthermore, taking the train is cheaper than the bus if you avoid the expresses. Furthermore, rail timetables are almost invariably easier to understand than those for buses: most stations have a board with a full list of departures from 0.00 to 23.59.

DRIVING

If you aren't tempted by the idea of taking your own car into Eastern Europe (see *Getting There*), you may consider the option of hiring a car once you have arrived. Given the relative low cost of public transport within the region, car rental is uneconomic. On the other hand, it may be the only realistic means by which you can reach the more isolated spots in the region.

Car Rental. The standard conveyances in Eastern Europe are the Lada and the Skoda — subjects of considerable mirth in the West. 'Q: Why are Lada drivers such good philosphers? A: Because they think they own a car.' Nevertheless, these are sturdy vehicles which can cope with freezing temperatures better than most Western models can.

Locally-made cars are invariably the cheapest to hire, but you won't often find them on offer by the international rental agents, which now operate in most of Eastern Europe. Hiring a Western model incurs the risk of attracting thieves: Skodas and Ladas blend into the background.

For a list of Hertz and Avis outlets call 081-679 1777 and 081-848 8765 respectively. These multinationals are geared mainly for those planning ahead, with the price for prebooked rental invariably cheaper than on the spot deals. Unlike local dealers, the big international companies will usually allow you to drop a car off in another country (as long as they have agents there).

Hiring on the spot is best done through a local company. Renting at the airport will enable you to avoid driving around strange and confusing cities, but rates tend to be higher. Rates vary enormously, but $300-400 for a week is not unusual. You must generally be over 21, and you'll need to show your passport and leave a deposit — usually $100 or your full credit card details. See page 16 for information on petrol.

Rules and Regulations. All traffic travels on the right. In most European countries it is an offence to drive even with a trace of alcohol in your blood. Lesser misdemeanours, such as breaking the speed limit, are punishable by on-the-spot fines, usually of less than £5. Enforcement is sporadic, though traffic police are not averse to picking on tourists. Seat belts must be worn at all times throughout Eastern Europe. Children under 12 are not allowed to sit in the front seat of a car in the Czech Republic; in Bulgaria, the age is ten, in Hungary six.

Look out for local idiosyncrasies, such as being able to turn right against a red light. Watch what local motorists are doing, though not to the extent that you imitate their reckless habits: few drivers have adapted to the fact that there is more traffic on the roads. The sight of an oncoming vehicle overtaking on your own side of the road is distressingly common. Quick reactions are a huge asset and defensive driving is advisable at all times. Local motorists are not the only ones to blame; Western motorists driving too fast on poor roads are another source of danger.

Accidents. One easy way to enhance your chance of avoiding an accident, is to drive only by day. Road markings and street lights are scarce, and there are still a lot of old cars about which do not have dipped headlights, or perhaps any headlights at all.

If you're involved in an accident, the obvious rules apply: administer first aid or summon help for the injured; call the police; and take names and addresses of other drivers and any independent witnesses. If possible, don't move any of the vehicles, but if you have to because you're obstructing the traffic, mark their positions, and take some pictures if you have a camera.

HITCHING

The increased number of private vehicles on the road means that hitching is easier than it used to be. Tourists cruise around in their thousands, though neither the Germans nor Austrians (who make up the bulk of foreign drivers) are particularly keen on giving lifts.

Most of Eastern Europe has never really had much of a holiday industry, hence the current shortage of hotels. Historic buildings are being converted and new hotels constructed, but demand still far outstrips supply. In high season, vacancies are scarce in the most popular tourist centres, though you can always fall back on private accommodation. You might consider booking a room in advance, but be prepared to pay extra for the privilege. Accommodation will almost certainly be your biggest single daily expense in Eastern Europe. You'll be hard pushed to find a hotel room for less than $20-30 for two, and most cost a good deal more than that. There is a general shortage of single hotel rooms.

Whether you stay in a smart or lowly establishment, you can usually rely on towels, soap and loo roll being provided. But take your own bathplug: there seems no good economic or cultural reason why Eastern Europe should have a chronic shortage of bathplugs, but they do.

Private Accommodation. Staying in a private house will give you the chance to experience ordinary culture and lifestyles. Most families are extremely welcoming, though in cities you'll usually be given a key to your room and the flat and left to get on with your own thing. In rural areas, you'll feel much more at home, and will probably be asked to share family meals.

The local tourist office is the most reliable source of private accommodation, though special agencies have sprung up all over the place. People also approach you direct, most commonly in transport terminals, or put up signs advertising vacancies. Given the competition for hotel rooms, going private is the most reliable way to find accommodation on the spot in the high season. It is also cheaper. Rooms cost an average of $10-15.

Youth Hostels. Most Eastern European nations can boast at least a few hostel-type establishments and several are associated with Hostelling International. A lot of places don't seem to care if you're not a member, though, and a card doesn't always entitle you to an automatic discount. In fact, the hostels which are open all year round are often more like cheap hotels, with more private rooms than dormitories. Most hostels of a more traditional — i.e. basic — and cheaper nature open in summer only. Beds get booked up by school and college parties, so try to phone ahead.

For membership details or other advance information, contact one of the following national youth hostelling associations:

England and Wales: YHA, 8 St Stephen's Hill, St Albans, UK (0727-55215).
Scotland: SYHA, 7 Globe Crescent, Stirling FK8 2JA (0786-51181).
Northern Ireland: YHA, 56 Bradbury Place, Belfast BT7 1RU (0232-324733).
Ireland: IYH (*An Oige*), 61 Mountjoy Street, Dublin 7 (01-304555).
Australia: AYHA, Level 3, 10 Mallet Street, Camperdown, NSW 2050 (02-565-1699).
Canada: HIC, 1600 James Naismith Drive, Suite 608, Gloucester, Ont. K1B 5N4 (613-748-5638).

USA: AYH, 733 15th Street NW, Suite 840, Washington, DC 20005 (202-783-6161).

Camping. Like hostels, campsites can be good places to meet people, and are by far the cheapest form of accommodation: you will rarely pay more than a few dollars per person. In areas popular among hikers, in the Czech and Slovak Republics for example, the facilities and locations are often extremely good; elsewhere, however, you may find yourself under a flight path and with nothing but a couple of cold showers and evil-smelling lavatories. In the Baltics, where campsites barely exist, you'll probably end up in a field (though you should ask around first).

Health and Hygiene

Travellers can take comfort from the fact that a trip to Eastern Europe need not entail immunisations against a range of dreaded diseases. Few travellers fall ill, the most common complaint being a bout of diarrhoea or a bad hangover brought on by some lethal local liquor. But no one should take their good health for granted. While you are extremely unlikely to encounter any but one or two of the hazards listed here, by following the advice given below and taking sensible precautions, you can help prevent illness from spoiling your visit.

Travellers' Health: How to Stay Healthy Abroad by Richard Dawood (Oxford University Press) is the most up-to-date and comprehensive guide for anyone concerned about their health.

NATURAL HAZARDS

Heat. You may not be in the tropics, but whether you're sightseeing in Bratislava or sunbathing by the Black Sea — you should respect the sometimes intense summer heat. Wear a hat and drink plenty of non-alcoholic fluids even if you aren't thirsty. If you experience headaches or giddiness after a long day outside, you probably have a mild case of heat exhaustion; drink plenty of water and sit in the shade until the symptoms subside. Heatstroke brings on more severe headaches and delirium, and must be treated immediately; remove all your clothes and cover yourself with a wet sheet in order to prevent the body temperature from rising further.

Sun. The most effective protection is to stay out of the sun between 10am and 3pm. The next best precaution is to expose yourself to the sun gradually and use a lotion with a high protection factor. Sea water, perfume and after-shave increase the rate of burning.

If, like most sun-starved travellers, you ignore this advice and get burnt, apply calamine lotion or cold cream liberally, or soak a towel in cold water and place it over the most tender areas. For severe burns use a mild antiseptic and keep the skin clean and dry.

Mosquitoes. While these hateful creatures are not carriers of malaria in Eastern Europe, they can still be a darned nuisance: their bites itch a lot and can make summer nights a misery in areas such as the Hungarian plain and along the Danube (especially in Bratislava). At nightfall, cover your limbs and apply insect repellent to exposed parts. For the best protection, choose a repellent which contains the chemical called Deet, such as Jungle Formula. Eating copious amounts of garlic is also said to repel mosquitoes, as well as other people. Soap, calamine lotion or any of the sting relief creams on the market help to ease itching. Applying ice to the bites can also soothe irritation.

DISEASES AND OTHER HEALTH HAZARDS

European Tick-Borne Encephalitis (TBE). This is a viral infection which can cause inflammation of the brain and is picked up from the bite of an infected animal tick or, less commonly, through unpasteurised milk. The disease occurs from June to September, mainly in the wooded regions of Hungary, Romania, Bulgaria and the Czech and Slovak Republics. It causes flu-like symptoms, which begin with a fever about a week after a bite. In very rare cases a coma can result. A serum exists for treatment, but this is not readily available in Eastern Europe.

Walkers and campers, the category of people most at risk, should consider being immunised against the disease (two shots one month apart), but prevention is equally important: wear long trousers tucked into your socks, apply insect repellent and avoid pasteurised milk. If you find a tick, remove it carefully. Applying a lighted cigarette sometimes works, but nail polish remover or strong liquor is more effective. If you use tweezers, ease the tick out very carefully to avoid leaving the beast's jaws in your flesh.

Gastric Problems. Much of Eastern Europe's food is so bland that you may conclude that the risk of gastric trouble is low. Any food, however dull, can carry bacteria, though in practice cases of food poisoning are rare. Romania has the worst reputation for upset stomachs, but wherever the standards of hygiene are obviously low it is wise to avoid eating meat. Contaminated water (see below) is an equally common cause of gastric problems. Some travellers to the Baltics have returned home with giardiasis, which is caused by an intestinal parasite picked up from contaminated food or water.

Diarrhoea is likely to be the first clue that you have eaten something you shouldn't have. If left to its own devices it should clear up in a couple of days. Rather than take drugs, drink as much (bottled) water as possible and eat only dry bread, rice, pasta, etc. Lomotil, codeine and immodium alleviate the effects of the diarrhoea (and will block you up if you are going on a long bus journey), but do nothing about the cause. Antibiotics can have a detrimental effect, and they are best avoided unless fever or serious infection is suspected. In this case you should seek medical advice.

Water: a disturbing number of Eastern Europe's waterways have been polluted by industry, and many people throughout the region choose to boil their tapwater. The quality of the drinking water is particularly bad in the Baltics and Romania, where you should seriously consider buying bottled water or purifying tapwater with tablets or iodine.

Hepatitis. A viral infection of the liver, hepatitis comes in various forms. The one which is most likely to affect travellers is Hepatitis A. It is easy to catch from contaminated food and water and Romania is the country where you are most likely to pick it up.

Incubation takes two to six weeks and symptoms include loss of appetite, lethargy, fever, pains in the abdomen, followed by nausea and vomiting. The whites of the eyes and the skin turn yellow, urine turns deep orange and stools become white. If you suspect infection, rest and seek medical advice immediately. Do not smoke or drink alcohol, nor eat fat. Some people are only mildly affected, but hepatitis can sometimes take six months to clear up; therefore you are strongly advised to go straight home and recover in comfort.

The gamma globulin vaccine offers good protection against Hepatitis A. Since the effect of the vaccine wears off gradually after it is administered, have the injection shortly before departure. If you plan to be away for more than six months or are a frequent traveller, you should think about having the new vaccine, Havrix, which gives immunity for ten years: it is administered in three doses, two a month apart before a trip, followed by a further one about three months later.

Pollution and Smoking. It may not seem fair to lump pollution and smoking together, but both are so widespread that asthmatics could face serious problems. The areas worst affected by industry include parts of Poland and northern Bohemia in the Czech Republic, but most capital cities in Eastern Europe have a serious pollution problem exacerbated by increasing traffic. An overwhelmingly large proportion of the male population smokes. Smokers from the West will be delighted at the lack of restrictions. Only the odd tourist-oriented restaurant has a non-smoking room; in bars and restaurants frequented mostly by local people, you can expect to sit in a smoky haze.

Other Diseases. The standard inoculations apart from those mentioned above are typhoid, tetanus and polio. Typhoid, like Hepatitis A, is caught by consuming contaminated food or water. The typhoid vaccination is administered in two doses, though travellers who have already had a course need only a booster injection. Polio and tetanus require a booster every ten years.

AIDS

The Acquired Immune Deficiency Syndrome (Aids) is caused by the Human Immunodeficiency Virus (HIV). This can damage the body's defence system so that it is unable to fight certain infections and other diseases. Statistics for Eastern Europe are scarce, and it is difficult to discover the extent of Aids and the virus which causes it. While there is a comparatively low incidence of intravenous drug abuse, prostitution is on the rise and hospitals strapped for cash cannot always maintain high levels of hygiene. Even so, for visitors who take sensible precautions against contracting the virus through unprotected sexual intercourse or intravenous drug abuse, risks are minimal.

You are strongly advised to avoid contact with male or female prostitutes and to take your own supply of condoms if there is a chance that you will have sex with somebody whose sexual history is unknown to you. In much of Eastern Europe condoms are hard to find or of poor quality. Infection through contaminated blood transfusions is less easy to control. Although screening is now common, this is not always done effectively. In addition, hypodermic syringes may be reused and may not always be adequately sterilised. If you are in an accident and require a blood transfusion, try to get in touch with your nearest consulate or embassy; the staff there will know the nearest source of 'clean' blood. You should also consider taking an Aids Pack. A normal kit contains hypodermic needles, suture material (for stitches), intravenous drip needles and alcohol swabs. Your doctor should be able to make a kit up for you; ask him or her to supply a letter explaining that the kit is for medical use only — this will save you potential hassle at Customs among officials convinced you are a possible drug-user.

Sources of Information. For up-to-date information on the extent of Aids, contact the Panos Institute at 9 White Lion Street, London N1 9PD (tel

071-278 1111, fax 071-278 0345). It publishes various books and a bi-monthly magazine called *WorldAIDS*. The Terrence Higgins Trust (52-54 Grays Inn Road, London WC1X 8SU; tel 071-831 0330, fax 071-242 0121) is the UK's leading Aids charity and offers good general information and advice on HIV and Aids. You can call its Advice Centre on 071-242 1010. You can also talk to trained advisors by ringing the National Aids Helpline on 0800-567-123: calls are free and confidential.

MEDICAL TREATMENT

Most countries in Europe have a Reciprocal Health Agreement with Eastern European nations, which entitles their citizens to free medical treatment, though prescription charges must be paid for. Even so, you should still take out full medical insurance. Doctors throughout Eastern Europe are generally well trained, but so short of money that the medicines and equipment at their disposal are severely limited. For the best treatment you may need to have recourse to a private (and very expensive) clinic.

Medications. While medicines are easier to buy in Eastern Europe than they used to be, as a general rule you should bring with you all the medicines you are likely to need. Cures for indigestion and headaches can of course be purchased over the counter, but some pharmacies do not have a sufficient range of drugs to make up complicated prescriptions. Nevertheless, pharmacists can be very helpful, and can save you a trip to the doctor if all you have are minor and easily recognisable symptoms. Furthermore, if you can overcome language problems, medicines are very cheap.

OTHER HEALTH MATTERS

Women's Health. If you are planning to travel while pregnant, check carefully the effects of any vaccinations you might require. It is advisable not to be inoculated with a live vaccine such as polio, especially during the first three months of pregnancy.

While you can buy tampons and sanitary towels, prices tend to be high and supplies erratic in some areas. You are advised to bring all you need with you.

Contraception. Take all the contraception you think you may require. Locally-produced condoms are best avoided, and sophistications such as spermicidal jelly or oral contraceptives are difficult or impossible to obtain. Note that the effectiveness of the contraceptive pill is reduced if you have a stomach upset, or if you take certain types of antibiotics.

INSURANCE

While most people are scrupulously honest, there is a small contingent of thieves who are never happier than when robbing foreigners. So insurance is essential for your possessions as well as for your health. The cover provided by most policies is fairly standard: delay and cancellation insurance of up to £2,000; £1 million for medical expenses; the same amount for personal liability; £20,000 for permanent disability; and lost or stolen baggage up to about £1,000 (sometimes valuable single items are excluded). Most now also offer an emergency repatriation service.

Every airline, tour operator and travel agent is delighted to sell you insurance because of their high commission (sometimes over 40%). Shopping around can save you money or get better cover for the same premium. Endsleigh Insurance offers good rates for its worldwide insurance scheme. Information is available direct from the head office in Cheltenham (tel 0242-223300) or from any youth travel specialists. North American travellers should check what provisions their own insurance policy makes before purchasing a new one.

If you're unfortunate enough to have to claim on your insurance, the golden rule is to amass as much documentation as possible to support your application. In particular, compensation is unlikely to be paid for lost baggage or cash unless your claim is accompanied by a police report of the loss.

Eastern Europeans have no culture of lawlessness, partly because of the oppressive regime under communism. Your average Eastern European doesn't break laws: they don't cross the road against the light, they don't write on walls and they keep out of trouble. However, economic crises of varying severity and the incursions of capitalism have resulted in an increase in crime at all levels across Eastern Europe. The incidence of murder and robbery has risen sharply, and gambling and prostitution are increasingly common. Organised crime is thriving, with activities ranging from small-time racketeering to high-level corruption.

Most casual visitors will be completely unaffected by (and oblivious to) crime of this nature. Dodgy moneychangers can be a danger (see *Money: The Black Market*), but the main threat is from pickpockets and other petty thieves. As a Westerner, you could be carrying in cash what for the average Eastern European represents several months' wages. Therefore theft of a wallet or purse presents understandable temptation.

But take heed of the fact that most travellers feel safer in Eastern Europe than in their home countries. Violent crime against foreigners is virtually unknown; you may be unfortunate enough to have your bag snatched, but it is most unlikely that you will be physically injured.

How to Avoid Robbery. There is no need to feel paranoid about crime in Eastern Europe, but by taking a few precautions you can greatly reduce the chance of being robbed. Western visitors displaying ostentatious wealth in darkened backstreets are asking for trouble. It pays to try not to look too much like a tourist. Do not carry a shoulder bag that can be easily swiped. Cameras symbolise Western wealth and can be a major temptation too. Leave as much money as possible in your hotel and conceal what you take with you in a moneybelt beneath your clothes. Keep a small amount of change in your pocket, so you don't have to undress just to buy a coffee or a newspaper. Some hotels have a bad reputation for security, and you are advised to put your funds in a safety deposit box.

When in cities frequented by a large number of tourists, treat anyone you meet on the street with caution, initially at least. Avoid revealing where you are staying until you feel you trust your new friend. Be particularly wary of gypsy children. One may approach you alone after a few pennies but will then try to distract you while accomplices pick your pockets.

The Law. It used to be the case that foreigners were automatically regarded with suspicion by the security forces. It was believed that a large proportion of visitors were there to subvert the state. These days, that view no longer prevails, and there is little reason for you to have any dealings with the police, but that doesn't mean you are free to do exactly as you please.

Drugs: potentially, the market for drugs in Eastern Europe is huge. The Colombian cartels have already taken to shipping cocaine through Poland and the Czech and Slovak republics. Most is directed towards the EU countries, but inevitably a market is growing within the region. The Turko-Bulgarian border is one of the strictest in Europe, simply because of the amount of drugs passing across.

The use of illegal drugs is still very limited compared with more developed countries, but the authorities are anxious to keep their subjects off anything stronger than vodka. Penalties for possession always include a fine, plus a term in prison of up to five years. In reality, in the case of foreigners sentences tend to be shortened, followed by deportation. Sentences for selling and smuggling range from five to ten years.

Drunkenness: don't get overly drunk in public places. While over-indulgence is tolerated in the privacy of your own home, if you wander drunk around the streets you run the risk of being arrested and locked up until you sleep it off. If you are robbed while drunk, expect little sympathy from the police.

Photography: formerly communist regimes may have a more relaxed approach towards security, but there are certain subjects which are still not considered suitable for photographs. As is the case in nations around the world, you should not take photographs of military or police installations or equipment, airports, power stations, border crossings, etc.

When it comes to taking pictures of local people, not everyone enjoys being photographed. It is good manners always to ask your subject for the go-ahead first.

Help and Information

Gay Travellers. Romania is the only country where all homosexual acts are still against the law (though anal sex is forbidden in Lithuania). The thirst for personal freedom has meant that most post-communist governments of Eastern Europe have relaxed the laws regarding homosexuality and reduced the age of consent. This is now 18 in Bulgaria, Hungary and Latvia, 15 in Poland and the Czech and Slovak Republics, and 16 in Estonia (14 for women).

Even so, most Eastern Europeans share a generally conservative attitude towards homosexuality, particularly in Bulgaria and (Catholic) Poland. There are still relatively few visible gay movements, with no real 'scene' as you'd find in Western Europe. Only a small number of bars cater overtly for the gay community, these being concentrated in the more developed capital cities like Prague and Budapest.

The best source currently is the *Gay Guide: Eastern Europe*, published by Softpress in Poland but available from gay bookshops abroad, including Gay's The Word at 66 Marchmont Street, London WC1N 1AB (071-278 7654). It is not much more than a booklet, but at £2.25 is better value than *Spartacus*, published in Germany by Bruno Gmunder, price £14.95. This country-by-country directory gives information about current laws on homosexuality, gay movements, etc., but it is not particularly accurate and is aimed primarily at gay men. In some towns, more research appears to have gone into locating cruising areas and public lavatories than in seeking out gay bars and clubs.

Women Travellers. Statutory equality between the sexes is well advanced, but women remain the traditional homemakers while the men pile down to the local bar. The average Eastern European male has a serious penchant for alcohol, particularly in Poland and Romania. There is a high divorce rate.

No amount of laws can dislodge male chauvinism, but harassment of women travellers is not common. The main aggravation may be the over-protective solicitude some local men display. The lobbies of smart city hotels are often a gathering place for prostitutes, so female travellers would be wise to avoid sitting alone in such places.

Young and Student Travellers. Anyone under the age of 26 should obtain an ISIC or FIYTO card, for students and other young people respectively. They are available from youth travel agencies or student unions and will entitle you to discounts on everything from museum admission fees to certain bus or train journeys.

Business Travellers. Business travellers are advised to contact the East European Trade Council, 25 Victoria St, London SW1H 0EX (071-222 7622). The council can supply booklets on trading arrangements with each nation, and has an extensive library which is open to the public: phone in advance to arrange a visit.

Hints for Exporters, published by the Overseas Trade Board and covering Bulgaria, the Czech and Slovak Republics, Hungary, Poland and Romania are available for £5 each from the DTI Export Publications, PO Box 55, Stratford-upon-Avon, Warwickshire CV37 9GE. Country profiles are also available, price £10. Write for a catalogue so you can check publication dates; some are shamefully out-of-date.

Travellers with Disabilities. The former Eastern bloc countries lag behind the rest of Europe in their provisions for people with disabilities, and financial constraints mean that this situation is unlikely to change in the near future. Those with wheelchairs will face constant impediments to mobility, and blind and partially sighted travellers will find it hard to get around. At present, the help of an able-bodied companion is, unfortunately, essential.

Anyone who is keen to travel around Eastern Europe should try contacting the tour operators listed under *Getting There,* since these have some experience of circumventing the problems confronting travellers with disabilities. Useful source books include *Nothing Ventured: Disabled People Travel the World,* by Alison Walsh (Penguin, £7.99), available from bookshops, and *Holidays and Travel Abroad: A Guide for Disabled People* by John Stanford, available from the Royal Society for Disability and Rehabilitation (RADAR) at 25 Mortimer Street, London W1N 8AB (071-637 5400), currently priced at £4.50 including postage. In the United States, you should contact the Society for the Advancement of Travel for the Handicapped at 345 Fifth Avenue, Suite 610, New York NY 10016 (tel 212-447-7284, fax 725-8253).

Electrical Items. Most sockets are standard Continental two-pin jobs, with an optional earth. Take an adaptor. The supply in all Eastern European countries is nominally around 220v at 50Hz AC, roughly the same as in the UK. Voltage drops and frequency fluctuations are usual, however, so be prepared for equipment such as hair dryers and radios to function below normal, and think twice before connecting sensitive equipment such as portable computers.

Weights and Measures. Eastern Europe uses the metric system. Distances are measured in millimetres (25.4mm 1 inch), metres (0.3m 1 foot) and kilometres (1.6km 1 mile). Volume uses the millilitre (550ml 1 Imperial pint) and the litre (4.5l 1 Imperial gallon). Weights are given in grams (27g 1 ounce) and kilograms (0.45kg 1 lb).

SOURCES OF INFORMATION

Maps and Books. While the best travel guides are published in the West, in Eastern Europe new, independently-produced books are gradually replacing the turgid, authority-approved volumes of the past. Maps are easily available once you're in Eastern Europe. No town or city plan will be 100% accurate, many street names have been changed since 1989, but in some places you'll be offered street plans which have been knocking about for years. Check the publication date carefully.

If you want to buy country maps before you leave home, the best ones are published by GeoCenter International, Freytag & Berndt, Bartholomew and Kummerley & Frey. Some specialist shops stock maps imported from Eastern Europe, including the excellent Cartographia series from Budapest. Falk Verlag publishes maps of most capital cities, price £4.95.

Books written about specific countries are mentioned in the relevant chapters, but there are numerous books recounting the experiences of writers who have travelled through several Eastern European nations. Pick any of the following to raise enthusiasm before a trip or to entertain and inform you on the road.

Death of the Dark Hero: Eastern Europe 1987-90 by David Selbourne (Cape, 1990) is a beautifully crafted, lyrical book by a keen observer.

Balkan Hours: Travels in the Other Europe by Richard Bassett (John Murray, 1990), describes a visit to Bulgaria, Romania and former Yugoslavia. It is a learned and atmospheric book in which Bassett's travels and impressions are overlaid with history.

From Berlin to Bucharest: Travels in Eastern Europe by Anton Gill (Grafton, 1990) chronicles a series of journeys made through Poland, Czechoslovakia, Hungary, Romania and Yugoslavia in 1988 and 1989. The author's observance of detail is unrepentant but somehow endearing, with the emphasis on eating and drinking.

Ticket to Latvia, A Journey from Berlin to the Baltic by Marcus Tanner (Dent, 1989). The descriptions of East Germany are perhaps the highlight, but Tanner also provides a well-observed and entertaining insight into Lithuania and Latvia before the dismemberment of the Eastern bloc.

Bookshops: Daunt Books at 83 Marylebone High Street, London W1M 4DE (tel 071-224 2295, fax 071-224 6893) stocks a good collection of guides and travelogues as well as related literature — from biographies to cookery books. A similar approach can be found at the Travel Bookshop, which also sells secondhand guidebooks and literature. Another specialised shop is Stanfords at 12-14 Long Acre WC2E 9LP (tel 071-836 1321), which has some of the more obscure guidebooks and is the best source of maps in London. In the USA, Hippocrene Books at 171 Madison Avenue, New York, NY 10016 (718-454-2366) keeps a good section on Eastern Europe.

Tourist Information. While tourist offices as we know them have begun to open up, most national tourist boards in Eastern Europe are still unaccustomed to dealing with independent travellers. Their function is primarily to make bookings for accommodation, theatre seats, train tickets and so on, not to tell you which bus to catch to visit the local zoo. For this type of information, you'll do better at one of the private tourist organisations, which are already well-established in several capital cities and are gradually opening branches in smaller towns and cities. Failing that, of course, try asking any local person. Most people will try their best to help.

Embassies. If you get into difficulties, whether caused by theft, ill-health or involvement with crime, your first point of contact should be your Embassy (or the Embassy of the country which represents you). The staff have a thorough understanding of the way things work — or fail to work — in Eastern Europe. In a real emergency, the staff will do their utmost to help you out; however, if your problem is that you've sprained your ankle while drunk, don't expect too much sympathy. Addresses of Embassies and Consulates are given in the text.

Estonia

Tallinn

Population: 1.6 million   **Capital: Tallinn (population 490,000)**

Remember Ronald Reagan and Mikhail Gorbachev? Their 1987 summit in Reykjavik took place aboard the ship Georg Ots, which now sails between Helsinki and Tallinn, the capital of Estonia. Instead of Presidents, these days its load is drunken Finns seeking cheap beer. Tallinn is just 50 miles from Helsinki, and even as part of the USSR, Estonia's proximity to Scandinavia made it more Westernised than any of the Soviet republics. Most Estonians still seem to consider themselves the *crème de la crème* of the Baltic states (of which it is the smallest), and they are confidently ahead in terms of opening up to Western economics and tourism.

Despite the ravages of state communism and weekend visits by marauding Finns, Tallinn retains great charm, with some superb architecture dating from its days as an old Hanseatic port. The other trading centres, such as Narva, have survived less well. The Estonian countryside is flat and consists mostly of forest and marshy plains dotted with lakes, with few particularly attractive towns. If you really want to explore, try visiting some of the country's 1,500 coastal islands. The largest, Saaremaa, is easily accessible and offers rural scenes that have more appeal than most sights in the country.

Estonia is an excellent introduction to Eastern Europe. In the elegant and bustling streets of Tallinn, it is extraordinary to think that it was so recently a (reluctant) paid-up member of the Soviet Union.

CLIMATE

Winter can be very cold with frequent heavy snowfalls. It lasts from November to mid-March: you sometimes see trees in blossom as late as June.

In summer, the average temperature is 17°C/62°F; July and August are both the hottest and wettest months. Try to visit in June, when the days extend well into the night — the so-called *White Nights.*

HISTORY

Estonia has had a chequered history, subject to a succession of invasions from expansionist neighbours. In the 11th and 12th centuries it was dominated by German crusading knights, who suppressed the local language but never managed to eliminate national consciousness. Sweden took over the occupation in the 17th century, but in 1721 the country was annexed by Russia. Only then did Estonia really begin to develop as a nation, though it had to wait until 1919 before the country could enjoy autonomy. Estonia was independent until 1940 when it was annexed again, this time by the USSR. Having borne the damage wrought by the German invasion during the Second World War, the Estonian people went on to suffer even more at the hands of Stalin. The Soviet leader was responsible for the deportation and execution of more than 60,000 Estonians from 1945 to 1949. After such harrowing events, Estonia did well to recover and become one of the richest republics in the Union.

Independence. Estonia was the first of the Baltic states to set up a People's Front, which began calling for autonomy and democracy in October 1988. A broad unity was established between the reformist majority of the Estonian Communist Party leadership and the popular movements. While supposedly in support of Gorbachev's *perestroika,* the reformists gradually eroded the powers of the Russians and their Soviet institutions and independence was eventually declared on 20 August 1991, shortly after the failed coup against Gorbachev.

Elections in 1992 landed the country with an unstable coalition government led by President Lennart Meri, head of the right-wing Fatherland Party. Like other former Soviet republics struggling to make a go of independence, the country still faces severe economic difficulties, including high unemployment and growing debts. And although Tallinn has the aura of a boom town which has swept aside its Soviet past, as long as Estonia is dependent on Russia for oil, the country will continue to feel vulnerable.

THE PEOPLE

Estonians make up 61% of the population. Russians, who number a substantial 30%, are in the majority in several towns and cities, including Tallinn itself. With Estonian nationalist feelings aggravated by the number of Russian immigrants, some people have demanded a stop to immigration and even the repatriation of Russians. In 1993, only intense political and economic pressure from Russia forced the Estonian parliament to revise a controversial law to limit the rights of Russian citizens. It is not for fun that police are now stationed around the largest Russian neighbourhoods in Tallinn.

Language. Estonian, which replaced Russian as the national language in 1989, is totally different from Latvian and Lithuanian, which are Indo-European languages. With its large number of vowel sounds, Estonian is close to Finnish and Hungarian. Here are a few basic rules about the pronunciation of consonants:

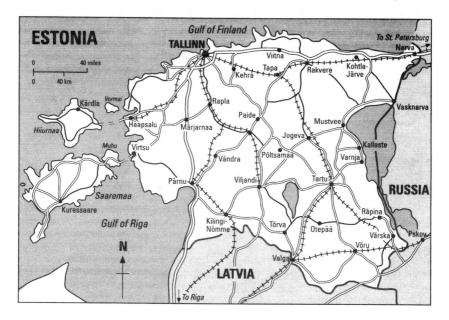

č — ch
š — sh
ž — s as in measure
g — more like a k
j — y as in yes
r — usually rolled

Estonians speak more English than their Baltic neighbours, but the most common second language is still Russian — though given the racial tension, it's best to avoid using it in conversations with an Estonian. Bookshops sell English-Estonian phrasebooks, and a short list of useful words and phrases follows.

yes — *jah*
no — *ei*
hello — *tere*
goodbye — *head aega*
thank you — *tänan, aitäh*
please — *palun*
where? — *kus?*
how much is it? — *kui palju see maksab?*
Do you speak English? — *Kas teie räägite inglise keelt?*

train station — *raudteejaam*
bus station — *autobussijamm*
street — *tänav (tn.), tee*
avenue — *puiestee (pst.)*
highway — *maantee (mnt.)*
square — *väljak*
hospital — *haigla*
market — *turg*

Several agencies have particular experience in dealing with travel to the Baltics from Western Europe. Most can arrange tours as well as book flights. They include:

Canterbury Travel, 248 Streatfield Road, Harrow, Middlesex HA3 9BY (tel 081-206 0411, fax 206 0427).
Finlandia Travel, 223 Regent St, London W1 (071-409 7334).
Gunnel Travel Service Ltd, Hayling Cottage, Stratford St Mary, Colchester, Essex CO7 6JW (0206-322352).
Instone Travel, 83 Whitechapel High Street, London E1 7QX (071-377 1859).
Progressive Tours, 12 Porchester Place, London W2 (071-262 1676).
Regent Holidays, 15 John St, Bristol BS1 2HR (0272-211711).

Air. You can reach Tallinn from Britain or North America on SAS via Stockholm four times a week. Other airlines serving Tallinn include Finnair, Malév and Lufthansa. The national carrier, Estonia Airlines, has a limited network only, with flights from Frankfurt, several cities in Scandinavia (including Helsinki) and the CIS. Scope for expansion is slim because the airline still relies on old Aeroflot planes.

The cheapest option from the UK may be to fly to Vilnius on Lithuanian Airlines and travel overland from there: for further information see *Lithuania: Getting There.* Helsinki is also an easy jumping-off point for Estonia, but Finland is not cheap to reach, and hideously expensive once you're there. Finlandia Travel has flights to Helsinki for around £250, with the short extra hop to Tallinn costing an additional £50 or so return. An advantage of Finnair and SAS flights is that you can fly into Tallinn and back from Riga or Vilnius for little or no extra cost.

Train. Trains from Minsk in Belarus run daily to Tallinn (17 hours) via Vilnius, Riga and Tartu, with another more comfortable service starting from Riga. There is also a daily service from Warsaw (30 hours). From Russia, trains serve Estonia from Pskov, southeast of Tartu, and St Petersburg.

Bus. Services run daily from Riga to both Tallinn (6 hours) and Tartu (3 hours), and from Vilnius to Tallinn (12 hours). Buses also run every day from St Petersburg (8 hours) and Pskov (3 hours), and once a week from Warsaw (22 hours).

Boat. *From Stockholm:* Estline's *Nord Estonia,* a car and passenger ferry, sails three times a week (all year round) between Stockholm and Tallinn. The journey takes 14-15 hours and costs $70 one-way: the cost of taking a car is about the same again.

From Helsinki: the advantage of travelling via Finland is the short crossing time and the frequency of services, currently running at about ten a day in summer. Ferries take four hours, the hydrofoils two. If you fly to Helsinki, your agent should be able to book a ticket for you. Try to travel during the week, since fares increase at weekends.

Ferries are run by Tallink, with six sailings a week between April and September, three in winter. The *Georg Ots* is passenger only ($15-20 one-way), while the *Tallinn* also takes cars ($20-40 one-way, plus about $40 per car). The central booking agency in Helsinki is Saimaa Lines, with offices at Fabianinkatu 14 (65 87 33) and at the harbour.

Helta Line hydrofoils operate from Magazine Terminal, and Estonia New Line (ENL) from Olympia Terminal. Helta hydrofoils currently leave Helsinki at 8am and 3pm daily, while ENL operates five trips a day. You can buy tickets at most travel agencies or at the port itself. A one-way ticket costs around $30. ENL also operates a car ferry, *Linda 1.*

Driving. The M12 between Riga and Tallinn is a reasonable road, following a picturesque route along the coast as far as Pärnu. In contrast with this fairly pleasant drive, the highway from St Petersburg is in a poor state (though it improves markedly west of Narva) and is flanked by a pipeline carried on concrete pillars. Tallinn lies 224 miles/358km west of St Petersburg, a comfortable day's drive with time for stops en route. From Finland it's easier to put your car on a ferry than to drive all the way around via Russia.

Many nationalities, including British, American and Australian citizens, can now enter Estonia without a visa. On arrival, you will normally be granted a stay of 30 days. If you require a visa (price £10), this will be issued on the spot if you go in person to an Estonian consulate, or by return post if you apply in writing. You can also obtain a visa on arrival at Tallinn airport, but it is easier to do all the paperwork in advance. Note that a visa for Estonia is also valid for the other Baltic Republics.

The addresses of Estonian missions abroad are as follows:

UK: 16 Hyde Park Gate, London W11 2RB (071-589 3428).
USA: Suite 142, 9 Rockefeller Plaza, New York, NY (tel 212-247-1450, fax 212-262-0893).
Canada: Suite 202, 958 Broadview Avenue, Toronto, Ontario M4K 2R6 (tel 416-461 0764, fax 416-461-0448).
Finland: Fabianinkatu 13 A, Helsinki 13 (17 95 28).
Russia: Sobinovsky pereulok 5, 103009 Moscow (290 50 13).

1 kroon (kr) = 100 sents
1994: £1 = 20kr   US$1 = 13kr

Estonia introduced its own currency in 1992. This has made life easier for visitors in that it has reduced the ramifications of the two-tier price structure, in which Estonians paid less (in roubles) than tourists (in hard currency). Prices have risen, and visitors must still pay for some things in hard currency, but Estonia remains cheap.

Currency. Notes are issued in denominations of 1, 2, 20, 50, 100 and 500 kroon, and coins in denominations of 1, 2, 5 and 20 sents and 1 kroon.

Changing Money. You'll find it easiest to change dollars or Deutsche Marks in cash, though travellers cheques are accepted in a growing number of places. For the best deals rely on the banks (*panki*) — Tartu Kommertspank usually offers the most competitive rate. Other exchange bureaux (*valuutavahetuskontor*) have appeared in Tallinn, but these offer a poor deal, as do the hotels.

Credit cards can be used at flashier hotels and restaurants.

Telephone. There are payphones for both local and long-distance calls, but the latter are scarce and both are unreliable. When calling an Estonian number from Tallinn, dial 8 and wait for the second dialling tone. If calling long-distance within Estonia, however, you'll do better at a local telephone office (usually attached to the post office). The same goes for calling abroad. When phoning from a hotel, you'll probably have to book the call with the operator (dial 007), who will then call you back. At a telephone office, give the number to the person at the counter and then wait — for anything up to an hour.

Currently, charges are cheap, around $0.20 a minute within Europe, $0.40 a minute to the USA. Estonia is two hours ahead of GMT, three hours from March to September.

Useful numbers: Fire Brigade 01, Police 02, Ambulance 03.

Mail. To send a postcard within Europe costs about $0.22 and takes 10-14 days. Poste restante is available at Tallinn's central post office (*postkontor*) at Narva maantee 1, but the delivery of inbound mail cannot be relied upon.

Maps. The Cartographia map of the Baltic Republics (£5.95) is commonly available abroad and features street plans of all three capitals. Within Estonia, look out for the *Eesti Maanteed,* a reasonably up-to-date road atlas. You can find street plans to most sizeable towns, though some of these are still Cyrillic.

Bus. Buses are cheaper, faster and more frequent than trains. The fast (*kiir*) buses are slightly slower than the express (*expres*) services, but you'll not notice a huge difference in the journey time. Try to book your ticket a day in advance.

Train. The often crowded trains are most useful if you want to save a bit of money or if you simply prefer rail travel. Book two days in advance whenever possible, particularly when heading abroad, though hops to Riga are normally possible without reservation on the daytime services.

Taxi. Cabs charge such low fares that it isn't outrageous to use them for long-distance journeys if you are in a group or in a mad rush. You would pay $20-25 for the 12ʋ-mile ride between Tallinn and Tartu, for example. It's not unusual for people to travel between the Baltic capitals by taxi.

Driving. Road accidents are common in Estonia, mostly due to drink-driving and the poor condition of minor roads. The speed limit on most roads is a highly theoretical 55mph/90kmh. Unleaded and four-star petrol are virtually unheard of outside the capital.

Several international car rental agencies are represented in Tallinn, including Hertz (Baltlink Ltd, Tartu maantee 13; tel 42 10 03) and Avis (International Airport; tel 21 56 02), and a few local firms have started up operations. The top hotels and tourist offices can also provide information.

City Transport. Buses and tram fares are ridiculously low, usually less than $0.05. Buy a ticket (*pileteid*) in advance from a kiosk, then punch it when you board.

You'll probably only need to take a cab in Tallinn or Tartu, Estonia's second city. Fares are low if you avoid the ranks outside the smart hotels. Yellow state taxis are the most reliable, and usually turn on their meter without any prompting.

Hotels tend to be either expensive Soviet-style blocks with no character or scruffy Soviet-style blocks with no hot water, an interesting repertoire of insect life and few home comforts. A new breed of joint ventures in Tallinn has smartened up establishments at the top end of the market. For a comfortable room expect to pay at least $50. A cheap room costs anything from $5 to $25. The fledgling Estonian Tourist Board publishes a booklet giving the addresses of over 100 hotels.

Homes and Hostels. The main alternatives to hotels are private rooms or hostels. The number of families renting out rooms or whole flats is fast increasing. Several agencies can arrange this, including the Family Hotel Service in Tallinn (Vanu-Viru 13; tel/fax 44 11 87). The average price is around $10 a night per person, but can rise to more than $20.

The ESP (Room 608, Kentmanni 20, Tallinn; tel 44 10 96, fax 44 69 71) is the local version of the YHA and runs most hostels in Estonia. These are generally open in the summer only and are in country areas. You'll pay around $5 (no Hostelling International membership card is necessary). Try to book ahead in mid-summer. BATS (Baltic Accommodation & Travel Service) at Sakala 11, Tallinn (68 18 93), can also provide information on hostels.

Estonia has a few campsites (*kämpingud*), mostly near Tallinn and in the resort of Pärnu. Some have chalets as well as space for pitching tents.

Old habits die hard, and restaurants rarely offer everything listed on the menu, though some of the new places in Tallinn do a better job of offering only what they've actually got. Fish is widely available, particularly trout and herring (try *rossolye,* herring served with vinaigrette). Veal is popular: *sult* or jellied veal is the most typical. As a rule, however, meals start well and then tail off, so pigging out on the hors d'oeuvres is often a good move.

Make the most of the restaurants in Tallinn because those in the provinces are extremely poor by comparison. You'll find it difficult to eat after 10pm outside the capital.

Here are a few terms to help you interpret a menu:

hors d'oeuvres — *külmad road*	snack bar — *einelaud*
main course — *teised road*	drink — *joogid*
meat dish — *liharoad*	ice cream — *jäätis*
fish — *kala*	water — *vesi*
trout — *forrell*	tea — *tea*
vegetables — *köögiviljad*	coffee — *kohv*
fruit — *puuviljad*	

Drinking. The most common drink is beer (*õlu*), which is imported in cans. For variation, try mulled wine (*hoogvein*), available in a few bars. Avoid Vana Tallinn, a dark, ruby firewater made locally, unless you want to end up like a Finn.

Tea and coffee are both easily available, the café scene being a long-established part of life in the capital.

Help and Information

The Estonian Tourist Board is still fairly new and few tourist offices have been set up as yet. Hotel staff can usually help with simple enquiries — go to the expensive hotels, where the staff are more likely to speak English. Several books, all published since the revolution, are available. *Tallinn — A Practical Guide* contains general information about Estonia and the main provincial towns as well as the capital. So too does *Tallinn — This Week* which, curiously, is only published every couple of months. *The Baltic States: A Reference Book* (last edition published in 1991), with remarkably thorough listings, maps, useful words and phrases and even a Who's Who section, is available in some travel bookshops abroad.

Estonian embassies will send you some photocopied information by post if you send a large stamped addressed envelope.

TALLINN

The Estonian capital, on the shores of the Gulf of Finland, started out as a small fortified town at the crossroads of trade routes. With the development of commerce, it grew into a large community of merchants and artisans and by the fourteenth and fifteenth centuries was a major Hanseatic port — some of the city's finest architecture is Gothic, dating from this period. Plague and war brought decline, but with annexation to Russia in the 18th century there was further expansion. Tallinn is still a big trade and fishing port, with a population approaching half a million.

The quiet cobbled streets, gently decaying palaces and elegant spires in the centre of Tallinn are a world away from the busy port and grim concrete blocks built to house Russian workers, but the different atmospheres combine to generate a relaxed and cosmopolitan capital. A twinning link with Venice may raise too many hopes, but Tallinn is well worth seeing: go now before foreign investors and tourists take over completely.

CITY LAYOUT

The centre of Tallinn is compact and easy to get around on foot. The oldest part of the city, known as Upper Town, centres on Toompea Hill, topped by a castle; down below is the walled Lower Town, with Raekoja plats as its focus. Both districts make up the Old Town or Vanalinn, where you'll probably spend most of your time. Lai is one of the main streets through the centre, running from the foot of Toompea Hill north to Oleviste church, whose tall Gothic spire is a useful landmark. The New Town developed outside the city walls: with the old fortifications so well preserved, it is easy to keep track of which part of the city you are in. The focus of the more modern district is Vabaduse väljak, just south of the old town. From here Estonia puiestee runs east to Viru väljak, overlooked by the high-rise Viru Hotel (appallingly ugly, but another useful reference point).

Maps. Several city plans are available, including a tourist map with information in English as well as Estonian and Russian. You can buy it from kiosks for $0.15.

ARRIVAL AND DEPARTURE

Air. The airport (*lennujaam*) is the easiest in Eastern Europe for links with

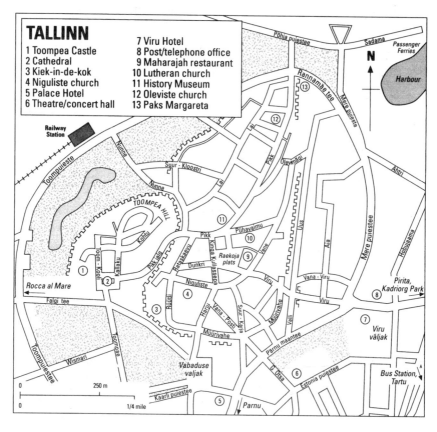

TALLINN

1 Toompea Castle
2 Cathedral
3 Kiek-in-de-kok
4 Niguliste church
5 Palace Hotel
6 Theatre/concert hall
7 Viru Hotel
8 Post/telephone office
9 Maharajah restaurant
10 Lutheran church
11 History Museum
12 Oleviste church
13 Paks Margareta

the city. It lies just a couple of miles southeast of the centre along the Tartu road. Bus 22 runs every 30 minutes between the airport and the railway station, also calling at the bus terminal and Viru väljak. The Estonian Airlines office is at 10 Vabaduse väljak. For flight information call 21 10 92.

Train. The railway station or *Balti jaam* is on Toompuiestee (44 67 56), northwest of Toompea Hill and about ten minutes' walk from the centre. You can also buy tickets in Hotel Viru.
Bus. The main bus station or Maaliinide Autobussijaam (42 25 49) lies about a mile southeast of the centre on Lastekodu, off Tartu Maantee and a 20-minute walk or a short tram ride from downtown. For information and tickets, it is easier to go to the office at Pärnu maantee 24. Local buses leave from the station next to the rail terminal.

Boat. Passenger ferries arrive at the dock (44 94 27) at the end of Sadama, northeast of the old town. Follow the locals to the nearby bus and tram stop, from where several services (including trams 1 and 2) head into the centre. You can buy tickets for the *George Ots* from the port and for the *Tallinn* from the Tallink office by Hotel Palace. Hydrofoil tickets are sold both at the port and in the Viru Hotel. Information about ferries to Stockholm is available from the Estline office at Aia 5a (66 65 79).

There is an acknowledged shortage of hotels in Tallinn, particularly at the lower end of the market. The Family Hotel Association (Vanu Viru; tel/fax 44 11 87) in the old town can arrange private accommodation. The nearest camping facilities are at the Kloostrimetsa campsite (23 86 86) near the cemetery in Pirita, 7 miles/11km around the bay northeast of the city and accessible on bus 34 from Viru väljak.

The following hotels are listed in ascending order of cost.

Lembitu, Lembitu 3 (44 12 91). Basic, but with rooms for under $5.

Agnes Youth Hostel, Narva maantee 7 (43 88 70). About $13 per person, open April to September. Reservations recommended.

Vitamiin, Narva maantee 7 (43 85 85). Clean, comfortable rooms above the Vitamiin shop. $30 single, $40 double.

Kungla, Kreutzwaldi 23 (42 14 60). A Soviet relic with resident mice helping to control the cockroach population, and double rooms for around $40. A last resort.

Viru, Viru väljak (65 20 81). A former Intourist establishment better known as Hotel Virus. All the drunken Finns wash up here, as do the city's prostitutes. Still, it's comfortable if you can get a room; even though the standard rate is $115 for two, the place is usually full of Finns on package tours. Besides several bars and restaurants (the view from the one on the 22nd floor is better than the food), it has a sauna and useful information desks.

Palace, Vabaduse väljak 3 (44 47 61). A 19th-century gem restored with Scandinavian money and now the best of Tallinn's hotels. If you can't afford the $200-a-night rooms, splash out in the restaurant, which is dazzlingly good; it used to be the very best in the Soviet Union. Hard currency or a robust credit card essential.

EATING AND DRINKING

If there's one thing to thank the Finnish tourists for, it's that their custom has helped make Tallinn the best place to eat in the Baltics. In addition to spectacular cuisine — in terms of taste and price — at the Palace, there are plenty of atmospheric places in the old town, and an increasing number of new places.

Vana Toomas, 8 Raekoja Plats (44 58 18). In a tastefully decorated cellar oozing with atmosphere and delicious food. A good place to try local specialities. Friendly waiters and jazz at weekends.

Maharajah, Raekoja plats 13. An English-Indian restaurant serving superb Asian food — the best between Pakistan and the East End of London. Moderately expensive (currently hard currency only) but probably the best in town.

Eeslitall, Dunkri 4, off Kullassepa. A small, friendly and buzzing restaurant with better-than-average Estonian food; the cellar bar down below is open late.

Reeder Restoran, Vene 33. Decent, meat-oriented menu. Reasonable prices, novel décor, less grasping waiters than elsewhere.

Bistro, Narva maantee 6. A partly Swiss-managed fast food bar, serving a mix of salads, pasta and other simple meals. Good value, closes early.

Drinking. Old Tallinn is full of cosy cellar bars, where you can while away a pleasant evening; some double up as restaurants. Particuarly recommended are Karikabaar, at the corner of Kuninga and Suur-Karja (with dancing later on) and Bar Viarosse at Lai 23, in a gorgeous 15th-century building. Western-style bars tend to be pricey: one such is the Mundi (Mundi 3), which attracts a young and trendy crowd and is very busy at weekends.

Tallinn is famous for its cafés (*kohvik*); indeed its first one opened in 1702, before even Paris had one. There are a couple of good examples on Pikk and another at Harju 48, which has a garden; try also the Moskva in Vabaduse väljak.

EXPLORING

Tallinn's old town is a superb example of medieval urban architecture, with a mixture of styles reflecting German, Russian and Scandinavian influences. Many of the buildings have been converted into museums, offices, cafés and souvenir shops, but the squiggly cobbled streets still exude atmosphere.

Lai and Pikk are particularly rewarding streets to explore. Along Lai, the houses at numbers 23 and 29 are characteristic of the burgher residences of the 15th century and still have the pulleys used to raise goods to store rooms. Pikk, which runs parallel, has many interesting medieval buildings too, notably numbers 17, 24 and 16. The first is a gem of the Northern Gothic style: visit the History Museum inside just to get a closer look at the marvellous interior. Beyond the Oleviste church, a 16th-century bastion called Paks Margareta (Fat Margaret) commands the northern end of Pikk near the seafront; it was used as a jail for political prisoners at one time. Near the bottom of Pikk on Pühavaimu, Tallinn's most notable Lutheran church (Pühavaimu Kirik or the Holy Trinity Church) has a superb altar, painted by Bernt Nothe in the 15th century.

Raekoja plats, the main square in the old town, is dominated by the Town Hall (Raekoda), completed in 1404 and one of the greatest Gothic buildings of its kind in Northern Europe. Its weathervane (the 16th-century original of which is in the City Museum) represents a soldier, Vana Toomas, who guards the city and is the symbol of Tallinn. There is also an apothecary's shop in the square, in operation for more than 500 years and said to have been used by Peter the Great.

For some of the best views of Tallinn, climb the Kiek-in-de-Kok (Peek-into-the-Kitchen) Tower, part of the old city wall at the southern edge of the centre. The museum inside traces the history of the capital from the 13th century onwards, with a few good models of the old town.

Toompea Hill. At the southern end of Pikk, Pikk Yalg and Luhike Yalg ('long leg' and 'short leg') connect the lower town to Toompea Hill. Climbing through the medieval townscape to the summit is like walking through a Gothic fairytale. Pastel-washed houses merge with jocular twirls of iron, and ornate gutters droop from steep red roofs.

Toompea itself is on a limestone plateau which, according to legend, is the grave mound of the folk hero Kalev, made by his mother whose tears formed the lake beyond. Toompea Castle presides over the hill and the republic — it is the seat of the Estonian parliament. The bulky Alexander

Nevsky Cathedral, at the top of Pikk jalg, is a rather more incongruous sight: the 19th-century Russian Orthodox church comes complete with onion domes. Walk up Kohtu east from the cathedral to a platform, which provides yet more panoramic views of Tallinn's roofs and spires.

Kadriorg Park. About a mile east of the centre along Narva maantee, Kadriorg Park is an excellent place to watch the locals relaxing. You can also visit the Kadriorg Palace (Kadrioru Loss), a delicious 18th-century Baroque mansion, built at the request of Peter the Great in honour of his wife Catherine. It is now an art gallery, open daily except Tuesdays. Traditional and popular song festivals take place periodically in the park, including a folk festival every year towards the end of July. Tram 1 or 3 from Pärnu maantee runs along Narva maantee, within spitting distance of the park.

Ethnography Museum. At Rocca al Mare, 4 miles/6km west of the city, the Ethnography Museum has exhibitions of rural wooden architecture, mostly dating from the 18th and 19th centuries. It opens daily from May to October; folk and dance concerts are staged on weekend mornings. Take bus 45 from Vabaduse väljak.

Pirita. To most locals, Pirita (north of Kadriorg Park) means beaches. If you consider the sea too dirty or too rough for bathing (most people do), you can hire boats at the Yachting Centre built for the 1980 Olympic regatta, or stroll in the nearby pine forest. Take buses 1, 8 or 34 from Tallinn.

ENTERTAINMENT

Tallinn has its own accomplished opera company which performs at the Opera and Ballet Theatre on Estonia puiestee. The Estonia Concert Hall, next door, has a fairly full programme, and smaller concerts are held in the old Town Hall in Raekoja plats and the nearby St Nicholas (Niguliste) church. A free handout called *What? Where? When? In Tallinn* provides a fairly comprehensive list of cultural events.

Several of Tallinn's beer cellars metamorphose into discos late at night, or have a club attached: one such is the Eeslitall Baari, perhaps the liveliest place in town and with a mixed clientele (including sailors). It is open into the early hours.

SHOPPING

Cultural freedom is not completely new to the Estonian capital, and the shops were always far better stocked than in rest of the old Soviet Union. Even so, shopping in Tallinn is still a good deal more rewarding than it used to be, with a growing number of places selling things you might actually consider giving to friends. Most arts and crafts shops are in the old town, with several along Pikk including numbers 9, 18 and 27; amber can be a good buy and is not too expensive. One of the city's best bookshops is Lugemisvara at 1 Harju, which has English-language titles and guide books. You can buy traditional Estonian music at the record shop in Raekoja plats.

Most shops open 9am-6pm, Monday to Friday, with slightly shorter hours on Saturday.

HELP AND INFORMATION

Tourist Information: the city tourist office (Kinga 6, near Raekoja plats) is fairly new but tries hard to meet the new demand for tourist information. Or try Estonian Holidays, a travel agency at Viru väljak 4. *Tallinn This Week* is a good source of general information, with listings, etc.

Communications: the main post and telephone office is at Narva maantee 1, on Viru väljak. The post office opens 8am-8pm Monday to Saturday, but you can make calls daily 7am-10pm.

Money: good rates at Tartu Kommertspank at Dunkri 9, open 9am-5pm. American Express is represented by Estonian Tours at Roosikrantsi 4B (44 20 34).

Central Hospital: Ravi 18, south of downtown.

Embassies and Consulates. *UK:* Kentmanni 20 (tel 45 53 28/53, fax 29 81 07).
USA: Kentmanni 20 (45 50 05, 45 53 13).
Canada: Tolli 3 (44 90 56).
Latvia: Tõnismägi 10 (68 16 68).
Lithuania: Vabaduse väljak 10 (44 89 17).
Finland: Liivalaia 12 (44 95 22).
Russia: Pikk 19 (44 30 14).

NARVA

Some 125 miles/200km east of Tallinn on the Russian border, Narva was once a moderately important trading town. Devastation in the Second World War means little of its medieval architecture has survived, though some restoration work has been done. Industry is Narva's main *raison d'être* these days. There's not a lot to detain you, but the town makes a useful stopping-off point if you are heading into Russia. Indeed Narva may as well be in Russia, the homeland of the majority of the town's inhabitants. In 1993 a controversial referendum in the town voted for autonomy from Tallinn.

The main attraction is Narva Castle, by the river, which dates from the 13th century and contains a modest museum. Art festivals are held in the castle grounds, and painters display their work in the open air. There is a pleasant café in the roofed gallery of the Western Citadel.

Narva lies on the main road and rail route to St Petersburg (90 miles/144km east) and is therefore easy to get to by bus or train. There is little to choose between the town's two hotels, the Narva (Pushkini 6) and the Vanalinn (Koidula 6), both a short walk from the castle.

TARTU

Situated 110 miles/176km southeast of Tallinn, Tartu is the oldest — and undoubtedly the most interesting — of Estonia's provincial towns. The large and lively student population is a great asset to the city's atmosphere too. Despite having been razed to the ground more than 50 times, Tartu retains some fine architecture, much of it classical in style.

The centre of the city occupies the west bank of the river Emajogi, with Raekoja plats the focus of the old town. Splendid classical buildings flank the square and include the 18th-century Town Hall. Just to the north is the heart of Tartu's ancient university, founded in 1632 and housed in another magnificent classical building on Ullkooli. There is an art museum inside.

Toomemägy Hill, to the west, marks the site of the first settlement and is topped by the 13th-century Vyshgorod Cathedral, a partial ruin containing a museum which traces the history of the university. You can enjoy good views over the town below.

Arrival and Departure. Four trains a day serve Tartu from Tallinn, taking three or four hours, but buses are much more frequent and slightly faster. The bus station is also more central — on Turu, four blocks southeast of Raekoja plats. The train station lies southwest of Toomemägy Hill on Vaksali, just under a mile from the main square.

Accommodation and Food. Hotel Park (Vallikraavi 23; 234-336 63), at the southwest foot of Toomemägy Hill, is the best place to stay. It has a modicum of character and rooms are comparatively cheap at around $30. Hotel Tartu, at Soola 3 (234-320 91), is just around the corner from the bus station and also cheaper.

For a relaxed evening, you can't do better than go to the Püssirohukelder at Lossi 28 (234-342 24), a wonderful cellar bar on Toomemägi Hill. The food is unexceptional but the décor and atmosphere provide ample compensation. Groups performing traditional song and dance entertain punters at weekends.

SAAREMAA ISLAND

To leave the beaten track, head for Saaremaa, Estonia's largest coastal island and once the favourite haunt of Soviet party officials. It is an attractive blend of pine woods and grasslands, with comparatively little modern development. The main town of Kuressaare feels thoroughly rural but has some interesting architecture, including a 14th-century castle.

To get to Saaremaa, take the ferry (which runs several times a day) from Virstu, 80 miles/130km southwest of Tallinn, to the island of Muhu, from where a three-mile causeway leads to Saaremaa. You can travel to Kuressaare direct by bus from Tallinn, which takes about five hours. There are buses also from Pärnu (3 hours) and Tartu (5 hours).

The tourist office in Kuressaare's main square can help with everything from accommodation to currency exchange (though you would do well to have changed money before your arrival). The best small hotels include Hotel Lossi (Lossi 27; 544 43) and Hotel Panga (Tallina 27; 577 02), a clean place close to the bus station. Don't leave town without visiting Café Veski at Pärna 19, in an old windmill just east of the main square.

PARNU

This town of 55,000 lies 80 miles/130km southwest of Tallinn, where the Pärnu river flows into the Gulf of Riga. Archaeological finds in the local museum show that Pärnu was inhabited in the Stone Age, although the 'modern' town dates from 1251. It retains a few interesting medieval features from its days as a Hanseatic port, but most Estonians are attracted more by the beach and the local health-giving mud than the architecture.

The resort area is deserted and rather forlorn out of season, but perks up when rich Scandinavian tourists arrive. Many people are still reluctant to swim through fear of pollution. The liveliest area is the promenade along the beach, where there are some pleasant bars and cafés and a few small parks.

Arrival and Departure. Pärnu is served by frequent buses from Tallinn, which take about two hours. There are daily buses also to Tartu, Riga and Vilnius. The bus station is slightly east of the centre on Ringi. Riga is four to five hours away by rail, with departures from the train station east of the bus terminal.

Accommodation. Given that Pärnu is a resort, it's no surprise that budget accommodation is limited. Hotel Pärnu at Rüütli 44 (244-421 45) is a characterless but convenient Soviet affair, located close to the bus station. Further east, Hotel Emmi (Laine 2; 244-220 43) is friendly and has hot water, though you'll find cheaper rooms at the Kajakas (Seedri 2; 244-430 98), just north of Rannapark and the beach.

Calendar of Events

January 1	**New Year's Day**
February 24	**Independence Day**
March/April	**Good Friday, Easter Monday**
May 1	**May Day**
May	Cultural Days, Tartu
June 23	**Victory Day (Anniversary of the Battle of Vonnu)**
Late June	**Midsummer Day**
June	Estonian Song Festival, attracting 30,000 performers and staged in both Tallinn and Tartu; held every five years, with the next in 1994
July	Music Festival, Pärnu
September	Flower Fair, Tallinn
October	'Tartu Autumn' Rock Festival, Tartu
November	International Music Festival, Tallinn
December 25	**Christmas Day**
December 26	**Boxing Day**

Public Holidays are shown in **bold**.

Latvia

Riga

Population: 2.7 million   **Capital: Riga (population 917,000)**

Latvia, about the size of Scotland, will never win any prizes for scenery: pine and birch forest covers well over a third of the land, punctuated by over 4,000 lakes and a staggering 12,000 rivers. The rest is often dull wide open space, given over to agriculture or industry. Under Soviet rule, Latvia produced some of the finest consumer goods in the USSR and earned itself the title 'workshop of the Baltic'.

Latvia has found it harder than the other Baltic Republics to shake off its Marxist past. This is due to both economic mismanagement — exacerbating the huge drops in salaries and industrial output and rising unemployment — and political considerations: given that almost half of the population is Russian, there is a large body of people that is not entirely keen on a total divorce from all that the old Soviet Union stood for.

Most of Latvia has changed little since independence. The biggest advances have been made in Riga, visible in both the reconstruction work and the rise in organised crime, which has won the capital a reputation as a Wild West city. For most visitors, however, Riga is one of the loveliest cities in Europe; before the war it was known as the 'Paris of the Baltic', not altogether unreasonably. There are other historical towns worth exploring too, and the wooded gorge of the Gauja National Park is one of the most scenic spots in the whole region.

CLIMATE

Latvian weather is invigorating, changeable and wet. The best time to visit is in August or September, when the wind drops and the sea is warm. June and July tend to be rainy: go prepared as you would for a capricious English summer. Winters are harsh and long, with thermals essential.

HISTORY

The people of Latvia have shared with the Estonians the burden of occupation by foreigners. In the 11th and 12th centuries they were dominated by crusading Teutonic Knights, who left an indelible mark on the country in the form of solid merchant houses and the Lutheran faith. Half the population was German even in the early 20th century, and German agricultural practices persist in the orderly farms that stretch across the country.

Like its Baltic neighbours, Latvia was ruled by Sweden in the 17th century and annexed by Russia in the 18th, but then refused to associate with the Bolsheviks in 1919. The country was devastated in the First World War, losing about a fifth of its population. Ever-resilient, however, Latvia was one of the most prosperous countries in Eastern Europe by the 1930s. 'Sovietisation' after 1940 set the country back initially, but the construction of factories gradually brought comparative prosperity, as well as shocking pollution and a huge influx of Russian immigrants.

Independence. Latvia's Communist Party was always more loyal to Moscow than others in the region. Even so, Party officials made up about a third of the members of the Popular Front which was formed in July 1988 and led Latvia into independence. Following victory for the Popular Front in elections in March 1990, an alliance of communists and the military began a propaganda campaign against the government. Events came to a head with an attempted coup in January 1991, when Soviet troops began seizing key buildings in the capital and barricades were set up outside the Communist Party headquarters. The coup failed and Latvia declared independence in August of that year.

Independence did not bring political stability to Latvia and the first elections were held only in June 1993. Latvian Way, a coalition of moderate nationalists won a surprisingly comfortable victory — surprising because it was led by Antolys Gorbunovs, once a secretary of the Communist Party. The more radical National Independence Movement coming a poor second. Support for the Popular Front totally collapsed — as elsewhere in the region, it had been a broad coalition useful for ousting but not holding onto power.

THE PEOPLE

Letts, the native people of Latvia, make up 54% of the population, Russian-speaking minorities around 45% and other Slavs (mostly Poles) a mere one in a hundred.

With such a large number of Russian inhabitants (they are the majority in the country's six biggest cities), the issue of race has kept a high profile in Latvian politics. One in three Russians voted for independence (the idea of returning home certainly doesn't hold much appeal), and many have made an effort to learn the official language — this is the only way they are likely to be successful in business or government. But they continue to campaign for increased rights: in the 1993 elections only about 40% of non-Latvians had the vote. Concord, the single multi-ethnic political grouping in Latvia, came third.

Language. Latvian has been the official language since 1988, but far more

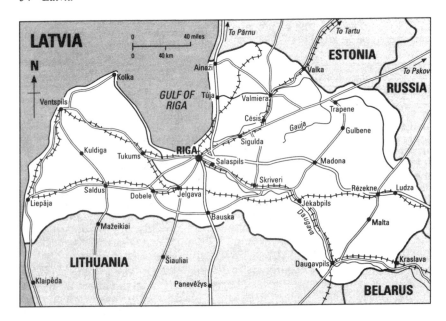

people speak Russian than the native tongue. This is due both to the number of Russians in the country and the fact that most native Latvians speak good Russian (though they may not like to admit it). The correct pronunciation of consonants should enable you to deal adequately with most Latvian words:

c — as ts
j — as y
ĝ — j
ņ — ny
č — ch
š — sh
ž — s as in measure

Useful words and phrases include:

yes — *jā*
no — *nē*

hello — *sveicināti*
goodbye — *uz redzēšanos*
please — *lūdzu*
thank you — *paldies*

how much? — *cik?*
do you speak English? — *vai jūs runājat angliski?*
airport — *lidostu*
train station — *dzelzcela staciju*
market — *tirgus*
hospital — *slimnīca*

Air. Baltic International Airlines and Latvian Airways provide a service between London Gatwick and Riga on alternate days. SAS (071-734 4020) flies to Riga from the UK and North America via either

Copenhagen or Stockholm. Finnair offers regular flights, but these require an overnight stop in Helsinki. Connections from Germany are better, with Lufthansa flying from Frankfurt and Hamburg Airlines from Hamburg and Berlin. Conti-Flug operates from London City via Berlin.

Direct flights also operate from New York on American Trans Air, via Belfast in Northern Ireland (but Irish travellers should note that the airline is not permitted to sell tickets between Belfast and Riga only).

As well as the Eastern European specialist agents listed in the introduction, try Amber Travel at 10 Victoria Terrace, Royal Leamington Spa CV31 3AB (tel 0926-431134, fax 431040), which specialises in flights to Riga.

Train. There is a daily train from Berlin to Riga via Warsaw and Vilnius, with several additional trains from the Lithuanian capital. Direct trains also run from Kaliningrad and Kiev. The journey from Moscow takes 13 hours; from St Petersburg, 11 hours. There are three or four trains a day from both cities. If you are heading to Russia, check visa requirements before you travel.

Bus. Travelling by bus is faster than by train, and usually less crowded. There are four or five buses a day from Tallinn and Vilnius, taking six hours from both cities, as well as from other Estonian and Lithuanian towns. The Warsaw-Tallinn bus stops in Riga too, but runs just once a week.

Driving. The quickest route from Tallinn to Riga takes about six hours, along the M12 via Pärnu and crossing the border at Ainazi. The M12 between Vilnius and Riga (via Panevėžys) is not quite as fast but still direct and straightforward.

Boat. If you are travelling by car, you can save long waits at the border (but not any money) by taking the *Mercuri-I* car ferry from Kiel in Germany. Journey time is 40 hours. The cheapest one-way passenger fare is $160, plus $140 for a car.

Ferries run once a week from Stockholm, taking 18 hours. The cheapest fare on the *Ilich*, operated by Baltic Express Line, is $140, but most fares are in the region of $200.

Red Tape

UK citizens do not need a visa, but at the time of writing US and Australian nationals do. Note that a Latvian visa is also valid for Estonia and Lithuania.

The usual cost of a visa is £7 (£10 for postal applications), though Americans pay no fee. You may apply for one on arrival at the airport, but are advised to obtain one in advance from a Latvian mission abroad:

UK: 72 Queensborough Terrace, London W2 3SP (tel 071-727 1698; fax 071-221 9740), open 11am-3pm Monday to Friday.
USA: 4325 17th Street NW, Washington DC 20011 (tel 202-726-8213, fax 202-726-6785).
Canada: 230 Clemow Avenue, Ottawa K1S 2B6 (613-238-6868).
Russia: ul. Chaplygina 3, Moscow 103062.

Upon arrival, most travellers are granted a stay of three months.

£1 = LS0.90 $1 = LS0.60
LS1 = £1.11   LS1 = $1.66

The lats (LS) has been in circulation since May 1993, but you'll still find a few Latvian roubles (an interim currency) and even older Russian roubles knocking about. If you have dealings with a black marketeer, you can guarantee to be given out-of-date notes.

Life for visitors remains fairly cheap, despite the fact that prices previously in roubles have shot up and that there are still hotels and other establishments which insist on charging a 'foreigners' price' of two or three times the locals' rate.

Changing Money. US dollars or Deutsche Marks in low-denomination notes are the things to take. Travellers cheques are an even bigger problem in Latvia than in Estonia, and you can rely on a credit card only in a few top hotels and restaurants — certainly not for withdrawing cash at a bank.

Try to change money in Riga, where branches of the Bank of the Republic of Latvia tend to offer the best rates. Bureaux de change have opened up in hotels, stations and so on, but watch out for high commission charges.

Teaching prospects are still fairly limited, but improving all the time. The English Language Club in Riga (c/o Rita Liepina, Riga district, p.n. Ragana 10-7, 2144-Latvia) teaches five to ten year olds and any native speakers willing to fund themselves in Riga would be very welcome to take some classes.

Voluntary work is also a possbility. The International Exchange Center in Latvia recruits English-speaking volunteers for its summer projects near the capital Riga. Participants are needed to work on farms, restore castles and to work as leaders and sports instructors at children's camps; it even has opportunities for au pairs. No special qualifications are required. It is possible to apply direct to the IEC in Latvia at 2 Republic Square, 226168 Riga (registration fee around US$100) or through Concordia in the UK (8 Brunswick Place, Hove, Sussex BN3 1ET; tel 0273-772086), which also charges a fee.

Telephone. Latvia may be independent, but most international telephone calls are still connected via Moscow. The least stressful way to phone, either within or from Latvia, is to do it through your hotel. Going to the nearest public telephone office is likely to involve a wait of several hours, even if you are phoning within Latvia. In Riga, if you are willing to pay slightly over the odds, there is a new telecommunications office which can connect your call almost immediately.

Some payphones can be used for long-distance calls, but until the telecommunications network is given an overhaul (foreign companies are competing for the privilege), using them is likely to lead only to frustration. Most take tokens known as *žetoni*, available at the post office, though you still find some demanding 15-kopeck coins.

Useful numbers: fire brigade 01, police 02, ambulance 03.

Mail. Sending an airmail letter or postcard abroad from Latvia doesn't cost more than about $0.10, but delivery can take 10-14 days. The Latvian for post office is *pasts*, usually with a *telegrafs* office attached for the sending of telegrams.

Getting Around

The rail network serves most main towns, but — as in the other Baltic states — buses are the best way to explore the country, being more frequent and faster than the trains. For short journeys covered by few buses, you could consider taking a taxi.

Driving. Petrol shortages have become a feature of everyday life since independence, so fill up whenever you can and be prepared to queue. You'll have no trouble finding four-star or diesel, but unleaded petrol is uncommon outside Riga. The speed limit is 80km/h (50mph) in the country and 50km/h (32mph) in built-up areas.

Rented cars are in big demand, and you should try to arrange this in advance. In Riga, the main car rental desk is in the Hotel Latvija (21 25 05), although Avis has an agent at the airport (20 73 53). Car theft is a problem in the capital, so consider picking up a vehicle at the airport and heading straight out of town.

Accommodation

The hotel (*viesnīcu*) scene in Latvia is similar to that in Estonia, with wide-ranging and unpredictable prices, whether you're staying in high-class or simple places. While many hotels in Riga have been spruced up with the aid of foreign cash, in provincial towns you'll still often find charming hotels and pensions which have been around since before independence.

The Latvian University Tourist Club (LUTK), at Raiņa bulvāris 19 (tel 22 31 14; fax 22 50 39), offers information about youth hostels open in summer, but the network is still small. Campsites are also scarce (and basic), though in rural villages you should be able to pitch your tent in a field.

LUTK, as well as the tourist board, can arrange private accommodation in Riga and elsewhere, and the number of homes renting out rooms is growing.

Eating and Drinking

Eating is not a delight in Latvia. Hard rye bread, tinned sprats and unappetising cucumbers are depressingly common. Even so, you should get the chance to have at least one feast. Traditionally, Latvians prefer fish to meat, one of the best local dishes being *Riga Tel'noe,* deep-fried fish fillets stuffed with a mushroom and anchovy mixture. Smoked salmon (*lasis*) can be good too. Fish aside, pork and chicken dominate restaurant menus, though hare and rabbit are also popular: a traditional way of cooking them is with mushrooms, cheese, wine and herbs. Sausages (*desa*) tend to be of uncertain provenance and gristly. If none of the above sound tempting, try the soups (*zupa*), which are often a meal in themselves, or fill up on cakes such as *biezpienmaize*, bread with curd, or Alexander Torte, a wonderful raspberry-filled pastry.

café — *kafejnīca*

snack bar — *bufete*

menu — *ēdienkarte*

starters — *uzkoda*

meat/main dishes — *gaļas ēdieni*

fish — *zivis*

vegetables — *saknes*

bread — *maize*

cheese — *siers*

fruit — *augli*

ice cream — *saldējums*

drinks — *dzērieni*

tea — *tēja*

coffee — *kafija*

(fruit) juice — *sulas*

water — *ūdens*

Drinking. Latvia, particularly the Aldaris brewery in Riga, produces the only good beer (*alus*) in the Baltics. Mērnieku Laiku is delicious though quite bitter. Bauskas Tumsais, also brewed locally, is a dark beer.

Kvas, fermented ryebread water with a taste of honey sounds and looks unappealing, but is ideal for quenching summer thirst (despite being slightly acoholic). Riga's Black Balsam, on the other hand, is dark, thick and very potent, flavoured with ginger, oak bark and cognac among other things. Most people also consume vodka in large quantities.

You're advised not to drink the tapwater. See the general introduction for information on water purification.

RIGA

As you first approach, the Latvian capital resembles a typical Soviet city, with hulking great apartment blocks, muddy grey and dismal, scattered as far as the horizon. Hideous housing is punctuated by towers belching poisons and linked by an artless network of cracked concrete highways. Not only does the city look Russian architecturally: more Rigans are of Russian descent than Latvian. Ten miles/16km inland from the Baltic Sea, on the banks of the broad Daugava river, Riga was a major military and shipping centre in the former USSR. With a population of over 900,000, it is bigger than Stockholm and Helsinki and almost twice the size of the other Baltic capitals.

Now that the main street is named after Freedom rather than Lenin, a certain colour has returned to the cheeks of Riga. Its heart has never been less than handsome, with the austere good looks of Lutheran architecture. Many streets are pedestrianised and now dotted with smart shops, new cafés and restaurants. You can walk off the coffee and cakes by exploring bulky churches clad in silvery grey tiles and the Baroque mansions of Hanseatic merchants.

Despite restoration and reconstruction, there is an appealing shabbiness about old Riga, though this also acts as a timely reminder that the new prosperity has benefited only a minority of Rigans and has been achieved at a cost. Appalling poverty persists and the capital boasts some of the most notorious gangsters in Eastern Europe. But don't let this put you off. Riga offers a fine combination of old architecture, well-kept parks, culture and fun, which is enjoyed by surprisingly few tourists. Furthermore, some of the best things in Latvia can be visited as day trips from Riga.

CITY LAYOUT

Riga straddles the Daugava river, but its heart occupies the east bank. The main October Bridge (Oktobra Tilts) leads from Pardaugava, the industrial

RIGA
1 Three Brothers
2 Pūt Vējini restaurant
3 Guild Hall
4 Rīdzene Café
5 Reitern House
6 Freedom Monument
7 Post/telephone office
8 Latvija Hotel
9 Hotel Riga
10 Opera House
11 Hotel Saulīte
12 Hotel Aurora
13 Post Office
14 St Peter's church

quarter on the left bank, into Kalku iela, which bisects the old city (Vecrīga). This is a compact area — you can walk from one side to the other in quarter of an hour — bound on the eastern side by a tree-lined canal (Pilsētas kanāls) which was once the old castle moat. Doma laukums, overlooked by the cathedral, is the heart of the old town. Beyond the canal are predictable modern boulevards, principally Brīvības bulvāris which continues into Brīvības iela.

Maps. *Riga City Map*, a post-independence street plan showing transport routes, is available from kiosks and some bookshops: try Centrālā Grāmatnīca at Aspazijas bulvārus 24.

ARRIVAL AND DEPARTURE

Air. Spilva airport lies 5 miles/8km southwest of downtown. It is poorly equipped, though there is at least a currency exchange desk. Bus 22 runs into the centre every half hour.

Train. The main train station or *centrālā stacija* (23 21 34) is at the southern end of Raiņa bulvāris, on the edge of the new city. Information is also available from the travel desk in the Latvija Hotel.

Bus. The bus terminal (*autoosta*) is on Prāgas, a short walk southwest of the train station. Call 21 36 11 for information.

Boat. The boat landing stage in Riga is at Eksporta iela 1 (32 98 82), about a mile north of October Bridge.

CITY TRANSPORT

Buses and trams are decrepit but just manage to hold together a reasonable service; buy tickets from kiosks before boarding. There is also a waterbus service, most active in summer — the Daugava freezes over in winter. The most useful boats go to Mežaparks (see below), though it's worth taking any boat just for the fun of the ride. Boats leave from Piestantne (Pier) 1 by October Bridge.

Taxis fares are moderately high due to fuel shortages. Some drivers seem to take tourists only if they wave dollars or Marlboro cigarettes around.

ACCOMMODATION

Riga has a fairly good range of hotels, though some of the cheaper places have been spruced up. In summer, try to book in advance.

> *Latvija,* Elizabetes iela 55 (tel 21 26 45, 21 25 03; fax 28 35 95), by Brivības iela. A former Intourist hotel and an ugly 27-storey hulk of glass and plastic. Double rooms go for around $120.
> *Riga,* Aspazijas bulvāris 22 (21 60 00, 21 67 00). A stately 19th-century building in the old town, but noisy, decaying and poor value (around $120 for two). It also has a miserable restaurant.
> *Tūrists,* Slokas iela 1 (61 54 55). Big Soviet-style place in Agenskalus on the west bank, about 1km from October bridge. Clean and well-priced double rooms for about $25.
> *Saulīte,* Merķela 12 (22 45 46), near the train station. Drab but clean rooms for $25 for two.
> *Aurora,* Marijas 5 (22 44 79), opposite the train station. Most central of the cheap options, but definitely no frills.
> *Victorija,* A. Caka 55 (27 23 05). Just over a mile northeast of the old town, bus 23 from the train station. Basic but cheap and better than the Aurora.

Hostels and Private Rooms. The Youth Hostel Interpoint (33 21 31), run by the YMCA at Kalnciema iela 10-12, is open in summer only. It is on the west bank and accessible on bus 22 (same as for the airport). Facilities are simple but cost less than $10 per person. The BATS hostel at Grecinieku iela 28 charges a similar rate.

The LUTK, the Latvian University Club (Raiņa bulvāris 19) has information about student residences open as hostels in the summer. It also arranges accommodation in a family home, as does Koop Viesis at Merkela iela 12 (22 28 02).

EATING AND DRINKING

Riga's selection of restaurants and cafés improves almost daily. The pick of the city's best restaurants follows:

> *Pūt Vējini,* Jauniela 18 (22 88 41), just south of Doma laukums. A small

cosy place offering quality cooking and good service. It's popular so book to be sure of a table.

Rostock, Tērbatas 13. Pleasant atmosphere, reasonably tasty Latvian dishes, mostly meat.

Astorija, 16 Audeju iela, on top of a department store. Specialises in local dishes.

Forum, Kalku 24. A café-cum-restaurant, with predominantly young clientele, live music and passable food at good prices. Hard currency only at present (as is the casino upstairs).

Latvija, the restaurant on the 25th floor of the hotel isn't bad and there is a good view of the city.

Cafés. There are a few old-fashioned cafes in the old city, particularly near the cathedral square. The Doma, at the top of Smilšu iela, serves great pastries and other snacks. The Rīdzene at Skārnu 9, on the other side of the cathedral, has conspiratorial booths where lovers sip and simper. The Peter Gailis (Skārnu 21) is a pleasant enough place for a coffee break but the Balta Roze, at the southern end of Meistaru iela is much better: the coffee and cakes generate queues, so allow plenty of time.

EXPLORING

Unless you have a penchant for Latvian architecture of this and the last century, you should spend most of your time in the old part of town, where architectural styles from Romanesque and Gothic to Renaissance and Baroque rub shoulders. Narrow alleys link spacious squares, some of them so narrow that they can only just take two people.

Overlooking Doma laukums, a pleasant cobbled square with stalls and buskers, the Dome Cathedral is a magnificent building that was begun in the 13th century but took over 500 years to complete. The result is a conglomeration of styles which yet remains remarkably simple. The interior, with a towering Romanesque nave, is decorated with beautiful woodcarvings and portraits of Lutheran worthies. The cathedral also houses the fourth largest organ in the world, with a total of 6,768 pipes. You'll find a museum about the history of Riga in the cloisters.

A short walk northwest is Pils laukums and Riga Castle, built in the 13th century but added to since. It contains the Latvian History Museum, the Foreign Art Museum and the Rainis Literary Museum (the latter dedicated to Latvia's most famous poet, Jānis Rainis). But you'll have more fun strolling the streets. East along the nearby Maza Pils iela, a trio of houses (numbers 17, 19 and 21) known as the 'Tris Brali' or Three Brothers have lavishly decorated facades and are typical of Rigan medieval architecture.

On the other side of Kalku iela, Skārnu has a fine collection of churches, the gem being the Church of St Peter, a large Gothic building constructed mostly in the 15th century: it was the tallest building in the old city until Intourist built the Latvija Hotel. There is a viewing platform 72 metres above ground which gives a wonderful panorama over the rooftops of Vecrīga. The Museum of Applied Arts in the church opposite contains an excellent collection of Latvian arts and crafts. Following Skārnu around towards the river, you turn into Mārstalu iela, with two fine 17th-century houses: the mansion of Reitern at no. 2, named after a wealthy merchant and a Baroque mansion at no. 21, built by a burgher called Dannenstern. In nearby streets, Sarkanas Gvardes iela and Veepilsetas iela, several 17th-century warehouses still have their original hoisting equipment.

The compulsory sight in the new town is the Freedom Monument (Brīvības Pieminkelis) near the southern end of Brīvības iela. Erected during independence in 1935, the monument has been a focus for political activity since the late 80s and is the nearest thing Riga has to 'Speaker's Corner'. Outside the former Communist Party headquarters, there is a fragment of the Berlin Wall alongside pieces of the barricades which were set up in January 1991 in defiance of Soviet troops. While in the new town, it's also worth strolling along Elizabetes and Alberta streets, where there are several fine Art Nouveau houses.

Mežaparks. The city's largest park is set among pine forests on the shore of Lake Kišezers, 4 miles/7km north of the centre. There is an amusement park, several boathouses and sandy beaches, but strolling or sitting about usually provides ample entertainment, particularly when the park is busy at weekends. You can reach Mežaparks by waterbus along the Daugava or on tram 11 from Kr. Valdemāra iela.

Ethnography Museum. Situated by Lake Jugla and dedicated to rural Latvian architecture, this is the best open-air ethnographic museum in the Baltics. The buildings (of which there are more than 100) and artefacts date mostly from the 17th to 19th centuries. To get there catch bus 1, 18 or 19 from the bus terminal and get off at the Balozi stop. Lake Jugla is also connected to Lake Kišezers by a canal which is plied by boats in summer. The museum is open between May and October.

Motor Museum. Located at S. Eizenšteina iela 6, 5 miles/8km east of downtown, the Motor Museum (Motor muzejas) is the whackiest thing in Latvia, containing cars that once belonged to some of the most hated men in the world. In one corner, seated at the wheel of a damaged Rolls Royce, is a wax effigy of a panic-stricken Brezhnev: he crashed the car in 1980 and for years it was kept hidden in a garage at the Kremlin. In another, Stalin sits in the back of a Zil limousine which weighs seven tons and has windows 8cm thick. The museum opens 10am-8pm Tuesday to Sunday. To get there take the special bus which leaves from outside the Orthodox church on Brīvības bulvāris, most frequently at weekends.

ENTERTAINMENT

The Opera and Ballet Theatre on Aspazijas bulvāris (22 88 34) is Riga's greatest venue. Wagner was resident conductor at the opera house until he had to flee his creditors, and Schumann gave concerts here — though he wrote home once saying that Rigans knew nothing about music. Whatever the truth, there is plenty of choice as far as music is concerned. Regular and well-attended concerts and organ recitals are staged in the Dome Cathedral. The German choral traditions are still very much alive here and any concert in the cathedral could be one of the highlights of a stay in Riga. High calibre recitals are also staged at the Wagner Concert Hall (R. Vāgnera 4) and in the old Guild Hall (Amatu iela 6), home of the Latvian Philharmonic Orchestra where concerts are held in the splendid Gothic banqueting hall.

Several restaurants in Riga double as dance halls, where you can usually choose between enjoying a spot of live music, usually jazz and rock, or bopping to songs that your parents probably danced to. All kinds of music, from classical to traditional folk, are performed in the open air during the summer, including in Komunāru Park near the Latvija Hotel, at the Ethnography Museum and in Mežaparks.

SHOPPING

You can spend a surprising amount of time in Riga shopping, or at least window-shopping. Souvenir shops usually have a good line in cheap woollen socks and gloves as well as very cheap amber jewellery. Most of the best crafts shops are along Kalku iela, Brīvības iela and Aspazijas bulvāris, though you can also buy crafts at the Ethnography Museum, particularly when special fairs are laid on. There is a fabulous daily market held in and spilling out of old zeppellin hangars behind the bus station; most stalls sell fresh produce and other food.

CRIME AND SAFETY

Riga is much troubled by organised crime — there are said to be at least five drug-dealing mafia groups and bomb attacks while not common are not unheard of. The ill-lit city-centre streets are unsafe after dark and few people venture out. On the other hand, petty theft seems no worse than in any other Eastern European capital.

HELP AND INFORMATION

Tourist Information: the tourist office is at Brīvības bulvāris 36 (tel 22 99 45, fax 28 45 72). *Riga This Week* (published every three months) and the *Riga Success Guide* both have listings and other information.

Central Post Office: Brīvības bulvāris 21, open 24 hours. You can also phone or fax abroad and send telegrams from here. There is another office at Stacijas laukums 1 by the train station.

American Express: represented by Latvia Tours, Grecinieku Str. 22/24 (882 0020).

Hospital: Maskavas iela 122 (24 17 70).

Embassies and Consulates. *UK:* Elizabetes iela 2, 3rd floor (tel 883 01 13, 32 07 37; fax 883 01 12).
USA: Raiņa bulvāris 7 (22 70 45, 22 05 02).
Canada: Elizabetes iela 45 (33 33 55).
Poland: Elizabetes iela 2 (32 22 33).
Lithuania: Elizabetes iela 2 (32 15 19, 32 17 44).

AROUND RIGA

Jūrmala. Just half an hour by suburban train from Riga, the thought of a Baltic Riviera sounds appealing. The sandy beaches, backed by dunes and pine trees, are very pleasant. Sadly, being so close to the polluted Daugava river, swimming is not recommended. Still, it's a nice day out, with plenty of scope for strolls along the beach or through the woods.

Jūrmala consists of a string of resorts, the best of which is Majori, with lively shops and cafés along the main street. In summer, take the one-hour hydrofoil journey from Riga, which adds to the fun of the trip.

Jelgava. This is a sizeable town, with a population of 75,000, 25 miles/40km southwest of Riga. The only reason to visit is to see the fabulous Rundale

Palace, one of the finest buildings in the Baltics and once the residence of the Dukes of Courland (an order of Teutonic knights). It was built in the 18th century according to a design by Bartolomeo Rastrelli, the architect of the Winter Palace in St Petersburg. It sustained damaged in both the world wars, but has been rebuilt. There are more than ten buses a day to Jelgava, taking about an hour. Allow a day if you can since there are extensive grounds to explore.

Salaspils. Ten miles/16km southeast of Riga, Salaspils was the site of one of Hitler's death camps. Virtually all Riga's 45,000 Jews died here, as well as perhaps another 40,000 brought from other countries. A moving monument has been erected amid pine forest, the large stone figures the epitome of Soviet sculpture at its most potent. To get there, take the train to Dārziņi from where you can walk to the monument.

SIGULDA AND GAUJA NATIONAL PARK

Sigulda lies 30 miles/48km northeast of Riga in the gorgeous Gauja valley. A large area running northeast from Sigulda to beyond Cēsis has been designated as the Gauja National Park, taking in woods, caves and lakes as well as several old castles. For a dramatic view of the gorge, take the cable car from Sigulda across to the north bank of the river. Nearby are the ruins of Krimulda Castle and, at the bottom of the gorge, the Gūtmaņa Cave, with graffiti dating back to the 17th century. You can carry on east up the hill to Turaida Castle (past stables where you can rent horses), founded in the thirteenth century but heavily restored: not great to look at but the views from the main tower are magnificent.

Served by regular buses and trains from Riga, Sigulda can easily be visited as a day trip; but since the surrounding scenery is — by Baltic standards — more than just pleasant, you should consider staying overnight. The Sigulda Hotel at Televizijas iela 19 (97 31 21) offers cheap bed and breakfast.

Cēsis. If you want to explore further up the valley, take the bus to Cēsis, 25 miles/40km northeast of Sigulda. Parts of this old walled city, once a member of the Hanseatic League, have survived a turbulent history, and the castle houses a museum. Hotel Tērvete at Vienības laukums (223 92) offers simple accommodation.

WEST OF RIGA

Kuldīga. This town, 100 miles/160km west of Riga, was briefly capital of the German Dukes of Courland. There are many well-preserved buildings in the centre, dating mostly from the 16th to 18th centuries. Hotel Kursa at Pilsetas laukums 6 (33-224 30) has adequate rooms and an attached restaurant.

Liepāja. As Latvia's second port (with a population of over 110,000), Liepāja would not seem to have a lot going for it. But it is surprisingly provincial, has a few interesting old buildings and is a good place to stop off if you want to follow an alternative route to Lithuania. Buses run every couple of hours from Riga and take about four hours. You can stay at the Hotel Liva on Liela, with doubles for $20.

Calendar of Events

January 1	New Year's Day
March/April	Good Friday
May 1	Labour Day
June 23-24	St John's Day (Jāni). The summer solstice is Latvia's most important festival. Beer is brewed specially and people don flowers and greenery and sit around bonfires all night singing traditional songs.
July 2-4	Latvian Song and Dance Festival, Riga
November 18	**National Day**
December 25-26	**Christmas**
December 31	**New Year's Eve**

Public holidays are given in **bold**.

Lithuania
and Kaliningrad

Vilnius

Population: 3.7 million   **Capital: Vilnius (population 595,000)**

The largest Baltic republic once commanded a huge slab of Eastern Europe, stretching as far south as the Black Sea. Now, however, Lithuania's frontiers have shrunk to enclose a slice of territory the size of Ireland. The countryside, consisting mostly of plains and forest cut through by innumerable rivers, is about as dull as that of its neighbours, though inland from the dunes and pine woods, gentle hills bring some added interest. Trakai and Kaunas are both pleasant historical towns and the beaches around Klaipėda are better than in both Latvia and Estonia. But Lithuania's saving grace is Vilnius. More relaxed and friendly than Tallinn and Riga, the capital is set apart from its Baltic neighbours also by the strong Catholic bias of both the city's architecture and its people. The religious allegiance of most Lithuanians recalls the country's long-standing political and cultural links with Poland which, along with Kaliningrad — a curious, lost corner of Russia — flanks Lithuania's western border.

CLIMATE

The coastal climate is milder than that inland, but Arctic currents can bring frost as late as June. The hottest period runs from June to August, July being the warmest month. While August is the wettest inland, on the coast the heaviest rain falls in October. For the most pleasant conditions, travel in the spring or autumn.

HISTORY

The first known state of Lithuania was recorded in 1293, when a number of tribes joined together to resist the threat of invasion by the Teutonic knights. In the 14th century, under Grand Duke Gediminas (now recognised as the founder of Lithuania), the state's borders were gradually extended until they reached as far as the Black Sea. In 1410 a joint Lithuanian, Russian and Polish force defeated the Teutonic order, but it was the Poles who gradually established control. Following the Union of Lublin in 1569, a Polish-Lithuanian feudal state was formed, known as the *Rzeczpospolita.* This did not provide for long-term peace or tranquillity, however, and spates of plague and war brought decline. In 1795 the state was split up among its neighbours, with Lithuania being handed to the Russians, who held onto it until 1915, when the Germans drove them out. Lithuania was independent between the wars, then occupied by the USSR following the 1939 Nazi-Soviet Pact. Under Moscow's control, there was the inevitable process of industrialisation and colonisation, though not on a scale seen in the other Baltic states.

Independence. Sajūdis, Lithuania's main nationalist group formed in June 1988, led the country into independence with a haste which both outpaced the more tentative approach favoured by Estonia and Latvia and also greatly disturbed the Kremlin. Economic sanctions imposed by the USSR forced the suspension of independence for a time, but in January 1991 Vytautas Landsbergis, the leader of Sajūdis and effectively Lithuania's president, redeclared independence. A bitter battle with Moscow ensued, with an attempt by Soviet troops to take over key buildings in Vilnius, including parliament. But the coup against Gorbachev brought the Kremlin's resistance to Lithuania's independence to an end.

Landsbergis made a series of blunders after independence which resulted in divisions within his right-of-centre party and the loss of the parliamentary majority in 1992 to Agirdas Brazauskas and his Democratic Labour Party. The economic crisis had exacerbated the already shaky position of Landsbergis, but Brazauskas — former leader of the Latvian Communist Party — also won respect for his toughness over the handing back of land taken into collectivisation. In elections held in Februry 1993, in which Lithuanians chose the first president of an independent nation, Brazauskas won a sweeping victory. But while Lithuania now enjoys surprisingly good relations with Russia, the republic remains the poorest of the three Baltic states. Inflation, an unstable currency and an industry still trapped in a timewarp are pressing problems for the government.

PEOPLE

About 80% of the population is Lithuanian, 10% Russian and 7% Poles. Many Poles live in the southern Vilnius region, where they are actually in the majority, with their own schools and newspapers. While Lithuania has faced its own problems with its Russian and Polish minorities, anti-immigrant feeling has never matched that in neighbouring Baltic states. In 1992, Lithuania settled an ongoing border dispute with Poland and also gave a commitment to safeguard the rights of the Polish minority.

Language. Lithuanian is an Indo—European language like Latvian, with similar pronunciation but very different vocabulary. In Vilnius, a surprising number of people know English. A few useful words and phrases are as follows:

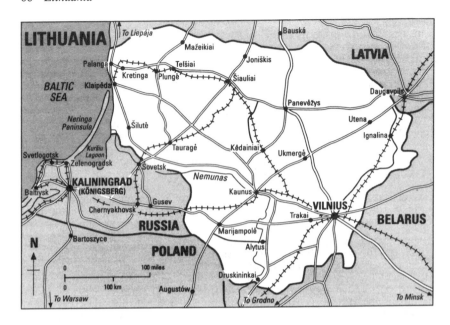

yes — *taip*
no — *ne*
please — *prašom*
thank you — *ačiū*
hello — *sveiki, labas*
goodbye — *viso gero*
how much? — *kiek?*

where? — *kur?*
do you speak English? — *ar kalbate angliškai?*
airport — *aerouostą*
train station — *geležinkelio stoti*
hotel — *viešbuti*
hospital — *ligonine*
street — *gatvė (abbr g.)*

Air. LAL or Lithuanian Airways (Lietuvos Avialinijos) flies to Vilnius three times a week from London Gatwick. A so-called Instant Purchase fare, which is non-refundable, currently costs about £250 return: call 0293-551737 for information. LAL also flies from other European cities, including Berlin, Frankfurt, Copenhagen and Budapest. SAS flies daily from Copenhagen, Lufthansa three times a week from Frankfurt, Hamburg Airlines twice weekly from Hamburg (via Berlin) and Lot three times a week from Warsaw.

See page 40 for a list of agencies in Britain specialising in travel to Lithuania and the other Baltic Republics.

Rail. Vilnius, the rail hub of the Baltic region, and the towns of Kaunas and Klaipėda are easily reached by rail direct several times daily from Riga (6-8 hours) as well as St Petersburg (14 hours), Moscow (13 hours) and Warsaw (12 hours). A sleeper train runs every day from Berlin (22 hours) via Warsaw, with services daily also from Prague (36 hours) and Tallinn (14 hours on the 'Chayka' bound for Minsk) and twice-daily from Kaliningrad (6 hours). Note that most trains from Warsaw go via Grodno in Belarus, in which case you will almost certainly need a transit visa: check before departure.

Bus. There are daily international services from Tallinn (12 hours) and Riga (6 hours), Warsaw (9 hours), Berlin (17 hours), Kaliningrad (5 hours) and Minsk (4 hours). Book as far in advance as possible, particularly if you're travelling from Poland. Some buses from Warsaw go via Belarus, so check visa requirements.

Driving. The main border crossing from Poland is via Ogrodniki/Lazdijai, but delays are notorious. You may find it quicker to travel via Belarus or to take a ferry from Germany.

Boat. A boat (mostly cargo, few cabins) operates daily from the German port of Mukran, near Sassnitz on the island of Ragen, to Klaipėda, taking about 20 hours. Book at least a month ahead, preferably more in high season. For further information, contact Deutsche Seereederei Rostock (DSR) in Sassnitz (tel 38392-452 21). Another ferry (*Mercury I*) connects Kiel, also in Germany, with Klaipėda every Thursday, taking nearer 30 hours. It has many more cabins than the other boat, but these are booked up sometimes months in advance.

Red Tape

British passport holders do not require a visa, but most other foreign nationals do. Transit visas are issued free of charge, but a normal tourist visa costs £10. This may be obtained either at the border or from a Lithuanian consulate abroad, and is also good for visits to the other Baltic states. You can extend your stay at the Emigracijos Tarnyba, Verkių 3 in Vilnius (75 64 53). Lithuanian consulates abroad are as follows:

UK: 17 Essex Villas, London W8 7BP (tel 071-938 2481, fax 071-938 3329).
USA: 2622 16th St NW, Washington DC, 20009 (tel 202-234-5860, fax 202-328-0466).
Canada: 235 Yorkland Blvd, Willowdale, Ont. M2J 4Y6 (416-494 4099).
Australia: 26 Jalanga Crescent, Aranda, ACT 1614 (06-253 2062).
Poland: aleje Ujazdowskie 13-23, Warsaw (62-3194).
Russia: ul. Pisemskogo 10, Moscow 121069 (291 2643).

Money

lita = 100 centu
1994: £1 = 6 lita   US$1 = 4 lita

The Lithuanian currency, the lita, was introduced in 1993. The two-tier system of prices in the local currency for Lithuanians and in hard currency for visitors has not completely disappeared, but the system has certainly been simplified.

Changing Money. While US dollars in cash are easily the most useful (though deutschmarks are the accepted currency in the resorts around Klaipėda), changing travellers cheques is not as difficult in Lithuania as it is elsewhere in the Baltics. Big tourist hotels and several banks handle cheques, both in Vilnius and in large towns such as Kaunas. The main drawback is the commission, which can be as much as 5% in some banks.

Work. Opportunities for earning cash are limited in Lithuania, but are likely to expand as the economy becomes more westward looking. For teaching possibilities, try contacting the Siauliai Pedagogical Institute Lithuania, P. Visinskio 25, 5419 Siauliai (tel 370-143 4736, fax 143-5459), which employs teachers of business English; or the American English School, a/d 731, 2038 Vilnius (tel 12-265087).

Telephone. Telephone calls are easier (though more expensive) in Lithuania than in the other Baltic states, thanks to a newly improved system. In Vilnius, you should be able to dial direct from your hotel. You'll probably have to wait for at least an hour in a public telephone office. If you have an urgent message and don't have the time to waste, send a telegram from the nearest post office (*paštas*).

While the majority of payphones are worse than useless, the new cardphones, found only in Vilnius so far, are great — particularly for international calls. When making a long-distance internal call from the capital, dial 8 and wait for the dialling tone.

Emergency numbers: fire brigade 01, police 02, ambulance 03.

Fax. Some hotels offer this service. Expect to pay about $3 a page within Europe, $5 to the USA, plus a hefty fee of about $4.

Mail. Try to post all letters in Vilnius, from where they should reach European destinations in a week or ten days; within Lithuania the postal service is poor.

As elsewhere in Eastern Europe, buses are generally the best way to get about. Nevertheless, there is a well-developed rail network, the *greit* or fast services being the best for long journeys. For overnight trips, the four-person *coupe* compartments are recommended. Timetables in stations are minimalist, giving the starting-point and destination but rarely stops in between.

Driving. Roads are quiet since there are still comparatively few private cars and petrol is prohibitively expensive for those on local salaries. Unleaded petrol is available only in the main cities, but even then you'll have to hunt for it. The speed limit is 80km/h (50mph) on the open road and 50km/h (32.5mph) in built-up areas.
Car Rental: you can hire cars in Vilnius. Balticar has offices in Vilnius (tel 46 09 98; fax 75 89 24) and Kaunas (75 92 45), and rents out both Western and Eastern European models. International agents are conspicuous by their absence, but are sure to set up sooner or later.

Book ahead in summer if you want to be sure of a room. Hostel and private accommodation is only in its infancy. While this means you'll be restricted to hotels in most places, the situation can only improve (and the range of hotels is already reasonably good).

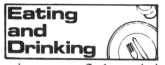

Eating and Drinking

Cuisine is rarely limited by political boundaries and Lithuanian cooking shares dishes with both Poland and Western Russia. *Zrazy* — roulades of beef or veal — are found all over the Baltics, but in Lithuania you may find a variation which is made with chopped meat, shaped like a burger and spread with a filling of, for example, grated horseradish root and sour cream. In winter the most common things on a menu are pork, sausages and pickled salads.

As in the other Baltic Republics, the cabbage is ubiquitous but cooked with great versatility e.g. with bacon, apples and lots of black pepper. A favourite dish is *golubtsy* (stuffed cabbage leaves), which dates back to the 14th century and was probably brought north by the Tartars. Potatoes also abound in many different forms, such as *bulvinai blynai* (potato pancakes) or *vedarai* (potato sausage), and even as a pudding (*kugelis*). A particular favourite is the *zeppelin,* a type of potato cake stuffed with meat and shaped like an airship (and usually saturated in grease). *Virtinukai,* similar to ravioli, are popular too, usually stuffed with meat but sometimes mushrooms (*grybai*) and cheese. Lithuania is not a bad place for vegetarians, though ostensibly meatless dishes are often fried in pork fat.

café — *kavinė*
menu — *valgiaraštis*
soup — *sriuba*
meat/main dish — *mėsos patiekalai*
fish — *uvis*
vegetables — *daržovės*
fruit — *vaisiai*

bread — *duona*
ice cream — *ledai*
drinks — *gėrimai*
beer — *alus*
tea — *arbata*
coffee — *kava*
(mineral) water — *(mineralinis) vanduo*

Help and Information

Lithuanian embassies abroad can send limited tourist information, actually photocopied pages from *Vilnius in Your Pocket,* an excellent guidebook published every two months, which you can pick up once you're there. It concentrates on the capital, but has general information too.

VILNIUS

The capital of Lithuania, draped over terraces in the broad, wooded valley of the river Neris, was founded as a fortress by Grand Duke Gedinimas in 1323. By the 16th century, Vilnius was one of the biggest and most important cities in Eastern Europe. Now the old and new town are closely merged, with towers and churches mingling with residential blocks and newly-planted trees.

Vilnius differs from Tallinn and Riga in that the architecture has been shaped by Catholic rather than Germanic tastes — more specifically, by the Italian branches of the Gothic, Renaissance and Baroque styles. Along the labyrinthine cobbled streets of the old town, imposing churches and palaces rub shoulders with more humble cottages painted in pastel shades. Impressive restoration work has succeeded (on the whole) in preserving the

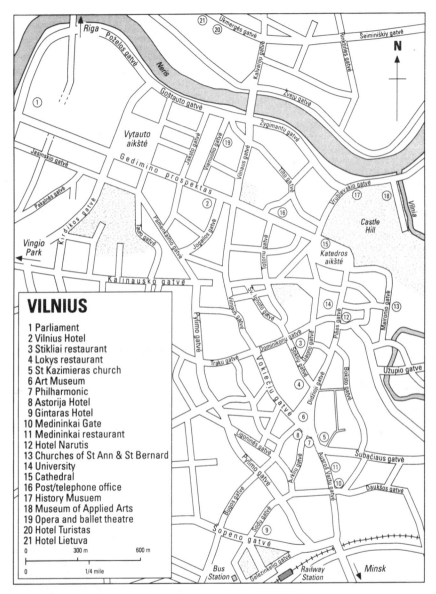

VILNIUS

1 Parliament
2 Vilnius Hotel
3 Stikliai restaurant
4 Lokys restaurant
5 St Kazimieras church
6 Art Museum
7 Philharmonic
8 Astorija Hotel
9 Gintaras Hotel
10 Medininkai Gate
11 Medininkai restaurant
12 Hotel Narutis
13 Churches of St Ann & St Bernard
14 University
15 Cathedral
16 Post/telephone office
17 History Musuem
18 Museum of Applied Arts
19 Opera and ballet theatre
20 Hotel Turistas
21 Hotel Lietuva

integrity of the exteriors while converting the interiors into shops, galleries and cafés.

The gap between the rich and poor is as wide as in the other ex-communist capitals, but the city centre lacks the *nouveau riche* atmosphere that afflicts some of its counterparts. Vilnius is lively and relaxed, and the local people seem to enjoy living here. There is a romantic air about the city and it is easy to get attached to the place.

CITY LAYOUT

The ancient and modern centre of Vilnius occupies the south bank of the Neris (all the less attractive workings of the city have been shunted across the river) and this is where you'll spend the vast majority of your time. The river Vilnia joins the Neris at the northeastern edge of the centre: Castle Hill (Piles Kalnas), which rises above the confluence, is a useful reference point. At the base of the hill, Katedros aikštė marks the heart of the old town, which spreads south from the square. Gedimino prospektas strikes west from Katedros aikštė as the principal road through the modern town.

Maps. There are maps in *Vilnius In Your Pocket,* available from news stands and decent bookshops (of which there are several on Pilies gatvė).

ARRIVAL AND DEPARTURE

Air. The airport (63 02 01) is 5 miles/8km south of the centre, linked to the train station downtown by bus. Facilities have improved greatly with the recent renovation; there is an exchange desk and duty-free shop. Lithuanian Airlines has an office at Ukmergės 12 (tel 75 25 88, fax 35 48 52).

Train. The railway station (63 00 86/88) is on Geležinkelio, due south of the old city. Trolleybus 2 runs to Katedros aikštė. You can book international tickets at Sopeno 3 (62 30 44), near the station, or in the Lietuva Hotel on Ukmergės, north of the river.

Bus. The main bus terminal (Autobusų Stotis) is at Sodų 22, next door to the train station. The timetables are pleasantly comprehensible. You can call for information on 66 04 81.

CITY TRANSPORT

You can easily walk around the city centre, but there is a good system of buses and trolleybuses, with a few battered yellow trams. Buy tickets before boarding at kiosks marked *spaudos.*

State taxis (with a green sign) are most easily hired from the official ranks, which are dotted all over the centre. Cabs hailed in the street are likely to be private (with a chequered signs), since these are more accustomed to looking for business. Don't be persuaded to pay in hard currency, often the habit of private cabs.

ACCOMMODATION

Hotels in Vilnius have been slow to shed their Soviet atmosphere, but there are a few new joint ventures, catering to the top end of the market. A few cheap hotels charge around $20 a night, though the easiest way to pay less than this is to arrange bed and breakfast privately or through an agency.

Astorija, Didžioji 35 (tel 62 99 14, fax 22 00 97). A good, partly Scandinavian-owned hotel in the old town, with rooms from $40 to $100.

Turistas, Ukmergės 14 (tel 73 31 06, fax 35 31 61). On the north bank (a 15-minute walk from the old town or take trolleybus 2 from the train station), next to the 23-storey ex-Intourist Lietuva Hotel. Large and ugly but comfortable, and not bad value with rooms for $70.

Vilnius, Gedimino pr. 20 (62 41 57, 62 36 65). In the old town, with annex down the road. The rooms are best in the main building, $30-60 for two.

Narutis, Pilies 24 (62 28 82). Characterful place in good location in old town, but restoration has increased room rates to over $30.

Gintaras, Sodų 14 (63 44 96). Gloomy, but convenient for the train station. Room prices range from $10 to $35.

BATS Backpackers' Hostel, Geležinio Vilko gatvė 27 (66 16 92), west of downtown. Usually open only in summer, $14 per person.

Litinterp, Vokiečių 10 (tel 61 20 40, fax 22 29 82). Can arrange bed and breakfast accommodation ($15 per person), plus flats to rent.

Norwegian Information Office, Didžioji 14 (22 41 40). Arranges rooms for $15-20 a night.

EATING AND DRINKING

There is a reasonable choice of cafés all over the town, particularly along Gedimino prospektas, but most cellar bars (*alaus baras*) are in the old town. One of the best is the Rudininkai, at Rūdininkų 14 south of the main square. The city's best restaurants are also concentrated in the historic quarter:

Medininkai, Aušros Vartų gatvė (61 40 19). In a restored 16th-century building with cellar. Reasonable food and café attached.

Lokys, Stiklių gatvė 8 (62 90 46). Also in the old town, with interesting interior. Specialises in game, including moose and wild boar.

Stikliai, Stiklių gatvė 7 (62 79 71). The best place in town, with a long-standing reputation dating from pre-independence days. Mitterrand is among the rich and famous to have dined here. It closes at 10pm and a reservation is essential.

Viola, Kalvarijų 3, on the north bank (just across the main bridge). Wonderful Armenian restaurant serving delights such as kebabs and meat salads.

EXPLORING

In Katedros aikštė, the most natural starting-point for a tour of Vilnius, the most striking sight is the squat and rather cumbersome Catholic cathedral (Arkikatedra Bazilika), dating mainly from the 18th century and with a facade lifted straight from the Parthenon. Until 1988 it was an art gallery and concert hall, but now it is once again a place of worship. Inside, the highlight is the Chapel of St Kazimieras, a Baroque confection of marble, stucco and granite.

A path leads from the square up Castle Hill. All that remains of the castle is the Gothic tower, from which you can survey the mosaic of steeples and roofs. It houses a branch of the History and Ethnography Museum, whose main building is at 1 Vrublevskio gatvė, at the bottom of the hill just north of the cathedral. The latter's collection covers Lithuanian history from the Stone Age up to the 20th century. Following the road east around the foot of the hill, you'll come to the Museum of Applied Arts (Taikomosios Dailės Muziejus) at Arsenalo gatvė 2, with a superb collection of Lithuanian decorative arts including furniture, jewellery and ceramics. About five minutes' walk further east, in the new town, the graceful Peter and Paul church sits marooned above a particularly arcane road layout by the junction of Kosciuškos and Olandų. Probably the finest example of late baroque architecture in Lithuania, its simple white exterior contrasts with the interior, which is like a wedding cake turned inside out and iced with stucco — a riot of frescoes, reliefs and life-size sculptures.

The key streets of the old city are Pilies and Didžioji, which run one after the other south of Katedros aikšte. Near the top of Pilies gatve, a narrow little street leads east to St Ann's church, a stunning example of 16th-century Gothic architecture. The church of St Bernard next to it is much more austere but has some beautiful frescoes. Occupying the block on the other side of Pilies is Vilnius university, dating back 400 years and retaining its charming courtyards and arcades. There is also an extraordinary Astronomical Observatory, built in the 17th-century and with a facade decorated with signs of the zodiac. Didžioji, which contains many interesting 16th-century buildings, finishes up at the former town hall — now the home of the Lithuanian Art Museum (Lietuvos Dailės Muziejus), dedicated to 20th-century works; the legacy of state-approved art still lingers. The Jesuit church of St Kazimieras, a huge Baroque creation, marks the beginning of Aušros Vartų, which is an attractive street running southeast to the Medininkai Gate (Aušros Vartai), the only city gate to have survived intact. On top perches a white madonna, dirtied by pollution.

All the streets around Katedros aikšte are worth exploring. The area southwest of the square once formed the heart of Vilnius' Jewish quarter. One synagogue (at Pylimo 39) and a Jewish museum (Pamenkalnio 12) recall the city's Jewish population — half that of the entire city before the second world war.

Gedimino prospektas runs west from Katedros aikšte right to the river. You can still see evidence of the 1991 independence struggles, though the barricades erected to defend the Parliament Building (at the western end) have been pulled down and the anti-tank ditches filled in. South along the river, Vingio parkas is the city's main park — a very pleasant place to stroll and with a huge open-air theatre where festivals are held.

One of the few things to tempt you north of the river is the Lithuanian State Museum (Lietuvos Valstybės Muziejus), near the western end of Ukmergės gatve. The collection includes folk costumes and crafts as well as superbly carved crosses and other religious artefacts. Other displays relate to 20th-century events, from the deportations of the Stalinist era to the 1991 nationalist uprising. Further west from the museum you can see the TV tower where 15 Lithanians were killed by Soviet troops in 1991; crosses commemorate those who died.

ENTERTAINMENT

If the opportunity arises, don't miss a performance by the Lithuanian State Dance and Song Company, the Lithuanian Chamber Orchestra or the Galve Village Choir; they are all renowned throughout the region. The main concert hall is the Philarmonic at Didžioji gatve 45. The Opera and Ballet Theatre is a modern building at Vienuolio gatve 1, northwest of the main square, and there is a puppet (Lele) theatre at Arklių 5, south off Didžioji.

For a more energetic night out, try one of the local nightclubs such as the Erfurtas (Architektų 19) and the Dainava (Vienuolio 4); both sometimes put on variety shows which can be good for a laugh.

SHOPPING

Amber, or fossil tree resin, is found throughout the world. However, the largest deposits are found along the Baltic coast, in sands which are 40-60 million years old. Lithuania has for centuries been the main source, and in ancient times was known as the 'Land of Amber'. You can buy amber jewellery in many shops in Vilnius, but try not to be palmed off with amberoid, which is small pieces of amber fused together. You also see imitation amber knocking about, but it is not a patch on the real thing and rarely fools anyone.

For this and other souvenirs, try the shop in the Art Exhibition Centre, at Vokiečiu 2 near the Lithuanian Art Museum, or Dailė (Gedimino prospektas 1). Folk craft festivals are staged periodically in Vingio parkas too.

HELP AND INFORMATION

Tourist information: there are several offices now dispensing information to visitors. Of longest standing is the Lithuania Travel Company at Ukmergės 20 (tel 35 65 26, fax 35 62 70), attached to the Lietuva Hotel. The *Norwegian Information Office,* at Didžioji 14 (22 41 40), is rather more convenient and does not deal solely with travellers from Norway. *Vilnius In Your Pocket* includes information on everything imaginable, from train timetables to the location of petrol stations.

Post Office: the central post office is at Gedimino prospektas 7 (61 66 14), with facilities for telephoning too, though the newer office at Vilniaus 33 (61 99 50/60) is generally more efficient and open 24 hours for telephone calls and telegrams. A fax service is available at the Foreign Tourists Service Bureau in the Hotel Lietuva (35 60 74).

Money: several banks on Gedimino prospektas will change money, including the Bank of Lithuania at no. 6 (open in morning only). Good rates also from Vilniaus Bankas: the branch in the main post office is the best one to use. American Express is represented by Lithuanian Tours at Selmyniskiu 18 (35 39 31)

Hospital: Siltnamiu 29 (26 90 69).

Embassies and Consulates. *UK:* Antakalnio gatvė 2 (tel 22 20 70/71, fax 35 75 79).
USA: Akmenu gatvė 6 (tel 22 27 24, 22 30 31; fax 22 27 79).
Estonia: Turniškiu gatvė 20 (tel/fax 76 98 48).
Latvia: Tumo-Vaižganto gatvė 2 (22 05 58).
Poland: Aušros Vartu gatvė 7 (22 44 44).
Czech Republic: Gediminio prospektas 54b-2 (62 97 13).
Russia: Juozapavičiaus 11 (26 16 37).
Romania: Turniškiu 25 (77 98 40).

TRAKAI

In the days when the Grand Duchy stretched from the Baltic to the Black Sea, Trakai was capital of Lithuania and one of the most important cities in Europe. Located on a peninsula between two lakes, 15 miles/24km west of Vilnius, Trakai is now a tranquil town with just echoes of its former life — including two castles north of the main square: one in ruins near Lake Luka, the other on an island in Lake Galvės. The latter is a magnificent red-brick Gothic complex dating from the late 14th century. It has been restored and contains an historical museum, with portraits of the Grand Dukes (the last pagan rulers of Europe) and a curious assembly of other objects. On summer Sundays, folk groups perform in the courtyard. You can also hire rowing boats, and other sports facilities for riding, etc. are being developed.

Look out for hot meat-filled pasties called *kibinai*, a local speciality: the surest place to find them is at the Kibininė restaurant. Although almost certainly Central Asian in origin, the pastie recipe was reputedly brought from the Crimea by a number of tradesmen employed as servants and bodyguards by the dukes. About 200 of their descendants, known as the Karaimes or Karaites, still live in Trakai. One of their few remaining prayer houses is at Karaimų 30, north of the main square.

Buses and trains serve Trakai frequently from Vilnius, journey time around half an hour.

KAUNAS

Sixty miles/96km west of Vilnius, Kaunas is Lithuania's second largest city, with a population of 440,000. Founded in the 11th century and at one time a major trading centre, Kaunas was the country's capital for most of the inter-war period. There are plenty of interesting buildings and several museums, and a pleasantly relaxed atmosphere. In addition, some of the best musical events in Lithuania are held in Kaunas.

The centre of the city lies in the triangle of land formed by the confluence of the Nemunas and Neris rivers, the historic quarter situated near the western point. The main street through the new town is Laisvės alėja.

Arrival and Departure. Buses run every 30 minutes or so from Vilnius (journey time two hours), with services also from Klaipėda and other main towns. The bus station is at Vytauto 26 (22 79 42), southeast of the centre. The train station (22 10 93) lies a couple of blocks further out, with frequent services to Vilnius.

Accommodation and Food. Hotel Baltija at Vytauto 71 (22 36 39), near the transport terminals, is comfortable and good value at under $30. There are several smarter places on Laisvės alėja, including the Nemunas at no. 88 (22 31 02). This street also has some of the town's best restaurants, or try Medžiotoju Užeiga on the old town square.

Exploring. The focus of the old town is Rotušes aikštė, lined with some beautifully restored German merchants' houses dating from the city's peak trading days in the 15th and 16th centuries. The most important buildings in the square are Baroque, including the old city hall and the cathedral (though the latter was originally Gothic). Kaunas castle, a short distance north, is in ruins, the 11th-century tower one of the few bits to have survived.

The city's best museums are on Putvinskio, north of Laisvės alėja. The Ciurlionis Art Gallery (closed on Mondays) at no. 55 contains works by Lithuania's most famous artist, M. K. Ciurlionis (1875-1911), who some say influenced Kandinsky and therefore indirectly had a hand in the development of abstract art. Opposite, at no. 64, is the Museum of Devil's Sculptures (officially the A. Zmuidzinavičiaus muziejus), which has a compelling collection of Lucifers from around the world, though most are wooden figures carved in Lithuania.

The former Russian Orthodox cathedral, at the eastern end of Laisvės alėja in Nepriklausomybės aikštė, is in a fairly poor state inside despite its handsome exterior. It functions as a concert hall and also houses a Gallery of Sculpture and Stained Glass. Further east still is Vytauto Park and, adjacent, Europe's largest and oldest city forest, Ažuolynas. The presence of the latter has been good for the town since there are heavy restrictions on construction and air pollution in an effort to preserve the centuries-old trees.

KLAIPEDA AND PALANGA

From Kaunas, the A228 follows the wide Nemunas valley 140 miles/224km west to Klaipėda, a major port with a population of around 200,000 but also a major destination for holidaymakers, particularly from Germany: while swimming in the murk of the Baltic Sea may not sound very appealing, the nearby beaches are some of the region's cleanest. Klaipėda was badly damaged by the Red Army in the war and little old architecture has survived (what remains is mostly south of the Danės river), but it is a cosmopolitan place and has about the liveliest nightlife in the country.

Buses serve Klaipėda from Vilnius, Kaunas and also Kaliningrad and the Latvian town of Liepāja. Trains run twice daily from Kaunas and the capital. Boats from Germany also dock here: see *Getting There.*

Hotel Klaipėda at Naujo Sodo 1 (199 60) is central and has good facilities including a fine restaurant. Rooms ($40 upwards) are often booked up in season. Less central but good value is the Vėtrungė at Taikos prospektas 28 (548 01).

Palanga. Fifteen miles/24km north of Klaipėda, this is the supposed gem of the Baltic coast, with its broad sandy beach, dunes and shallow sea. Locals gather on the long wooden pier in the evening to watch the sunset. Most accommodation is in the form of sanatoria, so you'll do best to visit on a day trip. There is an amber museum in the botanical gardens in the main town, north of the Ronze river.

Neringa. Klaipėda faces the Neringa peninsula, a narrow spit of land which extends 30 miles/48km and separates the Kuršių lagoon from the Baltic Sea; only the northern half belongs to Lithuania, the rest being part of Kaliningrad. Most of the peninsula, made up mainly of dunes and pine trees, is protected and the entry fee seems efficient in keeping a lot of Lithuanians away.

A road stretches the length of Neringa, giving access to fishing villages along the lagoon side and deserted beaches on the Baltic side. At the southern end is Nida, where the home of Thomas Mann, who lived here in the 30s, has been turned into a museum. The best way to reach Nida from the mainland in summer is to take a motorboat from Kaunas, a fun four-hour ride along the Nemunas river.

Boats take foot passengers and cars from Klaipėda across to the peninsula.

Calendar of Events

January 1	**New Year's Day**
February 16	**Restoration of Lithuanian State (1918)**
March/April	**Easter Monday**
March	International jazz festival in Birštonas in even-numbered years

May 2	Labour Day
May (1st Sunday)	**Mothers' Day**
June 14	Day of Mourning and Hope
July 6	**Day of Statehood (Anniversary of Coronation of Grand Duke Mindaugas in 13th century)**
Mid-July	Baltika international folklore festival, held in each republic in turn. Next in Lithuania in 1996. Well worth seeing, with many people wearing traditional costume.
November 1	**All Saints' Day**
December 25-26	**Christmas**

Public holidays are listed in **bold**.

KALININGRAD

The size of Northern Ireland, Kaliningrad is an anomaly, separated from the rest of the Russian Federation by the Baltic Republics and flanked on the west side by Poland — a pocket of the old Soviet Union marooned among changing Eastern European nations. From the 13th century until 1945, when Stalin annexed what was then part of East Prussia, Kaliningrad was a German province. But the expulsion of most Germans after the war and intense Russification means that little remains of its German past.

Home of the Baltic Fleet, Kaliningrad was always of too much strategic importance to be given over to any of the Soviet republics and was sealed off from the West completely for almost fifty years: foreigners have been allowed in only since 1991. It is still dominated by the military who, compared with a civilian population of about 800,000, number anything from 100,000 to 300,000 — as a result of the influx from former communist countries in Eastern Europe, no one really knows. The Kremlin could have a problem on its hands, given the restlessness of military commanders, the reluctance of thousands of troops to return home and the number of unused weapons which has spawned what is said to be one big arms market. A possible split between Lithuania and Poland has been discussed, though autonomy is also a possibility. For the moment, however, talk is mainly of a new free trade zone, and some optimists have already called Kaliningrad the 'Hong Kong on the Baltic'.

Not surprisingly, Kaliningrad does not have much of a tourist trade, though the number of German visitors is growing all the time and approached 200,000 in 1993. As one of the most curious places in Eastern Europe, Kaliningrad is a huge temptation just waiting to be explored.

Kaliningrad Town (Königsberg)

British bombing and the Soviet assault wiped out most of Königsberg, the old capital of East Prussia, during the war. Now it is mostly new, with spiritless open spaces flanked by grim concrete blocks — ugliest of all the House of Soviets, begun in the 1960s but never finished and known locally as either 'the Monster' or, less imaginatively, the 'Uncompleted Project'; there is a Danish scheme to cover it with green glass and turn it into offices. The few remaining old buildings include the former stock exchange by the filthy Pregol'a river, and the ruined red-brick Gothic cathedral where

Immanuel Kant is buried. The desire among some Kaliningraders to rediscover the German roots of the town has led to a few restoration projects, but these are almost totally dependent on foreign (mainly German) investment. Even so, some pre-war monuments have already been resurrected.

There is a severe shortage of accommodation in Kaliningrad and you can count the number of hotels just about on one hand. If the flow of German tourists continues, however, this situation should improve. Take dollars in cash to spend or exchange for roubles — in the banks or with one of the many moneychangers. Other street traders peddle amber. Kaliningrad has more than 80% of the world's amber, and you can pick up an amber necklace for under $10.

Help and Information. Note that virtually all nationalities require a visa to visit any part of the Russian Federation. For further information, contact the nearest Russian consulate or branch of Intourist, addresses below:

> *UK:* Consulate, 5 Kensington Palace Gardens, London W8 4QS (071-229 8027). Intourist, Intourist House, 219 Marsh Wall, Meridian Gate II, Isle of Dogs, London E14 9FJ (071-538 8600/5902).
> *USA:* Embassy, 1125 16th Street, NW, Washington, DC 20036 (202-628-7551). Intourist, Suite 868, 630 Fifth Avenue, New York, NY 10111 (212-757-3884).
> *Canada:* Consulate, 52 Range Road,, Ottawa, Ontario K1N 8J5 (613-236-7220). Intourist, Suite 630, 1801 McGill College Avenue, Montréal, Quebec H3A 2N4 (514-849-6394).

Poland

Old Market Square, Kraków

Population: 39 million　　　**Capital: Warsaw (population 1,700,000)**

In 1993, the communists made a comeback in Poland — retrieving some of the power they lost when the world of state socialism collapsed. This event is all the more remarkable given that the Poles never took to communism. Even when the Cold War was at its most frigid, and repression of rights at its most severe, the spirit of the Poles was never crushed. Stoicism seems to be a national trait. For much of its history the country and its people have suffered dreadfully, but the future at last seems to be bright.

Even under communism, the number of visitors to Poland was relatively high. In the main, however, they were not attracted by the best vodka and herrings in the world, nor the historic cities of Warsaw, Kraków and Gdańsk, nor the near-medieval rural life. Most tourists are of Polish descent, and visit the country to see relatives or search out their roots. Poland attracts few independent travellers. Poland, however, is a remarkable place to visit. Society is conspicuously open. The locals are friendly, and well-informed about Western affairs: during the 1980s, it was said that the only difference between Poland and the USA was that not every American approved of President Reagan. The ordinary Pole has long been allied to Western culture and ideals.

If Western visitors did suddenly descend upon the country *en masse*, tourist facilities in the country would be immediately swamped. But while numbers remain low, Poland is a rewarding place to travel. The rail and bus networks are extensive and inexpensive, if not exactly frequent. Above all. the locals are happy to offer friendship and accommodation; the openness and generosity of the people is startling. Be prepared to sample more varieties of vodka than you believed existed.

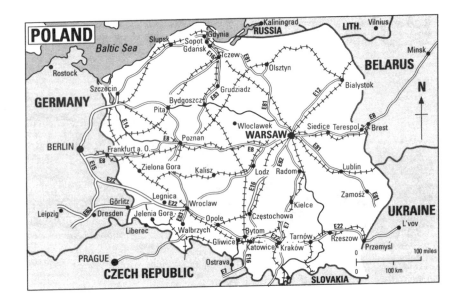

History. Poland's tortured history is largely the result of geographical location: a large plain, lying between acquisitive neighbours with seemingly insatiable appetites for territorial conquest. The nation is scarred by the fighting of a thousand years. The first Polish state was founded in AD 966, when the Polanie tribe, based in the area around present-day Poznań gained superiority over the surrounding Slavic tribes; their leader, King Mieszko I embraced Western Christianity, and the millenium was marked by the founding of a number of bishoprics around the country.

The 13th century saw the first waves of invaders to seriously threaten the Polish lands: two waves of Mongols were followed by the Teutonic Knights, who were not finally defeated until the Battle of Grunwald (1410). By this time, Poland had created a partnership with the neighbouring Grand Duchy of Lithuania through the marriage in 1386 of Prince Jagietto of Lithuania to the Polish Princess Jadwiga; by the 16th century, the Jagiellonian influence extended to Bohemia and Hungary. This was Poland's 'Golden Age', the zenith of the country's independent history, during which Polish territory included large areas which now belong to Belarus and Ukraine.

Decline soon followed: in 1655, the Swedes invaded and conquered most of Poland; the Turks invaded in 1672, but were defeated by the Polish army led by King Jan Sobieski at the gates of Vienna in 1683. In 1733, Russian armies deposed the King chosen by the Polish nobility and in 1764, still under the influence of the Russians, the last King of what is now accepted as an independent Poland — Stanisław August Poniatowski — was elected to the throne. By 1772, Poland had been cut dramatically in size in the 'First Partition'. A third of its territory was annexed in a carve-up by Prussia, Russia and Austria. Polish government continued to function in the remainder of the country: the Constitution of the Third of May, passed by the Parliament in 1791, was only the second such in the world, after the United States of America.

Russian and Prussian forces, however, fearful of a powerful Poland once more, invaded again. The 'Second Partition' (1793), and the 'Third Partition' (1797) wiped Poland from the map for over 120 years.

Polish culture, religion and language flourished despite the partitions. Although Napoleon created a puppet Duchy of Warsaw in 1807, it lasted just six years. Anti-Russian risings in 1830-31 and 1863-64 both ended in defeat. The outbreak of the First World War was soon followed by intense diplomatic activity by Polish nationalists, eager to impress upon the British, American and French in particular the importance of an independent Poland. The massive changes taking place in Russia were also used to the Poles' advantage, with the opposing factions more concerned with the internal power struggle rather than further territorial expansion into Polish areas.

Polish independence was achieved on Armistice Day, 11 November 1918, ahead of the Treaty of Versailles. The Hanseatic port of Danzig — attached to Germany for many years, but historically Polish — was declared a 'free city', giving Poland access to a sheltered Baltic harbour. Under the new Head of State, Jozef Piłsudski, Poland rapidly established distinct statehood and became an industrial nation. The chaos within the newly-formed Soviet Union led to an opportunistic war against the USSR between 1920 and 1921. Poland won significant parts of Lithuania, Belarus and Ukraine, much to the displeasure of the Soviet government. The Red Army retaliated, and Poland was delivered from Russian domination only by an eleventh-hour counter-attack — the 'miracle on the Vistula' — which drove the Soviets back to Brest. There followed a period of domestic instability, culminating in virtual martial law under Piłsudski in the 1930s, before international issues once more pressed on Poland.

A Non-Aggression Pact between Poland and Nazi Germany had been signed in 1934. Its terms were undermined, however, by the Nazi-Soviet pact of 23 August 1939, which contained a secret provision for independent Poland to disappear from the maps once more. A week later, on 1 September, Germany invaded Poland. This was the event which drew Britain and France into World War II, but their involvement did nothing to help Poland.

The Nazi occupation of Poland during World War II was horrific. Attempts were made to extinguish the Polish intelligentsia. Cities were destroyed, great numbers of people were pressed into forced labour or sent to internment camps. Resistance fighters, known by the insignia 'AK', were hunted in the country and ruthlessly suppressed in the cities. From the eastern territories of what was previously Poland, the Russian forces transported many hundreds of thousands of Poles to labour camps in Siberia and other remote corners of the Soviet Union. By 1942, the Nazi-Soviet alliance had collapsed following Hitler's march towards Moscow. Slowly, many Poles found their way back to the West under the banner of the Soviet-organized Polish Army. Men and women in the ranks of this scratch force fought alongside the Allies on every front of the war.

Inside Poland, the Nazi purge of the Jews led first to the establishment of the ghettoes. In these the evils of appalling food shortages were compounded by raging epidemics of typhus and other diseases. Then came the construction of the extermination camps. At first, hundreds of thousands of Jews, as well as Poles, were moved by trainloads and shot. In the winter of 1941/2, gas chambers were installed at many of the camps, such as Sobibor, Chełmno, Treblinka, and, most notoriously, Auschwitz south of Katowice. In Auschwitz alone an estimated four million people, from all the countries under Nazi occupation, perished. In all, some six million Polish citizens — half of them Jews — were exterminated by the Nazis.

In 1944, as the Nazi hold on Europe was loosening, the Polish Resistance saw its chance to strike at least one blow for freedom. As the allied Red Army approached from the east, the Poles in Warsaw planned to confront their liberators with a city already freed from its Nazi bonds: a Polish capital in Polish hands. Their underlying fear, based on an historical suspicion of Russian motives, was that if Soviet troops took possession of their principal city they would be unlikely ever to give it up.

The Warsaw Uprising began on 1 August 1944. It was an attempt to disrupt the Nazis from within as the Red Army advanced from the east. The Soviet troops, however, remained encamped on the east bank of the Vistula; the Uprising, after a two-month-long struggle that spawned tales of heroism that have assumed near-legendary status, eventually failed. Over 150,000 people lost their lives in those two months. Nazi vengeance was harsh. With dynamite and fire they set about obliterating what remained of the war-scarred capital. By the time the Red Army entered Warsaw to liberate its people, 93% of the city's buildings were either completely destroyed or ruined beyond repair. The rebuilding of Warsaw and Poland's other cities became a passionate mission in the decades following the War.

The ending of the War gave birth to a new Poland: a Soviet-galvanized People's Republic. The boundaries of the country, so often tampered with in the past, again took on an unfamiliar look. 'Poland' had moved some two hundred miles to the west. The Potsdam agreement between the Allies and Stalin still fuels bitter memories amongst some Poles. The western corridor, incorporating the cities of Szczecin and Wrocław, became part of Poland; thousands of Germans were forced to move. Meanwhile the eastern territories, occupied at the beginning of the war, remained in Soviet hands. The Poland that resulted was populated almost entirely by ethnic Poles, many of whom were moved west from areas taken over by the USSR to occupy the formerly German areas.

The People's Republic — a one-party state in all but parliamentary constitution where satellite parties of the majority communist (PZPR) had a thin veneer of independence — was to last over 40 years. Throughout this time, demonstrations against declining economic conditions were brutally put down by the authorities: June 1956 — Poznań, nearly 80 demonstrators killed; December 1970 — Gdańsk, 13 murdered; Szczecin the same month, scores dead. These clashes led to leadership changes: Gomułka replacing Bierut in 1956; Gierek taling over from Gomułka in 1970).

The election of the Archbishop of Kraków, Karol Wojtyła to the Papacy as John Paul II in 1978, led to a surge of confidence in the country and a new wave of agitation against the authorities. Proposals to raise food prices in 1980 led to nationwide strikes and the rise of the first independent trades union in eastern Europe: Solidarity (*Solidarność*). The movement, headed by Gdańsk shipyard engineer Lech Wałęsa, swept through the country on a wave of emotive support. The Government was forced to play for time and negotiate with a movement which pressed for greater civil liberties and a consequent reduction in the power and influence of the ruling party. For a year, Poland captured the headlines as no Eastern European nation had done before.

But the concessions gained by Solidarity were swept away by the imposition of martial law by the new leader, General Wojciech Jaruzelski, in 13 December 1981. Jaruzelski maintains he took this action to save Poland from outside invasion — Erich Hönecker and Leonid Brezhnev, leaders of

East Germany and the Soviet Union respectively, were making threatening noises — but many Poles believe it was merely the knee-jerk reaction of totalitarians. Martial law was relaxed in July 1983, although a number of stringent laws were implemented to maintain many of its effects.

It is not surprising that the effects of the ascendance of Mikhail Gorbachev in the Kremlin were felt in Poland ahead of the other Soviet satellites. Round-table discussions between the government, Solidarity and the Church in 1989 led to free elections. Many of the seats in parliament were reserved for the communists, but while Jaruzelski continued as president, the first non-communist prime minister was Tadeusz Mazowiecki.

Lech Wałęsa's hand was never far from the tiller, though, and he was elected president in November 1990 in a dismal economic climate of rampant inflation and rising unemployment. His first prime minister, the economist Jan Krzysztof Bielicki, implemented a series of austere and unpopular measures to try to rein in the economy. He was replaced by Jan Olszewski, who in turn gave way to the first woman prime minister, Hannah Suchocka.

The general election in September 1993 resulted in the electorate turning once more towards the former communist parties. A coalition between the former communists and the peasants' party led to the appointment of 36-year-old Waldemar Pawlak to the premiership. It is difficult to explain the renewed attraction of the communists to a people which spent 40 years under the state socialist yoke, but the notion that capitalism could provide an instant salve is thoroughly discredited. Together with coolness in the West towards Polish attempts to join institutions such as the EU and NATO, disillusion is rife in Poland.

CLIMATE

Although Poland lies in the temperate zone, the climate is continental in character: prolonged cold spells in winter, and hot in summer. Unusually, however, the year can be split into no fewer than six different seasons: a snowy winter; a milder period leading into a warm, sunny spring; a hot summer; the warm (usually) and dry (ditto) 'Golden Polish Autumn', and a colder and wet late autumn. Average temperatures in January vary between 0°C and minus 4°C; in July, 18°C is the norm, although 24°C is regularly achieved.

THE PEOPLE

As a result of the Nazi genocide, and the territorial changes and population dispersal which followed World War II, Poland has one of the most uniform ethnic structures in Europe. Non-Polish people — including Ukrainians, Jews, Germans, Russians and gypsies — account for only 1.3% of the total population; the remainder are all ethnically classified as Poles.

Meeting the People. Many Poles will regard you with fascination, and with most young people learning English, not to mention the spread of English-language popular culture, they seize every opportunity to converse in English (often with an American twang). The shadow of the last war still hangs heavily over the country. The Poles are sometimes accused of being over-sentimental, but considering the turbulence of their history this is hardly fair; 22% of the population perished, the heaviest proportional toll of any nation. War memorials are numerous but discreet, and it is striking to note that, half a century on, fresh flowers are still laid daily in remembrance on the graves of those who fell. There is, after all, hardly a single family in Poland that was not touched by the horrors of the war.

Language. Polish is a Slavonic language based on a phonetic (but initially terrifying) Roman alphabet. Whilst terms such as 'eksport' and 'disc-jockey' have transcended international boundaries, the vast majority of words will be completely alien to English-speakers. Any attempts to converse in Polish, however clumsy, will be welcomed by your hosts. Russian is taught as the second language in schools, although the majority of the populace is determined to ignore it. Even if you speak good Russian it may be injudicious to use it; try to converse in Polish or English first. German is spoken in many western parts of the country, but English is now gaining ground, particularly among the younger generations.

A good introduction to the language is *Say it in Polish* by Maria Grala (Warsaw, 1982), which is obtainable through specialist bookshops such as Collets and in Poland itself.

There are more letters in the Polish alphabet than English, and two letters together in a word can also change pronunciations:

ą	a nasal *on,* as in the French maiso*n*
c	*ts* as in ra*ts*
ć *or* cz	*ch* as in choose
ch	a gutteral *ch* as in lo*ch*
dz	*ds* as in car*ds*
dź	*j* as in *j*ump
dż	dg as in brid*ge*
ę	nasal *e*
ł	*w* as in *w*ork
ń	*n(y)* as in o*n*ion
ó	*oo* as in r*oo*k
w	*v* as in *v*at
ź	*zh,* roughly like *s* in plea*s*ure
ż	soft *z* as in a*z*ure

The symbols rz, ś and sz are all pronounced roughly as *sh* as in *sh*op; non-native speakers are unlikely to be able to differentiate between each.

Useful words

One	Jeden	Jeh-den
Two	Dwa	Dva
Three	Trzy	Chi
Four	Cztery	Chtehri
Five	Pięć	Pee-ench
Six	Sześć	Shesh
Seven	Siedem	Sheh-dem
Eight	Osiem	O-shem
Nine	Dziewięć	Dzhyeh-vyench
Ten	Dziesięć	Dzh-syench
Hello	Cześć	Cheshch
Goodbye	Do widzenia	Do vee-dzen-ya
Yes	Tak	Tak
No	Nie	Nyeh

Excuse me	Przepraszam	Pshare-Pra-Sham
Please	Proszę	Pro-sheh
Thank you	Dziękuję	Dzhen-koo-yeh
How much?	Ile kosztuje?	Eeleh kosh-too-yeh?
Left	Lewy	Levy
Right	Prawy	Pravy
Cheers	Na zdrowie	Naz drovier
Today	Dziś	Geesh
Tomorrow	Jutro	You-tro
Restaurant	Restauracja	Restauratsya
Hotel	Hotel	Hotel
Hot	Górąca	Go-ron-tsa
Cold	Zimny	Shimny
Tea	Herbata	Herbarta
Beer	Piwo	Peevo
Toilet	Toalety	To-a-leh-ti
Water	Woda	Voda
Hospital	Szpital	Shpeetal
Pharmacy	Aptekę	Aptehkeh
Market	Rynek	Rinek
Station	Stacja	Stay-Sha
Airport	Lotnisko	Lotneesko
Good	Dobry	Dobree
Bad	Niedobry	Needobry
Do you speak English?	Czy pan mówi po angielsku?	Chi pan moovee po angyelsku?
Entrance	Wejście	Vey-sh-che
Exit	Wyjście	Viy-sh-che
Attention	Uwaga	Oo-vaga
Letter	List	Leest
Postcard	Pocztówka	Poch-tuf-ka
Stamp	Znaczek pocztowy	Zna-check poch-tovy
Arrival	Przyjazd	Pshee-yazd
Departure	Odjazd	Od-yazd

Women in Poland. Old-fashioned social values still hold sway in Poland. Men rarely help with the housework, women drivers are regarded with some suspicion, and grandmothers are expected to look after children. While most women go out to work, this is born of economic necessity rather than sexual equality. Upon meeting a woman, a man is expected to kiss her hand while raising his hat with his other hand.

Whether because of the strong Catholic tradition or the good nature of the people, single women travellers need not fear harassment.

Jewish Poland. The first Jewish settlers arrived in Poland in the late 11th century, one hundred years or so after the first merchants had made contact with the locals. In 1264, Bolesluas the Pious granted Jews special privileges, extended by Casimir the Great and successive Polish rulers, which allowed them to practice their religion, build communities and adhere to their own laws. Prior to the outbreak of the Second World War, Poland was arguably the centre of European Jewry. Three and a half million Jewish people lived in the country, and Hebrew and Yiddish culture flourished.

The Nazi invasion of September 1939 was quickly followed by the establishment of ghettoes and concentration camps, to which Jews and other victims were sent from all over Europe. Five million were put to death in these camps, including over three million Polish Jews as the Nazis sought their 'Final Solution'. The end of the war saw fewer than 10,000 Jews remaining in Poland, yet even with such a small number, official and spontaneous harrassment against them continued. In the central town of Kielce in 1946 for example, a number of Jews were killed in a pogrom, and as recently as 1968, the government encouraged a number of leading Jews to leave the country. There is an alarming number of examples, from street graffiti downwards, of a latent anti-Semitism among some people.

The main centres of Jewish interest are in Warsaw, Kraków and Oświęim (Auschwitz), and fuller descriptions are given under those headings.

RECOMMENDED READING

Perhaps the best single book on the history of Poland is *Heart of Europe* by Norman Davies (Oxford University Press), an edited version of his more detailed two-volume set *God's Playground* from the same publisher. Neal Ascherson's *The Struggles For Poland* (Michael Joseph) concentrates mostly on 20th century Poland; Ascherson outlines the impact of the two world wars, the fortunes of the Polish people under communism and the roots of Solidarity. Stewart Steven's *The Poles* (Collins) is a collection of chapters each dealing with a particular Polish institution, ranging from the Church to the Press.

The UK has some excellent travel agents specialising in travel to Poland. These include:

Fregata, 100 Dean Street, London, W1V 6AQ (tel 071-734 5101).
Polorbis Travel, 82 Mortimer Street, London W1N 7DF (tel 071-636 2217).
Inter-Poland, 30 Sheen Park, Richmond, Surrey TW9 1UW (tel 081-332 2293).
Bogdan Travel, 5 The Broadway, Gunnersbury Lane, London W3 8HR (tel 081-992 8866; fax 081-896 9044).

All these operators have details of coach, air and rail travel, accommodation and package offers.

HOLIDAYS IN POLAND
INTER-POLAND LTD.
30 Sheen Park, Richmond,
Surrey TW9 1UW.
Tel: 081-332 2293

Exquisitely Poland, deliciously Polish and we are talking about a people and its hospitality. From Gdansk to Krakow, from Zapopane to Warsaw, from The Tatras mountains to the Great Mazurian Lakes, the natural beauty stretches for miles and rolling miles. This great country of Poland which has been the envy of every invading nation, invites you to experience an unforgettable holiday of diverse interests and charm.

All enthusiasts of nature will enjoy the golden sands of the Baltic coast; the rocky crags of the Tatras mountains; the wonderful network of the Muzurian Lakes. So if your interest is in swimming, water skiing, boating, fishing, riding the rapids, mountain climbing, hiking, or just lying on a slow moving boat with not a care in the world, then Poland awaits.

Why not try a horse riding excursion with meals by an open fire, ideal if you are a beginner or an advanced horseman. For those with a camera and a taste for history and its mementoes, many of Poland's old towns have been painstakingly restored. The Royal castles, palaces, museums, all holding the memory of many bygone centuries. Music and Art is plentiful, from Chopin to Penderecki, from The International Jazz Jamboree to Folklore.

AIR

LOT Polish Airlines and British Airways have a monopoly on the air travel market between the UK and Poland. BA has a daily mid-morning service between London Heathrow Terminal 1 and Warsaw. LOT matches this from Terminal 2, and also flies to Kraków (Fridays throughout the year, also Sundays and Wednesdays from March to October), and Gdańsk (Saturdays throughout, and also Mondays between June and October.) In addition, LOT has regular Saturday summer flights between Manchester and Warsaw. Discount fares to all destinations cost around £200.

There are also direct flights to Warsaw from Edmonton, Montreal, New York, with connections to and from Australia. In addition, Lufthansa flies from Frankfurt to Katowice, and Eurowings operates between Frankfurt and Wrocław.

TRAIN

Journey time from London averages 31 hours. There are early morning departures via Harwich and Hook of Holland or via Dover and Ostend, connecting to Berlin, Poznań and Warsaw. There are also direct services to Szczecin and Gdańsk from Berlin; Frankfurt to Wrocław and Kraków; and Vienna to Kraków and Warsaw.

BUS

Several low-cost bus services ply between the UK and Poland. London-Warsaw services are frequent throughout the year, and there are other routes to Poznań, Łodz, Wrocław, Kraków and Gdańsk. It is well worth phoning around to compare fares and schedules. Try:

Europol (Unit 20, Victoria Green Line Station, Colonnade Walk, Buckingham Palace Road, London SW1; tel 071-828 9008).
Fregata Travel (100 Dean St, London W1V 6AQ; tel 071-734 5101; fax 071-494 1567; plus offices in Manchester and Nottingham).

The London-Warsaw journey takes around 36 hours, with a return fare below £100.

CAR

The Polish Motoring Association (PZM) has offices at all border crossings, and they can supply details of their service centres throughout the rest of the country. PZM is affiliated to the AA and the RAC, whose members may use PZM's free breakdown service — although this only applies within 15 miles/25km of a PZM base. Opening hours in the larger centres are 0700-2200. The assistance offered includes towing and one hour's free mechanical help, but spares are charged to you. The national emergency number for PZM is 981.

Visas. Citizens of most countries, including the UK, Ireland and the USA, do not require visas so long as their stay in Poland does not exceed ninety days.

Polish Embassies and Consulates abroad include:

Australia: 7 Turrana Street, Yarralumla ACT 2600 (tel 06 273 1208); 10 Trelawney Street, Woollahra NSW 2025 (tel 02 363 9816).
Canada: 1500 Avenue de Pins Quest, Montreal, PQ H3G 1BB4 (tel 514-937-9481); 2603 Lakeshore Blvd West, Toronto M8V 1G5 (tel 416-252-5471)

UK: 19 Weymouth Street, London W1N 3AG (tel 071-580 0476); 2 Kinnear Road, Edinburgh EH35 5PE (tel 031-552 0301).
USA: 2224 Wyoming Avenue NW, Washington DC 20008 (tel 202-234-3800) 1530 North Lake Shore Drive, Chicago IL 60610 (tel 312-337-8166) 233 Madison Avenue, New York NY 10016 (tel 212-889-8360).

At the Polish border or point of entry, you must sign a form confirming you have enough funds to cover your stay. Don't lose this form; you will be expected to present it to the customs officers when you leave the country.

Registration. You are expected to register in your place of stay within 48 hours of entering Poland. In hotels and camp sites, this takes the form of your passport being kept by the receptionist, but if you are staying with friends or family, the procedure is usually ignored.

Customs. Visitors can bring the following into Poland duty-free:

Gifts to a total of $200; a camera and ten rolls of film (and the video equivalent), and those over 18 years old may also bring in up to two litres of wine and one litre of other alcohol and 250 cigarettes or 50 cigars or 0.25 kg of tobacco.

You can take out everything you brought in duty free, plus gifts to the value of $200 (the European Union will allow you to bring only $50-worth into your home country, however), up to 250 cigarettes or 50 cigars or 0.25 kg of tobacco, five litres of alcoholic drinks, and works of art etc., produced after 9 May 1945. Articles produced before this date can only leave the country with an export licence issued by the Ministry of Culture and Arts.

£1 = 30,000 złoty $1 = 20,000 złoty

The Polish currency is the złoty (literally 'gold' — an irony not lost on the locals.) The złoty is technically divided into 100 groszy, although no-one has seen a groszy for at least a decade, given the rampant inflation since the late 1980s. Although the government claims that price rises are under control, the 1994 rate is expected to touch 25%, and hence the value of the złoty will fall by about a quarter.

Złoty notes, which are all, confusingly, the same size, are available in denominations of 50, 100, 200, 500, 1,000, 2,000, 5,000, 10,000, 20,000, 50,000, 100,000, 500,000, 1,000,000 and 2,000,000.

The złoty is not yet freely traded on currency markets, but is easily exchangable for other major currencies in the country. All banks have foreign currency exchange counters. Opening hours are 9am to around noon Monday-Friday: some larger branches are open for a couple of hours on Saturday mornings. More numerous, and with longer hours, are the 'kantor' shops found just about everywhere, and quite reliable. Rates may differ marginally, but not by too much.

The black market for currency is all but dead in Poland. You may be approached in the street and offered a slightly better rate for your dollars and marks (the majority of black market vendors look confused when you mention the pound — or 'funt' as it is known) — but don't bother. There are numerous cases of travellers being swindled through folded notes or counterfeits. And don't accept 200,000 zl bills from them — they are no longer legal tender.

There are no limits on the amount of foreign currency you can bring in or out of Poland, but the importing and exportation of złoties is, for the time being at least, prohibited. The amounts of foreign currency you are carrying should be noted on the form given to you on entry, and checked on departure.

Tipping. Tips are usually expected in restaurants and by taxi drivers — a few thousand złoties or 5% is reasonable — 10% is more generous. When paying your bill in a restaurant don't hand an overly large amount to the waiter and say 'thank you' — he'll assume this includes a mammoth tip!

Credit and Charge Cards. Credit cards belonging to the Visa and Mastercard/Access groups as well as American Express are welcome in an increasing number of outlets — particularly the higher class hotels, restaurants and shops.

Memorise your PIN number if you have one — many outlets will ask for it when you use your card. Cash may be obtained through your credit cards at ORBIS hotels (officially to guests only, but sometimes the rules are bent) or at the following ORBIS offices in Warsaw: ul Bracka 16, pl. Konstyucji 4, ul. Marszalkowska 99a, and ul. Marszalkowska 142.

Loss of credit cards can be reported to PolCard Ltd on Warsaw 274513 (24 hours) and to American Express on Warsaw 635 2002, 635 3061 or 264460.

Work. Poland is a particularly popular place in which to teach. Students seem almost unfailingly friendly, open and keen to learn. Furthermore, the Poles have a great sense of humour and crack good jokes even with only elementary English. Another advantage of working in Poland is that there are no red tape hassles. Work permits are needed for anyone staying longer than three months but, with the help of an employer, can be arranged in one day (only after arrival in Poland). The procedures are made more complicated by the difficulty in many cases of getting a letter from landlords to confirm your accommodation, due to the fact that they do not wish to declare tenants for tax reasons. If you are lucky enough to have accommodation provided by your school, it is a simple matter of taking letters from your employer and landlord to the local foreigners' registration office.

Prospects for English teachers in Poland, western Poland in particular, remain more promising than almost anywhere else in the world. While Warsaw is full of native speakers looking for teaching work, the historic university cities of Wrocław, Kraków, Poznań and Gdańsk are still good bets, not to mention the many lesser-known towns and cities of Poland.

Numerous possibilities exist in both state and private schools. School directors are usually delighted to interview almost any native English speaker who turns up, though the best schools are as demanding as elsewhere. If you base yourself in Warsaw and wish to advertise your availability for private English tuition, try placing a notice just to the right of the main gate of Warsaw University.

The private language school market has overtaken those of Hungary and the former Czechoslovakia. There is still an enormous demand for English from the state sector which depends heavily on the steady stream of volunteer teachers supplied by the main agencies. The old state exam in English has been replaced by the Cambridge First Certificate creating a large demand for British teachers of English who have some experience of those exams.

The organisation Teachers for Poland is the largest supplier of professional volunteer teachers to any East European country. It places over 50 volunteers a year, mostly in *liceums* and technical schools. The primary target group are retired school teachers from Britain, but increasingly Teachers for Poland have been accepting young UK graduates with a TEFL qualification. Contact Teachers for Poland, Hereford Education Centre, Blackfriars St, Hereford HR4 9HS (tel 0432-353363, fax 276969).

Other useful sources of information include:

Batory Foundation, 9 Flory St, 00-586 Warsaw. Administers the Soros Foundation's English Teaching Program.

Ministry of National Education, ul. I Armii Wojske Pol. 25, Warsaw. Oversees placements in state schools.

State schools: The Polish educational system is undergoing massive reforms. Many teachers face serious shortages of materials, huge classes of 40, and insane timetables and syllabuses. A large measure of independence and self-reliance is essential.

There are over 60 foreign language teacher training colleges or NKJO *(Nauczycielskie Kolegium Jezyków Obcych)* with a dire need for qualified, experienced TEFLers. Pay is poor. Virtually every institute of higher education has a *Studium Jazykøw Obcych* (Foreign Language Department) which is where the students who aren't language majors fulfill their foreign language requirements. The learners are less advanced than at the NJKO, and they may be prepared to accept less well-qualified native speaker assistants.

English Language Centres (usually degree, RSA or Trinity and experience) at University of Silesia, Katowice; Jagiellonian University, Kraków; Adam Mickiewicz University, Poznań; University of Technology, Warsaw; University of Wrocław, Wrocław.

Although there are a few big-name Western schools like International House, the majority of private language schools are Polish-run. Freelancing is popular in Poland. Banks are good prospects and often pay ridiculously well by Polish standards. Others include:

American English School, Skrytka pocztowa 3, 04-141 Warsaw (tel 192-774).

English Unlimited, Podmlyńska 10, 80-855 Gdańsk (tel/fax 58-313-373).

International House, Ul. Gliwicka 10, 40-079 Katowice (tel 32-599-997, fax 598-404). Also at ul. Czapskich 5, 31-110 Kraków (tel 12-219-440/226-482, fax 218-652).

Lingua Studium Jezydow Obcych, Ul. Jazmogórska 6, 42-200 Często-chowa (tel/fax 34-243-368).

Modern English School, ul. Bonifraterska 6/3, 00-213 Warsaw (PO Box 4, 00-096 Warsaw 83). Tel 22-311-887.

Perfect, ul. Krakówska 51, 45-075 Opole.

Polanglo, Prywatna Szkola Jezyków Obcych, ul. Zurawia 24a, 00-643 Warsaw (tel 2-625-4994).

Program, ul. Fredry 7, Poznań (tel 61-536-972, fax 789-740).

World School of English, Basztowa 17, 31-193 Kraków (tel 12-229-098/161/193.

TELEPHONE

Parts of the Polish telephone system still belong to a bygone age, and are only being brought up to date slowly. To bypass this, many companies in Warsaw use satellite links to communicate with the outside world.

Local calls are quite easy to make, but city to city or international calls can test the patience in all but the biggest cities.

Tokens and phonecards rather than coins are used in public callboxes. 'A' tokens are for local calls, 'B' and 'C' tokens for longer and international calls, with phonecards available from main post offices the best bet.

During 1993, 'A' tokens cost 600 zł., 'C' tokens 6,000 zł. and phonecards 30,000 zł. When using these, remember to tear off the tab in the top right-hand corner to validate your card before inserting it in one of the few phones to accept it. Most of these phones are situated within main post offices in the larger towns. One minute to the UK costs 13,500 zł. direct — more if you make the call through the international operator.

To dial city to city, dial zero, and then a 2 digit code as follows:

Gdańsk 0-58; Kraków 0-12; Lublin 0-81; Poznań 0-61; Szczecin 0-91; Wrocław 0-71.

For 6 digit Warsaw numbers dial 0-22; for 7 digit numbers, ring 0-2.

The international prefix is 00 (add 44 for the UK, 1 for North America). Alternatively, ring 901 for the international operator.

For a reverse charge call to the UK, or a call using your British Telecom Chargecard, ring 0-044 009948 and speak to the BT operator direct.

Other important telephone numbers are:

997 Police; 998 Fire Brigade; 999 Ambulance; 981 PZM Auto Assistance; 900 Long Distance Operator; 901 International Operator.

Telegrams, Telex and Fax. Telegrams are easy to send from main post offices. The minimum charge is 12,000 zł. Many of the larger post offices now have fax machines alongside their telexes.

Mail and Courier Services. Postal services have improved dramatically in recent years: letters to and from the UK now take a matter of days, though if you are posting money it still makes sense to wrap it inside some leaflets to escape prying hands. Postcards and light letters cost in the region of 4,500 zł.

International forwarding companies are now established throughout the country. In Warsaw, DHL is at al. Jerozolimskie 30 (tel 263292); UPS at ul. Stycznia 39, H Pavilion (tel 606 6350); and TNT at ul. Potocka 1 (tel 330215).

Newspapers. International editions of British and other European newspapers are available in all larger towns and cities. In Warsaw, they usually reach the newsstands by the afternoon on the day of publication; in other centres, newspapers are usually one day old by the time they are sold.

The English language weekly *Warsaw Voice* (15,000 zł) is sold from newsstands from Friday onwards. It contains a resume of the weeks events, and articles aimed at businessmen. The *Voice* is also available on subscription from PO Box 28, 00-950, Warsaw.

The monthly *Warszawa What, Where, When* is glossier, and features a comprehensive listings section. It is available free of charge from all leading hotels and ORBIS offices in the capital.

Most of the Polish language papers carry columns of what's on listings — particularly cinema, theatre and museum programmes. The only truly national morning paper is *Gazeta Wyborca* (literally 'Election News' — it was started by Solidarity at the time of the first democratic elections). It has regional supplements daily which have comprehensive local listings particularly on Fridays and Saturdays.

Across the country, each major centre has one or two morning papers, and often an evening edition as well. General newspapers cover sport only sketchily: this is the province of specialist papers such as *Tempo* in Kraków, *Sport* in Katowice, and *Przeglad Sportowy* in Warsaw.

No newspapers are published on Sundays.

Broadcasting. Foreign series such as *Dynasty* and the abysmal *The Brittas Empire* still form the backbone of Poland's two state television channels. Moves are afoot to set up a network of regional television stations, but in the meantime, many Poles supplement the local fare with satellite or cable channels such as Sky News and Eurosport.

Two other Polish stations are available throughout most of Western Europe on satellite: TV Polonia and Polsat are broadcast from the Eutelsat II F3 (16 degrees east) satellite.

Polish Radio Four on medium wave retransmits BBC World Service news at 10.05 each morning, and BBC World Service and RFE transmissions can also be picked up on short-wave.

Independent radio stations are often the best bet for rock music: each city has at least one, and the Kraków based RMF FM also broadcasts on the Astra satellite. Poland's FM frequencies differ from those used in most of Western Europe and North America, so FM radios from home will be useless here.

Getting Around

Maps. The state cartographer, PRWK, produces an excellent range of city, regional and national maps which are available throughout Poland for around $1.50 each. A selection is also available (though at a higher price) in Stanford's, 12/14 Long Acre, London WC2E 9LP (tel 071- 836 1321). Geo-Centre International maps and guidebooks, with their distinctive bright red covers, are also recommended.

AIR

LOT has a restricted domestic service to and from Warsaw, timetabled for the business traveller, and it is only a time-saver if you are flying to somewhere remote like Rzeszow. The most frequent services are to Gdańsk (three or four daily.) Other centres have only one or two flights each day. Student standby fares are available on domestic routes.

LOT offices in towns served by its domestic routes are at:

GDANSK: ul. Waly Jagiellonskie 2/4 (311161,314026); airport: 413141
KATOWICE: al. Korfantego 36 (580684,585891); airport: 853487
KRAKOW: ul. Basztowa 15 (225076,227078); airport: 116700
POZNAN: ul. św. Marcin 69 (522847); airport: 481701

RZESZOW: pl. Ofiar Getta 6 (33550); airport: 32721
SZCZECIN: ul. Wyzolenia 17 (339926, 335058); airport: 182708
WARSAW: al. Jerozolimskie 65/79 (952, 953, 6281009); airport: 461143
WROCŁAW: ul. Pilsudskiego 36 (31744, 39032, 39031); airport: 574788

TRAIN

Poland's rail network, operated by PKP, is extensive and cheap, but slow. Trains are categorised, and tickets priced, in three degrees of slowness:

OSOBOWYCH (slowest); POSPIESZNYCH (quicker, but still slow); EXPRESOWYCH (fastest, but still only medium pace)

Where possible, use express or Inter City services which are designed for relatively quick city to city travel. Inter City services also include a 'little something extra', as it is enticingly described. Unfortunately, this only takes the form of a free newspaper and snack. Tickets for expresses must be booked in advance. Booking opens 90 days in advance at ORBIS offices and main rail stations.

Pricewise, an *expresowych* ticket costs 33% more than a *pospiesznych* ticket, which in turn is 50% more than an *osobowych* ticket. First class costs 50% more than second class. For example, a first class *expresowych* ticket from Gdynia to Warsaw in 1993 (a distance of 220 miles/350km), cost 231,000 zl; a *pospiesznych* ticket cost 173,300 zl, and an *osobowych* ticket 115,500 zł.

There are many sleeper and couchette services at night, particularly during the summer months to the holiday destinations. Booking is essential, and the prices are higher than those for seats.

Arrival and departure timetables are displayed at all major stations: arrivals *(przyjazdy)* on white paper, and departures *(odjazdy)* on yellow paper. *Peron* means platforms.

Left luggage facilities *(przechowalnia bagazu)* are provided at all big stations — there is a standard charge plus 1% of the declared value of your luggage as insurance.

BUS

The state bus company — PKS — operates a countrywide service. Prices are lower than on trains, but with a few exceptions, the service is slower. On the Kraków — Zakopane route though, the coach service is more frequent and quicker than all but the fastest express train.

A number of private services, using luxury coaches, are starting up. Fares are more expensive, but standards of comfort higher than on PKS services.

CAR

A car is essential if you need to visit really out of the way places. Polish roads are generally quiet (except of course in city centres) and in reasonable condition. Motorways are rare, and those that are under construction will probably open as toll roads to repay the costs.

Petrol stations are quite numerous in the built-up areas, but practically non-existent in rural areas. Petrol and diesel grades are usually identified by colour at stations:

86 octane (for Trabants) BLUE *(niebieska).*
94 octane YELLOW *(złota)*
98 octane RED *(czerwona)*
diesel BLACK *(czarna)*
unleaded GREEN *(zielona)* — not available at all stations.

In 1993, unleaded was 9,000 zł. per litre; 94 octane 11,000 zł., and diesel 8,000 zł.

Always carry a spare gallon with you, and also have a basic repair kit containing some spares, and have your driving licence, car registration document and Green Card available for inspection. A red warning triangle in case of accident is also compulsory.

Rules and Regulations. Drive on the right-hand side of the road; international traffic signs are used. Unless otherwise shown, the following speed limits apply:

60 km/hr (37 mph) in built-up areas, though sometimes as slow as 20km/hr (12 mph).
70 km/hr (46 mph) for cars with trailers on highways and expressways.
90 km/hr (56 mph) for cars outside built-up areas, and for motorbikes on highways and expressways.
110 km/hr (69 mph) for cars on highways and expressways.

There is a minimum speed limit of 40 km/hr (24 mph) on highways.

Dipped highlights must be used during daylight hours between November and February, and seatbelts must always be worn by drivers and front passengers. A left- hand outside rear mirror is also compulsory.

Drinking and driving carries the possibility of imprisonment.

If you are involved in a motor accident, contact the police, and don't leave the scene until you are satisfied that everything is OK. Contact with your own insurance company can be made through Warta Insurance, ul. Chalbinskiego 8, Warsaw (tel 300330).

HITCH-HIKING

Poland has relinquished its place at the top of the hitch-hiker's list. In 1992, the official hitching scheme — which involved the most generous drivers winning prizes — ended. This was Europe's only government-sponsored hitch-hiking enterprise, and was administered by the Social Autostop Committee.

Its demise has not affected chances too adversely. The main handicap to swift progress is the poor road system — most Polish motorists are prepared to give foreigners lifts, and usually waive the contribution of a few thousand złoties which is expected from local hitchers.

TAXIS

Ranks bulging with Mercedes cabs can be found outside all airports, stations and big hotels. Taxis have meters, but these are rarely adjusted to keep pace with price increases, so agree a set price before you get in. Rates rise by 50% from 2300 to 0500 and outside city boundaries. Only ever use taxis carrying a proper sign, particularly at airports.

If you need to book by phone, look in the local newspaper or under 'radiotaxi' in the telephone directory.

BUSES AND TRAMS

Most cities and large towns have good networks operating from 0500 to midnight: big cities also have a limited number of night services. A flat-rate price system is used, with tickets costing about 4,000 zł. for each journey. Buy a number of tickets from a kiosk before boarding, and cancel it in the machine aboard the vehicle. Failure to do so can result in a fine. Express and night services, together with those that go beyond city limits usually attract surcharges: normally double the rate. Excess luggage (at the driver's discretion) costs the same as a normal fare.

Hotels. Most top hotels are part of the ORBIS chain — a former state monopoly which for decades was the sole hotel operator at the business end of the market. Many of the hotel renovations and new constructions throughout the country are being funded privately.

Accommodation prices are up to the levels charged in other European countries even if the slightly dated facilities are not. However, a number of specialist travel agents such as Fregata and Polorbis offer reduced rates if you book and pay in advance through them. For example, two nights sharing a twin bedded room in the four-star Hotel Hewelius in Gdańsk during 1993 cost $120 for two people.

Youth Hostels. The Polish Society of Youth Hostels (PTSM) runs the country's *schroniska młodziezowe.*   The PTSM headquarters are at ul. Chocimska 28, 00-791 Warsaw. (tel 498354 or 498128; fax 498354.) There are over a thousand hostels, most of which are only open from the last week of June to the end of August. Preference in the hostels is given to Hostelling International; the international handbook lists the most reliable 200 hostels in Poland.

International Student Hostels. Open only during the college summer holidays, these student hostels are overseen by the Almatur organisation. The head office is at ul. Ordynacka 9, 00-364 Warsaw (tel 262356, fax 262353.) Hostels open in twenty or so cities, with booking priority given to ISIC card holders. Almatur also offer discounts on rail, coach and air travel for card holders, and its offices often constitute the best bet for information in each town.

Camping. It can't be too much fun pitching your tent in the middle of winter, and thus the vast majority of campsites are open only in midsummer. Those in the most popular tourist areas like the Baltic coast and the mountains are heavily booked in advance. You can make reservations through 'Camptur', ul. Grochowska 331, 00-838 Warsaw (tel 106050).

Private Accommodation. Perhaps the best way to meet ordinary Poles, accommodation in flats and houses is arranged by the Biuro Zakwaterownia in each town. Expect to pay around $8 per person, per night, and always ascertain the proximity of your accommodation to public transport.

Polish culinary traditions are shaped by those of its neighbours and conquerors. Jewish, Hungarian, Russian and German dishes have all found their way onto the table, while shish kebabs betray the influence of the East. Pork, chicken, potatoes, freshwater fish and berries seem, on first appearances, to predominate. Certainly there is a marked lack of a variety of vegetables and sauces on the menu.

Many Poles work from 6 or 7 am until mid afternoon, so the day starts with a light breakfast (sniadanie) of rye bread and butter, ham, cheese, jam, tea or coffee. The main meal of the day (obiad) is usually taken after 3 pm. The meal very often starts with a chilled soup: *barszcz* is beetroot soup, particularly popular at Easter and Christmas, while *chlodnik* consists of garden vegetables.

Among the national dishes are *bigos* — hunter's stew — made of sauerkraut, onion, cabbage and meat, and *pierogi* — little 'ravioli' filled with either meat or cheese. Roast pork loin — *pieczony schab* — is an expensive delight, and pork generally finds its way on to every menu both in hot cutlet form and as cold sausages and hams such as Krakówska and Soposka.

Christmas is a particular culinary feast. The evening meal of Christmas Eve marks the end of a day-long fast, and starts when the first star appears in the sky. The meal is traditionally meatless, and consists of twelve courses (one for each of the Apostles). The centrepiece is a large carp, usually brought home live in a bucket of water, kept in the bath until the appointed hour, and then killed by the head of the household. The fish is boiled, stuffed and served in its own juices, with jellied vegetable garnish.

DRINKING

The British-style public house does not exist in Poland, but many restaurants serve beer and spirits for consumption at the table. Licensing hours are generally open-ended, although wines and spirits may not officially be sold before 1 pm.

Theatre. Drama is flourishing. One of the most important roles played by the popular theatre in Poland was to provide an outlet for the passions aroused by political and social unrest. Experimental theatre fostered a vigorous tradition in which the dissident voice was clearly heard. This tradition has stood Poland in good stead, and the country has about a hundred full-scale playhouses. The leading ones are in Warsaw: the Narodowy, the Dramatyczny and the Ateneum.

Tales are still told of the manner in which the wartime resistance movement kept theatre alive underground, hidden — like its many other activities — from the not quite all-seeing eyes of the occupying Germans. In Kraków, a promising young actor and playwright named Karol Wojtyła performed regularly underground. He is today better known as Pope John Paul II. Wrocław is perhaps the leading centre for international drama in Poland. Leading Western writers and directors, such as Peter Brook, gathered there in the 1960s to tap fresh and energetic talent. From that time onwards, Wrocław played host to the biennial International Festival of Student Theatre.

Tickets should be booked well in advance if possible. Expect to pay between $1 and $2.50, or more if you are obliged to buy from the touts who hover outside every sold-out theatre.

Cinema. The long queues outside most of Warsaw's fifty or more cinemas indicate the popularity of movie-going in Poland. There are cinemas in most towns and cities throughout the country. Seats cost around $1 per person and can be booked in advance.

Big British and American films can be viewed, with subtitles, sometimes within months of their original release. The Polish tradition of film-making has a long and respected pedigree. The most famous Polish film-makers known to the West are Roman Polanski and Andrzej Wajda. Together they combine the best of the Eastern and the Western styles as they have evolved since the war. Polanski, brought up in Poland and a graduate of the Polish film school, began his career in films as a twenty-one year old actor in Wajda's *A Generation* (1955). He acted in two more Wajda films before becoming an assistant to another respected director, Andrzej Munk. He made a couple of highly acclaimed shorts, in Polish, before moving to the West. Wajda, who still lives in Kraków, began making films in the 1950s. From the beginning he displayed an original ability to express on film the frustrations and injustices in the history of his own people. The people in Wajda's films are invariably trapped, either literally in prisons or cellars (as in his wartime films), or by the system at large. Wajda, himself a Resistance fighter in the war, went on to portray the predicament of his compatriots in post-war Poland in the much-admired *Man of Marble* (1977) and *Man of Iron* (1980).

SPORT AND RECREATION

Poland is the largest of the nations in Eastern Europe, so there is a great deal of space to enjoy outdoor recreation. Horses still play an important part in Polish social and economic life, and a planned breeding policy ensures the continuation of thoroughbreds such as English and Arab full-bloods. If you are planning to ride, take out third party insurance before you leave home. Polorbis runs a number of holidays during the summer based on equestrian centres in the Poznań area.

Horse racing is also popular. All betting takes place on course. In Warsaw, the racetrack at Sluzewice holds regular weekend meetings throughout the summer, and racecards and details are printed in the *Zycie Warszawy* and *Przeglad Sportowy* newspapers. The course in Sopot has its most popular meeting of the season in June.

Hunting. Killing animals, under the auspices of the Polish Hunting Union (PZL), is popular with a minority. Deer, wild boar and small game are the most common victims of a blast from a shotgun. PZL is based at ul. Nowy Swiat 35, 00-029 Warsaw (tel 267949, fax 266242).

Skiing. The season extends from November to April. Zakopane, the largest town in the Tatras, is the skiing capital of Poland. In summer, it serves as the hiking capital. The Beskid Slaski range, around Szczyrk, is also popular. Skiing is average to good, but facilities are more primitive than in other European centres.

Hiking. Walking in the nearby Tatras keeps Zakopane busy throughout the summer months — details are given in the Zakopane and the Tatras section, and the Bieszczady highlights are noted in that section.

Beaches. The sandy beaches of the 524km-long Baltic coastline are popular with native Poles, but due to the polluted waters, bathing from a number of beaches has been banned by the authorities. Long-stay foreign tourists are few and far between, due to the rather rudimentary facilities available there. Centres such as Sopot, near Gdańsk, make few concessions to Western holidaymakers.

Spectator Sport. Football is the most popular sport in the country, although attendances at most of the top matches rarely top 5,000. The Polish soccer season starts in late summer, takes a winter break from December to mid March, and continues until early June. Tickets are cheap — usually about 30,000 zł. Silesia is the soccer hotbed of the country, with Gornik Zabrze, Ruch Chorzow and Katowice among the leading teams. While there are two First Division teams in each of Poznań, Łodz, Warsaw and Kraków (including the *non-pareils* of the mighty Hutnik Kraków), the teams from the Gdańsk area languish in the regional Second Division.

Polish League football is at present under a cloud. The 1992-93 season ended in scandal with four clubs, including the champions Legia Warsaw stripped of points for match-fixing on the final day of the season. Hutnik Kraków are above that sort of thing.

Speedway is one of the few sports where top overseas stars compete in Poland on a regular basis, with Motor Lublin leading the way.

Nowhere is the change from a planned to a free market economy more noticeable than in the shopping streets. Where once queues formed outside empty, soulless shops, passers-by can now gaze at all manner of Western goods — at Western prices.

The sight of Benetton and Levis shops opening was, for many, conclusive evidence that things would never quite be the same again. Prices in these shops match those in other European cities, but there are still a nunmber of bargains to be gained — although these are diminishing quickly. Books and maps are still good value, being exempt from the VAT introduced in 1993. Leather and linen goods bought in ordinary shops, rather than in the tourist traps, are still reasonable. Silver and amber jewellery predominates, particularly in Baltic towns — the Desa shops have the widest variety. The best Polish-owned fashion shops are in the Moda Polska chain.

Popular brands of films, particularly Kodak and Fuji, are easily available in big towns and cities — there is even the luxury of one-hour developing in some places if you are prepared to pay for it.

Poland is, by and large, a safe country, and you should not encounter too many problems. The domestic water supply has heavy doses of chlorine in it: it is safe to brush your teeth in, but unpleasant to drink. Stick to bottled mineral water where you can. The main problems are the heavily polluted rivers and the Baltic. Many people won't bathe in the Baltic because of all the effluent that enters it through rivers like the Vistula — nowadays more like a giant cesspit than an important waterway. Indeed, a significant minority won't even set foot on a beach or eat locally caught fish.

The coastline from Świnoujście to Hel is reasonably clean. From Gdańsk eastwards, the picture worsens. Generally speaking, the open coast is cleanest the further west one travels, but the coastline surrounding the Bay of Gdańsk is polluted.

Public toilets are a problem. If you're caught short, head for a decent hotel or restaurant and use theirs — it is well worth the 3,000 zl or so you will have to pay the (invariably wizened) cloakroom attendant. Universal pictograms depicting a man with his legs apart and a woman with one, central, fat leg are being used more and more, but many toilets are still marked with a circle for women and and a triangle for men.

Smoking. Poland still has one of the biggest proportion of smokers per head of population, and supports its own large cigarette manufacturing industry. But the tide is turning, and an increasing number of cafes and restaurants have a no-smoking policy.

MEDICAL TREATMENT

Poland and the UK have reciprocal free medical care arrangements, with treatment available upon production of your passport and E111 form which you should get in advance from a Post Office or DSS office. Hospital and dentistry work is covered by this, but a modest charge will be levied for prescription medicines and minor dental work.

Recent reports suggest that the state health service is facing severe problems, with shortages of medicines and bandages, and patients' beds overflowing into hospital corridors. In addition, anaesthetic is not widely used for minor dental work. Be sure to take some aspirin (or vodka) with you. If you require emergency treatment, dial 999 for an ambulance.

Pharmacies (*apetka*) are open 8am to 8pm, and each city has one open around the clock; hospitals or police stations can tell you where it is. Queues are often long; to avoid wasting time, ask first at the counter whether or not the item you need is in stock. Some pharmacies sell Western health products in exchange for hard currency.

The despised militia metamorphised into the caring, gentler, softer *policja* during the revolution of the late 1980s, but they are still basically the same, albeit under a much greater degree of accountability and parliamentary control.

The main points to remember concern motoring law: it is illegal to drink any amount and drive; always use your headlights from November to February, and don't exceed the speed limit: the police can be trigger-happy with their radar guns. Try to adhere to the other rules too, however silly or pointless they may seem. Crossing an otherwise deserted street in the 'wrong' place could earn you a dressing-down and cost you a $5 fine.

Most Poles are honest, but, as elsewhere, a small minority preys upon vulnerable tourists.

The tourist information industry is in a bit of a state of flux at present. ORBIS — the State Tourist Organization — owns hotels, runs tours and provides some information, but the loss of its monopoly means it has started to function rather more as an ordinary travel agent than an impartial source of advice. The best advice is to seek out the tourist information offices specifically mentioned in the regional section of this chapter.

Travel Agents. A few British travel agents have offices in Poland. Fregata Travel is at 'Dom Chopina', pl. Powstancow, Warszawa 2 (tel 274304, fax 274333); and ul. Szpitalna 32, Kraków (tel 224144, fax 211290). Thomas Cook/Wagons Lits is represented through ORBIS at ul. Marszalkowka 142, Warsaw (tel 276766, fax 271123); and American Express is at Krakówskie Przedmiescie 11 (tel 635 2002).

Travellers with Disabilities. Individual wheelchair-bound travellers, and those with pronounced walking difficulties will, unfortunately, face a frustrating time. Escalators and lifts are few and far between, and the majority seem to be permanently out of service. Specially adapted entrances and exits are only slowly being provided: the constant assistance of the able-bodied will have to be relied upon in many places.

Embassies and Consulates in Warsaw.
Australia: ul. Estonska 3/5 (tel 176081).
Canada: ul. Matejki 1/5 (tel 298051, fax 296457).
Ireland: ul. Lenartowicza 18 (tel 446440, 480140, fax 177065).
UK: al. Róż 1 (tel 6281001/5, fax 217161) (Commercial, consular/visa section at Warsaw Corporate Centre, 2nd. Floor, Emilii Plater 28, tel 6253030, fax 6253472).
USA: al. Ujazdowskie 29/31 (tel 6283041/9, fax 6289326); the USA also has Consulates in Kraków (ul. Stolarska 9; tel 227793, 220345, fax 218292) and Poznań (ul. Chopina 4; tel 529586, 529874, fax 530053)

Public Holidays

New Year	1 January
Easter Monday	March/April
Labour Day	1 May
Corpus Christi	ninth Thursday after Easter
National Day	22 July
All Saints' Day	November
Christmas	25-26 December

WARSAW (WARSZAWA)

The rather grey, functional capital may appear disappointing at first glance, but when you consider that most of the city was little more than smouldering rubble in 1945, its renaissance is remarkable. Indeed, such was the extent of its devastation that serious consideration was given to leaving the city in this state as a permanent war memorial. Instead, it was decided to reconstruct the historic centre as a reminder of what the city had been before the start of the Second World War. As the Nazis had systematically destroyed virtually all the architectural and planning documents belonging to the city, the new planners had, in many cases, only photographs and sketches to guide them. The successful reconstruction of the Old Town is a lasting tribute to them, and also the support of Poles throughout the world, who partially funded the work.

A 'new town' inasmuch as the first reference to it dates from only 1321 (Kraków was the major Polish town at the time), Warsaw grew in importance until, in the early 17th century, King Sigismund III transferred the capital of the Polish state to the town. Through good times and bad, Warsaw has remained a resilient symbol of nationhood to all Poles.

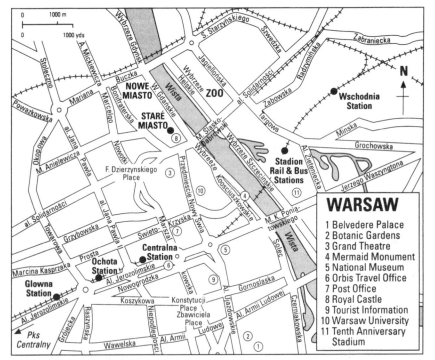

WARSAW

1 Belvedere Palace
2 Botanic Gardens
3 Grand Theatre
4 Mermaid Monument
5 National Museum
6 Orbis Travel Office
7 Post Office
8 Royal Castle
9 Tourist Information
10 Warsaw University
11 Tenth Anniversary
   Stadium

Getting Around

ARRIVAL AND DEPARTURE

Air. Okecie Airport is only six miles/10km west of the city centre: services to and from the former 'Iron Curtain' countries use Terminal 2; all other airlines use Terminal 1.

There is a frequent bus service from both terminals: no 175 to and from Terminal 1, and no 114 to and from Terminal 2. Buy your ticket (4,000 zł. in 1993) from the Ruch kiosk in the terminal building, and punch it at both ends in the machine on board the bus.

There's also a faster (yellow) bus linking the airport with the main hotels in the city centre. Tickets can be bought from the driver. It's less crowded, but tickets cost 25,000 zł. The service runs between 6am and 11pm. The Marriott Hotel also runs a minibus service between the hotel and the airport. It costs 100,000 zł., and like all the other services, calls at the main Warszawa Centralna railway station.

There are plenty of taxis as well, but only use official cabs licensed by the airport, or provided by the hotels. Unmarked, unlicensed taxis are often potentially dangerous rip-offs, so steer clear of them.

The main rail station, Warszawa Centralna, is slap bang in the centre of the city, alongside the LOT/Marriott Hotel skyscraper on al. Jerozolimskie, the main east-west road in the city. It's got a pretty bad reputation for muggers and pickpockets, and although the authorities are trying to clean up its act, hang on to your belongings and don't loiter there too long.

Centralna is in fact only a transit stop. Trains to and from the south and west (Kraków, Poznań and Wrocław for example) start and terminate across the river at Wschodnia station, while those from the north and east (e.g. Gdańsk) use Zachodnia as their terminus.

Bus. The main coach station — Dworzec Centralny PKS — is west of the city centre alongside the Zachodnia railway station. International services, as well as those serving the south and west use this station, while services for the north, east and south east use the Stadion station across the river near the massive Tenth Anniversary Stadium (Stadion Dziesieciolecia.)

Both bus stations are on the local rail network. From Srodmiescie station alongside Centralna, go to Zachodnia for Dworzec Centralny, and Stadion station for Dworzec Stadion. It's about fifteen minutes from Zachodnia to Stadion, with Srodmiescie halfway.

Driving. Car Hire. Local on 090216193 claim the cheapest prices; Budget are on 630 7280; Europcar at ul. Moliera 4//6 (tel: 263344) and Airport (tel: 504453); Avis in the Marriott Hotel (tel: 6307316) and Airport (tel: 6504871); Herz in the Victoria Hotel (tel: 274185) and Airport (tel: 469896), and if you fancy cruising in a Chevrolet or a Pontiac, call in at Americana, al. Zwirki i Wigury 32 (tel: 257275).

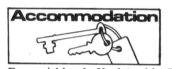

The top hotel is the Bristol on ul. Kraków-skie Przedmieście 42/44 (tel: 263241) — part of the Forte chain. Expect to pay over £100 per person per night for a touch of fin de siècle luxury. Across the road, the Europejski, ul. Krakówskie Przedmieście 13 (tel: 264081) is marginally cheaper.

Downtown, the Marriott on al. Jerozolimskie 65/79 (tel: 306306) dominates the city centre. Nearby the Victoria, ul. Królewska 11 (tel: 279271) and the Holiday Inn, ul. Złota 2 (tel: 206534) are also handily placed for the city centre.

A cheaper option may be the Saski at pl. Bakowy 1 (tel: 204611), but you will need to book in advance. Warsaw is poorly served by hostels: the most central is at ul. Smolna 30 (tel: 278952) (bus 175 from the airport); the National Museum tramstop is nearby. The other is at ul. Karolkowa 53a (tel: 32829), on the 24 tram route. Almatur at ul. Kopernika 23. 00-359 Warsaw (tel: 263512, fax: 263507) has details of summer hostels. The office is hidden away: from ul. Nowy Swiat, turn into ul. Ordynacka, then first left.

A regular during the summer vacation is 'Zaczek', ul. Wołowska 141 (tel: 451648), but check first with Almatur. For private rooms, try the 'Syrena' bureau at ul. Krucza 17 (tel: 217864 & 6287540).

The most popular camping site is midway between the airport and the city centre at ul. Zwirki i Wigury 32 (tel: 254391). It's on bus route 175 and open May to September. The largest is at ul. Połczyńska 6a (tel: 366716) (May — September) and the nearest to Wilanów is at ul. Idzikowskiego 4 (tel: 422192) (June — August only.)

The city boasts one of the few vegetarian restaurants in the country: the Nowe Miasto in the New Town Square (Rynek Nowego Miasto 13) (tel: 314379). It has a menu of Polish and international dishes.

Apart from in hotels. foreign flavours may be sampled at the Tsubame Japanese restaurant, ul. Foksal 16 (tel: 265127), and the Valencia Spanish restaurant at ul. Smocza (tel: 383217).

Traditional Polish dishes are served at the Rycerska, ul. Szeroki Dunaj 9/11 (tel: 313668j) and the Fukiera, Rynek Starego Miasta 27 (tel: 311013) among others.

Fast food addicts are well served. There's a McDonalds on Ul. Świetokrzyska, ten minutes walk north of Centralna station, and a Taco Bell, Pizza Hut and KFC at al. Solidarnosci 68.

If you've got a sweet tooth, head for the ice-creams in the Hortex cafes in the Rynek and on ul. Świetokryzyska, and keep and eye out for Wedel chocolates — amongst the best in the world.

For the best tourist itinerary of Warsaw, it is best to keep to the straight and narrow, and follow a direct route — the 'Royal Way' — from the Old and New Towns in the north to Wilanow, 6 km. away in the south.

When starting from the Centralna station/LOT Marriott Hotel skyscraper on al. Jerozolimskie, either walk eastwards to its junction with ul. Nowy Swiat, or take trams 7, 22, 24 or 25 three stops to the National Museum (Muzeum Narodowe). Bus 122 will take you north to the Old and New Towns, and south to Wilanow. This itinerary starts from the northern end.

THE OLD TOWN AND NEW TOWN (Stare Miasto and Nowe Miasto)
Castle Square (plac Zamkowy) is the central point of the area. Overlooked by the 70-feet-high Column of King Sigismund III Vasa (Kolumna Zygmunta III Wazy — the King who moved the capital from Kraków), the east side of the square is taken up by the Royal Palace (Zamek Krolewski).

Blown up by the Nazis in 1944, it took a further 27 years for restoration work to commence, and it reopened forty years after its destruction. The Ball Room and the Canaletto Room are the showpieces, Canaletto's paintings of Warsaw from the eighteenth century helping the architects reconstruct the rebuilt city. The castle is closed on Mondays, and on most days, you have to be part of a guided tour.

Opposite the palace, the narrow ul. Swietojanska leads via St. John's Cathedral to the Old Town Square — Rynek Starego Miasta — completely rebuilt to its original 17th and 18th century designs during the 1950s, a successful operation marked by an UNESCO award.

The Historical Museum of Warsaw (Muzeum Historyczne Warszawy) at number 42 features the destruction of the city (Closed Mondays). The streets on the east side of the Rynek are worth a detour — the steps in the northeast corner leading down to ul. Bzozowa lead to a quiet corner, while the cracked bell on the pavement of pl. Kanonina dates from the 17th century.

Re-entering the Old Town Square, ul. Nowo Miejska in the northwest corner leads to the semi-circular Barbican (Barbakan) with its summer art gallery. Passing through the Barbican, pause at ul. Freta no. 16 — the Museum of Maria Sklodowska-Curie marks the family home of the double Nobel prizewinner, and discoverer of radium and polonium. Ul. Freta leads to the New Town Square (Rynek Nowego Miasta), historically not much younger than the Old Town, and also restored after destruction during the War.

THE ROYAL WAY (TRAKT KROLEWSKI)

Returning to the Sigismund Column via the Old Town, the four mile/ 6km 'Royal Way' has its northern end at Krakówskie Przedmiescie, a wide,impressive avenue leading to the heart of modern Warsaw. Walking south, look out for the Adam Mickiewicz Monument, the Potocki Palace, Radziwill Palace (both now Government buildings), the Princ Jozef Ponitowski Statue and the plush Bristol and Europejski hotels. Beyond the Warsaw University, the road becomes ul. Nowy Swiat, and the palaces and churches are replaced by high class shops and boutiques. The Zamoyski Palace, home of the Foksal Art Gallery, lies in ul. Foksal, just off Nowy Swiat.

The Rondo Charles de Gaulle marks the intersection of Nowy Swiat and al. Jerozolimskie. Slightly to the east is the National Museum (Muzeum Narodowe), a rather disappointing looking building, but with a priceless collection of art and artefacts — well worth a visit (closed Mondays). The Polish Army Museum is next door. The Royal Way continues southwards down al. Ujazdowskie; the Parliament House (Sejm) is nearby on ul. Wiejska.

Warsaw's botanical gardens and palaces are not too far away. The *Belvedere Palace* (Palac Belweder) — the home of the Polish President — dates from the eighteenth century, and is surrounded by Botanical Gardens which separate it from Lazienki Palace.
by Łazienki Park, which attracts Varsovians and tourists alike in their thousands. (Łazienki incidentally is another Polish term for bathroom, just in case you're ever caught short.) Łazienki was the summer residence of King Stanisław August Poniatowski. The Palace Upon The Water (Pałac na Wodzie) was his actual residence, and is open daily to the public except Mondays.

In the Park, Chopin recitals are given in the shadow of the Chopin Monument on Sundays during the summer at 12 noon and 4pm.

Wilanów Palace (Pałac Wilanów is further down the Royal Way- bus 122 links it with the rest of the route — and was the summer residence of Jan III Sobieski. It's a gem, and tours are held daily except Tuesdays. Surrounded by well-manicured gardens, one special attraction is the Poster Museum (Muzeum Plakatu) which holds the largest collection in the world.

Compared with the riches of the Old and New Towns and the Royal Palaces, the city centre itself is something of a disappointment. Two skyscrapers dominate the area around Centralna station. The yellowy grey Palace of Culture and Science (Pałac Kultury i Nauki) was a 'gift' from the Soviet Union in the 1950s — a symbol of their then pervasive influence in the country. Today it houses halls and a museum. The area outside is to be avoided at night, the province of ne'er-do-wells and haggard prostitutes.

At least you will never lose your bearings in Warsaw — the Palace and the nearby Marriott Hotel/LOT glass-fronted skyscraper can be seen from virtually everywhere in downtown Warsaw.

Northwest of the skyscrapers, the Saxon Gardens (Ogród Saski) comprise a pleasant oasis. Northeast of the Palace of Culture, the site of the former Jewish Ghetto is now occupied by the districts of Mirów and Muranów. There are few visible reminders of the area's history remaining — the Nazis saw to that — but the Nożyk Synagogue on ul. Twarda still functions today. The world-renowned Jewish Theatre close by on pl. Grzybowski (Cmentarz Zydowski) on ul. Okjopowa is a reminder of the city's Jewish legacy.

All of these places are on the west bank of the Vistula, the river that cuts Warsaw in two. Over the river, the district of Praga was spared much of the wartime destruction of its neighbours. It is mostly residential, but the

Zoological Gardens (Ogród Zoologiczny) are here, as is the large market held in the grounds of the Tenth Anniversary Stadium (Stadion Dziesieciolecia): great fun, but a notorious haunt of pickpockets and worse, as is the whole riverbank area.

The British Embassy is at al. Róz 1 (tel: 6281001); the USA Embassy at al. Ujazdowskie 29/31 (tel: 6283041) and the Irish Embassy at ul. Lenartowicza 18 (tel: 446440).

American Express are opposite the Bristol and Europejski hotels at Krakówskie Przedmieście 11 (tel 6352002) and have a cash dispensing machine.

There's an IATA bonded 24-hour travel agency — Int. Express — at ul. Stołeczna 19/21 (tel: 337136). Twenty-four hour chemists are at the Centralna Station; ul. Freta 13/15 and ul. Widok 19. The *kantor* at Centralna never closes, and 24 hour shops operate at al. Jerozolimskie 65/79 (Marriott Hotel) and ul. Solec 32/34.

Car broken down? Ring 981 around the clock. Ring 997 for the police, 998 for the fire brigade and 999 for an ambulance.

The *Zycie Warszawy* newspaper carries a full list of night-time services in each edition.

DAY TRIPS FROM WARSAW

Chopin's birthplace at Zelazowa Wola, 32 miles/55km from Warsaw, is always popular with tourists. It lies on the outskirts of the Kampinos Forest, and has a museum and Sunday piano recitals in summer. Buses leave Warsaw for the town, and organised trips often fit in with the recitals.

Companies such as Mazurkas Travel at the Forum Hotel and ul. Długa 8/14 run tours to other beauty spots, as well as city tours. As many of the main rail services radiate to and from Warsaw, it is possible to take day trips to many of the other tourist centres from the city, as long as you are prepared to leave early in the morning. It is feasible to spend a reasonable amount of time in Kraków, Lublin, Poznań or the Gdańsk area on a day trip.

GDANSK

Gdańsk, with a population of 480,000, is the largest and most important commercial centre in northern Poland. Together with its neighbours Sopot and Gdynia, it is known as the Tri City. The whole urban sprawl of 800,000 inhabitants is the vibrant heart of the region, with each city complementing each other.

Gdańsk's history as a commercial hub dates back to Roman times, when merchants descended on the town for its 'Baltic Gold' — amber. The port grew at the mouth of the Vistula River, and was an importnat commercial and military base of the Teutonic Knights and the Hanseatic League.

The town was once again incorporated into Poland in 1454, yet maintained its cosmopolitan air, welcoming traders from Flanders — and architects too, as can be seen today in the streets of the Old Town. At the start of the 19th century, the ownership of the city switched between Prussia and the Napoleonic forces, but the Prussians regained the city under the terms of the 1815 Treaty of Vienna. When Poland reappeared on the map of Europe at the end of the First World War, Danzig, as the area was known to the Germans, became a free city under the auspices of the League of Nations. It was on the outskirts of the town that the first shots of the Second World War were fired.

The war hit Gdańsk hard: 90% of the centre was devastated, and over 60% of the suburbs. Work on reconstructing the Main Town commenced in 1946, but some work is still continuing. More recent 'warfare' took place outside the Main Town. In December 1970, a strike in the shipyards over huge food price rises was liquidated by troops opening fire on the demonstrators, leaving over thirty dead.

A similar disturbance in 1980, triggered by more price rises, led to the mobilisation of the workers by a group led by shipyard electrician Lech Wałęsa. The 'Gdańsk Agreements', signed by workers and the government in August 1980, allowed the formation of the first free trade unions in the Eastern Bloc, known under the name *Solidarność* — Solidarity.

It was to Wałęsa that the country looked during the days of military rule in the 1980's and Gdańsk was again at the forefront of the democratic process, when free elections were held for the first time in July 1989 — Wałęsa becoming President of Poland in 1991.

Arrival and Departure. LOT runs a direct service from London Heathrow each Saturday, and a Monday service during the summer. The LOT office in town is at ul. Waly Jagiellonskie 2/4 (tel 311161 and 314026), and at the airport on 413141. There are up to four return journeys daily to Warsaw.

The airport is at Rebiechowo, nine miles/14km west of the city centre. Facilities at the terminal are extremely limited, and often the only way to reach town without złoties is to haggle with a taxi driver — $25 was the going rate in 1993. Bus 110 does, however, link the airport with Gdańsk Wrzeszcz bus and rail station for the city centre for approx. 4,000 zł.

Wrzeszcz rail station is three stops up from Gdańsk Główny — the main station — and a further 4,000 zł. rail ticket. Services also leave Wrzeszcz for Sopot and Gdynia.

The PKS bus stations at Gdańsk and Gdynia are alongside the main Główny station.

Getting Around. The best way to get around the area is by train; there are frequent services on the rail line which links Gdańsk with Gdynia and Sopot.

Accommodation. The leading (and most expensive) hotels are all run by ORBIS and bookable in advance from overseas: the Hewelius (ul. Heweliusza 22, tel 315631); the Marina (ul. Jelitkowska 20, tel 532079); the Novotel (ul. Pszenna 1, tel 316241); and the Posejdon (ul. Kapliczna 30, tel 530227).

A good, and smaller, option is the popular Mesa Hotel at ul. Waly Jagiellonskie 36 (tel 318052), the ex-Communist Party headquarters, now run by a group of Christians. The Jantar on Dlugi Targ 19 (312716) is just about the only hotel in the Main Town, but it is basic and noisy.

For accommodation in private houses, call in at the Biuro Zakwaterownia on ul. Elzbietanska 10/11 (tel 312634 and 313849) near Gdańsk Główny.

The Central Youth Hostel at ul. Walowa (tel 312313), a 15-minute walk from Główny, between the Hewelius Hotel and the Shipyard, is supplemented in high summer by Almatur hostels elsewhere in the city for approximately 120,000 zł. per night: the Almatur office in the Main Town has full details from spring onwards.

There are three camp sites in the area — all operating from June to September, and all heavily booked in advance. The nearest (Brzezno) is 6.5 km. from the city centre at al. gen Hallera 234 (tel 566531), a short distance from the coast. Trams 7, 13 and 15 pass the front door. The Jelitkowo site is at ul. Jelitkowska 23 (tel 532731) is near Sopot (bus 143), and near the tram terminus for numbers 2 and 4, and ten miles/16km east away is the Orle site at ul. Lazurowa 5 (tel 380739) in Sobieszewo.

Advance bookings for all sites can be made at MPT Gdańsk-Tourist at ul. Heweliusza 8 (tel 319444 and 318946.)

Eating and Drinking. Gdańsk does not have the same spread of snack outlets as, say, Kraków, but it does have a number of good restaurants. The most famous (and probably the priciest), is the Pod Lososiem at ul. Szeroka 52/54 (tel 317652). The Tawerna, just off Dlugi Targ at ul. Powroznicza 19/20 (tel 314114) is good value, and the Milano at ul. Chelnicka 49/51 alongside St. Mary's Church has Italian dishes. The Tan-Viet at ul. Podmlynska 1/5 (tel 313355) near the Jacek Tower serves a variety of national cuisines.

Exploring. The city centre is split into three parts: the Main Town (Glowne Miasto) in the centre, the Old Town (Stare Miasto) to the north, and the Old Suburb (Stare Przemiescie) to the south.

From the main rail station Gdańsk Główny, the Old Town is immediately across the dual carriageway. The most interesting part — the Main Town — is a ten-minute walk along Wały Jagiellonskie. Enter the Main Town through the Upland Gate (Brama Wyzanna) which is alongside the LOT office. The Gate was built in 1574 and was the ceremonial gateway to the town. Rebuilt in 1588 by William van der Block, a Flemish master, the Gate marks the start of the Royal Way — the route traditionally taken by the Kings on their visits to the town.

In front of the Upland Gate stands the House of Tortures (Katownia), and the tall Prison Tower (Wieza Wiezienna). Restoration is proving to be particularly tortuous, and a museum including a working medieval torture chamber is currently being built inside. Further on is the Golden Gate (Złota Brama), the wider entrance to the Main Town. Built by Abraham van der Block between 1612 and 1614, the gate is adjoined to the left by the Court of the Fraternity of St. George (Dwor Bractwa św. Jerzego).

The broad street ahead is the carelessly named Long Street (ul. Długa), which seems almost as wide as it is long. As elsewhere in the Main Town, keep your eyes on the upper storeys of the houses. Each one tells its own tale, and all buildings in the Main Town have been meticulously restored since the end of the Second World War.

The town hall *(ratusz)* marks the end of the street: the Historical Museum of Gdańsk *(Muzeum Historii Miasta Gdańska)* is based here (closed on Mondays.) The most impressive room in the Town Hall is the Red Room, with its ornate ceiling stealing the show.

Beyond the Town Hall stands the Neptune Fountain *(Fontana Neptuna)* and the Long Market *(Dlugi Targ)*. The fountain dates from the early years of the seventeenth century; its ornate railings from 1634. To the left of the Fountain is the Artus Court *(Dwor Artusa)*, a banqueting hall which is still being renovated. Dlugi Targ ends with the Green Gate *(Zielona Brama)*, which marks the extent of the Royal Way.

On the other side of the Gate runs the Motlawa River. It is only worth crossing the bridge to take photographs, as all the sites of interest lie on the Gate side of the river. This was once the bustling quayside area of Gdańsk, and is now a popular tourist promenade. All the streets of the Main Town reached the riverside through a gate — the first of which as you turn right after recrossing the bridge into ul. Dlugie Pobrzeze is the Breadselters Gate *(Brama Chlebnicka)*. Boats to and from Westerplatte, Sopot and Hel leave from here. At the end of the quayside is the large wooden Gdańsk Crane *(Zurak Gdański)*. When it was built in the mid-15th century, it was the biggest in Europe. Inside lie two huge wheels and an equally impressive pulley system. The Crane is now part of the Maritime Museum *(Muzeum Morskie)* on the site.

At this point, the present-day metal cranes of the Gdańsk Shipyard pierce the sky, so retrace your steps past the Holy Ghost Gate to re-enter the Main Town through St Mary's Gate *(Brama Mariacka)* into ul. Mariacka, one of the jewels in the crown of Gdańsk. The street, with its ornate stairways and doors is home to many high class jewellery shops specialising in silver and the local amber.

The end of the street is dominated by the back of St. Mary's Church *(Kościół Mariacki)*, the largest brick-built church in the world (the nearest rival is in Medéllin, Colombia). It can hold 25,000 people, and its blackened exterior is in sharp contrast to its whitewashed, even plain, interior. While the main part of the church may appear relatively uninteresting, there is much to admire in the side chapels. The astronomical clock, for example, dates from the 1460s.

The Royal Chapel, nestling to the north of the church, is a rare example of Baroque architecture in the town. Leaving St. Mary's by Brewery Street (ul. Piwna) to the left, the Great Arsenal *(Wielka Zbrojownia)* with cannons in the street in front of it, dates from the early seventeenth century. Today it houses a modern shopping arcade.

Walking away from the Main Town, along ul. Kołodziejska and ul. Weglarska, the architectural gems become fewer. Crossing over to ul. Panska, the Church of St. Nicholas (Kościół św. Mikolaja), built by the Dominicans, is on the right, and beyond this, the Market Hall *(Hala Targowa)* bustles with traders and shoppers on weekdays. Opposite the market stands the Jacek Tower *(Baszta Jacek)*, and a little further on, the shell of St. John's Church (Kościół św. Jana) is now being turned into a high class shopping mall.

Turning left here, Waly Jagiellonskie runs left to right: the rail station is to the right.

Solidarity Gdańsk. Two places of interest attract visitors. To the north of the Old Town, ten minutes walk from Gdańsk Główny, lies the Monument to the Shipyard Workers *(Pomnik Poleglych Stoczniowcow)* outside the shipyard entrance on ul. Jana z Kolna. Three tall towers commemorate the massacre of 1970, and were erected a decade later.

Not far away, St. Bridget's Church (Kościół św. Brygidy) — destroyed in 1945 and rebuilt between 1970 and 1976 — became known as the Solidarity Church on account of its support for the movement. There are many remainders of the struggles in the church.

Old Suburb. On the opposite side of the Old Town this contains just one place of interest: the local branch of the National Museum (Muzeum Narodowe) at ul. Torunska 1 (tel 317061) (closed Mondays), one of the best museums outside Warsaw.

The suburb of *Oliwa*, to the northwest of the city, is a favourite day out for the people of Gdańsk. It has a cathedral set in parkland with an adjoining Diocesan Museum and Art Gallery. The cathedral is a ten-minute walk from Gdańsk Oliwa rail station.

Help and Information. By far the best Information Centre is the Gdańsk Osrodek Informacji Turystycznej at ul. Heweliusza 27 (tel 314355 and 316637), just past the Hewelius Hotel, ten minutes walk from the Główny stations. Opening hours are 8am-4pm, Monday to Saturday.

The PTTK tourist shop at ul. Długa 45 (tel 314751) is also very good; the Almatur office on the first floor of Dlugi Targ 11 (tel 312424) specialises in ISIC travel.

Sopot. The central town of the Tri City, Sopot developed as a fashionable seaside resort in the nineteenth century. Today it is rather shunned owing to the polluted waters of the Baltic. Still, it makes a pleasant half-day trip from Gdańsk, and it has a reasonable spread of accommodation. The town's pride and joy is its pier (molo) — at 512 metres, the longest on the Baltic coast. Each summer the town hosts an International Song Contest, and there are other concerts from May to September. In 1992, Sonia rather bizarrely shared top billing with Marillion, and in 1993 Boney M did the honours with LaToya Jackson.

Horse racing takes place during the summer: the racecourse adjoins Sopot Wyscigi rail station to the south of the town. The ORBIS office at ul. Bahaterow Monte Cassino 49 (the main street leading to the seafront) has details of accommodation. The swishest hotel, the Grand, is well worth a serious overspend if you are on a tight budget, being reminiscent of Sopot's fashionable past. The hotel is on ul. Powstancow Warszawy 8/12 (tel 510041) on the seafront.

Private accommodation can be booked at the Biuro Zakwaterownia at ul. Dworcowa 4 (tel 512617) near Sopot station; and there are campsites at ul. Zamkowa Góra 25 (tel 518011) and ul. Sepia 21 in the north of town; and to the south at ul. Bitwy pod Plowcami 69 (tel 516523), all open from June to September.

Gdynia. The worst face of Gdynia is immediately presented to tourists after leaving the main Glowna rail and bus stations: an ugly grey vista resembling a partial bomb-site, but the city — now one of Poland's leading ports may well be an accommodation option in high summer, and things do improve as you leave the confines of the station area.

Gdynia is also a leading ferry port with services to Scandinavia, and, once a week, to Tilbury in the UK. There is an Oceanographic Museum at the end of the southern pier *(Molo Poludniowe)* for nautical fans. The tourist office inside the Glowna station (tel 285378), and the private accommodation bureau at ul. Dworcowa 7 (tel 218265) have details of budget options in the town.

The top hotels are the ORBIS Gdynia, ul. Armii Krajowej 22 (tel 206661), and the Baltyk, ul. Kielecka 2a (tel 210649), and the youth hostel is at ul. Czerwonych Kosynierow 108c (tel 270005), north of the city centre.

Westerplatte. A peninsula to the north of Gdańsk, Westerplatte is the place where the Second World War started — at 4.45 a.m. on 1 September 1939 when the Nazi battleship Schleswig-Holstein shelled the Polish garrison here. The 182 Poles surrendered seven days later.

A popular visiting place for Poles, though marred nowadays by an ugly monument, bus 106 links Gdańsk with Westerplatte. If you have more time to spare though, boats also leave the Green Gate quay from May to November, and some also go from Sopot Pier. Book at the quay or Sopot Pier or telephone 314926.

Hel Peninsula. Another popular holiday spot, and best reached from the Tri

City by train or boat. A small number of direct trains reach Hel from the Tri City, otherwise change at Reda. In the summer, there is a direct service from Warsaw.

Only a kilometre or so in width, the peninsula has a number of old fishing villages like Jurata and Jaslarnia — some hardy souls walk the entire 20-mile/35km of the peninsula. If you fancy a dip, stick to the seaward side of the peninsula. The south side which faces the Bay of Gdańsk is especially heavily polluted.

THE MAZURIAN LAKE DISTRICT

This part of northeastern Poland is often described as the 'lungs' of the country. Probably the least industrialised region of Poland, the area is a popular holiday destination. It is heavily wooded, with a number of big forests: Augustówska, Piska, Knyszyńska and Białowieska, which is Europe's last remaining primeval forest. Amongst the forests are the Great Mazurian Lakes, of which the largest, Śniardwy, covers 114 square kilometres.

The Lake District is classic hostelling and camping territory. Hostels recommended by Hostelling International include:

BARTOSZYCE — ul. Bohaterow Warszawy 16 (July-August); tel 2012.
LIDZBARK WARMINSKI — ul. Poniatowskiego 3 (July-August); tel: 3147.
GOLDAP — ul. Wojska Polskiego 16 (July only); tel 150266.
SZCZYTNO — 'Pod Kasztanem', ul. Pasymska; tel 3992.
MIKOLAJKI — Szkola Podstawowa (July-August); no phone.
POLOM — p-ta Wronki (July-August); tel 75469.
PISZ — ul. Gizewiusza (July-August); no phone.
ELK — ul. Sikorskiego 7/8; tel 872514.

Registered campsites include:

GIZYCKO — ul. Moniuszki 1 (June-September); tel 3410.
KRETOWINY — Zabi Rog (May-September); tel 1618.
KOSEWO — (May-September); tel 8521.
KAMIEN — (May — September); tel Utka 22.
MRAGOWO — ul. Jaszczurcza Góra 1 (June-September); tel 2533.
PIECKI — (June — September); tel 25.
WEGORZEWO — (June — September); tel 2191.
PASYM — ul. Kosciuszki 2 (June — September); tel 152.
STARE JUCHY — (June — September); tel 142.
SZELIGI — ul. Elcka 27 (June — September); no phone.

Forests cover over 30% of the region, with both the Augustów and Pisz Forests each commanding areas of over 1,000 square kilometres. Pine and spruce predominate, but oak, hornbeam and beech also grow here.

The Augustów Forest (Puszcza Augustówska) borders Lithuania and Belarus. The northern section of the forest is separated from the more marshy southern part by the Augustów Canal, built between 1824 and 1839. The 60 mile/100km canal was intended to open up the interior with a port on the Baltic, but the idea came to little. Tourist boats ply the canal in high summer. There are a handful of trains daily from Warsaw to Augustów. PTTK have a camping site at ul. Sportowa 1 (tel 3455), close to Augustów Port rail station. There is also a hostel on the site.

Canoeing. There are two popular kayak trails here. The Krutynia River Trail (56 miles/91km) starts at Sorkwitz on Lake Lampacki, and leads to Lake Beldany, via the Krutynia River. There are a number of hostels en route at Sorkwity, Bienki, Babiety, Spychowo, Utka and Nowy Most.

The Czarna Hancza Trail (60 miles/97km) leads from Lake Wigry to Augustów, using the Augustów Canal for part of its journey. There are hostels along the way in Wysoki Most, Fracki, Jalowy Rog and Serwy.

Sailing. The Mazurian Lakes are extremely popular with yachtsmen. If you book in advance, it is possible to charter a five-person Venus yacht for about $50 a day, plus a helmsman for an extra $5 per hour.

Angling. Lake Sniardwy is the largest in Poland, and has a number of peninsulas and islands. Many types of fish are caught here: pike, eel, beam, bass, tench and roach are the most numerous.

Elbląg. Entering the region from Gdańsk in the west, the first big town is Elblag, historically an important Polish seaport. The town is a handy staging post for two more interesting centres: Frombork and Malbork, both of which may be reached from Elblag by rail and bus.

Frombork. A small town on the Vistula Bay (Zaleew Wiślany), Frombork is totally dominated by its 14th century Cathedral on the hill. This contains a Gothic tower, known as the Copernicus Tower, after the famous Polish astronomer. He worked here between 1512 and 1516, and again from 1522 to 1543, and it was here that he wrote his famous treatise *De Revolutionibus* which asserted that the sun, rather than Earth, was at the centre of the solar system. There is a Copernicus Museum in the Cathedral complex.

The Tourist Office is at ul. Katedralna 10 (tel 7352) and the PTTK hostel lies in the shadow of the Cathedral at ul. Krasickiego 3 (tel 7252). There is another hostel at ul. Elblaska 11 (tel 7453) — extra accommodation is available here during July and August.

Malbork. This town is home to Poland's biggest castle; apart from the Wawel in Kraków and the Royal Palace in Warsaw, it is the nation's best known site. The castle was built by the Teutonic Knights at the end of the thirteenth century. The complex is closed on Mondays.

Rail and bus stations are a 15-minute walk from the castle, and a summer hostel operates at Szkola Podstawowa 1, ul. Zeromskiego 45 (tel 2511) during the school holidays.

Olsztyn. This is the easiest centre to reach by public transport from the rest of the country. Trains run to and from Warsaw, Gdańsk and Elblag, and buses connect with Warsaw and smaller towns within the region.

The Hotel Kormoran, pl. Konstytucji 3 Maja 4 (tel 335864), is big and expensive. It has a reasonable restaurant and a café. PTTK runs a hostel on the edge of the Old Town (tel 273675), and during July and August, Almatur runs a hostel in the Agricultural College in nearby Kortowo (tel 278824). There is also a hostel at ul. Kopernika 45 (tel 276650). The campsite at ul. Sielska 12 (tel 271253) is open from May to October.

The Tourist Office, near the High Gate (Wysoka Brama) at ul. Warszawska 13 in the town centre (tel 273090 or 272738), is good. There is another office at ul. Staromiejska 1 (tel 275156).

Battlegrounds Around Olsztyn. For such an apparently peaceful area, the Lake District is, surprisingly, the home of two massive battles, one medieval and one more recent.

Gently rolling meadowland on the outskirts of the village of Grunwald, 25 miles/40km southwest of Olsztyn off the E77, marks the site of the most famous medieval battle in Polish history. Here on 15 July 1410, the Polish and Lithuanian Armies defeated the Teutonic Knights and thus laid the foundations for a revival in the power and prestige of Poland. The site of the battle is today marked by a few crosses, but there's not much else to see.

Fifty miles (80km) or so northeast from Olsztyn, and 500 years on from the Battle of Grunwald, the town of Gierloz was the home of Hitler's main Polish headquarters during the Second World War, and the site of the 'Wolf's Lair' complex — known in Polish as Wilczy Szaniec and in German as Wolfsschanze.

Buses run here from the nearest big town Ketrzyn, which in turn is connected by rail and bus to Olsztyn.

Eighteen hectares of partly destroyed concrete buildings meet the eye. Construction started in early 1940, when Hitler decided to attack the Soviet Union. The original buildings included eighty bunkers, with walls up to six metres thick, and ceilings up to ten metres tall. The complex was surrounded by bunkers and minefields, with full communications to all the battlefronts. Hitler was based here from June 1941 to November 1944. Despite all these precautions, Hitler narrowly escaped assassination when Colonel Claus von Stauffenberg's bomb attempt on his life failed. Von Stauffenberg and up to 5,000 others paid for it with their lives.

Hitler only fled to the Chancellery Bunker in Berlin when the Soviet Army approached, and the complex was partially destroyed in January 1945 by German Army sappers. The complex is open during daylight hours. There is a short film show depicting its history, and guides are available from May to October.

SZCZECIN AND WESTERN POMERANIA

The largest city in northwest Poland, Szczecin (pronounced roughly as the Germans spell it, Stettin) — and its seaport Świnoujście (Svinoosh) — has had a colourful history. Over the years, the city has been under the control of Poland, Denmark, Sweden, Brandenburg and Prussia. The latter occupier developed the city as the port for Berlin, linking both cities by canal.

Most of the city centre was destroyed during the Second World War by RAF carpet bombing and the fleeing Nazis, but unlike similar projects in Warsaw and Gdańsk, the centre was rebuilt without too much historical attention and so it is not quite as attractive as its rivals.

Arrival and Departure. The airport is 28 miles/45km away at Goleniow, and has just one early morning flight to Warsaw, with the return touching down late in the evening. LOT's office in town is at ul. Wyzwolenia 17 (tel 339926 and 335058). The LOT office at the airport is on 182708.

Szczecin's main rail and bus stations are close to each other south of the city centre, and there are good connections to Warsaw, Gdańsk, Kraków, Poznań and Berlin.

Accommodation. The best hotels in town are the Arkona, ul. Panienska 10 (tel 36061); Neptun, ul. Matejki 18 (tel 240111); and the Cukrowa, in Gumience to the south of the city (tel 822461).

There are three Hostelling International recommended hostels in the city. Unislawy, at ul. Unislawy 26 (tel 232566) is open all year round. It's north of the city centre on tram routes 2, 3 and 12 and bus route B. Two other hostels open their doors during July and August: at ul. Monte Cassino 19a (tel 224761) and ul. Grodzka 22 (tel 89424) — the most basic of the three.

There are two campsites in the area, both open from June to September. The Dabie site at ul. Przestrzenna 23 (tel 613264) boasts a swimming pool. The other site, 'Plonia' at ul. Szosa Stargardzka 45 (tel 612188) is even further away from the city centre.

Exploring. With the suburbs comprising mostly tower blocks and industrial units, sightseeing can be confined to the Old Town area. The big attraction here is the Castle of the Pomeranian Princes (Zamek Ksiazat Pomorskich), dating from the mid fourteenth century and rebuilt by the ruling Prussians in the nineteenth century. Virtually destroyed during the Second World War, it has been largely rebuilt in its original style — a snub perhaps to its later Prussian influence, although almost modern-looking wings give its courtyard a confused look. Complete with museum, the complex follows standard Polish opening hours — it's closed on Mondays.

The Town Hall (Ratusz Staromiejski), just off ul. Panienska, was also rebuilt after the War: the Historical Museum of Szczecin (Muzeum Historii Miasta Szczecina) is housed within (also closed Mondays.)

Perhaps the most interesting of the rebuilt houses in the Old Town is the Palace Under The Globe on pl. Orla Bialego in the centre of the area. For a number of years in the 1730-40s, it was the home of the infant Russian Empress Catherine II, whose father, a major-general in the Prussian Army, was promoted to Governor of Szczecin. The fountain which stood in the gardens of the house has been removed to its present position near the Holdu Pruskiego Gate.

Help and Information. ORBIS has two offices: at Boleslawa Krzywoustego 13/14 (tel 42251 and 80275) and pl. Zwyciestwa 1 (tel 44425 and 45154); Almatur is at al. Bohaterow Warszawy 84 (tel 44355) and PTTK at pl. Batorego 2 (tel 36267 and 37089).

Świnoujście. To the north of Szczecin, this port is linked to its larger neighbour by rail and bus. It is an important shipping and fishing centre, with passenger ferries to and from Ystad and Copenhagen. And if you fancy nipping over to Germany, the border is only two miles from town — take bus A to the pedestrian-only checkpoint, with Ahlbeck the neighbouring town on the German side of the border.

ORBIS is at ul. Armii Czerwonej 2 (tel 2393), and their office at Boleslawa Chrobrego deals with ferry tickets. PTTK's office is at ul. Paderewskiego 24 (tel 2613). The leading hotel in town is the Albatros, ul. J. Kasprowicza 2 (tel 2335 and 2336); there is a campsite at ul. Slowackiego 6 (tel 3912). Private rooms are available from the Biuro Zakwaterowan at ul. Armii Czerwonej 2.

Matelots and anglers alike should head for the Museum of Sea Fishing on pl. Rybaka 1, but not, of course, on Mondays when it's closed and the staff presumably put up the 'gone fishing' notice.

Kolobrzeg. A seaside resort and port at the mouth of the River Parseta, Kolobrzeg is a popular holiday destination. Originally built around its salt reserves, the town was virtually razed to the ground by the Nazis before being reconstructed. The 14th century cathedral and the town hall are the only buildings worth investigating in the town, but Kolobrzeg's *raison d'être* nowadays is as a proper resort. The seafront is punctuated by a pier and surrounded by cafés and hot dog stands, with an open lighthouse another attraction.

The ORBIS-run Hotel Solny at ul. Fredry 4 (tel 22400) on the outskirts of town, and the Skanpol, ul. Dworcowa 21 (tel 28211), near the ORBIS office and train station are both pricey. Private rooms are available from the local Biuro Zakwaterowan at ul. Lenin 2. (This is one of the few remaining streets named after the founder of state communism, and may well have changed).

PTTK at ul. Dubois 20, inside the Gunpowder Tower (Baszta Pochowa) (tel 22311 and 23287) is the best source of tourist information, although ORBIS has an office at ul. Dworcowa 2/4 (tel 23869).

Słupsk. Twenty-five miles/40km inland, Słupsk serves as a big regional centre. Trains and buses link the town with Gdańsk, Warsaw and Szczecin. The most important sight is the 16th century castle, which houses the regional museum. Opposite the castle is the 16th century mill. In Poland, the town is best known for its Festival for Yuong Polish Pianists, held each September. It is safe to assume there will be some Chopin on the repertoire.

The best hotel is the Staromiejski, ul. Jednosci Narodowej 4 (tel 2846465); the local Dom Turysty is at ul. Szarych Szeregow 1 (tel 22902). The ORBIS office is at ul. Wojska Polskiego 1 (tel 23614), and there is another office at ul. Jednosci Narodowej 4 (tel 24326).

POZNAN

Sited in central Poland, Poznań is an important trading centre and junction on the main Berlin-Warsaw-Moscow routes. It isn't the prettiest place in Poland, but you'll probably end up passing through here.

Arrival and Departure. The main rail station — Poznań Główny — lies just outside the city centre, and the PKS bus station is a five minute walk away from the rail station. The airport is at Lawica, four miles/7km from town. LOT flies direct to Warsaw and Szczecin only. The LOT office in town is at ul. św. Marcin 69 (tel 522847) and at the airport on 481701.

Accommodation. Poznań has an accommodation shortage, particularly when it is hosting one of its regular Industrial Fairs, which results in the top hotels being block booked, particularly in the middle of June when the International Fair hits town. The leading hotels are the Poznań, pl. Dabrowskiego 1 (tel 332081), the Novotel at ul. Warszawska 64/66 (tel 770011), the Polonez, al. Niepodleglosci 36 (tel 699141) and the Merkury, ul. Roosevelta 20 (tel 470801).

Down the price scale, the PTTK Dom Turysty in the middle of the Old Town at Stary Rynek (tel 528893) is popular, and private rooms can be booked through the Biuro Zakwaterownia at ul. Glogowska 16 (tel 666313) across the road from the main rail station. The closest hostel to the station is ten minutes away at ul. Berwinskiego 2/4 (tel 663680).

There are three seasonal campsites: at Strezszynek (tel 483145), accessible on bus 95; Lawicka, towards the airport (tel 143501), on bus routes Z and P); and Baranowo (tel 476894), reached by bus 61, all on the western outskirts of town.

Exploring. The modern, functional city centre lies between the stations and the main attraction, the Old Town (Stare Miasto). Take tram no. 5 to see the sights.

The Old Town Square (Stary Rynek) is a 450-foot-square expanse. It was laid out in 1253 with the rest of the Old Town. The Town Hall (Ratusz) dominates the scene, and was constructed in the Renaissance style between

1550 and 1560. The tower was added two centuries later. In front of the
building stands the pillory *(pregierz)*, the scene of medieval punishments.
Inside the Town Hall is the Historical Museum of Poznań *(Muzeum Historii
Miasta Poznańia)*, and the impressive Renaissance Hall which has served
the city for over 400 years.

The gabled houses of the Square merit a visit: at no. 45, the Museum of
Musical Instruments specialises in instruments from Chopin's era, and the
third museum at no. 3 highlights the Solidarity influence on the city. The
local branch of the National Museum at al. Marcinkowskiego 9, to the west
of the Old Town, has a collection of Old Masters.

A more modern remnant of history is the monument to the workers killed
during demonstrations against higher food prices in 1956: it was unveiled
at the height of the Solidarity movement in 1981 and is outside the immediate
city centre at pl. Mickiewicza on tram route 5.

Help and Information. The main tourist office is at Stary Rynek 59 (tel
526156) in the heart of town: the Almatur office is at ul. Fredry 7 (tel
523645 and 528001).

KARKONOSZE

The other main tourist area of Silesia is the Karkonosze Mountain range,
which form the border between Poland and the Czech Republic. Popular
with hikers and skiers alike, the range is tucked in the south west of the
country, and has an average height of 4,550 ft.

The area is watered by numerous small rivers with waterfalls and rapids.
The Lomniczka River has the longest cascade — 488 feet — and the highest
waterfall at 88 feet is on the Kamienczyk River.

Jelenia Góra is the transport junction for the Karkonosze, and the gateway
for the area. The ORBIS office at ul. 1 Maja 1 (tel 26206) has details of the
town and the surrounding region. PTTK are at al. Wojska Polskiego 40 (tel
22000). Their hostel is at ul. 1 Maja 88 (tel 23059). The Jelenia Góra is the
best hotel for miles around. It's at ul. Swierazewskiego 63 (tel 24081). The
'Bartek' youth hostel at ul. Bartka Zwyciezcy 10 (tel 25746) is open all year,
while the hostel at ul. Wirejska 86a (tel 24155) is open July to mid August
only. The summer only campsite is at ul. Swierczewskiego 42 (tel 26942).

The main towns of the Karkonosze region proper are Karpacz and
Szklarska Poreba. Karpacz is ten miles/16km from Jelenia Góra, the nearest
large town. Three trains daily and a similar number of buses link the two
towns. There are some direct services from Warsaw and Wrocław to Jelenia
Góra. Karpacz lies close to Mt. Sniezka popular with hikers and skiers.
Accommodation is in good supply, with numerous small hotels and pensions.
The Skalny Hotel at ul. Obrońców 3 (tel 19721) is worth a look, and the tourist
office at ul. 1 Maja 8 (tel 19453) also deals with private accommodation.

The camp site at ul. 3 Maja 8 is open from June to September, as is the
other site at ul. Obrońców Pokoju 4.

The strangest sight in town is the Wang Chapel — not a relic of a computer
company, but a pine church, moved here and reconstructed from its original
home in Norway by Prussian King Friedrich Wilheim IV. There are regular
tours for groups.

Szklarska Poreba lies at the foot of Mt. Szrenica. Again, the town is best
reached by rail and bus from Jelenia Góra, and there are direct trains from
Gdańsk and Warsaw in the summer.

The Sudety Hotel at ul. Krasickiego 10 (tel 172225) is the biggest in town and also has a restaurant. The youth hostel at ul. Piastowska 1 (tel 172141) is slightly out of town, and there's a small campsite at ul. Demokratow 6, near the rail station.

The tourist office at ul. Jednosci Narodowej 6 (tel 172123) keeps details of many of the small pensions in the area; private accommodation bookings can be made at the Biuro Zakwaterownia at ul. Maja 4 (tel 172393) near the bus station.

There's a chair lift to the top of the mountain. Look out for the waterfall at the junction of the Szklarska and Kamienna rivers — the waterfall is just off the main road from the small town of Piechowice.

WROCLAW

Wrocław, with a population of 650,000, is the largest city in Silesia, and the fourth biggest in Poland. The city returned to Polish control only after the end of the Second World War, having been the property of Bohemia, Austria, Prussia and Germany for the previous 600 years.

Any Germanic feeling which might therefore be expected in the area has been severely depleted by the postwar settlement policy of moving the population from the former Polish territories in the east, particularly from around L'vov in the Ukraine.

Arrival and Departure. The bus and rail stations are next to each other, a short distance from the city centre. If you can't bear the walk, trams 2 and 9 run from the stations into town.

There are frequent rail express services to Warsaw, and also direct services to Gdańsk, Bialystok, Poznań, Szczecin, Lodz and Kraków. International services link Wrocław with Munich, Frankfurt, Leipzig, Dresden and the border town of Gorlitz — some services carry sleeping accommodation.

Likewise, coach services serve the same centres — services from London to Kraków also stops at Wrocław.

LOT flies to and from Dusseldorf via Poznań: the LOT office is at ul. Pilsudskiego 36 (tel 31744 and 39032), and at the airport on 574788. Eurowings flies direct to and from Frankfurt. Bus 106 runs between the Airport and Swiebodzki rail station.

Accommodation. The leading hotels are the Dwor Wazow, ul. Kielbasnicza 2 (tel 441633); ORBIS Wrocław, ul Powstancow Slaskich 7 (tel 614651) and the ORBIS Panorama, pl. Dominikanski 8 (tel 443681).

The Grand Hotel, ul. Pilsudskiego 100/102 (tel 36071) is cheaper; the Piast I next door at no. 98 (tel 30033) is cheaper still. Biuro Zakwaterowania at the Piast I (tel 444101) looks after private accommodation.

The hostel at ul. Kollataja 20 (tel 38856), just north of Główny rail station is open all year, as is the 'Sleza' campsite at ul. Na Grobli 16/18 (tel 34442). It is slightly more centrally located than the bigger AWF site at ul. Paderewskiego 35 (tel 484641) on tram routes 9, 12, 16 and 17 in the grounds of the Olympic Stadium.

Exploring. Like most large Polish centres, much of Wrocław was destroyed by the fleeing Nazis, with the carefully reconstructed city centre being ringed by dull tower blocks. The centre of the city — the Rynek — is virtually an island, circled by the Odra River and the Foza Miejska. Indeed, the fourteenth century Church of St. Mary on the Sand (Kościół NMP na Piasku) is built on an island — Piasek Island — on the Odra.

Back in the Rynek, the Town Hall (Ratusz), started in 1327, is the focal point of the large square, its ornate galleries drawing attention to the astronomical clock in its centre. In front of the building is the punishment post — a replica of the fifteenth century original. The Town Hall has a Historical Museum (closed Monday and Tuesday), the centrepiece of which is the Knight's Hall.

South of the Rynek, the Arsenal is a reminder of the city's medieval fortresses; while to the east of the Rynek, the vast St. Dorothy's Church (Kościół św. Doroty) marks the 1351 summit between King Kazimierz Wielki and Charles V of Bohemia which resulted in the region being handed over to Bohemia. The Church of St. Mary Magdalene (Kościół św. Marii Magdaleny) is famous for its exotic flying buttresses. Walking further north along ul. Wita Stwosza, the Museum of Architecture (Muzeum Architektury) (closed Monday and Tuesday) is the appetiser for the Raclawice Panorama behind it.

Painted on the walls of a rotunda, this 400ft long by 50ft high spectacle depicts the Battle of Raclawice (a village near Kraków) in 1794 between the Polish peasant army and the Russians. The Poles won the battle but lost the war — the Third Partition of 1795 wiped Poland off the map until 1918. The painting, along with many thousands of refugees, made the long trek westwards from the Ukraine in the 1940s, but was only restored after pressure from Solidarity in 1986. Guided tours take place daily except Monday.

Help and Information. The ORBIS tourist offices are at Rynek 29 (tel 32665 and 34780), and ul. Pilsudskiego 62 (tel 33082 and 38745); Odra Tourist is down the road at ul. Pilsudskiego 98 (tel 30037). Almatur are at ul. Kosciuszki 34 (tel 443003 and 443951).

KATOWICE

An ecological diaster area with the whole of the region polluted by all sorts of emissions. If you have to linger here, the (optimistically concieved) tourist information centre is at ul. Mlynska 11, near the rail station; the youth hostel at ul. Graniczna 27a (tel 519457), 15 minutes from the rail and bus stations on tram routes 7 and 15, and the best hotel is the Katowice at ul. Korfantego 35 (tel 598021).

KRAKOW

If you only have a few days in Poland, head for Kraków. The tourist capital of the country, it simply abounds with character, museums, monuments, churches and stunning buildings.The original capital of Poland, Kraków escaped the Nazi destruction of the Second World War — the advancing Soviet Army catching the occupiers by surprise before they could dynamite it — and there is history around every corner. To do justice to the city, you'll have to set aside a few days, particularly if you want to visit all the museums and the Castle.

Arrival and Departure. *Air:* The airport is at Balice, 11 mile/18km away (LOT airport office tel 116700). There are regular LOT scheduled flights from Warsaw, London (Fridays throughout the year, Sunday and Wednesday during the summer season), Cologne, Frankfurt, Paris and Rome. The LOT office in town is at ul. Basztowa 15 (tel 225076 and 227078). Bus no. 208 runs between the city's bus station and the airport at 45 minute intervals throughout the day — journey time is around 45 minutes.

Bus: The main coach and bus station is on pl. Kolejowy, just northeast of the Old Town, and also services national and international routes from Warsaw, Zakopane, Italy, Germany, Austria and the United Kingdom.

Train: Kraków Główny, the main rail station, lies alongside the coach station, while the other main station, Płaszów, is less conveniently placed to the south of the city. Główny is currently being rebuilt, with the booking offices in the original station buildings a good five minutes walk from the new platforms to the north (the left luggage office is near the new platforms.) Give yourself enough time to walk between the two parts of the station. There are direct trains daily to Warsaw, Gdańsk, Zakopane, Wrocław, Poznań, Szczecin, Kraków — Lublin, Częstochowa, Bucharest, Dresden, L'vov, Kiev and Frankfurt.

Accommodation. There's a good range of accommodation, but during the high summer, it can be difficult to find a room. The top hotels on the outskirts are the Holiday Inn (on bus routes 139, 173, 208, 238 and 258) on al. Armii Krajowej (tel 375044). Rates start at $80 per night; Cracovia on al. Focha 1 (tram 15 and 18 heading for Cichy Kacik) (tel 228666) — both to the west of the city.

The best hotels in the Old Town are the Grand, ul. Slawkowska 5/7 (tel 216695), and the Francuski, ul. Pijarska 13 (tel 225122). Cheaper city centre options are the Europejski, ul. Lubicz 5 (tel 220911) and the Polonia, ul. Basztowa 25 (tel 221233), both near the rail and bus stations. Count on around $40 per person per night.

The PTTK Dom Turysty, ten minutes walk south of the stations at ul. Westerplatte 15/16 (tel 229566) has 630 rooms and is a popular medium-priced choice, although more basic than the other hotels. All-year hostels are at ul. Oleandry 4 (tel 338822 and 338920) (tram 15 and 18), and at ul. Złotej Kielni (tel 372411). From July to mid September, a hostel operates at the AWF college at al. Jana Pawla II 82 (tel 482027). A double room costs $12 per night, a single room $8 per night. Take trams 4, 5, 9 10 or 44 eastwards towards Nowa Huta.

Private accommodation is dealt with at the 'Waweltur' Biuro at ul. Pawia 8 (tel 221921) across the road from the stations.

All the camping sites are on the outskirts of Kraków, and open during summer months only. The most popular is the 'Krak' at ul. Radzikowskiego 99 (tel 372122), out towards the airport — airport bus no. 208 passes nearby. Off the main road south towards Zakopane is the site at ul. Zywiecka Boczna 4 (tel 664191) (on bus route 119, tram routes 8, 19, 22, 24 or 42). The third site is at ul. Kamedulska 18 (tel 211255) (bus routes 109, 209, 229.)

Eating and Drinking. The best and most famous restaurant is the centuries old Wierzynek at Rynek Główny 15 (tel 221035). Prices are smack up to date, though. Local gourmets say however that the restaurant in the Hotel Francuski, ul. Pijarska 13 (tel 225122) is snapping at its heels. The Grand Hotel restaurant at ul. Slawkowska 5/7 (tel 216695) and its adjoining cafe are also recommended.

There's no shortage of cafes in the Old Town — try the French cafe in the bakery on ul. Slawkowska, or the cafe in the Sukiennice.

Exploring. From the stations, the Old Town (Stary Rynek) is only five minutes walk away. Passing the tourist office and private accommodation bureau at ul. Pawia 8, turn right into ul. Basztowa until you reach the Grunwald Monument celebrating the victory of the Polish and Lithuanian forces over the Teutonic Knights in 1410. It was erected in 1910, destroyed by the Nazis in 1939, and rebuilt in 1976.

Barbica (Barbakan). Crossing the main road, the brick- built circular towered Barbican is, with the Florian Gate (Brama Florianska), all that remains of the foureenth and fifteenth century town fortifications. Built in 1498, it is one of the few remaining examples of this medieval defensive structure.

Planty. The band of parkland, 'Planty', that runs alongside the Barbican extends around the Old Town, and was laid out in 1822 to replace the old town walls and provide some greenery for the crowded city.

Florian Gate (Brama Florianska). Standing next to the Barbican, the gate is the only one remaining of the eight that once ringed the town. Royal processions would enter Kraków through this gate — the base dates from the thirteenth century, although the upper parts were added later.The busy ul. Florianska runs to the Market Square (Rynek Główny). Look out for Jan Matejko's House (Dom Jana Matejki) (no. 41), the birthplace of the famous Polish painter. It is now a museum featuring his work (closed Wednesday and Thursday).

Nearer the Florian Gate, though, is one of the prime attractions of Kraków — the *Czartoryski Museum* on ul. św. Jana 19. Created at the beginning of the 19th century by Princess Izabela Czartoryski, pride of place goes to Leonardo da Vinci's painting 'Lady With Ermine' (no matter that it's probably a ferret — the museum is one of only six in the world displaying a da Vinci.) The museum is closed Wednesday and Thursday, but admission is free on Fridays.

Take time, too, to examine the many churches in the immediate vicinity. The Piarist Church at the top of ul. św. Jana mixes Baroque style with a Rococo facade, and further down the road, St. John's Church (Kościół św. Jana) dates from the seventeenth century.

Market Square (Rynek Główny) — The biggest medieval market square in Europe, measuring 650 feet square, this is the heart of Kraków. Laid out in 1257, and surrounded by burgher houses, the centre of the square is dominated by the Cloth Hall (Sukiennice).

Cloth Hall (Sukiennice) — The original building, the biggest of its kind in the world, was originally built in the thirteenth century, gutted by fire in 1555, and then rebuilt in Renaissance style.
   Further additions in the nineteenth century, such as the entrances and arcades add to its charm. Inside the Hall are numerous stalls selling handicrafts (although look out for pickpockets in the gloom.) The Hall also has cafes, a pub, a tourist office and a branch of the National Museum.

St Mary's Church (Kościół Mariacki) — Standing in the eastern corner of the Square at a slight angle, the church is one of the spiritual centres of the nation.
   Construction started at the beginning of the fourteenth century on the site of an earlier temple destroyed by the Tatars in 1241. The twin towers were completed by 1406, the taller tower acting as a watchtower, and it is from here that a lone trumpeter sounds his call (hejnat) on the hour. This call is truncated — legend has it that a similar call was stopped in mid-blast by a Tatar arrow — and the call is now broadcast on Polish radio at midday.
   The church interior at first appears quite dark, but the centrepiece is the

magnificent wooden Gothic altar, the largest in Europe, lovingly crafted by Wit Stwosz, a master craftsman from Nuremberg, between 1477 and 1489. Nearly ten feet high, it contains 200 different figures, including one reputedly of Stwosz himself, an early forerunner of Hitchcock perhaps. The altar is opened on non- Church days at noon. The fourteenth century stained glass windows are also a feature of the Church.

Alongside the Church, the charming St. Mary's Square (pl. Mariacki) with its fountain, leads to St. Barbara's Church (Kościół św. Barbary), and the quieter, smaller Small Market Square (Maly Rynek.)

The Statue of Adam Mickiewicz — Polish poet and playwright — is a focal point back on the main square. Each December, a competition to find the best decorated crib or 'szopki' is held here. And in the south corner of the square, the small, domed St. Adalbeert's Church (Kościół św. Wojciecha) dates from the twelfth century. St. Adalbert is supposed to have preached here before his missionary journey to Prussia.

In the western corner of the square, the tower of the old Town Hall (Wieza Ratuszowa) is all that remains of the original building. The Historical Museum is here (closed Monday and Tuesday), and in the basement, formerly the torture chamber and gaol, the 'Maszkaron' Satirical Theatre now has its base.

Jagiellonian University. The second oldest university in central Europe, founded in 1364 by King Casimir the Great, the University soon settled in the western part of the Old Town. Famous students include Nicolaus Copernicus and Pope John Paul II. The oldest building — Collegium Maius — at ul. Jagiellonska 15, is a hidden treasure, a square Gothic court with high arcades and buildings — the University Museum is based here.

The Road to Wawel. The Royal Way starts again in the western corner of the Market Square alongside the Wierzynek House at Rynek Główny 15, now one of the best restaurants in the country. Proceding down ul. Grodzka, the road is crossed by ul. Dominikanska, with the Dominican Church (Kościół Dominikanow) on the far left (much used by the city's students), and ul. Franciszanska, crowned by the Franciscan Church (Kościół Francisz-kanow), on the right. Continuing down ul. Grodzka, SS. Peter and Paul's Church, with its stone replicas of the twelve apostles outside, stands opposite the lane leading to ul. Kanonicza, one of the most beautiful of Kraków's streets (at least it will be when the extensive renovation works are completed), which runs parallel to ul. Grodzka.

Wawel The royal castle and cathedral of Wawel rises at the end of ul. Grodzka and ul. Kanonicza. The original coronation setting and royal residence before the court moved to Warsaw, the castle during its history has been used as stables by the Austrian Army and the centre of government by the Nazis. The first settlement was built on the high limestone hill along the Wisla River in primitive times. A regal seat since the sixth century, a bishopric was established here in 1000 AD.

The castle was rebuilt in Renaissance style in the early 16th century after a fire in 1499 destroyed Casimir the Great's castle. The present cathedral was built between 1320 and 1364. The cathedral tower houses the massive 'Zygmunt' bell which takes eight people to ring.

The cathedral museum is closed on Mondays, as is the castle itself. The 'Lost Wawel' exhibition showing fragments of previous castles is closed on Tuesdays.

Kazimierz. Once a separate town lying to the west of Wawel, Kazimierz's importance of old can be gauged by the size of its town hall on pl. Wolnica, just off ul. Krakówska in a straight line from Wawel. Today the town hall houses an Ethnographic Museum displaying Polish folklore artefacts. It opens daily except Tuesdays.

But Kazimierz is more on the tourist trail for its Jewish past. Before the Second World War, almost 70,000 Jews lived here. Today there are fewer than 250 in the whole of Kraków. The district has an old feel to it — Steven Spielberg used it as the setting for his film *Schindler's List*, and there are seven synagogues in a small area, only two of which are used for prayer today.

ul. Jozefa cuts through the area: the Old Synagogue is now a Museum of local Jewish history (it's usually closed Mondays and Tuersdays, but this is liable to change around the time of Jewish holidays). The Remu'h Synagogue on ul. Szeroka is open for worship, and is surrounded by a large Jewish cemetery dating from the late middle ages.

Concentration Camps. The nearest Nazi concentration camp to Kraków was at Płaszów where 80,000 people of various nationalities were exterminated. Buses 103, 104, 164, 173 and 194 pass close by the monument marking the site.

But horrors on an even greater scale can be sensed at Oświęim, 42 miles/ 60 km west of Kraków, and better known by its German name of Auschwitz. It was here — and at the neighbouring Birkenau camp — that around four million people, including 2.5 million Jews, were killed after passing through gates cruelly inscribed 'Arbeit Macht Frei' — 'work makes free'. The camp opens daily from 8 am to sunset, and there is no charge for entry. There is an irregular train service from Kraków, with no departures between mid-morning and lunchtime, but a number of coach operators run day tours. Check with Point Travel at the Hotel Cracovia in Kraków (tel 219880.)

Wieliczka. For Wieliczka, read 'salt.' This small town, ten miles southeast of Kraków, and now virtually a suburb of its large neighbour, is dominated by a large 1,000 year-old salt mine with museum. It's a very popular tourist attraction, with subterranean galleries stretching for 3 miles, and including an underground chapel and sanitorium. Open daily, follow the signs from the town centre to 'Kopalnia Soli'. There's a regular train and bus service from Kraków Główny, and a number of private operators offer coach tours complete with guide.

ZAKOPANE AND THE TATRAS

Zakopane, the Polish winter sports capital nestling in the Tatra Mountains in the far south of the country, is re-emerging as a leading winter sports centre after a long period of neglect. The 1993 Winter University Games were held here, and the area looks likely to put in a joint bid with Slovakia to stage the Winter Olympics in 2002 or 2006.

The standard and range of facilities are being improved, but there is still a long way to go if the resort is to match those offered by its European rivals. The town is packed in winter and summer, when hiking holidays take over, but is more relaxed in autumn and spring. A number of British coach holiday operators specialise in package trips to the area — the biggest company is New Millenium.

Zakopane. The main thoroughfare in the town is ul. Krupowki: the bus and rail stations on ul. Jagiellonska are a ten minutes walk away. The Museum of the Tatras is located at ul. Krupowki 10.

The most expensive, and largest, hotel in town is the ORBIS Kasprowy on ul. Polana Szymoszkowa (tel 4011), a kilometre or so away. The Giewont, ul. Kosciuszki 1 (tel 2011) is a cheaper option. PTTK has a hotel, 'Dom Turysty' at ul. Zaruskiego 5 (tel 63281). Private accommodation and pensions are handled by ORBIS at ul. Krupowki 22 (tel 4812). The popular youth hostel is at ul. Nowotarska 45, ten minutes from the stations. The campsite at ul. Zeromskiego (tel 2256) is open throughout the year: the smaller Harenda site (tel 4034) is open May — October, and lies a mile north of the town on a main bus route.

The Tatra Mountains. The Tatrzanski Park Narodowy map shows all routes, and those published by the Slovakian State Cartographers are also easy to understand and accurate.

The nearest mountains to the town are Mt. Gubalowka (1120 m.) and Mt. Kasprowy Wierch (1,985 m.). A funicular runs up Gubalowka — the journey takes five minutes, and the lower station is just off ul. Krupowki, and there is a restaurant at the top.

A cable car goes up Kasprowy Wierch. The lower station is two miles from Zakopane in Kuznice — there's a bus service from Zakopane. If you book a return ticket, a seat will be reserved for you on the departure two hours after your outward journey. The mountains are traversed by a series of hiking trails: one of the most popular of which leads to Lake Morskie Oko (Eye of the Sea), one of 121 lakes in the area, and almost 51 metres deep. As the crow flies, it is nine miles/14km from Zakopane; by road it is 20 miles/32km., with a regular bus service. Nearby is Mt. Rysy, at 2,499 Zakopane is connected to Warsaw, Kraków and Nowy Targ by train and bus. Unless you catch an express train, it is likely that the more frequent coach service will be quicker — the slowest train services can be painfully slow.

LUBLIN

Slightly off the tourist trails, the eastern city of Lublin is worth a visit. Site of the 1569 Lublin Union which united Poland and Lithuania, as well as the centre of government in the early days of Polish independence after the First World War, and also at the end of the Second World War, it is today best known as the home of the Catholic University. Many of the buildings in the centre are still awaiting restoration after being damaged in the Second World War.

Arrival and Departure. There are express rail services to Kielce and Warsaw, and a few to Kraków. Bus 158 runs between the rail station and the Old Town, a mile or two away.

Accommodation. The leading hotels in town are the ORBIS Unia, al. Raclawickie 12 (tel 32061) and Victoria at ul.Narutowiczka 58/60 (tel 27011). Almatur at ul. Langiewicza 10 (tel 33237) has details of summer hostels in the city. The 'Europa' PTTK hostel at ul. Krakówskie Przedmiescie is central and reasonably priced.

There are three summer-only campsites on the outskirts of the city. West of the city, the site at ul. Nad Zalewem 12 (tel 40831) (bus route D) has a swimming pool; the others are at ul. Kreznicka 6 (tel 41070) (bus route 25) south of the city, and west of the city again at ul. Slawinkowska 46 (tel 712231) (bus route 18). All are open from July to September.

Exploring. The small Old Town (Stare Miasto) has the usual Town Hall (Stary Ratusz), Cathedral and Gate (Brama Krakówska): the Historical Museum of Lublin is in the tower (closed Monday and Tuesday.) The 19th century Castle is just outside the Old Town off ul. Zamkowa.

BIESZCZADY

A lightly travelled region in the southeast of Poland, bordered by Ukraine, Bieszczady is a superb hiking area which has the reputation in Poland of being virtually 'frontier territory' — a legacy of its recent history.

At the end of the Second World War, Poland and the Soviet Union agreed upon a border which effectively divided the region into two. The inhabitants, many of whom shared characteristics with their neighbours on the Ukrainian side of the border, bitterly opposed the division. The Ukrainian Resistance Army (UPA) fought a guerrilla campaign for two years after the war ended. Dozens of villages were completely razed, with their inhabitants slaughtered. Many of the survivors were forcibly resettled in Ukraine or other parts of southwestern Poland, particularly the Wrocław area.

The area still bears witness to this forced depopulation. Traces of former villages can be found in orchards, and outlines of buildings, including Orthodox Churches, can be seen in the overgrown grass.

The train journey from the Polish border town of Przemysl to Kroscienko and Ustrzyki Dolne to the north of the area mirrors the frontier mentality, cutting through a corner of the Ukraine before re- entering Poland. No visas are required for this trip, as the train does not stop in Ukraine.

SANOK

The main town of the area, Sanok lies to the northeast of the Bieszczady Mountains. Stock up here for the mountains, and while in town, enjoy the Ruthenian icons in the Historical Museum (Muzeum Historyczne), housed in the castle which is open from April to mid October daily except Mondays.

Arrival and Departure. There is one fast train to Warsaw departing daily at teatime, and also one to Kraków. Local services run to Krosno and Jaslo. Up to a dozen buses daily run to Ustrzyki Dolne. Half go further to Ustrzyki Gorne, and four fast buses go to Kraków.

Accommodation. The Hotel Turysta (tel 30922) at ul. Jagiellonska 13 is adequate, but pricy, and like all other places in town, space is likely to be at a premium in midsummer. The Youth Hostel at ul. Lipinskiego 34 (tel 31980), right opposite the bus station is open in July and August only.

Exploring. The open air museum (Muzeum Budownictwa Ludowego), a mile north of the town has the reputation of being one of the best of its kind in Poland. Opening times are generally similar to those for the museum in town, and buses 1 and 3 run from the Rynek in Sanok to the Museum.

Help and Information: the PTTK office is just off pl. św. Michala in the centre of town; the ORBIS office is on ul. Pilsudskiego, virtually opposite the main church in the town centre.

Ustrzyki Dolnet. This town is the likely stopping point for travellers heading towards the mountains. There's really not much to do here except stock up and move on. The best hotels in town are the Strwiaz, fifteen minutes walk from the bus and train stations at ul. Sokorskiego 1 (tel 303), and the Hotel

Bieszczadzki (tel 69 — the phone numbers indicate the size of the town!) on the Rynek.

The PTTK office at Rynek 14 (tel 247) has details of hotels and also a small amount of private accommodation.

The Bieszczady Mountains. The mountains are particularly popular for walking and winter skiing. Buy a good map before you set out: the best is the Bieszczady Mapa Turystyczna (scale 1:75,000) published by PRWK).

The area is noted for its wildlife, with eagles, bears, lynx and wolves numerous. The tallest mountains reach only 4,000 feet on average — the very highest is Mt. Tarnica (4,100 feet).

The Beskid Niski (Low Beskid) runs for 55 miles/90km along the Slovakian border. The Niski is particularly good for walking. Chief town of the region is Krosno, famous for its glass, and also, unbelievably, for being at the heart of the Polish oilfield. Buses and trains run to Kraków and Rzeszow.

The Beskid Sadecki, south of the town of Nowy Sącz, are slightly more testing. The tourist office in Nowy Sącz is at ul. Jagiellonska 46 (tel 23724), and the youth hostel is at ul. Batorego 72 (tel 23241) near the rail station.

The town of Krynica, in the heart of the Beskid Sadecki, is Poland's best known mountain resort and spa, and busy throughout the year. Try the healing waters in the pump room (Pijalna Glowna) on al. Nowotarskiego. Krynica mineral water is bottled and sold throughout Poland. Close by is the terminus of the funicular railway which makes its way to Góra Parkowa.

The PTTK tourist office is at ul. Kraszewskiego 14, and their hostel is at ul. Jaworzyna 18 (tel 5409). Pensions include the Jozefa at ul. Cicha 10 (tel 5420), and the Mewa at Bulwary Dietla 5 (tel 2051). Buses and trains connect the town with Nowy Sącz, Kraków and Tarnow.

CZESTOCHOWA

One of the primary tourist centres in the country, the town is world famous in Catholic circles for the Black Madonna relic in the Jasna Góra monastery. Indeed, Jasna Góra is one of the five leading pilgrimage centres in the world for Roman Catholics.

Arrival and Departure. *Air:* Częstochowa has no airport, but the LOT office in town is at al. NMP 64 (tel 43429 and 43749).

Bus: The bus station is close to the main rail station, and has direct services to Kraków, Warsaw and Opole.

Train: Częstochowa suffers from a lack of regular services to and from other centres other than Katowice and Warsaw. In many cases, it is necessary to change trains in Opole.

Accommodation. Częstochowa is badly equipped for tourists. The city is unremarkable, with accommodation at a premium. The main hotel, the Centralny (tel 44067) at ul. Pilsudskiego 9, is moderately expensive. The youth hostel at ul. Waclawy Marek 12 (tel 46795) is a good 15 minutes walk from the rail station. Most pilgrims stay at om Pilgrzyma (tel 43302) beside the monastery: it's usually block-booked. The youth hostel at ul. Jasnogorska operates in July and August only (tel tel 43121).

Exploring. The Black Madonna metaphorically overshadows the town. Tradition has it that it was painted by St. Luke on wood from the Holy Family's house in Nazareth. It's more likely, though, to emanate from Italy.

The painting was presented to the Pauline Order in 1384, and quickly grew in fame as a provider of miraculous occurences. It, and the monastery, escaped the Swedish sieges of 1655-56, a feat attributed to the protection of the Madonna, and in 1717, the Madonna was crowned Queen of Poland.

More recently, throughout the Communist era, the Madonna was revered as a symbol of a free (Catholic) Poland, and today as many as 100,000 pilgrims a day descend on Częstochowa and the monastery at Jasna Góra, many of them walking for up to 19 days and nights from all over Poland.

There is more to see at the monastery. Sculptures and paintings abound, and the monastery's book collection numbers over 10,000 volumes, many of them priceless. Two rooms, the Old Treasury and the Treasury-Arsenal are open daily apart from lunchtime, and display many church vestments and ecclesiastical treasures. The collection also includes ornaments owned by King Jan III Sobieski, and there are also reminders of Pope John Paul's visits to Jasna Góra since 1979.

The monastery is west of the city at the end of a straight two-mile road — Najswietszej Marii Panny (always abbreviated as NMP). The route is always busy — on the Marian feast days of 3 May, 15 August, 26 August, 8 September and 8 December, the crowds are overwhelming.

The Madonna is housed in the Chapel of the Blessed Virgin, and is on view from 6am until 9.10 pm except between noon and 3.30 pm, 4.40-7pm and 7.45-9pm.

Help and Information. ORBIS is at al. NMP 40/42 (tel 47987), and there is another tourist office at al. NMP 63 (tel 41380). Almatur is at ul. Zawadzkiego 29 (tel 54106 and 57375).

PIENINY MOUNTAINS

This small range of Jurassic limestone, 60 miles south of Kraków on the border with the Slovak Republic, covers just thirty square kilometres, with the highest peak Trzy Korony (Three Crowns) only 3,000 feet above sea level. Hiking is moderately easy — all the routes are shown on the Pieninski Park Narodowy map (scale 1: 22,500).

Krościenko, a small town at the northern end of the Pieniny is the tourist base for tourists. The PTTK office at ul. Jagiellonska 28 (tel 3081) has lists of accommodation. There is no train station in the town, but buses run frequently to Nowy Saécz, and a number go to and from Zakopane.

The big attraction is not the mountain range, but the Dunajec River, and more particularly the Dunajec Gorge (Przelom Dunajca). Rafting has been popular here since at least the beginning of the 19th century, although a painting dating from 1589 in the small church at Krościenko depicts the pastime.

The rafts, five canoes strapped together with the floor covered with spruce and fir branches, seat ten people and depart from Kąty on their ten-mile journey to Szczawnica. At one point, the gorge narrows to only 40 feet between cliff heights of 1,000 feet. At times, it is difficult to guess which way the raft will turn next. Upon arriving at Szczawnica, buses return to Kąty, but be sure to purchase your ticket before boarding the raft at Kąty. Up to 250 rafters ply their trade. The journey takes between two and three hours, depending on the conditions, and the season lasts from May to October, although operating hours shorten in the autumn, and usually finish at lunchtime at the end of the season.

If you wish to stay in Szczawnica, check accommodation prospects at the Podhale tourist office at ul. Szalaya 84. Buses run to and from Nowy Targ and Zakopane.

Czech Republic

Hradcany, Prague

Population: 10.5 million   **Capital: Prague (population 1.3 million)**

The Czech Republic is home to two of the world's finest beers — Budvar and Pilsner — which the local people like to drink in large quantities. But the Czechs are a well-educated and cool-headed people. When regimes in Eastern Europe began to tumble in 1989, the most glorious revolution was in Czechoslovakia. Escaping the bloodshed of Romania and the Deutschmark craving of the East Germans, in 1991 the people of Prague simply said 'Enough'. Limbs were bruised and broken by vicious police; but compared with the violence in recent history, the velvet revolution was a soft-focus coup. Under communism, visiting Czechoslovakia required heavy planning that deterred many tourists. Nowadays, visitors pack into the Tupolevs — the Skoda of the skies — in a kind of velvet invasion.

The Czech Republic lies at the heart of Europe, a land of natural and manmade beauty blighted by communism. With the dividing up of Czechoslovakia, the western half lost the spectacular Tatra mountains but kept much fine scenery of its own — the wooded hills and mountains, lakes and picturesque valleys form a comfortable, rather Heidi-esque landscape. Nevertheless, this is a country where the human influence (of the past, at least) holds equal and maybe greater appeal. Few nations are so rich in culture and history, with hundreds of castles, medieval towns and elegant spa towns that were left virtually unscathed during the Second World War. The communists made up for this by erecting swathes of concrete apartment blocks and factories — the latter mostly in Bohemia, where acid rain has devastated more than 50% of the forest. Scarred industrial landscape contrasts rudely with the countryside and historic towns that are a traveller's goal.

Prague too has suffered immeasurably from this pollution, and now has to cope with a newer phenomenon of tourist overkill. Each year, more than 80 million visitors descend on the Czech Republic and Prague, which is now the most popular tourist destination in the world, let alone Europe. Visitors either pop over only for the day or else barely set foot outside the capital. The magnetic appeal of Prague's superbly preserved architecture is irresistible, but don't miss out on the rest of the country. While close links with Germany have brought greater Westernisation than you'll find in most of Eastern Europe, you'll discover that the commercialisation of Prague has left behind most Czech towns, which are unspoilt and, in some cases, still surprised to see visitors. Furthermore, the Czech Republic is only about a quarter of the size of the United Kingdom, thus pleasingly compact.

CLIMATE

The Czech climate is temperate, with warm summers and cold winters. The average summer temperature is 20°C/68°F, with humidity often high. Winters are harsh (thermals are recommended), with frequent snowfalls which can make getting around difficult. Most rain falls in late autumn and winter.

Late spring and early autumn are the best times to visit: this holds particularly for Prague, where the overcrowding is unbearable in July and August — although there's not one month of the year when you could describe the capital as quiet. In winter, grey skies are common all over the country, but the appalling air pollution creates the worst winter smogs in the capital.

HISTORY

The history of the Czech Republic has never been anything but eventful thanks to its centrality within Europe. Early Celtic settlers were conquered by Germanic tribes who, in turn, faced an invasion of Slavs from the fifth century. The latter brought the Slav alphabet, adopted Christianity and created an independent nation which was appropriated by the Holy Roman Empire in the 14th century. Thus began a cultural boom, with the magnificence of Prague a lasting testimony to the city's temporary status as capital of the Empire.

The first serious attempt to attain independence from foreign domination came in the 17th century, when the Czech nobility rebelled against Habsburg hegemony and the Catholic Counter-Reformation. They were roundly defeated at the Battle of White Mountain in 1620, shortly after the start of the Thirty Years War, and the Czech lands remained within Habsburg control. Only at the end of World War One did the Czechs achieve independence with the founding of Czechoslovakia: the Czechs and Slovaks — living in different parts of the old Austro-Hungarian empire (with the Czechs under Austrian rule) — were lumped together largely because they spoke similar languages. Yet the new country, with Tomás Masaryk as its first president, became a stable democracy — until, that is, Hitler chose to occupy the country in 1938. The Red Army liberated Prague and the rest of what had become a German protectorate in 1945. By 1948, a reconstituted Czechoslovakia was a People's Republic operating along Soviet lines. Stalin's man in Prague was Klement Gottwald, who imposed totalitarian rule and favoured rigged trials, repression and all the other hallmarks of Stalinization.

In 1968, the country's new leader, Alexander Dubcek, tried to give

communism 'a human face'. But the so-called Prague Spring was short-lived and quickly defused by a massive influx of Warsaw Pact: Soviet tanks rolled through Prague and Moscow drew its satellite sharply back into orbit. Under Milos Jakes and President Husák, Czechoslovakia became one of the Eastern bloc countries most resistant to liberalisation. In 1988, a huge demonstration on the 20th anniversary of the Soviet invasion took the country by surprise and rekindled the ardour extinguished at the time of the Prague Spring. Sporadic demonstrations culminated in a student march in Prague in November 1989, calling for the removal of the entire government. The violence used by the police against the students sparked larger demonstrations and a general strike, followed closely by the resignation of the Communist Party's Politburo.

Václav Havel — playwright, philosopher, dissident — became interim president. Civic Forum, the main opposition group of which Havel was a leading member, won the country's first free elections in June 1990.

After the Revolution. Considered one of the most promising of the fledgling democracies and with the romantic figure of Václav Havel at the helm, Czechoslovakia seemed to embody the dreams of those hoping for a new Europe. But despite having a stronger social democratic tradition and better infrastructure than its neighbours, a smooth transition from a communist to a capitalist system was by no means automatic.

In 1991, Civic Forum divided into two factions, with rightwingers under the Finance Minister Václav Klaus splitting off from the main group to form the Civic Democratic Party. Within a short space of time Klaus was

Prime Minister, with responsibility for both the economic and geopolitical future of the Czech people. Discussions about autonomy with Slovak leaders resulted in an unexpectedly rapid agreement to split the country in two, announced in June 1992. According to a poll conducted on the eve of the separation, just over half the population in both republics said they would have preferred unity. But the break-up has been peaceful — a 'velvet divorce' to follow the velvet revolution.

Václav Havel was elected president of the Czech Republic, which officially came into being on January 1 1993 as a federation consisting of two republics, Bohemia and Moravia. However, political power remains with Klaus, a smart Thatcherite who has set about embracing free market policies (and foreign investors) with enthusiam. *Razantní* — going forward quickly — is his watchword. The people respect him for his strong leadership and his skills as an orator, although they are less enamoured of his arrogance and penchant for ridiculing the opposition.

The Czech ecomony was in a poor state prior to the revolution, with the usual problems of low efficiency, imbalanced supply and demand, and so forth. But inflation and unemployment figures remain comparatively low — partly through keeping wages down — and massive foreign investment has also provided a much-needed boost.

THE PEOPLE

The vast majority of the people are Czechs, with small communities of Hungarians, Poles and Ukrainians, among others. Prior to Hitler's invasion in 1939, a quarter of the Czech population was Jewish. Now only about 15,000 Jews are left, living mostly in Prague. A further demographic change came after the war, when two million Germans (about a quarter of the population at that time) were thrown out of the country; about 40,000 still remain. More recent arrivals are the expats, who have arrived by the plane-load since the revolution. It is estimated that 10,000 Americans (a mix of entrepreneurs, business consultants and English language teachers) are already living in Prague.

Religion. Religious expression has boomed since the revolution, but agnosticism remains common. Catholicism is still the principal religion — accounting for about 46% of the population — although it has never had such a strong following as in Slovakia. About 15% of Czechs are Protestant.

Meeting the People. The Czechs are a well-educated, traditionally liberal people — certainly in comparison with their conservative neighbours in Slovakia. Homosexuality, for example, is more open than in other Eastern European countries (though there are still very few exclusively gay bars).

In Prague, you'll find it hard to make friends unless you head out into the tourist-free suburbs. Generally, tourists have a reputation for flaunting money and being loud and intrusive. You don't have to venture far off the beaten track to find more traditional hospitality, however. Having a few drinks at a local beer or wine cellar is a good way to get talking to people, although these tend to be male-dominated places.

LANGUAGE

While you wouldn't want to be taken for a German (young Germans seem to treat the Czech Republic like the British do the Costa del Sol, i.e. as a place to get drunk cheaply), you'll have more chance of holding a conversation in

German than in English. The latter is very much the vogue language, but is not spoken widely outside Prague.

The Czech language is hard on the eye but is phonetic and fairly unproblematic once basic sounds and their symbols are mastered. Phrasebooks are hard to find, but you can pick up Czech-English dictionaries for a couple of dollars. Keen linguists should buy *Colloquial Czech* by James Naughton, which contains intensive grammar and conversation and comes with a cassette.

Pronunciation. In Czech, stress always falls on the first syllable. Vowels may be pronounced short or — when accented — long. Short vowels are as in English, and you simply stretch them to produce the sound of long vowels. Some consonants are also marked with accents. The more difficult ones approximate to the following sounds:

c   is ts as in lo*ts*
c   is ch as in *ch*in
ch is ch as in lo*ch*
j   is y as in *y*ellow
n   is nnyee as in o*n*ion
r   is a rolled Italian 'rrrr'
r   is a forceful buzzing sound, combined with an 'r' sound, pronounced (very) roughly as *rzh*; try Dvorak
s   is sh
z   is zh, pronouced as s in mea*s*ure

There are many subtleties and variations to the above, but these are only for the studious or fearless.

Useful Words and Phrases

hello — *dobrý den*
hello *or* goodbye (informal) — *ahoj*
goodbye — *na shledanou*
please — *prosím*
thank you — *dekuji* (less formal — *dik*)
yes — *ano*
no — *ne*
sorry — *pardon*
excuse me — *prominte*
cheers! — *na Zdravi!*
how much? — *kolik?*
today — *dnes (ka)*
tomorrow — *zítra*
tonight — *dnes vecer*
when? — *kdy?*
toilet — *záchod*
water — *voda*
hospital — *nemocnice*
pharmacy — *lékárna*
airport — *letiste*
hill — *kopec*

square — *námestí*
street — *ulice*
avenue — *trída*
bridge — *most*
station — *nádrazi*
entrance — *vchod* or *vstup*
exit — *vychod* or *výstup*
closed — *zavreno*
open — *otevrený*

0 — *nula*
1 — *jeden*
2 — *dva*
3 — *tri*
4 — *ctyri*
5 — *pet*
6 — *sest*
7 — *sedm*
8 — *osm*
9 — *devet*
10 — *deset*

FURTHER READING

The Czech Republic has nurtured many great authors, who are famous both nationally and internationally: none more so than the President. *Václav Havel: Living in Truth* (Faber, 1988) is an excellent introduction to the man himself and also gives a good insight into Czech history over the last few decades. Ludvik Vaculik, another founder member of the human rights movement Charter 77 wrote an interesting collection of essays called *Cup of Coffee with my Interrogator: the Prague Chronicles* (Readers International, 1987). They form a pithy, sad and funny observation on life in pre-revolutionary Prague. Milan Kundera, exiled under communism, and extremely popular in Western Europe during the 80s, combines sensuality with politics. *The Unbearable Lightness of Being*, probably his most famous work, has the Prague Spring for its background and conveys the struggle of the individual under communism. Last but not least is Kafka, who spent most of his life in Prague: *The Trial* (Penguin) and *The Castle* (Minerva) are both set in the capital during Austro-Hungarian rule.

Many foreign authors have written about the Czech Republic too: from Ivan Turgenev — who uses the former Czechoslovakia's polite spa society as a backdrop to his classic *Torrents of Spring* — to Bruce Chatwin, whose *Utz* (Picador, 1989) is set in Prague prior to the 1989 revolution.

Getting There

AIR

Prague's airport has seen a huge increase in the number of flights in recent years. The scope of Czechoslovak Airlines (CSA) widens almost monthly, particularly within the USA and the Far East. Since joining forces with Air France, CSA has acquired Boeings and Airbuses, which supplement the former fleet made up of antiquated Tupolevs and Ilyushins.

British Airways and CSA (071-255 1898) operate daily between London Heathrow and Prague. The cheapest return fare is around £150 in winter, £200 in summer, but not usually direct from the airlines. Try Cedok (071-378 6009) or the agents listed on page 11. If you want to visit just Prague, there are plenty of package deals available, often advertised in the national press.

CSA (545 5th Avenue, Suite 1101, NY 10017; tel 212-682-5833, fax 212-682-5836) has nonstop flights from New York, but you'll usually get a better deal on a Western airline such as British Airways. For information on flights to Prague from Canada, call CSA on 514-844-6376 (Montréal) or 416-363-3174 (Toronto).

TRAIN

Prague can be reached in less than five hours from several of Europe's main cities, including Berlin, Munich, Vienna and Budapest. The Czech capital is well placed on the main line from Berlin to Budapest and Vienna, with several daily services along the route. Berlin-Budapest trains also stop in Brno, the capital of Moravia, and Bratislava. The best train from the Hungarian capital is the Amicus Express, which runs overnight and takes about nine hours. There are frequent services also from Frankfurt via Narnberg and the Czech border town of Cheb, and from Munich via Plzen. Other possible routes from Austria are to Ceské Budejovice from Linz or to

Breclav in southern Bohemia from Vienna. Direct services run from Sofia and Bucharest, the Pannonia train serving both capitals. Express trains to Prague from Warsaw take about 12 hours.

If you are travelling a long distance and don't plan to explore outside the Czech republic, it will almost certainly be cheaper to fly. British Rail International (071-834 2345) charges £210 return between London and Prague; a change in Paris is necessary, and the journey takes 30 hours. Other routes from London Victoria are via the Dover-Ostend ferry and Stuttgart or via the Dover-Ostend jetfoil and then to Nürnberg; the latter is the faster and more expensive of the two.

International rail tickets bought within the Czech Republic may have to be paid for in hard currency (cash), particularly if you go through Cedok, though the rules are gradually being relaxed.

BUS

Private bus companies are opening up new services to the Czech Republic all the time. There are already buses from Linz and Vienna to Brno and Prague, and from Munich and Nürnberg to both Plzen and the capital. Most importantly for British travellers, services between London and Prague are expanding too. If you have the stamina for a 23-hour journey, the £47 (one-way) or £85 (return) fares charged by Kingscourt Express (15 Balham High Road, London SW12 9AJ; tel 081-673 7500; fax 081-673 3060) offer excellent value. It is also worth checking out the services offered by Eurolines (071-730 0202).

DRIVING

Several international European highways pass through the republic:

E7: Vienna — Brno — Warsaw
E12: Paris — Prague — Warsaw
E15: Brno — Prague — Berlin
E84: Vienna — Jihlava (E15 Prague)
E50: Nürnberg — Plzen — Prague — Brno — Bratislava — Uzhgorod
E55: Dresden — Prague — Ceské Budejovice — Linz
E65: Harrachov — Mlada Boleslav — Prague — Brno — Bratislava —
     Gysr

The most convenient route into the Czech Republic from Germany is via Narnberg to Plzen. If you travel from Britain to Prague from a channel port through Belgium and Germany, it will be a journey of about 700 miles/ 1,150km: driving flat out, you should be able to cover it in about 12 hours. The two best routes from the UK to Prague are:

Dover — Oostende — Brussels — Aachen — Koblenz — Mannheim — Heilbronn — Nürnberg — Waidhaus/Rozvadov (border) — Plzen — Prague

Harwich — Hamburg — Berlin — Dresden — Zinnwald/Cínovec (border) — Teplice — Prague: *this involves the least driving.*

Red Tape

British passport holders and US and most European nationals do not require a visa to visit the Czech Republic. Australians are among those who are currently not exempt, though you should check at the nearest consulate:

UK: 28 Kensington Palace Gardens, London W8 4QY (tel 071-727 9431; fax 071-727 5824). Open 10am-noon, Monday to Friday.
USA: 3900 Linnean Avenue NW, Washington DC 20008 (tel 202-363-6315; fax 202-966-8540).
Canada: 50 Rideau Terrace, Ottawa, Ontario K1M 2A1 (tel 613-749-4442; fax 613-749-4989).
Australia: 169 Military Road, Dover Heights, Sydney, NSW 2030 (371-8878).

Tourist visas usually cost £14 (though Canadians, for example, must pay a hefty £29) and can be obtained on the spot at any Czech consulate abroad. Visas are issued to motorists at limited border points, but are more expensive.
   Tourists can stay in the Czech Republic for an initial period of 30 days, but it is possible to extend this through the Passport and Visa Office in the capital (Olanská 3, Prague 3), at any regional passport office, or at a police station (department *Pasove oddeleni*). The maximum stay for British citizens, for example, is 180 days. Forty-eight hour transit visas are also available.

IMMIGRATION

In 1993 the Czech Republic introduced passport controls for those entering the country from Slovakia to help stem the flow of migrants through to Germany. Border procedures remain exceedingly cursory for non-Eastern Europeans from whichever direction you arrive, though if you change trains at the border you can expect to queue. A search by Customs officials is rare, though increased fears about drugs smuggling (see *Crime and Safety*) mean that there is greater vigilance than at the start of the 90s.

Duty free allowances include 250 cigarettes, two litres of wine and one litre of spirits. The importation of pure alcohol and pornography is prohibited. Works of art may be taken out of the country only if they have been purchased at an approved shop which can do the necessary paperwork. There is a fairly well established black market in antiques and prints, and transgressors may face a hefty fine.

100 haléru (h) 1 koruna (Kcs)
1994: £1 = Kcs 45 $US = Kcs 30

Currency. The Czech currency is the crown or *koruna*, which is divided into *haléru* (singular *heller*). Coins come in denominations of 5, 10, 20 and 50 haléru and 1, 2, 5 and 10 korunas; and notes to the value of 10, 20, 50, 100, 500 and 1,000 korunas. Since the division of Czechoslovakia, banknotes have been undergoing a gradual process of renewal, so that all manner of notes are in circulation, including old ones which have been overstamped: this has been done to distinguish them from the crowns used in Slovakia, so check carefully that you have been given the correct currency.

Changing Money. Hard currency and all brands of travellers cheques and Eurocheques can be exchanged in the Czech Republic. Rates vary enormously, but you get the best deals at the state banks. The main drawback with these is the opening hours (8am-3pm Monday to Friday, often with a break at lunchtime) and the queues, though in central Prague some banks operate special exchange desks which close later and deal quickly with most transactions.

Outside the capital, the main alternative to the banks is Cedok, which usually charges 3% commission, as opposed to the 1% demanded at the banks. Bureaux de change (look for the sign *Smenarna*) have sprung up all over Prague and are gradually catching on elsewhere too: these often advertise a very competitive exchange rate, but then charge an outrageous commission. Some hotels have 24-hour exchange bureaux (as does the Ruzyné airport and the main border posts) but the rate offered is poor, day or night.

Credit Cards. All the principal credit and charge cards, including Diners Club, MasterCard, American Express and Visa, are accepted in middle to top range hotels, restaurants and shops. Some banks, such as Zivnostenská Banka, allow you to withdraw cash on a credit card.

Black Market. There is little financial advantage to dealing on the black market. All the classic tricks are practised by the Czech Republic's few remaining (and desperate) black marketeers, including palming you off with Polish zloty notes (which are easily mistaken for Czech crowns), Slovakian crowns or with Czech Kcs100 bills to which an extra nought has been added.

Tipping. This usually involves rounding up the sum you are asked to pay - most commonly when paying for a meal or a ride in a taxi. The tradition of tipping petrol station attendants seems to be gradually dying out.

Work. To get a work permit in the Czech Republic, you need a contract (preferably long-term) from the school and proof of an address. This can be arranged before or after your arrival in the country.

State schools tend to provide the best teaching conditions. Recruitment of qualified teachers for secondary schools (mostly in small towns) takes place through the Academic Information Agency (AIA) in Prague, usually on a one-year contract with low-cost or free accommodation and a salary of about $140 per month. The minimum requirement is a university degree, preferably in English. Additional qualifications in TEFL and teaching experience give an applicant priority. Applications should be submitted before the end of April. The AIA also appoints some teachers to well-established private language schools. AIA's information for English teaching applicants is also available from the Embassies of the Czech Republic in London and Washington. Otherwise, contact the Academy direct at Dum zahranicních styku, Senovázné nám. 26, 111 21 Prague 1 (tel 2-267010, fax 267009).

People teaching at private institutes in Prague, where there is a definite glut of foreign teachers, have been called the 'sweat shop labourers' of the TEFL world because of the low wages employers can get away with. There is a high turnover of teachers, especially at the cowboy end of the market. Many people find the appeal of Prague hard to resist, but Brno, the attractive capital of Moravia, is a good alternative. Schools sometimes advertise vacancies on the notice boards of the American Hospitality Center in Prague (see page 163) and the American-Moravian Cultural Center in Brno (Radnicka 10). The schools below employ 10, 20 or even 50 teachers. All require both a TEFL qualification or degree as well as experience.

Bell School, Nedvezská 29, 100 00 Prague 10 (tel 2-781 5342, fax 782-2961).
Et Cetera Language School, PO Box 37, 130 00 Prague 3 (tel/fax 2-89 44 84).
Jazykova Skola Prague 4, Bítovská 3, 140 00 Prague 4 (tel 2-420595).
London School of Modern Languages, Belgicka Ulice 25, 12 000 Prague 2 (tel 2-256859, fax 250073).
Prague 8 Language School, Buresova 1130, 18 000 Prague 8 (tel 2-858 8028).
Statní Jazykova Skola, Narodni 20, 116 72 Prague 1 (tel 203814, fax 203820).

Communications

Telephone. The Czech Republic is one hour ahead of GMT (with clocks going forward one hour between March and September).

Like everywhere else in Eastern Europe, the Czech Republic is giving its telecommunications system a much-needed overhaul. Facilities in Prague have been vastly improved, but it will take years for the nationwide network to function efficiently. Until cardphones (see below) spread to the whole of the country, you'll do best to make long-distance calls from a post/telephone office. In Prague, you simply pay a deposit and then dial direct from a booth: you can talk for as long as you like, provided you don't exceed the amount you've paid upfront. In provincial towns, the number will usually be dialled for you. Collect calls are possible to most countries.

Payphones: the old yellow payphones, which take one crown coins and are for local calls only, are maddeningly unreliable. Stick to the newer grey ones, which take Kcs1, 2 and 5 and 10 pieces. One crown is the minimum charge for a local call, three crowns for a long-distance call within the Republic.

The new blue cardphones are a joy to use, with instructions in English, German and French as well as Czech, and ideal for making international calls. Phonecards (*telekarty*) are currently issued to the value of Kcs50 and Kcs150: the latter will allow a decent conversation of more than six minutes within Europe. It also gets around the three minute minimum rule that applies when calling from a public telephone office. Phonecards are best bought at post offices since news kiosks add a small commission. If you need assistance, contact the international operator: dial 132 for western Europe, 138 for North America.

Useful Numbers: directory enquiries 120 (for Prague), 105 (elsewhere); police 158; fire brigade 150; ambulance 155.

Telegrams and telex. The charges for international telegrams are inexplicably high: $0.60 per word, with a minimum of seven words. Telex facilities are available to visitors in most of the larger hotels.

Mail. The Czech postal service is excellent, both internally and internationally, letters within Europe often reaching their destination in five days; writing LETADLEM or PAR AVION can speed up delivery too. Mailing a postcard to the UK costs $0.18 (a letter $0.28), to the USA $0.22 and $0.35 respectively. Stamps (*známky*) for local mail can be bought at news stands as well as at post offices (*posta*). The latter usually open 8am-6pm, though some central town offices stay open later.

For important or urgent letters or packages, you can use DHL, which has several branches including one Na poríčí in Prague (tel 35 42 42).

MEDIA

Newspapers. *Lidové Noviny,* set up during the communist years and still run by former dissidents, is the country's most influential paper. *Rudé Pravo,* formerly the official paper of the Communist Party, survived the 1989 revolution and is to the left of the more centrist *Lidové Noviny,* but a duller read.

English-language newspapers are easy to pick up from news stands and hotels in Prague. In addition to the usual *Herald Tribune* and *USA Today,* you can find all the main European dailies: from Britain these include anything from the *Daily Mail* to the *Independent,* all costing around $2.50 each. *Prague Post* and *Prognosis* are weekly papers published by the local American community, both priced at about $0.75. The latter is the better of the two, with a reasonable digest of national and international news, as well as information aimed at tourists, including entertainment listings. The *Central European Business Weekly* ($1) has a rather more limited readership.

Broadcasting. Being so centrally located, the Czechs have always been able to pick up television from their Western European neighbours, which meant a wide choice of programmes and resulted in a fairly well-informed population. Nowadays, satellite TV has boosted the supply even further, and dishes are scattered liberally amongst Prague's ancient rooftops. The burst of new radio stations has been particularly marked in the capital as well: two of the better music channels are Kiss (98MHz) and Radio 1 (91.9MHz), the latter also broadcasting news bulletins in English.

Getting Around

Maps. Country maps are available (for a charge) from Cedok offices abroad (see *Help and Information*), but town and city plans are best bought on arrival. Street maps (*plan mesta*) exist of all the main towns, and you can buy them from tobacconist's shops (*tabac*) or from good bookshops, such as branches of Orbis Pictus.

AIR

The national airline, CSA, controls domestic flights. The main routes link Prague to Karlovy Vary, Brno and Ostrava: since the first two towns are only about four hours by bus from the capital and Ostrava is an unappealing industrial city, you should find little need to fly, though fares are cheap. Tickets can be booked at Cedok or CSA offices.

BUS

Buses, operated by CSAD, are more expensive than the trains but are generally faster: for example, Prague to Brno takes about three hours by express bus and four hours by train. On the whole, you can simply pay the driver, though you should book in advance if you are going on an express or long-distance bus, or if you just want to be sure of getting a seat. Timetables are usually incomprehensible and station staff rarely speak English, so you'll usually just have to write down your destination and departure time (make a guess if necessary) and hope for the best. Some town stations have a surprisingly efficient computerised system, but since most bus routes are still organised on a regional basis it can be difficult to get information about services in other parts of the country. The local Cedok office may have a copy of local timetables.

TRAIN

The rail network (operated by CSD) is extensive, but Czech trains are renowned for being both slow and uncomfortable. They are best taken only if you are heading out of the country, are short of money or just enjoy rail travel for its own sake. *Expres* (Ex) trains are the quickest; they are often international services and stop only at the main towns. The *rychlík* (R) are fast and cost about the same as the express trains, but stop at more stations. The *spesný* (Sp) trains are one notch down. Take the *osobný* (Os) or milk train only if you want to observe the countryside.

Station staff rarely speak English. If you have serious problems communicating, you can buy your ticket (*jizdenka*) at Cedok, paying a commission, of course. If you want a seat, then you should make a reservation (*mistenka*) when travelling along a busy line and in high season; this will cost a few crowns. Reservations are compulsory for first class travel (not available on all trains and costing half as much again as second class) and on some international services. Sometimes, however, when picking up an international train in a provincial town, you will not be allowed to make a reservation.

DRIVING

The main roads in the Czech Republic are reasonably good despite a large increase in traffic since the revolution. In summer German and Austrian tourists crowd some routes in southern and central Bohemia, but country roads are still fairly quiet. There is a small network of motorways, the best being the Prague-Brno-Bratislava route which has a few petrol stations and cafés. Driving standards vary, the Czech propensity for overtaking without due warning before bends being the main hazard.

Most good bookshops sell a decent road atlas, with petrol stations and sites of interest marked, as well as a glossary of Czech road signs.

Documents. You must have a valid national driving licence and, if you take your own car, the vehicle registration document and evidence of vehicle insurance. Third-party insurance is compulsory and the Green Card is recommended. Visiting motorists must also carry a first-aid kit and a warning triangle and a set of replacement vehicle bulbs.

Rules and Regulations. The Czech Republic has stringent drink-driving laws, and those found guilty of driving with even a trace of alcohol in their blood can be sent to jail for several years. For lesser misdemeanours (such as driving without a seatbelt), fines are issued on the spot. The speed limits for cars are as follows:

Built-up areas: 40km/h (27mph) 5am-11pm, 60km/h (37mph) 11pm-5am.
Open roads: 90km/h (56mph)
Motorways: 110km/h (70mph)

Fuel. There are two quality grades of petrol (*benzín*), 90 octane (special) and 96 octane (super). A litre currently costs about $0.65. Unleaded petrol (95 octane), known as *natural,* is available mainly along the principal roads from the German and Austrian borders and in and around Prague, though the number of garages selling it is increasing. Cedok produces a list of towns with unleaded petrol stations. Diesel is known as *nafta.*

Motoring Organisation. The National Motoring Club (Ustredni Automoto-klub) has a special agency, Autoturist, which provides all services for tourists, including breakdown numbers, maps, etc. Its head office is at Opletalova 29 (22 35 44, 22 48 28), near Prague's main train station.

The standard emergency breakdown number throughout the country is 154.

Car Rental. Several international car rental agents now operate in the republic, though most are represented only in Prague and Brno. Europcar has more offices than most, including in Plzen and Ceské Budejovice. The main Czech agency is Pragocar (head office at Stepánská 42, Prague; 235 28 09), which has desks in smaller tourist centres too, including Karlovy Vary.

Renting a car is one of the few things in the Czech Republic which isn't comparatively cheap. Expect to pay $40-50 a day for a Skoda Favorit, compared with $50-60 a day for a Fiat Uno or $75 for a Ford Sierra. Some private garages have begun renting old saloon cars, including smart Russian Tatras formerly used by Communist Party officials.

HITCHING

Thumbing lifts is fairly common, but competition can be intense. Although there are not that many local private cars, lorries thunder continuously along the main routes. Holidaying Germans and Austrians are mostly disinclined to pick up hitchers, but businessmen and lorry-drivers are more generous.

CITY TRANSPORT

Public Transport is efficient and easy to use. Tickets for buses, trolleybuses and trams must almost always be bought in advance, from newspaper kiosks, tobacconists (*tabac*) or any shop showing the sign *Predprodej Jizdenek*; larger towns also have ticket machines, usually located by major bus or tram stops. You punch your own ticket once on board. Transgressors pay an on-the-spot fine if caught.

Official taxis (identifiable by their stencilled numbers and 'taxi' signs) have meters, which you should insist the driver uses. If you travel in an unofficial private taxi, haggling over the fare in advance is strongly advised.

There is a severe shortage of hotel beds in the Czech Republic, especially in Prague. If you want to be sure of a room in a particular hotel or hostel, advance booking is essential in summer and recommended at other times. The opening up of private houses since the revolution has helped ease the pressure on hotels, however, and anyone willing to 'go private' should always be able to find a bed on the spot.

Hotels. The majority of Czech hotels are three-star or higher, and increasingly so as old establishments are renovated and upgraded, well out of reach of the average traveller's budget. In the country, hundreds of castles and chateaux, many wrecked and abandoned by the Soviet army, have already been earmarked for luxury hotels. You'll rarely find a double room for less than $30. In Prague the average price for two is $45-50. Single rooms don't cost much less.

You can book in advance through Cedok, but the tourist board tends to deal only with the moderate to expensive hotels and charges as much as $10 extra per room per night. The biggest problem with calling direct to a cheap hotel is that staff may not speak English; furthermore, a room not booked through Cedok is less likely to be held for you.

Hostels. CKM, the youth travel bureau, runs hostels in the main towns, though these so-called Juniorhotels charge about the same as cheap hotels. Nevertheless, they are good places to meet people and much better value if you have an ISIC or IYHF card (available from CKM if you don't already have one), which should get you a discount of 20-25% on the standard price.

In July and August student dormitories are converted into hostels known as *junior-strediska*: the location of these seasonal hostels changes every year, so contact CKM when you arrive. The standard price for a dormitory bed varies from $5 to $10. Priority tends to be given to groups, but staff will do their best to find you a place if you are persistent. In the larger towns, you should approach the CKM office first rather than go direct to the hostel. Staff should be willing to book you a bed in a hostel in another town, but may charge a small fee for doing so. The CKM head office in Prague is at Zitná 12 (299 94 17).

Private Accommodation. Staying in a Czech home is a good (and cheap) alternative to staying in either drab or expensive hotels: in the capital it may be your only option. Lots of private agencies in Prague can arrange this, but elsewhere you'll usually have to rely on Cedok. Expect to pay $10-20 per night if you go through an agent (more in Prague), but you can pay much less if you arrange accommodation through people who approach you on the street or in transport terminals. Some local people put up signs (e.g. *Zimmer*, 'room' in German) outside their homes; in some cases these have become full-blown guest houses, offering an increasingly viable alternative to the hotels.

Camping. You'll find campsites (*autokempink*) in all corners of the republic, most usefully in southern and western Bohemia, and generally open between May and September. While often spartan, sites usually have a good water supply and basic facilities, and you'll never pay more than about $2 per person. As with hostels, the location of some sites can change from year to year, although the ones listed in this book are permanent unless otherwise stated: Cedok has a full list. Campsites usually cater for caravans as well as tents, and many have chalets of some description which you can rent for around $10.

Eating and Drinking

Gastronomically, Austria has had the strongest influence on the cuisines of Bohemia and Moravia. This is no great recommendation, however, since restaurant meals in the Czech Republic are often bland and montonous; meat is poor-quality and fatty, often served as a soupy stew; decent fresh vegetables are also scarce. Dumplings (*knedlíky*) seem to come with everything, even stewed fruit, so that at least the meals are filling. A typical meal consists of roast pork with dumplings and Sauerkraut or some other pickled vegetable. A couple of dishes to look out for are *Segedinský gulás* (Hungarian goulash) and *Svíková na smetane* (beef tenderloin served with a sour cream sauce), and fish can also be good, though expensive. *Kapr na cerno,* carp served in a special black sauce (made from raspberry juice, beer, honey and raisins) is a traditional Bohemian Christmas Eve dish.

Restaurants come in all shapes and sizes. *Bufets,* also called *samoobsluha,* offer only a small choice but are great for a quick and filling hot lunch for $1 or less. In the evening, you'll usually be better off eating in a beer or wine cellar, where you can eat proper meals or simply a plateful of rye bread, smoked meats and cheese. Similar food can be eaten on the hoof during the daytime: shops which advertise themselves as a *jídelna* (literally 'dining room') or *lahudky* (delicatessen) offer snacks such as salads, open face sandwiches, cheese, cold meats and bread, which the Czechs eat for both breakfast and lunch. For cakes and coffee head for the local *kavárna* or *cukrárna*. Shops are the best source of a balanced meal for vegetarians, though Prague has seen a mushrooming of specialized restaurants, and pizzas are all the rage; some of the larger hotels will lay on special meals for non meat-eaters.

As in most of Eastern Europe, restaurants tend to close early. If you enjoy staying up late, you'll probably have to rely on hotel bars and dining rooms or on local beer and wine cellars.

Below is a list of some general words to help interpret menus (*jidelní lístek*), which are generally incomprehensible to the untrained eye.

beef — *hovezí*
beer — *pivo*

meat — *maso* (without meat, *bez maso*)
open sandwich — *chlebícky*

bread — *chléb*
cheese — *kýr*
chicken — *cure*
chips (greasy) — *hranolky*
duck — *kachna*
egg — *vejce*
fish — *ryba*
fried — *smacený*
fruit — *ovoce*
ice cream — *zmrzlina*

pastry, cake — *pecivo*
pork — *veprové*
potatoes — *brambory*
sauerkraut — *kysele zelfi*
(smoked) sausages — *uzeniny*
soup — *polévka*
veal — *telecí*
vegetables — *zelenina*
wine (white) — *bíla vina*
wine (red) — *cervena vina*

DRINKING

Beer. It is with some justification that the Czechs are great beer-drinkers: the republic's beer is amongst the best and strongest in the world. The most famous brews are *plzenský Prazdroj* and *Budvar*. The former, known abroad as Pilsner Urquell, is the original Pilsener and has been brewed for more than 700 years in the town of Plzen in Western Bohemia. It is many times better than the Pils you can buy in the West. Budvar, on the other hand, is the original Budweiser and comes from the town Ceské Budejovice (originally Budweis). According to the Czechs, an ex-employee of the Bohemian brewery emigrated to the States towards the end of last century and began brewing what we now know as Budweiser. Not surprisingly, there has been quite a battle between the Americans and Czechs over who has the right to market the name. The Czechs, quite rightly, regard American Budweiser as a pale and sweet imitation of their own version, which is dry and slightly bitter.

You find some good dark beers too, such as *Braník* which is brewed in Prague. Many towns have their own beers, and the Czech Republic is the one place in Eastern Europe where locally-brewed beers outnumber imported versions. Imported canned beer (mostly from Germany) is naturally more expensive than local brews and not half as tasty.

Beer is served both on tap (with a large head) and in bottles. The place to drink it is in a beer cellar, of which you'll find several examples in most towns; look for the sign *pivnice*, though some call themselves *hostinec* or *hospoda*. Many sell just one type of beer, served in half-litre mugs which are brought around the tables by the trayful — continuously, until you say 'stop'. For foreign visitors, the cost of beer is tantalisingly cheap, around $0.50 a glass.

Wines and Spirits. The Czechs are far less crazy about wine than they are about beer, but it is still drunk in special bars: *vinárny* are less raucous versions of beer cellars. There are a few vineyards in Bohemia but southern Moravia is the country's main wine-producing area. Most Czech wines are dry, white and light: unsophisticated but pleasant.

Locally-made spirits include *Slivovice* (plum brandy), which can be lethal; *Becherovka*, an aperitif made from herbs and said to be flavoured with petrol (nicer than it sounds); and *Kord,* a Czech vodka which has a gin-like flavour and is strong (but doesn't burn the throat).

Soft Drinks. Fruit drinks and lemonade tend to be made up from powder and are nothing like Western equivalents. Tea (*caj*), if you can find it, is poor. Coffee (*kava*) is usually Turkish coffee, very strong and full of grounds, served without milk. You'll find *kapucino* in places catering for the Western palate.

If not the beer, the Czech Republic's greatest appeal has to be its architectural heritage — particularly the medieval towns in central and southern Bohemia, such as Kutná Hora and Telc, and the castles which perch dramatically atop rocky crags. The most popular castles have compulsory guided tours (usually in English and German as well as Czech) which still suffer the relentlessly dull treatment of the pre-revolutionary era. Some contain museums, which occasionally eclipse the interest of the building itself. Castles are generally closed from 1 November to 31 March. Opening hours for the remaining months are roughly 9am-noon and 1-5pm, daily except Monday. Most other monuments and museums are open 10am-5pm and also close on Mondays. Admission costs are generally low.

Spas feature greatly in Czech tourist brochures, but a full cure — with massage, mud baths and professional medical supervision — costs at least $60 a day. For the average traveller, the main reason to visit the spas, particularly those in western Bohemia, such as Karlovy Vary, is to admire the elegant Victorian architecture and watch everyone else taking the waters.

THE GREAT OUTDOORS

Hiking. The Czechs love hiking, not surprisingly given their country's undulating landscape. Among the best places to walk are the Krkonose mountains in northern Bohemia and the somewhat quieter Beskydy range in Moravia. Both areas are busy in summer, but their popularity means that there are numerous campsites and the hiking routes are well-marked. Try to get hold of the *Soubar turistických* series of 1:100 000 maps, which show all the trails and have a key in English; note that some areas have two maps, one for hiking and one for skiing.

Skiing. People ski in the Krkonose ('Giant Mountains') of northeast Bohemia, but you would do far better to nip over the border to the Tatras in Slovakia, which is where all the best pistes are located.

Entertainment

There is a great cultural tradition in the Czech Republic, and the performing arts enjoyed substantial financial support under the communist regime, although this went hand in hand with censorship. Since the revolution, however, audiences have drifted away from the more traditional arts, with the old theatres, opera houses and concert halls no longer able to rely either on state subsidies or on people's passive acceptance of whatever is churned out. But while attendance at mainstream performances has fallen dramatically among the Czechs (tourists have made up the short fall in Prague), there is still an enormous amount on offer. By far the greatest choice of entertainment is in Prague — all good provincial performers tend to gravitate towards the capital.

Cinema and Theatre. The range of films you can see in the Czech Republic has improved greatly since 1989. Western — particularly American — films are in great demand, but they are usually dubbed. Those shown in the original will be listed as *Ceské titulky* (i.e. with Czech subtitles). The billboards advertising films are often impossible to decipher, however, and you'd do best to ask around or go to the local Cedok office.

Theatre companies have taken up the challenge to adopt more imaginative repertoires and mime and comedy are both enjoying a boom in Prague. Outside the capital, the choice is still fairly limited.

Classical Music and Opera. The Czech composer of greatest international renown is Antonín Dvorák (1841-1904), though almost equally famous at home are Bedrich Smetana (1824-84) and Leos Janacek (1854-1928). Someone (or some orchestra), somewhere in Prague gives a performance of at least one of these three on most days, although Mozart is always the favourite. The Czech Philharmonic has the best reputation, with the Prague Symphony Orchestra a close second (though the latter has many of its top players pinched by the former). The PSO is an umbrella for other smaller ensembles, including the Swingle Singers and Musica Bohemica, which plays a range of music from medieval to folk. Many other ensembles have sprung up since the revolution, but the majority play classics for the tourists.

Most musical events are still cheap by Western standards. You can buy tickets in advance from the box office or from Cedok (you may be asked to pay in hard currency) or one hour before direct from the theatre. In the summer there are open-air concerts, many of them free, and also festivals. Some of these attract Western orchestras, in which case the tickets are in high demand and may cost over £10.

Contemporary Music. Since 1989 the Czechs have been making up for lost time and there is an apparently insatiable demand for live rock music. President Havel has long been a fan of the Rolling Stones, though many young Czechs seem to prefer Heavy Metal. A whole range of big international acts, from Pat Metheny to Motorhead, play to packed audiences in Prague, in addition to local bands who entertain small crowds in bars and clubs.

Don't miss out on jazz, which came to occupy an extraordinary position in Czech culture under the communists, who tried desperately to suppress it and thereby turned the genre into a focus of dissent. The Czech Republic has some fine bands of its own — such as Naima, which plays mostly original music — and several clubs in Prague host international groups on a regular basis.

SPORT

While the most famous Czech sports personalities abroad are tennis players, football and ice-hockey are the national sports back home. The football season runs from February to November, with a break during July. Sparta Praha tops the national league (*první liga*), their main rivals being Slavia Praha. The Czech and Slovak football teams still compete within the same league tables, but this is likely to change. The country's top ice hockey team is also called Sparta Praha. Rugby was considered bourgeois by the communists, but the sport has been rejuvenated since 1989. There are already six teams active in Prague alone.

In Prague, you'll see a lot of familiar names, such as Benetton, but don't expect bargain prices. If you want to buy clothes, you may as well go for the souvenir T-shirts with slogans such as *Czech It Out,* though friends back home may prefer a bottle of real Pilsener or a compact disc. Locally-recorded CDs sell for as little as $4 (Suprafon, Popron and Panton are the main Czech labels, all with their own shops), with imported ones costing $10-12.

Souvenir shops don't purvey quite so much tourist tat as they did, though you may become sick to death of the sight of Bohemian glass (*sklo*). Some of the vases, bowls and ornaments are positively hideous, but the wine glasses and tumblers are often superb and a good buy if you can stand the stress of carrying breakables around.

Tap water is drinkable, but given the country's pollution problems, you might choose to stick to bottled water or use purifying tablets. The Czech Republic has one of the worst pollution records in the world, and even official figures admit that 70% of the country's rivers are polluted. Heavy industry and open-cast mining in Bohemia are the chief cause.

Crime has risen dramatically since 1989, a trend which has affected all the former communist nations. With such a central location in Europe, Prague has become a gathering point for criminal gangs trading in drugs and arms, bringing with them the additional menace of contract killings, extortion and prostitution. The worst gangsters come from Russia and Italy, but also from elsewhere in Eastern Europe, and the Czech police are unable to cope. There has been a boom in private 'security firms', self-styled vigilante groups which feed on the fear of growing criminality in the capital and other parts of the country. Most companies are run by the old secret police who seem to spend most of their time persecuting gypsies. There have already been cases of unlawful killing by these so-called security officers.

The main dangers for tourists are the con artists, pickpockets and cab drivers, who have millions of potential targets to choose from in Prague. It is still safer to walk around Prague at two in the morning than in most Western European cities, but use your common sense and don't carry around unnecessary amounts of money. Outside the capital, the dangers are negligible by comparison.

Drink and Drugs. Do not try and out-drink the natives. While over-indulging in a beer cellar is common practice, don't expect much sympathy from the police (or anyone else) if you make a public nuisance of yourself. Drinking alcohol in public places is not appreciated either, and you may be told to desist by the police. A law passed in 1993 introduced fines of up to $7,000 for those caught selling alcohol or tobacco in public places (because it's considered 'unhygienic and unaesthetic').

The inevitable result of drug trafficking through Prague is an increase in local custom too: there are said to be as many as 10,000 drug addicts in Prague. Be extremely wary of anyone peddling drugs in the streets; like black marketeers, they are probably out to fleece you.

Cedok, the National Tourist Board, has been privatised and no longer holds the monopoly on tourist information, but is still the main authority in most towns. Cedok is principally geared to booking hotel rooms, theatre tickets and so forth, but also exchanges money and can reserve seats on international trains and buses. Don't expect much joy if you turn up asking questions about what bus to catch to the local zoo. The main Cedok offices abroad are as follows:

UK: 49 Southwark Street, London SE1 1RU (tel 071-378 6009; fax 071-403 2321).
USA: Suite 1902, 10 East 40th St, New York, NY 10016 (tel 212-689-9720; fax 212-481-0597).
Canada: Suite 201, 1212 Pine Street West, Montréal, Québec H3G 1A9 (tel 514-849-8983; fax 514-849-4117).

British residents can benefit from the new Czech Centre, which opened at the beginning of 1994 at the Czech Embassy in London (28 Kensington Palace Gardens, London W8 4QY (tel 071-727 9431; fax 071-727 5824).

PRAGUE

Prague's unremitting beauty finds little competition among other European cities. The city is majestic at every turn: glancing up at the castle from the river, peering down from the castle at the city, looking around the streets at ground level. It contains elements of the quaint, the ornate, the gently crumbling and the hi-tech. Every corner brings some new surprise. Despite the destruction around the city during the Second World War, Prague emerged almost unscathed, with one of the world's greatest collections of Gothic, Renaissance and Baroque palaces and churches. But the city's architectural heritage spans many centuries, a portfolio of all the great European styles.

Charles IV, King of Bohemia and Moravia in the 14th century, made Prague the seat of his empire when he became the Holy Roman Emperor. He was responsible for creating much of the city's greatness, building many of the fine Gothic monuments you see today. The Hussite Wars, during which religious reformers fought against the crusading Holy Roman Empire, were bad for Prague's prosperity. But when Habsburg power was finally reimposed in the 17th century, the city found a new lease of life, reflected in the grand Baroque architecture.

Such a city should never have suffered the indignities of state socialism. The communist bulldozers were less busy in the centre of Prague than in other Eastern European cities, but shapeless factories and suburbs still encircle the capital. A neo-Stalinist television tower, looking like a relic from *Thunderbirds,* punctures the medieval skyline. A more serious communist legacy is pollution: grime and coal dust from industry in northern Bohemia descend on the city. Quite apart from the unpleasantness of the atmosphere, the damage to buildings has been considerable, and is now exacerbated by ever-worsening traffic pollution.

Prague pursues the tourist trade with a vigour which visitors of the old guard might find shocking: one new visitor arrives, on average, every few seconds. Massive building projects are underway, mostly in the form of reconstruction, though controversial modern buildings are filling the few empty spaces. The best time to enjoy the capital is in the evening, when the streets are (relatively) empty and the pneumatic drills silent.

The five-star hotels, Benetton shops and advertisements for M&Ms and Playboy do not mask the realities of a decrepit city. Out in the suburbs shops have little to offer, and people appear ever poorer as the new rich make their fortune from tourism or crime; and back in the centre the air of prosperity blends with an atmosphere of sleaze created by gangsters and prostitutes.

Prague is irresistible, but how will it possibly cope with all the attention? The city is being suffocated, gracefully but perhaps irrevocably, by the onslaught.

CITY LAYOUT

Prague sits astride the Vltava River, draped, like Rome, over seven hills. The city consists of four distinct districts, which were originally separate towns: Malá Strana, Hradcany, Staré Mesto and Nové Mesto. The first two are divided from the others by the swirl of the Vltava, with Malá Strana (Lesser Side) strewn liberally with Renaissance and Baroque mansions, once the homes of nobility but now mostly embassies and museums. Above them Prague Castle is a useful landmark and the heart of Hradcany, the former seat of Czech royalty and now of the President.

The Gothic Old Town (Staré Mesto), the original city, lies in the bend of the river across the Charles Bridge (Karluv most) from Malá Strana. Its focus is the Old Town Square or Staromestské námestí. The Jewish quarter (Josefov) occupies a small area just to the north. The New Town (Nové Mesto), also founded in the time of Charles IV, forms a ring around Staré Mesto. The focus of this largely commercial district is Wenceslas Square (Vaclavské námestí), a broad boulevard rather than a square. This and its surrounding streets have the biggest concentration of shops, hotels and restaurants. Na príkope, running northeast from the square, is the city's main shopping street.

Most sights are concentrated in the areas close to the river, all within easy walking distance of each other.

Maps. The yellow and blue *plán streda mesta* is sold at most kiosks, bookshops and tourist offices, price $1; it has a street index and is also the best guide there is to city transport routes. A larger city map in the same series costs $1.25.

Getting Around

ARRIVAL AND DEPARTURE

Air. Ruzyné airport (36 77 60) lies 10 miles/16km west of the centre. A taxi ride to town is steep at around $7 and it's much cheaper to take the CSA bus, which runs every 30 minutes 7am-7pm to its office on Revolucni (235 26 71), not far from nám. Republiky. Otherwise, catch city bus 119 to Dejvická metro station, and take the train into town.

Despite renovation, the airport is still too small to cope with the numbers passing through it: expect chaos and queues on departure. For arriving passengers, there are bureaux de change, an accommodation office, and car rental and tourist information desks.

Train. There are four main railway stations but no fixed pattern as to which regions they serve, with trains to Brno and Bratislava leaving from three of them. You can phone for information on 235 38 36.

Praha-Hlavní: Wilsonova 80, a short walk from Wenceslas Square. This is the main station, where many international and some national trains terminate (though these may stop at one of the other city stations too). It's a huge place, with several tourist, exchange and accommodation offices, some open until 11pm. You can pick up

Letenské n.

Milady Horákové

N

HOLEŠOVICE

Bubenská

Mariánské hradby

Chotkova

nábřeží kpt. Jaroše

Vltava

Švermův most

HRADČANY

Pod Bruskou

Valdštejnská

most Svatopluka Čecha M.

Na Františku

Kozí

nábřeží Luduika Svobody

Strahov Monastery

Manesův most

Pařížská

Bílkova

Dlouhá

Revoluční

Klimmenstská

NOVÉ MĚSTO

Nerudova

Letenská

㉘

㉗

㉙

㉛

㉚

STARÉ MĚSTO

Dlouhá

Dlouhá

Rybná

Na Poříčí

Mal

Vlasská

Mostecká

Karluv most

Karlova

Staroměstské nám.

⑥

Celetná

Ovocný trh

②

③

①

⑤

④

MALÁ STRANA

Ulezd Karmelitská

Vltava

Husova

Jilská

Rvtířská

⑦

Na příkopě

⑧

Nataklanka

Panská

Jindřišská

Politických Vězňů

⑩

Růžová

Opletalova

Hybernská

Praha-Hlavní Station

Petřín Park

Karlova

㉖

㉕

Smetanovo nábřeží

㉔

STŘELECKÝ ISLAND

Národni

㉒

㉓

Jungmannova

Václavské Náměstí

Vodičkova

Štěpánská

⑫

⑫

Wilsonova

Vítezná

most 1 máje

Ostrovni

Spálená

㉜

VINO-HRADY

⑪

Holečkova

Štefánikova

Zborovská

nábreží

SLOVANSKÝ ISLAND

DETSKÝ ISLAND

Opatovicka

⑲

㉑

⑳

Myslikova

Zítná

Ve Smečkách

Sokolská

Škrétova

⑬

⑭

Vinohradská

Rimská

Anglická

nám. Miru

Smíchov

Janáčkovo

Jiráskuv most

J..kovo nám.

⑱

Zítná

Lipová

Ječná

Anglická

Jugoslávská

⑮

Lidická

Palackého most

Palackého nám.

NOVÉ MĚSTO

U nemocnice

Katerinská

⑯

Ke Karlovu

nám. Pavlova

Bělehradská

Fügnerovo nám.

PRAGUE

1 Nám. Republiky	17 Police Museum
2 Municipal Hall	18 CKM hostel/hotel
3 Powder Tower	19 U Fleku
4 Florenc bus station	20 U Kotvy
5 Masarykovo train station	21 Hotel Koruna
6 Týn church	22 Reduta jazz club
7 Stavovské Theatre	23 National Theatre
8 Prague Information Service	24 Betlemské nám.
9 Čedok	25 Anenské nám.
10 Post Office	26 Klementium
11 Smetana Theatre	27 St Nicholas church
12 Europa Hotel	28 U Kocoura
13 AghaRTA jazz club	29 Dvořák Hall
14 National Museum	30 Jewish quarter
15 Luník Hotel	31 Decorative Arts Museum
16 Dvořák Museum	32 U Pinkasu

Wenzigova

⑰

Horská

Sokolská

Bělehradská

Jaramirova

Kresomyslova

0   500 m

0   500 yds

printed timetables of main rail routes from the CSD information office.

Holesovice: across the river north of Staré Mesto, with its own metro station. International services not terminating in Prague, including Berlin-Budapest trains, tend to stop here.

Masarykovo: near nám. Republiky metro. Serves mostly Brno and Bohemia, with the odd international train.

Praha-Smíchov: on the west bank, by Smíchovské Nádrazí metro. Serves mostly domestic routes in the southwest.

Bus. There are four bus terminals, but the majority of international and main domestic services, including those to Brno and most western towns, leave from Florenc station (22 14 45), just east of the Wilsonova flyover and north of Hlavní nádrazí, with its own metro station. Facilities are scanty, the lavatories abominable, the timetables incomprehensible, and no one speaks English. The other bus terminals are in Smíchov, Pankrác and Holesovice, all near metro stops of the same name. Seats on the most popular routes get snapped up fast, so book as far ahead as possible. Agents for international bus tickets include:

Bohemiatour, Zlatnická 7, off Na poprící (232 38 77, 232 39 89).
CSD, pasáz Sevastapol, Na prikope 31 (216 170 84/85).
Cedok, Na prikope 18 (212 71 11).

Driving. Most Czech roads lead to Prague. The problems start when you reach the outskirts (confusing signposting, intimidating trams) and peak when you reach the centre — not so much because of the traffic, but because of the number of one-way or pedestrianised streets. Parking anywhere in the city centre is a nightmare too, since it is prohibited in many areas, or else you need a permit. Illegally parked cars are routinely towed away: you must pay about $10 to reclaim your vehicle, but the time involved is the biggest drag. You are recommended to use car parks outside the city centre and take public transport from there.

Car Rental: in view of the headaches involved with driving downtown, you would do well to arrange rental at the airport. In the centre, Pragocar is based near the main train station at Opletalova 33 (22 23 24) and Hertz at Karlovo nám. 28 (297 836), southwest of Wenceslas Square, although a smaller agent such as Prague Car Rent (Malá Stepanská 7; 691 03 23) will be cheaper.

CITY TRANSPORT

The efficiency of Prague's public transport has been seriously tested by the vast increase in the number of visitors, but the network remains cheap and, for the most part, easy to use. The same tickets (*lístek*) are used for all transport systems and can be bought from street kiosks and yellow machines (found in all metro stations and at the odd bus stop). The standard fare is about $0.15. One-day travel cards are available from red machines, but the special tourist passes (*turistická sítová jízdenka*) can be purchased only at tourist offices and central metro stations; these are valid for one day (price $1) to five days ($3.50).

Metro. Prague's metro is probably Eastern Europe's most efficient. The three metro lines (A, B and C) operate from 5am to midnight, cover most areas of interest and connect all transport terminals. Tickets are valid on the metro for 60 minutes, allowing you to change lines as frequently as you like. *Prestup* is the word for 'connection'.

Buses and Trams. The trams are much more useful than the buses. The main services for both run 5am-11pm, though there are a few 24-hour routes. Night tram services are shown by the number at the stop being white on blue instead of the usual blue on white. Red badges indicate all-night bus routes.

Taxis. If Prague got rid of half its taxis, the city's traffic problem would probably disappear overnight. Taxis are everywhere, with ranks in most main squares and outside the major hotels. To book by phone, dial 20 39 41 or 20 29 51.

Fares are fairly cheap ($0.20 initial charge plus $0.30 per kilometre) if you deal with an honest driver. But Prague's cab drivers are notorious for ripping off tourists. Insist that the driver turns on the meter (*taxametr*) and make sure it's not set at some ludicrous amount.

Finding somewhere to stay is potentially the biggest problem you'll have in Prague, especially in the summer high season, when most central hotels are fully booked. Sadly, virtually all of the great old hotels, including the Pariz (see *Eating and Drinking*), have been refurbished and priced well out of reach of most visitors. There is very little in the way of cheap hotels, making private accommodation the only sensible option for those on a low budget. Low-cost rooms, whether in a private house or a hotel, may well be slightly out of the centre, but this is no great problem given Prague's transport system. Your chances of finding a vacant hotel room or being able to pick and choose among the private options will be greatly enhanced if you arrive early in the morning.

Hotels. There is nothing to stop you from approaching hotels direct, though if you don't fancy traipsing around, you can reserve through an agency. Cedok has a special accommodation office at Panská 5 (22 56 57, 22 70 04), open 9am-9.45pm on weekdays, 9am-2pm at weekends, but deals mostly with moderate to expensive hotels. See also the list of agencies under *Private Accommodation*.

Top Range: the number of hotels charging well over $200 a night is increasing at a ridiculous rate, although there seems to be unlimited demand for the type of luxury they offer. Few places offering good facilities and comfort charge under $100. There are hardly any hotels in Malá Strana, though some old mansions are being done up.

> *Hotel Europa,* 25 Wenceslas Square (236 52 74). An Art Nouveau delight with original features and the perfect place to immerse yourself in Central European nostalgia. An outright bargain at $90 for two, but usually full.
> *Central,* Rybná 8 (tel 232 43 51; fax 232 84 04), near thecorner of Jakubská, a short distance from the Old Town Square. Three-star, good restaurant, rooms for around $85.
> *Koruna,* Opatovická 16 (tel 29 39 33; fax 29 24 92). In a quiet street three blocks south of Narodní, $90 for two.

Luník, Londýnská 50 (tel 25 27 01, fax 25 66 17). Newly done up hotel in a leafy street in Vinohrady, near I.P. Pavlova metro. $50 single, $90 double.

Opera, Tesnov 13 (tel 231 56 09; fax 231 25 23). About $80 for two, pleasant restaurant.

Cheap Range: most of the following charge around $50 for a double room ($35-40 for a single).

Axa, Na porící 40 (232 72 34), between Florenc station and nám Republiky. Pleasant hotel with a 60s feel and a vinárna popular among locals. Swimming pool and sauna open to non-residents ($3.50).

Balkán, Svornosti trida 28 (54 07 77), near Andel metro in Smíchov district. One of the cheapest, from $35 a night.

Hybernia, Hybernská 24 (22 04 31/2), opposite Masarykovo train station. No frills, mildly seedy.

Juniorhotel Praha, Zitná 12 (29 99 41), off Karlovo nám. Run by CKM but not to be confused with the hostel next door.

Juventus, Blanická 10 (25 51 51/52). A pleasant two-star hotel located just east of nám. Miru in Vinohrady, ten minutes from Wenceslas Square and well placed for untouristy bars and restaurants.

Merkur, Tesnov 9 (231 68 40). Modern and unexceptional, but convenient for the main bus and rail stations.

Hostels. Out of the main season, you should be able to get a bed on the spot at the CKM hostel at Zitna 12 (tel 29 29 84, fax 235 12 97) in the centre, but otherwise you'll need to book. A bed costs $15, or $12 with a card. The CKM Student Travel office in the same building has a list of permanent and summer hostels in and around Prague, mostly some way from the centre. The most improbable accommodation is to be found at Na Vlachovice Autocamp, which puts guests up in huge old beer vats converted into little chalets. You can also book a hostel bed through the CKM office at Jindrisská 28 (22 42 51).

CKM has information about private rooms, but these are no cheaper than those offered by any other agent.

Private Accommodation. In the face of escalating hotel prices, Prague's private accommodation scene is thriving. There are numerous agencies which arrange this, charging fairly standard (and high) prices: typically, $20-40 per night for a room in a private house (less if you stay out of the centre), and $50-70 a night for a two-roomed flat. You can pay up to 60% less if you do deals with the people who approach you directly, usually at Hlavní nádrazí or one of the other transport terminals. Whether you deal privately or not, you can usually pay in any currency.

Hlavní nádrazí has the main concentration of accommodation agents, and there are others scattered about the city. In view of the growing competition some now open daily, but most open Monday to Saturday until 6 or 7pm. Some agencies can deal with advance bookings over the phone, but reservations aren't really necessary.

AR Tour, Karolíny Svetlé 9, near the National Theatre (tel/fax 235 83 89).

AVE Ltd, several offices, including at Hlavní (tel 236 25 60, fax 236 29 56) and Holesovice stations and at the airport.

Hello Ltd, Gorkého nám. 3 (22 42 83), a short walk west of the main train station.

Pragotur, U Obecního domu 2 (tel 232 22 05, fax 232 22 16), off Republiky nám. Open 8am-7pm weekdays, 9am-3pm at weekends.

*Top Tour,*Rybná 3 (229 65 26 or 232 10 77). Efficient, helpful, with good rooms and apartments. Open 9am-8pm weekdays, 10am-7pm at weekends.

Camping. Pragotur should be able to book you into one of the seven campsites around Prague, but try calling direct if you're told a site is full. The best facilities are at the Sokol Dolni Pocernice (Dolni Pocernice, Nad rybnikem; 89 90 34). A more convenient site, however, is the Sport Camp (V Podjáji; 52 16 32, 52 18 02), a short ride on tram 9 from Andel metro station on the west bank.

Eating and Drinking

Food tends to be a disappointment in Prague. The opening-up of new restaurants has improved your chances of finding a decent meal, but many of these serve Western cuisine. Drinking a few mugs of good Czech beer is usually much more fun.

Cheap restaurants are scarce downtown, so don't expect many Czechs for company. If you're staying in private accommodation slightly out of the centre, hunt around for bars and restaurants in your area, where prices are much lower and the clientele strictly local. This way you'll also escape the trials and tribulations of finding a table, a problem which dogs tourists downtown; you'll need to book in advance to be sure of eating at most downtown restaurants. Beer halls and wine cellars are a much better prospect if you don't want to bother with booking. Wherever you end up, watch out for rip-offs. Beware of menus without prices and waiters quoting unlisted dishes which turn out to be the most expensive on offer; and always check your bill carefully.

For a quick and easy snack in the middle of the day, you can't do better than go to one of the city's numerous delicatessens (easily spotted, their windows crammed with salamis and sausages of every imaginable size and shape). Look out for those selling *Prazska sunka* (Prague ham) or *Prazsky klobás* (Prague sausage), delicious when grilled. For a bigger choice, visit the food hall in the basement of the huge Kotva department store on Republiky nám. Pizzas are all the rage in Prague and make cheap snacks too: a whole pizza can cost under $2, but you can also buy it by the slice. Fast food has made inevitable inroads (there is a McDonalds in Wenceslas Square), but is positively scarce by Budapest's standards.

The best choice of restaurants, bars and cafés is on the east bank. Try to avoid the main squares and pedestrian streets in favour of quieter areas, such as around Dlouhá (north of the Old Town Square) or south of Národní. Seeing whether the menu is only in Czech is a good enough guide to the number of expected tourists. Most of Malá Strana's beer and wine cellars have been smartened up, but a few good ones survive and are pleasant in the evening; there are several along Nerudova and in Malostranské nám.

Restaurants. Some of the best of Prague's poor range of restaurants are listed below:

Prazske Restaurace, Závod Obecní Dum. Part of the Art Nouveau

Municipal Hall at the top of Na príkope. One of the few restaurants in this area not to have been tarted up. The Moravská Vinarna downstairs serves delicious Moravian specialities but is expensive: spaghetti for $4.50 is about the cheapest thing on the menu.

Indický Restaurace Mayar, Stepanská 61 (236 99 22). One of the few chances you'll have to eat Indian: Tandoori is the speciality. Main dishes cost $4-6, but you can get lentil curry for $2 or soup for $1 at the snack bar next door.

Jewish Restaurant, Maiselova 18, in the Jewish Town Hall in Josefov. Serves a three-course kosher lunch or dinner for $14: a high price to pay for the sake of being different.

Pizzeria San Pietro, Benediktská 16, off Revolucni. Small, unpretentious place, with better-than-average pizzas.

Nebozizek Restaurant, Petrin Hill (53 79 05). The best place for a proper meal, though the cuisine is not as haute as they would have you believe: moderately expensive (about $10 a head), mostly meat-oriented Czech dishes. You can eat either inside the elegant old house or on the terrace. If you're counting your pennies, just buy a beer and enjoy the fabulous views. To get there take the funicular (see *Exploring*) as far as the halfway station, from where it is only a short walk.

Beer and Wine Bars. These are almost invariably the best bets for wholesome Czech food. The ones listed here are mostly cheaper and more authentic than the flash, overpriced places along Celetná, for example, though the bars catering for tourists tend to stay open later. Those on the east bank are listed first below, followed by those in Malá Strana.

U Fleku, Kremencová 11, three blocks south of Národní. Vacationing Germans are drawn like a magnet to this huge 15th-century beer hall. It's always packed in the evening (with some locals too) — not least for the dark Flek beer, which has been brewed on the premises since 1499. You can eat fairly well on typical fare, from goulash ($3.50) to roast goose and dumplings ($6).

U Supú, 41 Spalená (29 93 10). Small wine bar opposite Národní metro, serving reasonable food at average prices (a few dishes are less than $3). Open until midnight.

U Kotvy, Spalená 11, a short walk south of U Supú. Mostly locals, buzzing and friendly, with a big open-air courtyard. Unadventurous menu but reasonably cheap: the atmosphere makes up for any shortcomings in the culinary department.

U Pinkasu, Jungmannovo nám. Down-to-earth, with a surprising number of locals given its proximity to Wenceslas Square. Pilsner beer and homely food at good prices.

Slovanská Hospoda, about the only place on Na Príkope worth trying. Its huge open courtyard, down an alley beside the PIS tourist office, is well shaded by trees and provides a good place to rest your feet without being hassled by the staff (who are rather inattentive). Not cheap though, $1 for a coke.

U Mécénase, Malostranské nám. A huge vaulted beer cellar beneath the arcade by St Nicholas church. The best of the smartened-up places in Malá Strana.

U Kocoura, Nerudova 2. The most convivial of the pivnice on this street. Not much food (Prague ham and sausages) but good dark beer.

Vinárna U Kolvrata, Valdstejnské nám. Quiet, menu in Czech only, reasonable choice of wine and beer.

Olympia, Vitezna, west of Legii bridge. An ideal place to sample good, ordinary food in an atmosphere of enlightened gloom. The smoke-stained ceiling and crude grafitti in the loo certify its authenticity.

Cafés. Street cafés fill the pedestrian streets of Staré Mesto in fine weather, almost taking over the whole of the Old Town Square. But even on a summer's day, you would do better to head indoors: if you can't afford to stay in one of the top hotels, at least treat yourself to a coffee.

Most locals nip into a stand-up café for breakfast, but if a slice of bread with egg and gherkins on top or a calorific but not particularly tasty cake doesn't appeal, seek refuge in one of the newer cafés-cum-bakeries, where you can get good though not especially cheap pastries: Bonal has several branches, including one on the Old Town Square. Otherwise, choose from one of the following:

Hotel Pariz, U Obecního domu 1, Staré Mesto. A Neo-Gothic cum Art Nouveau confection dating from 1907. Heavy restoration has reduced the atmosphere, but still a great work of art. And the coffee's good too.

Hotel Europa, Wenceslas Square. Retains more of the turn-of-the-century aura than the Pariz. The ground-floor café is a soufflé of marble, mahogany and mirrors, rather like drinking in a library. Put up with the surly waiting staff and the tourists, and soak up the elegance.

Café Slavia, west end of Národní. This large café has long been popular among intellectuals and artists (Václav Havel used to drink here), although the clientele is more mixed these days, including businessmen and tourists. Located across from the National Theatre and open until midnight, it is ideal for a pre- or post-performance drink. Numerous types of coffee and reasonable cakes are on offer. The faded charm of the Art Deco interior was under renovation at the time of going to press.

Kavárna Velryba, Opatovická 24. Tucked away in an unadorned basement west off Spalená. Popular among students who drink coffee, munch snacks and chat until the early hours.

Jo's Bar, west side of Malostranské nám. A small café-cum-bar. Best for a drink, but has a limited menu of vegetarian and Mexican dishes.

Exploring

Exteriors rather than interiors are the highlight of Prague, but some insides should not be missed. Museums and buildings usually open 10am-5pm daily except Monday, and most charge for admission, ranging from $0.50 to $3. The so-called Matilda card ($8), available from tourist centres, gives free admission to most museums in the city.

Nové Mesto. The broad, sloping boulevard of Wenceslas Square is the focus not only of the Nové Mesto, but also of some of the worst developments since 1989; an excessive number of striptease joints, casinos and fast-food restaurants divert attention from some fine Art Nouveau architecture.

Nevertheless, the square is still impressive, with the huge National Museum looming at the top (and providing the best views back down the slope).

Wenceslas Square was a focal point for political action, both in 1968 and 1989. Near its southern end, the spot where the student, Jan Palach, set himself alight in protest at the crushing of the Prague Spring has become a memorial to the victims of communism and is often piled with flowers. Nearby, King Václav I (St Wenceslas) watches over the square from astride his horse: a devout Christian murdered by his own brother in the tenth century, the mythical Good King has a special place in the heart of the Czech people. Overshadowing the statue, however, is the National Museum (Národní Muzeum), the former royal palace with its green and gold topknot standing out above the blackened edifice. Visitors sometimes wonder what they must be missing here, since it defeats normal expectations of a national museum. The room full of rocks, for example, is jolly interesting for geologists, but you're likely to end up simply enjoying the airy grandeur of the 19th-century building rather than its contents. You might like to seek out the skulls of Bohemian kings and queens, however.

One of the most rewarding parts of Nové Mesto to explore lies southwest of Wenceslas Square. A few blocks away, the huge Karlovo námestí is busy with traffic, but the blackened church of St Ignatius has a sumptuous Baroque interior and the shaded grassy area in the middle is a good place to sit quietly. Heading east, you'll find yourself surrounded by students who pour in and out of several university faculties located on or near U nemocnice. The streets in this area are particularly pleasant just to stroll along, but if you hunger for a museum, continue east to Ke Karlovu, where there are two: the Dvorák Museum near the corner of Katerinská is mainly for Dvorákophiles, but the cultured atmosphere and background music are worthwhile; concerts are held in the wonderful frescoed room upstairs. The Police Museum at the bottom of Ke Karlovu is not what it once was; but while you can no longer gawp at a stuffed dog responsible for catching people trying to escape to the West or read unadulterated praise for the communist regime, it's still quite fun.

You should also explore the back streets west of Karlovo nám., wending your way gradually to the National Theatre, a hulk of a building at the end of Národní. Cross the road to the bridge, from where there are good views across to Hradcany and south along the riverside.

Staré Mesto. Na príkope, a busy pedestrian street, runs northeast from Wenceslas Square as a boundary between the New and Old Towns. The 15th-century Powder Tower (Prasná Brána) stands at the top, its back to nám. Republiky; climb it for a good view of the oldest part of the city. The adjacent Muncipal Hall is a fabulous Art Nouveau building, currently undergoing much needed renovation. You can wander freely through parts of it and the Smetana Hall (see *Entertainment*) is open for tours 10am-3pm.

Celetná, a much-restored pedestrian street with upmarket shops, wine bars and barely a Czech in sight, runs west straight to Starometské námestí, the centre of the Old Town. Architecturally, the square is the most impressive in Prague, surrounded by a beautiful and rather higgledy-piggledy assembly of well-preserved medieval buildings. But visit as early in the day as possible, before the tourists, street traders and horse-drawn carts arrive in all their force.

Dominating the square on the south side is the Town Hall (Staromestské radnice), with a 15th-century astronomical clock around which tourists gather to watch Christ and the Apostles emerge as it strikes the hour. While you're waiting, you can climb to the top of the tower, which affords a wonderful panorama of the Old Town's skyline. The twin-towered Týn Church monopolises the view, although the baroque church of St Nicholas is also impressive: both have rather more impact from outside than in. The National Gallery, which occupies the cream and pink baroque-cum-rococo building on the north side, is currently open for exhibitions only. The views from the second floor are good for a different perspective on the square. Nearby, the monument to Jan Hus, the religious reformer and Czech nationalist burnt at the stake in 1415, is a popular resting place for both foreign visitors and the local homeless.

The southern part of Staré Mesto is well worth exploring, and suprisingly quiet in places — though not along the narrow Zelezná, which runs from opposite the clock southeast to the Charles University (or Karolinium), founded by Charles IV and the first in Central Europe. It has been much amended, but you can still see a few old features. Nearby is the Stavovské Theatre, where the first ever performance of Mozart's *Don Giovanni* took place in 1787. The restored cream and green building is hemmed in on two sides and is best viewed from Rytirská, which runs west. From here, you can wander along some of the Old Town's prettiest streets, including the broad Havelská, parallel to Rytirská, and the contrastingly narrow Husová beyond, with gabled houses set at interesting angles along the curving street. The latter has been extensively smartened up recently, however, and the streets and squares further west — particularly Betlémské nám. (with a huge gothic chapel where Jan Hus once preached), Liliová and Anenské nám. — are much quieter.

Karlova runs across the top of Husová, linking Staromestské nám. to the 14th-century Charles Bridge. The Klementinum, a huge 17th-century walled complex, houses the State Library, but the oldest and most interesting rooms are closed to the public. Before crossing the Charles Bridge, head north to Jan Palach nám., a rather characterless square but with perhaps Prague's best museum, the so-called UPM or Decorative Arts Museum. The collection, from both the Czech Republic and Europe and spanning the 16th to 19th centuries, includes the most superb Bohemian glass you are ever likely to see and outrageous Baroque and Rococo clocks and cabinets in almost mint condition. All rooms have notes in English and other languages. There is a pleasant café downstairs, popular with arty (and rich) locals.

Jewish Quarter (Josefov). From the Old Town Square, Maiselova leads north to the old Jewish Quarter. Much of the area was destroyed at the end of the 19th century to make way for new buildings (it is full of wonderful Jugendstil facades), but it wasn't completely obliterated.

The State Jewish Museum (Státní Zidovské Muzeum) incorporates the most important buildings in the area. The gorgeous 13th-century Staronová synagogue is on Maiselova itself, but most buildings are along nearby Hrbitova. In the main museum (where you can buy a ticket giving admission to everything in the quarter), exhibits include moving drawings done by children in the concentration camp at Terezín and treasures looted by the Nazis from synagogues throughout Europe — brought to Prague with the idea of creating a 'museum of an extinct people'. The most atmospheric place in Josefov is the cemetery, the oldest Jewish burial ground in Europe, its jumble of tombstones scattered haphazardly among the sprinkling of trees. Confined within a tiny ghetto, even the dead (an estimated 100,000 of them) had to struggle for space. Arrive early (the cemetery opens at 9am, daily except Saturday) since the one-way path through the graveyard will otherewie be jammed with camera-wielding tourists.

Malá Strana. Connecting the east and west banks is the magnificent Charles Bridge, topped with large stone saints. It's one big bazaar, where traders peddle everything from Soviet army surplus to hippy earrings and bootleg cassettes, and buskers play jazz or the Beatles. Tourists weary after a day's sightseeing, and local sweethearts gather here as the light fades at dusk.

The Charles Bridge forms a bottleneck forcing tourists to proceed in hordes up Mostecká, on the other side. In contrast with this souvenir shop-ridden street, the sloping main square of the quarter (Malostranské námestí) feels more authentic, though it is hardly beautiful: trams rattle past and recycling bins form a curious centrepiece. Most striking is the 18th-century church of St Nicholas, a Baroque extravaganza of marble and gold with statues perching impossibly on the pillars and a skilful *trompe l'oeil* ceiling.

Nerudova runs steeply up the hill from Malostranské nám. With its cobbles and ochre-coloured houses, it is typical of the district and a far more pleasant prospect than Mostecká. It is hard not to resist the attraction of Hradcany, but the area south of Nerudova is probably the best part of Malá Strana. (To avoid reclimbing too many hills, you could explore this area on your way down.) Follow the steps down Jánský to the labyrinth of streets between Nerudova and Vlasská, where exquisite architecture greets you at every turn.

Hradcany. This district contains the capital's greatest churches, some of its best palaces and museums, and also the largest number of tourists. Lording it over Hradcany (and the country) is Prague Castle, a large complex of buildings which includes the official residence of the president. Before the Velvet Revolution, President Husak lived in almost total isolation and the castle was an ominous place. Under Havel, however, it has been transformed into a buzzing centre, with a refreshing lack of security. The main entrance is on Hradcanské nám., accessible up Ke Hradu from the top of Nerudova. It is open to the public 10am-6pm daily except Monday and a $2.30 ticket provides admission to everything. Go as early as possible, perhaps visiting Hradcany before exploring Malá Strana in order to avoid the worst crowds.

Prague Castle was originally built in the ninth century, but what you see now dates from the 16th century, with later additions. The first two court-yards are dull, faceless affairs, with little to stop you making a beeline for the third, all purple and ochre and almost filled by St Vitus' Cathedral. If the castle has a heart, this is it. The superb edifice was six hundred years in the making, but the neo-Gothic touches of the people who completed it in 1929 have the upper hand. The soaring nave creates a wonderful perspective through to the east window, but the gem is the Chapel of Wenceslas, where the tomb of Václav I and even the walls are decorated with a dazzling array of semi-precious stones. Other kings, including Charles IV, are buried in the crypt. Other highlights include several monuments with fine relief carving in the south aisle and the white Imperial mausoleum in the centre of the choir. Unmissable if only for its gall, is the hideous silver monument plonked unceremoniously in the ambulatory.

The Old Royal Palace faces you as you leave the cathedral from the south aisle. The chamber next to the main Vladislav Hall is of historical interest; it was from here that the cult of defenestration — throwing from windows — began, when Protestant nobles ejected two Catholic councillors in 1618, thus sparking off the Thirty Years' War), but most rooms in the palace are empty and lacking in atmosphere. Not so the St George's Basilica opposite, whose Baroque facade hides a stunning Romanesque building. The unadorned walls and smooth curves of the arches are a soothing contrast to the elaborate cathedral. The adjacent convent houses a wide range of Bohemian art from the Middle Ages onwards.

From St George's you can walk down Jirská and then cut left into Golden Lane (Zlatá ul), a cul-de-sac lined on one side with almost miniature medieval houses built into the castle wall and once the home of alchemists and craftsmen. Franz Kafka lived at no. 22 for a time and this, like most other houses in the street, is now a souvenir shop. If you've had your fill of Hradcany, you can leave the castle complex here (Malostranská metro is nearby), but there is more to see. Retrace your steps to Hradcanské nám., turn right in the second courtyard and visit the Royal Gardens: immaculate, and definitely not a place to lounge on the grass, but it's worth walking to the Belvedere palace at the far end.

An alley off the spacious Hradcanské nám. runs down to Sternberský Palace, which houses the National Gallery. Its superb collection of 19th- and 20th-century European art, includes the works of Goya, El Greco and many French Impressionists. Rather than following the well-trodden path along Loretanská west from here, keep to the northern side of the square (past the decorate house used as Mozart's home in the film *Amadeus*) and take a slightly longer route along Kanovnická and Novy Svet, both quiet and comparatively unspoilt streets. You can rejoin Loretanská near the fancy Loreta church and huge Cernin palace (now the foreign ministry).

The second least missable sight in Hradcany after the cathedral is the Strahov Abbey, around the corner from Loretanská nám. Founded in 1140, the monastery is a glorious muddle of Baroque, Romanesque and Neo-Classicisal styles. Following the eviction of the monks by the communists in 1948, the main part of the monastery was converted into a museum of literature. This is of only scant interest compared with the two libraries, which are decorated with superb murals; the so-called Theological Room resembles an illustrated Baroque underground station. Monks are gradually reclaiming Strahov, so the future of the museum- if not of the libraries- is in some doubt, but guided tours are still available. An opening in the east wall of the monastery leads through to tranquil gardens and one of the best views over Prague. You can walk from here down to Petrin Park (see below), or else join Uvoz, an interesting street which runs all the way down to Nerudova. If your feet are worn out, there is a taxi rank in the square by Strahov monastery, though you'd do better to take tram 22, which clatters down the hill like a geriatric rollercoaster, as it loops around the castle. Stay on it across the river, and alight when it reaches Karlovo nám.

An alternative approach to Hradcany is by way of Svatopulka Cecha bridge to the Summer Gardens. A grand terrace, with a mobile metronome sculpted by a Russian, affords excellent open views over Prague. There is also a very enjoyable tea house en route.

Petrin Park (Petrinské sady). This is a fine place to stroll and escape the stress of crowded streets. If you haven't the energy to walk from Hradcany, take the funicular from Ujezd, south of Malostranské nám., although there can be quite a queue in summer. There is a station halfway up, if you can be bothered to walk part of the way. As you ascend, the views behind get steadily better and the splendour of the castle becomes overwhelming. The carriage deposits you in a patch of woodland at the top. Amble along to the modest miniature of the Eiffel Tower, a relic from the Universal Exhibition of 1891.

Villa Bertrámka. The house where Mozart finished *Don Giovanni* (and where scenes from *Amadeus* were filmed) is open to the public and is also used for performances of the composer's work. It is at Mozartova 169 in Smíchov district of Praha 5, within walking distance of Andel metro station.

Vysehrad. Perched atop a cliff above the Vltava, south of Nové Mesto, Vysehrad is a natural fortress which has inspired artificial reinforcement from a variety of rulers: the country's first royal seat was founded here in the 11th century. You can still see some old fortifications, though these are mundane compared with other parts of Prague and with the excellent views up and down the river. Next to the church of Saints Peter and Paul is the immaculate Slavin Cemetery, a spiritual centre for the Czech Republic. In 1989, a crowd of 50,000 students gathered at the cemetery to mark the 50th anniversary of a student hero killed by the Nazis. Though their march to Wenceslas Square was halted by the last stand of the communist riot police, they had won the argument; within days, Czechoslovakia was free. Slavin cemetery (open 9am-4pm daily) is a peaceful tribute to great Czechs. Anton Dvorák's covered memorial takes pride of place, directly opposite the entrance, usually covered in fresh flowers. The grave of his compatriot Janacek bears five bars of an Intermezzo.

The most obvious way to get there is to take the metro to Vysehrad station, the world's best situated metro station but for the bleak Palace of Culture. If it's the end of the day, you should consider walking back to town, just as the sun drifts slowly over the river.

Boat trips. The main departure point for trips on the Vltava is between Jiráskuv and Palackého bridges, on the east bank. You can take a four-hour boat trip to the Slapy dam, for example: the countryside is beautiful as you approach the dam, but it's a full day's outing. The one-hour trips are best avoided unless you enjoy views of tenement blocks and warehouses, interrupted by the occasional burst of greenery.

Show business is booming: theatres, clubs and cafés stage shows from traditional jazz to time-delayed punk. Theatre and concert tickets for the top performers can be difficult to book at short notice. Of the many ticket agencies, the PIS (Na príkope 20) is the best source of information in English about mainstream cultural events, and can also make reservations. For listings see *This Month in Prague* or one of the English-language papers such as *Prague Post*. The latter also list films shown in the original language.

Theatre, Classical Music and Opera. The choice of performances is daunting, with scores of good venues. With so many tourists to cater for, the quality of musical performances varies widely. Ten dollars for attending a top-notch opera is still a bargain, but most things cost less than half that. Concerts take place in churches and all manner of other buildings on both the east and west bank, with some of the best at St Nicholas church in the Old Town Square. During the Prague Spring Music Festival from 12 May to 2 June, you can enjoy an orgy of concerts — usually four or five a day.

The main venues are as follows:

Smetana Theatre (Smetanovo Divadlo), Wilsonova 4 (26 53 53), north of the National Museum. Prague's lavish state opera house, with a traditional but high-quality repertoire.

Stavovské Divadlo, Ovocný trh (26 86 58). The oldest opera house in Prague. Given its associations with Mozart, the demand for tickets is high.

Dvorák Hall, Jana Palacha nám. Home of the excellent Czech Philharmonic, but too small for such an orchestra.

Smetana Hall (Smetanovo sín), a lovely Art Nouveau auditorium inside the Municipal Hall on nám. Republiky. The Prague Symphony Orchestra is based here. Tickets from the adjacent office at U Prasné Brany 2 (232 25 01).

National Theatre (Národní Divadlo), Narodní 2 (20 53 64). One of the most sumptuous theatres in Europe, staging opera, ballet and some drama.

Nová Scéna, Národní 40. A fly's eye of a building alongside the National. The main stage for the popular Laterna Magika, performing a mix of drama, mime and music.

Disk Theatre, Karlova 8 (26 53 77). The Panoptikum school of drama performs here.

Divadlo na zábradli, Anenské nam. (234 604 49). Mime and straight theatre from Havel and Dario Fo to Alan Bennett.

Studio Gag, Národní 25 (236 86 11). Some of the best comedy mime around, daily from 8pm. Admission steep at $10.

Popular Music and Nightclubs. Prague has a lively jazz scene and bands do the rounds of the city's various clubs. Choosing a nightclub is a more hit-and-miss affair. Those around Wenceslas Square cater for tourists and are ghastly for the most part, with outdated music and men in search of prostitutes (or vice versa). New places are opening up, however, so ask young locals you meet.

Reduta Jazz Club, Národní 20 (20 38 22/25). One of Europe's oldest jazz clubs. Looks like a split-level airport lounge, but good Czech and international bands are featured, from 9pm Monday to Saturday. Almost exclusively tourists. Admission $3.25, and $1.80 for a can of beer.

AghaRTA Jazz Centrum, Krakovská 5 (26 58 34). Cosy and friendly club-cum-bar, with attached shop with a good selection of CDs. Associated with ARTA, which publishes some of the country's top jazz acts. Open until midnight. Admission $2.25.

Malostranská Beseda, Malostranské nám. 21 (53 90 24). Jazz, folk, country and other music daily in upstairs club. Shop attached.

Lucerna, turn-of-the-century ballroom on Vodicková off Wenceslas Square. International acts from Suzanne Vega to Fairport Convention perform here.

Mamma Klub, Elisky Krásnohorské 7, north of Old Town Square. Good mix of people, lively, decent music to dance to.

Exodus Club, Národní 25 (16 10 85). Newish reggae disco, open 9pm-5am.

Sport. The biggest and best football matches (including international matches) are held at Stadión Sparta, near Hradcanská metro station. Games are usually on Tuesdays, Fridays or Sundays and you can buy a ticket on the day. Ice hockey is played at the stadium in Holesovice, on different days of the week, and you can watch horse racing (mostly steeplechases) at Velká Chuchle, 3 miles/5km south of the city.

Downtown Prague is in danger of becoming one big shopping centre, though most shops have priced themselves outside the range of most Czechs. Souvenir shops greet you at every turn, many of them peddling much the same kind of stuff. Western shops are found mainly in the pedestrian streets between Staromestké nám. and Wenceslas Square. You'll certainly have no problem picking up Bohemian glass and other crafts, if that's what you're after; there is a good choice in the shop on Havirská right by the Stavovské theatre. The Kotva department store in nám. Republiky, once one of the best shops behind the Iron Curtain, is a more interesting place to buy souvenirs, such as Spartak Prague mugs and hats, from the ground floor. The American Hospitality Center on Na mustku, just north of Wenceslas Square, sells 'Czech It Out' T-shirts for $12.

Head into the suburbs and you'll see the gloomy shops which your average citizen must still contend with. This is also where you'll find open-air markets selling fresh produce; fruit is easy to buy in the centre, but the stalls charge higher prices.

Books and Records. Cizojazycna Literatura at Na príkope 27 sells books in English and other languages as well as a well-chosen selection of postcards, maps, posters, prints and T-shirts. Celetná has several bookshops, including a branch of Orbis Pictus, and an excellent secondhand bookshop at no. 31, which sells prints and has been known to price first-edition Graham Greene novels at just $5; you can also pick up a dog-eared Desmond Bagley or similar for under $2.

The main recording companies have shops all over the centre, including a branch of Panton on Karlova, which has headphones for listening to tapes and CDs. For cheap records unwanted in the West (Blondie or Shakin' Stevens go for under $3), try Albatros on the corner of Na Persýne and Národní.

It used to be said that Prague was the safest city in Europe. It may still be so, but crime has probably doubled: see the *Crime and Safety* in the introduction. Wenceslas Square is a popular hang-out for pickpockets (as well as a growing contingent of prostitutes).

With the black economy as good as dead, black marketeers now resort to straight swindling. New arrivals off the airport bus are offered temptingly good deals on currency transactions, but take a good look at their notes before parting with yours.

Tourist Information: the Prague Information Service or PIS is the best source of general information, with English-speaking staff. It has offices at Na príkope 20 (54 44 44), Staromestské nám. and Hlavní nádrazi, open 9am-7pm weekdays, 9am-6pm Saturdays. Cedok is useful for information about international trains and buses, but not much else. Its head office is at Na príkope 18 (212 71 11), with others at Parizská 6 (232 72 16) and Rytírská 16 (26 58 67). The *American Hospitality Center* on Na mustku (tel 236 74 86; fax 26 97 38) has helpful, English-speaking staff (you don't have to be American), plus information on international buses.

Money: good rates at banks on Na príkope. Zivnostenská Banka, next to PIS, will give cash advances on some credit cards, including MasterCard and Visa, open until 9pm. Cedok and private exchange offices, such as branches of Chequepoint, tend to charge at least 3% commission (make sure the advertised rates are the ones you get).

Post Office: main office at Jindrisská 14 (26 41 93), open 24 hours. You can make international telephone calls and send telexes or faxes (receive on 232 08 78 or 232 09 78) from here too.

American Express: Wenceslas Square 56 (24 22 9883). Open 9am-6pm Monday to Friday, 9am-noon on Saturday.

Thomas Cook: Opletalova 1, corner of Wenceslas Square.

Medical Treatment: the Fakultní Poliklinika at Karlovo nám. 32 (29 93 81) is a special foreigners' clinic. There is a 24-hour pharmacy at Na príkope 7 (22 00 81). Dental emergencies are treated at Pstrossova 10 (29 43 26), south of the National Theatre.

Gay Switchboard: 52 73 88, 6-8pm, with English-speakers.

Embassies and Consulates. In Malá Strana unless stated otherwise.

UK: Thunovská 14 (tel 53 33 47/8/9, fax 53 99 27).
USA: Trziste 15 (tel 53 66 41, fax 53 24 57).
Canada: Mickiewiczova 6 (tel 31 20 251, fax 31 12 791).
Bulgaria: Krakovská 6, Nové Mesto (26 43 06/10).
Poland: Valdstejnská 8 (53 69 51).
Hungary: I.V. Micurina 1 (36 50 41).
Romania: Nerudova 5 (53 30 59).

AROUND PRAGUE — CENTRAL BOHEMIA

Bohemia was once the heart of the Central European industrial revolution. Despite its present industrialisation, the region has a wealth of castles, palaces and churches, reminders of the country's feudal past. Prague is a perfect base for exploring Central Bohemia. All the following destinations can be seen on day trips, although it can be rewarding to stay longer and sample the very different atmosphere of some of the provincial towns.

MELNIK

The town of Melník sits on a hillside above the confluence of the Vltava and Elbe rivers, 20 miles/32km north of Prague. Surrounded by vineyards, it is the centre of the Bohemian wine industry, a white wine called *Ludmila* being the most famous local vintage. Dominating the old town is a Renaissance-style castle (open March-September), which houses a museum of viticulture and an art gallery of moderate interest. Concentrate on trying the local wines in the (passable) restaurant and enjoying the views over the Elbe. Don't miss the church next door, which contains a bizarre Gothic ossuary with thousands of human bones arranged into weird and wonderful patterns.

Buses to Melník leave regularly from outside Prague's Holesovice station.

KARLSTEJN

This large walled fortress, 20 miles/32km southwest of Prague, was built by Charles IV and is the best known hilltop castle in Bohemia. It looks magnificent as you approach, but heavy restoration has made it more Disney than history. Furthermore, the chapel in the Big Tower, the gem of Karlstejn, has been closed for many years. But while the superb 14th-century murals are hidden from view, there are good displays outside and the Church of Our Lady has impressive frescoes. The castle is open all year.

Karlstejn village is 40 minutes by train from Praha-Smíchov station: it's a 20-30 minute walk up to the castle from the village. You can eat reasonably well at U Elisky restaurant.

KONOPISTE

Thirty miles/48km south of Prague, Konopiste castle is less dramatic but more interesting than Karlstejn. Founded in the 14th century, the castle's most famous occupant was Archduke Ferdinand, whose assassination at Sarajevo in 1914 sparked off the First World War. The state rooms are luxurious and there is a macabre collection of stuffed animals — the trophies of Ferdinand, an obsessive hunter — and the weapons used to kill them. You can clear your head by strolling through the lovely wooded grounds of the castle. Konopiste is open April-October.

The castle overlooks a lake just over a mile west of Benesov village, which is served by buses from Florenc terminal and trains from Hlavní nádrazí; the journey takes about an hour. There is a well-trodden path up to the castle from Benesov. You can stay at the Hotel Posta in the main square.

KUTNA HORA

If you have time for just one day trip from Prague, make sure it's to Kutná Hora, in the flat plains 42 miles/68km east of the capital. The town sits in the lovely Vrchlice valley, its clifftop cathedral a striking sight as you approach. About 500 years ago Kutná Hora was the second largest town in Bohemia after Prague. Following the discovery of silver deposits nearby, Václav II founded the Royal Mint here in the 13th century. Kutná Hora prospered until the early 1700s, after which time it went into decline. The town has remained largely unspoilt and Gothic and Baroque buildings of singular beauty line the labyrinthine streets and the main square, Palakého námestí.

Arrival and Departure. Kutná Hora is on the Prague-Brno railway, with trains from Prague's Masarykovo and Hlavní stations; the main station is a couple of miles and an easy bus ride northeast of the centre. You may need to change trains at Kolín, a pleasant, untouristy town just north of Kutná Hora. If you're heading east afterwards, go back to Kolín. Buses are less regular than the trains, although the terminal is at least central.

Accommodation. An overnight stay in Kutná Hora is strongly recommended: the town is busy with tourists in the daytime and the atmosphere improves tenfold as the light begins to fade and the visitors head home. You can stay at Hotel Medínek on Palackého nám., and there are several pleasant beer and wine cellars in which to while away an evening.

Exploring. Kutná Hora is a fine place in which to stroll around and there are certain buildings of particular interest. Just off the main square, the Italian Court (Vlassky Dvur) is the site of the old mint. It has been much mucked about by restorers, but you can still sense an atmosphere of faded glory. The palace gardens provide superlative views across to the cathedral. Beyond the high-steepled church of St James, you reach the 15th-century Stone House (Kamenny Dum) at Radnická 24, said to be the oldest house in Kutná Hora. It has a marvellous carved facade and now contains an historical museum. The tour through the medieval mine shafts beneath the town should not be missed.

The jewel of Kutná Hora is the Gothic St Barbara Cathedral (Chrám Svatého Barbory), one of the finest churches in the country. The architect responsible for St Vitus' cathedral in Prague, Peter Parler, was involved in the design, although the church was not completed in his lifetime; begun in 1388, the cathedral took almost 180 years to finish. The exterior, with its soaring flying buttresses, towers and spires is staggering. The interior is less impressive but still contains much of interest, particularly the 15th-century frescoes in the Minter's Chapel.

SOUTHERN BOHEMIA

The area stretching to the south of Prague is scattered with charming towns and wooded mountains, including the unspoilt Sumava range along the German border. There are also many lakes and rivers, and the Vltava virtually splits the region in two, with castles dotted through the valley. Several medieval walled towns are virtual museum pieces, surprisingly untouched given the country's turbulent past. Compared with northern Bohemia, this region is pleasantly free of industry but not of tourists: Germans and Austrians pour in during the summer.

TABOR

Fifty-five miles/88km south of Prague, Tábor sits in an attractive spot on the banks of the river Luznice. It was founded by the Hussites in 1420 as a centre of religious resistance, a Protestant island in a sea of Catholicism. It was captured only in 1452; the crooked medieval streets which survive today were designed to confuse Catholic attackers. Baroque and Renaissance burgher houses and a 15th-century Gothic church overlook the main square, Zizkovo námestí. But the town's most interesting feature is the network of underground tunnels built as a safe refuge for the Hussites; they have been in frequent use during the town's colourful history as a focus of peasant rebellions and, later, the working-class movement and anti-fascist revolt. They lie beneath the Hussite Museum on the main square, but are open in summer only. For a panoramic view of Tábor climb up the tower of the old Kotnov Castle, southwest of the square by Bechyne Gate.

Trains from Prague (some en route to Vienna) take two hours to Tábor, and there are also good bus and train services to Ceské Budejovice. As such, Tábor is an easy stop-off on the way south. There are a few hotels, the best being the Slovan at trida 9 Kvetna (0361-236 97).

CESKE BUDEJOVICE

The capital of Southern Bohemia, 105 miles/168km south of Prague, Ceské Budejovice is large and moderately industrial. But the old town, whose prosperity was built upon its position on a major trade route, is beautifully preserved — particularly nám. Premysla Otakara II, one of the largest squares in Europe. Ceské Budejovice was founded in the 13th century, but most of the buildings and the handsome arcades around the square date from the 1600s. Climb the 250 steps of the Black Tower (Cerná Vez) for a magnificent panorama of the town and surrounding area. The streets running off the square also boast fine burgher architecture. The town's oldest surviving building is the 14th-century Dominican monastery by the river.

It won't take long to explore the best of Ceské Budejovice, but the town is an ideal base for exploring southern Bohemia, with good bus and train connections. A visit here will also give keen beer-drinkers a chance to sample Budvar beer in its home town. (The brewery is not really geared up for visitors, but Cedok can usually arrange a tour.)

Arrival and Departure. There are daily trains from Prague (2½-3 hours), although the bus is quicker, taking about two hours via Tábor (an hour northeast). Both trains and buses run south to Vienna via Linz, with the frequency of these last services increasing all the time.

Accommodation and Food. Hotels are few, considering the summer crowds. There are a couple in prime sites on the main square, including the atmospheric and friendly Hotel Slunce (038-36 755) charging $45-50 for a double. You'll find cheaper options by the train station, including the Malse at Nádrazní 31 (038-27 631). There is a caravan-cum-campsite a mile southwest, and CKM (Karla IV 12; 038-36 138) has information about accommodation in and around the town, though there is no permanent hostel. The Cedok office is on the main square (038-38 428).

For food and drink, stick to the beer halls: the lively Masné Kramy, in an old meat market on the corner of Hroznová just north of the main square, is *the* place to drink Budvar. Also try the U Zelezné Panny around the corner on Ceská.

Around Ceske Budejovice

Ceský Krumlov. The small town of Ceský Krumlov, 15 miles/24km south of Ceské Budéjovice, is a medieval gem on the banks of the winding Vltava River and the best sight in Southern Bohemia. The atmosphere of the town has suffered with the ever-increasing influx of tourists, but the beauty of the place remains as staggering as ever.

On a ridge on the west bank of the river, the magnificent castle is the second largest in the country after the one in Prague. Though medieval in origin, like many buildings in the town it has been altered in the intervening centuries. The palace in the upper castle contains a collection of pictures, furniture and tapestries and is open in summer; the gardens lie across a bridge west of the main complex. Impressive as the castle is, however, it is the old town across the river which is the town's main attraction. Winding cobbled streets converge on nám. Svorností, with many alleyways and nooks and crannies to explore. There is a good regional museum, and the 15th-century St Vitus church contains fine woodcarving inside.

Ceský Krumlov is best reached by bus from Ceské Budejovice because the bus terminal is more central than the rail station and also offers the best views over the town. A day trip is recommended, since the hotels are usually full. If you can book in advance, stay at the Krumlov Hotel in a wonderful Gothic building on nám. Svorností (0337-2255); rooms cost around $40. Cedok (0337-2189) is also on the main square.

Trebon and Jindrichuv Hradec. Twenty-two miles/36km east of Ceské Bude-jovice, Trebon is a pleasant spa town surrounded by lakes full of carp: the fish are harvested in September and October, when they are served up in all the local restaurants. Of more enduring interest than Trebon, however, is Jindrichuv Hradec, 17 miles/28km east and a typical self-contained medieval town. The tranquillity is a perfect antidote to the crowds that characterise Ceské Budejovice and Cesky Krumlov. Not much goes on, but the atmosphere is thoroughly relaxing. The castle is an architectural hotchpotch but impressive all the same, with pleasant gardens. There is also a moderately interesting museum with an exhibition commemorating the composer Smetana, as well as some folk sculptures. As it is just an hour by train from Ceské Budejovice, Jindrichuv Hradec can be visited comfortably in a day, although there are hotels both here and in Trebon.

WESTERN BOHEMIA

The proximity of Germany is felt more heavily in Western Bohemia than in any other part of the republic — an influence that dates back to the twelfth century, when Germans first colonised the region (most resident Germans were expelled after the Second World War), and continues in a different fashion with the thousands of tourists that flood over the border. Express trains from Munich and Narnberg zoom through the region ten to the dozen. Industrialisation has marred some parts of West Bohemia, but has left the famous spa towns untouched, and these are the region's main attraction.

PLZEN

The capital of West Bohemia is a large industrial city 50 miles/80km southwest of Prague. It was an important trading centre during the Middle Ages, but since then industry and wartime bombing have had a detrimental effect on the town. The heart of Plzen has a small but impressive collection of Baroque, Renaissance and Classical buildings, albeit against a backdrop of ugly industrial and residential developments, and with a heavy coating of grime.

Plzen is most famous for two products: the first (Pilsner beer) is exported worldwide, the second (the Skoda car) is not. For keen beer-drinkers the fact that Plzen produces the original Pilsner beer is likely to be the city's only appeal. Much of the insipid lager poured down Western throats goes by the name of Pilsner, but has little in common with this town's fine beer — Plzensky prazdroj — which started the fashion for top-fermented brews. Teetotallers should treat Plzen as a jumping-off point for Western Bohemia's other sights, although if you have a few hours to spare, the old town is worth exploring.

Arrival and Departure. Plzen lies on the Prague-Munich railway and all international trains to and from the capital (four or five a day) stop here. Trains arrive from all other directions too, including from Ceské Budejovice. Most trains arrive at the Hlavní nádrazí, 20 minutes' walk or a short tram ride southeast of the main square, nám. Republiky.

Buses from Prague (2 hours), Ceské Budejovice and other towns arrive at the station nine blocks west of the main square.

Accommodation and Food. Plzen's hotels are on the expensive side. Oldest and most characterful are the Slovan at Smetanovy sady 1 (019-335 51), just south of nám. Republiky, with doubles for around $30; or the cleaner Continental at Zbrojnická 8 (019-330 60), which charges nearer $40. Cedok, at Presovská 10 (019-352 77), can arrange private accommodation. There is a pleasant lakeside campsite at Bílá Hora, 3 miles/5km north of the city.

Skip Plzen's mostly mediocre restaurants in favour of its beer halls. The Restaurace Prazdroj, built into the brewery (see below), serves wonderful beer and local cheese. Or try the buzzing *pivnice* on Veleslavínova, by the brewing museum, or U Zumbery (Beucova 14), the best place in the centre.

Exploring. The pick of Plzen's historic buildings are situated on the large nám. Republiky, dominated by the Gothic church of St Bartholomew, whose tower provides fine views. Also on the square is the Renaissance Town Hall and the Ethnographical Museum, which provides a reasonable background to the region.

The Museum of Beer Brewing (Pivovarské Muzeum) is in an old malt house on Veleslavínova, northeast of the main square. The tours are uninspiring but there's a lot to look at. For an insight into the modern beer-making process go to the brewery, a short walk southeast across the river from the museum. They prefer visitors to go as part of a tour organised by Cedok, but individual (and mildly pushy) callers can usually be accommodated.

Around Plzen

Domazlice. Southwest of Plzen, not far from the West German border, Domazlice is home to a minor Czech ethnic group called the Chods, who have a rich folk heritage. The town boasts a fine collection of Renaissance and Baroque houses, an attractive arcaded square (nám. Miru), and a 13th-century castle. You still see people in traditional costume — particularly women in their colourful skirts, short jackets and red stockings. The town museum (open April-October) on the main square provides a summary of Chod history and folklore. There are a few small hotels and a tourist office in the main square, but this is a sleepy town which attracts few tourists.

THE SPA TOWNS

The towns of Karlovy Vary, Mariánské Lázne and Frantiskový Lazne form the West Bohemian spa triangle. They are among the oldest spa towns in the world and during their heyday in the 19th century attracted royalty and the rich or aristocratic from all corners of Europe. Under communism the spas became shabby, with the smart old hotels taken over by party officials or converted into rest homes for workers. They are now gradually being restored, and the towns generally cleaned up. The old pre-communist names of Karlsbad, Marienbad and Franzensbad are back in fashion too. All three towns are linked by regular bus and train services, bus being the best way to get around.

Taking a full cure (the waters are said to help with a variety of ailments, from constipation to infertility) is expensive and must generally be arranged in advance; but you can still enjoy the tranquillity, the old-fashioned elegance and the genteel cafés. Tourists (mostly German) probably outnumber patients, but when the sight of so many ill people and hypochondriacs begins to depress, you can head into the hills; each spa town nestles in a picturesque valley surrounded by pine forests. Prices are uncharacteristically high for the Czech Republic — on a par with Prague.

Karlovy Vary. Founded by Charles IV in the 14th century, Karlovy Vary is the oldest of the spas and has boasted numerous illustrious visitors in its time, from Beethoven to Karl Marx. It is also the biggest spa and probably the best to visit in terms of facilities and things to do — although in fact just strolling around or sitting about is probably the most fun. Much of the centre is pedestrianised and the Teplá river is lined with handsome fin-de-siècle houses. Have a peek inside the sumptuous 18th-century Grand Hotel Pupp on Stará louka, where the crass communist alterations are gradually being obliterated.

There are several colonnades where people amble about taking the steaming waters from spouted mugs: you can buy your own plastic tumbler from local shops, but the waters are very rich in minerals and taste unpleasant. The busiest colonnade, at the bottom of Trziste, was built in 1975 and is named after the cosmonaut Yuri Gagarin, who came here in the Sixties. The only place you can immerse yourself in the waters — unless you go for a full-blown cure — is at the open-air swimming pool on the hill above the thermal sanatorium, a hideous 60s creation. The best walks are southwest of the centre — several trails begin near the top of the hill above Grand Hotel Pupp and can be reached by the funicular railway from Marianská.

Arrival and Departure: buses run every hour from Prague's Florenc terminal, and slightly less frequently from Plzen. Buses serve the other spas too, although Mariánské Lázne is also accessible on local trains from the station (dolní nádrazí) on Konevova, opposite the main bus station. Most trains to Prague (3+ hours) and west into Germany leave from the station (horní nádrazí) north across the Ohre river.

Accommodation: expensive rooms are plentiful, cheap ones are not. The Atlantic Hotel at Trziste 23 (017-247 15) is very central, elegant and good value. Otherwise try the Wolker, nearby at Trziste 19 (017-277 15). Hotel Adria at Konevova 1 (017-237 65), opposite the main bus station, is one of the cheapest but fills quickly. The Turist at Davida Bechera 18 or the Jizera at no. 7 are other possibilities in this area. CKM runs the Junior Hotel Alice at Petiletky 1 (017-248 48), 20 minutes' walk or a short bus ride south of town. There is a campsite attached to the nearby Motel Brezová (017-252 24), operational in summer only. Cedok at Trziste 23 (017-267 05) can arrange private rooms, but these are oversubscribed too.

Eating and Drinking: Karlovy Vary's choice of restaurants is disappointing, though some of the hotels serve reasonable food, and the riverside cafés are better. The Continental M-Bar at Trziste 27 is always buzzing and serves wonderful cakes and ice cream, which can be enjoyed with either coffee or beer. Wherever you go, look out for two local specialities: the herbal liqueur *becherovka* (an acquired taste) and *oplatky,* wafers with a sugar or chocolate filling.

Mariánské Lázne. Situated in a beautiful valley 30 miles/48km south of Karlovy Vary, Mariánské Lázne's position was inspiring enough to have prompted Goethe to write his poignant *Marienbader Elegien.* Grand architecture attests to 19th-century prosperity and the ornate, wrought-iron colonnade is superb, following restoration. The musical fountain is another popular attraction, playing several times a day. While busy, Mariánské Lázne is much quieter and less commercial than Karlovy Vary; there are far fewer pedlars and most people find this the more attractive resort.

When Edward VII visited Marienbad, he used to stay in the Hotel Kafka

(Kavkaz) on Goethovo nám.: you can too if you want to splash out, but there are lots of other hotels along Hlavní trida, the main street where you'll find most cafés and restaurants. The Europa, just off the main drag at Trebízského 101 (0165-2063/4) and with doubles for around $30, is particularly recommended. The CKM Krakonos at Zádub 53 (0165-2624), in a lovely spot on a hill above the town, is a hotel more than a hostel: $25 to IYHF members but twice that for everyone else.

Mariánské Lázne is two hours by train from Karlovy Vary, but buses take half that time. Some international express trains on the Prague-Nürnberg line stop here too, calling also at Plzen (47 miles/76km northeast).

Frantiskovy Lázne. The least interesting of the three, Frantiskovy Lázne still has some handsome architecture, including houses painted in ochre or pale yellow with white stucco decoration.

CHEB

The German border (and one of the main crossing points into the Czech Republic by road or rail) is just 5 miles/8km west of Cheb. Germans used to form the majority in the town, which was incorporated into the Third Reich in 1938, and they have left their influence — increased by the number of daytrippers flooding across the border. There are a few small hotels and Cedok can help with private rooms. But with Marianske Lazne and Karlovy Vary both a short train ride away (and Frantiskovy Lázne is just 4 miles/7km north), Cheb is easily visited on a day trip: a few hours are all you need here.

Within the unpleasant outer fringes, Cheb retains an interesting centre of Gothic and Baroque buildings, particularly around the spruce main square. They include a charming group of 16th-century houses once used by Jewish shopkeepers and now the Spalicek restaurant. The local museum nearby has a room dedicated to Wallenstein — the Habsburg general made famous in the Thirty Years' War, who was assassinated in Cheb in 1634. The 12th-century castle northwest of the square is delapidated but you can climb the tower for a panoramic view.

NORTHERN BOHEMIA

This region is the most industrialised part of the country and one of the most polluted in Europe: acid rain has massacred whole swathes of forest, and all manner of gruesome emissions have done untold damage to people's health. The Krkonose mountains and the hills of the Cesky Raj in the northeast have not gone unscathed, but still provide some of the most beautiful natural scenery in the republic.

CESKY RAJ

Northeast of Prague, towards the Polish border, Ceský Raj — the 'Bohemian Paradise' — is an extremely beautiful area with castles and dramatic sandstone rock formations. Being within fairly easy reach of both Prague and Germany, the region sees many visitors, but don't be put off. To explore the region properly, buy the *Ceský Raj Podebradsko* map, available in any decent bookshop.

The main town of Ceský Raj is Turnov, a mediocre place about 60 miles/96km northeast of the capital. Malá Skála is a better place to stay, situated

in a valley surrounded by fir-covered mountains. You can walk up to a
ruined chapel, perched on rocks high up above the village. A bus leaves
Prague for Malá Skála daily from the station at Holesovice and takes about
two hours. You should be able to organise accommodation in a private
house quite easily, and you can also camp. Opposite the campsite is a typical
Czech beerhouse which serves food, stays open into the early hours and is
always lively.

Jicín, southeast of Turnov, is more easily accessible (but therefore busier)
than Malá Skála. From there you can reach some of the best sights in the
region. Supreme among these is Prachovské Skály, just a couple of miles
from Jicín, where massive rocks soar above the trees. There are two good
castles in the area. Trosky (open on summer weekends only) is a ruin in a
dramatic position offering fine views; it is a two-mile walk from Ktová, on
the Turnov-Jicín railway line. Further west, Kost Castle, near the village of
Podkost, is one of the best preserved medieval castles in Bohemia.

THE KRKONOSE MOUNTAINS

The Krkonose (Giant) Mountains, in northeastern Bohemia along the Polish
border, provide the best hiking country in the republic. It is also a preposterously photogenic area, with colourful wooden houses scattered among the
woods and meadows. This area is fast being developed, but it is still possible
to find some secluded spots. Maps available locally show all the main
footpaths, which are well marked on the ground as well. Accommodation
in the mountains is in the form of *boudas,* wooden huts, varying from the
basic to the luxurious and generally accessible on foot only. Information on
these is available from local tourist offices. Be warned that the weather is
notoriously changeable in the Krkonose: rain and snow are common and
arrive without warning: go well prepared for all conditions. Although Slovakia is better for downhill skiing, cross-country skiing can be fun here.

Vrchlabí, 80 miles/128km northeast of Prague, is the main gateway to the
mountains, with good transport connections and a reasonable amount of
accommodation (including a campsite). The town is beautifully situated and
has some magnificent Renaissance monuments. The Cedok office can help
with arranging accommodation in the mountains, but demand often outstrips
supply in the summer. Buses from Vrchlabí serve all the main resorts.

Spindleruv Mlýn, 10 miles/16km north of Vrchlabí, is one of the best
starting-points for walks. Situated on the banks of the river Elbe, it's a
pleasant blend of old and new architecture, although the latter is on the
increase. There are chairlifts up a couple of nearby mountains and a choice
of walking trails: the six-mile hike along the Elbe to its source at Pramen
Labe is wonderful. Hotels in the town are likely to be full, but there are
campsites and you should be able to find a private room without too much
trouble.

One of the best walks in the region is from the top of Mount Snezka
(1,602m/5,255ft), the highest peak in Bohemia and accessible by chairlift
from the resort of Pec pod Snezkou, in the Upa valley, northeast of Vrchlabí.
You can walk down to Spindleruv Mlýn through a beautiful pine forest.

MORAVIA

The Moravians, separated from the Bohemians by the Bohemian-Moravian
Highlands, claim to be distinct from their fellow Czechs to the west. They

seem more relaxed and open than their neighbours. The northern areas are industrial, but Moravia is known more for its thriving agriculture (and its wine). There are picturesque towns and valleys in the southwest, a smattering of castles here and there; and Brno, the capital, is a lovely city well worth crossing the country for. While there is plenty to see, perhaps the fact that not many people bother to explore Moravia is one of the region's chief attractions. It is an ideal place to experience both the people and their pleasant, unassuming little towns, without feeling the pressure to do heavy-duty sightseeing.

The first town you come to if you're taking the motorway from Prague to Brno is Jihlava. The most noteworthy fact about it is that it was the childhood home of Gustav Mahler, but industrialisation has destroyed the town's charm. It is well worth stopping off here, however, in order to catch a bus south to Telc.

TELC

Surrounded by beautiful countryside, 18 miles/29km southwest of Jihlava, Telc is an absolutely idyllic Renaissance town which has few rivals in Europe. Considering its beauty, it sees surprisingly few visitors, although coaches periodically deposit groups here for an hour or two. The cream of Telc's architecture is clustered around the main square, nám. Zachariáse z hradce, where fine Baroque facades preside over older arcades. At one end is the impressive castle, founded in the 14th century by the Hradec family and rebuilt in the 16th. You can go on a tour of the sumptuous interiors and stroll through the gardens. There is also a museum, with a scale model of the town dating from the 1890s. For a different perspective, climb the tower of the nearby St James church.

The most regular buses to Telc come from Jihlava, but Ceské Budejovice-Brno buses also stop off. The U Nádrazí hotel at Nádrazí 164 (166-96 25 72) near the transport terminals is cheap, but for greater comfort go to the Cerny Orel Hotel (066-96 22 21) on the main square.

If you enjoyed Telc, don't fail to visit Slavonice, another Renaissance relic 15 miles/24km south.

ZNOJMO

Znojmo is big and disappointing after Telc (40 miles/65km northwest). But the town's location above the deep Dyje valley is stunning, and the old town picturesque, though shabby. Znojmo has long been the centre of the Moravian wine industry, and most of the old houses in Masarykovo nám., the main square, were once owned by local wine magnates. Their cellars were connected by passages, and you can explore the underground network from Kamarská, just east of the Town Hall. The latter was rebuilt following damage during World War Two, but its Gothic tower has survived and provides excellent views. The tower at the southern end of the square belongs to a Capuchin monastery, although it was originally part of the town's fortifications. The churches of St Václav and St Nicholas lie west of Masary-kovo nám., side by side on the cliff above the river. You can walk along the old fortifications, and paths also lead down into the forest and beside the river beneath the castle. You can't go inside Znojmo Castle, but the views along the valley from there are magnificent.

Znojmo lies just inside the Austrian border, on the Prague-Vienna road. Trains run from Prague, Brno and Vienna, and Jihlava and Brno are both about 90 minutes away by bus. If approaching from Telc, you'll normally have to change buses at Kasárna. Buses also head south into Austria. A few hours in Znojmo should suffice, but if you need to stay overnight, try the Cerný medved (0624-42 71) on the main square; the Znojmo Hotel, by the bus and train stations southeast of the centre; or the Huberius Pension, nearer the centre. There is no shortage of reasonably-priced restaurants.

BRNO

The capital of Moravia, with a population of more than 400,000, is the second largest city in the Czech Republic. (To do as the locals, pronounce Brno with the stress on the final 'o'.) The city's trade fairs are well-known in international business circles, but Brno has been neglected by travellers. While primarily an industrial centre, and a fairly run-down one at that, it is a relaxed and buzzing city, with a lively student population and lots of good bars and restaurants. Business visitors don't really explore the town, preferring to stick to their four-star hotels. As a result, you can eat and drink largely in the company of local residents, generally a warm and friendly people.

Brno has long been an important cultural centre: the birthplace of the exiled author Milan Kundera and the home for most of his life of the Moravian composer, Leos Janácek. The city also has two of the best museums in the country and some architectural gems. Unlike most other Czech towns, the best buildings date from the last century, although some more avant-garde buildings were erected between the wars. As in Prague, every street holds a surprise, with handsome doorways or curious carved figures. Both the damage of World War Two and pollution have wrought havoc, but the decay adds to the atmosphere. Restoration work gathers pace but after Prague, where the noise of reconstruction is constant, Brno comes as a relief.

City Layout. The centre of Brno is fairly compact. The main shopping street leads north as Masarykovo from the train station to nám. Svobody — Brno's triangular central square — continuing as Ceská to Jostova, the northern boundary of the old town. Most of the streets running off this main artery are pedestrianised (although the odd tram rattles through nám. Svobody) and people go for leisurely promenades in the early evening. Of the other squares in the centre, Zelný trh, west off Masarykovo, is the most important. The twin spires of the church of Saints Peter and Paul rise above it and are a more striking landmark than the rather distant Spilberk castle, perched on a ridge west of the centre, but only just poking up above the trees.

Maps: you can buy a good town plan ($0.70 from tourist offices and bookshops), which has a street index and lists monuments and interesting buildings.

Arrival and Departure. *Train:* there are regular trains from Prague (3-4 hours) and Bratislava (2-3 hours). All Berlin-Budapest trains stop at Brno, with services to other European cities including Warsaw. There is the odd direct train to Vienna, otherwise change at Breclav.

The train station (05-275 62/64) is well equipped, with exchange desks and so on. You can buy tickets either from the main counters or from Taxatour, the 24-hour information office near the left-luggage lockers.

Bus: frequent buses run from Prague, taking about 3 hours ($2.50), some en route to Budapest. There are good services also from Bratislava, with less frequent connections with smaller Slovakian towns such as Banská Bystrica and Poprad. You can pick up buses to all sorts of other places, including Linz and Salzburg in Austria (daily) and a number of cities in Germany, Italy and France (weekly); most of these are operated by private companies. Buses also penetrate most corners of Moravia, particularly in the south, making Brno a good base from which to explore the region.

The bus station (05-33 72 81, 33 03 93) is on Opustená, five minutes' walk south of the train station.

Car: Taxatour runs private cars to various European cities, including Vienna ($5.50), Munich ($18) and Frankfurt ($23). A blackboard outside its office in the train station lists how many seats are available in each car.

If you want to hire your own vehicle, Europcar has an office at Pruchodní Str. 2 (05-255 46) off Radnická, open 8am-5pm Monday to Friday.

Accommodation. Hotel accommodation in Brno is stretched (and more expensive) during trade fairs, although business visitors stay mostly in the top-notch places. The nearest campsite is 7 miles/12km south of town, within walking distance of Popovice train station.

> *Avion,* Ceská 20 (tel 42 21 50 16; fax 42 21 40 55). Central and friendly, with doubles for $20-40.
>
> *Astoria,* Novobranská 3 (42 21 69 83). Lovely old place with doubles for $25-45 and a reasonable restaurant.
>
> *Europa,* Janská 1 (266 21). A rundown place with doubles for $25-35 without breakfast. Good location but poor value.
>
> *Pegas,* Jakubská 4 (tel 101 04; fax 112 32). Clean, comfortable and excellent value at $50 for two. Lively bar downstairs, where they brew their own beer.
>
> *U Jakuba,* Jakubské nám. 6 (229 91). Not as good as the Pegas, with a rather drab atmosphere redolent of pre-independence days. Doubles from $50.
>
> *Slavia,* Solnicní 15 (tel 42 21 50 80; fax 42 21 17 69). Better outside than in, but with four-star doubles for under $100 it's better value than other smart places.
>
> *Private Rooms:* the quickest way to arrange a private room is to go to the Taxatour office in the train station. They offer rooms in the centre for around $10, less if you're willing to travel further out. The Cedok office nearby at Divadelní 3 can also arrange accommodation, as can CKM at Ceská 11.

Eating and Drinking. Brno has a fine selection of beer and wine cellars and a growing number of cafés, several of which spill out onto the street in summer. Try Pizzeria Adria, on the corner of Masarykovo and Josefská, which serves reasonable food, but is more pleasant just for a drink. Of the old-style cafeterias, Sputnik — a large place on the corner of Ceska and nám. Svobody — is undoubtedly the best: the shop at the front serves cakes and open face sandwiches, with a buffet for hot meals at the back. When it comes to eating out, don't neglect the area north of the old town where, in the quiet streets off Veverí, you'll find some of the liveliest places in the city. The pick of the city's bars and restaurants are as follows:

> *Vinárna Pod Radnicním Kolem,* Mecova 5. In the vaulted cellar of Brno's oldest medieval building. Excellent food (particularly the liver)

and Moravian wine served in mugs or elegant Bohemian glasses. Civilised but usually quite lively by the end of the evening. Good music, often traditional and sometimes live: impromptu by customers, if not by actual groups.

Restaurace Spalícek, west side of Zelný trh. Few frills, buzzing and friendly. Closes at 10pm.

Cerný Medved Vinárna, Jakubské nám. 1. Dates back to the 15th century, though you wouldn't think so. Smartish and quiet, but a good place to splash out on goose liver paté and caviar. Main dishes cost $5-8.

U Lucerny, corner of Slovakova and Veverí. Looks shabby and unpromising from the outside but good food and exclusively frequented by locals.

Restaurace U Capa, corner of Gorkeho and Obilní trh (a pleasant square), west of Veverí. Similar to U Lucerny in style but livelier.

U tri knízat, Minoritská 2. Attractive Gothic vaulted ceiling, family restaurant open until 6pm, the bar until 9pm. Serves local Starobrno beer.

Smíchovská pivnice, Starobrnenská 7, up the road from Zelný trh. A popular student watering hole, with Staropramen beer (from Prague).

Memphis Bar, Dominikanské nám. Main gathering place for local artists, musicians and intellectuals, open into the early hours. Good filter coffee, beer and various liqueurs.

Exploring. Námestí Svobody is rather lacking in cohesion and atmosphere. Most people simply pass through it, but there is a pleasant outdoor café behind the handsome 17th-century plague column. The ugly green Komercní bank on the west side rather dominates the square, but opposite is the extraordinary Dum u ctyr mamlasu (House of the Four Ninnies), built in 1901 by a wealthy Jewish industrialist. The 'four ninnies' in question are the huge, muscular stone figures who hold up the building, their faces twisted into agonised expressions. Opposite is Schwanz's Palace, Brno's finest Renaissance building but much blackened and in dire need of repair. On the north side of nám. Svobody, the superb Ethnographical Museum (open 9am-5pm) contains a visual feast of 19th-century traditional costumes and gorgeous painted furniture, often in mint condition. Scattered among the artefacts are old photographs of Moravian peasants and traditional rural architecture.

West of the square is the sloping Dominikánské nám., where you should at least have a peek at the New Town Hall (Nová radnice). The 16th-century building, now housing offices, is nothing special from the outside, but there are some quite handsome frescoes and staircases inside. South along Radnická, the Old Town Hall (Stará Radnice) is rather a hotchpotch of passages and courtyards built at different times, although it has a fine Gothic doorway. You can climb the 172 steps to the top of the tower for a view of the city's skyline: dirty rooftops, aerials and cranes, and also over Zelný trh, immediately south.

Zelný trh means Cabbage Market, which is what it was originally. The trade in fresh produce was decidedly meagre under communism, but the market has revived considerably in the past few years. The bustle around the stalls is the most pleasing thing about the square, which is lined with a haphazard collection of buildings and has for its centrepiece a hideous jumble of concrete and stones claiming to be a fountain. The Baroque Dietrichstein Palace on the southwest side contains the Moravian Museum (open daily 9am-6pm), where fossils, stones and minerals illustrate the long history of the area. The third floor — with reconstructions, old bones, pots and some fine jewellery — is the most interesting.

A short hike up the hill west from Zelný trh will take you to the Cathedral of Saints Peter and Paul (Dóm na Petrove) — a stylistic mess (mostly Baroque and neo-Gothic) with not a great deal to admire, but in a pleasant, tranquil part of town. Note the wall opposite the east end of the church covered in graffiti in memory of John Lennon. Heading down Biskupská you pass Denisovy Sady, a small park with a few benches and a nice enough place to sit. Starobrnenská will take you back to Zelný trh. but you can make a short diversion, by joining Husova and walking the short distance north to the Moravská Galerie (open 10am-5pm Tuesday to Sunday), near the plush International Hotel. The ornate building is of interest in itself, but the decorative arts on the second floor are absolutely superb. The collection dates from the Middle Ages to the present day and includes artefacts from all over Central Europe (though mostly from the Czech lands and Germany). No single object should be missed, but possible high points are the Bohemian glass and the Baroque, Rococo and even Cubist furniture. The Art Nouveau collection is also impressive and includes stunning glassware.

Back at Zelný trh., head south to the Capuchin Monastery (Kapucínsky Kláster), open 9am-noon and 2-4.30pm Tuesday to Saturday, 2-4.30pm on Sunday. The crypt contains the most bizarre sight in Brno: the mummified remains of Capuchin monks and various nobles, dating mostly from the 17th and 18th centuries; the bodies have been preserved by the constant stream of air which runs through the rooms. Best (or worst) are the monks laid out in rows on the dirt floor, some with horrified expressions.

There's not much of interest east of Masarykovo, although several buildings have been well restored on Minoritská, including some striking Art Nouveau houses. Near the junction with Janská two churches sit side by side. On the right, St John's has the city's finest Baroque interior, with fantastic (though poorly restored) trompe l'oeil frescoes; the gold and wooden confessionals are great too. Double doors (sadly, not always open) in the north aisle link St John's to the next door church, where the high point is the Loreto chapel. Orlí, another pleasant street, runs east to Malinovského nám. and the City Art Gallery (Dum umení). It is a shabby and rather spiritless venue, but stages some good exhibitions.

Villa Tugendhat: about a 20-minute walk north of the centre, at Cernopolní 45, Villa Tugendhat was the most famous building ever designed by Ludwig Mies van der Rohe (1886-1969), the last director of the Bauhaus. The minimalist white box, constructed 1929-30, is set into a slope and most of what you can see (not very much) is actually the third floor. The house belongs to the city and while not open regularly to the public, you may be able to arrange a tour there at the tourist office. It's worth walking up to it in any case: this is a quiet, leafy part of town and you get an unusual perspective over Brno's spires and up to Spilberk Castle.

Spilberk Castle: strolling around the centre of Brno is so pleasant that it's hard to feel tempted by Spilberk Castle, perched on its uninviting hill west of the old town. Founded in the 13th century, the castle resisted numerous assaults before its capture by Napoleon after the Battle of the Three Emperors nearby. It was later converted into a prison which is said to have been one of the worst in Europe (and was used much later by the Nazis). The castle is undergoing restoration, but you can go on a rather gruesome guided tour of the dungeons; the views are available at any time. To get to the castle, walk up one of the roads heading west off Husova.

Entertainment. You can't do much better than spend an evening in one of Brno's wine or beer cellars, but there are a couple of theatres which stage high-quality performances. The Mahen Theatre in Malinovského nám. is the finest 19th-century building in Brno (and was also the first theatre in Europe to enjoy the benefit of electric light). Recently restored, the interior is sumptuous. Go in the evening to have a proper look: the lobby and staircase are magnificent enough, even without the auditorium. Most of Janácek's operas opened here, but now it is largely plays that are staged at the theatre. The Janácek Opera House (Janáckovo divadlo), further up Rooseveltova 1 and by contrast an ugly modern building, devotes itself for the most part to opera and ballet. Operetta is popular in the city too.

Help and Information. *Tourist Information:* the city tourist office at Radnická 4 (open 8am-6pm Monday to Friday, 9am-5pm on Saturday) is the best source of information about Brno, and stocks a range of publications and maps. *Brno City Guide* covers the history and sights in great detail and also has a short listings section at the back. Cedok's most useful office is the one at Divadelni 3 (05-233 03), although there is another on nam. Svobody. Taxatour in the railway station (05-258 82/90) is also very useful: it sells maps, has a CSD information desk and accommodation service, and is open 24 hours. CKM at Ceská 11 (05-236 41), open 9am-5pm Monday to Friday, can exchange money and sell tickets as well as arrange accommodation.

Post office: the main office at Postovská 5, east of nám. Svobody, opens Monday to Saturday, but the one attached to the railway station is open 24 hours.

Money: there are several exchange bureaux, but the Komercní bank usually offers the best rates. Its main office, on the north side of nám. Svobody (10am-5.30pm), will also change money back to hard currency if necessary. It runs a counter in the train station too, open 7am-6pm Tuesday to Friday, 7am-noon other days.

MORAVSKY KRUMLOV

About 25 miles/40km southwest of Brno and served by regular buses, the town of Moravský Krumlov can easily be visited in a day. There is a 16th-century castle but most of it is off-limits, except for the gallery devoted to the work of Alfons Mucha (1860-1939) — Art Nouveau painter and one of the Czech Republic's most famous artists. In the West he was most famous for his posters, but pride of place is given to the so-called Slavonic Epic, a cycle of paintings commissioned by a wealthy American and completed in 1928. The gallery is open in summer only, 9am-noon and 1-4pm Tuesday to Sunday.

MORAVSKY KRAS

The Moravský kras (Moravian Karst) is an area north of Brno remarkable for its limestone formations, caves and rivers. Four caves are open to the public, the best (and busiest) being the Punkva Caves (Punkevní Jeskyne): a tour takes you past a series of spectacular stalactites and stalagmites to the magnificent Macocha abyss (you can see the sky through the hole 460ft overhead), and then in a boat along the underground Punkva river. Arrive as early as possible in summer to avoid the longest queues. All the caves close in the early afternoon, but there are some lovely trails through the woods and gorges. You can go on particularly good walks from Adamov, on the railway line between Brno and Blansko. To make the most of the area, look out for the Moravský kras map in Brno.

Blansko, 10 miles/16km north of Brno, is the jumping-off point for the Moravian Karst, the main area to explore being east of the town along the Punkva river. There are hotels, but it is easy enough to do a day trip from Brno. Another starting point is Jedovnice, a small resort accessible by bus from Brno and Blansko, and just a couple of miles southeast of the Punkva caves.

NORTHERN MORAVIA

Northern Moravia is the least inspiring part of the region. The area around the town of Ostrava is known as the 'steel heart of the Republic'. The chief attraction is the Jeseník and Beskydy mountains along the northern and eastern borders, which offer plenty of scope for walking.

Olomouc. After Prague, Olomouc has the best-preserved centre in the Czech lands. Strangely, however, it is not a particularly beautiful place. Founded in the 11th century, Olomouc was the capital of Moravia until the 17th century, when it was virtually destroyed during the Thirty Years War. Despite being a sprawling industrial town (the local chocolate factory spews out a rather sickly and nauseating smell), Olomouc has a lively student population. While not worth crossing Europe (or even the Republic) for, it's a pleasant enough place to break your journey. The most interesting sight in the main square (Horní náměstí) is the town hall, which has an astronomical clock and a tower you can climb. Most of Olomouc's churches, including St Wenceslas Cathedral, are gloomy affairs.

Buses speed up the motorway on a regular basis from Brno, 50 miles/ 80km southwest, although there is also a rail service. The simple Hotel Morava at Riegrova 16 (068-296 71), close to the main square, offers the best value for money, around $20 for a double. Olomouc's top hotel is the Národní Dum at 8 kvetna 21 (068-248 06). The Cedok office on the main square can arrange private rooms.

Roznov pod Radhostem. In ancient times, the Wallachians (from what is now Romania) lived in the Beskydy mountains, a low range in northeastern Moravia along the border with Slovakia. Their descendants still maintain the traditional wooden cottages, churches, *salas* (shepherds' huts) and granaries. Wallachian folk costumes are among the most colourful in the Czech Republic.

The town of Roznov, at the foot of the mountains 40 miles/64km east of Olomouc, has the oldest and largest open-air folk museum (*skansen*) in the country. The wooden buildings, moved here from villages in the area, are all furnished with original artefacts. In summer you can watch local artisans making traditional crafts. There are a few hotels in Roznov, including the moderately cheap Tesla Hotel, plus a campsite with chalets. Don't expect much elbow room in summer.

The surrounding hills are dotted with wooden houses and churches; you can see some fine examples at Velké Karlovice, which is within easy reach of Roznov and also has a campsite.

Calendar of Events

January 1	**New Year's Day**
March/April	**Easter (velikonoce)**
May 1	**Labour Day**
May 8	**National Day (Anniversary of Liberation)**
May-June	Prague Spring Music Festival
mid-June	International Festival of Mime, Mariánské Lázne
end June-early July	International Folk Festival in Stráznice (Moravia), the most important festival of its kind in the country
July 5	**Day of the Apostles St Cyril and St Methodius (commemorating the introduction of Christianity)**
July 6	**Jan Hus Day (Anniversary of his death)**
July	International Film Festival, Karlovy Vary
mid-August	Chod Folk Festival, Domazlice, well worth a diversion
October 28	**Anniversary of Independence**
late September-early October	International Music Festival, Brno
December 24-26	**Christmas (*Vánoce*),** celebrations are much more restrained than at Easter. Christmas Eve (*Stedrý vecer*) is traditionally a day of fasting.

Public holidays are shown in **bold**

Slovak Republic

National Theatre, Bratislava

Population: 5.3 million   **Capital: Bratislava (population 445,000)**

On New Year's Day 1993, the Slovak Republic's divorce from the Czechs became absolute. As an independent country, it has attracted more outside attention than ever before, but the fledgling state is still neglected by travellers. This is a country full of colour, with a rich folk culture and some of the best scenery in Europe.

From a visitor's point of view, Slovakia's most obvious asset is the Carpathian mountains. They cover much of the republic (apart from the Danube plain, which stretches from Bratislava east into the Ukraine) and include the spectacular Tatras in the north. Slovakia has far fewer historic buildings than the Czech Republic, but there are still many architectural gems — particularly in the eastern region, where unspoilt medieval towns and villages have survived in semi-isolation and where rural communities have maintained their traditions to a greater extent than anywhere else in the country; in the more out-of-the-way villages you still see people wearing folk costumes.

Most people seem to treat Slovakia as somewhere simply to pass through: Bratislava is a natural stopping-place between the Czech Republic and Budapest, which is just down the road. But those who restrict their travels in this way are doing the Slovak Republic — and themselves — a serious injustice. This small nation (it is not much bigger than Denmark) comes as a breath of fresh air after the increasingly busy Czech Republic, even though the Slovak people are quite reserved (some would say dour). Bratislava, which is trying to adjust to being a capital city, is unassuming and thoroughly provincial compared with Prague. The difference symbolises the much broader picture: while the Czech and Slovak republics still have much in common, Slovakia has been left behind, both politically and economically. But at least it isn't burdened with some of the worst tourist overcrowding in Europe.

CLIMATE

Slovakia is cooler and wetter than the Czech Republic, with extremes of temperature in the mountains where harsh winters can last for five months. Temperatures are pleasant between May and September, but you'd do well to avoid visiting in July and August, when the heat can be unbearable in Bratislava and the Danube plain. Conditions are more pleasant in the mountains.

HISTORY

The former Czechoslovakia only existed as one country for a span of 74 years, from 1918 to 1992. Prior to that, the history of Slovakia was almost completely separate from that of Bohemia and Moravia.

As in the present Czech Republic, Celtic settlers were booted out by Germanic tribes who, in turn, faced an invasion of Slavs in the fifth century. They formed their own principality which by the end of the eighth century became the Great Moravian Empire, under which the Slovak and Czech people were united. Unlike Bohemia and Moravia, however, Slovakia never became part of the Holy Roman Empire. The dominant influence came from Hungary: the Magyars first occupied southern Slovakia in the tenth century and made Bratislava their capital in 1536. The Slovaks were absorbed into the Habsburgs' Austro-Hungarian empire, ruled from Vienna, but when the empire split in 1867 (with Austria and Hungary as independent states but united under one Habsburg ruler), Slovakia was ruled by a much more oppressive regime in Budapest.

Independence followed the defeat of the Habsburgs in World War One. Twenty years later the Czechoslovak Republic was invaded by Adolph Hitler. Soon after the war started, Jozef Tiso established an independent Slovakian state (the first ever), but the people rose up against what was more or less a puppet Nazi regime. The 1944 Slovak National Uprising or SNP (an acronym after which many a main square is named) was disorganised and lasted only two months. About 30,000 Slovaks were killed by the Nazis in the reprisals. However, it was held up by the communists afterwards as a heroic act against fascism.

After the war, Slovakia developed rapidly under communism, the most visible sign of which is the number of huge steel and armaments factories scattered about the fertile Danube plain, which is far better suited to agriculture.

Independence. There were calls for Slovak independence from the time of the 1989 revolution. Public Against Violence, a sister party to the Czech Civic Forum, proposed self-determination, but wished to stay within the federation. The Slovak people's desire for autonomy, however, led them in June 1992 to vote for Vladimir Meciar, leader of the Movement for a Democratic Slovakia (HZDS). This proved to be the greatest impetus behind the eventual split between the two republics, as discussions between the Czech and Slovak leaders reached a total impasse.

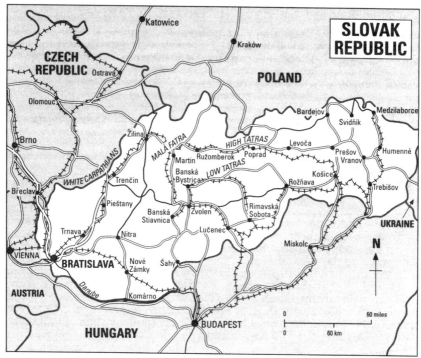

The transition to independence since January 1993 has been much harder for Slovakia than for its neighbour. Local frustration has been shown only too clearly by extremists who have been caught in possession of explosives to be used in an anti-Czech bombing campaign. Many Slovaks are suspicious of Prime Minister Meciar, a communist-turned-nationalist and an authoritarian, who has placed many of his own people in positions of power and has undermined opponents. But while the appointment of former communists causes political unease, Slovakia's economic vulnerability is a much more urgent problem. The country's industry is outdated, uncompetitive and ill-suited to the new order and has attracted comparatively few Western investors, who have largely favoured the Czech Republic. Unemployment has risen inexorably, there is a huge budget deficit and a radical economic overhaul is required if the country's prospects are to improve.

THE PEOPLE

Slovaks make up over 85% of the population, with small communities of Romanians, Poles, Ukrainians and around 65,000 gypsies. The largest minority group, however, is Hungarian, accounting for over 10% of the population and living mostly along the southern borders of Slovakia. The Hungarians have felt the brunt of the nationalist feelings which have erupted since the revolution, and fear discrimination with some justification: a new constitution has been drafted reducing their already limited rights.

Unlike the more urban and liberal Czechs, the Slovaks are a rural and conservative race. They are also fervently Catholic — not to the degree that you'll find in Poland, but you can still expect to find packed churches.

Language. To those unfamiliar with it, Slovak (*slovenský*) is indistinguishable from Czech. Everyone will understand if you use Czech words and pronunciation (see page 133). Vocabulary differs frequently but usually only slightly.

yes — *áno, hej*
no — *nie*
please — *prosim*
thank you — *d'akujem*
goodbye — *do videnia*

train station — *železničná stanica*
bus station — *autobusova stanica*
ticket — *lístok*
do you speak English? — *hovoríte anglicky?*

AIR

As yet there are no direct flights to Bratislava from the UK. The easiest way to reach the Slovak capital from Britain is by flying to Vienna and taking the direct shuttle bus from the airport 30 miles/48km north to Slovakia: the journey takes 80 minutes and costs about $15. Cheap flights are readily available on British Airways, Austrian Airlines and Lauda Air; expect to pay around £150.

Direct international flights link Bratislava with many Eastern European cities, including Berlin, Warsaw, Sofia, Moscow, St Petersburg and Kiev, operated either by the Czech airline CSA, or Aeroflot. Slovakia's own Tatra Air links Bratislava with Prague, Munich, Zurich and Stuttgart. There are several non-stop flights from Prague every day (journey time 50 minutes), with services also direct to Košice and Poprad.

TRAIN

Bratislava is an important railway junction, with frequent trains from Prague, Budapest and Vienna as well as more distant European capitals, including Paris and Warsaw. There are good services along the Berlin-Prague-Bratislava-Budapest line. Trains from the Czech capital are mostly direct, though you may need to change at Brno. Express trains direct between Prague and Budapest currently stop in Bratislava three times a day. The journey from Vienna takes two hours by express (the more frequent local trains being much slower). Services from Bucharest and Sofia also run daily.

International train services to Košice in eastern Slovakia include the Cracovia train from Krakow to Budapest.

BUS

Bus can be the best way to travel overland into Slovakia, although the private companies which have flooded Prague with new services have mostly ignored Bratislava. Many international buses tend to be en route either to or from Prague and Budapest, which at least means that services to both these cities are frequent; the journey to the Czech capital takes only slightly longer than the express trains. There are also direct links to other Slovakian towns, including Košice and Poprad.

Driving. The main international E-routes to Slovakia are:

E16: Vienna — Bratislava — Gdynia

E50: Narnberg — Plzen — Prague — Brno — Bratislava — Košice — Uzhgorod
E65: Harrachov — Mlada Boleslav — Prague — Brno — Bratislava — Gysr
E75: Bratislava — Katowice
E85: Hranice (E7) — Košice — Moscow

See page 136 of the chapter on the Czech Republic for information on driving to Slovakia. The route by motorway from Prague to Bratislava is blissfully easy, with reasonable traffic and surfaces.

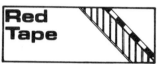

Most European nationals do not require a visa to visit the Slovak Republic. Australasians and Canadians do, while US nationals may enter visa free for visits of up to 30 days. The tourist visa, which costs £15-30 depending on your nationality, is valid for six months from the date of issue and permits an initial stay of 30 days.

The Slovakian Embassy in the UK is at 25 Kensington Palace Gardens, London W8 4QY (tel 071-243 0803, fax 071-727 5824). In the USA and Canada, the Czech and Slovak embassies still operate from the same premises: see page 136 for addresses.

Since the Czech Republic introduced passport controls for those crossing from Slovakia, it must only be a matter of time before the Slovaks follow suit — but at the time of going to press, the two countries had not agreed on a joint border administration.

Slovenská koruna (Sk) = 100 haléru (h)
1994: £1 = Sk50 $1 = Sk33

Earlier this century, the Slovak crown was a thoroughly dependable currency, like the Swiss franc. Nowadays, it is one of the weakest in Europe, with inflation consistently higher than in the Czech Republic.

The Slovak crown currently in circulation is still the old Czechoslovak version, with notes overprinted with the nation's insignia. New coins are already being introduced and proper Slovakian notes are sure to follow — but for the moment you still come across black marketeers in Bratislava trying desperately to offload onto innocent Westerners banknotes lacking the overprint; do not be tempted, since they have no value.

Changing Money. Private exchange bureaux haven't really taken off in the Slovak Republic yet, and when it comes to changing money, you'll have to rely on the banks, the smarter hotels and branches of the tourist organisations Slovakoturist or Cedok. Look for the sign *zmenáreñ*. Banks offer the best rate.

It is increasingly easy to obtain a cash advance on a credit card, although this is still best done in Bratislava. Tatratour acts as an agent for American Express, and offers most Amex services.

Work. The chances of finding a good teaching job in Slovakia are rather higher than in the Czech Republic, simply because the supply of prospective employees is much lower. The rules remain basically the same as they were before Czechoslovakia split up. To get a work permit, you need a contract from the school and proof of an address. This can be arranged before or after your arrival in the country.

Recruitment of qualified teachers for secondary schools (mostly in small towns) takes place through the Academic Information Agency (AIA) in the Slovak capital, usually on a one-year contract with low-cost or free accommodation and a salary of about $140 net per month. The minimum requirement is a university degree, preferably in English. Additional qualifications in TEFL and teaching experience give an applicant priority. Applications should be submitted before the end of April.

The AIA also appoints some teachers to well-established private language schools. Its address is Slovak AIA, Hviezdoslavovo nám. 14, 813 29 Bratislava (tel 7-333010, fax 335827).

Schools worth approaching directly include the following:

Akadémia Vzdelávania, Gorkého 10, 81517 Bratislava, Slovakia (tel 499-580).
Jazyková skola, Palisády 38, 811 06 Bratislava (tel 332-437).
ASPEKT Jazyková skola, Damborského 7, 949 01 Nitra, Slovakia (tel 26829).

Telephone. Slovakia's telecommunications network is distressingly bad and making international phone calls can be a nightmare. If you have to, try to do so from Bratislava, where the public telephone office is more used to dealing with international calls. When it comes to domestic calls, you could try your luck with a public telephone. Phonecards haven't reached Slovakia, but there are new orange and black payphones, which are ten times more reliable than the old ones. These take 1, 2, 5 and 10 crown coins (minimum Sk2).

The main area codes within Slovakia are as follows:

Banská Bystrica 088	Košice 095	Poprad 092
Bratislava 07	Levoča 0966	Prešov 091

Useful Numbers: Fire 150; Ambulance 155; Police 158.

Fax. Public fax facilities are scarce, so you'll probably have to go to a top hotel in Bratislava or other major towns.

Mail. Faced with the frustration of calling home, you could try writing instead. Outbound letters and cards shouldn't take more than a week to destinations within Europe. Great Britain in Slovak is written 'Velky Británia'.

MEDIA

The demise of communist rule has not brought an end to dull state-run television, but if you like pop, new FM stations have improved the radio scene. The lucky inhabitants of Bratislava and southern Slovakia can also tune into Austrian radio and television.

Pravda, the old Communist Party paper and still the most widely read daily, is better than it once was, but journalists are still under pressure from the government to apply self-censorship. There are few foreign newspapers available: thetop hotels in Bratislava sell the *Herald Tribune* but not much else.

Since the Czechoslovakian transport system was largely developed to serve Bohemia, and more specifically Prague, the network of public transport in Slovakia is not as extensive as in most Eastern European countries.

AIR

Both CSA and the domestic airline Slov Air link Bratislava with Košice and Poprad and a few other towns, but internal flights are likely to be of little use in a country as small as Slovakia.

TRAIN

Travelling by train (*vlak*) is a viable option between the main towns, but the network is limited and services are fearfully crowded in summer and at the height of the skiing season. One advantage of using the trains is that timetables are easy to understand: most stations have the entire national timetable on display, with services specific to that station on a separate board. If you pick up an international express from a provincial town, you will probably be unable to make a reservation.

BUS

Unlike the trains, buses (run by the old Czechoslovak company CSAD) reach most corners of the country and are generally the best way to get around, although services are infrequent between smaller towns. Rural buses are often schoolbuses, running early in the morning and then in mid-afternoon only. Timetables tend to change completely at weekends, with services much reduced on Sundays, even between main towns. Inter-city journeys take longer than they should because of rest stops en route.

DRIVING

Roads in Slovakia are generally lightly travelled and easy to negotiate — the hair-raising antics of Slovakian drivers less so. New petrol stations are appearing all the time, but it's still wise to fill up whenever you get the chance. The price of fuel is cheaper than almost anywhere else in Europe, and unleaded petrol is frequently available on the main routes.

Car rental is best arranged at the airport in Bratislava, although Hertz, for example, also has a desk at Košice airport. Cedok offices anywhere should be able to arrange something, but in provincial towns this may involve a car being sent from the capital. Prices are similar to those charged in the Czech Republic.

Hotels tend to be drab Soviet-style blocks, whether they are at the top or bottom of the range. If there is a spirit of hospitality in the local people, it hasn't as yet infiltrated hotel management. You won't find much for under $20-25 for two, particularly in Bratislava; and in the Tatras, hotel prices often double in the high season (December to March and June to September).

Hostels. Slovakia's hostels are still run by the old Czechoslovak youth organisation, CKM. The permanent ones are more like cheap hotels and charge $10-15 per person. You can get a list of temporary (and cheaper) summer hostels from the CKM office at Hveizdoslavov nám. 16 in Bratislava.

Private Rooms. Word is gradually spreading through the republic that renting out a room to visitors is a good way to supplement poor wages. You can arrange private accommodation at some Cedok and Slovakoturist offices, but local people will also approach you directly; look out for signs in windows too.

Eating and Drinking

Slovakian food has been strongly influenced by the nature but unfortunately not the quality of Hungarian cuisine. It's not that Slovakian food is inedible, but simply monotonous and uninspiring. Restaurant menus don't vary much at all, with pork the most popular meat. There is little scope for vegetarians unless you choose to live off *halŭsky*, stodgy potato dumplings made with sheep's milk cheese — though the least dull version (*bryndzové halŭsky*) is cooked with bacon. In eastern Slovakia, a stew of mushrooms and sour cream is popular, and reasonably tasty and filling when served with rye bread. Soups (*polievka*) are a good idea if you can't face the endless choice of meat or stodge: some are quite filling (particularly when accompanied with lots of the excellent local bread), and they are always good value: even in a smart restaurant soups rarely cost over $0.50. Most meals in Slovakia are at least cheap.

Bratislava has none of the stalls that fill the centre of Prague. Street food in Slovakia is usually limited to ice cream, though you sometimes find piping-hot sausages or corn-on-the-cob. Fresh fruit remains fairly scarce.

Drinking. Slovakia has produced its own wine for centuries, the majority of the vineyards being in the Danube Plain and on the slopes of the Carpathians near Bratislava. While inferior to most Moravian wines, there are some perfectly good dry white wines and sparkling wines. In winter, wine is often served mulled (*varené víno*).

Slovaks have always been wine drinkers first and foremost, but beer became popular during unification with the Czechs, and most bars now offer both. As in the Czech Republic, drinking beer is an exceedingly cheap habit. Bratislava even makes its own local brew — not a patch on Pilsner Urquell, but perfectly palatable. The most common spirit is *borovička*, a gin-like concoction from the Spiš region. Slovaks also swear by the local plum brandy (*slivoviča*); when home-distilled it can be 60% proof and highly dangerous, though you are likely to come across it only if you are invited into someone's home.

Beer cellars (*pivnica*) and wine bars (*vináreň*) are the best (and often the only) places to eat or drink. In rural areas, these are also the best place to hear traditional music, whether formally or during a communal singalong.

Hiking. The Slovaks are mad about hiking, and at weekends and during the holidays trains overflow with people laden with knapsacks and mountain gear. The Slovakian Tatras provide some of Eastern Europe's best walking country. Trails are mostly well maintained and marked, and particularly well-trodden in the High Tatras (Vysoké Tatry). To avoid crowds in high season, head for the Low Tatras (Nízke Tatry) or the Malá Fatra mountains further west, though the scenery is not as spectacular. In the summer you can go white-water rafting on the Dunajec river.

Skiing. The Slovakian mountains provide better skiing than in the Czech Republic and facilities are improving slowly. You can ski in the Malá Fatra, but the Tatras are more rewarding, the main resorts lying within easy reach of Poprad.

The republic's national tourist board, Slovakoturist, exists alongside Cedok, but is gradually taking over all the country's tourist offices. For information prior to your departure, contact the nearest Slovakian embassy or consulate or any branch of Cedok: for addresses, see page 148.

BRATISLAVA

Lying on the edge of the Carpathians, the capital of the Slovak Republic is rather pushed to the corner of its own country. But it is plumb in the middle of Europe: you can walk to Austria in an hour and to Hungary in ninety minutes. With a comparatively small population of 445,000, Bratislava feels solidly provincial and lacks the appearance of a place that people once thought it worth bartering and battling over.

The capital looks overwhelmingly functional, composed mainly of gaunt chimneys and graceless tower blocks. The Danube, which washes the scum of Central Europe through Bratislava, looks as dull as the ditchwater it contains. But the Magyar occupation, which marked the city's heyday, left a smattering of Baroque palaces and churches which now dominate Bratislava's old town. Not much of this is left, and it is far inferior to the architectural wonders of nearby capitals. But visitors to Bratislava can at least enjoy a sense of discovery: for decades overshadowed by Prague, the Slovak capital is finally coming into its own. The influx of new foreign influences has brought branches of Benetton and the usual upgrading of hotels and restaurants, but Bratislava remains a relaxed place where a large student population brings life to the streets.

CITY LAYOUT

Aside from Bratislava's rather ugly castle, the city's most obvious landmark is the Slovak National Uprising Bridge (Most SNP), perched like a wanton alien astride the Danube. It is a piece of decidedly uncivil engineering. Worse still, the approach roads gouge a concrete scar through the old city and link the centre to the hideous suburb of Petržalka, a sea of grey apartment blocks on the south bank. The Jewish quarter was obliterated in the process.

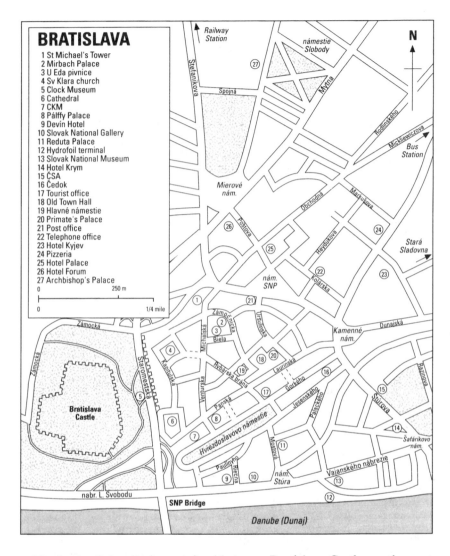

BRATISLAVA

1 St Michael's Tower
2 Mirbach Palace
3 U Eda pivnice
4 Sv Klara church
5 Clock Museum
6 Cathedral
7 CKM
8 Pálffy Palace
9 Devín Hotel
10 Slovak National Gallery
11 Reduta Palace
12 Hydrofoil terminal
13 Slovak National Museum
14 Hotel Krym
15 ČSA
16 Čedok
17 Tourist office
18 Old Town Hall
19 Hlavné námestie
20 Primate's Palace
21 Post office
22 Telephone office
23 Hotel Kyjev
24 Pizzeria
25 Hotel Palace
26 Hotel Forum
27 Archbishop's Palace

0   250 m

0   1/4 mile

The heart of the city is contained between Bratislava Castle, on the west side, nám. SNP to the north and the Danube (Dunaj) to the south. Nám. SNP is the closest thing Bratislava has to a main square, but it is not much of a focus for the city. There are a couple of cafés, a few trees and a sculpture of a Hero, his Mother and Sweetheart (a touch more subtle than most Communist bloc monuments), but precious little else. Hviezdoslavovo nám., to the south, is grander but more of a boulevard than a square. It is usually quiet and not a place you're likely to spend much time.

Maps: you can pick up maps and guidebooks from the BIPS city tourist office (see *Help and Information*). The best bookshop for maps and guides is at the corner of Michalská and Biela. Look out for *Bratislava: Guide* (1992, price $1.20), which gives a good background to the sights.

ARRIVAL AND DEPARTURE

Air. Ivanka airport is 6 miles/10km east of the city, with a few facilities including a bureau de change and car rental desk. Bus 24 serves the main railway station, and airport buses run to and from the CSA office at Sturová 13 (33 07 88) to coincide with flights: there is a schedule by the bus stop outside. While this office deals with domestic flights, for international information go to Gorkého 5 (33 07 90).

Train. Most trains arrive at Hlavná stanica (482 75), almost a mile north of the centre. Tram 1 from the station's lower level runs every 20-30 minutes into town (the most central stop is at the corner of Obchodná and Poštova, near Hotel Forum) and bus 23 goes to Safárikovo nám., southeast of the centre near the Danube. There is no exchange desk at the station, so if you've just arrived from abroad you may have to travel without paying.

Some rail services (mostly from western Slovakia) leave from Bratislava-Nové Město station (60 74 78) on Tomášikova, over a mile northeast of the centre and served by tram 6.

Bus. The bus station (Autobusová stanica) is at Mlynské Nyvy (21 27 34, 632 13), some way northeast of the centre. Trolleybus 217 will take you in four stops to the Hotel Forum in Mierové nám. Buses serving the area immediately around Bratislava leave from the station on Bajkalská (21 40 80).

Boat. Hydrofoils from Vienna (journey time one hour) arrive at Fajnorovo nábrežie by the National Museum. There is no direct link with Budapest, but Raketa runs a regular ferry to Esztergom, where you can change. If leaving for Austria, try to book a seat as far in advance as possible. Blue Danube Travel (tel 595 01, fax 33 39 05) operates a variety of excursions, including to Budapest, though the cheapest is a one-hour trip for about $2.

Car. International car hire agencies operate at the airport and Hotel Forum, but a good local firm is Recar at Stefánikova 1 (33 34 20, 33 39 13), which hires out Skoda Favorits for less than $40 a day.

CITY TRANSPORT

Trams (*elekricky*), buses (*autobusy*) and trolleybuses (*trolejbusy*) are fast and moderately efficient. You must buy tickets in advance ($0.20 each), either from kiosks or yellow machines found near some bus stops. A 24-hour tourist pass is available from the transport office in the subway beneath Mierové nám.

Taxis are most easily picked up near the smart hotels. All are metered and charge a fixed rate.

Between March and November there is a ferry across the Danube from nám. Stúra: a brief ride but reasonable fun.

ACCOMMODATION

You shouldn't have a problem finding a room on the spot, but ask at the BIPS or Slovakoturist office if you need help. Both cheap and pleasant medium-priced hotels are scarce, so anyone on a low budget will almost certainly have to stay with a family; these same agencies can help with private accommodation.

The main hotels to choose from are as follows:

Palace, Poštová 1 (tel 33 46 01; fax 33 32 00), just north of nám. SNP. A traditional Eastern Europe (i.e. shoddy) hotel, but in the heart of the city and the cheapest around, costing $20 single/$25 double including breakfast. Rooms are gloomy and noisy but the upstairs restaurant is good, considering.

Krym, Safárikovo nám. 6 (554 71). The next cheapest option, charging $65 for two, but likely to be revamped.

Carlton, Hviezdoslavov nám. 5 (582 09). A huge place near the theatre, currently undergoing massive (and much needed) renovation. Likely to be middle to top range.

Kyjev, Rajska 2 (tel 32 20 41-4; fax 32 68 20), just east of the centre. A multi-storey affair, with more than its fair share of spivs hanging around outside. About $80 for two.

Devín, Riecna 4 (33 08 51), overlooking the Danube. Overpriced at $128 for two, but more characterful than the other top hotels.

Hostels and Camping. For information on youth hostels open in summer, ask CKM at Hviezdoslavovo nám 16 (33 16 07). It also runs the CKM Juniorhotel Sputnik at Drieňová 14 (23 43 40), by a small lake in the suburbs east of downtown. The standard rate is around $16 (single), $25 (double), with discounts for card-holders. To get there take bus 34 from the centre.

The Zlaté Piesky complex (21 41 22), by a lake 5 miles/8km northeast of Bratislava, has a couple of campsites, bungalows and a hotel. Take tram 4 from the train station.

EATING AND DRINKING

Restaurants.

Mozartov Dom, Ventúrska 10. An 18th-century palace where Mozart stayed as a child, which now houses two restaurants and a café. Closes at 6.30pm.

Madharská reštaurácia, Hviezdoslavovo nam. 20 (33 48 83). Serves the best Hungarian food in town. Expect to pay $5-10.

Pizzeria, Spitálska 31, just beyond Hotel Kyjev. Popular among young Bratislavans and has a surprising range of toppings.

Terno, on the fourth floor of Dom Odievania store on Nám SNP. Wholesome Slovak food, though the view is the highlight.

Beer and Wine Cellars.

Stará Sladovňa, at the far end of Cintorínska, five minutes' walk east of Kamenné nám. In an old malthouse with a huge courtyard, this claims to be the largest beer hall in Europe. At its best at weekends, when long lunches culminate with singing sessions. Traditional Slovak food and live music on Thursdays, Fridays and Saturdays.

Smichovsky dvor, Markušova 6, five minutes northeast of nám. SNP. Cheap, full of students and open until 11pm.

U Dežmára, Klariská 1, down an alley west off Venturská. Lively atmosphere and decent food.

Pivnica U Eda, Biela. Excellent Slovak food, with good house specials. Always buzzing, closes at 10pm.

Klub VSVU-Friedl, Hviezdoslavovo nám. 18. A bar-cum-café in the basement, ideal for after-hours drinking and with live music and discos on some nights. The liveliest thing to happen along the boulevard after dark.

Cafés. The pavement cafés along Venturská can be touristy in high season, but on term-time evenings they are busy with students and good for post-dinner drinking. Bratislava seems to go in for combined art galleries and cafés; try Ars Presso at Prepoštská 4, Espresso U Liszta, next to U Dežmára, or the Gremium Café Gallery at Gorkého 11. More elevated only in the physical sense is the Bystrica, in the tower of the SNP bridge: it's worth paying the lift fee for the view but certainly not for the coffee.

The décor of the newish Roland Café on Hlavné nám. doesn't live up to the restored Art Nouveau exterior, but it's a genteel place for a drink. The coffee's not great, though some of the combinations (such as an 'Algerian' mixture of advocaat, coffee and cream) are at least novel. You'll find a more interesting clientele — mostly local arty types — at Café Krym at Safárikovo nám. 7.

EXPLORING

The monstrosities put up by the communists have undoubtedly marred the Old Town, but three-quarters of the Staré Mesto has survived. A startling mix of architectural styles has converged, a rich muddle of Gothic, Baroque and Ottoman, narrow streets full of crumbling cottages and pastel-shaded churches. Many of the old palaces are now museums, mostly open 10am-5pm daily except Monday.

A good place to begin a tour is at St Michael's Tower (Michalská Veža), at the top of Michalská, the only remaining part of Bratislava's medieval fortifications. The museum inside is not half as good as the view from the top or the Pharmaceutical Museum opposite. The stern, heavy shelves in this old chemist's shop are crammed with ornate jars which used to conserve remedies such as cannabis and something called pulverised purgator.

You can follow Baštova west down to the Convent of sv Klara (closed to the public), which has a fine Gothic tower and is surrounded by some of the centre's most crumbling and atmospheric streets. Zámonička, curves east from St Michael's Tower to the lovely Franciscan Church (founded in 1297) and the Mirbach Palace, a beautiful late Rococo building. It houses some of the country's best pre-20th century Slovakian paintings. The Jesuit church a little further down is worth a look for the extraordinary pulpit, all black and gold with knobs on. It overlooks Hlavné nám., the old town's main square but a thoroughly sleepy affair.

The Old Town Hall (Stará Radnica), founded in the 15th century but rebuilt in the 19th, is a splendid structure overlooking Hlavné nám. Beneath its multi-coloured roof and fine tower is a lovely galleried courtyard with animals carved in stone around the windows. Inside, the city museum begins with a gallop through the history of Bratislava, the highlight of which is the map exhibition: a 1637 map of Europe provides the prospective traveller with stereotypical illustrations of each nationality; Belgians are shown as fat, Poles dour and Greeks knavish. Then you move into a collection of municipal memorabilia, such as faded photographs of football teams and pictures of musical worthies (Bratislava was bang in the middle of the

European tour circuit for composers such as Bartok and Mozart), before being beckoned down to the basement. This contains a fully equipped torture chamber, full of manically crafted machines for settling scores or extracting confessions. The walls are draped with all-too-graphic diagrams of the sadist's methodology, showing how to carry out castrations or fry feet.

The town hall backs onto Primaciálne nám., a strangely spiritless square despite the imposing presence of the neoclassical Primate's Palace — a monument in pink with magnificent gilded decorations, sculpted eagles, giants and other extravagances. Inside, you can see the Hall of Mirrors where Napolean signed the Pressburg peace treaty with the Austrian Emperor, Franz I, in 1805. Heading southwest along Laurinská and Panská you reach the Pálffy Palace, which contains some of the republic's best 20th-century art, including the peasant scenes of Martin Benka (1888-1971) and the dreamier compositions of Janko Alexy (1894-1970). Ludovít Fulla and Miloš Bazovský are other names to look out for.

If you continue to the end of Panská, you'll end up by the Cathedral (Dóm sv Martina), just a few fume-filled feet from a trans-European superhighway, the E-65. The towering Gothic building is best seen early on a bright Sunday morning, when the sun streams through the stained glass, softening the raw, austere interior. The fact that ten Hungarian kings and eight queens were crowned here at least adds a touch of majesty.

Across the flyover from the cathedral (steps lead to a bridge nearby), a duet of museums huddle together at the base of the hill. The Clock Museum (Múzeum Hodín) occupies a charming Rococo house which narrowly missed obliteration by communist bulldozers. Both the house and museum deserve a quick visit; many of the clocks were made locally or in Vienna. The Folk Museum opposite contains a small collection of decorative arts. From here, you can walk up Beblavého and a sequence of staircases to Bratislava Castle.

From the river, the fortress looks imposing and impregnable, but it has few redeeming features. During its turbulent history, each wave of invaders seems to have demolished the existing castle and put up a new one. A fire in 1811 left it in ruins until the present palace was erected inexpertly after Soviet troops swept in at the end of World War Two. It now contains mostly offices, with a dull museum and a café, but the views offer some compensation for the climb: even on a murky day, you can see across into Hungary and Austria, though the army of apartment blocks across the river dominates.

The Waterfront. Bratislava's position by the Danube is not a patch on Budapest's, but there are a few cafés and a couple of museums near the waterfront. The Slovak National Gallery on Rázusovo nábrezie is housed in an 18th-century military barracks with an extraordinary modern wing of red and white painted metal. Inside, the rows and rows of 19th-century portraits are best skimmed, in favour of the exhibitions, though a lot of rearrangement is currently going on. The Slovak National Museum further east is not worth a wander unless you have a fascination for ineptly stuffed animals. You'll find something far more unusual beyond Safárikovo nám. on Bezručova, where Odsn Lechner — more famous for his Art Nouveau creations in Budapest — designed a church called Modrý Kostolík. With a glossy blue topknot and voluptuous curves, it is more like a cake than a building. Lechner's unmistakable style continues with the nearby grammar school.

Námestie Slobody. Communism's legacy of monumental architecture is best seen in and around nám. Slobody, a 15-minute walk northeast of the centre.

The square, designed to include the former archbishop's summer palace, now the seat of the Slovak Republic, was completed only in the 1980s. Compared with other such squares in Eastern Europe, it is moderately pleasant, with benches for sitting about and a fountain for cooling off. The telecommunications HQ on the northeast side successfully hides the upside-down pyramid of the Radio Building, more space-age design to rival the SNP bridge.

Viewpoints. Trolleybus 213 whines as it climbs up to Slavín, a tribute to the heroes of socialism. At the crown of the city's highest hill, northwest of the centre, a cemetery has been laid out for the war dead of a former superpower. Seven thousand Soviet soldiers perished while Bratislava was taken in 1945. Each tomb bears a faded sepia portrait of a brave young Russian or Ukrainian, who died fighting somebody else's war. The quiet beauty of the location makes it all the more poignant. The same bus 213 continues north to Kamzík Hill, topped by a TV tower with a revolving restaurant providing more views.

ENTERTAINMENT

The state opera and ballet companies perform at the Slovak National Theatre (552 28) on Hviezdoslavovo nám.; the opera is of a particularly high standard and is well worth seeing. The Slovak Philharmonic Orchestra is based in the Reduta Palace (33 33 51), a voluptuous building nearby on Mostová. Classical and other concerts are also held in various buildings in the Old Town, including in the church of sv Klara and the castle. Bratislava's jazz festival, held each October, features many of the bands which perform in Prague's own jazz week.

You're likely to see the best theatre either at the Hviezdoslav Theatre at Laurinská 20 or Studio S on nám. 1 mája (525 52). Cerný havran café, at the east end of Biela, hosts a mixture of plays, small gigs and poetry readings. The café, popular among local artists, is a pleasant place for an after-dinner coffee.

The pick of Bratislava's clubs are the New Model Club at Obchodná 2 and the Rock, Pop, Jazz Club at Jakubovo nám. 12. For jazz and blues you'll do best at the Mefisto Club in the U panny wine bar at Panenská 24.

Sport. The country's top football matches take place at the Slovan stadium: look out for games featuring Slovan Bratislava, the country's best team, or its closest rival Inter Bratislava.

SHOPPING

Bratislava isn't a great shopping city, though you'll find a few gift shops and bookshops around the Staré Město. There is a reasonable range of good-quality folk arts and crafts in the shops next door to Café Roland on Hlavné nám., though if you're going to eastern Slovakia then you'd probably do better to wait.

CRIME AND SAFETY

Crime grows but is not yet a big problem in Bratislava. Particularly dark and quiet streets in the Old Town, around the cathedral and in Hviezdoslavovo nám. are the main potential trouble spots.

HELP AND INFORMATION

Tourist Information: BIPS, the city tourist office at the corner of Laurinská and Rybárska brána (33 37 15, 33 43 70/25), is the best source of information about Bratislava. It opens 8am-4pm Monday to Friday (until 6pm in summer), 8am-1pm on Saturday. For more general information about the country go to Slovakoturist at Panská 13 (33 57 22, 33 16 07), in the passageway between Panská and Hviezdoslavovo nám. Cedok, at Jesenkého 12 (816 40), has been somewhat marginalised.

Money: you can change money at a lousy rate at the big hotels. Rely rather on Všeobecná úverová banka, which has branches at nám. SNP 19 and Dunajská 24. Tatratour on Frantiskanské nám. is an American Express agent and also changes money.

Communications: the main post office is at nám. SNP 35 (open 7am-8pm Monday to Friday, 7am-6pm on Saturday, 9am-1pm on Sunday). Telephone and fax facilities are upstairs. There is a telephone office at Kolárska 12 (a block east of nám. SNP), which is open for calls 24 hours a day.

Medical Assistance: U Salvátora pharmacy at Panská 35 (33 01 29) has English-speaking staff.

Embassies and Consulates. *UK:* a building was being sought at the time of going to press. Ask at the tourist office.
USA: Paulínyho 1, overlooking Hviezdoslavovo nám.
Bulgaria: Kuzmányiho 1 (31 53 08), west of Mierové nám.
Hungary: Palisády 54 (33 56 01).
Poland: Hummelova 4 (31 52 22), northwest of the castle, accessible on trolleybus 213.

WESTERN SLOVAKIA

The Little Carpathians (Malé karpaty) extend northeastwards from Bratislava, their slopes smothered with vineyards and providing reasonable walking country close to the capital. Trnava, 30 miles/48km northeast of the capital, marks the beginning of the Central European plain and was once the religious heart of the country. Most of the churches used to be boarded up, but gradually they have reopened, and there are some interesting Renaissance buildings.

The broad valley of the Váh, one of Slovakia's principal rivers, is not particularly dramatic, but there are some pleasant towns and even one or two castles dotted along the banks. Piešťany, about an hour by train northeast of Bratislava, is the country's biggest and most famous spa, but it doesn't have much going for it when compared with the spas of Western Bohemia. You would do better to head straight to Trencín, 25 miles/40km beyond.

Trenčín. The Váh valley's most pleasant town is dominated by a huge castle, which was built in the 15th century and once guarded an important route between the Danube and the Baltics. Like most of the town, the castle was destroyed by a fire in 1790, but parts have been restored and the tower provides magnificent views. There's not much else to detain you in Trenčín, but it's a convenient place to stop off if you're heading for the mountains. Hotel Laugaricio on Vajancského nám. (0831-378 41) is the most comfortable of the cheaper hotels. Some Bratislava-Košice trains go via Trenčín, but bus links are better.

CENTRAL SLOVAKIA

The main attraction of this region is the Malá Fatra mountains and the Low Tatras. The hiking, climbing and skiing is less spectacular than in the High Tatras, further east, but this gives you more chance to get off the beaten track, particularly if you're camping. Most towns are linked by both road and rail.

THE MALA FATRA

Zilina, north up the Váh valley from Trencín, is an industrial town and an important rail junction. It has the best supply of hotels in the area (try the Metropol opposite the train station) and is the main jumping-off point for the mountains. But Terchová, 15 miles/24km east, is a much better base for hiking; in winter you can ski from here too. Terchová itself is an attractive village which marks the beginning of the Vrátna Dolina valley, one of the most beautiful spots in the country. There is a campsite and a fair number of households advertise private rooms. You can also walk from Dolný Kubín, east of Terchová in the Orava valley, but it's not nearly such a pleasant place.

BANSKA BYSTRICA

A population of around 85,000 coupled with the smells and eyesores that go hand-in-hand with industry, don't make Banská Bystrica sound very promising. But the town lies at the heart of a lovely region and the old centre still has considerable charm, with attractive buildings dating from the 15th and 16th centuries, when the nearby silver and copper mines brought great prosperity to Banská Bystrica. The town's greatest fame, however, stems from its role as the birthplace in 1944 of the Slovak National Uprising (SNP), in which thousands of local people rebelled against the Germans and their country's pro-Nazi government.

You won't need much more than an afternoon to explore the town itself, but from Banská Bystrica you can reach several other interesting towns.

Arrival and Departure. The bus and train stations are next door to each other, about 15 minutes' walk east of nám. SNP, the main square. There are a couple of trains a day from Bratislava and one from Košice, but buses follow a more direct route (and are the only way to reach the High Tatras); for international rail connections, you'll do better at nearby Zvolen. Buses link Banská Bystrica with most towns in the region as well as with Bratislava (almost hourly), Brno (several times daily) and with Budapest (three times a week).

Accommodation. The cheapest deal is offered by the CKM Hotel Junior at Národna 12 (088-233 67), just south of the main square, which charges $10 per person. Narodny Dom, opposite at Národna 11 (088-237 37), is a combined theatre, hotel and restaurant with double rooms for $25-30. Hotel Urpín, around the corner at Cikkera 5 (tel 088-245 56, fax 238 31), charges a similar rate, with singles for around $18. The Lux, a modern characterless place at nám. Slobody 2 (088-24 14 18) has doubles for $55.

There is a campsite attached to the Turist Hotel, 2 miles northwest of the centre along Tajovského, open all year. Bus 7 runs there from the railway station.

Eating and Drinking. Most cafés and restaurants are concentrated in the main square and along Dolná and Horná, which run west and east of it respectively. Cechova Restaurant serves the best food in nám. SNP, but you'll do better at Slovenská pivnica on Lazovná, a couple of blocks north of the square. With shiny pine tables and crisp checked tablecloths, it looks positively twee, but most dishes cost less than $1 and helpings are large. The food is strictly Slovak, with little in the way of vegetables or salads.

Horná has the best choice though. There is a reasonable pizzeria not far from the post office, and Piváren Perla occupies a lovely restored building a couple of blocks further east; its smart outward appearance conceals a simple, buzzing restaurant upstairs (open until 11pm). Almost opposite, Café Atom looks like a cross between a hairdresser's salon and a stage set. It's about the trendiest place in town, with beer strictly in bottles ($1). Food is more expensive than average, but includes unusual dishes like nasi goreng (Indonesian fried noodles). Another young and hip place for a drink is the Melod Klub, down a passageway near the posh Bystrica restaurant at the western end of Horná; it is one of the few places to stay open until midnight.

Exploring. The main square has some impressive Renaissance mansions and various Gothic and Baroque buildings. A couple are open to the public, including Thurzo's Palace, which houses a good municipal museum with an array of religious sculpture, tatty old costumes, weapons and furniture. The Renaissance Bernického Dom on the other side has a painted facade with a coat of arms featuring two miners in ceremonial dress and a delicate arcaded loggia for views over the square and along Dolná, an attractive street retaining much of the original architecture. At the top of nám. SNP, a jumble of old buildings and towers mark the site of the original mining settlement. The old barbican, with its crumbling butterscotch-coloured tower, and the town hall opposite are both art galleries. The nearby Panny Márie church, built by the German founders in the 13th century, contains a superb Gothic altarpiece by Master Pavol of Levoča, featuring painted figures with wonderful expressive faces.

Banská Bystrica's most famous landmark is the Slovak National Uprising Museum (open daily 8am-6pm), housed in an extraordinary building looking like two halves of a badly made cake. With the reassessment of the events of 1944, the whole *raison d'être* of the museum has been questioned. There is virtually no mention of the SNP at all, with most space given over to military memorabilia; a slide show (available in English) describes the birth of Czechoslovakia.

Help and Information. The Cedok office in nám. Svobody, just east of Hotel Lux, can help with accommodation in the Low Tatras, and sells hiking maps (also available from Knihy Obuv, at the west end of Horná). You can change money at Agrobanka, at the bottom of Kuzmányho, near the bottom of Dolná.

Around Banská Bystrica

Zvolen. Twelve miles/20km south of Banská Bystrica, Zvolen is a place to change buses or trains rather than a destination in its own right. But between connections, you can usefully stroll around the castle — a white, heavily restored block at the end of nám. SNP — or the museum, which has good folk displays. The town is an unassuming, buzzing little place and you can see a few real country types in the small market hidden away off the main square. For food, try Modranská vináreň, on the square west of the church, or the restaurant in Hotel Polana. The latter charges $50 for a double room, but for a room at less than half the price, go to the quiet and friendly Hotel Na Námestí (nám. SNP 37; tel/fax 0855-261 38).

Zvolen is served by regular bus and train services from Banská Bystrica, including buses bound for Budapest. There are numerous trains to Fil'akovo, the last town before the Hungarian border, and the Warsaw-Budapest express passes through daily at about midnight. If you're waiting for a late departure, Café Paris (between the bus station and nám. SNP) stays open beyond 10pm.

Kremnica. This picturesque town west of Banská Bystrica was formerly the site of the imperial mint. It is still full of old wooden miners' houses and there is a mint museum in the old town hall on the main square. Kremnica's medieval castle was badly damaged during World War Two and is only now undergoing restoration.

Trains from Zvolen to Kremnica take about an hour. There is a small and friendly campsite, and you can swim in the neighbouring open-air thermal pool.

Banská Stiavnica. In its prime, this quiet old community in the hills southwest of Banská Bystrica was the most important mining town in the Hungarian kingdom. Banská Stiavnica's crumbling architecture spans many centuries, its enchanting streets winding about the jumble of steep hills. The heart of the town, ten minutes up the hill from the bus stop, is clearly marked by the Town Hall, with a clock tower, and the golden-coloured archive building nearby. The sloping main square behind has been partially restored but is usually deserted. A large and impressive plague column (seen in many Catholic towns, erected in gratitude for deliverance from the Black Death) provides a focus, flanked by several fine houses.

The small mining museum on the right is of only minor interest compared with the handsome Hellenbachov Dom next door, with 16th-century frescoes on the facade and an art gallery (with some good Gothic sculpture) and restaurant inside. Steps near the town hall lead to the old castle, a rather forlorn complex constructed around a large Romanesque basilica. Visible through the trees and accessible west up Slákovičova, are the 17th-century Klopačka tower, whose clapper was once used to wake the miners, and the new castle. The latter is a sparkling white toytown affair, in a well-chosen spot for guarding against impending Turkish attack and, nowadays, for sitting in the shade. There are several cemeteries in this area, including a small Jewish graveyard among the trees beneath the castle. About a mile beyond the old town gate nearby is Banská Stiavnica's main mining museum (open 8am-3pm Tuesday to Sunday), a fascinating exhibition featuring a trip down a mine shaft.

Like Kremnica, Banská Stiavnica is best approached from Zvolen, with buses about four times a day. It's a lovely journey by road, but by train it's even better — though much longer. Having to change at Hronská Dubrava means the journey can take a couple of hours, compared with 40 minutes by bus. The last bus back leaves at about 4pm, but check the timetable when you arrive.

You can stay at the Grand Hotel on Kammerhófska (0859-211 91) for $8 per person or at the Matej Restaurant on Akademická (0859-239 60), close to the Cedok office, for $25 (double). A few private homes advertise rooms.

THE LOW TATRAS

The closest base to Banská Bystrica for hiking in the Low Tatras (Nízka

Tatry) is Donovaly, 16 miles/26km north and with plenty in the way of accommodation. But Liptovský Mikuláš, further north on the Váh river, gives access to arguably the best sections of the Low Tatras. The town retains some typical Slovak houses but it's a fairly lacklustre place. Some traditions survive, including delicacies such as the local Lipto cheese, known as *bryndza*. There is a choice of hotels, though none is outstanding; try El Greco or the Kriváň, both on Stúrova. The nearest campsite is a short bus ride north in Liptovský Trnovec.

South from Liptovský Mikuláš, Demdnovská dolina is probably the most beautiful valley in the Low Tatras, with a couple of impressive caves; regular buses carry visitors about the valley in summer, with services sharply reduced at other times. East of Liptovský Mikuláš, the village of Východná has a strong folk tradition and is famous throughout the republic for its folk festival, held each year in July.

EASTERN SLOVAKIA

This is the land of the High Tatras (Vysoké Tatry), the highest mountains in Europe bar the Alps. The landscapes are among the most magnificent in Central Europe and attract understandably (and distressingly) large crowds, both in summer and winter. In contrast, the regions east of the Tatras are overlooked by most travellers, but the historic towns and idyllic medieval villages are well worth exploring; and the local people, still comparatively unused to tourists, are often disarmingly friendly.

THE HIGH TATRAS (VYSOKE TATRY)

The High Tatras extend for less than 20 miles, peaks soaring either side of dramatic valleys. Mount Gerlach, at 2,655m above sea level, is the highest mountain in the whole Carpathian range.

Most of the mountain region is part of the Tatra National Park (TANAP), and trails are well-marked. But walking in the Tatras is an adventure which should be taken seriously. Climbs are not always easy: use proper footwear and clothing, take local advice before attempting anything tricky, and beware of the sudden changes in weather that are a feature of these mountains. It usually starts snowing by November, from which time on avalanches are a potential hazard. Make sure you have detailed maps and find out about local weather conditions before setting off.

You can reach the three main resorts — Starý Smokovec, Strbské Pleso and Tatranská Lomnica — from Poprad, on the main Bratislava-Košice train line and accessible by bus from all over the country. Buses also run direct to the resorts, including from Bratislava and Banská Bystrica. An electric railway connects the resorts and there is a network of cable cars and funiculars.

In the high season, you must be prepared to take whatever you're offered as far as accommodation is concerned: local tourist offices should be able to fix you up with something. Cheap rooms are scarce, and during ski tournaments there may be no spare rooms at all. The limited number of chalets are usually booked up months in advance. Try to stock up on food in the main towns, since local shops in the mountains can't usually cope with the demand.

Where to go. Some of the best walking country is in the Mengušovká Valley, which is accessible from both Starý Smokovec and Strbské Pleso. Most of the walking trails in the Tatras are well-trodden, none more so than the Tatranská Magistrála, a 40-mile/64km route across the southern ridge of the mountains which you can join from all the main resorts. Guides (these can be hired from local tourist offices) are necessary for some peaks, but two routes you should be able to handle without are up Slavkovskú štít (2,452m) from Starý Smokovec and Rysy Peak (2,499m) from Strbské Pleso.

For the best skiing, go to Tatranská Lomnica or Zdiar, about 10 miles/16km north and served by regular buses (some of which continue to the Polish border at Javorina, 10 miles west).

Poprad

At the foot of the High Tatras, Poprad is a largely industrial town with little of interest. But as the main jumping-off point for the High Tatra resorts (to which it is connected by an electric railway built early this century), you'll find Poprad hard to avoid.

Express trains link Poprad with both Zilina (a stunning journey taking about two hours) and Košice, with departures roughly every two hours. Buses arrive at the terminal opposite the railway station from most corners of Slovakia and also from Budapest, Brno and Prague. The bus and train stations are a 15-minute walk from the centre.

The best hotel in Poprad is the Európa at Wolkrová 3 (092-327 44), a decrepit but characterful old building opposite the railway station. Basic rooms cost around $15 a double. The high-rise Gerlach, not far away on Hviezdoslavovo nam. (092-337 59), charges $20-25 but offers only marginally more comfort and much less atmosphere. There is no campsite.

The tourist office is at nám. Dukelských hrdinov 60.

The Resorts

Starý Smokovec. Just 8 miles/13km north of Poprad, Starý Smokovec is the Tatras' main resort. The turn-of-the-century Grand Hotel (0969-2501) is a splendid place to stay and has a range of rooms: in low season you can pay as little as $25 for a double, but generally prices are nearer $50. Hotel Tatra and Hotel Sport are among the cheaper deals. Most hotels will be full in the high season and you'll often do better to go one or two stops on the train to the adjacent resorts of Horný Smokovec or Nový Smokovec. There is a CKM hotel in Horný Smokovec (0969-2661), but you'll need to book in advance in summer. The nearest campsite is Tatracamp in Pod Lesom, on the railway a couple of miles south towards Poprad.

Strbské Pleso. Ten miles/16km west of Starý Smokovec, this resort has much less character than its neighbour, despite its lakeside position. Strbské Pleso gets crowded because it is a major ski resort (international competitions are held here), with good facilities. The best slopes are on Solisko Hill.

In addition to the electric railway, normal trains serve Strbské Pleso from Poprad and Košice. Accommodation is surprisingly limited and you'll probably do better in nearby Tatranská Strba, which has a campsite and the excellent Rysy Hotel (a bargain with rooms for $10-15), though the main resort is best for restaurants and shops. Tatranská Strba, accessible by a 19th-century cog-wheel railway from Strbské Pleso, offers marvellous views of the highest Tatra peaks. And since it is on the main rail line, you could use this as an access point to the Tatras and avoid Poprad altogether.

Tatranská Lomnica. Four miles/6km east of Starý Smokovec, Tatranská Lomnica is not so good for hiking, but you can take the cable-car up Lomnický štít (2,632m), not for the faint-hearted. The resort's most chic hotel is the Grand Hotel Praha (967-607), close to the cable-car terminal, with the best of the cheaper deals — the Hotel Lomnica and the Hotel Mier — both near the railway station. A couple of miles east and accessible on the Poprad train, Eurocamp FICC is a massive complex made up of a campsite, bungalows, restaurants, shops and virtually everything else you could possibly need. The four-bed bungalows are very comfortable and cost around $40 each.

SPIS REGION

Spiš describes the area east of Poprad, where Saxon settlers came in the 12th century, mostly to work in the nearby mines. Their communities remained almost totally cut off from the rest of the country and several towns and villages have survived in a remarkable state of preservation, retaining an unmistakably German air. The mix of artisans' cottages, merchants' mansions and Gothic churches provides the best architecture in the country. Anyone travelling between the Tatras and Košice should not fail to stop off, though Spiš also warrants a major diversion.

Levoča. If you have time to visit just one place, make sure its Levoča, which lies at the foot of the Tatras 15 miles/24km east of Poprad. The town has retained its medieval street layout together with the old walls. The main square, Mierové nam., has much of interest including the superb medieval church of St James, which has the tallest altar in the world — a 61ft Gothic masterpiece in wood. For the background of the making of the altar and its creator, visit the museum in the house of Master Pavol, opposite the church. Various other houses in Levoča are open as museums, all worth visiting just to see the interior.

Buses link Levoča frequently with Poprad, Košice and Prešov, and arrive at Slobody nám., northeast of the centre just outside the city walls. The town is also served by train from Spišská Nova Ves, 8 miles/13km south, an uninspiring town on the Poprad-Košice line.

Levoča currently has just one hotel, the scruffy Družba at Cesta Slobody 22 (0966-25 59), southeast of the main square and just outside the city walls. There is a campsite (Levočská Dolina) a couple of miles northwest of town, which is open in summer only.

Spišské Podhradie. Seven miles/10km and 30 minutes by bus east of Levoča, this town is not of great interest in itself. But it provides access to two of the region's most interesting sights. You can stay at the Spiš Hotel, near the main bus stop.

Spišský Hrad: towering over Spišské Podhradie, Spišský Hrad is the largest castle in Slovakia. Founded in the 13th century, rebuilt in the 15th and badly damaged by fire in the 18th, it is now a ruin. But what remains and its position high on the ridge are breathtaking. You can walk up to the castle in about 30 minutes from the town. It is open only May to October (9am-5pm Tuesday to Sunday) but you don't have to go inside to appreciate this mighty structure.

Spišská Kapitula: situated about a mile north of the town, Spišská Kapitula was built as a religious centre. It went into hibernation under communism, but there is a chance that it may function again in the future. Enclosed within old city walls, Spišská Kapitula consists of little more than a single street. Along it are ranked fine Gothic houses plus a magnificent Cathedral, built in 1273.

SLOVENSKY RAJ (Slovak Paradise)

The 'Slovak Paradise' is a protected area of dramatic caves, cliffs and ravines southwest of Spiš. Try to get hold of the *Letná Turistiká Mapa: Slovensky Raj* no. 23, an essential companion to the region available most reliably from the tourist office in Poprad.

A good place to walk from is Cingov, a collection of chalets rather than a village, 5 miles/8km southwest of Spišská Nová Ves. A number of trails run from here, including up the Hornád Gorge (the most popular route, linking Cingov and Podlesok) and to Hrabušice. Podlesok is another chalet camp and gives access to the Suchá Bela Gorge. The glorious landscapes make it worth stomaching the crowds of local hikers.

The Dobšina Ice Cave is one of the largest ice cave systems in the world. Only a comparatively small part is open to the public (May to September, 9am-3pm daily except Monday), but it should not be missed. If you are driving, the entrance is on the Poprad-Rožňava road south of Vernár, but you can also reach the cave by train: the Banská Bystrica-Kosice railway has a station called Dobšinská Ladová Jaskyňa, about 20 minutes' walk away. Alternatively, you can walk from Podlesok, but allow four hours each way.

KOSICE

This is the second largest town in the country (with a population of 250,000) and the economic and political centre of Eastern Slovakia. At first sight, Košice appears to have been consumed by urban sprawl and pollution, but the steel factories and drab apartment blocks conceal an historical town with plenty to explore. Behind streets lined with imposing facades you'll find alleys with hidden markets and atmospheric cafés and wine bars. Košice is a lively cultural centre and well worth a stop of a day or two.

Links between Košice and Hungary go back hundreds of years, and this century the town has changed hands between Hungary and former Czechoslovakia several times. Nowadays, Košice is culturally diverse, with large communities of gypsies and Hungarians.

Arrival and Departure. Trains serve Košice from all directions, including overnight sleepers from Bratislava. There are also numerous international connections, including daily express trains from Budapest and Kraków; Prague-Moscow services stop here too. Košice lies 10 miles/16km north of the Hungarian border and there are local trains daily to Miskolc in Hungary. The railway station is a short walk east of the centre, with the bus station next door.

Accommodation. The best deals in Košice are the Európa on Mlynská (095-221 42), just across the park from the railway station, and the Imperial, a couple of blocks nearer the centre at Mlynská 16 (095-221 46); both charge less than $20. Hotel Slovan (095-273 78), at the southern end of Hlavná ulica (the main street-cum-square), charges around $60 for a double and is poor value; the food is dreadful too. Cedok, in Hotel Slovan, can help with private rooms and CKM at Hlavná ul. 82 (095-278 58) offers information about summer hostels. There is a campsite with bungalows 3 miles/5km south of the city, open just in summer.

Eating and Drinking. The choice of restaurants comes as a relief for those fresh from a stint in the provinces. The best place in town is Ajvega at Orlia 10, just east of the main square. The vegetarian food is as popular amongst the locals as it is among tourists. More run-of-the-mill places are dotted along Hlavná ulica, including Miskolc, an Hungarian restaurant in a Renaissance house on the square. Anyone fresh from Hungary is likely to be unimpressed, but the setting is pleasant. It is open for lunch only.

Exploring. Life revolves around the main square (Hlavná nám.), which takes up about half the length of Hlavná ulica. The architectural highlight here is the Cathedral of St Elizabeth (Dom Svdtej Alžbety), completed in 1508 and one of the most beautiful Gothic churches in Central Europe. Just to the north is the handsome State Theatre and, beyond, the Technical Museum, which has some early examples of factory robots and numerous displays of wrought-iron work, for which the region is famous. The prize for best museum, however, goes to the East Slovak Museum (Vychodoslovenské múzeum), on Maratónu Mieru nám. at the northern end of Hlavná ulica. Its proudest possession is the collection of gold coins kept in the basement. Dating from the 15th-17th centuries, they were discovered only in the 1930s. The displays illustrating the cultural background of Košice are complemented by those in the dungeons of Miklušova Väznica, the former prison a block east of Hlavná nám.

NORTH OF KOSICE

Prešov. Situated 22 miles/35km north of Košice, Prešov is a buzzing place where the past and present blend comfortably. The town centre is of great architectural interest, reflecting Prešov's status as the cultural heart of Slovakia's Rusyns or Ruthenians, a Ukrainian-speaking people absorbed into Czechoslovakia in 1918 and mostly peasants living in the hills. There are decorative burgher houses and a number of attractive churches: best of these is the 14th-century church of St Nicholas in Hlavná ulica, the main street/square. Nearby, a museum illustrates the history of the town.

Buses serve Prešov hourly from Košice, and there are also links with Levoča and other towns in the region. Trains are less convenient, though the express service between Krakow and Budapest stops here.

Located in the centre of Eastern Slovakia, Prešov makes a good base for exploring the region. There are various hotels on Hlavná ulica. The Dukla (091-227 41), opposite the tourist office at the southern end of the street, is overpriced at $25 for a double, but clean. The Savoy (091-310 62) at no. 50 is much dingier but less than half the price. You can camp or rent a bungalow at the motel 3 miles/5km south of town.

Bardejov. About 30 miles/48km north of Prešov, Bardejov is a purer historical relic than its neighbour. Founded in the 13th century, the town grew into an important trading centre which peaked in the 15th to 17th centuries. Parts of the old city walls remain and you can amble along medieval streets lined with Renaissance burgher houses. The beautiful main square, Osloboditel'ov nám., is overlooked by the Gothic church of St Egidius, which contains eleven carved altars dating from the late 15th century and including one by Pavol of Levoča. In the middle of the square, the Renaissance town hall contains an excellent museum illustrating the history of medieval Bardejov. The Icon Museum nearby is worth a visit too.

Buses serve Bardejov hourly from Prešov and there are services direct from Košice and Poprad too. The local hotels aren't great, the best of a poor choice being the Dukla (0935-2721) just north of the main square.

Bardejovské Kúpele: this small town is just 3 miles/5km northeast of Bardejov and accessible on a town bus service. While one of the region's most pleasant spas, Bardejovské Kúpele is worth visiting primarily for its *skansen* or open-air museum of traditional wooden buildings. There are trails into the hills around the spa, so allow a whole day to explore.

Medzilaborce. Tucked away in Slovakia's northeastern corner, Medzilaborce seems an unlikely place for a museum dedicated to Andy Warhol, but the artist's Rusyn parents lived in the area before emigrating to the USA in the early 1900s. The museum, opened following the artist's death in 1987, doesn't contain great works of art (most of what you see is on loan), but is a touching tribute. There is a shop selling wacky Warhol souvenirs and books about Rusyn culture. The museum opens 10am-noon and 2-4.30pm Monday to Friday and 2-5pm at weekends.

Medzilaborce is 30 miles/48km northeast of Prešov as the crow flies, but the train journey from Prešov takes about four hours. If approaching from Bardejov, you'll have to change buses at Svidník. There is a hotel if you need to stay overnight.

Calendar of Events

January 1	**New Year's Day**
March/April	**Easter** (*Velká noc*), much more important than Christmas, particularly among the Orthodox and Uniate churches in eastern Slovakia
May 1	**Labour Day**
May 8	**Liberation Day**
June	International Folk Festival, Košice
July 5	**Day of the Apostles St Cyril and St Method**
September	Bratislava Jazz Festival
October 28	**National Day, Anniversary of Independence**
December 24-26	**Christmas** (*Vianoce*)

Public holidays are shown in **bold**.

Hungary

Pest, from Gellért Hill in Buda

Population: 10.4 million   **Capital: Budapest (population 2 million)**

Hungary conforms little to the image of unmitigated Warsaw Pact grimness. Even under communism, you could enjoy luxuries found nowhere else in the region. Eastern Europeans regarded Hungary as a comparatively good place to live, and it was always the most popular holiday destination within the communist bloc. Being the most Westernised, Hungary therefore had a head start over its neighbours following the changes of the late 80s, with capitalism being grafted more easily onto the system already in existence. Western tourists will feel surprisingly at home, but Hungary has not proved immune to the ills that afflict other former communist nations. An estimated three million people are said to be living either below or only just above the poverty line. And sanctions against Serbia, which have had a dramatic effect on trade along the Danube, have hit Hungary badly.

The number of tourists visiting Hungary has multiplied since the fall of the communist regime, but many are Austrians, who flood across the border to go shopping and enjoy cheap meals or to join the summer hordes in the Lake Balaton resorts. The Great Plain, which takes up two-thirds of the country, is bleak — though orchards bring welcome splashes of colour in summer — and you'll find few idyllic rural communities such as those in Slovakia or Romania. But the country is not short on history or culture. Despite having been repeatedly invaded and annexed by enemy powers, Hungary retains a culture which is quite distinct from those of its occupiers and its neighbours. This is undoubtedly due partly to the unassimilability of the Hungarian language, but also to a fiercely nationalist pride among its people. Magyar horsemen and violin-playing gypsies are nowadays associated only with tourist entertainment, but the romance of Hungarian history has survived all assaults, including four and a half decades of Soviet control.

As the crossroads for both traders and invaders from East and West, Hungary boasts historic remains from Roman baths and Turkish mosques to medieval churches and opulent Baroque palaces. Many of these have benefited from the state's generous programme of restoration — nowhere more so than in Budapest, a fabulous and lively city which is undoubtedly the best thing the country has to offer. And while not as cheap as say Romania or Slovakia, Hungary remains an inexpensive place in which to travel.

CLIMATE

Hungary has a continental climate, bringing hot summers (a peak of 30°C/86°F is not unusual) and cold winters. In January the temperature usually hovers around freezing point, and the nights are still fairly cold in April. There is not much climatic variation, though the extremes are more pronounced in the Great Plain, which can be especially humid in summer.

Hungary is relatively dry, enjoying an average of over five hours of sunshine a day. Heavy showers occur in spring and autumn, but these two seasons are still the best time to visit: due to both the balmy temperatures and to the comparatively small number of tourists.

HISTORY

After the Romans had colonised Hungary (then known as Pannonia), the Huns invaded in the fifth century and set up their own kingdom. It is strenuously argued that the name Hungary does not derive from Hun but rather from the Magyar word *Onogur* meaning 'the ten peoples'. The Magyars arrived from the steppes of the Ural Mountains at the end of the ninth century, converting to Christianity about 100 years later. The Arpád dynasty reigned until the end of the 13th century, when Hungary suffered devastation at the hands of the Mongols. The Magyars survived, but were later defeated by the Turks, who controlled Hungary from 1526 to 1686. They had little impact on the culture apart from building mosques and baths, a few of which survive.

With the help of the Habsburg dynasty in Vienna, the Hungarians finally managed to drive out the Turks, only to once again become a colony. There was nationalist resistance to domination by the Austrians over the next 150 years, but no outright success until an uprising on March 15, 1848. The revolution was defeated but it forced a compromise, resulting in the dual Austro-Hungarian monarchy. Virtually every town in Hungary has a square or street which is called Március 15 or is named after the romantic radicals and reformers involved in the resistance: including its leader Lajos Kossuth and Sándor Petőfi, a poet who delivered a famous speech from the steps of the National Museum in 1848 and whose premature death during the fighting turned him into a folk hero.

Following the First World War, Hungary gained independence from Austria, but ceded vast expanses of territory to Czechoslovakia, Yugoslavia and Romania (including Transylvania, which is considered the cradle of Hungarian culture). A right-wing regime under Miklós Horthy held sway during the ensuing period and took Hungary into World War Two on the German side in 1941. Budapest suffered terrible damage during the conflict, especially in the final year of the war, when the Red Army besieged the castle where the Germans had barricaded themselves. Liberated by the Soviet Union, Hungary soon became a nominally communist state.

In October 1956, the Hungarian people, under the leadership of Imre Nagy, revolted against the Soviet-dominated government. Nagy abolished the one-party system and called publicly for free elections and the withdrawal of Soviet troops. Red Army tanks didn't take long to move in and install a puppet government under János Kádár. More than 65,000 troops were subsequently stationed in Hungary, the first of which were withdrawn only in 1989. The uprising lasted a fortnight and was mercilessly crushed, resulting in the death of 3,000 Hungarians and the exile of 200,000 others. Nagy refused to repent publicly and was executed in 1958.

Kádár, hated initially, gradually earned more respect for his comparatively enlightened government. He allowed more personal freedom than in other Warsaw Pact countries, and even introduced a few free market policies — by the end of the 80s Hungary was ahead of its Eastern European neighbours in terms of economic reform. Hungary's brand of communism increased industrial production and improved the standard of living for millions of peasants. Private ownership of farms and businesses was much more common than in neighbouring countries, and there were even a few fee-paying schools. Political change was minimal, however, limited by Kádár's distrust of a multi-party system.

Károly Grósz, who took over from János Kádár in mid-1988, was a more natural political as well as economic reformer. He was a self-confessed admirer of Margaret Thatcher, though his watchwords 'compromise' and 'tolerance' were not notable characteristics of the former British prime minister. Under him, workers were given the right to strike and political parties other than the Communist Party were allowed into the political forum. It was Hungary that sparked off the upheavals affecting the whole of Eastern Europe: in the spring of 1989, the Hungarian authorities began dismantling the fence along the Austrian border, thus enabling freedom seekers from the Eastern bloc to simply travel to Hungary, walk across the border and reach the West. The rest is history.

Hungary since 1989. The process of democratisation in Hungary was fairly open, with televised round-table talks between the communist leadership and non-communist opposition. In multi-party elections in 1990, a fairly new opposition coalition, the centre-right Hungarian Democratic Forum (MDF), took the most seats and formed Hungary's first post-communist government under the leadership of József Antall. In the same year, Hungary became the first former communist country to join the Council of Europe.

At the time of going to press, Prime Minister Antall headed a deeply unpopular government. In addition to divisions within the ruling MDF, moving the country towards a market economy has brought runaway inflation, high unemployment and an ever-widening gap between the rich and poor. Many voters hold the governing coalition responsible for the economic misery that Hungary, once a comparatively prosperous country, is now enduring.

THE PEOPLE

The vast majority of Hungarians are Magyars. There are small pockets of Germans, Slovaks, Romanians, Serbs and Croats, and Gypsies make up about 4% of the population. Thanks to Hungary's late entry into the war, there was no time for the Nazis to deport the country's Jews. However, 80%

209

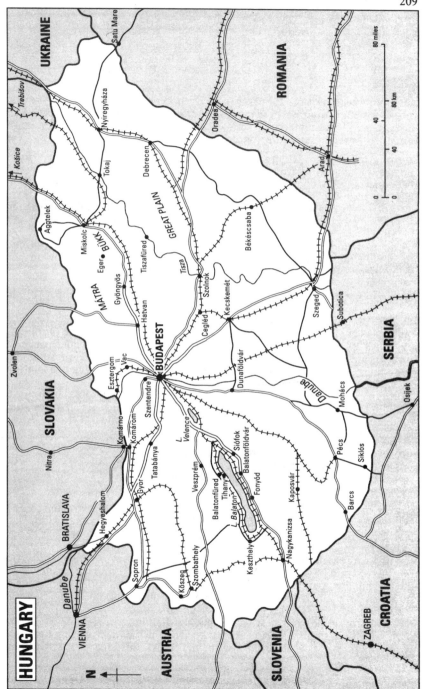

of them died from starvation and disease, or else fled. Virtually all those who survived live in Budapest. As elsewhere in Eastern Europe, Gypsies and Jews have been victims of a new patriotism. The authorities have taken small steps to address the problem, but mostly on a very superficial level — including the prohibition of extremist symbols (aimed primarily at the swastika).

Religion. About 65% of Hungarians are Catholic, though Protestants (mostly Lutherans and Calvinists) are fairly numerous in eastern Hungary. Freedom of religion is guaranteed under the constitution, so church attendance remained fairly constant during the communist years.

Meeting the People. Hungarians are a generally relaxed and friendly race, though they tend to be reserved towards strangers. While they will usually respond easily and courteously to any approaches you make, they are unlikely to initiate conversation unless they want to practise their English. Hungarians are not in the least reticent with one another, however, and they can be surprisingly expressive in public: affection is demonstrated warmly and openly.

Life in Hungary is very family-oriented. Many young people continue living with their parents even after marriage, and the stresses show in one of the highest divorce rates in Europe.

LANGUAGE

It's hard to come to terms with the Hungarian (Magyar) language, even if you're staying for a couple of weeks. This terrifying tongue is one of the few languages of Europe which is not Indo-European, being related only to Finnish and Estonian. Hungarian words look like bad hands at Scrabble, made up of letters which fail to behave as they should. The one consolation is that Magyar at least uses the Roman alphabet.

Pronunciation is a nightmare, and the simplest words will sound incomprehensible to the natives unless you master a few basic rules, e.g. that the first syllable is always accented. The pronunciation of the most difficult letters is as follows:

c   is ts, so *útca* (street) is pronounced *oot*-sa
cs is (ts)ch, so *csirke* (chicken) is pronounced *chir*-kay
s   is sh, so Budapest is pronounced *Boo*da-pesht
gy is dy or dj, so *ágy* (bed) is pronounced aadj

Vowels also cause problems, though the main surprise is that an unaccented a is pronounced like the o in hot: as in Magyar (which becomes *Mody*-or), or in the socialist party newspaper *Népszabadság*, which becomes Nape-soh-bod-shahg.

While some Hungarians may know German and a few English words, on long bus or train journeys you'll probably have to resign yourself to silence — unless you are happy to get involved in mad gesticulations or complex drawings. If you are keen to do more than just muddle along, several Hungarian universities, such as Debrecen, run summer courses for foreigners. Otherwise, do your best with a pocket dictionary (available for about $1 in local bookshops), a great asset when it comes to deciphering menus.

Here is a basic vocabulary (with the most difficult pronunciations explained):

yes or okay — *igen* (*ay*gen)   shop — *bolt*

no — *nem*
hello — *szia (see*ah)
sizasztok (to more than one person)
goodbye — *viszontlátásra (vi*sontlatashro)
please — *kérem (kay*rem)
thank you — *köszönöm (ker*sernerm)
next please, what can I do for you? — *tessék*
    (*tesh*shek)
excuse me — *bocsánat (boh*chahnot)
how much is it? — *mennyibe kerül (menn*jibe *ke*rul)
cheers! — *egészségédre! (eg*gesshaigehdry)
today — *ma*
tomorrow — *holnap*
I am English — *angol vagyok*
prohibited — *tilos*
ticket — *jegy* (yedge)

open — *nyitva*
closed — *zárva*
toilet — *ferfi* (men's)
nīu (women's)

1 — *egy*
2 — *kettő*
3 — *három*
4 — *négy*
5 — *öt*
6 — *hat*
7 — hét
8 — nyolc
9 — *kilenc*
10 — *tíz*

Getting There

AIR

The Hungarian national airline, Malév, is one of the best Eastern European carriers — partly thanks to the involvement of Alitalia, which holds a 35% stake. It is certainly the most profitable, with comparatively high fares.

There are daily flights from London on Malév to Budapest. You can book directly through Malév (10 Vigo St, London W1X 1AJ; tel 071-439 0577) or though an agency. Other airlines serving Budapest from London include Air France, KLM and Lufthansa. Hungarian Air Tours (071-437 9405) can offer good deals on fares from London, e.g. around £240 return, £160 single.

If you can't get a cheap deal direct to Hungary, you might consider flying to Vienna, which is just 130 miles from Budapest. Bucket shop fares go for around £140 return, £100 one-way. See below for how to get to Hungary overland from the Austrian capital.

The only direct flights from North America go from New York. Malév shares an office with the Hungarian Travel Bureau in the Rockefeller Center in New York (Room 1900, 630 Fifth Avenue; tel 212-757-6480).

TRAIN

Train fares from London to Budapest for those under 26 cost around £110 single and £200 return, roughly half the regular fare. The quickest way to Hungary from London by rail is to take the Ostend-Vienna Express and then connect with a train to Budapest: this journey takes about a day and a half altogether. If you don't book a through ticket, be sure to find out which of Vienna's stations your connecting service leaves from. The international *Wiener Waltzer* from Basel, the *Orient Express* from Paris and the *Arrabona* from Vienna depart from the Westbahnhof, run daily, take about 3½ hours and arrive at Budapest's Keleti station. The *Léhar Express,* which is slightly faster, leaves from Vienna's Südbahnhof and terminates at Budapest's Déli station. There are also daily services to Budapest from Prague (via Brno and Bratislava) and Bucharest.

Note that if you require a visa to enter Hungary (see *Red Tape,* below), you must obtain this in advance since there are no facilities to buy one at the border.

BUS

International coach services to Hungary are reasonably frequent and efficient from the Czech and Slovak Republics, Germany and Italy, with established links also with Croatia and the Ukraine. There are at least two buses a day from Prague, the fare around $30. A ticket from Bratislava costs about $10, from Bucharest $50. The weekly Eurolines service from London (071-730 0202) runs in summer only, costs around £60 single, £110 return and takes about 48 hours. From Vienna, buses leave several times a day from the Mitte Autobusbahnhof and take 4½ hours (allowing 30 minutes at the border).

BOAT

The most romantic (and by far the most expensive) way to enter Hungary is along the Danube — though if the controversial Gabcikovo-Nagymaros dam is completed, a 15-mile stretch of the Danube east of Bratislava will be diverted into a concrete ditch and will detract considerably from the aesthetic appeal of this approach. It will also do untold harm to the balance of nature, particularly the breeding habits of fish, and even jeopardise the supply of drinking water for all of Western Hungary. Protests from conservation groups, scientists and politicians have induced Hungary to withdraw from the project, but Slovakia hopes to continue. The International Court of Justice in the Hague has been called to settle the dispute by deciding whether or not it was legal for Hungary to pull out of the project; this could take several years.

The main service from Vienna is the fast and comfortable hydrofoil, operated daily from April to October by the Hungarian shipping company Mahart. With drinks and a tourist commentary, it's more of a cruise than a means of public transport (though the windows are often too grimy to afford good views). The fare, in either direction, is payable in hard currency only: $70 one-way, $110 return. Budapest-bound hydrofoils leave from the dock (*Shiffsstation*) at Vienna's Mexico Platz, where you can also buy tickets. The journey takes around 4½ hours. For reservations and information in Vienna call 010 43 1 21 75 00.

DRIVING

Driving to Hungary is straightforward, though it's a long haul from Britain: the distance by road from London is 1,100 miles/1,760km. The fastest route takes you through Germany, where the autobahns make for a relatively high speed. Navigation is also painless: the E-5 goes from Ostend direct to Budapest via Brussels, Frankfurt, Linz and Vienna.

There are many points of entry into Hungary. Nickelsdorf/Hegyeshalom on the E-5, on the Austrian border, and Komárno/Komárom (a city divided by the Danube between Slovakia and Hungary) are two of the busiest and you may well encounter delays at weekends and in summer. Border posts are open 24 hours a day, so you can avoid the queues by crossing early or late; otherwise, choose a more minor route once you near the border.

See *Getting Around: Driving* for details of documents required by motorists.

HITCH-HIKING

Traffic is heavy on the E-5, but weekending Austrians are not famed for their willingness to give lifts: you'll almost certainly be picked up by other foreigners or by lorry-drivers.

Red Tape

British passport holders and citizens of the USA, Canada and many Western European nations do not require a visa to visit Hungary as a tourist. Australians are among the nationals that currently still do. Tourist (30 days) and transit (48 hours) visas both cost the equivalent of about $18. Neither can be arranged at the border, so apply in advance to a Hungarian consulate abroad, allowing at least 48 hours for processing. Addresses of Hungarian consulates are as follows:

UK: 35B Eaton Place, London SW1X 8BY (tel 071-235 4462; fax 071-823 1348). Open 10am-12.30pm Monday to Friday.
USA: 3910 Shoemaker St NW, Washington, DC 20008 (tel 202-362-6730; fax 202-966-8135) or 8 East 75th St, New York, NY 10021.
Canada: 7 Delaware Avenue, Ottawa, Ontario K2P 0Z2 (tel 613-232-1711/1549; fax 613-232-5620).
Australia: Unit 6, 351a Edgecliff Road, Edgecliff, Sydney, NSW 2027 (328 7859).

The initial stay of 30 days granted to tourists can be extended once you're in Hungary. In Budapest you should go to the Police Aliens' Registration Office at Andrássy út 12, open weekday mornings only.

IMMIGRATION

Whichever way you enter or leave Hungary, border formalities are negligible. With the collapse of black market trading, customs officials can no longer fill their time keeping a look-out for visitors taking in goods to sell for a profit.

You are allowed two litres of wine or one litre of spirits duty free, plus 250 cigarettes (or 250g of tobacco).

Money

1 Forint (Ft) = 100 fillér
£1 = 150 forints   US$1 = 100 forints

Notes and Coins. Coins are issued to the value of 1, 2, 5, 10, 20, 50, 100 and 200 forints. New coins were issued in 1992, but the old ones (with the communist star) will remain in circulation until 1995. You still see a few 50-fillér coins, but these have not been replaced and so will be obsolete by 1995, if not before. Notes come in denominations of 20, 50, 100, 500, 1,000 and 5,000 forints.

Changing Money. Exchange rates are published in various papers, including the national daily the *Magyar Hirlap*. Dollars and deutschmarks in cash or as travellers cheques fetch the best rates.

Most offices of Ibusz, the main national tourist agency, have an exchange counter (*Pénztar*) and are often the most convenient places to change money. Banks or bank-sponsored exchange kiosks offer better rates, however, particularly for travellers cheques. The Kereskedelmi és Hitelbank (known as K & H) has automatic exchange machines at its biggest branches. Banking hours are 9am-2pm Monday to Friday, 9am-noon on Saturday.

Hotels and tourist agencies other than Ibusz, such as Coopturist and Express, offer a poor rate and are best avoided. There are exchange facilities (many of them open 24 hours) at all border points, but don't expect a good deal. Note that wherever you change money, there should be no commission on the transaction.

Keep your exchange receipts in the event that you should need to reconvert forints into hard currency before you leave, which you can do at Ibusz. In theory, you may not take forints out of the country, bar some small change. Since you'll get only a pitiful rate if you try to exchange Hungarian currency abroad, there's little point in flouting this law.

Black Market. Black marketeers, who still hang around in Budapest's railway stations and in a few of the other main tourist haunts, offer an exchange rate slightly over the odds, but are an unsavoury bunch for the most part. Deal only with someone you think you can trust.

Credit Cards. The number of businesses that accept credit and charge cards, including Visa, MasterCard and American Express, has grown rapidly. Most average-to-smart restaurants, hotels and shops accept them nowadays.

Withdrawing cash on a credit card is straightforward at the larger branches of Ibusz and in main town or city banks.

Tipping. Giving a tip, usually 15-20% of the original bill, is done for virtually every service in Hungary. When settling up, say for a meal, tell the waiter the amount you are willing to pay, i.e. if you are told the bill is 400 forints and you want to tip about 15%, say '460 forints' when you hand over the money; if you haven't mastered Hungarian numbers, write it on the tab. Should you offer a 500Ft note and say *köszönöm* (thank you), he or she will probably keep the lot — particularly off the beaten track, where people aren't so used to tourists not knowing local habits.

Work. The EFL boom in Hungary continues unabated with a concerted effort to attract native teachers both to the private and public sectors. The invasion of foreigners has not been so overwhelming as in Prague. But like Prague, Budapest has a glut of teachers and the opportunities that do exist now both for qualified EFL teachers and for native speaker teaching assistants in state schools are mostly in the provinces. Certainly the demand for teachers continues strong. Teachers are poorly paid in Hungary, aside from the top-notch private schools and the British Council.

Hungary has work permit regulations which have more in common with Western European countries. Now it is necessary to arrange the paperwork before leaving your country of residence. And to apply for the working visa, applicants must have a labour permit (obtained by the Hungarian employer) from the appropriate Hungarian labour office stating that no Hungarian national is available to do the job.

The tourist organisation Tourinform in Budapest can provide the addresses of local schools to personal callers. Turning up in a staff room has led to more than one job offer in the past. English is compulsory for so many students that the demand is enormous. Native English speakers are eagerly sought by all state schools. The English Teachers' Association of Hungary (Dózsa György út 104. II. 15, 1068 Budapest (tel 132-8688, fax 131-9376) helps schools all over Hungary to find qualified English teachers. Queries passed on to schools.

The university towns of Debrecen, Miskolc, Szeged and Pécs are all better bets than the over-saturated capital. It is estimated that there are over 100 private language schools in Budapest alone and 300 around the country — mostly for business. The Department of Commerce employs teachers to train bankers, traders and top electrical engineers. Many professionals now need English as part of their work and are both able and prepared to pay for it. Schools taking on TEFL teachers include:

Bell School, Gyula u. 1, 1016 Budapest (tel 185-3460). BA/RSA Certificate/Diploma and several years' teaching experience.

International House, Language School & Teacher Training Institute, Bimbó út 7, 1022 Budapest (PO Box 95, 1364 Budapest). Tel 115-5275/4013, fax 115-5275).

Karinthy Frigyes Gimnázium, Thökoly utca 7, Pestlorinc, 1183 Budapest (tel 787-383).

Katona József Gimnázium, Dózsa György út. 3, 6000 Kecskemét (tel 327-436).

Living Language Seminar, Fejér György u. 8, 1053 Budapest (tel 135-6154, fax 117-9655).

London Studio, PO Box 1617, 1518 Budapest (tel 166-8137, fax 181-1959).

Communications

TELEPHONE

While the most advanced in the region, the Hungarian telephone system is by no means perfect. The old network is gradually being replaced, but millions of homes have been waiting months and even years to be connected. In fact you will usually find it easier to call home than to phone a local restaurant.

Hungary has several types of payphone, the oldest occupying antiquated yellow and green phone boxes which are a thrill to look at but not necessarily to use: you can sometimes wait 20 seconds for the dialling tone. Yellow phones take 5Ft coins and can usually handle only local calls. Red phones, which take 5Ft, 10Ft and 20Ft coins, are capable of both long-distance and international calls, but for the latter you would do better to find one of the newer blue or grey phones (see below). When calling long-distance within Hungary, dial 06, wait for the second tone, then dial the area code and number. For domestic calls the cheap rate operates 6pm-7am and all weekend. The area codes for the major centres are as follows:

Budapest 1	Eger 36	Sopron 99
Debrecen 52	Györ 96	Pécs 72

International Calls. Calling abroad from a public telephone office will be the only option in smaller towns. Generally, however, it is far easier to use one of the new grey public cardphones. Phonecards (*telefon kártya*) are available either with 50 units (*egység*) or 120 units. The rate for calls works out at about $0.76 per minute to the UK, $1.90 to the USA and $2.20 to Australia. For a brief conversation within Europe, the 50-unit card ($3) is perfectly adequate. Blue payphones can also be used for international calls, but you'll need a whole handful of coins.

For the international operator dial 09. The operator can be reached on 01, but you'll need to speak Hungarian.

Telegrams, Telex and Fax. These can be sent from the larger post offices and, in the case of telex and fax, from major hotels.

MAIL

Hungary's postal service is surprisingly efficient but not cheap. Stamps (*bélyeg*) for postcards sent airmail (*légiposta*) cost $0.35 to the UK, $0.70 to the USA. Mail to Britain takes an average of a week and to North America about 10 days. Post offices (*posta*) normally open weekdays 8am-6pm, plus 8am-2pm on Saturdays. Stamps are also on sale at tobacconists *(Trafik)*.

Receiving poste restante (*postá maradó*) can be hit-and-miss in Hungary, and you may prefer to use American Express, which has an office at Deak Ferenc 10 in Budapest.

MEDIA

Newspapers. The Press enjoyed a comparatively high degree of freedom under communism, though there was a tendency for self-censorship. Since the political changes even this has stopped, though *Népszabadság,* the Socialist Party paper and most circulated daily, still makes fairly dull reading. The other main national dailies are the *Magyar Hírlap* (*hírlap* means newspaper in Hungarian) and *Népszava.*

Two English-language papers, *Budapest Sun* and *Budapest Week*, are available in the capital, both costing about $0.70. While probably most useful for their list of exchange rates, weather reports and 'what's on' columns, each contains a digest of the most important national and international events of that week: not great works of journalism but useful if you can't understand Hungarian or don't want to spend $1.50 on a foreign paper. The latter are available in all shapes and sizes in Budapest, from the *International Guardian* to the *Daily Express.* Distribution of British, American and other major European papers to the provinces is limited to the main tourist centres.

Broadcasting. The government opened up local radio and television airwaves for the first time in 1993, though there are still no plans to lift the ban on the granting of licences for regional and national broadcasting.

The capital's Radio Petöfi and Danubius Radio (103.3 Mhz in Budapest) both broadcast news bulletins in English. Radio Bridge (102 Mhz), set up in 1989, was the first English-language commercial radio station in Eastern Europe. It seems to cater mainly for language students, but has a good range of programmes, from music to sport, with news bulletins every hour.

Reception of the World Service is poor, especially in low-lying areas (i.e. most of the country), while the Voice of America can be picked up much more clearly. The tuning scales of Hungarian radios are marked H   Long Wave; K   Medium Wave (AM); R   Short Wave; URH   VHF (FM).

According to most Hungarians, home-produced television programmes are abysmal. Satellite TV is widespread, and many hotels in Budapest have CNN and MTV on throughout the day. Private subscribers receive Sky and Superchannel in English as well as TV-5 in French.

Getting Around

Maps. The map produced by Ibusz is perfectly adequate for most general purposes. It shows all major roads, railways and towns, with Central Budapest and Lake Balaton on the reverse. If you plan to head off the beaten track, you would do well to buy a more detailed map, such as the one published by Hallwag, before leaving home. Once in Hungary, look for the blue *Magyarország Autótérképe* (road map) with a scale of 1:500,000 or the *Magyarország Autóatlasza*, with sketch maps of most towns and villages. If you're driving, ask in tourist offices for *Motoring in Hungary*, price $0.60.

AIR

Trains and buses between them offer a good service, but there is also a domestic airline, Danube Air, which links the capital with more than ten towns and cities around the country. Its fleet consists of small turboprop and jet aircraft.

TRAIN

The rail network, run by Hungarian State Railways (Máv), radiates from Budapest. The main advantages of trains over buses are that fares are generally cheaper and that there are more services per day to principal destinations, e.g. eight trains a day from Budapest to Pécs compared with three buses.

Fares on the express services (*gyorsvonat*) are about double those on ordinary stopping trains (*személyvonat*), with a small surcharge for a reservation (*helyjegy*), which is recommended on a fast train. Note that ticket counters at stations usually bear only the name of the express, not the time nor destination. Therefore you should check on the timetables in advance which service you want: Arrivals (*Erkezö Vonatok*) and Departures (*Induló Vonatok*) are posted up in white and yellow respectively. Specify that you want an express ticket, since otherwise you are likely to be sold the basic fare for a slow train. The only time you might be tempted to pay 50% extra for a first class seat is in summer, when the usual comfort of the ordinary carriages is adversely affected by the heat and crowds.

The Hungarian word for station is *pályaudvar* (with a silent l) usually abbreviated on maps and signs to 'pu'. The locals will think you mad if you ask directions to the pu, just as you'd react if a Hungarian asked the way to a stn. If you have problems communicating what you want at the railway station, or if the queues are terrible, you can book tickets through Ibusz, but this will be 5% more expensive. Note that international tickets must currently be paid for in hard currency.

Facilities. Trains are generally punctual, and long-distance services usually offer reasonably good buffet facilities. Most town stations have money-changers (official and unofficial) and a left-luggage deposit (*ruhatár* or *csomagmegörzö*). Waiting rooms can be a positive delight (the one at Debrecen station has shelves of books and newspapers), though using them for overnight kipping is technically illegal: whether or not you are moved on will depend on the demeanour of the station officials on duty.

Rail Passes. The comparatively cheap fares mean that the rail passes sold to tourists, and valid for 10, 20, or 30 days, aren't a particularly good deal, though they are worth buying if you plan to make several long trips by express. For details in advance contact Danube Travel (6 Conduit St, London W1R 9TD; 071-493 0263) or Eurotrain (52 Grosvenor Gardens, SW1W 0AG; 071-730 3402).

Special Tourist Season Tickets, valid for 7-10 days, are also available: ask at any railway station or Ibusz office.

BUS

Buses (operated by the national coach company, Volán) have the edge over the trains when it comes to city-to-city routes which bypass Budapest, since this avoids having to change. However, long-distance journeys for which there is a direct train tend to be slower by bus, partly because of stops at roadside cafés.

For short popular routes, such as from Budapest to Esztergom, there are dozens of services a day. For longer journeys, you tend to find a clump of departures between 5am and 8am and then no others until late afternoon. Long-distance buses can sometimes be flagged down away from bus stops. Normally, however, you'll do better to go to the bus station (*autóbuszállomás* or *autóbusz pályaudvar*).

DRIVING

While in Budapest traffic is heavy and standards of driving poor, elsewhere the roads are fairly empty and the drivers polite. Hungarians tend to drive fairly slowly and carefully, sticking conscientiously to the slow lane on a motorway unless overtaking.

There is a good road network, with reasonable surfaces along the principal routes. Single figure roads 1-8 are main highways (all but highway 8 radiating from Budapest), two and three figure roads secondary routes. A road number in, say, the 40s or 400s will lie between highways 4 and 5, though it may not necessarily branch off highway 4. The four motorways are gradually being extended: the M1 so far goes only as far as Györ (and has a single carriageway stretch which is notorious for head-on crashes), but will eventually reach Vienna; the M7, which is complete, extends from Budapest to Zamárdi on Lake Balaton; the M3 serves Gyöngyös, en route to the industrial city of Miskolc; and the M5 runs towards Kecskemét but is still unfinished. There is a ring road around Budapest, enabling you to avoid the downtown area.

Rules of the Road. Speed limits are as follows: built-up areas 60km/h, outside built-up areas 80 or 100km/h (watch for signs) and on motorways 120km/h. Minor offences, including speeding, are punished with on-the-spot fines. Driving with even a trace of alcohol in your blood is considered far more serious. Random breath testing is rare, but you will be in deep trouble if you are involved in an accident while even mildly drunk.

Note that cars may turn right on a red light: this is more a warning for pedestrians, who will also discover that zebra crossings are seldom taken seriously, particularly in Budapest.

Fuel. The price of petrol (*benzin*) is about $0.90 for a litre of 98-octane (extra, equivalent to 4-star) or 95-octane (unleaded) and $0.85 for 92-octane (super). Diesel is 30% cheaper than regular petrol. Unleaded petrol (*olommentes uzemanyag*) is available at an ever-increasing number of stations.

Documents. Driving your own vehicle into Hungary involves a minimum of red tape. If you have a Western European licence plate, officials often assume that you have third party insurance (compulsory in Hungary), and don't even bother to check. On the whole, however, if you don't have a green card, you will be required to purchase a third party policy at the border: this covers damage only to persons, not property.

Motoring Organisation. The Magyar Autóklub or MAK (Rómer Flóris út 4/a, Budapest) extends its services to members of foreign motoring organisations. The breakdown service (*segélyszolgálat*), available from yellow patrol cars, operates on main roads at weekends and around the clock daily on motorways. Help can be summoned by ringing from petrol stations or roadside phones displaying a yellow sign.

Car Rental. Do not be fooled by attractive-looking daily rates (payable in hard currency), starting at $20 for a small Lada. On top of this will be a charge per kilometre and 25% tax. Unlimited mileage deals are usually better value, with a daily rate including tax of around $60.

Several international rental agencies are represented in Hungary (including Hertz, Avis and Budget), some operating through different tourism organisations, such as Ibusz and Coopturist. Hertz has seven regional outlets besides three in the capital, but this is still the exception: while simple to arrange in Budapest and by Lake Balaton, renting a car on the spot can be difficult in smaller tourist centres: to play safe, make enquiries first in Budapest and pre-book if necessary. Otherwise, enquire at the nearest Ibusz office.

Accidents. Accidents involving injury should be reported to the police promptly (dial 07 in Budapest, 007 outside the capital). Theoretically, cars with damaged bodywork cannot leave the country without the driver producing a police statement about the circumstances, but this is rarely enforced.

HITCH-HIKING

Hitching is not wildly exciting if you don't speak Hungarian, though most drivers seem to prefer carrying hitchers along in silence anyway. Provided you are standing on a suitable stretch of road with a reasonable flow of slow-moving traffic, you shouldn't have to wait more than half an hour for a lift.

CYCLING

Conditions for cyclists are promising: the terrain is mostly flat and there is a good network of minor surfaced roads. The routes along the Danube and around Lake Balaton may seem ideal for cycling, but the traffic is heavy. For a more relaxed ride choose a quieter area, such as the valleys either north or south of Lake Balaton, or the vineyards surrounding Eger and Tokaj in the east of the country. Note that cyclists are banned from single digit roads.

The tourist authority produces a booklet called *Cycling in Hungary,* which provides suggestions for one-, three- or five-day routes, as well as a list of bicycle shops and repair outlets in Budapest and recommended routes for leaving the capital. Some long journeys are best covered by rail: most trains have a guards van where you can put your bike for a small charge. Larger stations can store bikes in their left-luggage offices.

Bike Rental: you can hire bikes at some train stations (usually in summer only), Balaton campsites and a few other rental outlets: the youth tourism organisation Express is a good source of information. Expect to pay $3-5 a day for a heavy bicycle with a minimum of gears.

BOAT

Several ferries operate on the Danube and Tisza rivers and on Lake Balaton.

River trips are seasonal: the navigation season on the Danube usually lasts from early April to late October, though boats run regularly only between May and early September.

Ferries are operated by the Hungarian shipping company Mahart, the most popular trips from Budapest being the 90-minute excursion to Szentendre on the Danube Bend or the five-hour trip to Esztergom. You can pick up a free copy of the Danube timetable from the national or international landing stations in Budapest: see page 231.

CITY TRANSPORT

As throughout Eastern Europe, urban transport systems are excellent and very cheap. Tickets must be purchased before you board the bus, tram or metro, usually from a kiosk or machine. If you intend to stay in one place for any length of time, monthly passes are a bargain.

Finding a bed for the night in Hungary is seldom a problem. You can approach the hotel, hostel, etc. independently, though in a large town you may prefer to go to Ibusz or another tourist agency: either to save you from traipsing around several hotels or to arrange private accommodation. They should also be able to reserve rooms for you in another town, though will charge you for the telephone call. Note that Ibusz offices outside Budapest open Saturday mornings only at weekends.

Hotels and Pensions. While hotels (*szállodák*) are given star ratings from one to five, pensions (*panziók*) are simply classed 1 or 2, with the occasional 3 in the provinces. A class one pension is broadly equivalent to a three-star hotel, with little difference in price or facilities; both include breakfast in the cost of a room. Hotels and pensions, whatever the category, should provide toilet paper, soap and towels.

A one-star hotel or second-class pension should be perfectly adequate if you don't mind sharing a bathroom: expect to pay $15-25 for a double, sometimes more in Budapest, sometimes less in the country. Note that accommodation in Lake Balaton is more expensive than in the capital. For a room offering greater comfort and a few more facilities, be prepared to pay $40-60 for a double, not much less for a single.

Booking in advance from abroad by mail, fax or telephone is no guarantee that a room will be kept for you, so try to get an acknowledgment in writing or by fax from the hotel. You can of course book through any Ibusz office abroad, though it is likely to offer only a limited choice of moderately expensive establishments. The Hungarian tourist board publishes a booklet called simply *Hotel* (available free from tourist offices), which lists hotels and pensions with their star ratings and facilities.

Hostels. Express, Hungary's youth tourism organisation, oversees the country's network of youth hostels. It runs several permanent hostels of its own, some of which barely differ from a one-star hotel (in looks and price). Most (cheaper) hostels open only in the summer, usually just from early July to late August. Coachloads of students from neighbouring countries can fill a hostel in a flash, so it's worth trying to book ahead whenever possible. The location of summer hostels changes each year. Express can give you the relevant addresses: the head office is in Budapest (see page 233) and there are offices in all the main towns.

Hostels rarely seem interested in seeing an IYHF membership or a student card, though you should always proffer both in case you qualify for a discount.

Private Rooms. The number of houses offering private accommodation has doubled in the last few years. More and more Hungarians are bypassing the booking agents, either by approaching travellers direct at transport terminals or, in the provinces, by putting up a sign in their window offering *szoba* (rooms). On the whole, however, the easiest way to arrange private accommodation is through one of the tourist organisations, principally Ibusz and Cooptourist. Ibusz grades rooms as first, second and occasionally third class. These categories can be misleading, however, since even a sofa in the sitting room can be called first class accommodation. As a rough guide, expect to pay $5-15 for a single, $10-20 for a double room: usually somewhere in between, veering towards the bottom in the provinces and towards the top in Budapest. Watch out for extras, such as a steep 30% charge for staying less than four nights at one address. Although breakfast is rarely included, the occasional hostess may offer you some sweet tea and cream cheese on a bread roll.

Camping. Hungary is well set up for campers, though many of the 140 sites run by the Magyar Camping & Caravanning Club (MCCC) are on the shores of Lake Balaton. It publishes a country map which lists all campsites on the reverse, with their category, facilities and dates of opening. The tourist board's *Camping* booklet includes a full list too. It is not normally necessary to pre-book, except possibly in July and August. Go either to a tourist office or, in Budapest, to the MCCC information office at Ullöi út 6.

Whereas three-star campsites tend to offer the kind of facilities you'd find in France (such as supermarkets and discos), one-star sites may have a café but not much else. Rates are calculated according to the space you occupy plus a per capita rate depending on the class of site. For an average tent you shouldn't expect to pay more than $5. Some of the larger campsites on Lake Balaton and elsewhere have bungalows, designed mainly for families or people travelling in a group of four.

Camping in the wild is forbidden but plenty of young people do it, especially in the forests of the Danube Bend.

Rural Accommodation. Farm cottages for rent and bed-and-breakfast style guest houses in the provinces can be booked through regional tourist offices, each of which should have a list of those in their area. The rustic furnishings, elderly folk in traditional costumes and horses are peddled as part of the attraction.

Eating and Drinking

Compared with other Eastern European countries, Hungary is a gastronomic delight. The range of dishes and restaurants makes other Eastern Europeans weep. Prices are not as low as they used to be, but still offer extraordinarily good value for money. It is hard to spend much more than $5 on dinner unless you want to push the boat out, and easy to fill up for $1-2.

Hungarians love their food and enjoy big, filling meals. This is definitely not a place to be on a diet: many savoury dishes are fried and based on a sauce made from melted pork fat and flour. Paprika is another ingredient that unites most Hungarian cooking, both in the more familiar powdered form and as whole peppers — red or green, hot or mild. A visit to any market will introduce you to the astonishing range available.

Hungary has a weird but often wonderful cuisine, dominated by meat. Brains, tripe and boar's head are not uncommon items on a menu, though the real regulars are pork and turkey breast. The famous goulash (*gulyás*) is descended from a thick Magyar soup. In Hungary it is still more like soup than stew, and is quite often less fiery than foreign imitations. While always tasty, there are plenty of other more unusual dishes. *Halászlé,* for example, is a soup-cum-stew made most commonly with carp (*ponty*): this is a bony fish, so be prepared to do battle. Battery-farming doesn't really exist in Hungary and you can rely on chicken being good: *paprikás csirke* (chicken paprika) is popular and tasty.

You usually have to order vegetables separately from your main meal, and a lot of locals don't seem to bother. Despite the long and often varied menus, vegetarians are not well catered for. Even soups and vegetable dishes usually include bacon or ham. Vegetarians should look out for *gomba* (mushrooms) or *rántotta* (scrambled egg, not to be confused with *rántott,* which means deep-fried), but you may well have to rely on cakes to fill you up.

Elongated doughnuts called *lángos* — served either plain or with garlic sauce, sour cream, etc. — are one of Hungary's most delicious snacks. Ice cream (*fagylalt*) is ubiquitous, and irresistible more because of the cost than the quality.

Restaurants. For a simple, filling snack, stand-up counters are ideal, though most open only during the day. You can usually choose from several kinds of sausage, salami and blood pudding served with bread; gherkins are extra. Coffee bars (*eszpresszós*) tend to offer fewer snacks, but have a bigger range of drinks and possibly somewhere to sit down. Self-service cafeterias (*önkiszolgáló étterem*) purvey delicacies like liver dumplings, often eaten by the locals for breakfast.

But since meals are so cheap, even budget travellers can eat out in some style. Most restaurants (*étterem* or *vendéglö*) offer a set menu, normally consisting of soup, a meat dish and a pudding, and typically costing around $2. Dining à la carte will be more expensive but probably also more interesting. 'Ready-to-eat' main dishes (which arrive at the table within minutes of your ordering them and are rarely piping hot) cost less than those which are made to order: menus usually list the two categories separately.

Most beer and wine bars serve at least some food, and are much more relaxed than your average restaurant. You can't expect such a good-quality meal, but the food is nearly always traditional. Bars tend to stay open later than restaurants too, particularly in Budapest, where they cater for Western tourists' drinking and eating habits. Hungarians eat their main meal at lunchtime and most restaurants close by 10pm. Note that few restaurants open on Sundays, even in the capital.

Menus: your first encounter with a Hungarian menu (*étlap*) can be daunting, since you probably won't recognise a single word other than *paprikás*. The most important words to master are the names of the categories on the menu. Common headings are as follows:

levesek — soups	*sajtok* — cheese
fözelekek — vegetables	*készételek* — ready-to-eat main courses

köretek — side dishes
saláták — salads
tészták — pastries and pancakes
hideg meleg elöételek — hot and cold appetisers
szendvics — sandwich

halételek — fish main courses
konyhafönök anjánlata — house specialities
frissensültek — light refreshments

Patisserie. Urban Hungarians while away many an hour enjoying coffee and pastries in a café, and you would do well to join them. Sour cream and other dairy products such as whey and curd cheese are used in many savoury dishes, but they appear with most dramatic effect in pastries and cakes, which in Budapest rival those of Vienna and cost a fraction of the price. Cake shops (*cukraszda*) are hard to resist wherever you are, though some provincial patisserie is absurdly sweet and artificially flavoured. Cakes to look out for include:

Gundel palacsinta — pancake with walnuts, chocolate and rum
dobostorta — sponge with chocolate and caramel
rakott metélt — noodles baked with sour cream, cottage cheese, nuts and raisins
retes — similar to strudel

Buying Food in Shops. Shopping for a picnic in Hungary is much like it is in the rest of Europe. Small delicatessens (*csemege*) and supermarkets with a delicatessen counter sell cheese and salami (another Hungarian staple, coming in all shapes and sizes), and often bread (*kenyér*) too; the latter is usually white. Good quality fruit (*gyümölcs*) is most abundant in season, but stalls selling a wide variety do a good trade at any time of year.

DRINKING

Hungarians do not seem to consume alcohol as single-mindedly as some of their Eastern European cousins, and many locals drink Coke with their meals. It is technically against the law to drink in public places, though no one is likely to object unless you go completely over the top.

Wine. Hungarian wine, once the favoured tipple of European monarchs, can be exceptionally good and is exported in large quantities. About three-quarters of it is white, mostly on the sweet side. The two most well-known wines are Egri Bikavér (the notorious Bull's Blood from Eger) and Tokaj, a sweet aperitif made from rotted grapes grown in eastern Hungary (better than it sounds). For a reliable table wine, try red Kadarka or white Olasz riesling, grown extensively on the Great Danube Plain. The other wine regions lie to the north of Lake Balaton around Badacsony, and around Pécs and Sopron.

A bottle of plonk in an ordinary restaurant will cost $2-3, sometimes less than that. Prices in shops start at under $1, rising to about $4 for a good Aszú Tokaj. *Minösegi* on bottle labels means 'best quality'. Wine bars (*borozó*) sometimes sell wine straight from the barrel.

Beer. Some beer (*sör,* pronounced 'shir') is made locally, such as Köbanyai in Budapest and Szalon in Pécs. Popular imported versions include Tuborg and Amstel, though most Hungarians prefer Czech beer, which is available almost everywhere and far superior to Hungary's own efforts.

Beer normally comes in bottles ($0.75-1.00 in a restaurant, $0.50 in a shop), but you can often get draught beer (*csapalt sör*) in a *söröző* (pub). In this case, you must simply choose the size of receptacle: *picolo* (small glass), *pohár* (medium glass) or *korsó* (jug).

Spirits. Locally-produced gin like Borovicka is a reasonable approximation to Beefeater or Gordon's, though you'd do better to try the Hungarian fruit brandies (*palinka*): the most famous is *barackpálinka*, an apricot brandy but more like schnapps. A mysterious dark brown drink called Unicum is sold in appealing round bottles but tastes disgusting: it is said to be good for stomach ailments.

Soft Drinks. Coffee (*kávé*), drunk strong, is good though not always piping hot. Cappuccino has made significant inroads, though only in Budapest's better cafés can you expect the real McCoy. The quality of tea is almost universally abysmal, which Hungarians try to disguise by serving it sweet.

Everyone seems to drink Coke and Pepsi all the time, even though a can costs around $0.60. Fruit juices such as plum, peach and tomato are good but not particularly cheap either. Orange juice (*narancs*) is cheaper but tends to be squash rather than fresh. You can buy bottled mineral water (*ásványvíz*), but the local tapwater is excellent and will probably taste better than what you're used to back home. In many town parks, fountains provide drinking water which the Hungarians use without hesitation.

Even under communism, the authorities devoted much time and money to the restoration of its churches, palaces and castles, not only in Budapest but throughout the country. The enthusiasm for preserving the past continues unabated. There is a tendency to over-restore, most easily noticed in the streets of old Buda, which look just too perfect. Pride in the past is also reflected in the large range of museums across the country. Most are best for a stroll-through rather than a detailed study, though labelling in English is increasingly common. Admission to museums and buildings is usually under $0.50; most close on Mondays.

THE GREAT OUTDOORS

Hiking and Riding. Hungary's dry summers provide an ideal climate for hiking. The best areas for this are in the north, including the woods around Visegrád and Badacsony, north of Budapest; the Mátra mountains near Eger, including the country's highest peak (Mt Kekes), a mere 1,014m above sea level; and the Bükk mountains west of Miskolk. Don't expect to explore any really wild country, though, partly because there is no network of hostels or huts for hikers, and most campsites are concentrated near towns.

A fine way to enjoy the hills is on horseback. Hungarians love horse-riding passionately, and you can arrange treks easily in the above-mentioned districts: ask at the tourist office locally or abroad. Ibusz organises riding tours in all regions of Hungary but only in the summer season. Expect to pay around £700 for ten days (not including flights), though shorter and longer trips are also available. Some experience is necessary.

For permits to visit protected nature reserves and bird sanctuaries, apply to the National Office for the Protection of Nature, Költö út 12, Budapest 12.

Swimming and Watersports. The most popular place to swim is Lake Balaton, where the large number of Western tourists is catered to by a steadily increasing number of officially designated nude or topless beaches. During the high season, when the lake resorts are full to bursting, seek refuge in the numerous public swimming pools (*uszoda*) or thermal baths, though the latter are far better in Budapest.

Watersports also thrive in the resorts around Lakes Balaton and Velence, especially sailing and windsurfing. Students are sometimes eligible for a 50% discount on the hire of equipment.

Skiing. In winter, even Hungary's modest mountains provide some scope for skiing between Christmas and April. In addition to the Buda hills near the capital, more challenging skiing can be found at Bánkút in the Bükk Mountains, where there are five runs and a tourist complex.

The language barrier puts most Hungarian theatre and cinema out of reach of visitors, but music can be enjoyed almost everywhere, from the gypsy buskers in Budapest's Vörösmarty tér to the chamber concerts in Baroque palaces in the provinces. For a reasonably complete listing of what's on in both the capital and elsewhere, pick up the free monthly tourist booklet *Programme in Hungary,* which covers both highbrow and popular events. While the bulk of good entertainment goes on in Budapest, other cities like Szeged and Békéscsaba have regular concerts and summer festivals.

Cinema. Films (*mozi*) are advertised everywhere on large cylindrical notice boards, as well as in the local press. In Budapest there are usually four or five English sound-track films (*mozi angol*) showing on any weekday and a few extra at weekends; these are more likely to be golden oldies like *Gone With the Wind* or newer stand-bys like *Raiders of the Lost Ark* than new and exciting films. Most movies, however, are dubbed into Hungarian, indicated by the word *szin* (short for *szinkronizált*) or 'mb'. *Feliratos* means subtitled. Interpreting the starting times can also be tricky: n6 = 5.15, f6 = 5.30, de = am, du = pm.

Music, Ballet and Opera. Music is taken very seriously in Hungary, the birthplace of Liszt, Bartók and Kodály. By Western standards, tickets are ridiculously cheap: you can pay less than $5 to see high quality productions. Light opera and musicals are almost as common as more high-brow works, and ballet also has a big following: the Györ Ballet Company has a particularly good (and well-deserved) reputation.

In terms of popular music, jazz and heavy metal (both indigenous and foreign) have the biggest followings. What is considered as traditional Hungarian folk music is really gypsy music, whose origins are a long way east of the Danube. Nowadays, it is almost impossible to hear gypsy music in the villages, so you will have to content yourself with the version heard in city restaurants, where the calibre of performers is highly variable. A typical band consists of at least one violin, drums and a cimbalom, a kind of dulcimer whose strings are struck with sticks.

SPORT

The present national soccer team is a shadow of the stunning side which dominated European football during the early 1950s. Even so, soccer (*futball*) is still the main spectator sport in Hungary, played with enthusiasm throughout the country. Ferencvaros and MTK-VM, both from Budapest, tend to dominate the first division of the league. The season runs from September to June with a break during January and February. Tickets for games — even internationals — are normally easy to obtain at the gate.

Continuing the Magyar tradition of horsemanship, racing has a big following in Hungary. Trotting, as popular as the *Galopp*, is a novel form of racing which is well worth seeing. Other spectator sports include motor racing. The first Grand Prix to be held in a socialist country took place in Budapest in 1987 and has become an annual event, held each August at a track 12 miles/20km northeast of the capital, in the hilly region of Mogyoród.

Under communism, people arriving from other Eastern bloc countries used to be dazzled by Hungary's brightly-lit and well-stocked shops full of luxuries like chocolate and Levis, unavailable in their own countries. Despite changes elsewhere, the choice of goods is still far better in Hungary than elsewhere — particularly in downtown Budapest, where shops don't look vastly different from those in a Western capital city.

While the cost of living has increased sharply for Hungarians, prices are still comparatively low for tourists from Western Europe. Austrians pour across the border in droves to buy not only cheap food and drink but also household goods and basic clothing.

Shops normally open 10am-6pm, plus Saturday mornings.

Gifts and Souvenirs. Classical records, cassettes and CDs are not much cheaper than in Western Europe unless you choose the local recordings, which are cheap but not necessarily good. An average imported CD costs $17, compared to $12 or less for a Hungarian recording. Cassettes go for about $6.50.

Good quality local crafts are probably best bought in Budapest, where you can also pick up embroidered linens and blouses sold by Romanian gypsies, who gather at the capital's most popular tourist sights. To see gypsy sellers outside the tourist context, visit any outdoor market where they can be seen selling flowers, herbs and other produce. For a novel but no less typical gift, buy a tin of ground paprika or a salami: $15 for a whole paprika salami may sound a lot, but it goes a long way and keeps for six months.

There is a new breed of antique shops in Hungary, but these cater mostly to local millionaires and very wealthy tourists. The average traveller will find more to buy in the secondhand bookshops, which often stock old books in English and other European languages at bargain prices.

Tobacco. Everyone seems to smoke, particularly in Budapest. Marlboro and Camel are the most popular foreign cigarettes, costing about $1.40 for 20. Among native brands, Sopianae are rather like filtered Gitanes, Sopianae Junior being slightly milder. The average Hungarian, however, favours Symphonia, which are fairly rough but not too strong; the filterless variety is only for the hardened smoker.

Health and Hygiene

Hungary carries few health risks for travellers, one of the biggest binds being the mosquitoes in summer — not carriers of disease but still a nuisance. Figures relating to the incidence of HIV/Aids are not completely reliable, but are comparatively low. All blood donations are screened.

Medical Treatment. The standard of health care is very high in Hungary, particularly when compared to what is available in neighbouring countries. (Budapest's famous Petö Institute leads the world in the treatment of handicapped children.) The number of Western Europeans who go to Hungary for dental treatment attests to the good quality (as well as affordability) of local dentistry too.

Most towns and cities have clinics with English-speaking doctors. If you have only mild symptoms, a visit to the chemists (look for the symbol of a pair of scales or the word *patika* or *gyógyszertár*) is often easier than going to see a doctor. But you'll be lost without an English-speaking friend or a dictionary. Guesswork won't help: the word for painkiller, for example, is *fájdalomcsillapító.*

Emergencies: dial 04 for an ambulance, or ask a taxi to take you to the nearest hospital (*kórház*).

Crime and Safety

Following the trend in the rest of Eastern Europe, crime has risen in the 1990s, though the scale of the problem is small compared with that faced elsewhere. All the usual rules apply as far as avoiding crime is concerned, however, particularly in Budapest after 10pm, when most people head home.

The police (*rendörség*) are generally helpful if you've been robbed.

Help and Information

Agencies designed to help tourists are springing up all over the place, particularly in Budapest. Most offer a similar range of services, including transport reservations, accommodation bookings and currency exchange, but few are designed to handle simple queries such as 'which bus do I take to get to. . .': whether you get an answer will probably depend on whether or not the particular member of staff happens to know that bus route. Look for the sign *Információ, Iroda* or *Idegenforgalmi* when you are seeking advice in stations or offices.

Ibusz, the largest (and now privatised) travel company in Hungary, has scores of offices throughout the country, including about a dozen in Budapest. Its offices normally open 7.30am-4.30pm Monday to Friday and 7.30am-12.45pm on Saturdays (though at weekends the range of services may be limited to currency exchange). Tourinform, affiliated to the Hungarian tourist board, is usually more helpful than Ibusz, though it has few information offices outside Budapest. The Mosaic series of small-format booklets published by Tourinform on specific topics (e.g. cycling, folklore, etc.) contain a degree of hard information, though are typically bland in style. Other competing agencies include Express (the youth travel agency) and Cooptourist.

In the regions, local offices are better sources of information than national agencies like Ibusz. In addition to Budapest Tourist in the capital, there are about 20 county tourist offices, whose names are taken from the region rather than the town in which they are located: Mecsek Tourist in Pécs, Ciklámen Tourist in Györ, etc. These offices sell detailed maps of the town and region, and can advise on local excursions by public transport, bicycle or on foot. They can also book accommodation outside their region.

Corvina, Hungary's main English-language publisher, produces a series of books about the country, including on history and food. The rather turgid style and format has yet to be shaken off.

Tourist Information Abroad. Danube Travel, 6 Conduit Street, London W1R 9TG (tel 071-493 0263; fax 071-493 6963) represents Ibusz in the UK. In return for a cheque for £2 and a stamped addressed envelope, they will send you an information pack.

Americans should contact the Hungarian Travel Bureau at Suite 1104, One Parker Plaza, Fort Lee, NJ 07024 (tel 201-592-8585; fax 201-592-8736) for advance information about travel in Hungary.

BUDAPEST

While Hungary's first city may not have the architectural kudos of its neighbours Prague or Vienna, Budapest enjoys a dynamism not found in any other Central European capital. Certainly, it has a much more genuine feel than other capitals, its broad streets buzzing with traffic and two million people going about their daily lives. Budapest receives more visitors than any other city in Eastern Europe after Prague, but it lacks the city-under-siege atmosphere. For a long time the most Western of all the communist capitals, Budapest has not been so utterly transformed by the new commer-cialisation that has had such visibly dramatic effects elsewhere.

The not-so-blue and fast-flowing Danube cuts the capital in two: hilly, charming Buda on the west bank, and flat, bustling Pest on the east. Clambering over the hills in Buda reveals fine views at every turn, while the more utilitarian parts of Pest are enlivened by glimpses of the west bank. In the fifteenth century Buda was one of the most important cities in Europe, but it declined after the Turkish siege, which destroyed large parts of it. Baroque reconstruction followed eventually, with more building after the siege of 1849. Most of Pest was built in the second half of the 19th century too, when the whole city vied with Vienna to be the shining jewel in the Austro-Hungarian crown.

Seventy percent of Budapest was destroyed during the Second World War, but the restoration of churches, palaces and houses has been painstaking, going a long way to recreating the city's past glory. The obliteration of the war is most evident in the close juxtaposition of old and new, but since many buildings in Pest are replicas of those destroyed it is not always easy to tell what is real and what isn't. Buildings exist in every imaginable architectural style from Baroque to Oriental, though it is the undulating, sinuous shapes of the Art Nouveau architecture which has left the greatest mark. Pock-marked walls are reminders of both the war and the 1956 uprising, and more recent damage has been wrought by the appalling pollution, which in summer casts a heavy cloud of smog over the city and has blackened many buildings. The city council's campaigns to try to reduce pollution have met with mixed success. Hundreds of Trabant owners have taken advantage of favourable credit deals to trade in their old bangers for cleaner new cars, but the offer to enjoy three years' free public transport in exchange for dumping a Trabant on the scrap heap has met with less enthusiasm.

Budapest has plenty of sights, but the city's greatest appeal lies in the outstanding architecture of Pest. Every street reveals some marvel, even the manholes are a work of art. Few things beat simply strolling the streets, stopping periodically for coffee and cakes in one of the elegant 19th-century cafés. The Hungarian capital is often compared adversely with Prague and Vienna, but Budapest can hold its own against any city in Europe.

CITY LAYOUT

The Danube (Duna) is a point of constant reference, whether or not you cross it: you are more likely to go under the river than over it. Pest, on the east bank, is the commercial heart of the capital and the area in which you are likely to spend most of your time. The centre of the district, known as the Inner City (Belváros), is enclosed by the so-called Nagykörút, a huge semicircular boulevard which crosses five districts and has five different names. Wide avenues radiate from it, the most important being Rákóczi út, a noisy commercial street, and Andrássy út, a grand thoroughfare modelled on the Champs-Elysées; the latter runs northeast from the centre to Hosök tere (Heroes Square), a grandiloquent patio backing onto Városliget, the city's main park. A short walk from the western ends of both streets Vörösmarty tér is the focus of Pest, with the newest and smartest shops here and in the surrounding streets, particularly along the pedestrian Váci útca. This last street runs south from the square and should not be confused with the broad Váci út which runs north from Nyugati train station.

Buda is the most historical part of the city. The Castle District, at its heart, is a peaceful haven after the bustle and traffic of Pest, but tourists usually outnumber locals, most of whom are trying to sell you something. Just south of the Castle District is Gellért Hill, a tree-smothered cliff and a useful landmark topped by a statue of liberty bearing a palm leaf.

Maps. Budapest has yet to kick away all the traces of tyranny; evidence is dotted around the capital in the form of shabby shops and monuments to miscellaneous communists. But street names have been changed with greater alacrity here than in other Eastern European cities. Check the date on any map before you buy it: roadname changes continue unabated, so no street plan will be completely accurate.

The most useful map for general purposes is the *Budapest: Stadtplan* or the *Budapest Belváros: Idegenforgalmi Térképe,* both of which cost about $0.50. The Cartographia city map, available for $2.50 from information offices and street traders, covers the whole metropolitan area and has a street index, but is not particularly easy to use and doesn't mark sights. All maps include a plan of the metro.

Getting Around

ARRIVAL AND DEPARTURE

Air. Ferihegy Airport (pronounced Ferry-hedj) is 9 miles/14km southeast of the city centre. Most international flights arrive at Terminal 1, but all Malév flights use the smaller and more cheerful Terminal 2, 4 miles/6km beyond. Ferihegy is one of the few airports in the world to have duty-free on arrival.

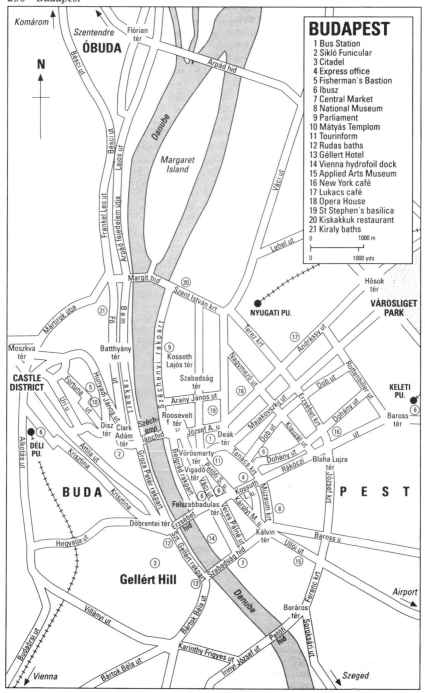

BUDAPEST

1 Bus Station
2 Sikló Funicular
3 Citadel
4 Express office
5 Fisherman's Bastion
6 Ibusz
7 Central Market
8 National Museum
9 Parliament
10 Mátyás Templom
11 Tourinform
12 Rudas baths
13 Géllert Hotel
14 Vienna hydrofoil dock
15 Applied Arts Museum
16 New York café
17 Lukacs café
18 Opera House
19 St Stephen's basilica
20 Kiskakkuk restaurant
21 Kiraly baths

0   1000 m

0   1000 yds

The 30-minute taxi ride into town should cost $8-10, assuming you don't get one of the many drivers who try to rip off new arrivals; insist that the meter is turned on. The Airport Administration or LRI (157-6283) runs a private minibus service from Terminal 1, offering a lift to wherever you like for about $5. But for less than half the price, you can take the regular airport bus, which serves both terminals and runs every 30 minutes to Erzsébet tér bus station downtown. To save a few more pennies, catch local bus 93 to the end of metro line 3 (Köbánya-Kispest), and then head downtown from there; this last journey takes about an hour.

Internal flights on Danube Air leave from Budaors Airport, 10 miles/ 16km from the city.

Rail. Budapest has three railway stations: the grand and imposing Keleti pu (Eastern Station), the smaller Nyugati pu (Western Station), both in Pest, and the Déli pu (Southern Station) in Buda. The destinations served by these stations can be quite illogical: it makes sense that trains to Eger and Miskolc in the east should leave from the eastern station, but none whatsoever that those to Debrecen, which is further east, leave from Nyugati pu; in fact most trains from the western station head east or north.

You can buy a ticket in advance at any station (and each has a full list of departures you can refer to), so make sure you know which one your train leaves from. The international ticket kiosks at Keleti and Nyugati are nearly always busy: arrive as soon after 8am as possible or go instead to Déli pu, which is much quieter. All train information is available 6am-8pm by phoning 227-860 or 429-150.

Stations have 24-hour buffets and luggage deposits, but not non-stop exchange or accommodation desks. Most such facilities have closed by 7 or 8pm.

Bus. Most buses (including international services) use the centrally located Erzsébet tér terminal in Pest. For international departures call 172-562 or 172-369, though you'd do better to go in person. The ticket office opens 8am-8pm. Information on domestic services is available 6am-8pm by calling 172-966, 172-318 or 187-315. Some services east of the Danube leave from the capital's second bus terminal on Hungária körút, near Népstadion metro station.

Boat. Mahart hydrofoils linking Vienna and Budapest dock at the Belgrád quay (*rakpart*) between Erzsébet and Szabadság bridges. You can buy tickets here between 8am and 4pm, until noon at weekends. The upstream trip to Vienna takes five hours.

Driving. Traffic congestion is a big problem in Budapest, alleviated only slightly by the park-and-ride service which operates at the metro termini. Cars are banned from the Castle District and a few streets around Vörösmarty tér, but traffic is heavy in most of the city. The elaborate one-way system in Pest is a nightmare for the uninitiated and on busy streets it is often illegal to turn left against oncoming traffic. If you insist on driving, careful planning is essential; try to obtain a map with directional arrows or else ask for specific instructions.

Parking is a headache which the locals solve by ditching their cars almost anywhere, usually on the pavement. Metered parking is cheap, but you're unlikely to find a place.

Car Rental: owing to the hassles of driving downtown, you would do well to hire or drop off your vehicle at the airport. Downtown, you can arrange rental at most tourist offices or direct from the car hire agent: Avis, for example, is based at Szervita tér 8 (118-4158).

CITY TRANSPORT

You can explore much of Budapest on foot, but the public transport network is cheap and easy to use. Services operate roughly 4.30am-11pm, with a few bus and tram routes running through the night.

You must buy tickets (about $0.25) in advance from news kiosks, tobacconists (look for the *Trafik* sign) and from machines in metro stations. At peak times, queues for tickets in stations are long, so buy several at a time. When buying a ticket from a machine, you must put in the exact amount of money. Yellow tickets are for trams and the metro, blue ones for buses. Cancel the ticket when you board a vehicle or enter a station. Inspections are not infrequent, the on-the-spot fine for fare-dodging being $4.50. If most people don't appear to have a ticket, this is because they carry a pass. Day passes are only worth buying if you plan to make at least eight journeys.

Metro. The oldest of the three metro lines, laid in 1896, was the first underground line built on the Continent. But the system has lasted well, and the metro is by far the best way to get around Budapest.

Line 1 (yellow) runs from Vörösmarty tér to Mexicöi útja, via Heroes' Square; Line 2 (red) is the only one to burrow under the Danube, going from Déli pu to Ors vezér tere, via Keleti pu; Line 3 (blue) runs from Köbánya-Kispest to Arpád hid, north of the centre. All three lines intersect at Deák tér, in the heart of Pest. Note that you must punch a ticket every time you board a train, including when you change lines.

Buses and Trams. Both forms of transport are often crowded and best avoided in the rush hour. One of the most useful (and scenic) bus routes is no. 16, which travels between Erzsébet tér and the Castle District across the Chain Bridge. Tram no. 2 also has a pretty route, rattling alongside the Danube from the Central Market to the Parliament building.

HEV. The suburban railway system, known as HEV, is useful for day trips north to Szentendre (from Batthyány tér) or south to Ráceve (from Vágóhid). You must buy a ticket before boarding the train.

Sikló Funicular. This runs to the top of Castle Hill from Adam Clark tér, named after the Scottish engineer who built the nearby Chain Bridge (Széchenyi lánchíd) in the 1840s. It runs continuously 7.30am-10pm. If there is a big queue, or if you want to save $0.70, the nearest steps to the top are to the right up Király lépsco: a sharp five-minute climb.

Taxi. You shouldn't need to make much use of taxis, which is fortunate since cowboy cab drivers have given Budapest a bad name. Beware of being charged exorbitant fares by private taxis and of stroppy drivers who refuse to use the meter. State cabs, such as Fö-taxi, as distinct from private taxis, can be recognised by the cross-hatching on the sides.

To ring for a taxi dial 666-666 for Volán-taxi, 222-222 for Fö-taxi and 249-000 for Buda-taxi.

River Transport. You can take a 60-minute pleasure ride for $8.50 from the Mahart boat station at Vigadó tér (118-1223) in Pest. Expect to pay at least twice as much if you go with one of the other companies. For information on the boat services to the Danube Bend, see *Further Afield* below.

Cycling. Riding a bike in Budapest isn't much fun, and few locals do it. There are no cycle routes and some roads are barred to bikes, including the Chain Bridge and its approaches, the tunnel under Castle Hill and the road to the airport.

There is no one area with a concentration of cheap accommodation. Buda is greener and quieter than Pest but less central and more expensive when it comes to lodgings. There is a much wider range of rooms available east of the river.

Hotels. If you have not prebooked a room (advisable in summer), try to go direct to a hotel rather than through an agency, therby avoiding having to pay commission.

Budapest has several fine Art Nouveau hotels, including the famous Hotel Gellért by Szabadság bridge and Hotel Nemzeti on Jozsef körút, but you don't have to pay $150 a night ($300 in the case of the Gellért) for a comfortable room.

> *Metropol,* Rákóczi út 58 (142-1175, 142-0922), near Blaha L. tér metro. Its rooms are not bad value considering the central location: the cheapest doubles go for $45.
>
> *Ifjúság,* Zivatar út 1 (tel 115-4260, 135-33311; fax 135-3989). A modern three-star hotel tucked away in a leafy residential quarter west of Margaret Bridge. Lovely views and doubles for $60.
>
> *Hotel Dominik,* Cházár A. 3 (141-5140), ten minutes' walk east of Keleti station. If you have $20 to spare, you can't do better than this place, which has friendly staff and spotless rooms.
>
> *Hotel Express,* Beethoven út 7-9 (175-3082), in a quiet residential street ten minutes' walk southwest of Déli pu station. This youth hostel is good value if you have a IYHF card. Otherwise, it's $18 per person.
>
> *Citadella Hotel,* Citadella sétány (665-794), in a fabulous but rather isolated position within the fortress on top of Gellért Hill. Dorm beds go for just $6, but the awkward access is a discouragement. Bus 27 serves the Citadella, but you must pick it up south of Gellért Hill. Alternatives are a steep, 15-minute hike from Döbrentei tér (not recommended with a heavy pack) or a taxi.
>
> *Hotel Bartók ESZV,* Bartók Béla út 152, Buda (851-188). Not a brilliant location, at the bottom end of Bartók Béla, so probably a last resort: $15-20 per person.

Youth Hostels. Apart from the Hotel Express, listed above, hostels in Budapest open up for the summer only. For the current list, go to the Express office at Semmelweis út 4 (178-600), near Astoria metro. Expect to pay around $8 for a bed. Express can also arrange private accommodation.

Private Rooms. Staying in a private house costs around $10 per person and will be the most reliable option in summer. To book private accommodation, go to any Ibusz office or one of the other tourist agencies. The railway stations have a choice of accommodation desks. Ibusz is the only agent so far at Ferihegy airport (open till 9pm), and deals mainly with hotels. See *Help and Information* for a full list of the main Ibusz offices, which include the only 24-hour office in Budapest. Other agencies are as follows:

Tourinform: Sütö ut 2, near the Deák tér metro (tel 117-9800; fax 117-9578).

Budapest Tourist: main office at Roosevelt tér 5 (tel 117-3555; fax 118-1658). Branches at Terez körút 41 and Baross tér 3, at the corner of Rákóczi út.

Coopturist: Bartók Béla út 4, near Gellért Hotel (125-1615) and Bajcsy-Bsilinszky út 17 (111-7034).

People offering rooms may approach you at the transport terminals or outside city-centre accommodation offices. Note that these rooms sometimes work out more expensive than if you'd booked through Ibusz, so you may want to make speculative enquiries at an agency before accepting.

Camping. Camping in Budapest is so popular that it can be difficult to find a space at the height of summer. The largest site is Rómaifürdö Camping (188-7167), on the road to Szentendre and visible from the HEV station of the same name. Hárshegy Camping at Hárshegy út 5-7 (151-482) is better, but open only from May to the end of October; to get there take bus 22 from Moszkva tér metro station. If you find Hárshegyi full, there are two other campsites in the same district near Budheszi út: Tündérhegyi Feeberg and Zugliget Niche.

Eating and Drinking

While Western food has made significant inroads into Budapestis' diet, it is easily avoided. For the most authentic meals (and to avoid inevitable gypsy music), head away from the heart of Pest and the Castle District. If you manage to find a genuine Budapesti restaurant, you will be amazed at the low prices. One area where the company will be mostly Hungarian is Obuda, the third town on the Danube to be amalgamated with Pest and Buda. Two restaurants to try, not far from the western end of the Arpád Bridge, are the fish restaurant Sipos Halászkert on Fö tér and the Hídvéndeglö at Mókus út 22. To get to Obuda take the HEV suburban train from Batthyány tér metro to Arpád híd mh.

Other, more central restaurants are listed below. To be sure of a table, book in advance. Always check your bill; 'inaccuracies' seem particularly common in the more expensive places.

Kispipa, Akácfa út 38 (142-2587), just north of Rákóczi út near Blaha L. tér metro. A superb place, offering a gourmet four-course menu for about $5, including delicacies such as cold cherry soup and chocolate and walnut *palacsinta* (pancake). Wild boar is just one of the many other specialities.

Kiskakkuk, Poszonyi út 12 (132-1732), a block east of Margaret Bridge. Housed in an airy and antiquated hall, this restaurant has excellent food (particularly the game), attentive service and good, discreet music.

Kisbuda, Frankel Leó út 34 (115-2244), near the Buda side of Margaret Bridge. If the restaurant is full, you might be able to squeeze into the adjoining bar, where a full and interesting menu is served. Good live bands play periodically.

Kárpátia, Károlyi Mihály út 4, just south of Ferenciek tér. A superb period piece, though slightly garish after restoration: worth a snoop (don't miss the huge room at the back) if not a meal. Coffee for $1.80

is a rip-off, but the menu is varied and includes everything from spaghetti for under $4 to fried goose liver for $15. The set menu for $10 is recommended.

Vegetarian Restaurant, Cukor út 3, around the corner from the Kárpátia. A newish place, serving salads, pasta and other dishes ideal for those seeking exile from the aggressively carnivorous menus elsewhere. Main dishes $3-4.

Háry Borozó, Bródy Sándor út 30 (138-4878), behind the National Museum. Strictly speaking a wine bar, but it's better for eating than for just drinking. The food is excellent, though not particularly varied: roast goose with cabbage cooked in wine for $4.50, goulash for $3.50. The atmosphere is low-key, the clientele mostly local. Open until midnight.

Gundels, Allatkerti körút 2 (121-3550), just north of Heroes' Square. Opened in 1904 and recently restored by Americans at a cost of £10 million, Gundel's is the crème de la crème of Budapest's restaurants. Its luxurious dining rooms and shady terrace were a gathering place for the rich and famous between the wars, including Charlie Chaplin; Mrs Thatcher was a more recent guest. If you've got money to blow, the $40 set menu is an unrivalled gastronomic experience; if you want to soak up the atmosphere more cheaply, have just a coffee instead.

Beer and Wine Bars. For a more impromptu meal, or a few drinks, you'll do better at one of Budapest's many sörözös or borozós. Again, the best are out of the immediate downtown area: for example, north of Parliament around Szt. István körút, a busy commercial street running east from Margaret Bridge. Most bars in this area are liveliest at the end of the day (they are generally closed by 8 or 9pm), so it's worth venturing out early. Try Club Borozó on Balaton út and, around the corner, Tokaji Borozó on Balassi Bálint, both a block south of Szt. István körút; at the latter a litre of wine goes for not much more than a dollar.

A whole new breed of 'pubs' has opened up in the form of smart bars serving imported beer. The John Bull pub on Bajcsy-Zsilinszky út, by Arany Janos út metro station, hasn't done a bad job of recreating the décor of an English pub; but with pints at $2.80 and a clientele made up mostly of expats and smart Budapestis, it is only for the cynical or the seriously homesick. If you're desperate for a Guinness, repair to the Fregatt at Molnár út 26, which also has a dartboard.

Angyal, at Szentkirályi út 8, east of Astoria metro station, is Budapest's most popular (and lively) gay bar, open 10pm-3am. There are discos/shows on some nights.

Cafés. Budapest has an enviable collection of cafés, many of which are ideal for soaking up the old-world ambience over breakfast or a mid-afternoon pastry.

New York Kávéház, in the black and crumbling New York Palace on Erzsébet körút, just north of Rákóczi. The cream of the capital's coffee houses, this glittering Art Nouveau café once functioned as Budapest's literary clearing house, where authors, publishers and agents gathered to write, edit and deal. The original café was turned into a sports shop during the Stalinist period, but was resurrected after the war. Dripping with gilt and scarcely faded opulence, the café is a visual feast not to be missed. You might even be tempted to splash out on a caviar sandwich. Open 9am-10pm.

Gerbeaud's, situated on Vörösmarty tér, is frequented almost purely by tourists: waitresses scurry about in comical white ankleboots but have no time to be friendly. The décor is disappointing too after the New York Café, but the cakes are supreme, oozing cream, chocolate and calories. Enjoy a coffee and a cake chosen from the counter display, though you may consider $1.25 for a cappuccino (wonderful though it is) a little steep. If it's just the cake you're after, head straight for the shop on the right-hand side, where *dobbestorte* (chocolate cake topped with caramel) and other house specials are on sale.

Müvész, 29 Andrássy út. Situated across from the Opera House and open until midnight, this is a good place for a pre- or post-performance coffee and cake.

Lukács, Andrássy út 70, near Oktogon metro. Formerly a canteen for the secret police, whose headquarters was at no. 60, and now popular among students from the College of Fine Arts opposite. Run by Gerbeaud's (waitresses wear the same boots), Lukács is simpler, cheaper and quieter than its cousin, and the brioches are wonderful. Open 9am-8pm.

Museum-Kave, next to the National Museum on the corner of Bródy Sándor út. The restaurant prices are high, but the genteel atmosphere is pleasant and the pianist's musical accompaniment unobtrusive. Open until 11pm.

Caffé Károlyi, towards the bottom of Károlyi Mihály. A new and lively café, full of students and open 9am-1am. Serves mostly drinks but also a few snacks.

Pardon Café, Szondi út, three blocks south of Nyugati pu. A great café-cum-bar, serving cakes, crêpes and piano music until 2am or beyond. In the small hours journalists hunch over their eszpressos, engrossed in the first editions.

Ruszwurm Café, an 18th-century coffee house on Szenthározag út. The best place for a pastry stop in the Castle District if you don't mind being in a confined space with only tourists for company.

Fast Food. Budapest is the fast food capital of Eastern Europe. There are several branches of McDonalds, including an aesthetic horror with a sickly purple ceiling by Nyugati pu. The world's biggest Burger King by Oktogon metro does a roaring trade too, with MTV blasting from video screens. Kentucky Fried Chicken, Pizza Hut, Dunkin Donuts and Dairy Queen have also joined the fray, outdoing Budapest's home-grown chain of fastfood restaurants, Paprika, which has a branch on Harmincad út by Vörösmarty tér, where a meal of thick meat stew and caraway potato costs under $2.

Buying Food at Markets. The covered Central Market (open from 6am Monday to Saturday) at the Pest end of the Szabadság Bridge is buzzing and has some of the best food in the city, including wonderful cheeses and cooked meats. It is especially good in summer, when the stalls groan with luscious cherries, raspberries, plums and every variety of mushroom. A visit in winter is also worthwhile if only to see the artistic displays of dried paprikas. While the old market building is under restoration (see *Exploring*), traders congregate in the old customs house nearby on Közraktár út.

Skála Csarnok, just north of Blaha Lujza tér, is a much-smartened up old market hall. It's more like a supermarket these days, but you can pick up fresh produce and tasty snacks upstairs. It is open until 8pm. The ABC on Batthyány tér in Buda is similar, though more downmarket.

Note that museums in Budapest are almost all open 10am-6pm daily except Monday. Most admission charges are less than $0.50, with entrance to some places free on certain days.

Castle District. Once the centre of government, castle hill is now the domain of tourists, with restaurants and souvenir shops galore. Few people actually live there, and the atmosphere is dead compared with Pest. Nevertheless, the lack of traffic is welcome and the museums give a useful historical background to the city. You should allow at least half a day to explore the castle district, more if you have the stamina for all the museums.

Szentháromság tér, a short walk north of the terminus of the Sikló funicular (see *City Transport*), is the focus of the Castle District, with the main concentration of tourists and gypsy musicians competing for their attention. The splendid mounted figure of Stephen I watches scornfully over the proceedings from one corner, but he too is overshadowed by the Mátyás Templom, a careful reconstruction of the most ancient church of Budapest, dating originally from the 13th century. The exterior, with its roof tiled in porcelain, is splendid, but nothing quite prepares you for the interior, where every inch of wall space is covered in colour — albeit dull in the gloomy light. The architect of Mátyás Templom was also responsible for the nearby Fisherman's Bastion, a phoney rampart that offers some of the best views over Pest, particularly of the Parliament building.

The streets running north from Szentháromság tér have been meticulously restored, but lack the quirky features that make Pest's architecture so interesting. Notable if only for its gall is the Hilton, which skulks at the bottom of Fortuna út and incorporates an old church: it's worth going inside just to get a closer look at this abomination. Almost opposite at no. 4, the Museum of Commerce & Catering has an unusual collection, including confectionery moulds in every shape imaginable. The ugly National Archive building, with its multi-coloured roof, ends the street off badly. Instead, cut west to Uri út, where the road's gentle swirls provide pleasant views of pristine architecture. At no. 9, you can head underground and explore a series of natural caves linked by passages originally dug by the Turks. The labyrinth has been in almost constant use ever since, including as a bomb shelter during World War Two. Admission is steep at $1.50 and the waxworks both comic and gruesome, but the extent of the tunnels is impressive and the whistle-stop tour of Hungarian history illuminating.

Tóth Arpád setany runs parallel to Uri út, skirting the western edge of castle hill. The views over Déli station aren't stunning, but the shady walk is peaceful, with usually just a few old folk pottering about. From its southern end you can stroll down to the 'castle' proper: Buda Palace or *Budavári Palota*. The original Gothic fortress was virtually destroyed by the army which liberated Buda from the Turks in 1686. A new palace replaced it, but this also sustained attack, most recently during the Second World War. It has been rebuilt once more, using new designs. A sizeable chunk of the building is taken up by the National Gallery, which contains many of the country's native art treasures. Of particular interest are the late 19th and 20th century works on the upper floors, though the medieval carvings in stone and wood on the ground floor and the late Gothic altars on the first are also worth seeing. (The Ludvig gallery, entered from the palace's west side, houses only a mediocre art collection.) Inside the nearby Budapest History Museum, you can descend into the bowels of the cliff, where what remains of the Gothic Palace has been reconstructed. An aura of history is somehow completely absent, however, and the displays of Roman jewellery upstairs hold just as much interest. From the museum lobby, steps lead down through quiet gardens to the base of Gellért Hill.

Gellért Hill (Géllert-Hegy). There are numerous ways up this hill, the quickest (and steepest) being from Döbrentei tér at the west end of Erzsébet bridge — a fairly painless, 15-minute climb. The Citadella at the top, built by the Austrians following the 1849 revolution, is not much to look at inside or out, and is barely worth even the small admission charge. The views — the main reason to climb the hill — are equally good from outside: either from the viewpoint just down from the entrance to the fortress or from by the statue of liberty, built in 1947. Steps near this typically communist heroic figure lead down through the trees to the Gellért hotel and baths, the latter's domes clearly visible from above: see *Thermal Baths.*

Pest. The inner city has an appealing shabbiness which has been little marred by modern development, apart from the glossy hotels which now line the Corzo, the riverside promenade between Vigadó tér and the Chain bridge: cafés here attract exclusively tourists, catered to in the evenings by a fair number of prostitutes.

The most striking building in Pest if only for its size is the Hungarian Parliament, north of the Chain Bridge. Partially modelled on Westminster in London, it was once described by a poet as 'a Turkish bath crossed with a Gothic chapel'. Hour-long tours are available, but only when the National Assembly is not in session: a shame, given that debates are livelier than ever before. The Ethnographical Museum opposite is another monster of a building which in many ways cuts a more impressive figure than Parliament, with statues along the top assuming a variety of arrogant poses. The entrance hall is stunning, its ceiling decorated with staggering intricacy. The collection of embroidered costumes and other folk crafts is impressive too, a testimony to the survival of rural traditions despite the traumas of the 20th century. The museum ventures beyond the frontiers of Europe for glimpses of rural Hungarian communities in Romania.

Amble south to Szabadság tér, quiet and shady and a good place to escape the noise of the city streets. The TV building (formerly the stock exchange) on the west side is the most overbearing but the least interesting sight in the square. The east side is taken up by the US Embassy and the Magyar Nemzeti Bank (hence all the cameras), the latter wrapped in fine reliefs. Walk around the back and up Hold út, where a splendid Art Nouveau building designed by Odön Lechner (see below) is topped by a cheeky wavy roof and brightly coloured tiles. A short distance south rises the grimy bulk of St Stephen's basilica, the city's largest church begun in the mid-19th century and completed in 1906. Outside, the forest of scaffolding has become an almost permanent fixture, so long has restoration work been going on. Inside, a strange orange gloom prevails.

Zrinyi út leads west from St Stephen's to the riverside Roosevelt tér. The highlight here is the Gresham Palace, a crumbling extravaganza built in 1906, with a fabulous frieze of figures above the third storey windows and gold that still manages to glisten. The most interesting feature of the Academy of Letters and Sciences on the north side are the figures of Descartes and Leibniz, perched precariously at two corners. South past the Atrium Hyatt hotel, it's only a short walk to Vörösmarty tér, where tourists pause for a coffee at Gerbeaud's café but eventually gravitate towards Váci útca. This street has been much restored, to the detriment of the atmosphere, and is now the domain of foreigners and nouveau riche Hungarians. Above the shops bearing big names like Reebok and Levis, however, there is still some fine architecture to be admired. South of the chaotic Ferenciek tér, streets like Molnár and Veres Pálné are more atmospheric, though less impressive architecturally.

The buildings south of Rákóczi are generally less monumental than further north, but there is still plenty of interest. The University Church, for example, on the corner of Károlyi Mihaly and Papnövelde út, is a fine Baroque structure, with charming woodcarving over the door and a pulpit laden with angels and cherubs, the gilt darkened by age and dust. Due east, on the other side of Muzeum körút, the National Museum houses a rather daunting collection. The military and other historical exhibits are of minimal interest to non-Hungarians, but you might like to join the throng of patriotic locals who gather round the Magyar Royal Crown — smuggled out to the United States during the war and recovered only in 1978.

Architecturally, other buildings in the area are far more rewarding. Firstly, the Ervin-Szabó Municipal Library, a couple of blocks south of the museum on Baross út. There is almost as much bustle inside the library as in the streets: you will cause little disruption by wandering through the small gilt-and-mirrored rooms. Leave your bag downstairs first. Southeast along Ullöi út, the Museum of Applied Arts was designed by Odön Lechner, the most famous Art Nouveau architect in Budapest. The elaborate porch has suffered less from pollution than the exterior walls. Inside, the architecture adds spice to the already considerable interest of the collection. Heading along the back streets west of the museum will deposit you in front of the Central Market (Vásárcsarnok), a cross between a church and a railway station created from brick, glass and cast-iron. While under much needed restoration, you can still see inside. The nearby university building, by the Danube, is an altogether more decorous structure.

Heroes Square and Városliget Park. A monument as grand as that overlooking Heroes Square is a fitting end to Andrássy boulevard. The Millenium Monument was begun in 1896 on the 1,000th anniversary of the Hungarian nation. The central column is topped by a statue of Gabriel, credited with a walk-on role in Hungarian independence — he is said to have offered King Stephen I the crown of Hungary in the first year of the new millenium. Around the base, dramatic mounted figures represent the seven chieftains who led their tribes to conquer Hungary. The statues in the colonnades behind allude to Work, Welfare, War, Peace, Knowledge and Glory. The memorial to Hungary's national heroes is a more recent addition, guarded by soldiers obliged to remain motionless before a constant clicking of cameras.

Two art galleries face each other across the square. The Museum of Fine Arts, on the north side, contains a mammoth collection of mainly foreign paintings, including important works by Goya and a collection of El Grecos which constitutes an admirable survey of the artist's career. You can easily get lost among the endless rooms of Dutch and Italian art, but it's worth seeking out the paintings by Breughel (room IX) and Raphael and Filippo Lippi (rooms I and III). The Múscarnok exhibition hall opposite is currently under renovation.

Beyond Heroes Square, Városliget is the city's largest park, ungracefully bisected by a main road and with metro trains rumbling disconcertingly underfoot. On fine days, there is a mass of people about, boating on the lake (or skating on it in winter), visiting the zoo, watching old men play chess or simply sitting about. A mock Transylvanian Castle (modelled on the original at Vajdahunyad in Romania) lurks in one corner, a bizarre complex worth a quick stroll. The Agricultural Museum was built to demonstrate the range of Hungarian architectural styles.

Margaret Island (Margit-Sziget). Situated between Margit and Arpád bridges, this is a favourite spot for Budapestis to stroll around on Sunday afternoons. During the week, it is a pleasant refuge away from the fumes of the city traffic. If you're feeling energetic, you can cover the whole island in about three hours, but on a fine day it's tempting just to take a picnic and lie in the shade.

Thermal Baths. Lolling around in one of the city's thermal baths (*gyógyfürdő*), in use since Roman times, is highly recommended — it is a way of life for many locals. The best baths date from the Turkish occupation and are concentrated in Buda, in the so-called Víziváros (Watertown) district along the Danube. Saunas, steam baths and bone-wrenching massages are just some of the more commonplace facilities at your disposal. The cost by western standards is small: as little as $1.50 for a straightforward steam bath. Note that some establishments have a men-only policy. Most open 6am until early evening.

> *Gellért,* attached to the Gellért Hotel and similarly opulent: the main pool has marble columns, potted palms, a sliding roof and even a wave machine. The majority of customers are tourists (often in large groups) and queues are long in summer. The main advantage is that all services are listed in English (from 'carbonic tub' to 'hygienical gymnastics'). Pool tickets are valid for three hours.
>
> *Rudas,* Döbrentei tér 9. In a peeling, dirty pink building beneath Gellért Hill, but probably the most impressive Turkish baths in Budapest. The beautiful echoing domes and arches with starlights are all virtually unchanged since the 16th century. The high mineral content of the water is good for arthritis. Why go to the Gellért?
>
> *Király,* in a crumbling green building at 82 Fö út (at the northern end of the street), popular with local shoppers. Second only to the Rudas and open to women on alternate days of the week.
>
> *Széchenyi,* in a fine turn-of-the-century building in Városliget Park. Said to be the largest thermal baths in Europe, and certainly the next busiest and grandest after the Gellért baths (particularly following recent renovation), though with a more mixed clientele. Middle-aged men wallow while playing chess on floating chessboards.

Aquincum. There has been a settlement on the site of Budapest for around 2,000 years. To go back to the city's earliest history, you should visit the Roman ruins of Aquincum, which date from around the birth of Christ and are named after the nearby thermal springs. You can wander around the baths, market and amphitheatre as well as the archaeological museum, whose most famous exhibit is an organ powered by water.

Aquincum is next to the HEV stop of the same name.

Buda Hills. From Moszkva tér metro you can take the cog railway to Széchenyi-hegy, a hill skiable in winter. From the station here you can go for a ride on the so-called Pioneer or Children's Railway, operated (though not driven) by earnest young teenagers. The train runs a gentle course for 7 miles/12km west through the forested Buda Hills, taking about 90 minutes. If you get off at János-hegy station, you can walk up to the János-hegy belvedere, the highest vantage point above Budapest.

If you like to spend every night clubbing, then you have probably come to the wrong place. The average city discotheque is best avoided. Some are thinly disguised sex shows, and new topless bars and peep shows are opening up all the time. Most clubs in the centre seem to exist solely for tourists and are often attached to international hotels. Your best bet is to get to know some local people and ask their advice.

But while the city has a desultory selection of clubs, you'll be spoilt for choice when it comes to more elevated forms of entertainment. There is a multitude of venues, though you would do well to avoid the tourist-oriented performances, such as those staged in the Dominican courtyard at the Hilton. *Pesti Müsor* (or 'PM'), available at most news stands, contains a complete listing of films, plays, concerts, opera, etc. The monthly *Budapest Panorama,* which you can pick up free in hotels and tourist offices, is less comprehensive but at least is translated into English, German and Italian. The newspapers *Budapest Week* and the *Budapest Sun* contain listings but not addresses. The bimonthly *Koncert Kalendarium* is by far the best source for classical concerts. For film programmes, check the red, white and blue posters in the streets.

The most convenient ticket booking office is in Vörösmarty tér, which has English-speaking staff — unlike the one at Andrássy út 18. If you have trouble getting tickets, it might be worth asking at Ibusz, which sometimes has a few seats reserved for tourists. Opera is very popular with Budapestis and tickets are hard to get hold of on the day. Touts do a fair amount of business, but you'll pay over the odds and could end up in the rafters. In the case of classical concerts, for all but the very top orchestras tickets can be bought at the door for very little money.

Opera, Ballet and Theatre. Most of the capital's best theatres are on or near Andrássy út, including the city's top opera house (Operaház) at no. 22. The interior is sumptuous but the dress surprisingly casual. The Erkel Theatre, on Köztarsaság tér off the eastern end of Rákóczi, is associated with the state opera house and also hosts top-quality performances including ballet. For a more light-hearted evening, get tickets for the Puppet Theatre (Bábszínház), at Andrássy út 69 in the basement of the College of Fine Arts, near Vörösmarty út metro station.

For straight drama, one of the best venues is the Arany János Színház on Paulay Ede út, on the other side of Andrássy from the Opera House. The quality of performances is good and the Art Deco building superb, both inside and out. The Vígszínház at Szt. István körút 14 also stages drama of a generally high calibre.

Classical Music. Budapest's musical life has a long and distinguished history, which remains vigorous around the calendar.

The premier venue for classical music is the heavily restored Vigadó Concert Hall (Vigadó tér), where Bartók gave his final performance before fleeing the Nazis in 1941. While one of Europe's top venues (it is the home of the Hungarian Philharmonic Orchestra), the acoustics are by no means perfect. The general public can also get seats for concerts at Magyar Radio, held in the hall on Pollac Mihály tér behind the National Museum. In the Castle District, free concerts are staged periodically at the National Gallery, and there is an organ recital every Friday at 8pm in the Mátyás Templom.

Contemporary Music. Good modern music can prove a little harder to track down, though there is plenty of it. Big rock acts, national and international, perform at the Petöfi Csarnok in the Városliget park (142-4327), a long-standing focus of the youth scene in Budapest. Small venues hosting more regular acts, particularly jazz, include the following:

> *FMK, Club of Young Artists,* Andrássy út 112 (131-8858) near Voros-marty út metro. Hosts a varied programme of concerts and has a pleasant open-air bar open any time.
> *Kassák-Klub,*Uzsoki út 57, six blocks beyond Városliget Park. Hosts informal jazz sessions on Wednesday and Sunday evenings.
> *Merlin Jazz Club,* Gerlóczy út 4 (117-9338), between Károly körút and Petöfi Sandor. Bands play every night from 10pm, in a room more like a gymnasium than a club.
> *Tilos az A,* Mizsáth tér, behind National Museum. A good variety of music and popular among students.
> *Go Jazz Studio,* Krúdy Gy út 6 (138-4281), along from the Tilos az A. An intimate venue for jazz and blues, with shop selling CDs and equipment next door.

Traditional Music. Live gypsy music of variable quality is common in restaurants in central Budapest, but for some of the best traditional music seek out a Táncház (originally, a 'village dance hall'). The Táncház movement got going in the 1970s as an antidote to ghastly folk-troupe displays, and has a strong following. Traditional Hungarian tunes accompany tuition in the finer points of folk-dancing. Many of the musicians and dancers have collected music in Transylvania and other outlying areas, and have managed to transpose it fairly successfully to an urban setting. You are free to participate or simply admire. Two recommended dance houses are the Teka Táncház on Almássy tér (Fridays) and the Kalamajka Táncház in Molnár út (Saturdays).

SPORT

The massive Népstadion (251-1222), on Stefánia út east of Keleti pu, seats 70,000 and seldom reaches capacity: you can be sure of obtaining a ticket for a football match at the gate. For a more unusual afternoon's entertainment, attend a trotting race at the Lóverseny Racetrack (134-2958), south of Kerepesi út, every Wednesday at 4pm and Saturday at 2pm.

It may be interesting to stroll along fashionable Váci út and the surrounding streets, but don't expect to pick up any real bargains or to see many things that you won't find back home: the small branch of Marks & Spencers at Váci út 10 charges only slightly less than its British counterparts. Folk art shops are dotted about both here and all over the centre, and Romanian women peddle traditional clothes in the street: avoid doing business with those in the Castle District, where they expect higher prices, in favour of those who hang around in the metro stations, particularly at Astoria.

Record Shops. Music fans who know their Liszt from their Kodály could spend hours at the music shop on the west side of Vörösmarty tér. It also has world music on CD from such exotic places as Azerbaijan, Tibet and Scotland. The other best shops in Budapest are Rözsavölgyi Zenemubolt, near Váci út on Szervita tér, and Kodály Zoltan at Múzeum körút 17-21.

Bookshops. You can't move for bookshops (*könyvesbolt*) in Budapest. The biggest and best all have a range of titles in English, including guides, cookery books and contemporary Hungarian literature in translation. The city's secondhand bookshops often carry a surprising selection of books in English and other languages, though you won't find too many cheap paperbacks suitable for whiling away the hours on a long train journey. For these you should go to the shop on Munnich Ferenc (between Vörösmarty tér and Parliament), where books are cheaper than in the UK. It's also well worth browsing around the shops at Múzeum körút 13 and Bajcsy-Zsilinszky út 34. The latter has a particularly good line in maps and guides. Another good shop for maps is a minuscule place in Parisi Udvar, a gloomy but magnificent arcade on Ferenciek tér.

Markets. The Central Market (see *Eating and Drinking*) is very entertaining, but the number of peasant traders frequenting this downtown market has diminished. The Lehel market, by Elmunkás tér metro station north of Nyugati, is a more authentic trading place. The mountains of fruit and vegetables are splendid, some the work of Bulgarians who bring their high-quality produce for demanding Hungarians. Other stalls sell new and secondhand clothes, and individuals stand about trying to sell personal possessions. But for real antiques and bric-a-brac, nowhere beats the Ecseri market, southeast of the centre at Nagykőrösi út 156, in XIX district. It is held 8am-3pm Monday to Saturday, but is best at weekends. While in the heart of the market experts with top-quality antiques (often bought from rural peasants strapped for cash) do deals with knowledgeable Western collectors, you also find proper junk alongside spanking new trainers, jeans and other fruits of capitalism. To get to Ecseri, take the metro to Határ út and bus 54 from there.

Help and Information

Tourist Information: the most reliable, helpful and impartial source of tourist information for Budapest and the whole country is Tourinform at Sütö út 2 near the Deák tér metro station (tel 117-9800; fax 117-9578). This is one office you can be sure of finding helpful, English-speaking staff, and a broad range of literature and advice. Open 8am-8pm.

Ibusz has offices throughout the city centre, in addition to those at the three railway stations. These include the head office at Károlyi körút 3c (142-3140), the 24-hour office at Petöfi tér 3 and others at Vörösmarty tér, Ferenciek tér 5, József Attila út 18 and Terez körút 6. Other agencies, such as Budapest Tourist and Cooptourist are best used only for arranging private rooms: see *Accommodation.*

Express, the youth travel agency, has an office at Semmelweis út 4 (117-6634), by Astoria metro, but for information about the whole country, go to the head office at Szabadság tér 16 (tel 131-777, 153-0660; fax 153-1715).

Post Offices: the main office is at Petöfi Sándor út 13-19, open 8am-8pm Monday to Friday, Saturday 8am-3pm. The telephone and fax office is in the smart new building next door, open 8am-8pm weekdays, 9am-3pm at weekends. Large post offices near Keleti and Nyugati stations stay open day and night.

Money: if you don't feel inclined to deal with dodgy-looking black marketeers, financial transactions are best done at Ibusz or one of the banks. K & H bank has 24-hour automatic exchange machines dotted about the city, including one at Sas út 3, on the corner of József Attila.

American Express: Deak Ferenc út 10 (tel 266-8680; fax 251-5220). An automatic machine outside allows you to withdraw cash with an Amex card.

Thomas Cook: 3 Dorottya út (182-788), off Vörösmarty tér.

Embassies and Consulates. *UK:* 6 Harmincad út, by Vörösmarty tér (118-2888). They have fairly up-to-date English newspapers and a small library. The British Council shares the same premises.
USA: Szabadság tér 12 (112-6450).
Australia: Délibáb út 30, Budapest VI (153-4233).
Canada: Budakeszi út 32, Budapest XII (176-7711).
Bulgaria: Andrássy út 115 (122-0836/0824).
Czech Republic: Stefánia út 22 (163-6600/6608), near the Népstadion.
Romania: Thököly út 72 (425-552/426-944/427-689).
Russia: Andrássy út 104 (131-8985).

Most day-trippers cling to the Danube when they venture out of town for the day and usually head north (see below). South of the main city bridges, the river forks around the 30-mile/48km long Csepel Island, a favourite recreation spot for Budapestis in the summer. The town of Ráckeve on the island, at the end of a HEV train line, has a frescoed 15th-century church.

Other places in the environs of Budapest may be worth a journey, especially for special events such as the series of Beethoven concerts held in summer in the park at Martonvásár, a castle about 25 miles/40km southwest of Budapest and accessible by train. Concerts are held on alternate Saturdays in July and August.

THE DANUBE BEND

The Danube Bend refers to one of the most scenic stretches of the river just to the north of Budapest. The mountain scenery and historic towns combine to make this an area not to be missed. There is the added bonus of easy access along the Danube to Szentendre, Visegrád and Esztergom, the three main towns of the Danube Bend — all highly recommended destinations for day trips or longer stays. You can travel by train or bus, but boat is the most fun. Mahart boats leave Vigadó tér in Budapest twice a day during the summer; most stop at Batthyány tér too. Buses to all the main towns leave hourly from the bus station on the Pest side of Arpád Bridge (accessible on metro line 3).

SZENTENDRE

The charming village of Szentendre totters high above the Danube, on the west bank of the river 12 miles/20km north of Budapest. Nothing beats simply strolling through the twisting streets and alleys or promenading beside the river, though don't expect much tranquillity or solitude: this is Hungary's main tourist centre. Some of the buildings date from the 17th century and have icons, dormer windows and other features which show the influence of Serbian merchants, who settled here to escape the Turks.

Szentendre has long been the Montmârtre of Hungary and still has a thriving community of artists. There are numerous galleries dotted about the town, the most interesting being the Kovács Margit Museum at Gyorgy út 1, which contains the unusual ceramics of Margit Kovács (1902-77), who took her inspiration from Hungarian folk art.

There is an Open Air Ethnographic Museum nearby (open April to October), with examples of early peasant architecture; a guide book in English is available. Try to visit on the first Sunday of the month, when artisans demonstrate old handicrafts such as milling, candle-making and honeycake preparation. Other special events include the Spring Days which coincides with the Budapest Spring Festival in March and brings concerts to the Blagovestenska Church.

Arrival and Departure. Though lacking the romance of the Danube ferries, the HEV train from Battyány tér costs less and is quicker, taking 40 instead of 90 minutes; there are several services an hour, running until late. The HEV station is about half a mile south of Fő tér, the main square. An excellent bus service is also available.

Accommodation and Food. There is a good choice of accommodation. You can book private rooms through Dunatours at Bogdányi út 1 or Ibusz, down the road at no. 11. For a cheapish hotel room, try the Coca Cola Panzió at Dunakanyar körút 50 (26-10 410), on the busy main highway but surprisingly quiet and pleasant. Bed and breakfast costs under $40 between two. Bükkös Panzió, at Bükkös-part 16 (26-12 021), just south of the centre, is more convenient but also slightly more expensive. In summer, the Duna Parti Diákhotel hostel is an excellent option, located at Somogy Bacsó part 12 (26-12 657), close to the river a short walk from the main square.

The Régimódi Kisvendéglo on Futo út is one of the best places to eat in town, with elegant turn-of-the-century décor and excellent fish dishes.

VISEGRAD

This is the next ancient settlement along the Danube Bend, lying about 15 miles/24km beyond Szentendre. Its main attraction is its setting, amidst the forested Visegrád mountains, but the town was also the home of Hungarian kings and queens for nearly 200 years; you can visit the remains of the 14th-century royal palace on Fő ut. The town's main hill (Várhegy) culminates in the ruined Citadel, built by the Hungarian kings in the 13th century. It's a strenuous 40-minute climb, though in summer you can take a bus, which leaves from just south of the riverboat wharf. The views over the Danube Bend are out of this world, and help you appreciate the value of the site as a fortress. From the citadel, trails continue into the wooded hills, providing scope for marvellous walks. Local bookshops sell hiking maps.

In addition to boats and buses from Budapest, you can also reach Visegrád direct by bus from Szentendre's HEV station. Szob-bound trains from

Nyugati station in Budapest stop in Nagymaros, on the north bank, from where ferries leave for Visegrád every hour, running all year except when the river freezes over.

There's not much in the way of conventional accommodation, but you can arrange a private room at Dunatours at Fő út 3 (26-28 330), located opposite the riverboat wharf. There are a couple of hostels open in summer, the best of which is the Salamon at Salamon tornya út 5. At other times of year, try Hotel Eötvös at Fő út 117, with doubles for around $30.

ESZTERGOM

Marking the western end of this beautiful stretch of river, Esztergom is the most urban of the Danube Bend towns. Yet it is also one of Hungary's most historic. It was the Magyar capital in the 11th and 12th centuries and has been the religious centre of Hungary throughout its history.

Esztergom is dominated by the largest church in the country, the Roman Catholic Cathedral, whose green dome is second only to St Peter's in Rome in size. You can walk around the rim of the dome for a stunning panorama over the Danube and across to Slovakia. The foundations of the church are very old, though the present imposing structure dates from the 19th century. There is a superb treasury in the crypt. Other highlights in the town include the Museum of Christian Art in the Primate's Palace, near the cathedral on Berényi Zsigmond út. It contains many priceless paintings, making up one of the best art collections in the country.

Esztergom can be easily reached by bus from Visegrád or direct from Budapest. There are also regular trains from the capital's Nyugati station. Esztergom is one of the busiest ports on the Danube, with a constant flow of boats and ferries. The latter include hourly services across to the Slovakian town of Stúrovo, opposite, though this border crossing is still open only to citizens of Hungary and Slovakia. The bridge across the Danube was bombed by the Germans during the war, but it has never been rebuilt.

Private accommodation can be arranged at Express at Széchenyi tér 7 (33-13 712), Ibusz on Lőrinc út (33-12 552) and Komturistat Mártirok út 6 (33-12 082). Among the most reasonable hotels are the Fürdő at Bajcsy-Zsilinskzky út 14 (33-11 147) and the nearby Alabárdos Panzió at no. 49 (33-12 640), both charging $30-40 for a double.

LAKE BALATON

If you are looking for the undiscovered Hungary, Lake Balaton is not it. The largest lake in Central Europe, 51 miles/85km long, has been heavily populated throughout history. Its shores were planted as vineyards by the Romans and villages in the area later became prosperous enough to build some impressive Gothic churches. European nobility, such as the Esterházy family, chose to build mansions and establish hunting grounds nearby. Lake Balaton is not so romantic these days, with a fair proportion of the 125-mile perimeter lined with holiday developments, but travellers who dislike or tire easily of swimming and watersports, can head up into the hills. The area north of the lake is much hillier than the south and is generally the most rewarding to explore. Roads leading away from the lake wind and climb into the Bakony hills and are well worth exploring. You could spend days visiting ruined forts, aristocratic palaces, Baroque churches and vineyards. There are clearly advantages in hiring your own transport, particularly as this will enable you to discover the seldom visited ruins which are scattered throughout the hills and valleys; if you ask the locals whether there are any *romok* (ruins) in the vicinity, chances are they will name a nearby village.

Most of the thousands of people who flock to Lake Balaton each summer, however, are attracted mainly by the warm water, good weather and the lively social life. Many Hungarians cherish fond memories of childhood vacations on the lake which perhaps exceed the reality a little, just as an adult who revisits his or her childhood haunts at Margate or Blackpool might be disappointed. The whole area is radically seasonal: the Ibusz statement that the Balaton is 'most alive in the summer' is a euphemism for 'completely dead in the winter'. The season officially opens on the last weekend of May.

Swimming and watersports are of course the main activities. Don't expect mile upon mile of sand. The more popular and developed southern shore boasts few sandy beaches, though the lake bottom is composed of fine sand. Instead there are concrete embankments, sometimes giving the (false) impression that the lake is artificial. The lake is so shallow that the summer sun quickly warms up the water — eventually to around 26°C/80°F — but only a few exceptionally hardy souls venture into the water in May. It is easy to arrange sailing or windsurfing from any of the resorts. Keep an eye on the weather and listen for the warning gun, since wind storms can brew up suddenly and stir up the normally smooth waters to dangerous levels.

Getting Around. The lake's accessibility, especially to Austrians, accounts for its immense popularity. Express buses from the Erzsébet tér station in Budapest use the fast M7 motorway to cover the 60 miles/96km to the lake in about an hour and a half. Rail lines run along both shores, bisecting resort towns such as Siófok, Balatonfüred and Badacsony. Trains leave frequently (hourly in summer) from Budapest's Déli pu and take about two hours to reach Siófok, the first of Balaton's resorts, and three and a half hours to reach Keszthely, the pleasant town at the far end of the lake.

One of the few places not spoilt by railway tracks is the Tihany Peninsula, a promontory which juts out deep into the lake from the north shore. It can however be reached by a frequent local bus service from Balantonfüred, a few miles to the east. Tihany is also one of the many *révs* or ferry landing places, though it is the only one of two to have a car ferry service. The 3-mile/5km trip across to Szantódrév opposite takes only a few minutes: this can save motorists a long drive round the lake. Travellers without cars have a much greater choice of ferry routes, though to travel from Siófok to Keszthely, for example, you'll need to change a couple of times: the whole journey takes about seven hours. All boat services on the lake are run by Mahart. You can pick up a timetable (*menetrend*) at any of the boat stations.

You can rent cars in Siófok and Balatonfüred.

Accommodation. Hotel prices tend to be even higher around Lake Balaton than in Budapest because of the resort tax, but there are numerous tourist agencies which can organise private accommodation — this is easy to find independently too: 'zimmer frei' ('rooms vacant') signs are everywhere. Beware of the overpriced *csárdas* or inns, which are heavily promoted by the agencies.

Dozens of campsites line the lake, where every amenity is offered from bicycles for hire to four-person bungalows. Express has large youth hostels at Kiliántelep (86-45 566) and Balatonföldvár (84-40 374).

If you can't stand the resort scene, consider staying in one of the villages inland from the shores, where the ways of the local people have not been dramatically altered by an influx of tourists and their money. Siótour or Balantourist can help arrange this.

Food and Drink. Western food is ever more popular, but you can still eat plenty of fish cooked according to traditional Hungarian methods. Lake Balaton is full of fish, especially carp, which turns up on most restaurant menus. Keep an eye out also for *fogas,* a delicious perch-like fish (which must be quite indifferent to climate since the only other places it is found are Egypt and Siberia).

Surrounded by vineyards, you'll be spoilt for choice when it comes to wine. If you prefer beer, be sure to specify in a pub or restaurant that you want it to be local (*helyi*), since otherwise it'll usually be assumed that you're willing to pay twice the price for a bottle of imported Tuborg.

Maps and Information. A Cartographia map of Lake Balaton with a scale of 1:80,000 is widely available, but it is not particularly clear and the legend is only in Hungarian. Furthermore, the town maps on the reverse are no better than the free Ibusz town plans featured on the Lake Balaton North and Lake Balaton South maps.

The two main regional tourist organisations are Siótour and Balantourist, both of which have offices in all the main resorts — as does Ibusz. All agencies produce huge amounts of bumpf. Whereas Tourinform's publication *Lake Balaton* contains a certain number of hard facts, Ibusz brochures push their own tours to the virtual exclusion of information useful to independent travellers.

The main places to visit around Lake Balaton are listed below, in anticlockwise order from Siófok.

SIOFOK

On the south coast of Lake Balaton, Siófok seethes with tourists in summer and has an almost raucous nightlife. It's not a particularly appealing place, but being the main gateway to Lake Balaton for most people arriving from Budapest, you may well at least pass through it. If you have a few hours to kill, visit Köröshegy — west of Siófok and just inland from Balatonfoldvár. The village has a fine 15th-century Franciscan church.

Accommodation in Siófok is about as expensive as it'll get around Lake Balaton. Furthermore, in summer, even private rooms can be in short supply. You won't find hotel rooms for less than about $70, which is what the Napfény Hotel (Mártírok út 8; 84-11 408) and the Vénusz at Kinizsi Pál utca 6 charge. To arrange a private room, try Siótur at Szabadság tér 6 (84-10 801) or Ibusz at Fő utca 174 (84/11-107). If you don't mind being thrown together with hordes of Austrians and Germans, brave the Ifjúsági campsite, a couple of miles southeast (in most other respects an excellent place to stay).

BALATONFURED

Across the water from Siófok (and linked by ferry in summer), Balatonfüred is a dignified old-world spa which has long been the most fashionable resort on the lake. Füred, as it is more commonly known, is a pleasant place to just hang out and soak up the atmosphere. Unlike most other resorts, it doesn't hibernate completely in winter. Furthermore, you can use the town as a base to explore the Bakony hills, which provide the best hiking country around Lake Balaton and include many picturesque villages: Dörgicse, north of Balatonakali, boasts simply a gorgeous setting, and Nagyvázsony, north of Balatonszepezd, has an over-restored but picturesque fort built during the reign of Mátyás. You could also make a slight diversion to Veszprém, an historic town about 12 miles/20km north of the lake.

Rooms in Balatonfüred are a bargain compared to what you pay in Siófok. A couple of cheap hotels to try are the UNI at Széchenyi utca 10 (86-43 085) and the Ring Pansió at Vörösmarty utca 7, both of which charge less than $40 for a double, with good rates also for single rooms. For private accommodation, go to Balantourist at Blaha Lujza utca 5 (86-42 438) or Ibusz at Petöfi Sándor utca 4/a (86/42-251). There are good campsites too.

TIHANY

The Tihany Peninsula is a teardrop of land famed for its interesting geology and wild lavender, but also for its stunning scenery. The main attraction in the village of Tihany is the Benedictine Abbey, which sits magnificently above the ferry wharf. The ornate Baroque church that you see now was built in the 18th century, but the original foundations and crypt, which date from 1055, have also survived. The first document to contain a significant number of Hungarian words interposed among the Latin came from the abbey at Tihany, but it is now housed in the archives at Pannonhalma near Gyor (see below). Organ recitals are held inside the abbey in summer. There's not much else to do or see in Tihany, but to find some peace and quiet you can walk west from the village, along the shores of Belsó Lake and beyond.

A giant Club Med-style tourist complex dominates the southern tip of the peninsula, but in Tihany village there is little accommodation. Instead, look out for signs in windows, or ask at the Balantourist office at Kossuth Lajos utca 20.

BADACSONY

The Badacsony Peninsula, west of Tihany, is the stump of a long extinct volcano, a miniature tableland whose soils are well suited to wine production. Badacsony has plenty of old wine cellars and hostelries in which to sample some of the excellent wines: watch for Furmint and Kéknyelü, and if you're in the area in September, don't miss the local wine festival. Whatever time of year you visit, make time to climb to the top of the volcano (437m), from where the views over the lake are superb; there are several trails you can follow.

There are a few pansiós scattered about the place and private rooms can be arranged by the usual agencies. The Balantourist office is just north of the train station at Park utca 10.

Szigliget. A short distance west of Badacsony and accessible by bus or ferry, Szigliget boasts a beautiful setting, a ruined hilltop castle and a relatively uncrowded beach. A few local people offer private accommodation.

KESZTHELY

At the western extremity of the lake, Keszthely is the second largest Balaton town after Siófok. It has its fair share of tourist tat, but Keszthely is not just a summer resort and can be enjoyed all year round. Some handsome architecture includes the Baroque Palace of the once-great Festetics family on Kossuth Lajos utca, the main street. It is now a museum, containing a varied collection of paintings and antiques; concerts are performed here in summer. The Balaton Museum (Múzeum utca 2, off the main street) gives an account of the natural history and geology of the lake region.

The best place to stay, the Amazon Hotel (84-12 248) on the corner of Kossuth Lajos and Georgikon streets, is unfortunately often full. Rooms go for $15-20 per person. Hotel Georgikon, a couple of blocks west, is not a bad second choice. For private accommodation and information, ask at Ibusz (Szechenyi utca 1-3; 84-12 951) or Express (Kossuth Lajos utca 22).

Around Keszthely. One of the best trips from Keszthely is along route 84 to Sümeg, 15 miles/24km north. Zalaszántó, about midway between the two towns, has an interesting 13th-century church and Sümeg has a picturesque ruined fort dating from 1210.

Out-of-season visitors can enjoy the water of Lake Hévíz, 4 miles/6km west of Keszthely: it is fed by hot springs which raise the temperature of the small lake to an impressive 32°C/90°F throughout the year.

TRANSDANUBIA

The vast area of Hungary west of the River Danube, which includes Lake Balaton, is often referred to as Transdanubia. The terrain is hillier than that to the east of the Danube, and on the whole the towns have more of historic interest.

GYOR

On the main rail line between Vienna and Budapest, Győr (pronounced Dure and known in German as Raab) is an obvious and easy stopover. Most tourists can't be bothered with it, but the city is well worth exploring. Győr is a major industrial centre, but at its heart lies a handsome Baroque town.

Győr straddles the confluence of three tributaries of the Danube, and the old town lies close to the junction of the Mosoni-Danube and Rába rivers. Széchenyi tér, the focus of Győr, is an almost intact Baroque relic; the Franciscan church of St Ignatius has some fine frescoes and a wonderful pulpit, and the pharmacy museum is also worth a visit. The streets just north and east of here are quiet and atmospheric, though Dunakapu tér fills with noise and bustle from the open-air market. Chapter Hill (Káptalan-domb), directly west of here, is the oldest part of the city, with winding narrow streets leading up to the Cathedral. This is a Baroque masterpiece, but is most famous for a medieval gold bust of St Ladislaus, said to be the most valuable of its kind; you'll find it in the Gothic chapel. To the south of Chapter Hill, Köztársaság tér has more fine Baroque architecture, including the 18th-century Carmelite church. You can also see the remains of old fortifications.

Arrival and Departure. Several trains a day stop at Győr, en route between Budapest's Déli station (2 hours) and Sopron (1 hours), though only a couple continue to Vienna. For Lake Balaton, go first to Veszprém. If you're heading north into Slovakia, the nearest border crossing is at Komárom (on the Budapest line), but you can also pick up buses to Bratislava. The main bus station is across the tracks from the rail terminal, both south of the centre.

Accommodation. Rooms are neither plentiful nor cheap. Hotel Szárnyaskerék at Révai Miklós utca 5 (96-14 629), by the train station, is one of the few places to charge under $25. If you can afford to pay nearer $50, try to book a room at the Hotel Klastrom, in the former Carmelite convent at Fürst Sándor utca 1 (96-15 611) by Köztársaság tér. For private accommodation contact Ibusz (Szent István utca 29-31), Express (Bajcsy-Zsilinszky útja 41; 96-18 853) or Ciklámen Tourist, the local agency at Aradi Vértanúk utca 22, near the train station. The Kiskút-liget campsite (96-18 986), a couple of miles northeast, opens in summer only.

For authentic food and drink, you can't do better than Halász Csárda at Rózsa Ferenc utca 4, where fish is the speciality. Várkapu on Köztársaság tér and Szürkebarát Borozó at Arany János utca 20 are two of Győr's best wine cellars, and both also serve food.

Around Győr

Pannonhalma. Just 11 miles/18km south of Győr, Pannonhalma has a monastery which is another of Hungary's ecclesiastical wonders. Superbly situated on a hilltop, it was established in about 1000 and is still a functioning Benedictine community. Vespers are sung at 7pm and Lauds at 5.45am. Visitors to the abbey are taken around in groups, so you may have to wait a while if you come during the week. The treasures in the ecclesiastical museum and the library are also impressive.

Pannonhalma is best reached by bus, with five or six departures daily from Győr.

SOPRON

The approaches to Sopron are inauspicious, as the gently rolling hills give way to ugly tenements and industry. But these conceal a charming town with a superb network of old buildings. Sopron is noticeably more Teutonic than elsewhere in Hungary and boasts architecture of most periods, including many medieval buildings which escaped destruction by the Turks (who never made it this far).

That Sopron attracts thousands of tourists every year isn't due only to the fact that it has more of historic and architectural interest than perhaps any other town in Hungary. Though much more pleasant than your average channel port, being so close to the Austrian border Sopron has begun to resemble Boulogne as a shopping paradise for day-trippers. The town has more than forty supermarkets and what was, at its opening, the only Marks & Spencer in Eastern Europe; most shop signs are in both German and Hungarian. The town's inhabitants refer to Austrians as their 'brothers-in-law' in jest, but this is literally true in not just a few cases.

Arrival and Departure. Express trains run regularly between Budapest (3 hours) and Vienna, just one hour north, stopping at Sopron. If you're heading south, to Keszthely for example, you'd do better to take a bus. The rail station is within walking distance south of the centre. The bus station is closer, on the northwestern edge of the old town.

Accommodation. If you can afford to pay about $50 a night, don't miss trying for a room at the Hotel Palatinus at Uj utca 23 (99-11 395), a friendly and characterful place with a superb restaurant. A notch down, with double rooms for around $35, is the equally welcoming Pannónia at Várkerület utca 75 (99-12 180); you can while away many an hour in the café, an elegant relic of the late 19th century.

For private accommodation, ask at Ibusz at Várkerület 41 (99-13 281) or Ciklámen Tourist at Ogabona tér 8 (99-120 40). You can camp at the Lövér Campsite (99-11 715), a couple of miles south of town and accessible on bus 12 from the train station.

Exploring. The inner ring — enclosed by Ogabona tér on the west side and Várkerület on the east side — is a virtually unspoilt vision of medieval townscape, yet not as twee as, say, Salzburg. The centre is small and fun to explore on foot, an ideal place to wander with no fixed itinerary, past exquisite Renaissance loggias and elegant Baroque palaces. A few unmissable sights include: the Dominican church on the south side of Széchenyi tér (which forms the southern edge of the old town); the Fire Tower (Tüztorony) in Fő tér, Sopron's main square; and a unique medieval synagogue in Új utca, which was not uncovered until the 1970s. The lovely Esterházy Palace in Templom utca houses an interesting mining museum, though its future is apparently in the balance.

Crossing into Austria. In addition to the express trains direct between Budapest and Vienna, six trains leave Sopron for Austria each day, three to each of Wiener Neustadt and Ebenfurth; both offer connections to Vienna. Trains to each destination depart almost simultaneously, enabling frontier controls to be carried out on both sets of passengers. You should arrive about half an hour early in order to pass through passport and customs formalities in the international departure hall (adjacent to the main booking hall). Expect to be surrounded by Austrians returning from shopping expeditions, who can cause delays at customs, but most nationalities receive only a cursory inspection. After these controls, passengers assemble in a small waiting room and are then escorted to the waiting trains. There are no further inspections once you've crossed the border into Austria. You buy your ticket on board.

FERTOD

The best excursion from Sopron is to Fertöd, 17 miles/27km east and site of the Esterházy Palace. The opulent Baroque chateau, invariably compared to Versailles, is one of the finest things you're likely to see in Hungary. It is open 8am-4pm all year round, daily except Monday. The fame of the Esterházy family persists because of their patronage of Haydn, who composed many of his best known works here. Concerts featuring his music are held at Fertöd in the summer.

Fertöd is accessible by regular bus from Sopron.

KOSZEG

Heading south from Sopron, the one place not to miss is Kőszeg, a lovely medieval town set among hills almost a stone's throw from Austria. It is teeming with tourists from across the frontier, but this is no reason to avoid the place. The main square, Jurisics tér, is lovely. Two of the most notable buildings are the old town hall, with a painted Renaissance facade, and the 15th-century church of St James, decorated with superb frescoes. You can then follow the narrow streets up to Jurisic Castle nearby, built in 1263 and in a superb spot; it contains a good history museum.

Buses to Kőszeg are not particularly frequent from Sopron, with much more regular connections (also by train) leaving from Szombathely to the southeast. Szombathely is not a place you'd really choose to go to (it was badly damaged in the war), but you'll find it hard to avoid. If you're heading south from Kőszeg, try to leave early in the morning, so that you have plenty of time to make onward connections the same day. In Kőszeg, private rooms can be arranged through Kőszeg Tourist at Kossuth Lajos utca 4 or Savaria Tourist at Várkör utca 57 (94-61 258). But there are several excellent hotels too, including the Park at Park utca 2 (94-60 366) and the Strucc at Várkör utca 124 (94-60 323), which charge $20-30 a night.

PECS

The fourth largest city in Hungary (pronounced Paitch) is one of the most interesting and attractive destinations in the whole country, and can be reached in just over three hours by train from Budapest. The surrounding region is known as Mecsek, after the range of gentle hills which rises north of the city. Pécs itself is set on a steep hill.

The Romans occupied Pécs (or Sopianae as it then was) for four hundred years, but nowadays you will see much more evidence of the Turkish occupation, which was more comprehensive than in other parts of the country.

This is a lively place, particularly during university terms and the July Summer Festival. With its fine architectural heritage and the appeal of the nearby hills, Pécs is well worth visiting.

Arrival and Departure. Trains run regularly from Budapest's Déli pu, with a daily service also to Szombathely. Buses serve most neighbouring towns. Local trains and buses head south to Osijek and Zagreb in Croatia. Both the bus and rail terminals are a short walk south of Széchenyi tér, the heart of the city.

Accommodation and Food. Hotel Palatinus at Kossuth Lajos utca 5 (72-13 322), is a superb building but expensive, with rooms for around $70. You'll pay less at the modern Főnix Hotel at Hunyadi János útja 2 (72-11 680), but for a cheap night you'll need to go private: see *Help and Information* for agency addresses. In summer, you can camp or rent a bungalow at the Mandulás Camping (72-15 981) in the hills north of town, accessible on bus 34.

You shouldn't have any trouble finding somewhere good to eat, but one place not to miss is the Barbakán Borozó, built into the old city walls at Landler Jenö utca 18, with great food and congenial ambience.

Exploring. A dozen roads converge at Széchenyi tér, a large and impressive square. The most unusual building here is the large Mosque of Gazi Kassim Pasha, the largest Ottoman building in Hungary. It now functions as a Catholic church but features a *mihrab* (Muslim prayer niche) as well as some not-quite-obliterated lines from the Koran. Also in the square is the fine turn-of-the-century County Hall and the Archaeological Museum, where you can trace the history of the Roman occupation.

Káptalan utca runs up the hill east from the top of Széchenyi tér. You'll pass several museums along the way, including the Zsolnay Porcelain Museum at no. 2: whether or not you like Art Nouveau porcelain, this is the oldest house in Pécs and worth seeing for that reason alone. Continuing up Káptalan utca, you'll end up in Dóm tér, backed by the bastion and crenellated wall of the old fortifications. The square is overlooked by the four-towered Cathedral, founded in the Middle Ages but thoroughly rebuilt in the 19th century; it has a highly ornate interior. In the southern part of the square you can visit a Roman Christian burial vault, dating from the 4th century and with traces of original frescoes.

The other great remains of the Ottoman occupation are the well preserved 16th-century mosque and minaret of Jakovali Hassan on Rákóczi utca, southwest of Széchenyi tér. You'll see more fine architecture, including the Baroque National Theatre, along Kossuth Lajos utca, a pedestrian precinct with many shops and cafés.

Taking a bus out of the main square uphill towards the university (the oldest in Hungary, though no old buildings survive) is just one way of enjoying a view over Pécs. You can walk downhill, past the city walls and the cathedral and back to the main square. Bus 35 from the train station goes to the TV tower north of the centre, from where trails penetrate the Mecsek hills in all directions.

Help & Information. *Tourist Information:* Mecsek Tourist is at Széchenyi tér 9 (72-14 866) and Ibusz at no. 8 (72-12 148). Express is based at Bajcsy-Zsilinszky utca 6, south of the square.

Communications: the main post and telephone office is at Jókai Mór utca 10.

THE GREAT PLAIN

By some miracle of marketing, the Great Plain of southern and eastern Hungry is considered a tourist attraction. There is an element of the Emperor's New Clothes in this, since once visitors have been persuaded to make the pilgrimage to the Great Plain, they feel obliged to sense its ancient mystery and to see the (incredibly rare) mirages in the sky. In fact, a great deal of the region is extremely dull, and if your time in Hungary is limited, you might prefer to skip the enormous prairie, which stretches east of the Danube and south of the Budapest-Miskolc highway.

The Romans didn't bother much with the land on the far side of the Danube, and the Great Plain is much more redolent of the Magyars. Peasants still follow a traditional way of life, though visitors passing through will be more likely to see mostly museums which preserve the folk traditions, such as in Kalocsa or Debrecen. The town of Csongrád, north of Szeged, has preserved the peasant architecture in the town centre.

At one time the great *puszta* or treeless grassland of Eastern Hungary might have had a wild and rugged appeal. But most of the Hungarian steppe has been tamed; like the Danube, the Tisza (the second great river of Hungary) has been brought under control, the marshy banks drained and much of the land planted or turned into grazing land. Hortobágy, the uniterrupted flat lands east of the Tisza, is the one area to have been preserved in its original state. Occasionally you may glimpse an evocative scene from a car or train, particularly early in the morning when the mist has not yet been banished from the rivers and lakes, and when small fishing boats can be seen lurking among the reeds on the opaque water. The Kiskunság National Park (between the Danube and the Tisza) also preserves unspoilt terrain, including expanses of reeds, wild flowers and swampy forests, particularly in the Bugacpuszta, near the village of Bugac south of Kecskemét. There is also a chance of seeing herds of ancient breeds, such as the long-horned grey cattle, racka sheep and curly-bristled pigs.

Soon the wildness of the landscape gives way to cultivation, especially of apricots around Keszkemét (home of the famous *barackpálinka* or apricot brandy) and of paprikas, mainly around Szeged. Houses are often adorned with strings of colourful drying peppers, and there is even a paprika museum in Kalocsa.

SZEGED

Situated on the banks of the Tisza river not far from the borders with Serbia and Romania, Szeged is a lively university town. It is also surprisingly attractive given that it was completely destroyed by a flood in 1879 and replaced by a planned city in a grid pattern. The semicircular boulevard which encloses the centre adopts a variety of names, a sign of thanks to the cities which provided help after the flood. Szeged is inundated with people during the town's famous festival in late July and August, but otherwise it is not a great tourist destination. Most foreigners in the city are students at the university.

Széchenyi tér, the centre of Szeged, has some fine buildings, but the best square is Dóm tér, dominated by the Votive Church. This is an extraordinary neo-Byzantine cum neo-Romanesque structure, with a huge dome and two 90m towers plus a heavily frescoed interior. The 10,000-pipe organ is used during concerts, which are held here regularly. Dóm tér is the main venue for events during Szeged Festival, though many other buildings are also used for plays, operas and concerts. Other buildings constructed after the flood are also well worth seeing, including the Art Nouveau Synagogue in Jósika utca, which has brilliant stained glass. There are a couple of good museums too.

Express trains run direct to Szeged from Budapest's Nyugati pu (2+-3 hours) via Kecskemét. From Pécs, the easiest route is by bus, with several departures daily. The train station is a 10-15 minute walk south, the bus station a shorter walk west. Pölös Panzis at Pacsirta utca 17a (62-327 974), an easy walk west of Széchenyi tér, has rooms for about $25. You can arrange a private room with Ibusz at Klauzál tér 2 (62-11 533) or at Szeged Tourist, nearby at no. 7 (62-11 711). The campsite on the other side of the river is very good and is within easy walking distance of the centre. Finally, don't leave town without trying the cake shop on Klauzál tér — it rivals Gerbeaud's in Budapest.

DEBRECEN

Not content with its role as capital of the Great Plain, for two brief periods of Hungary's unstable recent history Debrecen has been capital of the country — in 1849 and then in 1945. With a population of 211,000, Debrecen is the country's third largest city, only slightly smaller than Miskolc. It's untouristy and relaxed and a surprisingly pleasant place to spend a day or so.

Debrecen, a stronghold of Calvinism, has the largest Protestant Church (Református Nagytemplom) in the country — a stark neoclassical building in Kalvin tér. Across this main square is the Calvinist College, established in 1546 and still held in high regard. The historical museum and library inside are both worth a visit, though you should save plenty of energy for the Déri Museum, west along Péterfia utca. It has a good collection of modern Hungarian painting, including fine canvases by Munkácsy, as well as good displays of peasant crafts, such as ornately decorated shepherds' cloaks and brandy flasks, handmade rural implements and woven straw. The museum foyer carries an unusually good selection of postcards.

The broad avenue of Piac utca runs south from Kalvin tér, with the railway station at its foot and the Art Nouveau Aranybika Hotel and the County Hall decorated with majolica in between. The Aranybika Hotel (52-16 777) has an excellent restaurant, but it's not a cheap place to stay, with rooms from $70. More affordable nights can be spent at the Főnix Hotel at Barna utca 17 (52-13 355) or in a private house: ask at Ibusz in Hotel Aranybika (52-15 326) or Hadjú Tourist, the regional agency at Kalvin tér 2 (52-15 588).

Moscow-Budapest trains stop at Debrecen, the journey from the capital taking about 3+ hours. Buses serve most towns in the Great Plain from the station a short walk west along Arany János utca from Piac utca.

NORTHERN HUNGARY

With ruined border fortresses, lovely Baroque towns, vineyards, hills and caves, the appeal of Northern Hungary is more obvious than that of the Great Plain. The northeast of the country (loosely defined as the area north of highway 3 — now the E71 — but including Tokaj) is not as large and unwieldy as Transdanubia and the Great Plain: it's well worth making the effort to go at least as far as Eger.

EGER

The main rail line from Budapest to Miskolc bypasses Eger, which may partially account for its lack of industrialisation and modern (including 19th-century) development. Eger is one of Hungary's oldest settlements, having been made a bishopric by King Stephen in the early 11th century. The Turks managed to erase almost all signs of the town's medieval history, but there remain a few fine relics of the Ottoman occupation and some elegant and beautifully restored Baroque buildings. That Eger sees a lot of tourists is also due to the robust red wine, Egri Bikavér (Bull's Blood), for which the region is famous or infamous, according to your tastes. You can visit cellars in the area: some have been hewn from the porous rock of which the hills surrounding the town are composed.

There are several direct trains a day to Eger from Budapest's Keleti pu station, with frequent buses too, taking about three hours. Debrecen is accessible by train or bus.

Accommodation. Rooms fill quickly in summer, but there are several cheap options if you arrive early. Try the Mini Motel at Deák Ferenc utca 11 (36-311 388) or the Tourist Motel at Mekcsey utca (36-310 014), both wtih double rooms for around $15. Lots of agencies can fix up private rooms, including Eger Tourist at Bajcsy-Zsilinszky utca 9 (36-117 24), which also sells town plans. There is a choice of campsites.

Exploring. Szabadság tér is dominated by a huge neo-classical basilica (Nagy templom), but of greater interest is the nearby Eszterházy College, a handsome Baroque palace which contains a library with superb wood reliefs and a fresco showing the Council of Trent; there is also a reasonably interesting astronomy museum. You can climb up to the top floor for a view over Eger's rooftops.

Walking down Kossuth Lajos utca (a grand street lined with good Baroque architecture) and then veering north, will deposit you in Dobó István tér, the main square. Here, the Minorite church is one of Eger's best Baroque buildings. Up above looms the Vár, the old stone fortress-cum-castle built in the 13th century, extended in the 16th and restored in the 20th. Some original window frames survive and the foundations of the on-site cathedral have been excavated. The medieval bishop's palace nearby houses the Hall of Heroes, which particularly commemorates István Dobó, who held out against the Turks in 1551/2. The collection of objects in the museum is mostly martial in character though there are a few examples of pottery and traditional costumes. Down below the castle to the west you can see Eger's most important Turkish building, a 14-sided minaret (which would provide an excellent view of the town were it not locked). The Turks also built the thermal baths on the eastern edge of Népkert Park, a short distance south of the centre.

Szépasszony völgy ('Valley of Beautiful Women') is an easy walk southeast of the centre. Here, a group of 16th-century wine cellars have been restored and can be visited.

Around Eger

Eger is near several places worth exploring by car or bus. About 15 miles/24km north, the undistinguished town of Bélapátfalva hides a Romanesque church behind its cement works. The church was built in 1232 by the Cistercians, who claim to have introduced grapes and figs into the area. Locals will happily direct you to the road leading to the *templom,* which is set rather dramatically between fields and the abrupt rise of the Bükk hills. If you have your own transport, you can easily travel the few miles west to Mikófalva, where a furnished house and forge belonging to the Palóc ('blonde') ethnic group have been preserved and are now open to the public. There are many Palóc villages further west too, on the other side of the Mdtra mountains. The picturesque village of Hollókö is the most geared up to receiving tourists eager to catch a glimpse of traditional Palóc dress and architecture. Other villages are Buják and Rimóc.

TOKAJ

Situated at the foot of a stray branch of the Carpathian mountains, Tokaj is even more famous for its wines than Eger. But it's surprising to find that such renown is attached to so modest and unspoilt a place. There is very little industry in this far northeastern town and little provision for tourists, who come in small numbers to explore the cobbled streets still plied by horse-drawn carts and the mist-covered volcanic hills along the River Bodrog on which the vines grow so well. There is a small museum in the basement of an old house at Bethlen Gábor utca 7, with a collection made up mostly of icons and statues, and a tiny tourist office in the village square, which should be able to direct you to some private wine cellars open for tastings. Failing that, you can travel 14 miles/22km north to Tolcsva, where there is a large state wine-producing consortium; or simply taste good Tokaji Aszú (sweet) or Szamorodni (dry) in a village borozó.

The easiest way to reach Tokaj is by train from Miskolc, a large industrial city which you'll find hard to avoid if you want to explore this corner of Hungary or head north into Slovakia. Tokaj has a couple of hotels, the Tokaj at Rákóczi utca 5 (41-52 759) and the Makk Marci Panzió at Liget Köz 1 (41-52 336), and local people also advertise rooms.

AGGTELEK

Northwest of Miskolc and right on the Slovakian border is the massive cave system of the Aggtelek National Park. Baradla Cave stretches for about 14 miles/22km and contains the biggest stalactite system in Europe. Some of the stalactites are as long as 45m. There are three main entrances, at Aggtelek, Jósvafó and Vörös-tó, with guided tours available from each. The one from Vörös-tó is easily the most impressive. (Anyone with respiratory problems might be interested to know that the air in the caves is reputed to remedy chest complaints.)

Day trips are feasible from Miskolc: there is a daily bus in each direction, the return service leaving Aggtelek at about 5pm. A bus runs from and back to Eger every day too, taking about four hours, but this won't leave you much time to enjoy the caves. There is a hotel, youth hostel and campsite in Aggtelek.

SZATMAR

In the far northeastern corner of the country, Szatmár is the most remote and least visited area of Hungary. Nyírbátor, 45 miles/72 southeast of Tokaj (and 30 miles/48km northeast of Debrecen) has an enormous wooden belfry in the magnificent style of Romania just across the border, and there are fine frescoed Romanesque churches in Csaroda and Mánd further north. In a superbly isolated spot just south of the Tisza river northeast of Fehérgyarmat, the village of Szatmárcseke has a strange graveyard full of tall boat-shaped wooden grave posts, unlike anything else in Hungary.

Calendar of Events

January 1	**New Year's Day**
March 15	**Anniversary of 1848 Uprising**
March/April	**Easter.** One of the few occasions when the Hungarians throw themselves into a celebration of Christianity.
March 1	Mohács Carnival, renowned for processions and crowds of masked merry-makers.
March	Budapest's Spring Festival, celebrating music, drama and dance. It lasts for ten days from the third Friday in March and features both Hungarian and foreign performers.
May 1	**Labour Day**
July	Summer festivals around the country, including in Szentendre. Also Debrecen Jazz Days.
August 20	**Constitution Day.** There are parades in large towns all over the country, but the best place to be is Budapest, where there is a regatta and a superb firework display.
August 20	Bridge fair, Hortobágy, celebrating the skills of the Great Plain's horsemen.
September	Arts Weeks, Budapest, beginning on September 25 (the anniversary of Bartók's death) and lasting for about a month.
October 23	**Day of Proclamation of the Republic**
December 25-6	**Christmas**

Public holidays given in **bold.**

Romania

The Athenaeum, Bucharest

Population: 23.2 million   **Capital: Bucharest (population 2.2 million)**

Of all the countries of Eastern Europe, Romania should have the most to offer foreign travellers. Once one of the richest provinces in the Roman Empire, it has a fascinating history and culture plus the wonderful scenery of the Carpathian mountains. Yet during the corrupt regime of President Ceauşescu, Romania became the most repressed and backward nation under the Soviet sphere of influence. And although the revolution of 1989 put an end to the dictatorship of Ceauşescu, the past still weighs heavy. While people no longer live in a state of terror, it is likely to take years for the atmosphere of mistrust to dispel completely, particularly since the communists are still in power. Political stability has been slow to arrive and the transition from a police state to a democracy has been much harder than elsewhere in Eastern Europe. Despite the appearance of a few smart shops and higher prices in Bucharest, little seems to have changed. Shops are half empty, people still queue for bread, and with inflation and unemployment both soaring, most Romanians endure a wretched existence. The country has seen little of the Western investment enjoyed by countries such as Hungary and the Czech Republic, and the lack of change comes as a shock for anyone arriving from the north.

Urban Romania may not be as sad and shabby as it once was, but ostensibly it would still not seem to have much going for it as a tourist destination. Towns and cities were grotesquely re-modelled under Ceauşescu, with historic buildings replaced by neo-fascist monstrosities. Never more so than in Bucharest, which is perhaps Europe's least appealing capital city (though certainly interesting if only for that reason). The Westerners who do go to Romania tend to go in search of somewhere different (and affordable) to ski or lie in the sun. But the best thing about this country is the beautiful and unspoilt northern provinces, where it is still possible to glimpse traditional rural existence. In Moldavia and Maramureş, you will find charming villages where some of Europe's finest vernacular architecture managed to survive the scourge of Ceauşescu. Further south, Transylvania has the best scenery plus fascinating old German and Hungarian communities, and the added attraction of Count Dracula's old haunts.

For independent travellers, there is no doubt that Romania is hard work. But the often idyllic rural scenes, coupled with the experience of watching a people emerge from a terrible past, makes a visit highly rewarding. The cost of living is often ridiculously low and the people are extremely warm and still intrigued by tourists.

GEOGRAPHY

Romania, which is about the size of Great Britain or the state of Oregon, is divided into five regions. Wallachia consists of the flat lowlands in the south of the country with Bucharest at the centre. The Dobrudja region to the east takes in the Danube Delta, rich in birdlife, and the Litoral or coastal strip, stretching 170 miles/270km by the Black Sea. Transylvania, the massive plateau that occupies much of the north and west of Romania, is dominated by the southern end of the Carpathian mountain chain. Moldavia, in the northeast, borders its namesake republic in the former Soviet Union. Finally, Banat lies to the west of Transylvania, a flat area bearing much in common with Hungary's Great Plain.

CLIMATE

Romania's climate is archetypally Continental: hot summers and cold winters with short transitions in spring and autumn. The period from July to early September (when most Romanians take their holidays) is distinctly warm, averaging 21°C/70°F with highs of 35°C/95°F. The average temperature between November and March is just below freezing. In view of the precarious nature of the power supply, and the ordinance which restricts the temperature in most public buildings to 10°C/50°F, you are advised to dress warmly in winter whether indoors or out. As elsewhere in Eastern Europe, however, hotels for foreign tourists seem to be permanently overheated.

HISTORY

The first signs of a recognisable nation-state originated around 2000BC, when Indo-Europeans formed an advanced civilisation north of the Danube. After some difficulty, the Romans conquered the province of Dacia in AD106 and swamped the region with colonists and eventually with the Latin language, on which present-day Romanian is based. With the decline of the Roman Empire, there followed many centuries of invasions by Barbarians, Hungarians, Turks, Tartars and finally Austro-Hungarians. Romania was divided, ruled, then re-divided.

The last vestige of explicit foreign rule ended in 1918, when the Habsburgs lost control of Transylvania. Under the shaky leadership of Crown Prince Carol, Romania struggled through economic strife to come to terms with its new independence. Amidst the political instability, a fascist terrorist organisation called the Iron Guard gathered strength. Initially neutral during World War Two, Romania joined the war on Germany's side in 1941. But when the balance shifted against the Axis powers in 1944, the Iron Guard leadership was overthrown by anti-fascists and the nation changed sides to join the Allies. Falling within the part of Europe nominally liberated by the USSR, Romania came under Soviet hegemony and in 1946 became a communist republic.

In 1965, Nicolae Ceauşescu came to power and almost single-handedly led the Romanians to international isolation and domestic disaster. Known simply as *Conducator* (leader), he used and abused power for the benefit of himself and his family. The country's resources were used not to ameliorate the state of Romania, but to ensure the survival of the Ceauşescu personality cult. By means of his brutal secret police, the *Securitate,* the President ensured that freedom of speech was minimal. He didn't succumb to pressure exerted by Gorbachev and followed the Kremlin line only when it suited him. While its neighbours developed strong economies and showed signs of liberalisation, Romania remained little changed from the immediate post-war years.

The Revolution. Simmering resentment against the Ceauşescu regime finally boiled over in 1989, when the authorities in Timişoara tried to arrest Reverend Laslo Tokes after he had attacked the government in a sermon. The people who tried to stop troops from taking him away were dealt with brutally, and protestors elsewhere met with tanks, bayonets and water cannon; some estimates put the number of people killed during these uprisings at around over 3,000. But in Bucharest on 22 December 1989, the army for once refused to fire on demonstrators who had taken over the television and radio stations. Later, the newly formed National Salvation Front (NSF) announced that it had taken over control of the country. Ceauşescu and his wife tried to escape by helicopter but were captured and tried by a military tribunal. They were executed on Christmas Day 1989.

Romania since 1989. Ion Iliescu, founder of the National Salvation Front and a former communist, became the interim president of Romania. The NSF was meant to be only a caretaker administration, but ended up standing as a party in the 1990 elections and won an overwhelming victory. Many Romanians accused the communists of stealing the revolution. And while President Iliescu pledged to uphold fundamental human rights, even as interim president he had opposition party and newspaper offices ransacked. Dissatisfaction with the NSF grew, and prior to elections in 1992 thousands of anti-government protesters occupied the heart of Bucharest, demanding that former leading members of the defunct Communist Party should not be allowed to stand for office — most of all Iliescu (who dismissed the protesters as riff-raff). In the ensuing elections Iliescu and the NSF failed to obtain the high percentage of the vote they had in 1990, but still remained the most powerful party. The opposition group to win the most votes was the centrist Convention for Democracy coalition, which controls Bucharest city council.

The split in the NSF between the old communists, who want a slow pace of change, and the more liberal elements, has not helped Romania's democratisation process. Economic progress is painfully slow (output is actually falling), not least because the presence of former communists in the government has discouraged foreign investment. Few of the country's industries are worth investing in anyway. Nikolae Vacaroiu, prime minister,

is heavily criticised for his handling of the economy. Despite a massive sell-off programme, much scepticism remains as to whether privatisation will cure the country's ills. Ceauşescu's mania for heavy industry and for drawing people away from the land, was a disastrous policy in a country so rich agriculturally. Many fields have been overtaken by weeds. Romania has virtually no foreign debts, but it remains one of Europe's poorest countries. There is a severe shortage of water and electricity, and since subsidies on food were first removed in 1990, poverty has spread rapidly. Thousands of families cannot cope with their own babies, and there are said to be about 100,000 orphans in Romania. In Bucharest, the number of homeless children on the streets grows daily.

THE PEOPLE

According to the official statistics, most Romanian citizens (88%) are descended from the Romans and Dacians. This figure, however, includes gypsies and other non-Roman people who have Romanised their names.

There are around two million ethnic Hungarians in Romania, mostly in Transylvania, the cradle of the ancient Magyar civilisation which was handed over to Romania after World War One (because the majority of its population was Romanian). The long-established German community (numbering around 250,000) is also concentrated in central Romania, parts of which were colonised by the Germans in the 12th century. They have always been known as 'Saxons' and their dialect still includes medieval phrases understood by no other Germans. An official census puts the number of gypsies in Romania at 430,000, but the real figure is probably several times that.

The Hungarians and Germans bore the brunt of Ceauşescu's 'socialist territorial re-organisation', his campaign to eradicate ethnic differences in Romania. He did this mainly by resettling Romanians in areas that were densely populated with people of Hungarian or German origin, and many people fled the country. The situation of those who chose to remain has improved only slightly since the revolution: an explosion of ethnic tension has resulted in a series of violent clashes, particularly between Romanians and Hungarians, in which several people have died. The post-revolutionary government has permitted Hungarians to reopen their own schools, but has shown little interest in dealing with the broader implications of the ethnic tension.

Religion. The Romanians are a religious people, mostly following Orthodox Christianity. In Transylvania there are Catholic and Lutheran minorities, reflecting the ethnic diversity of that region. There was officially freedom of worship under communism, but only since the revolution has the phrase assumed any real meaning. Small Jewish and Muslim communities exist.

Orthodox churches are usually open all day, with a constant stream of people going in and out to light candles and say prayers. Inside, ancient frescoes have been turned black from the smoke. Outside, candles are placed in metal trays marked *Vii* and *Morti,* for the spirits of the living and the dead.

Homosexuality. The lot of gays in Romania has not improved hugely since 1989, though at least there is not the terror of persecution. At the time of going to press, homosexuality is still illegal, punishable by a prison term.

Women in Romania. Attitudes to women are determined largely by the male interpretation of Eastern Orthodoxy. Women are expected to run the home, go out to work and raise large numbers of children: Ceauşescu had a policy of rapid population growth, and both contraception and abortion were illegal. The attitudes engendered by such a policy cannot be eliminated overnight.

Since Romanians no longer feel so nervous about associating with foreigners, men approach tourists more than they used to. But single women travellers report few cases of explicit harassment.

Meeting the People. Romania is a Latin island hemmed in on north and south by the Slavic nations of Bulgaria and the Ukraine. Given the country's recent history, it is understandable that Romanians don't seem to possess much of the *joie de vivre* usually associated with Latin peoples. When aroused, however, they can exhibit tempers and exuberance more often associated with the Italians.

Under Ceauşescu, few Romanians risked being open with their compatriots, let alone with Westerners. Reactions to foreigners remain ambivalent in Bucharest, but for every Romanian that stares blankly through you, there is another who smiles or engages you in conversation. Expect to be particularly well received in rural areas, especially in the northern region of Maramureş, where Latin traditions of hospitality have been little affected by four decades of communism.

LANGUAGE

Although over the centuries it has absorbed influences from neighbouring countries and invading powers, the Romanian language retains its Latin roots. Anyone with a knowledge of Italian or Spanish will be pleasantly surprised at how many similarities there are, and should find it fairly easy to master the basics. German and Hungarian are spoken widely in Transylvania, but the foreign language most Romanians are likely to know is French. In the country's top museums, labels are usually translated into both French and English, but sometimes just the former.

Most Romanian words are pronounced more or less as they look, with the following variations:

ă is pronounced as the vowel sound in 'hurt' or 'merge'.
ce or *ci* is pronounced ch: ceai (tea) becomes *ch*ai.
ch before e or i is pronounced k: cheia (key) becomes *k*eia.
e at the start of a word is pronounced ye: Elena becomes *Ye*lana.
g is hard (as in 'go'), except before e or i when it is soft (as in 'gin').
i at the start of a word is pronounced yi: Ionesco becomes *Yi*onesco.
i at the end of a word is hardly pronounced; two together is a long *ee*.
î (or *â*, used only in România) is similar to the French pronunciation of 'u'; it lies between the vowel sounds of the English words r*ee*d and r*u*de.
o or *u* before another vowel is pronounced w: Timisoara becomes Timis*w*ara.
ş is pronounced sh: Braşov becomes Bra*sh*ov.
ţ is pronounced ts: Constanţa becomes Constan*ts*a.

Useful Words and Phrases

hello — *bună ziau*
goodbye — *la revedere*
my name is — *mă numesc*
yes — *da*
no — *nu*
excuse me — *scuzaţi-mă*
please — *vă rog*
thank you — *mulţumesc*
how much? — *cit costă?*
hot — *rece*
cold — *cald*
tea — *ceai*
beer — *bere*
wine — *vin*
toilet — *toaletă*
water — *apă*

hospital — *spital*
station — *gară*
airport — *aeroport*
closed — *închis*
open — *deschis*

1 — *unu* (masc.), *una* (fem.)
2 — *doi* (masc.), *două* (fem.)
3 — *trei*
4 — *patru*
5 — *cinci*
6 — *şase*
7 — *şapte*
8 — *opt*
9 — *nouă*
10 — *zece*

FURTHER READING

The number of books about Romania attests to the fascination Romania holds for travellers. Sacheverell Sitwell visited the country in the 1930s, before the advent of communism, and describes the trip in *Romanian Journey* (Oxford, £5.99); he is particularly good on art and architecture. *In Another Europe* by Georgina Harding (Sceptre, £4.99) is a sensitive description of Romania before the fall of Ceauşescu, experienced during a cycling trip through Europe. *Transylvania and Beyond* by Dervla Murphy (Arrow Books, £6.99), on the other hand, gives a good insight into Romania immediately after the revolution and is full of enthusiasm. For a more solidly political background, read *Romania in Turmoil* by Martyn Rady (I.B. Tauris, 1992).

 The principal travel specialists in the UK are Friendly Travel, Research House, Fraser Road, Perrivale, Middlesex UB6 7AQ (tel 081-566 9040; fax 081-566 8494) and East Coast Travel, 283 Archway Road, Highgate, London N6 5AA (tel 081-348 2000; fax 081-348 9938). Both can arrange tailormade trips for independent travellers and East Coast Travel also organises its own package tours. For winter sports, you can also try Inghams, Intasun or Ski Enterprise.

AIR

The national airline Tarom is gradually expanding its routes, but the bulk of its services link Bucharest with European capitals. There are four scheduled services each week on Tarom between London Heathrow (Terminal 2) and Otopeni airport in Bucharest, with three additional flights from Stansted which call at Timişoara in western Romania. A straightforward return flight, valid for three months, costs around £200; the cheapest fares are generally offered by Friendly Travel. Tarom has acquired several Airbuses and offers a surprisingly good service, in contrast with the dismal experience of taking an internal flight. Departure times often vary from those shown on tickets, so you are advised to check with the agent or Tarom (071-224 3693) a day or two in advance.

In the summer, charter flights link Gatwick and Manchester with Mihail Kogălniceanu airport, 20 miles/32km from Constanţa and convenient for Black Sea resorts. Seat-only arrangements can be booked through the agents above at the same prices as for London Heathrow to Bucharest, although Manchester flights incur a small supplement. Note, however, that for about the same price (and travelling on the same aircraft) you can have a week's half-board accommodation at a Black Sea hotel, for example on a package tour from Duggan Holidays, 20 Mount Pleasant, Liverpool L3 5RY (tel 051-709 3111; fax 051-709 0224).

Other European airlines to serve Romania are Swissair and Air France, both with connections from London. Tarom also operates a weekly flight between Bucharest and New York (tel 212-687-6013), calling at Vienna. A return flight costs $750-800, only marginally less for a one-way fare.

TRAIN

Many travellers arrive in Romania by rail from Budapest: this is certainly the best way to approach the northern and western areas of the country. Several trains a day link the Hungarian and Romanian capitals, which take 12-14 hours and include overnight services. The fare is $50, though students are eligible for a discount when travelling into Romania (not in the other direction). Four trains daily link the Bulgarian capital, Sofia, with Bucharest, taking 11 hours. There is one train a day from Warsaw (17 hours).

For the fastest journey direct from the UK to the Romanian border station of Curtici (on the Budapest-Bucharest line), first go to Paris and then take the Orient Express (not to be confused with the luxury *Venice-Simplon Orient Express*). It takes about 48 hours.

DRIVING

The fastest route from Britain is via Ostend, Brussels, Cologne, Frankfurt, Nürnberg, Passau, Linz, Vienna and Budapest. There should be no problems with the route except perhaps in winter when some mountain roads in Romania are impassable. Car drivers should ensure that the details of their vehicle are entered on the visa obtained for Romania. See *Getting Around: Driving* for full details of the documents required.

Note that if you drive to Romania from Hungary, the border route via Mako is notorious for long delays. Waits of up to 30 hours at the height of summer are caused mainly by the mass movement of Turks wending their way homewards from Germany and Holland.

HITCH-HIKING

The recommended route from Britain is the same as for driving (see above). This journey should be fast as far as the Austrian frontier at Passau, whereupon you can expect long waits and a generally unhappy journey.

Visas. Most visitors to Romania require a tourist visa, which is valid for a single visit of up to 30 days. The embassy or border official will want to know how long you wish to stay in the country; if your plans are vague, it's always best to ask for the maximum allowed. Visas may be extended once in Romania, for a maximum of 90 days in total.

The cost of a tourist or transit visa is a hefty £25 (or £18 if you book a flight and some accommodation through one of the agents listed above). You can apply for your visa directly at the Romanian frontier, but border procedures can be slow and considerable time will be saved if you get a visa in advance through a consulate abroad:

UK: 4 Palace Green, London W8 4QD (071-937 9667).
USA: 1607 23rd St NW, Washington DC 20008 (202-232-4747).
Canada: 655 Rideau Street, Ottawa (613-232-5345).

IMMIGRATION

Immigration and customs procedures have changed comparatively little since 1989, and are particularly time-consuming if you enter the country by land. When crossing the border by train, you may be visited by as many as four separate officials: one who takes your passport away for anything up to an hour, another who asks questions about the length of your visit, yet another who searches every possible hiding-place and another with a sniffer dog.

The authorities are well aware that drug-trafficking, mainly from Turkey and Bulgaria, is on the increase: don't even consider trying to bring drugs, however mild, into Romania. The more common and mundane attractions among customs officials are cigarettes and electronic goods (or anything else they think you might sell on the black market).

Customs. The duty-free allowance for alcohol is one litre of spirits and two litres of wine or beer. The tobacco allowance is 250g or 200 cigarettes. Even non-smokers might wish to take in their quota of Kent cigarettes; see *The Black Market,* below.

1 leu (plural lei) = 100 bani
1994: £1 = 1,600 lei   US$1 = 1,050 lei

Notes and Coins. Coins circulate in denominations of 1, 3, 5, 20, 50 and 100 lei, with the odd 50-bani coin — though inflation has rendered the latter virtually obsolete. There are 100, 200, 500, 1,000 and 5,000 lei notes. Try to avoid getting landed with too many large-denomination bills, though these are the only ones likely to be in decent condition: most 100 and 200 lei notes are in a pitiful state.

Changing Money. Banks offer the best rates of exchange. Their opening hours vary but are usually 9am-noon (Monday to Saturday) and 1-3pm (Monday to Friday). Outside these hours you will have to rely on tourist offices, hotels and the growing number of exchange offices (*casa de schimb* or *birou de schimb*), but these usually give an often appalling rate. The airport at Bucharest and at the larger provincial towns have exchange desks. If entering the country by train, a briefcase-wielding official will come and offer to change money at the border: the rate is fairly good, and it's usually worth changing $10, particularly if you are due to arrive at your destination in the early hours or late at night. Railway stations have no exchange facilities.

You should rely mainly on cash when exchanging dollars into lei. Travellers cheques aren't much use in Romania, particularly outside the capital, and banks take an age to deal with them. If you've run out of notes, it's easy to generate cash at a bank in Bucharest: when you ask to change cheques for lei, the bank will actually give you the equivalent in dollar bills (minus some commission): you are expected to take these to the bank's cash exchange desk, but there is no obligation.

Keep all your receipts. While few hotels and restaurants demand dollars, some will ask to see exchange receipts if you pay in local currency. And if you get landed with too many lei (try not to: there is nothing much to spend them on and Romanian currency cannot be exported), you can change them back to hard currency only against a receipt and normally only at the airport.

Credit Cards. Visa and Access/MasterCard are accepted at top hotels and restaurants, but are generally of limited use. It is not yet possible to withdraw cash on a credit card. ONT, the national tourist organisation, is the American Express agent in Romania (Bdul Magheru 7; 12 25 96).

The Black Market. The financial advantage of dealing with black marketeers is greater in Romania than in other Eastern European countries. The black marketeers or *bisnitas,* are one of the few groups to have benefitted economically from the revolution. Dealers seem to lurk around every corner in Bucharest, though the authorities have supposedly cracked down on the illegal trade. The main disincentive is the number of stories of rip-offs by street dealers, who pass worthless notes or devise other ways of cheating visitors. Be as careful and discreet as possible. Black marketeers will accept other currencies, such as Deutschmarks and Hungarian forints, but dollars fetch the best rates.

Cigarettes can still be used to open doors. Nowhere else has a packet of Kent cigarettes (a brand not held in high esteem by most of the smoking world) achieved the status of a gold standard.

Tipping. Gratuities are a well-established part of Romanian life. The 12% tax on restaurant meals is sometimes misleadingly called a service charge;

it is not paid to the staff, who expect an additional 5-10% tip. Porters and cloakroom attendants should be given a few coins; taxi drivers and hairdressers expect at least 10%.

Teaching English. The demand for English is enormous but the country has no resources to divert into EFL. There are virtually no private language schools; the demand that exists is in the state sector, where there is a handful of English medium secondary schools. Anyone prepared to travel to Romania and teach on an entirely voluntary basis would probably be able to find a niche without too much difficulty. Several voluntary organisations are active, including Teaching Abroad (10 Drew Street, Brixham, Devon TQ5 9JU; tel/fax 0803-855565), which places native speakers with no TEFL background as language assistants in local schools or summer camps in Romania for an all-in fee of around £500. You can work for a few weeks to a year.

The first private language school was opened in 1992 by International House in association with the Soros Foundation in Timisoara. The classrooms are located in the Technical University (17 Republicii St, 1900 Timisoara; tel: 61-11041). It's worth contacting Romanian universities direct as well as the British Council in Bucharest and the Ministry of Education (Strada Berthelot 30, 70749 Bucharest).

Voluntary Work. The publicity surrounding the plight of Romania led to the setting-up of numerous charities abroad following the Revolution. Most of these concentrate on fund-raising at home, but a few send volunteers too. Note, however, that Romania is almost saturated with overseas aid workers, and that what positions do arise are generally long-term (minimum six months). For a list of charities operating in Romania, send a large stamped addressed envelope to the Romania Information Centre (The University, Southampton, Hants. SO9 5NH; tel 0703-593406, fax 593939).

Telephone. Romanian telecommunications rely upon outdated (and abysmal) equipment, and the system often fails to function properly. Local calls can be made from ordinary street booths which take 10 lei coins. You can call long distance from newer payphones (marked *Telefon Interurban Automat*), but these are scarce and you would do far better to go to a public telephone office — most are attached to post offices. A cheap rate (30% off) applies 6pm-6am and all day on Sundays and holidays.

Note that most numbers in Bucharest are gradually being changed, though often this involves simply the addition of an initial 6. All area codes are prefixed 9; the codes for major towns and cities are as follows:

Bucharest 90	Constanţa 916	Ploieşti 971
Braşov 921	Mamaia 918	Sibiu 924
Cluj-Napoca 951	Piteşti 976	Timişoara 961

Calling abroad: international calls made from public telephone offices are astoundingly cheap, though you should beware of the bizarre system for charging: rates increase on a sliding scale, so that the second batch of three minutes costs more than the first. Therefore you should *never* make an international call lasting more than three minutes. Instead make a series of short calls, or ask your contact to call you back. A three-minute station to station call to London from Bucharest costs just $1.50, to New York or Sydney $3.80. A person-to-person call costs about 30% more. It's also possible to reverse the charges.

Once you've given the number and a deposit to the operator (to cover the cost of the three-minute minimum), you should not need to wait more than 10 or 15 minutes before being directed to a booth, though this can turn into an hour or more outside the capital: take a good book and a large amount of patience.

Useful Numbers: ambulance 961; police 955; fire brigade 981.

Telegrams and Telex. Telegrams sent from Romania can take a couple of days to reach their destination, but they are worth falling back on if you have trouble getting through by phone. The ordinary rate is $0.08 per word to the UK. Charges to North America are about 50% more.

You can use the telex facilities at luxury hotels upon payment of a surcharge. Rates for overseas telexes are the same as for telephones, including the increases for calls over three minutes.

Mail. Principal post offices open 7am-9pm daily except Sunday, 7am-noon on Saturdays. The time taken for letters and cards to reach addresses abroad depends to a large extent upon where you post them: a letter sent from the capital might reach the UK in three days or North America in five, but up to a week longer if posted in a rural area far from Bucharest. The cost of sending a postcard within Europe is $0.06 ($0.20 for a letter), $0.10 to the USA.

THE MEDIA

Newspapers. The press enjoys greater freedom than ever before and several papers have joined *Romania Libera,* the country's main and longest-established opposition daily, in criticising the government. One of the best new post-revolutionary papers is Bucharest's daily *Adevarul* ('The Truth'). The cartoons reveal that Ceaușescu did not succeed in eradicating the Romanians' sense of humour and taste for irony.

The party newspaper *Scintea* is hardly scintillating, though the tributes to Romania's leadership are less obsequious than in the past. The authorities produce several publications in English, including *Romania News,* but these are almost impossible to get hold of. Top hotels in Bucharest usually stock the *Herald Tribune, USA Today* and maybe *Time* and *Newsweek,* but the only places you will find other foreign newspapers are in the embassies.

Broadcasting. The BBC World Service (usually best on 9410kHz short wave) is the most entertaining radio network you can hope to find, unless your idea of entertainment is listening to music which even your parents would find dated. When it comes to television, many Romanians tune into Bulgarian channels. But Channel 2, transmitting since 1992 and the first commercial television network in the former Communist bloc, has also acquired a big audience. It broadcasts mainly news, current affairs, drama and light entertainment.

Maps. About the best foreign map is the Freytag & Berndt *Rumdnien — Bulgarien,* available at specialist bookshops abroad for £5.95. Once in Romania, you can buy the *Tourist Map* either from street stalls in Bucharest or from tourist offices; it costs $0.80 and includes street plans of all the main towns. The blue *Harta Administrativă Rutieră și turistică* (same price) is the best alternative.

Place Names. The only notable Anglicisations of Romanian place names are Bucureşti (Bucharest) and Constanţa, which is transliterated as Constantsa or Constanza. When pronouncing place names, pay attention to ţ and ş, which are pronounced ts and sh respectively. Thus *piaţa* (square) is pronounced 'piazza', and *şoseaua* (highway) is pronounced 'shoss-ayo'.

AIR

The national airline Tarom still uses mostly Soviet aircraft. All its flight numbers are prefixed ROT, which some travellers may see as singularly appropriate. Safety provisions are minimal, but fares are astoundingly cheap, e.g. $12 from Bucharest to Constanţa on the Black Sea. There are daily services to major cities outside the capital, but demand outweighs supply and cancellations are common. You will be told that many flights are full, although there are usually some seats held back for officials. You are strongly advised to buy tickets in advance from Tarom offices or agents abroad, or immediately upon arrival in Bucharest.

TRAIN

By far the best way to get around Romania is by train. Romanian State Railways (CFR) operates a comprehensive network, although speeds are low due both to the terrain and the poor condition of rolling stock: the fastest train on the 225-km journey between the capital and Constanţa takes three hours, an average speed of only 75km/h. Fares are phenomenally cheap.

Long-distance trains are classified either as fast (*Rapide*) or express (*Accelerat*). Local services are either moderately slow (*Cursa*) or extremely slow (*Personel*). Express services are usually reliable, but local trains may often be cancelled for no apparent reason: timetables have been reduced quite dramatically in some areas since the revolution. The demand for seats on direct services runs out of control in summer, and if time allows you would do better to piece together a few local trains. Whichever train you travel on, expect poor or non-existent sanitation.

Buying a ticket (*bilet*) for long-distance services within Romania can be a disheartening process, involving joyless queuing and persistence. Your best bet is to go to an off-station CFR ticket office or the tourist office (which may require you to pay in hard currency); do this at least one day before your planned departure. Try to get a reservation for fast or express services, for which you must pay a small supplement. Anyone staying in Romania for any length of time should buy a copy of the national timetable, which costs only a couple of dollars and is available at most stations. It looks terrifyingly complicated at first but is surprisingly accurate and will enable you to plan your route carefully.

You can buy tickets abroad through Thomas Cook and Friendly Travel (081-566 9040), and also use an InterRail pass. The latter is still quite a novelty, however, so be prepared for a certain amount of confusion, and you may have to pay extra to ride on express services.

BUS

Buses can be hideously crowded and are more expensive than the trains. Long-distance buses are fairly regular between the main towns, but long gaps punctuate the timetable of services to rural areas; there are often no buses at all on Sundays. Every city, town or village has some sort of central bus terminal known as an *autogara* (though Bucharest doesn't), but rarely a trustworthy-looking timetable. By asking around it is possible to establish fairly accurately when the next bus might depart.

DRIVING

On the plus side, Romanian roads are lightly travelled. Disadvantages include poor road surfaces (though the motorways are reliably asphalted) and police checks. Make sure your paperwork is in order, and don't touch a drop of alcohol. The principal hazard is other motorists, particularly in Bucharest. The Romanians are terrible drivers, often wandering all over the road. It is with some justification that pedestrians are cautious about stepping off the kerb at a red light, let alone a zebra crossing.

Motorways link the capital with Pitești and Ploești, and short stretches radiate from Constanța on the Black Sea coast; don't expect much in the way of service areas. Most other highways are single carriageway which, given the low volume of traffic, is quite adequate. Few roads penetrate the mountains, those that are close tending to follow the line of the valleys.

Foreign motorists arouse much interest and often generate a warm welcome, particularly in country areas. In urban areas, however, theft can be a problem: some visitors have taken to attaching massive chains to the car doors.

Speed Limits. The blanket urban speed limit is 60km/h (37 mph). On other roads, limits depend on the size of the car's engine: under 1100cc — 70km/h (44 mph); 1100-1800cc — 80km/h (50 mph); over 1800cc — 90km/h (56 mph).

Parking. Except in the centre of Bucharest, finding a parking space is rarely a problem. Be warned, however, that Romania's economic straits have induced some citizens to turn to petty theft to alleviate poverty. Foreign and rented cars are an obvious target, so you should remove items of value before you leave your vehicle. Unfortunately, it's hard to prevent the breaking up of the car itself: visitors have reported wheels being stolen in their absence.

Fuel. Petrol, sold by the state oil monopoly Peco, is cheap at around $0.30 a litre (though the price can fluctuate dramatically). Note that octane levels don't always correspond with what is written on the pump. Fuel is no longer rationed, but supplies are erratic (particularly in winter and in country areas) and queues often long.

Motoring Organisation. The head office of the Automobil Clubal Roman (ACR) is at Strada Chioschi 1, Bucharest (611 04 08). Red ACR vans marked *Assistentia Tehnica* patrol major highways during daylight hours. You can summon help by dialling the local number for the ACR, which is shown on roadside signposts. If you break down in the middle of nowhere, a local garage is unlikely to be much use if you're driving a foreign car. What spare parts are available are those for the ubiquitous Romanian car, the Dacia.

If you are involved in an accident in Romania, the ACR can be remarkably efficient in arranging legal advice and assistance. It also helps greatly if you are a member of a foreign motoring organisation.

Car Rental. The main international car rental firms to operate in Romania are Europcar and Hertz. Europcar works in conjunction with the tourist organisation, and vehicles can be hired through ONT offices in Bucharest,

Braşov, Timişoara and other large towns. Hertz has outlets in Bucharest (airport), Cluj (Velvedere Hotel), Mamaia (Siret Hotel), Oradea (Dacia Hotel) and Timişoara (Continental Hotel).

Car rental at first sight looks quite reasonable (around $20 per day for a Dacia saloon), but the distance charge is very high ($0.20 per km). If you want to explore rural Romania for a week, however, $350 for a Dacia with unlimited mileage is not such a bad deal. Insurance is included.

HITCH-HIKING

Thumbing lifts is not illegal, and many locals practice it on short journeys. The paucity of private vehicles contributes to the popularity of hitching but also means that you can expect long waits and short lifts (mostly in decrepit trucks). You may on occasion have to fend off persistent demands for dollars or Western goods, but you should expect to pay something, whoever you ride with: a pack of Kent cigarettes will cover most journeys.

It may help to know the coding system which indicates where a vehicle is registered: the letter or pair of letters in the middle of Romanian number plates indicate the province of origin. The most important codes are B (Bucharest), BV (Braşov), CJ (Cluj), CT (Constanţa), DJ (Craiova), IF (Giurgiu), PH (Ploesti), SB (Sibiu) and TM (Timişoara).

CITY TRANSPORT

Public Transport. Bus, trolleybus and tram services charge a flat fare of around 20 lei (currently worth around $0.03). Tickets must be bought in advance from special booths, usually found at major intersections.

Taxis. A variety of vehicles and colours are used, and the best clue to an available taxi is the sign on the roof. State-run taxis have a yellow licence plate and usually checks on the back fender. Expect to pay around $5 for a three-mile journey. Some private motorists earn a bit of extra cash by offering lifts. They'll usually charge twice as much as normal cabs and will often refuse to accept lei from tourists; but they can be easier to find than the regular taxis, particularly in Bucharest. A tip is expected whichever type of cab you take.

Maxi-taxis are vans which ply fixed routes, and pick up and drop off passengers anywhere along the way.

Hotels. Officially hotels are deluxe, first or second class. In practice, hotels can be broadly divided into large modern complexes (such as those on the Black Sea and in the ski resorts) devoted to the processing of tourists, equally charmless city hotels catering mainly for business travellers, plus a few no-frills establishments where rooms are pokey, beds hard and facilities minimal. Cold water and faulty light bulbs are part and parcel of staying in the cheapest hotels, but these have bags more character than most other places. No hotel is immune to plumbing problems and in 1993 water rationing was introduced in Bucharest as a result of the decaying supply system. Electricity supplies are also erratic.

Compared with the cost of other things in Romania, accommodation prices are fairly high (more than in neighbouring Bulgaria, for instance). Second-class hotels in Bucharest charge $20-25 for two, but most hotels are one notch up and demand at least $60 for a reasonable double. In the provinces, cheap rooms cost only a little less, but you shouldn't expect to pay more than $40-50 for a comfortable room. Breakfast is usually included in the price.

Hostels. There are no permanent hostels to speak of, but FJPT, Romania's youth organisation, can help anyone under 25 with finding cheap accommodation, whether in a student hostel, private home or hotel. It has offices in Romania's main cities.

Private Accommodation. Staying with a family is the best way to both cut your accommodation costs and gain an insight into the lifestyle of a Romanian family. Since the revolution, prior to which it was illegal for families to take in visitors, Romanians have been encouraged to open guest houses. The standard of room is almost invariably higher than in a cheap hotel, and you'll always be made to feel welcome. Most tourist offices have a list of families with rooms and there are even a few offices dealing specifically with private accommodation; otherwise just ask around. Expect to pay around $10 a night, though in Bucharest the charge can be three times that.

Monasteries and Shooting Lodges. Some monasteries have guest rooms, but in practice it is hard to get in. You must first approach the local tourist office, which is much more disposed to placing foreigners in hotels. Be persistent but prepared for disappointment.

The shooting lodges (*hijas*) dotted about the Carpathians offer surprisingly cheap accommodation, and are comparatively easy to book at short notice: ask at the local tourist office. Some of Ceaușescu's hunting lodges have been converted into hotels and foreign investors are competing to convert his other palaces and villas. When finished, these will almost certainly cater for the top end of the market, but should be worth splashing out on for the chance to glimpse one of the dictator's old haunts.

Camping. Facilities are poor and the official sites are not always easy to get to, but they are good places to meet people and you'll rarely pay more than a couple of dollars to pitch a tent. Some sites have bungalows, which cost in the region of $10. In theory you should camp only at the official sites, but in rural areas no one is likely to stop you pitching a tent in a field; it's always politic to ask local villagers first though.

Eating and Drinking

That Ceaușescu came close to wiping out Romania's foreign deficit was achieved partly by diverting much of the country's best food and drink production for sale abroad, by concentrating on industry rather than agriculture and by cutting imports to a trickle. Meanwhile, this policy reduced the inhabitants of one of Europe's most fertile areas to eating stewed nettles. With the country still strapped for cash, the food situation hasn't improved greatly since the revolution. Fresh fruit and vegetables are scarce out of season, particularly in the towns, though here you are more likely to find imported produce such as bananas: but $1 or more for a kilo of bananas is expensive compared with the cost of other foods. Queues for bread remain common, more out of habit than a result of shortages, though bakeries only bake bread at certain times of day. Look out for the darker and more expensive *pîine alba,* delicious and a much better buy than the blander white version. Food shops (*alimentaria*) don't have much to offer except rows and rows of bottled vegetables and pickles, cured meats and dairy produce.

Eating out in Romania is often a joyless experience. Romanians can't afford to eat out much, so restaurants are scarce. What restaurants there are close at 10pm or even earlier, and the same goes for bars: late-night eating and drinking will be confined to your hotel, where you are likely to have only tourists, businessmen and black marketeers for company. In a simple restaurant or cafeteria frequented by locals, you can eat for $1. You should expect to pay $5-10 for a two-course meal, including beers, in a higher-quality restaurant.

The only national dish that you are sure to sample is *mamaliga,* a bland corn dish with the consistency of porridge, which accompanies meat and fish. *Mititei,* a meat kebab which Romanians used to eat on street corners, is now found only in the odd smart restaurant. Pork is the most common meat, but beware of sausages and salami, which often contain an exotic variety of offal from all manner of animals. No establishment in Romania caters specifically for vegetarians, but the scarcity and expense of meat means that vegetable, egg and cheese dishes are fairly common. Try *ghiveci,* a kind of ratatouille. You can always fill a grumbling stomach at a *cofet ria* (café-cum-cakeshop). Pastries are a bargain at $0.15 a shot, though there is rarely any coffee with which to wash them down.

Fast food has made little inroads into Romania. A couple of American-style burger bars have opened in Bucharest, but this is one country where you won't find McDonalds or Burger King (not yet, at least).

DRINKING

Wine and Beer. Romania is one of Europe's main wine-producing nations. While its wine is not so well known nor as good as its Bulgarian counterpart, it is perfectly palatable — the reds from Wallachia and the whites from Transylvania in particular. The wine-making process is antiquated by most standards, but the climatic conditions are ideal; if investment is forthcoming, the potential for development is excellent — though the heavyweight, syrupy wines which go down well locally may have to be adapted to suit the overseas market. You can buy a bottle of reasonable wine for $1 in the shops (the same will cost $3 in a restaurant), though if you're really counting your pennies, you can find real plonk for $0.50. That Romania produces little good beer is borne out by the wide range of brews from other Eastern European countries on sale, particularly Hungary. Expect to pay about $0.80 for a bottle in a bar, less than that for the weak and watery variety made locally. *Tuica* is the potent local spirit, distilled from plums, cherries, apples or apricots. Romanian vodka is equally lethal.

Soft Drinks. Fizzy and other soft drinks come in unlabelled bottles (or are sold by the cupful in the street), their colour and taste variable: green is kiwi fruit flavour and sickly sweet. Coca Cola and Pepsi have both made it to Romania, and in cafés it's more common to have a coke with your cake than a coffee. You'll often have to hunt around for a cup of coffee, and will probably end up in a hotel café. Expect instant, which is known as *Nes* but bears little resemblance to Nescafé. If you can find it, the local stuff is drunk sweet, strong and Turkish style. Whichever type you end up with, get used to drinking your coffee black. Some places offer tea, but this will generally be a herbal infusion rather than a Typhoo-style cuppa. Both tea and coffee come ready sweetened, so say if you don't want sugar.

THE GREAT OUTDOORS

Romania's prime walking country is in the Fagaras mountains, an area of the Carpathians accessible from the Transylvanian town of Sibiu and which attracts hordes of local walkers in summer. The Romanians who don't spend their holidays hiking are most likely to be lounging on the beaches, which are washed by the calm waters of the Black Sea. Most resorts are uninspiring, but some of the beaches make up for the lack of atmosphere and the Danube Delta has rich birdlife. In the height of the summer season, observing Romanian holidaymakers en masse is experience enough.

Skiing. Romania's two main ski resorts, Poiana Brasov and Sinaia, are in the Carpathian mountains north of Bucharest. A few European tour companies still run package trips to Poiana Braşov (see *Getting There*), but many have shifted operations south to Bulgaria. This is largely because of the state of the facilities in Romania: cable cars may not be working, rescue provisions are minimal and evening entertainment is uninspiring. The advantages, however, include the ridiculously low prices (ski hire, instruction and pass cost around £80 a week), a good snow record and half-empty pistes free of the flash skiers found in most European resorts.

Performing Arts. Romanian theatre is an interesting entity. It is cheap, truly classless and during the Ceauşescu regime was regarded as one of the few mouthpieces open to the people to voice their disquiet. The most popular productions before the revolution were foreign plays with analogies in present-day Romania, such as *One Flew Over the Cuckoo's Nest,* dealing with the suffocation of individuality. This type of theatre remains popular, though there is a hunger for new plays too. Several works by Eugene Ionesco, the nation's best-known dramatist, have been staged since 1989: they were disapproved of by the communist regime because he depicted Romania in unflattering terms. Performances are often interrupted by spontaneous applause and cheering when the audience perceives parallels with modern life.

Classical concerts are best seen in Bucharest, which has its own accomplished symphony orchestra. Look out for performances of works by Bartok, born in Transylvania.

Cinema. Given the language barrier of theatre, you may prefer to spend your evening in the cinema. There is not enough money around to pay for dubbing, so foreign films are shown in the original language with Romanian subtitles. Don't expect too much comfort in return for the $0.30 (or less) admission fee: cinemas usually look more like a village hall and have hard seats. Most have morning as well as afternoon shows, with the final screening usually at around 6pm; some cinemas in Bucharest have an 8pm show.

SPORT

For a nation of its size, Romania produces numerous accomplished sportsmen and women (it finished fifth in the medals table in the 1984 Olympic Games). If you get a chance to attend an athletics meeting, take it.

Romanian football is dominated by Steaua Bucharest (pronounced *stay-ahwah*), the Romanian army team; they are often capable of going for a season without being beaten and routinely qualify for the European Champions' Cup. The closest challengers in the 18-team first division are usually Dinamo and Sportul Studentesc (both from the capital) and Argeş Piteşti. The consequence of Steaua's domination is that domestic games involving the team tend to be one-sided and dull, but conversely there is often the chance of seeing good European matches. Romania has some decent rugby players too, though the national team has never recovered the form it had when it defeated France 15-0 in 1981.

Greyhound racing used to be very popular but was banned under communism. It is gradually coming back to life and races are sometimes held at the Giulesti Stadium in Bucharest.

In Romania one shop window looks very much like another: most places seem to stock exactly the same range of goods, but rarely anything that you'd want to buy. Browsing is not much fun either, since the old-style shops, where you must stand and point at what interests you, still predominate. The amount of trading on the street increases slowly, but stalls are few compared with what you find elsewhere in Eastern Europe; and most sell essentials rather than luxuries such as fruit and tapes. You won't find much on which to spend your lei.

Some Romanian handicrafts are well worth buying, particularly the embroidery. There are several specialist shops in Bucharest, where you can find exquisite handmade tablecloths for anything from $20 to $90. Don't waste time hunting for CDs: though cheap at $12, the choice is minimal. Cassettes are a bargain at $1, but most have been simply recorded from tapes bought in the West: the quality is almost universally abysmal.

Health Hazards. There are no longer believed to be any vampires living in Romania. A more likely threat is seismic activity. An earthquake in 1977 registered 7.4 on the Richter scale and killed 5,000 people in Bucharest alone. Advice has been taken from Japanese consultants on measures to improve building standards, but Romania is just not rich enough to implement their recommendations. Consequently no high building should be trusted in the event of a tremor.

On a more mundane level, you're more likely to get diarrhoea (the 'Transylvanian Two-Step') in Romania than in any other Eastern European country. This is likely to be due either to impurities in the water or to dodgy food that hasn't been cooked properly. You are strongly advised not to drink the tapwater: sewage leaks into the water are run-of-the-mill in Romania's aging water supply system. The incidence of hepatitis has rocketed too, and immunisation against the disease is strongly recommended. See the general introduction for further information about health precautions.

Medical Treatment. There are few worse places in Eastern Europe to fall ill than Romania. The poor economic health of the country has had a dire effect on medical services — as was illustrated so graphically after the 1989 revolution, when horrifying pictures of emaciated patients in Romanian hospitals and young orphans suffering from Aids were shown on television around the world.

The best plan is to have an insurance policy which will fly you home should you become ill. Otherwise, cross the border into Hungary and seek help there. Hospitals providing accident and emergency care are designated *spitalul de urgenţa*.

State Security and the Police. Under Ceauşescu, the Securitate was perhaps the Eastern Bloc's most notorious secret police force, able to instill terror in most Romanians. During the 1989 revolution, however, the Securitate was transformed into an object of hatred rather than terror, and its headquarters was one of the buildings to be ransacked by protestors. After the fall of the President, the secret police apparently disappeared overnight, though some people believe it is still operational, albeit under a different guise and much toned down.

The absence of the military on the streets is one of the most noticeable changes in post-revolutionary Romania. This is all comparative, however, and in Bucharest you see far more men in uniform than in other Eastern European capitals. The police presence at political rallies is low-key, but you can still pick up a feeling of tension. Old habits die hard and trust between former enemies has been slow to materialise. While you should have no problems taking pictures of demonstrations, military installations are still illegal subjects for photographs (as they are in most countries).

Crime. While crime is definitely on the increase, this is usually on the level of mild swindling by black marketeers and remains miraculously low. You still need to look after your belongings, however, just as you would anywhere else in the world. Pick-pocketing is always a possibility in crowded buses, railway stations, etc. Gypsy children are particularly adept at this.

If you have been robbed, dealings with the police should be problem free, and they are often positively helpful.

The Romanian national tourism organisation, ONT, has offices in many European capitals. The branch in the UK is at 17 Nottingham St, London W1M 3RD (071-224 3692), and in the USA at 573 3rd Avenue, New York, NY 10016 (212-697-6971). In Romania it is divided into two regions: Carpaţi (serving the capital and the interior of Romania) and Litoral (for the Black Sea coast). The Carpaţi office and headquarters of ONT is at Bulevardul Magheru 5-7 in central Bucharest. ONT-Litoral is based at the Bucureşti Hotel in Mamaia. In addition to providing general information, maps, arranging accommodation and changing money, ONT organises a variety of trips, lasting one day or more.

BUCHAREST (Bucuresti)

The screen version of Orwell's *1984* was shot in desolate areas of London, but it could have been filmed almost anywhere in the Romanian capital. Bucharest's dark and decrepit streets are grim, even in the post-Ceauşescu era. While the West pours money liberally into Prague and Budapest, little finds its way to the Romanian capital, where the journey towards prosperity is distressingly slow. Coca Cola, Panasonic and a few other names light up the central Piaţa Unirii, but the colours look as out of place as the few affluent tourists who make it to this overwhelmingly grey place. Rural Romanians have been forced by poverty into the city, whose population has swelled since the revolution, but few find life to be much better in Bucharest. Destitution is most obvious in the suburbs though beggars are a common sight downtown.

Once upon a time, Bucharest was the epitome of elegance and grandeur. But much of its architectural heritage was erased in line with Ceauşescu's doctrine of modernisation, and quaint historic districts were replaced by drab streets and bleak apartment blocks. The construction of the vast Boulevard of Socialist Victory (now Bulevardul Unirii) involved the destruction of sixteen churches and three monasteries, not to mention several thousand private houses. The city centre is hollow, engulfed by soulless boulevards which create a thoroughly undesirable sense of spaciousness. A sense of community is hard to find in the Romanian capital.

Not all Bucharest's good points have been obliterated. You can still track down hidden treasures, including several old palaces, crumbling Orthodox churches and a few excellent museums. Some buildings in the centre still display the scars of the revolution, but the events of 1989 are evoked more emotively by the numerous monuments and shrines to the dead. Hard though it is to believe, the atmosphere in Bucharest is much less demoralised than it used to be, illustrated best at weekends when local people relax in the city's splendid parks. And while Bucharest has nothing of the richness of Budapest, Prague nor even Sofia, a stay of a few days can be rewarding.

CITY LAYOUT

The outer boundaries of the capital are defined by a ring road encircling the city about 7 miles/12km from the centre. The main streets (prefixed Bulevardul, Soseaua or Splaiul) run in from this orbital road to wide squares: Piaţa Victoriei to the northwest, Piaţa Romana to the north, Piaţa Universitaţii to the east, Piaţa Unirii to the south and Piaţa Operei to the southwest. Most places of interest lie inside this boundary and within easy reach of Calea Victoriei, the main thoroughfare through the centre flanked by a mixture of imposing nineteenth-century architecture and characterless modern developments.

Maps. There is a surprising choice of city maps, all of which have the new roadnames and a plan of the metro. The one produced by ONT ($0.80) and available from the tourist office is the easiest to use. Other maps are sold be traders outside the university building on Piata Universitatii, the most up-to-date of these currently being the yellow ACR map ($0.30), which has listings on the back. The names of streets continue to change, so don't expect any map to be 100% accurate.

Getting Around

ARRIVAL AND DEPARTURE

Air. Bucharest's international airport is Otopeni (code OTP), 10 miles/16km north of the city centre. For airport information call 633 66 02. Facilities at Otopeni have been improved but it remains one of Eastern Europe's worst airports. Progress through immigration and customs is slow and chaos rules in the arrivals hall, caused in part by the

Airports

Herăstrău Park

Kiseleff Park

N

Dinamo Stadium

Banu Manta

Bulevardul I Mai

Sos. Kiseleff

Str. Iacob Felix

Str. Paris

Str. Argentina

Bulevardul Aviatorilor

Str. Washington

Str. Londra

Str. Roma

Str. Bruxelles

Calea Dorobantilor

Str. Braziliei

Caracas

Piața Victoriei

Bulevardul Iancu de Hunedoara

Str. Polona

Str. Aurel Vlaicu

Nicolae Titulescu

Alexandru Ioan Cuza

Str. D'Sarou

Str. Buzesti

Str. Grigore Alexandrescu

Cladirea Bastilieu

Saraea Voda

Bulevardul Ana Ipătescu

Str. Sevastopol

Str. Frumoasa

Calea Victoriei

Bdul I. G. Duca

Gare De Nord

Calea Grivitei

Mihail Moxa

Piața Romana

G-Ral Gh. Manu

Str. Carol de Nord

Bdul Dinicu Golescu

Stefan Furtuna

Theodor Aman

Luigi Cazzavillan

Str. Popa Tatu

Str.

Piața Amzei

Berthelot

Str. George Enescu

Mendeleu

Str. I. Aman

Str. Polona

BUCHAREST

1 Tarom
2 Grivita Hotel
3 Hotel Dimbovita
4 Tarom/CFR office
5 Bulevard Hotel
6 National History Museum
7 Stavropoleos church
8 Hotel Rahova
9 Hanul Manuc
10 Airport bus stop
11 Municipal Museum
12 Piata Universitatii
13 National Theatre
14 Inter-Continental Hotel
15 US Embassy
16 Hotel Carpati/Post Office
17 Telephone Office
18 National Art Gallery
19 Piata Revolutiei
20 Tourist Office
21 Athenee Palace Hotel
22 UK Embassy
23 Market
24 Ceramics & Glass Museum
Ⓜ Metro Station

0 _____ 250 m

0 _____ 1/4 mile

Stirbei Voda

Cişmigiu Gardens

Schitu Magureanu

Brezoianu

Calea Victoriei

Nicolae Balcescu

Cimpineanu

M. Millo

Edgar Quinet

Bdul Republicii

Ion Ghica

Bulevardul I. C. Bratianu

Plevnei

Bulevardul Mihail Kogălniceanu

Doamnei

Calea Victoriei

Lipscani

Gabroveni

Iuliu Maniu

Dîmbovita

Splaiul Independentei

Smirdan

Selari

Națiunile Unite

House of the People

Bulevardul Libertății

Bulevardul Unirii

Piața Unirii

George Georgescu

Bdul George Coșbuc

Eroilor Cemetery, Gara Progresul

Calea 13 Septembrie

throng of taxi drivers; they expect hard currency, but don't be bullied into paying more than $8 for the trip downtown. You would do better to take bus 783, an hourly express service to Piata Unirii. The fare is the equivalent of about $0.12 and the journey takes no more than half an hour. The bus stops also by the Inter-Continental Hotel (at the top of nearby Bdul Bratianu when en route *to* the airport), which you may find more convenient.

Those leaving on an international flight will be told to arrive two hours ahead of departure. While this is a little excessive, you should plan to reach the airport at least 90 minutes before the scheduled departure time. There are two security checks, both before and after you check in, and it can take as long as an hour to reach the departure lounge. Late departures are not uncommon, however. Tarom has a substantial 'bucket shop' trade, carrying a large number of discount travellers via Bucharest to destinations such as Istanbul and Bangkok: delays awaiting late inbound aircraft are frequent. Don't expect to blow your last lei at the bar (there's no restaurant) or the duty-free shop: the airport is a dollar-only zone.

Most internal flights depart from Băneasa airport (code BBU), south of Otopeni and also accessible on bus 783 (though there is a short walk the other end). Some domestic flights are sectors of international flights, however, so you'll need to check in even earlier at Băneasa to allow time to be transferred by sealed coach to Otopeni.

The Tarom office dealing with international flights is upstairs at Strada Brezoianu 10 (15 04 99), open 7.30am-7pm Monday to Friday. Domestic tickets are sold at the Tarom head office at Calea Victoriei 96 (15 12 24), just off Piata Victoriei.

Train. Bucharest's main station is Gara de Nord (17 13 87), on Calea Griviței northwest of the city centre. The best way out is by metro: you'll need local currency for this, but the ONT information desk can change money. Other railway stations are used mainly for suburban services, though most trains to Bulgaria leave from Gara Progresul (85 63 85), south of the centre.

Gara de Nord can be thoroughly confusing and buying a ticket positively daunting (though renovation work currently under way should bring some improvement). Try to book your seat in advance from one of the two CFR ticket offices: either along the street from the station at Calea Griviței 139 9650 72 47) or in the centre at Strada Brezoianu 10 (613 26 44), in the same building as Tarom and open 7.30am-9pm Monday to Friday, 7.30am-1pm on Saturday. For general rail information call 952.

Advance reservations are required for the following express trains, which are part of international services:

Pannonia, running via Brașov to Arad and onwards to Budapest, Prague and Berlin.

Orient Express, following the same route via Arad to Budapest, thence Vienna, Munich and Paris (arriving a day and a half later).

Balt-Orient Express, travelling via Brașov to Oradea, then on to Budapest, Prague and Berlin.

Reservations (or a surcharge in lieu of a reservation) are also necessary for express services to Constanța (four daily, journey time 4-5 hours), *rapide* trains to Timișoara (four daily, 8 hours) and services to Oradea (twice daily, 9-10 hours). There are more frequent services from the capital to Ploești (45 minutes), Brașov (3 hours) and south to Giurgiu on the Bulgarian border

(90 minutes). The journey north from Bucharest becomes very scenic beyond Ploeşti, so you should try to take a train through the Transylvanian Alps to Braşov and beyond during daylight hours.

Bus. In general, you are ill-advised to travel by bus, but in summer when the trains are packed you may have no option. Since long-distance services are all run by private companies, finding out information is a nightmare. The only sensible solution is to ask at the tourist office.

Car. The broad boulevards through the capital make Bucharest something of a motorist's paradise. Road approaches to the city are mostly wide and fast, and navigating around the centre is fairly straightforward, with few one-way systems and restricted turns. Parking can be a problem, however, since an inordinate amount of roadside space is reserved for official vehicles. Try to obtain space at your hotel. Bear in mind also the earlier warning about the propensity of some of the locals to break into foreign-registered cars: don't leave anything of value behind. A gift of a cigarette or two should be enough to persuade someone to keep a watchful eye on your vehicle while you're gone.

There is a 24-hour petrol station at Strada Tudor Arghezi 7, near the Inter-Continental hotel.

Car Rental: Europcar has an office attached to ONT at Bdul. Gen Magheru 7 (tel 614 4058; fax 312 0915). Information on car rental is also available from the motoring organization ACR, Strada Chioschi 1 (611 04 08).

Hitch-hiking. For highway DN1 to Ploesti, take tram 3 or 4 to the terminus at Piata Scinteii, a couple of miles north of the centre. Going west to Piteşti, take tram 9, 11, 13, 25, 26, 35, 37 to the start of Bdul. Armata Poporului on the edge of the Botanic Gardens. For Constanţa and the Black Sea, take tram 1 to the point where it turns off Soseaua Colentina and hitch from there.

CITY TRANSPORT

Metro. The underground system (*metrou*) is the best way to get around Bucharest. Trains are decrepit but run fairly frequently. There are three lines, M1, M2 and M3, each following major roads. M2 is the only line to cut through the heart of the city and there are few stations apart from Piata Universitatii and Piata Unirii in the immediate downtown area. This presents no great problem, however, since you can do most exploring on foot, and the main places of interest out of the centre are all within walking distance of a station.

Instead of buying a ticket, you put money (currently two 10-lei coins) in a slot at the turnstile before you board; there are booths where you can get change. Not all stations have maps, and signs can be misleading: you may have to ask for help in finding the correct platform.

Buses and Trams. Bucharest has a slow and archaic network of trams, buses and trolleybuses, which follows a confusing route system and is exacerbated by appalling overcrowding. Before boarding a vehicle, you must buy a ticket in advance from a street kiosk and validate it once you get on. All public transport runs 5am-11pm.

Taxis. Bucharest is full of taxis, which are cheap when you can pay in lei. Most drivers, however, will try to demand hard currency from tourists. Always bargain a price before you set off since meters rarely work.

Hotels. Bucharest has a surfeit of posh hotels, from the high-rise Inter-Continental on Piata Universitatii to the Bucuresti and Continental on Calea Victoriei, where you must pay around $150 for a double room. If you can afford to pay over $50 between two, choose one of the following:

Atheneé Palace, Strada Episcopiei 1, a fine turn-of-the-century building just north of Piata Revolutiei. It charges $65 double, $50 single.

Bulevard, Bdul Kogalniceanu 1 (15 33 00). Another stylish old place, though the floor shows are excruciating. Rooms are good value at $35-60 single, $45-80 double.

Hanul Manuc, Strada Iuliu Maniu 62. Most famous for its restaurant, the rooms ($40 single, $60 double) are perhaps overpriced. But the huge galleried courtyard, with wooden verandahs carved by Maramureş craftsmen, is fabulous.

Among second-class hotels (which charge $20-40 for a double), the following are small, have at least some character and are fairly central:

Rahova: Calea Rahovei 2 (15 26 17/18). In an excellent location, just north of Piaţa Unirii. Cold water, mildly run-down but about as cheap as you'll get, with double rooms (more like apartments) for $20, singles for $13. Beware the grumpy owner.

Dîmboviţa, Bdul Schitu Măgureanu 2 (16 20 66/69). Between Izvor metro station and Cişmigiu Gardens, 10 minutes' walk from Calea Victoriei. $30 double, $22 single.

Carpaţi, Strada Matei Millo 16 (15 76 90). A couple of blocks north of Bdul Kogalniceanu, friendly and comfortable in a down-to-earth kind of way. $25 a night for double room with shower.

Negoiu, Strada Ion Cîmpineanu 16 (15 52 50). Turn-of-the-century décor and a buzzing bar which attracts a mixed clientele (including black marketeers). About $35 for two.

Grivita, Calea Grivitei 130 (50 69 95). If your main criterion is proximity to Gara de Nord, this is your best bet. Cheaper and grottier alternatives are the Bucegi (49 51 20) and the Cerna (49 32 50), both within spitting distance of the station.

Private Rooms. You can arrange accommodation with a Romanian family at the tourist office in Gara de Nord or at Bdul Magheru 7, but this is not always a cheap option: expect to pay $25-30 a night.

Camping. The nearest site to the capital is 6 miles/10km north in the Băneasa forest, east of the main Bucharest-Ploiesti highway (DN1). Although it has a picturesque setting, noise can be a problem since the site is sandwiched between the capital's two airports: you can walk there from either. Otherwise, catch a bus from Piata Universitatii.

The advantage of hotel restaurants is that they tend to stay open beyond 10pm, but on the whole they are dull places to eat. Wherever you go, reservations are unnecessary; few restaurants do what could be called a roaring trade.

The Caru cu Bere, Strada Stavropoleos 3, has one of the finest interiors in Eastern Europe, with the original turn-of-the-century wood panelling and fittings and well-restored paintwork. The atmosphere does not quite match the décor but the food is reasonably good; try the mixed grill, but beware the strange-tasting, offal-laden sausages. Expect to pay at least $5 for a good two-course meal. The adjacent bar has similar decoration but is spiritless and somehow dingy. The Casa Capsa, on the corner of Calea Victoriei and Strada Edgar Quinet, is not so splendid a Victorian relic, but is still recommended for a good meal out in civilised surroundings. The restaurant is unusual for having both a smoking and a non-smoking dining room, but the latter attracts few customers. Meals are good value, $4-5 for a two-course meal and a beer.

Romanian specialities are available more cheaply at Casa Rapsodia (Strada Selari 2), tucked away up an alley just north of Strada Lispcani and, more simply, at the Columbia Restaurant, at the corner of Selari and Iuliu Maniu; the latter is always lively in the evening, though it too obeys the 10 o'clock curfew. More cheap eateries are scattered the length of Bdul Kogălniceanu. Many of these are stand-up cafés and pastry shops, but you'll find a few restaurants, including a couple of pizzerias and the Three Stars on the corner of Magureanu, an attempt at an American-style fast food joint. Better than all these is the Gambrinus, a buzzing and cheap restaurant-cum-beer bar at the corner of Brezoianu.

Cafés and Bars. Bucharest is not the kind of place you'll spend a lot of time sitting around in cafés during the day or in bars late at night. The daytime scene has improved a little in the last few years, with several new open-air cafés, including one near the ONT office on Bdul Magheru and another opposite the Continental Hotel on Calea Victoriei. In winter you'll be confined indoors. Confet ria Victoria (open 7am-9pm), on Calea Victoriei just up from Lipscani, enjoys a steady stream of customers. Buy your cake (smothered in cream or soaked in something vaguely alcoholic) at the counter before sitting down. Most people drink Pepsi, but black coffee is available. The confeteria attached to the Continental hotel has a more stylish setting and better cakes (including good croissants), but doesn't even serve coffee. One of the few cafés in the city to stay open late is the Cafea at Bdul Bălcescu 33, a small but cheery place with a predominantly young clientele.

Hanul Manuc in the gypsy district (see *Accommodation*) has a celebrated but expensive restaurant, and you may prefer to simply enjoy a beer in the courtyard bar. Be warned that Hanul Manuc attracts more tourists than any other establishment in Bucharest, but this rarely means a crowd. You'll find more locals at Efes pub, a new Pilsner bar at the top of Bdul Magheru, with tables inside and out.

Exploring

The southeastern part of the centre is the most interesting area to stroll around. This is the core of the medieval city, where some streets survived the scourge of Ceau-şescu and are lined with dusty old shops with gypsies, Turks and Bulgarians doing a surprisingly (or at least comparatively) brisk trade. At the eastern end of Strada Iuliu Maniu, opposite Manuc's Inn, is Bucharest's oldest church, built in the 16th century. Busier than any church in the city, a steady trickle of people stops by to light candles and say a prayer. Nearby are the remains of the Curtea Veche, the Old Court built in the 15th century by Vlad the Impaler (Dracula, no less);

the modest and neglected ruins are visible through a rusting fence. Walking west along Iuliu Maniu and then north up Selari takes you up to Lipscani, the liveliest part of the gypsy district (though at night the streets are deserted), with stalls in the street and music blaring. In a much quieter corner, just a block or so west, Stavropoleos church has exquisite carvings in stone and wood, and retains the original 18th-century icons. The frescoes in the porch and beneath the eaves have survived far better than those within the church.

Around the corner, the imposing Museum of History (Muzeul de Istorie) dominates the lower end of Calea Victoriei. The entrance hall is gloomy and bare, but the basement conceals one of the finest collections of gold and jewels in the world, dating from pre-Dacian times onwards. The treasury, lined in purple and bathed in a yellowish light, is a startling and stunning sight that should not be missed. The dingy rooms upstairs contain dull displays relating to Romanian foreign policy in the 19th century and the independence struggle. The grim atmosphere is thoroughly depressing, but you may learn something. The second floor was closed at the time of writing; it can only be hoped that a reassessment of 20th-century events is being prepared. The museum opens 10am-5pm Tuesday to Sunday.

A few blocks further north up Calea Victoriei, Bulevardul Republicii strikes east to Piața Universitatii, where two buildings vie for supremacy: the Inter-Continental Hotel, a 300ft blight frequented mainly by businessmen and journalists, and the National Theatre, too large for the site but an improvement on its neighbour (its facade was torn down and rebuilt three times before President Ceaușescu pronounced himself happy with its design). The hotel and theatre together manage to dwarf the main university building opposite and the small square nearby, which has been a focus for rallies since the revolution. It was here that students established their so-called City of Peace which was broken up by the miners in 1990. Several crosses and plaques recall those who died, and the walls are smothered in graffiti and peeling posters. On the other side of Bdul Republicii, at the top of Bdul Brătianu, the Municipal Museum (open 10am-5pm Wednesday to Sunday) houses displays only mildly more interesting than those at the History Museum; there is no mention of events after 1939. Around the corner on Strada Ion Ghica, the onion-domed Russian church provides something of a haven; sadly, it is often closed.

Revolution Square. Some 300 metres north of Bdul Republicii, Calea Victoriei broadens out into Piața Revolutiei, the heart of the revolution of 1989. The pock-marked, burnt-out or reconstructed buildings generate a moving but eerie atmosphere. Several years after the event children still approach you selling postcards of the revolution, $3 for ten.

On the east side of the square rears the former home of the Central Committee of the Communist Party, a spiritless hulk of a building constructed in the 50s and from whose balcony Ceaușescu made his last speech. The headquarters of the hated Securitate, in front of it, has been rebuilt, while work continues opposite on the blackened shell that was once the central university library: the fire, started by the security forces, killed twenty students. A nearby ruin houses a small Museum of Resistance (open Saturday only 10am-6pm), though its future, like that of the building, is uncertain. The nearby apartment block resembles a slab of gruyère cheese, spattered with bullet holes.

The former royal palace stretches almost the entire length of the west side of Piața Revolutiei. Built in 1937 (and no beauty), it was latterly the seat of the State Council but was badly damaged in 1989. While the outer shell has largely been restored, inside there is much to be done. One wing contains the country's most important collection of paintings, but most of these have been placed in storage during the restoration work. Just three rooms on the ground floor are currently open to the public: the biggest and best room contains decorative arts including an impressive array of Gallé glass. Once the gallery's full collection is on show again, the foreign works — including paintings by Titian, Tintoretto, Rubens, Rembrandt, Monet and Renoir — overshadow the modern Romanian works in stature, though the latter are interesting as social documents. Next door to the palace, the red-brick Crețulescu church, built in the 18th century, sits rather isolated in the southwest corner of the square, but is highly distinctive with its twin towers. The frescoes in the domed porch depict scenes from the Apocalypse.

Across from the northern end of the royal palace is the 19th-century Romanian Athenaeum (Ateneul Roman), topped by a rather fussy grey cupola but magnificent inside. It's worth going to a concert just to get a peak at the auditorium; the theatre is closed during the day. Trees flank the small park in front of the Athenaeum, providing shade to old folk who gather to chat.

Beyond Piața Revolutiei, Calea Victoriei gradually becomes more leafy, with old mansions housing a variety of political parties and a couple of museums (including the excellent Ceramics and Glass Museum at number 111). Finally, it reaches Piața Victoriei, a huge open space with no character and not even much traffic.

Cişmigiu Gardens. West of Calea Victoriei, the Cişmigiu Gardens (Grădina Cişmigiu) are the city's most central park. There is a small lake for boating, but most people are content to just sit about and chat: the abundant trees give welcome shade in summer. Go at a weekend, when a military band plays to an appreciative audience and gypsies hawk sweets and drinks. Men gather to play chess in a small paved area near the southwestern entrance.

The Centru Civic. The area south of Splaiul Independentei shows the summit of Ceaușescu's 'achievement'. He didn't live long enough to see his project complete and monolithic buildings have been left unfinished, a permanent monument to his madness: supreme among them the colossal House of the People (Casa Poporului), which Ceaușescu was having built for himself and his cronies. With 17 storeys and hundreds of rooms, the palace is the second largest building in the world after the Pentagon in Washington, its magnitude almost incomprehensible. The future of the palace (outside it is as good as complete, inside it is not) remains undecided, with suggestions ranging from outright demolition to conversion into a casino; the latter option is said to be particularly popular with the authorities, who have already been in consultation with investors from Hong Kong. For the time being the palace remains guarded, though from the north (by Izvor metro) you can gain access to the surrounding parkland.

The scale of the Casa Poporului is almost matched by Bulevardul Unirii, which runs straight as an arrow eastwards from the palace to Piața Alba Iulia. Two walkways alternate with trees on either side of the road, with elegant but non-functioning lamp posts and fountains down the middle. The high-rise buildings north and south contain highly desirable flats (with an inordinate number of satellite dishes), smart shops and even a couple of cafés, which are helping to bring the street to life. But behind the row of immaculate blocks, you can see the devastation done to the old town in the name of progress.

Herăstrău Park and the Village Museum. Herăstrău Park, north of the centre, is Bucharest's biggest public garden. You can go boating on the lake or just stroll about, but don't miss the Village Museum (Muzeul Satului), situated at the western edge of the park and one of the best sights in Bucharest. The open-air complex preserves traditional rural buildings from all over the country, most of them furnished authentically. Created in the 30s, the museum managed to survive Ceauşescu's regime intact, despite his express desire to eradicate all traces of peasant life. If you don't plan to explore upcountry, this may be your only chance to glimpse the richness and variety of Romania's peasant craftmanship. Many buildings date from the nineteenth century, but some are older: of these, one of the highlights is the church from Maramureş, built in 1722 and donated by the village because it couldn't afford to rebuild it following a fire. The main body of the church is original and covered in frescoes, though these are mostly in a poor state.

The museum's setting among trees alongside Herăstrău lake is lovely, though a new research centre currently under construction promises to throw an unwelcome shadow over the old buildings. The entrance to the museum (open 9am-8pm Tuesday to Sunday, until 5pm on Mondays and in winter) is on Soseaua Kiseleff, near the Arcul de Triumf and a short walk west of Aviatorilor metro station. You can pick up a booklet and map at the entrance ($0.25), but the labelling is good enough to make this unnecessary.

Cemeteries. Many victims of the revolution are buried in Cimitirul Eroilor on Calea Serban Vod, close to Pieptanari metro station, south of downtown. It is a moving spectacle, in contrast to the more disturbing sight of Nicolae and Elena Ceausescu's graves in Ghencea Cemetery, west of the centre. The graves are close by the church — unmarked but easy to spot due to the profusion of floral tributes: an acknowledgement that some Romanians still hanker after the past.

The National Theatre (613 94 37) is the main venue for drama and operetta, but you would do far better to go to the Athenaeum, a splendid venue for concerts (see *Exploring*), or the National Opera House at the western end of Bdul Kogălniceanu, which stages both opera and ballet. Plays are staged exclusively in Romanian, except at the State Jewish Theatre (Strada Iulius Baras 15), where Yiddish-speakers will enjoy an art form unique in southeastern Europe.

Bdul Magheru has Bucharest's best cinemas, including the Scala at no. 2 and the wide-screen Patria at no. 12. Most mainstream films come here first, though the Victoria at Bdul Kogălniceanu 1 shows moderately up-to-date British and US films (all in the original language).

Sport. To see Romania's finest soccer team, watch Steaua Bucharest on their home ground at Calea Plevnei 114. Dinamo Bucharest play at their stadium on Soseaua Stefan Cel Mare (12 14 70), north of downtown by Stefan Cel Mare metro. Major club matches and international games are played at the Stadionul National (21 20 05) on Bdul Muncii, east of the centre near Piaţa Muncii metro station.

Victoriei, Bălcescu and Magheru are Bucharest's main shopping streets. A few posh clothes shops have opened up along Calea Victoriei but these are still the exception and stand out against the more drab and dusty shops which sell everything but nothing. There are a surprising number of department stores, such as the Victoria at Calea Victoriei 17, near Strada Lipscani. Branches of Romarta (which seems to have a monopoly on Bdul Unirii) sell mostly clothes, but at prices few people can afford.

Most local people rely on the small shops or the stalls in the metro stations, some of which have become veritable underground markets — Piaţa Universitatii even has a café and is one of the liveliest spots in town. For fresh fruit, go to the open-air market on Strada Piata Amzei, between Victoriei and Magheru. Supermarkets abound in this and neighbouring streets, so this is a good area to stock up on food.

You won't find a lot in the way of souvenirs, though there are a couple of good craft shops (Romartizana and Artizanat) on Calea Victoriei, just north of Lipscani. The tablecloths and other embroidery are the best buys. For a selection of more modern art forms, try Galeria Orizont at Bdul Bălcescu 23a, which usually has a fairly interesting range of paintings, ceramics and glass. Antique shops cater mainly for the occasional party of rich American tourists, none more so than Tiffany's on Calea Victoriei, though it's interesting to have a wander around.

You won't find much in the way of music, unless you're into ancient records and poorly-recorded cassettes. The best selection is at Muzica (Calea Victoriei 41). For both Romanian and foreign books, visit the Dacia bookshop next door or Sadoveanu Bookshop at Bdul Magheru 6.

Crime and Safety

By 10 o'clock the streets of Bucharest are almost completely deserted. Reports of street crime are surprisingly rare and the atmosphere is not in the least menacing, but even so it's best not to wander about too late. Given the poverty endured by many Bucharestis, some may find a prosperous Westerner too much of a temptation.

Help and Information

Tourist Information: ONT, Bdul Magheru 7 (14 51 60) is the best source of information for both the capital and the country as a whole. Books and maps are available, though stocks erratic. ONT also acts as the local American Express agent (tel 12 25 96). It opens 8am-8pm Monday to Friday, 8am-2pm at weekends. ONT has desks in Gara de Nord and the Inter-Continental hotel.

Money: private exchange offices (including in hotels) offer a poor rate of exchange and you'll do better to use the banks along Strada Lipscani. Banca Romana de Comert Exterior (open until 1pm), at the corner of Garada, changes both cash and (eventually) cheques.

Communications: for stamps and telegrams, go to the office at Mattei Millo 12 (614 40 54), open 7.30am-7pm Monday to Friday, until 2pm on Saturday. The telephone office (open 24 hours) is at the top of the same street and part of Bucharest's main telecommunications building.

Medical Treatment: the Spitalul de Urgenţa (emergency hospital) is at Calea Floreasca 8, on the corner of Soseaua Stefan Cel Mare (76 64 90).

Embassies and Consulates. *UK:* Strada Michelet 24 (11 16 34/35), off Bdul Magheru.

USA: 7-9 Strada Tudor Arghezi (12 40 40), just north of the Inter-Continental.
Canada: Nicolae Iorga 36 (50 62 90).
Hungary: Jean Louis Calderón 63, east of Bdul Magheru.
Bulgaria: Strada Rabat 5.

SOUTHERN ROMANIA — WALLACHIA

Whether or not you have enjoyed Bucharest, you are advised not to linger too long in Wallachia: there is much more of interest in Transylvania and eastern Romania. If you have just a day to spare, go to Snagov, a quiet village by a lake 22 miles/35km north of the capital. The attraction is the island monastery where Vlad the Impaler, aka Dracula, is buried; boats run from the village. Snagov is accessible by train from Bucharest, but be prepared for more than a mile's walk from the station to the lake.

Ploeşti and Piteşti, further north, vie for the honour of least appealing city in Romania; both are dominated by oil refineries and neither has any attractions of note. Tîrgovişte, 30 miles/48km west of Ploeşti, is blighted by industry too but at least has a history: it was the capital of Wallachia for over 350 years and at the forefront of the defence of the kingdom against the Turks. The royal seat remains as a mass of crumbling ruins known as the Princely Court. Vlad the Impaler was brought up here and there is a museum. Apparently Ceauşescu had plans to build a palace on the crumbling ruins: he seemed to like the idea of being identfed with the national hero (though probably not with a vampire). By some strange coincidence, it was in the military barracks at Tîrgovişte that the President and his wife were executed in December 1989. The Hotel Turist on the Parcul Central is moderately expensive, but the tourist office next door can usually arrange accommodation with a family.

From Piteşti, highway 7 runs northwest to the Olt Valley, where the road to Sibiu in Transylvania winds alongside the river in an area dotted with spa towns and small villages. Just north of Călimăneşti (accessible by rail), the Cozia monastery marks perhaps the high point of Wallachia. Built by Mircea the Old in the 14th century, the church shows a strong Byzantine influence and has unusual frescoes. There is a campsite in the nearby village of Brezoi.

TRANSYLVANIA

The Transylvanian plateau lies to the north and west of the Carpathian range, high above sea level. The scenic mountains, amounting to some of the prettiest landscapes in Romania, dominate the mainly agricultural region. It is dotted with picturesque villages, which are rich with peasant culture. Transylvania has a largely German and Hungarian population.

Horror movie fans are sure to be disappointed by the scarcity of violent thunderstorms and dark and broody castles. Yet Transylvania still has some of the romance and drama its name suggests. The towns of Braşov, Sibiu and Sighişoara have forbidding Gothic spires and towers, built in the Middle Ages by Saxon settlers, and it doesn't need much imagination to picture bats flitting twixt the turrets and cloaked figures scurrying in the shadows. Vlad The Impaler (or Vlad Tepeş), the Dracula of legend, is a hero to the

Romanians for his success in standing up to the Turkish invaders in the 15th century, even though he used brutal methods. But most Romanians have never heard of 'Dracula', nor Bram Stoker, author of the book to have planted the vampire firmly in the imaginations of the rest of the world: under Ceauşescu the book was never available.

BRASOV

With a population of over 200,000, Braşov is the second largest city in the country, with all the industry and suburbia to match. But within the swathe of anonymous apartment blocks, the historic centre founded by the Saxons has survived; the town still has a substantial German population. While the Saxon atmosphere is far more tangible in Sibiu and Sighişoara, Braşov is a very pleasant town with a fabulous setting. It also makes a good base for visiting the surrounding area (and for skiing).

Braşov lies about 100 miles/160km north of Bucharest, served by several trains a day which take about three hours. The station is some way from the centre: take trolleybus 4, having first bought a ticket from the kiosk. For a cheap (private) room you'll have to rely on students hanging about at the station or the tourist office. Otherwise, the best place is the old Hotel Postăvrul on Strada Republicii, the buzzing pedestrian precinct between Parcul Central and Piaţa 23 August.

Castle Bran. About 15 miles/24km southwest of Braşov, Castle Bran is the site most often connected with Vlad The Impaler. While history books recount that Vlad attacked the Saxons at Braşov in 1460, he doesn't appear to have conquered the castle at Bran, though some say that he lived here for a short time. (It is certainly a long way from Stoker's setting for the castle). The myth has been encouraged probably because Bran simply looks the part. From a distance the 14th-century castle is rather surreal, as though an attraction from Walt Disney World had been transplanted to the middle of the Transylvanian plateau. Perched on a rocky outcrop, the fortress is disappointingly small but still unforgettable. It has been reasonably well preserved and restoration work is ongoing. You can go on a guided tour (daily except Mondays), but there's not much to see inside. Bran has a small ethnographical museum, with a few traditional houses and farm buildings.

You can join a tour to Bran from Braşov, but there is also a regular bus which leaves from the stop near the library. Otherwise take a bus or train to Rîsnov, a lovely little place, and catch a bus from there. There is a hotel in Bran should you get stranded, plus a campsite at Rîsnov.

THE SKI RESORTS

Poiana Braşov. Several British tour operators run holidays to this purpose-built resort just south of Braşov. It has an excellent snow record but only a handful of runs, with considerable discontinuities between them: for example, beginners who master the 75m-rise nursery slope must make a leap to a 750m-rise blue run. The two black runs are often closed because the national Romanian team uses them for practice. The northwest-facing slopes also have a nasty habit of icing-up towards the end of the season.

Poiana Braşov is not a particularly appealing place, even though après-ski entertainments are improving gradually (i.e. bars stay open beyond 10pm). The small ice-rink provides a better prospect for an evening's entertainment than the often moribund atmosphere of the bars in the resort's hotels.

Sinaia. This resort, 25 miles/40km south of Brașov, is altogether more pleasant. The main part of the town is industrialised, but further up the slopes of the Bucegi mountains the atmosphere of a village ski resort predominates. The name of the town originated from a monastery founded in the 17th century by a priest following his visit to Mount Sinai; it is still there, a collection of churches and courtyards at the top of Strada Mănăstirii. The high point, however, is Peleș Castle, with its fairytale towers poking above the trees and overlooking the town. Formerly the summer home of the Romanian royal family and later a weekend residence for party officials, it is now a museum. The interior is fabulous, with sumptuous woodcarving and an extraordinary collection of objects from all over the world. It is open 9am-3pm Wednesday to Sunday.

A fairly slow cable car takes skiers up to 2,000m, with many runs accessible immediately and others reached by chair and drag lifts. Cross-country skiing is popular, and in summer colour-coded trails provide scope for some excellent hikes.

Downtown Sinaia is short on charm but does at least provide alternatives for evening entertainment, including a chance to enjoy the opulent surroundings (and fresh food) of the Palace Hotel. The five-star Spa & Casino Mara hotel opened in 1993, but the two standard tourist hotels are the Montana and the Sinaia, which charge around $70. There is a campsite a couple of miles south.

SIBIU

Ninety miles/140km west of Brașov and just north of the Făgăraș Mountains, Sibiu is one of the most pleasant towns in Romania, with an immaculately preserved medieval centre little spoilt by tourists or traffic. The cobbled streets and squares and old city walls are thoroughly Germanic, and hark back to the days when Sibiu played a leading role in the defence of Transylvania against the Turks. More recently, the town was a power base of the Ceaușescu family: Nicu, the President's son, was the local Communist Party chief until his arrest in 1989.

Sights not to be missed include the Orthodox Cathedral, styled after the Ayha Sophia in Istanbul, and the Brukenthal Museum, which has some interesting paintings and folk art. One of the most atmospheric parts of the lower town is down the steps from Piața Grivita, where you'll find a huge market with a wonderful array of stalls. Dumbrava Park, just southwest of the town and accessible on trolleybus 1 from the station, is also well worth a visit. The large park contains an ethnographical museum with a large number of traditional wooden buildings.

The journey by train to Sibiu from Brașov takes a good three hours. From the station, you can walk to the centre of Sibiu in about ten minutes: head straight up Strada Gen. Magheru to Piața Republicii. If you book ahead, you may get a room at Hotel La Podul Minciunilor (924 17259), one of the rare hotels to charge under $10. Otherwise, the favourite is the Imparatul Romanilor, a decorative 19th-century creation with doubles from $70. You can arrange cheap private rooms through the office down the passageway at Strada Nicolae Bălcescu 1, just off the main square. The campsite attached to the Dumbrava Restaurant a couple of miles southwest is poor.

SIGHISOARA

From Sibiu, Highway 14 curves round to Sighișoara, 55 miles/90km northeast. This medieval Saxon town is a stunning historical relic and boasts a fine setting among dramatic mountains and forest. High up on the south bank of the river lies a haven of cobbled streets where ancient churches and burgher houses have weathered the centuries well (though vandals have had a crack at some of them). The city walls are almost intact, with several towers including a lovely old clocktower with an ancient functioning glockenspiel; it offers good views and contains a small museum. Dracula fans may be attracted to Restaurantui Cetate in Piaţa Muzeului, where Vlad the Impaler lived for a while, but it's a fairly unimpressive house.

If you travel to Sighişoara from Sibiu by rail, you must change at Mediaş, on the main Braşov-Cluj line. The station is a ten-minute walk north across the river from the centre. Sighişoara has just one hotel, the Steaua at Strada 1 Decembrie 12 (950 71594), which is good value considering: around $40 a double. The tourist office on the same street may be able to help you find a room with a family.

The area east of Sighişoara, around the town of Odorheiu Secuiesc, is famous for the carved wooden houses and gates of the Székely people, who are related to the Magyars. Village dances and balls are almost weekly events, so ask around.

CLUJ-NAPOCA

Usually known simply as Cluj, this town lies 125 miles/200km north of Sibiu. It was the Magyar capital of Transylvania until 1918, and even now a quarter of the 400,000 inhabitants are Hungarian. There are many Magyar villages in the surrounding area too.

Cluj (still called Kolozsvőr by local Hungarians), is a large, busy town which feels much more Westernised, prosperous and relaxed than other Romanian towns. The town's historic centre and setting are disappointing by Transylvanian standards, but there are some excellent museums — none better than the Ethnographic Museum on Strada 30 Decembrie, which contains superb folk costumes and carpets. Piaţa Libertatii, overshadowed by the mighty church of St Michael, is a popular place to sit and watch the world go by. But for greater tranquillity, head out to the Botanical Gardens, just south of the centre along Strada Republicii. For the best views of the city, climb up to the old ruined citadel.

Cluj has a fairly good choice of hotels. The Hotel Pax opposite the railway station, north of the centre, charges about $20 for a double, but for the same price you can stay at the Hotel Central on Piaţa Libertatii, the heart of the old town. ONT is on Strada 30 Dicembrie, a couple of blocks west of the main square, but can't usually help with arranging private accommodation.

There is an excellent Greek restaurant on Strada 30 Decembrie, with a self-service beer hall opposite. For fresh fruit, go to the large town market on Piaţa Mihai Viteazul on the northern fringe of the centre, where local farmers sell their produce at very reasonable prices.

THE BANAT

The flat western marches of Romania have the least to offer in the country, though Timişoara is a great place — in spite of the memory of the events of 1989, which shot the town into the pages of the nation's history books. It is probably the most chic place in Romania, enjoying a relaxed, Westernised atmosphere. Having explored the lovely old squares and the fabulous cathedral in the centre, you can while away many an hour in the numerous parks. The best place to stay is Hotel Banatul at Bdul Republicii 5 (377 62), just east of the main square.

Oradea makes a reasonable stopover on the way to or from Hungary. It's a pleasant town, with some fine architecture and few tourists. For a cheapish and pleasant night, stay at the Parc Hotel at Calea Republicii 5 (116 99), close to the main square.

MARAMURES

Situated in northwest Romania between the Carpathians and the Ukrainian border, this is the least-visited yet most remarkable area of the country. High mountain passes have meant that the Maramureş have seldom had much contact with the outside world, be it the Roman Empire or communism, making it possibly the most untouched peasant region in Europe. Few other places can offer such idyllic rural scenes, where motorised traffic is scarce and many of the local people still wear traditional clothes: the men with their tunics and sheepskin waistcoats and women their stripey skirts and aprons. The people demonstrate a self-confidence rare in Romania and they are extremely hospitable, offering food and drink to passing travellers at the slightest opportunity.

Furthermore, the vernacular architecture of the Maramureş is unmatched in Europe. Houses with decorative eaves, doorways and windows line the village streets, each entered through a gateway elaborately carved with human or animal figures. Most impressive are the wooden churches (*biserici de lemn*), mostly built during the 17th and 18th centuries. Their tall spires still tower like Gothic sentinels over their humble muddy villages. Inside, many of them have byzantine wall paintings. Neglect has taken its toll, however, the price paid for the region's blissful isolation. Unlike Moldavia, the Maramureş has so far received little money to fund restoration work. In view of the interest in the area which has grown apace since the revolution, however, it can only be a question of time.

Public transport is minimal, so if you aren't driving you'll need to have plenty of time and flexibility to make a visit worthwhile. Exploring here is certainly an adventure, but one made much easier by the friendliness of the local people. The most interesting churches are on or off the road between Baia Mare and Sighetu-Marmaţiei (on the Ukrainian border) or in the Iza valley further east. Along this first route, the best churches are in Surdeşti (on a hilltop with a 180ft tower), Deseşti (good paintings) and Sat-Sugatag (built in 1642 and surrounded by a wonderful cemetery with carved wooden crosses). Along the Iza valley, the highlight is Poienile Izei, up in the hills and accessible from Bîrsana. The church contains extraordinary paintings, including of humans being gruesomely tortured by devils: a pair of bellows up the bottom seems to be the punishment for farting in church.

Baia Mare is served daily by train from Bucharest via Cluj. It has a tourist office (Strada Culturii 1), where you can arrange to hire a car, and a few hotels (though none are cheap). Five buses a day run north 40 miles/64km to Sighetu-Marmaţiei, a pleasant town with a couple of reasonably cheap hotels.

MOLDAVIA

The beautiful northeastern plateau of Romania is only marginally less isolated and wild than Maramureş. Moldavia also enjoys a living peasant culture, but best of all are the painted monasteries of Bukovina — the closest thing that Romania has to perfection. Dating from the 15th and 16th, centuries these churches are unique in Europe. The fortified monasteries were erected by Stephen the Great (1457-1504) — who for nearly 50 years defended Moldavia against the Turks — and his descendants. They bear frescoes on the exterior walls, created for the enlightenment of illiterate peasants and soldiers, who were not allowed inside. On the more exposed surfaces the paintings have weathered badly, but elsewhere they are protected by overhanging eaves. The Old Testamant scenes, saints and eternal damnations have survived remarkably well and are now under the protection of UNESCO.

The three best monasteries are Voroneţ, Moldoviţa and Suceviţa, with smaller chapels at Humor and Arbore. All are situated fairly close together in the peaceful valleys of southern Bukovina, west of Suceava. As in Maramureş access can be difficult. Tours are available only from Bucharest, though you may be able to attach yourself to a tour group in Suceava. There are irregular bus and train services, but without your own transport be prepared for delays or long walks. There is a hotel in the vicinity of most monasteries if you get stuck.

Suceava, 280 miles/450km north of Bucharest, is well served by train from the capital and also from Cluj in Transylvania and Iaşi. Owing to the number of tour groups, hotels fill quickly; try to arrive as early in the day as possible. There is a tourist office (Strada N. Bălcescu 2), but it doesn't have cars to rent. Suceava hasn't much going for it, so try not to waste too much time here.

Gura Humorului, a long (8-hour) but beautiful train ride from Cluj, is the best base for visiting Humor and Voroneţ. It's a small town with just one hotel (the cheap and basic Carpaţi), but is a great place to relax and enjoy the scenery. Crowded local buses leave every couple of hours for Humor and Voroneţ, but try to allow time to walk back: both monasteries are just 3 miles/5km from Gura, north and south respectively.

Vatra Dornei, on the rail line further west from Gura, is not a town worth crossing the country for, but can be a useful stopping-off place between Transylvania and Moldavia. It's an old spa town with a faded Victorian air and a superb mountain setting. There are a few cheap hotels across the river from the train station.

IASI

The old capital of both Moldavia and Romania, Iaşi (pronounced 'Yash') is the region's most interesting town. Known as Romania's 'literary' city, it is a thriving cultural centre with a lively quarter centred around the university. The soulless modern streets bear the unmistakable stamp of Ceauşescu, but parts of the historic centre survive and there are some fabulous museums. Few tourists bother to visit Iaşi, but there are enough sights to keep anyone busy for a day or two. Among the highlights is the Church of the Three Hierarchs, the outside of which is completely covered in intricate carving; it is at the bottom of Strada Stefan cel Mare near the Palace of Culture (the former Parliament). Coppu Park, north of the centre past the university, is the best place to lie in the sun or while away a few hours.

Iaşi is 8 hours by train from Bucharest, 5 from Suceava, and 3+ from Gura Humorului. The town has a miserable collection of hotels, the best of a poor bunch being the Hotel Continental on Strada Cuza Vodă (981-14320). You would do better to arrange a private room through the tourist office (Piaţa Unirii 2) or the agency near the Continental Hotel.

THE BLACK SEA COAST AND DANUBE DELTA

The coastline along Romania's Black Sea (Marea Neagra) used to attract thousands of holidaymakers from all over Eastern Europe. Since the revolution, however, the foreign tourist trade has decreased dramatically. While Romanian families still come here they do not fill the hotels, many of which now stand empty. The Western European tourists brought over on package tours do little to dispel the coast's air of abandonment. The resorts lining the coast have little to distinguish them, each struggling to create an impression of the French Riviera and most failing dismally. Furthermore, the beaches have been tainted by pollution scares, though the unlawlful dumping of waste now appears to be under control.

CONSTANTA

Charter flights bearing sunseekers from Western Europe land at the airport near Constanţa. An ancient settlement and today the country's chief port, Constanţa feels much more cosmopolitan than other Romanian cities, and is also a more relaxed and relaxing place than many. The city has its fair share of dirt and ugliness, but it is more than just a jumping-off point for nearby beaches: there is a buzzing historic centre, a lovely seafront boulevard and some good museums — including an excellent archaeological museum on Piaţa Ovidiu, which traces the history of the Greek and Roman occupations of Constanţa. Other Roman remains include a huge mosaic close to the museum. Most sights are on the spit of land sandwiched between the port and the sea.

Constanţa is at its best at night, and there is a refreshingly good choice of restaurants. The best hotel (and restaurant) is the elegant Casa Cu Lei by the seafront at Strada Titulescu 27 (916 18050), with doubles for around $50, but it's often full. For a grotty but cheap room go to the Hotel Victoria at Bdul Republicii 7. Tourist information is inside the Hotel Continental.

Constanţa is three hours by train from Bucharest, 140 miles/225km north, but services are heavily booked in summer. During this period, you may find it more convenient to travel with Tarom, which has flights to the city from all over the country. Bus services along the coast are reasonably good, particularly to the more southerly resorts, of which the best is Eforie Nord.

MAMAIA

Like Miami Beach and Surfers Paradise, Mamaia is a resort on a narrow isthmus with a lake on one side and the sea on the other. The white sand beach stretches for five miles and is very crowded in season. Conveniently, a tram links the hotels along the resort. Inconveniently, there is little to see in the immediate vicinity once you have had enough of sunbathing and watersports. You would do best to base yourself in Constanţa, a few miles south.

THE DANUBE DELTA

Having formed the southern border of Romania for most of its journey, the Danube suddenly turns north near the town of Cernavoda, 40 miles/64km inland from the coast. (In fact a canal links the Danube direct to Constanţa, saving nearly 200 miles on the journey to the Black Sea.) Close to the city of Tulcea the Danube divides, with its northern course forming the border with the Ukraine. The middle river cuts across to the port of Sulina, while the southernmost branch meanders to the coast at Sfîntu Gheorghe. The land enclosed by these channels is a swamp which, despite the pollution problem caused by sitting on Eastern Europe's main drain, manages to host a vast and varied wildlife population. The area is particularly rich in birdlife (there are over 250 species), and is the only place in Europe where pelicans breed.

The best way to explore the delta is to take the ferry to Sulina from Tulcea, itself accessible by boat from Galati and Brăila, both of which can be reached by train from Bucharest (about 125 miles/200km southwest); Brăila is the more pleasant of the two. Tulcea is a hideous place, but it's hard to avoid at least one overnight stop in the town. There are ferries and hydrofoils daily all year round to Sulina, but be sure to arrive in good time in summer (and take plenty of mosquito repellent).

Sulina, on the coast 45 miles/72km due east of Tulcea, is not exactly beautiful but boasts a preposterously romantic spot. Not served by road, vehicles are scarce and there is little to disturb the tranquillity. The journey by hydrofoil takes about 90 minutes, by ferry three hours. It makes more sense, however, to get off in the heart of the swamp, before you reach Sulina. The best facilities are at Crişan, though there are only a couple of hotels and a basic campsite. From Mila 23, just to the north, you can arrange trips to nearby lakes.

Calendar of Events

January 1-2	**New Year.** In some rural areas, celebrations continue until Epiphany.
March/April/May	**Good Friday, Easter Monday** (the Orthodox church is calculated according to the Julian calendar, which means that Easter can fall about a month later than in the rest of Europe, where the Gregorian calendar is used)
May 1-2	**Labour Day**
May	Pageant of the Juni, Braşov on first Sunday in May, attracting large and boisterous crowds.
August	Folklore and music festival at Călimănesti (Wallachia) in first week of August.
December 1	**National Day**
December 6	St Nicholas' Day. Marks the beginning of preparations for Christmas and New Year celebrations.
December 25	**Christmas**

Public holidays are given in **bold.**

Bulgaria

National Palace of Culture, Sofia

Population: 10 million   **Capital: Sofia (population 1.2 million)**

Bulgaria is quite unlike the rest of Eastern Europe. Its ten million people occupy a big chunk of the northeast Balkan peninsula, but only a marginal place in the average European's psyche. The country is easily overlooked by travellers, since it is a long way from the West and did not experience the kind of high-profile political change that its former Eastern bloc allies underwent. Yet anyone hoping to gain a real insight into Eastern Europe should visit Bulgaria, since it presents a different face to the thrusting entrepreneurship which seems to be turning its former Warsaw Pact partners into parodies of the West.

Bulgaria is also a very beautiful country. The mountains are especially handsome (and offer excellent skiing terrain), and there are still some unspoilt parts of the Black Sea coast. The cities are not renowned for their exuberance, but Sofia and Plovdiv are both well worth visiting.

Geography. Bulgaria is roughly rectangular. Serbia lies to the west, and the former Yugoslav republic of Macedonia to the southwest. Greece and Turkey share the southern border, while the barrier to the east is the Black Sea (Cherno More). To the north, the Danube forms a natural frontier with Romania. It is navigable from Ulm in Germany to the Black Sea, giving Bulgaria a maritime link — subject to political sensitivities — with Austria, Hungary, Slovakia and Serbia.

One third of the country is mountainous: the Balkan Range stretches right across the country, dividing it between north and south. Below the Balkans are the Sredna Gora mountains, one of which — Mount Vitosha — presides over the capital, Sofia. A third range, the Pirin mountains, occupies the southwest corner.

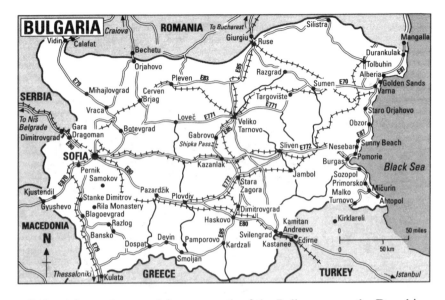

Bulgaria's two largest plains are north of the Balkan range: the Danubian in the northwest, and the Dobrudja in the northeast. This latter region is known as the 'bread basket of Bulgaria'.

Climate. For most of the year, Bulgaria manages to be comfortably warm. The Black Sea coast is mild throughout the year. Elsewhere, however, winters can be bitter. In the southern lowlands, the climate is Mediterranean. Above 3,000 feet (900 metres) it becomes Alpine, with cold winters and cool summers. The best time to visit is late spring and early summer, when the skies are usually clear and the flora at its best.

History. Bulgaria's history is most easily told by starting with events since the war. After it became a Communist People's Republic in 1946, Bulgaria began to imitate the Soviet style of government perfectly. East Germany, Poland, Czechoslovakia, Hungary and Romania were regarded by the Kremlin as potential delinquents; but Bulgaria could be relied upon to stick to the Party line. At one stage it was close to becoming the 16th republic of the USSR.

Even when the Eastern bloc fell apart in 1989, Bulgaria was slow to shrug off state socialism. The domino effect of tumbling communist regimes came to a halt in Bulgaria. In November, the hardline dictator Todor Zhivkov was forced to resign by a putsch of reformists in the Communist Party, and was replaced by his Foreign Minister, Mladenov. During demostrations calling for an end to one-party rule, President Mladenov was filmed asking 'shall we send in the tanks?'. Even so, he repackaged the party as the Socialists and won the election in June 1990. He was forced to resign only three weeks later after a general strike.

The centrist Union of Democratic Forces finally came to power in 1991. The new president, Dr Zhelyu Zhelev, has maintained the government's enthusiasm for whoever happens to be in control in Russia, throwing his weight behind Boris Yeltsin in the attempted Moscow coup in 1993. That

Bulgaria should show solidarity, bordering on slavish adherence to the ways of the old USSR, is not altogether surprising given its history. Soldiers of the Russian Empire have twice liberated Bulgars from their oppressors: most recently in 1944 when the Red Army crossed the Danube to defeat the occupying Germans, but earlier in 1878 when Russian troops drove out the Ottomans.

Bulgaria has claims to be a much more ancient Slavic nation than Russia. The country was something of a cradle of civilisation and letters while Russia was ruled by illiterate barbarians. Its location, between Turkey and the rest of Europe, has meant Bulgaria has been fought over repeatedly.

The first civilisation was the Thracians, who from about 1000BC occupied much of the Balkans and parts of Greece and Turkey. Most Bulgarians are — or, at least, claim to be — descended from the Thracians. From around 600BC, Persians, Macedonians, Romans and Slavs took turns to invade and conquer. The Bulgars, who originated in central Asia, arrived in the late 7th century AD. They gave their name to the country and installed a harsh regime, but gradually converted to Christianity and eased oppression.

The strategic location of Bulgaria, together with its agricultural potential, made it increasingly attractive to invaders. Successively, Byzantines, Mongols and Turks took control, the latter remaining in power for 500 years from the end of the 14th century. The struggle for independence was led by Vasil Levski (whose name, and image, is commemorated in every Bulgarian town). He died in 1873, but by then the momentum for insurrection had become unstoppable.

The Russians joined forces with Bulgarian partisans in the War of Independence in 1877-78, in the name of Slavic solidarity. They dislodged the Turks easily, and Bulgaria began to expand. This triggered tension with its neighbour, Serbia, and a number of bloody struggles were fought. Bulgaria also tested expansion into Turkey and Macedonia.

The ebb and flow of territorial gains was interrupted by World War I, in which Bulgaria joined the German side. In the Treaty of Versailles, signed in 1919, Bulgaria was 'punished' along with the other losing nations. Its frontiers shrank to approximately their present dimensions.

The 1920s and 30s were decades of political turmoil, involving monarchists, socialists and fascists. Bulgaria went into World War II initially neutrally, but then joined the wrong side again in 1941. The Red Army rolled in on 9 September 1944, and a one-party communist state was duly established.

Recommended Reading. For a fascinating account of both sides of the story of Bulgarian communism, read *The Porcupine* by Julian Barnes (Picador, £4.99). It is a fictional account of the trial of a Balkan communist leader called Stoyo Petkanov, but is modelled rigorously on Todor Zhivkov, the former ruler of Bulgaria.

Economy. Since the Second World War, Bulgaria has moved into the 20th century industrially and technologically, providing a reasonable standard of living in comparison with the unambitious achievements of Eastern Europe. Yet the label of being 'a nation of peasants' — stemming from Bulgaria's stolidly agricultural roots — has proved hard to shrug off. The farming which earned the country this description has blossomed since the free market came into being, but it is still difficult to get a good meal.

Tourism. On a visit to Bulgaria in 1956, the then Soviet leader Krushchev remarked that its tourism potential should be exploited. Since then, tourism has taken over the Black Sea coast, where the shoreline is blighted by a thread of spectacularly ugly mass-produced hotels. Resorts like Varna and Burgas do, however, provide many of the eight-million visitors each year with cheap sun, sea and sand.

Two million people a year go skiing here, too. Bulgaria is hardly a country at the top of everyone's (or anyone's) list, but it is moderately good at meeting modest expectations whether you come for the beach, the skiing or the culture.

The People. The late Georgi Markov wrote 'Of all the attributes one could admire in the character of one's countrymen, I am proudest of the Bulgarians' incredible sense of humour . . . I think this sense of humour has something in common with the striking absence of blind fanaticism in the Bulgarian people'. A good example of how a certain dry levity helped the people to endure the years of communism can be summed up by the factory worker's comment that 'we pretend to work, and they pretend to pay us'.

You can expect most of the people you meet to be open, friendly and courteous, providing you do not encounter them while driving. A Bulgarian behind a wheel is an unpredictable person.

Language. Alone of the countries in this book, Bulgaria uses the Cyrillic alphabet; indeed, it is a source of national pride that the alphabet, which originated in Bulgaria, should have been exported to Russia and Ukraine. (This is all the more surprising since the Cyrillic alphabet made the linguistic leap across Romania, with its strictly Latin roots.)

The single most useful piece of advice for anyone heading to Bulgaria is to master the alphabet. Those back-to-front Rs, and letters which you dimly remember from algebra lessons, and Hs which behave like Ns, are remarkably easy to master. In a short time you will be able to read local maps and timetables, and decipher shop and *PECTOPAHT* signs (that transliterates to *restorant*, and means restaurant).

The alphabet is given below, with pronunciation hints:

а	a as in hat	п	p
б	b	р	r
в	v	с	s
г	g as in gas	т	t
д	d	у	oo as in boot
е	e as in bed	ф	f
ж	zh, as s in leisure	х	kh, as ch in loch
з	z as in zoo	ц	ts as in its
и	i as in it	ч	ch as in church
ы	ii — a 'y' sound on the end	ш	sh
к	k	щ	sht as shed in pushed
л	l	ъ	short u as in gut
м	m	ь	'soft sign' — ignore it
н	n	ю	you as in youth
о	o as in hot	я	ya as in yank

Yes and No. Cultural differences in head movements cause all manner of confusion for Western visitors. Bulgarians move their heads from side to side to signify 'yes', and up and down to mean 'no'. To compound the problem, some locals deliberate adopt the opposite practice when dealing with Westerners, in order to help them. To be on the safe side, you should rely upon speech: *da* means yes, *ne* means no.

Religion. Eastern Orthodox is the main religion, with a Muslim minority among the Pomaks. Even as a secular state under communism, Bulgaria was tolerant of Orthodox religion. Church-going is especially popular in rural areas.

Islam, the Pomaks' religion, suffered along with its practitioners during Zhivkov's 'Bulgarianisation' of the Turkish minority. The mosques which were closed in the 1980s are gradually reopening.

Meeting the People. Some travellers have commented on a certain earnestness among Bulgarians, but any such impression is usually rapidly amended; most of the locals have an excellent sense of humour, and — like their neighbours in Greece and Turkey — a strong tradition of hospitality towards visitors. Leaving aside the traces of indifference bred by 40 years of state socialism, Bulgarians are among the most helpful people you could hope to meet.

Even in touristy areas, curiosity about foreigners is considerable — as is the locals' tolerance of Western eccentricities. About the only real offence you could cause would be to visit a church or mosque while dressed immodestly.

Air. Balkan Bulgarian Airlines has regular flights between London Heathrow and Sofia. The standard return fare to the Bulgarian capital is shocking, however: over £300 return for a three-hour flight. Discounted tickets for the London-Sofia trip alone are rare. There is, however, a simple-but-strange way to cut costs on the route: by buying a ticket to beyond Sofia. Plenty of agents will sell you a ticket to somewhere further afield via Sofia for a lot less than the standard round-trip. For example, the research for this chapter was conducted by using a London-Sofia-Larnaca (Cyprus) ticket, bought through Tradewings (071-631 1840) for £266. Balkan Bulgarian discounts extensively to numerous destinations through its Sofia hub, so you could take a side-trip to Athens or Istanbul.

If these fares are still too high, or you wish to travel from another British airport, try to get a seat on a charter flight to one of the Black Sea airports. Balkan Holidays (071-493 8612) sells charter tickets for around £200 return from several UK cities to Burgas and Varna. One more option is a charter flight to Greece (Thessaloniki is the closest), which can be as cheap as £100 if you book close to departure.

Package Holidays: given the relatively high cost of reaching Bulgaria, inclusive tours can represent extremely good value. For around £250 in summer, you get a flight to the Black Sea and a week in a tolerable hotel. In winter, flights operate to Sofia and Plovdiv to give access to the main skiing areas, for similar prices. The leading specialist is Balkan Holidays (071-493 8612), but many other operators include holidays in Bulgaria.

Train. Routes into Sofia from the west are problematic because of the war in the former Yugoslavia and the repercussions of United Nations blockades against Serbia. The only routes which are likely to be trouble-free are from Bucharest (crossing from Romania at Giurgiu-Ruse) and Thessaloniki (using the Promachon-Kulata crossing from Greece), though even this route will be jeopardised if trouble flares in Macedonia.

Driving. Similar problems with access apply to driving into Bulgaria. If you are entering the country with a rented car you need to show confirmation that you have permission to drive it. Any driver entering Bulgaria has to produce a copy of the Vehicle Registration Document. It is best to obtain green card insurance in advance; cover bought at the Bulgarian border is expensive.

Bulgarian motoring regulations require that your car be equipped with a fire extinguisher and a first-aid kit. It is illegal for a child under 12 years to travel as a front seat passenger. For other details on motoring in Bulgaria see *Getting Around: Car.*

Visas. Package tourists do not need visas; almost everyone else still does.

Tourist Visa: Anyone on business or travelling independently has to have a tourist visa (valid for 30 days). The quickest way to obtain this is to call in person at a Bulgarian Consulate, (in the UK at 188 Queen's Gate, London SW7 5HL; tel 071-584 9400). Opening hours are Monday to Friday 9.30am-12.30pm. You will need a full passport, one photograph and £20 in cash or postal orders. The visa issuing process takes 10 working days at any Bulgarian Consulate. You can also apply by post but allow longer for this and obtain an application form first. You may be able to persuade a travel agent specializing in Eastern Europe (e.g. Peltours, 071-637 4374) to fax you a form if you are in a hurry. You can then send the form to the Consulate with a stamped addressed envelope, photograph and £20 in postal orders. If you book a flight to Bulgaria with Peltours they will arrange the visa for you.

Alternatively you can wait until you arrive, and obtain a visa on the spot. This will cost a minimum of $66, unless you don't want to stay long and can persuade the authorities you are in transit.

Transit Visa: Single-entry visas valid for 30 hours are normally issued on the spot and cost £20 (£40 for a double entry). Expiry dates are three months from issue.

Visa Extensions: Visa extensions are possible in theory but in practice the bureaucracy involved is maddening; it is probably less hassle to cross over into Romania, Greece or Turkey and head straight back in.

US citizens should allow 2-3 weeks for obtaining visas from the Bulgarian Embassy at 1621 22nd Street, NW Washington DC 20008, USA. The fee is $30 plus $3 postage. In Canada, the Embassy is at 325 Steward Street, Ottawa, Ontario.

Carte Statistique. All independent travellers are issued on arrival with an exit card, called a *Carte Statistique* (presumably to reinforce the notion under communism that you are merely a number. This bureaucratic hangover is supposed to be stamped by the receptionist at the hotel or campsite where you are staying, every night. If you have gaps on your card, in theory at least, you are liable to a fine. In practice however you would be very unlucky to be caught as the *Cartes* are not usually scrutinized closely provided they have several stamps on them.

Staying with Bulgarians. No longer a problem; what may be more of a problem is dealing with the crowds of touts who greet incoming trains in Sofia.

Customs. Inbound checks on tourists are almost invariably cursory except at the overland frontier with Turkey, when drug searches are common. In case anyone decides to take a close look at your possessions on the way out, it is advisable to declare valuable items to facilitate re-export upon departure from Bulgaria. As well as personal effects, you may import 1 litre of spirits, 2 litres of wine, 250 cigarettes or 250 grams of tobacco products.

Frontier Posts. *From Serbia:* motorists coming by road E80 will cross at the checkpoint of Kalotina, subject to UN controls. Those coming by train from Belgrade will go through customs at Dragoman.

From Macedonia: the southern point of entry from Yugoslavia by road E770 is Gyushevo. Vrasha Chuka (E761) is the northwest border.

From Greece: The entry point is at the southwest corner of Bulgaria at Kalata.

From Turkey: Those travelling by road will go through the checkpoints of Malko Turnovo or Kapitan Andreevo and by train at Svilengrad.

From Romania: The usual border crossing for motorists is Ruse by way of the Friendship Bridge (Most na Druzhbata) and for the train customs formalities take place at Ruse railway station. In the northwest there is a regular ferry crossing from Calafat to Vidin. Silistra on the Danube is not a reliable border crossing as it is only open intermittently.

Airports: International flights serve Sofia, Plovdiv, Varna, Burgas and Ruse. For travellers arriving on charter flights, checks are cursory and searches rare. Those arriving on scheduled flights should expect more attention.

The currency is the lev (plural leva).
£1 = 42 lev
$1 = 28 lev
You can change money upon arrival at Sofia and Plovdiv airports, and at thousands of bureaux de change throughout Bulgaria. Stick to changing money in large towns and cities, since competition keeps rates highly competitive. Inflation is above 50%, which means you should not change too much at one time — the exchange rate improves in your favour by about 1% a week.

The easiest way to check current exchange rates is to look at the front page of the business newspaper *24 Hours*, which quotes the median rates against dollars, Deutsche Marks and sterling. Cash gets better rates than travellers cheques.

Credit Cards. All the usual credit cards are accepted in the main towns and resorts. Holders of Eurocard, Mastercard or Access can get a cash advance in Bulgaria equivalent to $100. In rural areas stick to cash.

The Black Market. There is no good reason for changing money on the black market, except for those hoping to offload counterfeit currency.

Work. The best opportunities are in teaching English. All teaching positions in Bulgaria are organised by the Ministry of Education & Science, precluding the possibility of signing a private contract (at least officially). Specialist foreign language secondary schools in Bulgaria are being provided with native speaker teachers on one-year renewable contracts by the Central Bureau for Educational Visits and Exchanges on behalf of the British Council and the Bulgarian Ministry of Education (18 Boulevard Stamboliski, Sofia). There is a demand for certified teachers of science, etc. to teach in one of the many English Language Medium Schools (ELMS). Language schools to contact (all require qualified teachers):

'Ivan Vazov' English Language School, 22 Bulgaria Boulevard, 4700 Smolyan (tel 301-23328).
'Simeon Radev' School for Foreign Languages, Blagoi Gebrev Str, 2304 Pernik 4 (tel 7-5487).
ELM School 'Aleko Konstantinov', Pravets 2161 (tel 7133-2183/2181).

Communications

Telephones. Public payphones are found in the foyers of hotels, offices etc., but functional problems are endemic. The best plan is to make calls from hotel rooms or telephone offices. At the latter, a direct-dialled call to the UK costs only $1 a minute. In Sofia, telephone calls can be made 24 hours a day at the main post office at 6 General Gurko Street. Telephoning involves queueing at the appropriate counter to give the assistant the telephone number you wish to call. You will then be allocated a booth and probably dial the call yourself. The international access code is 00.

Useful Numbers: 121 — long distance operator; 123 — international operator; 166 — Police; 150 — Ambulance; 160 — Fire; 170 — Telegrams.

Telex and Fax. International telexes can be sent from the Main Post Office in Sofia at 6 Gurko Street, and at all the major hotels in Sofia. For a small fee, business visitors can use the telex and fax facilities at the British Embassy during office hours: Boulevard Marshal Tolbukhin 65-67 Sofia (885 3651).

Post. Post Office opening hours are usually 8.30am-5pm Monday to Saturday. Postcards to the UK cost around $0.10. Stamps (*marki*) are available only from post offices. When posting mail at main post offices use *Burza Poshta* (fast mail) which appears on a red background above the box.

Newspapers. Bulgaria has a lively press, ranging from *Demokratsiya*, the newspaper of the ruling Union of Democratic Forces. The old communist paper, *Trud*, has survived, but — tellingly — the rates for dollars, Deutschmarks and Swiss francs are shown on the front page. *Kontinent* has fewer axes to grind, and has good foreign coverage. *Standart* is a tabloid printed on blue paper, and has excellent sports coverage. Unusually, it also has the headlines in English on the back page. For business people, *Pari* and *24 Chasa* (24 hours) have all the relevant numbers. Unfortunately for the visitor, all of these are published in Bulgarian. The only English-language publication is *Bulgarian Business News.*

Radio. American news and current affairs can be found on TNN (95.5FM). The Sofia station, at 99FM, plays the best music.

Television. Russian television is still broadcast in Bulgaria, but MTV is also widely available.

Water. The local supply of water *(voda)* is safe to drink everywhere, but if you don't like the taste of tap water there are various bottled spring waters (see *Eating and Drinking*). In Sofia, and spa towns such as Velingrad and

Sandanski, there are drinking fountains spurting spring water for public consumption.

Medical Treatment. British citizens and nationals of other countries having a reciprocal health agreement with Bulgaria can receive free medical treatment upon production of a passport. Medicines, however, have to be paid for. In Sofia there is a clinic especially for foreigners at Mladost 1, ul Evgeni Pavlovski (tel: 75361). If you are not in Sofia and you need to see a doctor (*lekar*) or dentist (*zabolekar*), ask to be taken to the nearest polyclinic. In an emergency telephone 150 for an ambulance.

Pharmacies. In Sofia there is a 24 hour pharmacy at ul Alabin 29. To find out which other pharmacies are open at night and weekends, call 178. Most pharmacies stock Western brand-name drugs, but check expiry dates carefully.

Aids. Bulgaria has been relatively lightly affected by Aids, even allowing for a certain underestimation in the statistics. There are no plans at present to introduce compulsory tests for foreigners.

Getting Around

Maps. It is difficult to buy a map of Bulgaria on its own, as it is usually combined either with Romania or the whole of Eastern Europe. The Bulgarian Tourist Office, 18 Princes Street, London W1R 7RE (tel 071-499 6988), hands out free motoring maps plus plans of Sofia and other big cities. Although not very detailed, they should be adequate for most purposes. In North America they can be obtained from Balkantourist at 161 East 86th Street, New York, NY 10028 (tel 212-722-1110).

AIR

The national airline Balkan flies between Sofia, Vidin and Ruse on the Danube, and Varna and Burgas on the Black Sea. The cost of these flights is about $70 one-way, regardless of destination. Seats can be booked at any Balkan office. If you know your requirements in advance, you can book through travel agents in the UK. Even though international services use the latest aircraft, expect no frills aboard the fleet of Russian Tupelov and Antonov (propeller driven) aircraft operated by Balkan on internal routes.

RAIL

Bulgarian State Railways (BDZh) has an extensive network centred on Sofia. You can get to most places by rail, but trains are slow by Western standards. There are three types of train: Express (*Ekspres vlak*) which operate on main routes, "fast" trains (*brzi vlak*) and finally the *patnicheski* (slow trains). Second class fares start at about $3 for 100km (60 miles), with a surcharge on expresses. The first class premium is 50%. Sofia to Burgas costs around $25 one-way in second class.

Regular express electric trains link Sofia with Varna and Burgas on the Black Sea coast. Others serve Plovdiv (the second city) and the Turkish border at Svilengrad. The route to Varna splits at Gorna Orjahovica, from where you can get trains to Ruse on the Danube and on to Bucharest. There are overnight trains to the Black Sea coast with sleeping cars and couchettes.

Buying Tickets. For express trains you will need a seat or sleeper reservation in addition to your ticket; if possible, book in advance. As well as at ticket offices in railway stations (where there are usually long queues) you can buy tickets from BDZh town offices.

Timetables. International timetables are in both Roman and Cyrillic, while all others are in Cyrillic only. Finding the right platform to depart from, let alone working out which station you have arrived at, may be a cause for celebration. If you haven't memorized Cyrillic, ask your fellow passengers or train staff for help. As expresses usually run on time you may find you can work out where you are from the *Thomas Cook* timetable.

BUS

Most places are accessible by bus in Bulgaria, but the more remote the area the less frequent the service. *Autogara* means bus station. To get a ticket (*bilet*), queue at the ticket kiosk (*gishe*) a short time in advance. For local buses in rural areas pay the driver. Make sure he or she knows where you want to get off.

CAR

Traffic in Bulgaria has displayed the same trends as elsewhere in Eastern Europe: greatly increased volume with hardly any improvement in roads. Therefore congestion, potholes and general aggravation are common on main routes. Off the main roads, watch out for farm animals, horse-drawn carts and gypsies on horseback.

Rules and Regulations. The speed limit in built-up areas is 60km/h (37mph) otherwise 80km/h (49mph) and 120km/h (74mph) on "motorways". Limits are lower for caravans 50km/h, 70km/h, 100km/h. It is illegal to have any alcohol in your bloodstream while driving. If you don't have Green Card insurance you can obtain a Blue Card at the border. Should you be unlucky enough to have an accident you are legally required to report it to the Militia and to wait at the scene for their arrival. To report an accident telephone 146.

Petrol. Garages are located on main routes at roughly 20-25 mile intervals. Petrol comes in 89, 93 and 96 octane grades, and unleaded is usually available.

Road Signs. Direction signs display place names in both Cyrillic and Roman alphabets on main routes only. Once off the main highway you will need to translate the Cyrillic.

Car Hire. Rentals are available through the usual multinational chains.

Motoring Organisation. The national motoring organisation is the Union of Bulgarian Motorists, 6 ul Sveta Sofia, Sofia (tel 878801). The UBM operates a nationwide breakdown scheme: dial 146 (the same number as used to report accidents). Main routes are patrolled in the summer season from early morning to about 10.30pm.

Motorways. A network of motorways is planned to link Sofia with Varna (the Hemus Highway) and with Burgas (the Trakia) with a branch to the Turkish border. Only certain stretches have been completed so far. A third motorway linking Varna and Burgas along the Black Sea coast is largely complete.

Motoring Offences and Confrontations with the Militia. There is a system of on-the-spot fines for motoring offences in Bulgaria. If you are Bulgarian you can choose instead to have a hole punched in your licence. Once there are three holes you are temporarily disqualified from driving, so not surprisingly most Bulgarians prefer to pay the fine. Foreigners have no choice but to pay up, although they can pay their fines at the border on leaving. Speeding fines are normally in the region of $5, although the maximum is abour $25. Usually oncoming motorists warn of a speed trap by flashing headlights. Militia posts at the roadside are marked by the sign KAT and motorists may be flagged down at them for a spot-check. Make sure that your vehicle is mechanically sound (e.g. that all lights are working), that your paperwork is in order, and that there is not a trace of alcohol in your body.

BOAT

Hydrofoils ply along the Bulgarian side of the Danube linking several of the towns from Vidin to Ruse (about 230 miles). The whole trip lasts about six hours, leaving Vidin early in the morning and arriving at Ruse around lunchtime. The trip can also be done the other way round, but takes longer. The once infamous (but no longer operational) Belene labour camp for political detainees is situated in the Danube estuary. Hydrofoils also link ports along the Black Sea coast, as do the more ponderous hydrobuses.

CITY TRANSPORT

Public Transport. In cities there is a standard fare of about $0.10 on all forms of public transport; buses, trolleybuses and trams. Tickets must be bought in advance from ticket kiosks found at most bus stops. Given the low cost, it is worth buying a lot at one go — especially since kiosks close in the evenings.

Taxis. Fares work out at $0.50 per kilometre if the driver is honest (most are). A three-mile cross-town journey should cost around $2.50. Fares increase by a third at night.

Cycling. Bicycles can be hired at the Black Sea resorts of Golden Sands and Sunny Beach. Cycling in Sofia is not recommended, due to the prevalance of tram tracks.

Prices range from just $5 for a room in a private house to $200 for a twin room at the Balkan Sheraton in central Sofia. Independent travellers pay more for hotel accommodation than package tourists, who get special rates. The individual rates for moderate tourist hotels are about $50 per double per night and motels cost around the same.

Youth and Student Hostels. The youth and student travel organisation of Bulgaria is Orbita, 45a Boulevard Stamboliiski, Sofia. It deals mainly with groups, but there may be scope for the independent traveller especially during the summer vacation (mid-July to mid-September). Orbita allocates rooms or dormitory beds in student accommodation blocks for about $6 per person per night. Orbita also operate hotels and hostels.

Hostelling International's affiliate in Bulgaria is the Bulgarian Tourist Union, Zentralrat, Boulevard Tolbukhin 18, Sofia (tel: 88 29 66). It runs basic, cheap and sometimes hard-to-find hostels, but the price — around $5 per night for a dormitory bed — is excellent.

Camping. A map of campsites can be obtained from Bulgarian tourist offices abroad. There are approximately 120 sites, about a third of them on the Black Sea coast. Some are in close proximity to the beaches which causes the official brochure to wax lyrical: "You just roll off your tent and go right into the clear seawater splashing by." Campers are charged around $4 a night. Popular campsites need to be booked in advance through Balkantourist offices. Camping outside official sites is prohibited.

Chalets. Fairly basic chalets for two or more people are found on all campsites in Bulgaria and cost from about $10 per night. In tourist areas such as the coast and the mountains, popular sites are full during peak periods so it is advisable to book in advance. Hikers wishing to use a mountain chalet (*hizha*) should obtain authorisation from the Bulgarian Tourist Union, Pirin Travel Agency, 30 Boulevard Stamboliiski, Sofia (tel: 87 06 87), which can make advance bookings. Hizhas vary from basic to comfortable hotel-style accommodation.

Eating and Drinking

Food similar to that in Bulgaria is found throughout the Balkans — in Yugoslavia, Romania, Greece, Turkey and Albania — so it is more accurate to talk about Balkan rather than Bulgarian cooking. A typical dish is a meat stew or thick soup made from beef, pork or lamb, with vegetables and spices baked very slowly in an earthenware pot (*guyvech*).

Bulgaria's main claim to culinary fame is as the home of yoghurt (*kiselomleko*). Usually made from cow's milk, it is naturally sweet. It may be drunk or eaten with a spoon (depending on consistency) and is used as an ingredient in many dishes. Bulgarian babies are often weaned on yoghurt. The famed sheep's milk variety is available for about a month in April/May when the lambs are slaughtered. It has a thick, creamy consistency and a taste which makes yoghurt fans drool.

For those for whom 'holiday' and 'gastronomy' are synonymous, Balkan Holidays in London (tel: 071-493 8612) runs wine and dine tours in Bulgaria. Some cynical visitors would say that the words 'Bulgaria' and 'good food' do not sit easily together, but standards are improving (or, rather, reverting to pre-commmunist norms).

National specialities include:

kevarma kebab — stew comprising pork and vegetables baked in an earthenware dish.
kebapcheta — minced spicy meat (usually veal or pork) served in rolls.
drob sarma — meat, rice and herbs topped with eggs beaten in yoghurt.
sarmi — cabbage or vine leaves stuffed with minced meat and rice.
shopska salat — cucumber, red pepper, onion, tomato and white cheese, served as an accompaniment to most meals.
imam bayaldu — literally *the priest burst* (from over-eating). Of Turkish origin. Cold vegetarian dish of aubergine stuffed with all manner of vegetables.
shkembe churba — tripe soup dressed with garlic and vinegar.
moussaka — minced meat, onions, carrot, cubed potatoes, baked with eggs and yoghurt topping. Usually as luke-warm as it is in Greece.

banitsa — pastry. Can be sweet or savoury.
sirene po shopski — cheese fondue with eggs cooked in a clay pot.

Desserts

mlyako s orez — creamy cold rice pudding sprinkled with cinnamon.
banitsa saralia — pastry layers filled with walnuts and syrup.
banitsa mlyaka — pastry baked in eggs and milk with semolina.
baklava — pastry filled with nuts and syrup.
strudel — apple pie (German but very common in Bulgaria).

Restaurants. The old Soviet-style catering establishments are out of favour these days. Ignore anywhere called the Mosskva, Praha or Budapest in favour of the newer, bistro-style places. There are plenty of folk-style restaurants known as *mehanas* or *hanches* where you can get most of the dishes mentioned above and many others, and hear Bulgarian music while lapping up the atmosphere. In mehanas and hanches you always get a small round loaf called *pitka,* baked on the premises. There is always a tiny bowl of salt and herbs on the table into which you dip the *pitka.*
Nearly every large town has a chicken restaurant (*Zlatno Pile*) where you can get only grilled chicken and chips, or chicken soup, very cheaply. Mostly the fare is disgusting. Spaghetti restaurants and pizza stands are popular. As some of the cheaper places only serve beer with the meals, it is considered quite acceptable to bring your own wine. The equivalent of the fast food joint in Bulgaria is probably the pastry shop where you can get coffee, sandwiches, cakes etc.

Vegetarian Travellers. In the main towns at least, vegetarian restaurants are on the increase. Other meatless places to dine are the milk bars and cafeterias where you can get savoury banitsas, sweet milk puddings, cheese and chips as well as the ubiquitous yoghurt. Vegetarian dishes include *gradinarska chorba* (gardener's soup) made from carrots, onions, celery, beets, green beans, peas, cabbage and yoghurt. *Zelen fasul* is a dish of simmered vegetables. *Manastirska chorba* (monastery soup) is based on beans and vegetables. *Parzheni chuski s sirene* are peppers stuffed with cheese and eggs, breadcrumbed and deep fried. *Fasoul* is a mixed bean and vegetable stew with paprika and wild mint, served hot or cold.

Buying Food From Shops. More accurately, you should try to buy from markets *(hali)* in big towns. The range of produce is as wide as it is colourful. More mundanely, you can save money by buying food in shops *(magazin)* and supermarkets *(gastronom).* Bread *(hleb)* can be bought either from a baker *(hlebarnitsa)* or a bread and pastry shop *(hleb i hlebni izdelia).*

DRINKING

Most Bulgarians like a drink. The café society which was subdued under communism has sprung up again with a vengeance, and in summer half the population seems to spend the afternoon and evening drinking beer or coffee at outdoor tables.
If there is a national pick-me-up, it is probably *slivova* — a plum-based spirit. *Grappa* (distilled from grape skins), *mastika* (aniseed based, like ouzo) and *raki* (general-purpose firewater) are also popular. For something a little more sophisticated, try the local cognac-style brandies with brand-names like Pliska, Pomorie and Preslav. A strictly Balkan drink is *bosa*: this is made from baked millet, wheat or rye flour, sugar and water. It is left to

ferment mildly (making it about 1% alcohol), and forms a greyish beige drink which is sweet when young, sour when mature. This is considered something of a delicacy, at least by Bulgarians, but has made little headway in impressing the rest of the world. Schoolchildren used to thrive on it, but nowadays they get their kicks from Pepsi.

Similar sounding, but much more powerful, is *rosa* — raki mixed with rose-petal syrup. This is promoted heavily in tourist areas, since it plays upon the Bulgarian rose tradition.

Beer. The export brew is AstikA (whose name appears on labels in that form), a tasty lager which is strong, but not as strong as the 12% in the label would seem to suggest; this refers to the proportion of sugar at commencement of fermentation, not the percentage of alcohol (about 5%) in the can.

Beer brewed for the local market is weaker and more insipid, but perfectly drinkable; a 500ml bottle (just under a pint) costs $0.30 in a shop, $0.50 when served in a restaurant. In flashier bars, you may be only able to get imported beers; European ones are much better than the unknown and highly dubious American brands which crop up frequently.

Wine. Although wines were introduced into Bulgaria thousands of years ago by the Thracians, winegrowing before 1948 consisted of peasant smallholdings and wineries. Since that year a thriving wine industry has been built up under state control. Grape-gathering is mechanized and processing methods are modern. The state monopoly Vinimpex controls all import and export of wine and spirits. Its considerable success may be measured in the way that Bulgarian Cabernet Sauvignon is one of the most popular wines in Britain. Most red wines are produced from the French grapes Merlot, Cabernet Sauvignon and Chardonnay. There is *Mavrud* which is dark and plummy and *Melnik,* a full-bodied wine from the south west. One of the reds, *Trakia,* won international acclaim in 1982; it has a coin showing the head of Philip of Macedonia on the label. There is also a white version which is a popular export to the US. Wines usually cost $1 a bottle in a supermarket, $3 in restaurants. Bulgarian "champagne" is drinkable and costs $5 from shops, double in restaurants. It is recognizable by its gold foil top.

Soft Drinks. There is a range of slightly sweetened fruit juices known as *nektar.* Some are juice, while others are puree mixed with water which makes a much thicker drink. Nektar is sold in the same green bottles as beer. Bottled mineral waters include *Gorna Banja* and *Hisar.* There are also some fruit flavoured drinks made from carbonated water and concentrates: *lozina* (grape), *krusha* (pear) and *yabolka* (apple).

Tea *(chay)* is usually served black with lemon, so take your own powdered milk if you prefer it that way. coffee is served Turkish style: sweet and strong in small cups *(Tursko Cafe).* If you want it with milk ask for *kafe s mlyako.* In some places *espresso* is served.

Museums and Galleries. Most of the nation's museums seem to be on a permanent electricity-conservation purge, so you'll have to get used to admiring paintings and relics in the gloom of a 20-watt lightbulb. Bulgarian museums range from the spectacular National History Museums of Sofia and Varna to some sad little house-museums, the latter usually featuring collections of folk costumes and memorabilia of historic events (particularly the struggle for liberation from the Turks). Generally museums are closed on Mondays and most open other days from 10am to 6.30pm. In winter they close an hour earlier. The big problem for Westerners is the lack of captions in English. Entrance to museums usually costs foreigners $1; you pay only one-quarter as much if they think you are Bulgarian.

Bulgaria suffers from a variety of shortages, but live entertainment is in all-too-plentiful supply — from the purest of the performing arts to the seediest striptease or the ersatz folkloric floorshows in tourist restaurants, all are thriving. Bulgarian audiences flock to new popular plays, and younger people fill the sports stadia for both sport and rock concerts. Ticket prices for cinema, theatre, opera and ballet are cheap by Western standards with a top price of about $2 for big-name performances of opera and ballet.

Cinema. In the big towns cinemas are prolific. Most films tend to be Russian or Bulgarian but if you can decipher the Cyrillic on posters you will also see Western films advertised (though they tend to be one or two years behind). Foreign films are usually in the original language with subtitles. Tickets cost about $1, and for hit movies like *Jurassic Park* and *The Fugitive* may be sold out weeks in advance.

Performing Arts. One providential legacy of communism is a thriving arts scene. Larger towns have at least two theatres (Sofia has twelve), showing a range of opera, ballet and drama. There are annual festivals of music featuring international opera and ballet stars and orchestras (see the *Calendar of Events* at the end of this chapter). In summer Bulgarians are especially keen on outdoor productions staged either in purpose-built open-air theatres or among atmospheric ancient ruins. Ballet and opera have a wealth of home-grown talent, notably the opera singer Ghena Dmitrova. New ballets often have a historical theme relating to Bulgaria's past, and modern music tends to be surprisingly traditional.

Plays by Alan Ayckbourn are very popular in Bulgaria, but all foreign drama is performed in Bulgarian. You should choose a musical and get someone to explain the basic plot, or go with an interpreter, or choose an Alan Ayckbourn play you've already seen in English. Popular contemporary playwrights include Stefan Tsanev.

Theatre performances usually start at 7pm and concerts at 7.30pm. Tickets can be bought direct from the theatre box offices (usually around the side of the threatre), or from ticket agencies — which often double as bureaux de change.

Skiing. Bulgaria does not have the cachet of French or Swiss Alpine resorts, but the skiing possibilities are excellent. A skiing holiday in Bulgaria is highly recommended, not least because two of the main ski areas are close enough to big cities to make for good outings. Furthermore skiing holidays in Bulgaria are extremely cheap compared with those in other countries.

The main skiing areas are blessed with good snow records, sunny days and only occasional fogs. They are described in more detail below:

Aleko: on Mount Vitosha, overlooking Sofia. Although this is the least challenging of the main resorts, the views over the capital — and easy access to it — make for a good, all-round holiday.

Borovets: challenging for good skiers, less than ideal for beginners.

Pamparovo: excellent for beginners and intermediate skiers. Close to Plovdiv, Bulgaria's second city.

Hiking. The skiing areas mentioned above are good hiking and climbing territory in summer. Leaflets on hiking and mountaineering can be obtained from Bulgarian tourist offices abroad, and also from the Bulgarian Hikers' Union, Pirin Travel Agency, 30 Boulevard Stamboliiski, Sofia (tel 87 06 87).

Beaches. Nude and topless sunbathing are officially forbidden on non-naturist beaches so it is rather surprising to see the latter depicted in the Bulgarian Tourist Office brochure. Every big resort has naturist beaches, but there are usually separate ones for men and women, known as Adamov Plag (Adam's beach) and Elvin Plag.

Spectator Sports. Bulgaria's national game is football and the main stadium is Vasil Levski in Freedom Park, Sofia. The season is from August to December and March to June, when you can see the leading Bulgarian teams in action. In winter, ice-hockey can be seen in the Druzhba Stadium which is also in Freedom Park, Sofia. There is an annual car rally from Albena on the coast to Sliven which is held in the first week of May. Bulgaria's first Formula-1 racing track is just outside Sliven on the route to Burgas. It incorporates motorcycling and karting tracks.

Good buys include silk skirts (around $20) and leather. For those unalarmed at the thought of provoking animal lovers back home, a fox fur muffler (just like our grandmothers wore) is all the rage in Sofia and will set you back $150.

For souvenir seekers, one of the more rarefied buys might be a vial of rose perfume in small painted wooden screw-top containers reminiscent of chess pawns; pay no more than $0.50 for one. Or try an imitation icon (exporting the real thing is forbidden).

Shopping Hours. Many shops in Sofia centre are open from 9am to 7pm. Elsewhere opening hours are 8am-1pm and 4-7pm from Monday to Saturday. Some variations may occur in the regions.

Tobacco. Bulgaria produces some excellent tobacco. Unfortunately, as with wine, the best is exported. If you are down on your leva, try Arda filters (the packet is marked *apga*), which are around $0.20 for 20. Upmarket is the only way to go from here, and the first stop is BT ($0.40). You look a little less unsophisticated if you smoke Victory ($0.60), but most people lash out with $1 to buy imported Marlboro or Rothmans.

Police. In Bulgaria the police are known as *milita* and are quite separate from the army *(armia)*. You are most likely to encounter them if you are motoring (see *Getting Around — Car*). The State Police

(Darzhavna Sigurnost) still enjoy a fearsome reputation, but you are unlikely to encounter them.

Photography. Taking pictures of airports, railways, bridges, highways (even petrol stations!) or anything military is theoretically forbidden, as is landscape photography in the immediate vicinity of international borders.

Crime. Most of the rogues are in Sofia, specifically around the main station. Crime levels have risen since the introduction of democracy, but Bulgaria is still relatively safe.

Help and Information

Embassies and Consulates. British: 65 Boulevard Tolbukhin, Sofia; tel: 88 53 61/ 87 83 25. US: 1 Boulevard Stamboliiski, Sofia; tel: 88 48 01/88 48 02.

Lost Property. Police in Bulgaria will not issue Statements of Loss for insurance purposes except where crime is involved, e.g. robbery direct from the person or if your room or car is broken into.

Tourist Information. Most tourist services in Bulgaria are dealt with by Balkantourist. Information bureaux can be found in the larger hotels and in city offices. Balkantourist offices in big cities and resorts are called Comprehensive Service Bureaux and organise accommodation and travel. Reception staff in the larger hotels will also supply you with town plans (if they have them), train and bus times etc. The quality of service is variable. Outside Sofia and the big tourist towns you cannot rely upon English being spoken.

Disabled Travellers. There are few facilities for disabled travellers. Even Balkantourist advise handicapped travellers to travel with an able-bodied companion.

American Express. MegaTours, Levski 1, Sofia (tel 82 25 67); MegaTours, Slivnitza 33, Varna (tel 23 21 15).

SOFIA

Bulgaria's capital has ancient origins. The original name of the city was Serdica, a name given by the Thracians about 5000 years ago. It later became Triadica (Byzantine for 'between the mountains'), then Sredec (Slav for 'in the centre' — indeed it does lie in the middle of the Balkan peninsula. The name Sofia means wisdom, and the name was taken from the 5th century church of St Sophia, which still stands in Alexander Nevski Square in the city centre.

This church apart, Sofia's rich history has not endured well. If you arrive expecting the city to be full of old and beautiful buildings, you will probably be disappointed by the profusion of new and ugly ones. Before 1880, whilst under the Turks, Sofia had a population of only 15,000. It comprised a collection of narrow twisting streets whose buildings by Turkish edict rose no higher than a man on horseback (an edict ingeniously circumvented in some cases by sinking buildings below ground level). The central part of the city was laid out after the liberation, bombed in the Second World War and

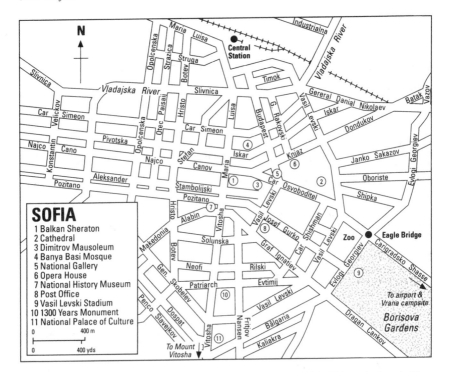

SOFIA

1 Balkan Sheraton
2 Cathedral
3 Dimitrov Mausoleum
4 Banya Basi Mosque
5 National Gallery
6 Opera House
7 National History Museum
8 Post Office
9 Vasil Levski Stadium
10 1300 Years Monument
11 National Palace of Culture

0   400 m

0   400 yds

rebuilt in the 1950s. Nowadays the population is 1,200,000 and the skyline is dominated by the grey skyscrapers of housing estates.

Sofia lies one-third of a mile above sea level in a great plain surrounded by mountains. Some might think that the capital's most attractive feature is its proximity to Mount Vitosha which dominates the view to the southwest and boasts excellent recreational facilities: in summer for hiking, and in winter skiing at the resort of Aleko-Vitosha. The Lyulin mountains lie to the west. The climate is pleasantly moderate in summer and autumn, with an average temperature of 20°C in June and July. Temperatures hover just below freezing in January, with frequent snowfalls. The biting wind that sweeps across the plain can make it seem much colder.

Unlike many important cities, Sofia is not situated on the banks of a great river. (It does however have hot springs which are still in use today and which must have been an attraction for the original Thracian inhabitants.) Instead, the centre of the city sits snugly between two modest rivulets, the Vladajaska to the north and the Perlovska to the south. Within this area are most of the main sites and shops.

Getting Around

ARRIVAL AND DEPARTURE

Air. Sofia airport is five miles/8km east of the city centre. From west to east, the terminals are international arrivals, international departures and domestic flights. There is a post office for making international calls, and a business centre, in the international departures hall.

The airport is not among the most sophisticated in Europe. Everything seems calculated to make an arrival, departure or transit an uncomfortable experience. Passengers are bussed on and off the aircraft. The arrivals hall (if that is not too grand a description) is flourescently floodlit, and packed with the kind of fake-veneer, mass-misproduced offices which sum up state bureaucracy.

Arriving passengers without visas must purchase them from the imitation-teak hut in the middle. Transit passengers with immediate connections (to use the term loosely) should follow the signs, and hope that someone turns up to issue boarding passes. You need to go through a passport and security check before entering the departure 'lounge'.

If you are intending to stay in Sofia, bus 84 takes about 30 minutes to reach Orlov Most (Eagle Bridge), on the edge of the centre. Travellers to Macedonia can take the direct bus that operates several times daily between the airport and Skopje, the capital of Macedonia.

Departing passengers should note that there are airports where formalities can be carried out swiftly, but Sofia is not one of them. Check in at least an hour before an international flight.

Train. Sofia Central Station is a mile north of the city centre. It is a huge and intimidating modern building, isolated from the rest of the city by an eight-lane road. Buses, trams and trolleybuses run from the far side of this highway. Also on this side is Eastern Europe's biggest collection of black market currency dealers. As mentioned in the introduction, there is no black market in currency, so it is a safe bet to assume that they are all swindlers. Fortunately there is a 24-hour bureau de change opposite the station.

Ticket offices for Ruse, Vidin and Varna are at ground level and tickets for other destinations are in the basement. Timetables are posted with main station names in Cyrillic and Roman, and electronic signs on the platforms give train details. There is a Balkantourist Office in the large waiting room on the ground floor.

Bus. Most international services run by private companies arrive at and depart from the Novotel Evropa, a five-minute walk south of the railway station. Buses to Modlova, Ukraine and Greece all leave from here.

Driving. The four main road approaches to Sofia are the E80 from Belgrade (Serbia); the E80 (coming in the other direction) from Edirne (Turkey); the E79 approaching from Greece and finally, from the direction of Romania and crossing at Ruse, the E83. There are several possibilities for accommodation near Sofia on these routes including the Vrana campsite 10km southeast on the E80.

Hitch-hiking. To enhance your chances of a lift out of the capital, get yourself to the appropriate hitching spot by public transport or on foot: none of these places is too far from the city centre. For the E80 west to Belgrade, head west along Valcho Ivanov to just beyond the bridge over the railway. The E79 southwest to Thessaloniki and Skopje begins in earnest where Boulevard. 9 Septemvri joins the ring road. For the E80 east to Plovdiv, try the Orlov Most, but expect a long wait; any bus to the airport turn-off could speed your departure. The E79 northeast to Ruse and Varna is most problematic: start walking along Botevgradsko Shose, until you hitch a lift or your legs give out.

City Transport. Buses, trolleybuses and trams comprise a unified system which uses the same tickets. These must be bought in advance from roadside kiosks, and can be hard to find after dark (the locals will advise you to travel without one). Assuming you have one, punch it in one of the machines placed at eye level once on board. Transfers are not allowed on one ticket — you have to cancel a new one each time you change.

Routes are show on the excellent Sofia Plan (in Cyrillic), price $1. Even if you do not read Cyrillic, you can use the map in conjunction with the one in this book to get your bearings.

Taxis. Dial 142 or 2121 to summon one. A two-mile journey in middling traffic should cost about $1.60.

Underground. The centre of Sofia is likely to be a mess for a few more years until the east-west subway line is completed.

Possibilities in Sofia city centre range from a room in a private home for about $10 to the Balkan Sheraton at up to $200 a night. Private lodgings for foreigners can be booked through Sofia Tourist (18a Ves-lets Street; tel 80 22 38), which specialises in the cheaper end of the market, including cut-price hotels. These include:

Hotel Hemus (3 star), 31 Boulevard G. Traikov (tel 66 14 15).
Hotel Pliska (3 star); (tel 72 37 21). A Balkan Airways hotel, handy for the airport. Passengers in transit who are obliged to make an overnight stop are billeted here.
Hotel Serdica, 2 Boulevard V Zaimov (tel 44 34 11).
Hotel Preslav, 3 ul Traiditsa (tel 87 65 86).
Hotel Sevastopol, 116 ul Rakovski (tel 87 59 41).

Camping. Between June and September there are three campsites open within a reasonable distance of Sofia: the Vrana site, sic miles/10km from the capital on the E80 towards Plovdiv (tel 72 37 20); Tcherniat Kos, six miles/10km out on the E20; and at Bankia off the E80 ten miles/16 km from Sofia near the thermal baths. This last site opens two weeks earlier, on 15 May.

Restaurants. Boulevard Vitosha, the main pedestrian and shopping street has many restaurants. Some of them are bizarre hangovers from communism, such as the Restaurant of the Bulgarian Field Sports Union which serves only game and if you've shot it yourself they will cook it for you. Others are new arrivals, and you can take your pick from a relatively appetizing selection. One warning: the recipe for pizza seems to have suffered in translation, and you should steer clear of most of the city's pizzerias.

The Forum Restaurant Complex, near the Palace of Culture, is an upmarket place. Its champagne bar serves low-alcohol cocktails, ice cream sodas and coffee as well as 'champagne.'

A couple of other slightly ritzy places which are reasonable are the restaurant of the Grand Bulgaria Hotel, an old building just of 9th September

Square, and the Grand Sofia restaurant in the hotel of that name opposite the National Assembly.

The best pastry shop in Sofia is the Kristal in the garden opposite the Russian Church in Boulevard Russki. All the pastries are baked on the premises.

 Sofia is in the middle of acquiring a welcome elegance. The city centre is spacious and is being developed sensitively, with the rougher edges of the excesses of communism being smoothed down. The centre contains many imposing public buildings and Stalinist architecture from the 1950s, a style which is not altogether unattractive, in a brutal sort of way. There are a few elaborate houses from the turn of the century; these are mostly embassies and are beautifully kept.

Sofia has more than its fair share of monuments, some of them hideous and some striking. Bulgarians are obsessed with their history; throughout the country there are statues and plaques commemorating all manner of revolutionaries, events, etc. Most of these have survived the fall of communism, though they are daubed in (often obscene) graffitti.

The centre of Sofia can be seen in a day as nearly all the main sites and main public buildings are grouped around the four main squares, all within reasonable walking distance of each other.

Ploshtad Sveta Nedelya and Boulevard Knyaginya Mariya Luiza. It is perhaps hardly surprising that Ploshtad Sveta Nedelya (formerly Lenin Square) is considered the centre of Sofia as it lies directly over the hub of ancient *Serdica,* including the crossroads running north-south and east-west. Beneath the site of the *Church of Saint Nedelia* the *Praetorium* was situated. *St. Nedelia* church dates from 1856 and replaces other churches on a site holy since the middle ages. In 1925 there was an unsuccessful bomb attack inside the church against King Boris III. On the south east corner you will find the *Theology Academy* (1900-1905) by the architect Petka Momtchilov. Built mainly of yellow brick it incorporates motifs from medieval Bulgarian architecture. It has a stunning facade and is four storeys high.

On the eastern side of Ploshtad Sveta Nedelya is the Balkan Sheraton, on the south of which is the Boulevard Stamboliiski. From this street you can enter the courtyard of the Sheraton to see the *Rotunda of Saint George;* the oldest edifice still standing in Sofia, it dates from the fourth century. Returning to Ploshtad Sveta Nedelya, descend into the undeground passage. At the centre is the *Church of Saint Petka Samardjiska* which dates from the early years of Ottoman domination and was built by the Guild of Saddlers. Extremely modest looking from the outside — so as not to excite the wrath of the Turks — it contains remarkable frescoes and other medieval art. Regrettably it is of such historical and artistic importance that it is not open to the public. The same underground passage also connects with TsUM (Central Universal Store), the Bulgarian equivalent of GUM in Moscow and still functioning.

Proceeding north along Boulevard Knyaginya Mariya Luiza, which is the continuation of Ploshtad Sveta Nedelya, you will come to the *Banyabashi Mosque* (1576) on the right hand side. This impressive building is the work of the illustrious Ottoman, Hadji Mimar Sinan who built the famous mosque of Sultan Selim of Andrinople in Turkey. The Banyabashi derives its name from the handsome Mineral Baths *(Banya)* (1913) which are close by, and have sadly fallen into dereliction. These are also the work of Momtchilov and are in renaissance style with a central building with two wings. The whole outside is decorated with ceramics. Built over one of the hot springs, they are reputedly shortly to be developed into a balneological and fitness centre.

Opposite is the market hall *(Hali)*. Built around 1909-1910 in National Revival style, the main entrance is a majestic deep archway surmounted by a clock tower. The windows of the facade are set in arched niches. Unfortunately the inside, having been insensitively modernised in 1974, does not live up to the exterior. Behind the Hali on the corner of Ekzarh Josef Street is the Sofia Synagogue (1910), an oriental looking building comprising a rectangular block crowned with a great cupola with smaller ones at the corners. Bulgaria has always showed religious tolerance of Jewish people, even during the alliance with the Third Reich. In the basement of the building situated at the corner of Boulevard Dmitrov and ul Ekzarh Josef is the partly preserved triangular tower and north wall of ancient Serdica.

Boulevard Vitosha. Heading south off Ploshtad Sveta Nedelya, you find yourself in the city's main shopping and eating street. At the beginning of the Boulevard is the National History Museum which occupies the former Palace of Justice built 1928-36. You cannot miss its imposing facade with a row of pillars and a flight of steps flanked by two black, standing lions which represent Bulgaria and which were later additions to the building. The fabulous gold treasures of the Thracians are on the ground floor and are named after the villages where they were discovered — Valchitran and Panagyrurishte — and they include ritual drinking vessels and personal items of adornment from tombs. There is also the silver treasure of Rogozen; the workmanship is exquisite. Continuing along Boulevard Vitosha (you can take a tram or bus) you arrive at the modern looking monument in *Baba Nedelya* Square that commemorates 1,300 Years of Bulgaria since the founding of the first kingdom in 681. At the top end of the Baba Nedelya Square you will see the building which probably more than any other represents the civic pride of Sofia, the National Palace of Culture (NDK). It is a vast black and white building with a stylised black sun on a white square above the main entrance. Covering an area of 17,000 square metres, it houses a complex of halls of various sizes used for concerts, congresses etc. There is a press centre plus an overpriced underground shopping arcade and refreshment area. The tourist office in the arcade is efficient and you can book most kinds of tickets there, including those for international travel. The NDK also has a coffee terrace where you can enjoy an excellent view of the city; there are lifts to it from the underground shopping arcade.

The Largo. The administrative centre is characterised by monumental buildings constructed 1952-57 around a great wide avenue known as the Largo. At the eastern end of the Largo the Communist Party House stands out as a landmark with its six-pillared portico and spire. The red star was removed in 1993, and the communist HQ turned into a cinema. In front of the main entrance of Party House you can descend into the subway for an experience of ancient civilisation, walking through the preserved East Gate of Serdica and walking on a 5th century Roman pavement. Both of these have been incorporated into the architecture.

Going east from here, you cannot fail to spot the Mausoleum of Georgi Dmitrov, a stark white block with rectangular niches. Dmitrov was the founder leader of the People's Republic of Bulgaria who died on a visit to Moscow in 1949. The mausoleum was erected in six days and nights in time for the arrival of his remains. They have been removed and buried, and nobody quite knows what to do with the building.

Opposite the mausoleum is the former Konak (Ottoman administration centre), the exterior of which was modified in Viennese style by the architects Rumpelmeier and Grunanger. It now houses the ethnographic museum. The first street on the right on the same side of 9 September Square as the mausoleum is Vasil Levski Street down which you will find the Ivan Vasov National Theatre. Originally built in 1907, it was destroyed by fire in 1923 and completely reconstructed. It has a neo-classical portico decorated with a relief depicting Apollo surrounded by the muses. Turning back towards the Largo, and turning right down Boulevard Russki you will see on your left in a shady setting the Russian Church of St Nicholas (1913). It was designed by the great Russian architect Prebrajenski. What it lacks in size it makes up for in style with its mustardy yellow exterior and five gleaming gold onion domes. After the monotony of the socialist architecture that precedes it, it is an extravagant treat for the eyes. It was paid for by the Russian diplomatic inhabitants of Sofia of that epoch who wanted their own church, as they disapproved of the differences in ritual between the Russian and Bulgarian churches.

Narodno Sabranie Square and Alexander Nevski Square. Continuing along Boulevard Russki you come to Narodno Sabranie Square. In the southeast corner is the Grand Sofia Hotel where you could have a rest and refreshment on the terrace, a superb vantage point from which to view Alexander Nevski Square. The Grand Sofia also does one of the best breakfast buffets in Sofia. The Grand Sofia looks out over the Liberator's Monument (1905), an equestrian statue of Tsar Alexander II of Russia.

Following the gaze of the Tsar and his mount you will see in front of you the National Assembly — seat of power and legislative body of Bulgaria. Between the National Assembly on the right and the National Academy of Sciences on the left you can walk into the vast oval space of Alexander Nevski Square. The Alexander Nevski Cathedral is dedicated to the 200,000 Russians who died liberating Bulgaria from the Ottomans in 1877-88 and is named after the Russian commander. Construction began in 1882 and took 40 years to complete. Built in the form of a cross it is in neo-Byzantine style. The exterior is characterised by successive rows of arcades leading up to the great cupola and belfry. The gold leaf on the domes was donated by the Soviet Union. The interior is decorated with frescoes painted by the leading Russian and Bulgarian masters of the time and is rich with Italian marbles and Venetian mosaics. The Crypt contains a superb collection of icons.

Museums and Galleries. *National History Museum,* 2 Boulevard Vitosha. Open 10.30am-6.30pm, Friday 2-6.30pm. Contains all the national treasures; if you are only going to see one museum this should be it.

National Archaeological Museum, 2 Boulevard Alexander Stamboliiski.

Military History Museum, 23 Boulevard Skobelov. Open Monday to Friday 9am-noon and 2-6pm; Sundays 1-7pm. Bulgarian military history is mostly concerned with their heroic struggle against the Turks in the 19th century.

National Art Gallery, 9 September Square. Open Wednesday to Friday 10am-6pm.

Sofia City Art Gallery, ul General Gurko 1. Open 10.30am-7pm.

Permanent Gallery for Sales of Art, ul Rakovski 133. Open 10am-6pm.

Graphic Art Gallery, ul General Gurko 62.

Theatres. There are over a dozen theatres showing drama, ballets, opera and concerts. The main ones are the Ivan Vasov National Theatre, 5 Levski Street; National Theatre of Opera and Ballet, 1 Yanko Zabounov Street; National Youth Theatre, 6 Boulevard Dondoukov; Operetta Theatre, 4 Boulevard Volgograd; National Theatre of Satire, 26 Stefan Karadja Street. There is a Puppet Theatre at 14 General Gurko Street. Tickets can be purchased direct from theatre box offices (usually round the side of the theatre), from the tourist office at the Palace of Culture, or Concert Bookings at 3 Boulevard Russki (tel 87 15 88). Performances of ballets and plays usually start at 7pm.

Music. Classical music can be heard at the Bulgaria Hall, 1 Benkovska Street, Georgi Kirkov Hall in the Party House, Slaveikov Hall in Slaveikov Square, and the National Palace of Culture. Sofia hosts annual music festivals: from 24 May to 30 June "Sofia Music Weeks", and a New Year's Music Festival in the Natinoal Palace of Culture from 26 December to 4 January. Concerts usually start at 7.30pm.

Rock concerts are popular (though Westerners may find the music dire) and are usually held in the various sports stadia in Sofia and in the National Palace of Culture. You should ask for details at the various tourist offices or at the NDK itself.

Nightclubs and Casinos. Sofia is not one of the world's liveliest capitals and nightlife is limited. There are folk-style floorshows in restaurants such as the *Boyansko Hanche* (reached by bus 63 or 64) in the Boyana suburb at the foot of Vitosha Mountain, and the *Vodenicharski Mehani* (bus 93) in the suburb of Dragalevtsi. The alternative is the live music in the dining-rooms of all the larger hotels where you can dance, but they can be tuneless and deafening. Some of these hotels — notably the Grand Sofia in Narodno Sabranie Square, the Park Hotel Moskva, 25 Nezabravka Street and the Vitosha New Otani — also have a night club. There are discotheques in the underground arcade at the Natinoal Palace of Culture and in the underpass at Boulevard Bulgaria. The New Otani and the Sheraton have casinos.

SPORT AND RECREATION

Spectator Sports. Sofia has two main stadia and both are situated in the *Park na Svobodata* (Freedom Park). The larger one is named after Vasil Levski and the other is Druzhba Stadion (Friendship Stadium). Football is played in both from March-June and August-December and the leading teams are *Sredec* and *Levski spartak.* In winter you can see ice-hockey at Druzhba Stadium.

Participation. Most of the action takes place on Mount Vitosha, which dominates the skyline southwest of Sofia. See *Day Trips from Sofia* for details of access.

Sofia's stores sell lots of dross, but there are several shops of the Union of Bulgarian Artists. The best are at 6 Boulevard Russki and 13 ul Rakovski where you can buy handmade clothes and embroidered table-cloths, pottery, silver, jewellery, etc. *Mineralsouvenir* at 10 Boulevard Russki has an interesting selection of jewellery and small articles made of Bulgarian marble. There is also a souvenir shopping centre in front of the Palace of Culture where you can buy articles carved from wood. The open air market is a bustling affair located in ul Georgi Kirkov, and especially good early in the morning.

Antiques. The Antiqwaren Magazin in ul Vasil Kolarov, which crosses Boulevard Vitosha about half way down, sells some interesting antiques.

Embassies. UK: 65 Boulevard Tolbukhin (tel 88 63 61). Open: Mon-Thurs 9am-12 noon and 2-3.30pm. Fri 9am-12 noon. Has telex and facilities open to business travellers.

Citizens of Canada, Australia and New Zealand should consult the British Embassy.

USA: 1 Boulevard Stamboliiski (tel 88 48 01). Open: Mon-Fri 8.30am-1pm. There is a library and selection of Western press publications in the American Centre next door.

Lost Property: If you have left belongings on public transport, make enquiries (or get an interpreter to) at the central tram station in front of the Hali and the Banya mosque.

Tourist Information: The central office is at 37 Boulevard Dondukov (tel 88 41 77) which is open until 10.30pm. Other main offices are at 1 Boulevard Vitosha (tel 43331; fax: 88 13 94); Ploshtad Sveta Nedelya and in the Palace of Culture underpass. The Union of Bulgarian Motorists' agency, Shipka, is at 6 Sveti-Sofia Street (tel 87 88 01) where you can get petrol coupons, arrange car hire, book accommodation and even arrange legal consultations in case of accidents.

English Language Churches: The Church of the Holy Sabbath and the Evangelist Church are both in ul Vasil Kolarov.

American Express: MegaTours, Levski 1 (tel 87 25 67).

Youth/Student Travel Offices: The youth tourism organisation Orbita is at 45a Boulevard Stamboliiski (tel 87 95 52).

DAY TRIPS FROM SOFIA

Mount Vitosha. The best trip you can make is up onto Mount Vitosha, a ramp of rock stretching along the city's south side. Fortunately, it is easy to reach by cable car or city bus. (It is possible to walk from the southern suburbs of Sofia, but most hikers choose the cable car or bus.) As an anti-pollution measure private cars have been banned from making the ascent up the steep winding road to Vitosha at weekends and it has been declared a National Park. Several buses, including 62 and 63, make the ascent when the cable car is not running.

In addition to other charms, Vitosha offers the most stupendous view of Sofia spreading out across the wide Sofia plain, with the Rila mountains as a backdrop. On a clear sunny day you can see the gleam from the gold on Alexander Nevski Cathedral's cupola and belfry in the centre of the greyish and white lunar-city skyscrapers of the housing estates that extend on either side.

From the Aleko station there are two more chair lifts to Mount Resena from where you can reach the highest peak, Mount Cherni, in about 45 minutes. To return to Sofia take the gondola to Simeonova suburb and take bus 123 to the tram terminal of tram 2, near Ploshtad Sveta Nedelya.

Hiking. The trails marked on the Sofia Plan are reliable, though you need some Cyrillic for these to correlate with the signposts on the mountain. You can walk for five miles along the ridge, before descending to Dragilevsky Monastery. Bus 66 runs from here down the mountain, terminating near the zoo from where you can catch a second bus to most parts of the city.

Skiing. The ski resort of Aleko on Mount Vitosha has a season of about 150 days and a ski school. The best hotel at Aleko is probably the three-star Proster, (tel 67 11 73) which also has a swimming pool. There are two other hotels at Aleko, the Chastlivetsa and the Kopitoto, both of which are two-star establishments.

The highest peak, Mount Cherni is 2,290 metres (7,513 feet). In summer it has fine woodland trails for hiking and in winter cross-country and downhill skiing from the ski resort of Aleko-Vitosha (1,803 metres).

Boyana Church. In the Boyana suburb at the foot of Mt. Vitosha — reached by bus 64 — is a medieval church, part of which dates back to the 11th century. The walls are painted with astonishingly well preserved frescoes dating from 1259. In another part of the church, its patron saints are depicted. There is also a scene of the Last Supper in which are contained details from the lives of the early Bulgarians, including their typical diet of bread, garlic and radishes.

Nearby is the *Boyana Hanche* restaurant complete with folkloric floor-show; you may find one of the newer cafés more to your liking.

Bankia. The quiet spa town of Bankia is 17km from Sofia and can be reached by road or rail. The hot springs are said to be beneficial for those suffering from cardio-vascular disorders and diabetes. There are plenty of hotels and restaurants, as well as a campsite.

Rila Monastery. Although only 55km from the capital, Rila is hard to reach by public transport in a day. It is therefore suggested that you do it more justice than a day trip would allow, and it is described in detail delow.

SOUTHWEST BULGARIA

Kyustendil. One of the oldest towns in Bulgaria, Kyustendil has been inhabited for millennia. It was conquered by the Romans in 46AD. Its warm mineral springs were revered by one of their emperors who was cured there, and who renamed the town *Ulpia Pautalia.* In the 15th century the town was renamed *Konstantinilli,* after the Ottoman ruler. Today Kyustendil is a modern town and fruit growing centre. There are several public baths where you can pay to swim in the sulphate rich, 74°C waters. On the Hissarluk hill above the town are the ruins of the *Asclepion* and a medieval fortress. Kyustendil has a three star hotel, the Pautalia and a one star, the Hissarluka.

Samokov. Going south from Sofia, following the Iskur river upstream, you pass the artificial lake created by damming the river. The road continues towards Samokov, famous in the past for its painters and woodcarvers who exercised their skills in monasteries and on the houses of the rich. The Metropolitan Church in Samokov contains some of their work. Zahari Zograf, one of Bulgaria's most prolific painters of religious frescoes was trained here. Also do not miss the attractive Bairakli Mosque a legacy of the Ottomans.

Borovets. Twelve kilometres south of Samokov is the resort of Borovets, originally the site of an aristocratic enclave. A former hunting lodge, Yastrebets is now a hotel. Fast developing as a major ski resort, Borovets is popular with experienced skiers and it is advisable to book accommodation in advance during the skiing season (or just take a package there). In summer Borovets is a starting off point for hikes organised by Balkantourist including an ascent of the highest peak of Rila and the Balkans, Moussala (2,925 metres). Hotels include the Rila, Edelweiss and Moura. There are two holiday villages the Yagoda and Malina which consist of wooden villas.

Rila Monastery. The eastward turn-off to Rila from the E79 is marked by a statue of Ivan Rilski, the founder of the monastery. Rila Monastery is the largest and best known monastery in Bulgaria. It is 55km from Sofia and can be visited from there by bus, but the timings are such that you would not be able to spend much time at the monastery. So it is worth considering hitching there or better still going on a Balkantourist excursion from Sofia. The road to the monastery passes through Rila town where there is an Orbita youth hostel in the centre on the main street. This is a convenient spot to take a meal break. The road to the monastery continues its upward climb, flanked on the right by the Rila river. Its isolation from the main highways was one of the reasons the monastery was able to keep its rights and privileges granted by both Bulgarian and Ottoman rulers, and it functioned as a major centre of Christianity throughout the Middle Ages.

   The founder, Ivan Rilski, was a hermit who preached against the injustices of feudalism and after his death in 946 he was canonised by the Greek Orthodox Church. Copies of portraits of Rilski can be seen in the Monastery museum. The original monastery was built 2km away from the present site. It was completely destroyed by brigands at the end of the 18th century and no sooner had it been reconstructed than a disastrous fire gutted the place. The present building bar the tower, the kitchen and the refectory dates from 1835. Enclosed upon itself, the monastery has high walls with small windows outside and inside red and white striped arcaded tiers.

   In the centre are the church and 14th century Hrelio's Tower reputedly the hiding place of a local boyar-turned-monk who was also a benefactor of the monastery. The church was built in 1835 and the outside resembles the churches of Mt. Athos in Greece. Inside there is the largest and arguably the greatest, iconostasis in Bulgaria which is partly the work of Atanas Teladus and Petar Filipovich Garka and is covered in gold leaf.

   At ground level you can see reconstructions of monks' cells and the kitchen whose roof which also serves as the chimney was inspired by a pine-cone. The museum contains icons, church treasures and the original 14th century gate of the monastery; also manuscripts from the 14th century and a copy of the 1762 seminal work of the National Revival. *The History of the Slavs* by Paissi of Hilendar. There is also a display of educational publications. Secular education in Bulgaria began around 1835, mainly as a result of the sons of rich Bulgarian merchants who were sent to study in Russia, bringing back books and ideas.

Westerners can stay at the three-star Balkantourist Hotel behind the monastery. There is also a primitive campsite in a meadow near the hotel. The Orbita hotel in Rila town will probably be booked out in summer. Between Rila and the monastery there is a restaurant *Mehana Ribarnika,* down a flight of steps next to a trout farm which resembles a concrete honeycomb. This is a good spot for fish *(riba)* but it is closed in winter.

Proceeding south on the E79, you pass through Blagoevgrad — the largest town in the southwest (population 55,000). Originally a Thracian settlement. It was rebuilt in the 15th century and became a trading centre on the route south along the valley of the river Strouma. Today it is an industrial centre and not of particular interest except as a stopover place. There are a couple of modern hotels: the Alen Mak (three stars) and Hotel Bor (two stars). Continuing south you come to Simitli, a small town with a lot of hot springs. From Simitli the road forks left to Bansko. This is a big tobacco-growing region

Bansko. In this charming old town in the foothills of the Pirin Mountains, do not be surprised to see older women wearing part of the old folk costume, the skirt and apron. The nearby ski resort is developing fast. Bansko is famous for such diverse reasons as being the birthplace of Paissi of Hilendar, the monk who wrote the *History of the Slavs* and for having the lowest divorce rate in Bulgaria. Other famous Bulgarians with Bansko connections include Nikola Vaptsarov, a poet and revolutionary whose house is now a museum, and Neofit of Rila who led the campaign to build the *Church of the Holy Trinity* in Bansko and was abbot of Rila Monastery in the 19th century.

The Church of the Holy Trinity was begun in 1835 after bribing the local governor. A wall was then used to disguise the fact that the church was bigger than Ottoman regulations allowed. The outside of the church is very plain, so as not to attract unwanted interest of the Turks. Inside it is tremendously ornate and everything is carved from wood. At the back of the church behind diamond-shaped lattice-work is the women's section of the church decorated with frescoes of female saints. The church icons are the work of the Bansko school and in particular the Molerov family. The Icon Museum in Bansko contains a Molerov icon of Jesus which makes him look like a Spanish *hidalgo.*

The Museum opens Tuesday to Saturday, 9am-noon and 2-5pm. Other museums keep the same hours and include the Ethnographic Museum in Velianov's House, containing pottery, costumes, rugs and furniture; the Birth-house of Neofit Rilski; and Nikola Vaptsarov's House.

In summer Bansko is a hiking centre. The Pirin range is wild and rugged and many of the 45 peaks are snow-capped for most of the year. Botanists come here to study the alpine flora. Accommodation is provided in *hizhas* (mountain huts and refuges).

You can return to Simitli and continue south by road or rail, following the course of the river Struma to the Greek border. The road passes through the Kresna Gorge. Rebellion broke out in the villages here after the Treaty of Berlin 1878 divided Bulgaria and handed Macedonia (as this part of the Pirin is known), to the Turks. The rebellion was unsuccessful and many inhabitants left for the liberated regions. Sandanski, the leader of the rebels, has his name commemorated by the next town which is named after him.

Sandanski. You breathe only the purest air in Sandanski. It is the hottest town in Bulgaria with no fog or daytime frost. A spa town with three hot springs, it was once a Thracian settlement called Zapara. The Romans who took it over renamed it Desudava and the remains of the Roman baths can be seen not far from the Sandanski Hotel; also fine mosaics in a museum built over them. In the middle ages Sandanski was called *Sveti Vrach,* meaning 'holy doctors' after two Russians who treated poor people free. In 1915, when Sandanski was killed, the town was renamed after him.

Sandanski (the town, not the person) is famous for its tobacco and hot-house tomatoes and cucumbers and for having been the probably birthplace of Spartacus, the slave who led a revolt against the Roman Empire. The Pirin mountains nearby are a source of the grey and white marble used for the statues in the park behind the Sandanski Hydro Hotel. There is an annual marble sculptors competition held in Sandanski. On Mondays there is an open market where you can buy honeys and hunks of pure beeswax, fruit, wool, knitted hats, agricultural implements and tatty horse harness, in an atmosphere of ferocious free enterprise.

There are two possibilities for accommodation: the Sandanski Hydro, a four-star establishment attached to a balneological treatment complex and boasting a superb naturally hot mineral water swimming-pool with an indoor and outdoor section, or the less exotic Spartacus hotel in the town centre where rooms cost around $15 for a single.

As the station is outside the town you will have to take bus 2, which takes around 15 minutes between the Spartacus hotel and the station. Sandanski is the last train stop before the Greek border.

Melnik. Eight miles (13km) south of Sandanski a left-hand fork takes you to Melnik, renowned for its red wines; apparently Churchill even ordered Melnik wine for his wedding. The approach to the village is stunning, winding as it does between golden sandstone peaks eroded into crumpled witch's-hat shapes. Melnik is now reduced to being the smallest town in Bulgaria, consisting of 623 souls, and is being got up for the tourists on the strength of its past glories. You can reach it on one of the frequent buses from Sandanski.

Thracians were the first inhabitants, and in the Middle Ages it was the residence of the local feudal lord, Alexi Slav. During the National Revival Melnik reached its peak of prosperity and a population of 20,000 was recorded. By the end of the 19th century this had declined to 13,000. After the Balkan Wars the Turks did not leave much standing and of the 60 houses that remained, about 40 have been rebuilt. The most important of these is Kordupolov's House. Kordupolov was a rich Greek merchant. His house, built around 1750, is the largest National Revival House in Bulgaria. Combining Bulgarian, Greek and Levantine styles, it has a reception room with 24 windows commanding views in every direction. The dining room downstairs is connected to the *Hammam* (Turkish Bath) heated by steam from the kitchen below it. The dining room has a false cupboard used as a hideaway by the family who were Bulgarian sympathisers. Downstairs are tables set out for winetasting, even though the huge wine casks are now empty. A labyrinth of tunnels cut into the sandstone were once used for maturing the celebrated, full-bodied dry red wine of Melnik.

In the square of Melnik flanked one side by the rather ugly Melnik Hotel, is a row of reconstructed shops. One is a bookshop where you can buy copies of a booklet (in English) on Yana Sandinski. Another is a wine shop where you can buy homebrew Melnik wine in screwtop bottles for $0.50. It bears a strong resemblance to vinegar. A better bet is to buy *Melnik Harsovo,* a light red wine, in a supermarket elsewhere.

The town museum, Pashov's House contains photographs from the life of Sandanski and records one incident in particular. At the turn of the century, Sandanski and fellow revolutionaries kidnapped an American missionary, Miss Stone, and her pregnant Macedonian maid, intending to hold them to ransom. In spite of the fact the ransom was not forthcoming (though a smaller amount was later handed over) the women were well treated and following their release by Sandanski, Miss Stone published a book in which she praised the rebels. The top floor of the museum has a collection of the belongings of turn-of-the-century Melnikians, and there is also a harem (formerly the house belonged to a Pasha). It was Sandanski's home from 1912-15 up to when he was assassinated on the orders of the pro-German Bulgarian ruler, Ferdinand. Pashov was the last owner of the house.

Two houses in the main street have been converted into a Mehana, where you can treat yourself to Turkish coffee and figs in syrup, a local speciality. The cheapest accommodation is in private houses; the Melnik Hotel charges around $30 double.

Rozhen Monastery. Four miles (6km) from Melnik is the Rozhen monastery founded by Alexi Slav in the 11th century and devoted to the birth of the Virgin *(Rozhen* means birthday in Bulgarian). In the 14th century the monastery was destoyed many times by the Turks. The present church dates from the 16th century and has three naves. The iconostasis is 18th century and is one of the best examples of the woodcarver's art in any Bulgarian monastery. The three-dimensional carvings depict birds, deer and the story of Adam and Eve. Straight ahead as you come through the entrance into the narthex, is a chapel dedicated to Cosma and Damian the two philanthropic Russian doctors of Sandinski. To the left of the narthex entrance is a fresco of The Judgement showing those who are not worthy to enter heaven being flung from a ladder into the jaws of a worm-like monster.

PLOVDIV

With a population of around 260,000, Plovdiv is Bulgaria's second city. Many visitors find it more attractive and livelier than the capital. Inhabited since Thracian times, it was first called Eumolpias which is believed to be the founder's name. It was then conquered by Philip of Macedonia in 341 and renamed Philipopolis. Lucian, the Roman writer, described Philipopolis as 'the largest and most beautiful town in Thrace'. Rome subsequently captured it and called it Trimontium after the three hills on which it was built. When the Ottomans took it over it was called Philibe. Today Plovdiv covers six hills which rise straight from the Thracian Plain. As well as being the venue for two important annual trade fairs, Plovdiv has an annual arts festival which resolves around *al fresco* classical drama performed in a partly restored antique theatre.

Arrival and Departure. Plovdiv's airport serves only to shuttle package tourists about, including skiers heading for Pamporovo (two hours south by road).

Arriving by train at the central station in the south of the city, or by bus at one of the two terminals nearby you will find the centre *(Tsentralen)* within easy walking distance down Ivan Vasov street. Trams and trolleybuses also go to the centre. There are express trains leaving Plovdiv for Sofia (2½ hours) and Burgas (4 hours) and Varna (6 hours). Tickets for the Istanbul Express can be bought at the Rila Agency, 13 General Gurko St, but if possible try to hitch to Svilengrad at the border as the ticket is expensive at about $20. The same agency sells tickets for internal destinations.

From the bus stations there are services to Asenovgrad, Haskovo, Kardzali, Smolyan, Pamporovo and Bachkovo Monastery.

Accommodation. The most picturesque accommodation in Plovdiv would be a private room in the Old Town. Touts descend upon new arrivals, but can usually be trusted. The cheapest hotels are the Bulgaria, 13 Patriarch Evtimii Street and the Leipzig, 76 Boulevard Russki, which are both two-star. There are plenty of three-star hotels like the Trimontsium and the Park Hotel, but these will cost upwards of £20 a night.

There are three campsites near Plovdiv which are open all year: Dveti Kolometer (motel and campsite) which has a swimming pool, 6 miles/10km from Plovdiv on the Sofia road; Trakia campsite, on the same road, and Chaya, 7 miles/11km out on the route to Svilengrad.

Eating and Drinking. There are a several restaurants with floor shows (in summer only) in the old quarter which is a pleasant walk up from the centre: *Trakiiski Stan,* Puldin St which occupies two 19th century houses; *Alafrangite,* 15 Nektariev St in another grand old house with wood carved ceilings, while the *Puldin,* Knyas Tseretelev St, has a summer garden.

Cheaper places to eat are the cafes, in particular around 19 Novembri Square just at the western edge of Old Plovdiv. There is also a vegetarian restaurant on 11 August St. There are plenty of hotel bars to choose from, and in the Trimontsium you might catch a glimpse of Bulgarian pop stars.

Exploring. The river Maritsa flows through Plovdiv and about three quarters of the city, including the original three hills and the Old Town, lie on its south side. There is much to see in Plovdiv but the old town should be a priority. It is part of the architectural conservation area that contains magnificent architecture from the National Revival period interspersed with the remains of medieval walls which are sometimes incorporated into the houses. The best place to start a sightseeing tour is from the Central Square (Tsentralen). This is a vast pedestrian square dominated by the solid-looking hotel Trimontsium, Party House and the Central Post Office. Next to the post office a viewing platform has been constructed around the ruins of a Roman forum.

From the Tsentralen you can stroll northwards along Vasil Kolarov Street, one of the main shopping areas, towards the old quarter eventually reaching Ploshtad 19 Novembri where another viewing platform enables you to look down on the gladiator's entrance and a small section of the Philipopolis arena. You can enter the old town from here where a fairly steep flight of steps leads upwards to the 2 AD Antique Theatre which has been partially reconstructed. This Amphitheatre commands a splendid view down the main highway; to the right you can see a red and white building not unlike an aircraft hangar which is the modern drama theatre.

The National Revival houses of old Plovdiv are bigger than those of Koprivshtitsa and are some of the largest in Bulgaria. The crafty mer-chantmen who built them got over the problem of restricted groundspace by building houses with overhanging upper floors known as oriels. It is difficult not to get lost in the maze of narrow cobbled streets of the old town as street names are not easy to spot. Several of the houses are museums. The Ethnographic museum is housed in Kojmudjioglu's House on ul Starinna built in 1847. The outside is painted navy blue and is decorated with yellow alafrangi panels. In the 19th century alafrangi meant anything from abroad but it is generally used to refer to painted panels inside and outside National Revival houses. Inside the museum is a magnificent collection of folk costumes of all the Bulgarian regions, all in mint condition. Not far from the Ethnographic Museum is the Hissar Kapiya, the ancient Eastern gate of the city.

The showpiece of the old city is probably Balbanov's House, which is a complete reconstruction as the original was destroyed by fire. Balbanov's House is used for Mayoral receptions and downstairs there is an art gallery for contemporary exhibitions. However, most of the furniture is imported and you will probably find some of the other houses with original frangipani painting and fittings more interesting. Among these are the Georgiadi House (1 ul Starinna), which is now the Museum of the National Liberation, and Lamartine's House (19 Knyaz Tseretelev, near the antique Theatre), so called because the French poet stayed there in 1833 while convalescing from cholera on his way back from Constantinople.

Theatres. As well as the Amphitheatre there is an Open air Theatre on Liberators' Hill, and the Masslitinov Drama Theatre at 36 Vasil Kolarov Street. The Cultural Information Centre, at 30 Vasil Kolarov Street, should be able to tell you what's on.

Music. The Plovdiv Philharmonic performs in a concert hall attached to Party House in the Tsentralen and in January puts on a Winter Festival of Music. Water music (a combination of fountains and lights with a sound-track) can be seen and heard in Freedom Park.

Nightclubs are located in the Park Hotel Leningrad, 97 Boulevard Moskva, the Novotel Plodiv, 2 Zlatyo Boyadjiev St and the Trimontsium.

Shopping. Descending from Georgiadi's House in the old town you will come to Strumna St, a row of renovated craftmen's shops where you can buy wares such as baskets, pottery etc. and watch them being made. In Vasil Kolarov St, which is a pedestrian precinct, there is a department store (number 11) and another, Neva at 1 Vasil Levski St.

Help and Information. The Comprehensive Service Bureau is at 34 Boulevard Moskva (tel 5 28 05). Another central tourist office is at 13 Patriarch Evtimii St in the Bulgaria hotel.

SOUTHERN BULGARIA

Barely ten minutes out from Plovdiv south towards Asenovgrad, the Rho-dopes begin to rise. For Bulgaria they are a rich source of non-ferrous ores. Asenovgrad, 12 miles (19km) from Plovdiv, was a defence fortress in the Middle Ages and nowadays it is a centre of the tobacco and food-processing industries. Just beyond the town is Asen's Fortress of which only a 7th century single-nave church remains, perched on a hill. A further 6 miles (10km) on is the monastery of Bachkovo and just before it is the 14th century Ossuary and Church of the Archangel Michael.

Bachkovo Monastery. The monastery is situated on the bank of the river Cheparlarska, and is the second largest in Bulgaria after Rila. Founded in 1083 by the Georgian monk Grigorii Bacurani it has been reconstructed many times and today is based around two quadrangles each containing a church. The larger of the churches was built in 1604. During the 18th century the monastery was extended and another church, St. Nicholas was built. It has murals by Zahari Zograf who always managed to include a self-portrait amongst his work. Arriving on a Saturday one traveller was interested to find a sheep tethered in the church porch and a lone chicken patrolling the courtyard. Apparently these were offerings from farmers whose prayers had been answered. Inside the church were less animate presents; bags of flour laid against the iconostasis and perhaps more surprisingly, bundles of underclothing. Near the monastery is a restaurant and campsite.

A further 8 miles (14km) into the Rhodope mountains is the Narchen Spa where the spring waters are radio-active. Hardly an advertisement you would think but nonetheless popular with several sanitoria and a Balkantourist Hotel with a coffee shop and restaurant. As the road climbs up towards Chepelare the scenery becomes typically alpine with vast forests of evergreen spruces in every direction, which provide a rich source of timber for Bulgaria. Bulgarians use Chepelare as a dormitory for the ski resort of Pamporovo, staying in private guest houses. Chepelare also has a two-star hotel, the Zdravets. Six miles (10km) on is Pamporovo, the nicest of Bulgaria's ski resorts.

Pamporovo. The resort is situated on the slopes of Mount Snezhanka (Snowhite) at an altitude of 1650 metres. A television tower rises from the top of the mountain and provides a splendid view from its cafe situated 93 metres up the mast. Pamporovo has a reliably sunny climate and a good snow record, with skiing from January to mid-April. There is something for all levals of skier and the beginners' slopes are close to the main hotels. There are four ski-hire outlets. Accommodation in Pamporovo is likely to be booked out in season by package tourists so you are advised to book ahead.

Of the hotels, the Orpheus, Panorama and Snezhanka are the cheapest and the Tourist Offices in the Murgavets and Perelik hotels will probably help with bookings. The Perelik is the best hotel with a swimming pool and sauna. The Murgavets has a rooftop cafeteria. Accommodation may also be available at the Malina Holiday Village. If you want a good meal there is plenty of choice but recommended are the *Chervermento* and the *Vodenitsata*. The former is a collection of rustic looking wooden buildings where the speciality is *cheverme,* spit-roasted whole lamb turned in front of a huge medieval looking fireplace. The Vodenitsata is a converted water mill which serves *maroudnitsi* (Rhodope pancakes) among other local specialities. It is four miles from the resort.

Other excursions include the Yagodinska Cave and Trigrad Gorge and a day trip to the Dospat dam to go fishing and rambling. In summer Pamporovo is a base for a variety of hiking excursions to historic sites (including nearby Smolyan) and botany trails.

NORTHWEST BULGARIA

Vidin. The Danubian port of Vidin is situated in the northwest corner of Bulgaria. It is a border crossing to Calafat, Romania which is reached by the Vidin-Calafat passenger and car ferry operating a daily service. Vidin is also one of Bulgaria's oldest towns having been settled by the Celts in the 3rd century BC. The Romans then built a fortress over the remains of the Celtic settlement and named it Bononia. During the Middle Ages, Vidin became the capital of the Vidin Kingdom under Ivan Stratsimir and it prospered as a trading centre. During the 19th century Vidin was the focus of a major uprising in 1850 against the Turks. Liberation finally came in 1878 with the help of Romanian troops. The main point of interest is the Baba Vida fortress which was greatly expanded during the Middle Ages and by the Turks, and whose walls border the Danube for about half a mile. It is now a museum.

VELIKO TURNOVO

With an estimated three million visitors a year, you might expect a lot from Veliko Turnovo ('Turnovo the Great') but nothing else you see in Bulgaria, or for that matter anywhere, will quite prepare you for the fabulous setting of this old capital city. As romantic as anything described by Byron or Coleridge, it has everything. It is girdled by the river Yantra which snakes back on itself at the bottom of a deep canyon, making the three hills on which the city is situated look like islands; it has a medieval citadel and a magnificent old quarter of beautifully homogeneous houses perched on a hillside and reaching down to the river in which they are reflected.

Turnovo has a long history going back to the 5th century when a Byzantine fortress stood on the Tsarevets Hill. In 1185 the uprising against Byzantine rule was announced by the Assen brothers of that dynasty, and from 1187 Turnovo became the capital of the Second Bulgarian Kingdom until it fell to the Ottomans in 1396. The first National Assembly of the newly liberated Bulgaria met in Turnovo to draft the Constitution in 1879.

Arrival and Departure. *Airport:* there are daily flights to Sofia. *Railway Station:* This is situated at the foot of Sveta Gora Hill, on the right bank of the Yantra. Frequent buses will take you to the city centre. *Bus Station:* The Terminal is on the left bank of the Yantra on Hristo Botev Street from where you can easily walk to the centre. You can get buses to nearby points of interest including several monasteries and Arbanasi village. There are also buses to Gabrovo.

Accommodation. The cheapest accommodation can be found at the *Bolyarski Stan* campsite just outside Turnovo on the E771. Buses go to it from Vasil Levski Street. The cheapest hotel in Turnovo is the Orbita, 15 ul Hristo Botev on the left bank of the Yantra, but in summer it is likely to be booked up. If this is the case try the Etur hotel (two star), a high-rise block in the same street, or in the same category the Yantra hotel, 1 Velchova Zavera Square in the old town. A splendid view of the old city can be had from the luxury (three-star) Veliko Turnovo hotel which costs around 90 leva per night. The Balkantourist office is at 1 Levski Street.

Eating and Drinking. For food with a view, the terrace of the Veliko Turnovo hotel is hard to beat, but it is expensive. The restaurants in other hotels, the Etur, and the Balkan are cheaper. There are also traditional *mehanas* like the *Hadzhi Mincho* on the Square of the Hanged and the *Slavanks* restaurant and cafe at 35 Levski Street.

Exploring. The citadel on Tsaravets Hill was the centre of medieval Turnovo which was approached by a stone causeway on which there were three fortified gates. On the top of the Tsarevets Hill is the almost completely reconstructed Church of the Ascension which now houses The Pantheon of Bulgarian Spiritual Culture. Inside the church the walls are covered with murals by Teofan Sokerov depicting the key events of the Second Bulgarian Kingdom. This church was reopened in 1985 to commemmorate the 800th anniversary of the liberation of Bulgaria from Byzantine rule. Parts of the fortress walls have also been restored and outlines of the many buildings within can be seen. On special national days, a light and sound spectacular with bell-ringing and *son et lumiere* is put on in the citadel. The view looking down over Turnovo and the river gorges from the Pantheon is breathtaking.

There are plans afoot to raise the level of the Yantra and use it for boat trips around the city. To the east of Tsarevets on the right bank is the Church of the Forty Martyrs, built in 1230 by Ivan Assen II to commemorate a great victory at Klokotnitsa. Still undergoing restoration it contains murals of the Turnovo school and columns with inscriptions in old Bulgarian and Greek. The Church of St. Dmiter (12th century) at the foot of Trapezitsa Hill is where Peter and Assen declared rebellion against the Turks.

After the Tsarevets Hill, the next most interesting area is the *Varosha* or Old Quarter of Ottoman times. Not to be missed is the Samovodska Market Place in Rakovski Street, where a row of artisans' workshops have been restored rather pristinely, and arts and crafts revived. You can shop and watch the craftsmen at work making baskets, pottery etc. In the old photographer's shop you can have your picture taken and drink delicious Turkish style coffee in the adjoining cafe. At 13 Ivan Vasov Street is the first Bulgarian pharmacy; founded in 1823, it is half museum and half dispensing chemist.

Museums. The following museums are in the Varosha district: The National Revival Museum in Suedinenie Square is housed in the old Konak (Ottoman town hall). A large pale green building, it is the work of the self-taught architect Kolio Ficheto. His work can be seen elsewhere in Turnovo, notably at the Hadji Nikoli Inn, 17 Rakovski Street which is now the Ethnographic Museum. Old Gurko Street is a typical street of the National Revival style. Of particular interest are no. 88 — *Kashasarafka* (Sarafkin House) — and no. 35, Granny Mota's House.

On the right bank of the river opposite the Veliko Turnovo hotel is a magnificent monument to the Assen dynasty comprising four black equestrian statues surrounding an obelisk.

Help and Information. *Tourist Information.* The Balkantourist Comprehensive Bureau is at 1 Vasil Levski Street. The Rila office for international rail tickets is at 1A Stamboliiski Street and for other rail tickets the Railway Office is at 12 Hristo Botev Street. The Balkan Airlines office shares the same address as the Rila office.

Excursions from Veliko Turnovo. *Arbanasi* is a picture postcard village three miles from Turnovo. Situated high on a plateau it overlooks the Tsaravets and Trapezitsa hills. The buildings date from the Middle Ages and the National Revival, and many of them are fortified, and beautifully decorated inside with murals and carved ceilings. The Konstantsalieva House contains a museum. The village also has five churches built between the 16th and 18th centuries. The 17th century Church of the Nativity contains a mass of frescoes from different periods. Arbanasi can be reached by bus 14 from Turnovo.

The Transfiguration Monastery. Otherwise known as Preobrazhenski Monastery, this is four miles (7km) north of Turnovo. You can get part of the way by bus, and walk or hitch from the turn off that leads to the monastery. Founded in the 15th century during the reign of Tsar Ivan Shishman, the monastery suffered the usual Ottoman destruction. Restoration began in 1825 and the main church was built in 1834, with murals from 1849 by Zohari Zograf. The iconostasis was carved by artists of the Tryavna school. Both Veliko Turnovo and the monastery have connections with Vasil Levski, the revolutionary who often kept undercover here.

Nicopolis Ad Istrum. This town is difficult to reach, but it is interesting enough to warrant a mention — and a detour. Ten miles north of Turnovo, Nicopolis ad Istrum was founded by Emperor Trajan in 106AD, and was an important military and administrative city on the route between the Danube and the Balkans. Although there is not much left (a pavement, stumps of columns, the odd statue), the scale of the town is impressive, as are the remains of a reservoir and 15-mile-long viaduct.

CENTRAL BULGARIA

Thirty miles (50km) south of Turnovo on route E85 is Gabrovo. There are a number of possible detours along the way including the monasteries of Kilifarevo and Plakolo. The village of Dryavno was once famous for its silk-worm industry, and Dryavno Monastery is two miles southwest of the town. During a local uprising in 1876 the monastery became a refuge for hundreds of rebels under siege from 10,000 Turks who hanged the leader Bacho Kiro when the rebels capitulated. Another detour worth making is the beautifully restored 19th century village and former crafts centre of Tryavna.

Gabrovo. This small town has become synonymous with a tradition of jokes to do with the miserliness of its inhabitants: 'they don't whitewash the walls so as not to make the room smaller,' and 'they dock the tails of their cats so as to close the door an instant sooner and conserve more heat'. With their customary inventiveness Gabrovians have turned their reputation to their own account by making themselves a tourist attraction, with their House of Humour and Satire opened on April Fool's Day 1972. It contains a collection of cartoons, paintings, photographs and satirical writing etc from a host of nations. A biennial Festival of Humour and Satire is held every four years in Gabrovo.

In the 19th century Gabrovo flourished as a centre of crafts (textiles, wood and iron) and with prosperity came cultural development. The first secular Bulgarian school was opened in 1835 in Gabrovo. Coming into Gabrovo from the direction of Turnovo you get a superlative view of the village and the crest of the Balkan range.

Etura. The open air museum of Etura is five miles south. You can see craftspeople at work spinning, woodworking, knifemaking etc. in workshops mainly powered by water-wheels (a Transylvanian innovation of the last century). There is also a bakery where you can buy bread from the oven and a kind of dried plum paste which is a very sustaining if not gourmet repast. There is a hotel and restaurant nearby, and buses run from Gabrovo to Etura fairly frequently.

Shipka Pass. Continuing south on the route to Kazanlak, few experiences in Bulgaria can compare with crossing the Balkans via Shipka Pass. You can take the bus from Gabrovo to Kazanlak which will take you across. At any time of year it is magnificent but in winter it is stunning. The leafless trees either side of the road near the top of the pass, have thick white outlines from the covering of snow and ice on their branches which almost meet overhead so you are passing through a translucent tunnel. With snow falling the effect is enhanced.

In August 1877 the pass was held by 6,000 Russians and Bulgarian volunteers against an Ottoman force over four times as great. Short of ammunition they were reduced to hurling stones and anything that came to hand, including corpses, at the Turks. When Pleven surrendered to the

Russians reinforcements released from besieging Pleven arrived and the war was all but over. At the top of the pass 1,000 steps lead to a monument to the Russians built in 1936. On the southern side of the pass is the Russian Memorial Church, unmistakable with its five gilded domes. Built by grateful Bulgarians it commemorates the Russian heroes of Shipka Pass. Inside are murals, also many icons, the latter brought as presents from Russia by veterans. The church is much visited by Russians who place flowers on the memorial stones inside which mark where the Russian remains are buried.

Kazanlak and The Valley of the Roses. The past of Kazanlak is inextricable from the growing of roses for oil of attar, the base for many perfumes of which Bulgaria produces most of the world's supply. Since about 400 years ago the growing of Kazanlak roses spread across the so called Valley of the Roses at the foot of the Balkans which includes the National Revival Towns of Sopot, Karlovo and Kalofer. Karlovo is the birthplace of Vasil Levski, the main organiser of the National Liberation struggle. Kalofer is the birthplace of the poet Hristo Botev and Ivan Vasov, author of *Under the Yoke* was a native of Sopot. Their dwellings are all museums. Every year a Festival of Roses is held on the day before the rose-picking begins, usually at the beginning of June. It is held in one of the towns in the Valley of the roses, with a "King and Queen" in Thracian dress, showers of rose petals and fireworks.

Koprivshtica. After Rosino, the road continues with the Balkan range to the right and the Sredna Gora chain to the left. These two ranges are separated by a narrow valley. A left hand turning leads to Koprivshtica in the Sredna Gora, where the April Rising began on April 20th 1876, and just about every house and street commemorates some heroic deed of the past. The houses are all from the National Revival period the oldest being Pavlikenska House which is 18th century. The tourist office in Koprivshtica can arrange accommodation in some of the old houses. The National Bulgarian Folklore Festival which attracts folklore enthusiasts from all over the world is held every five years in the mountainous area of Voivodenets nearby. The next one is due in August 1996.

RUSE AND THE NORTH

The Danubian port of Ruse is Bulgaria's fourth largest town with a population of 178,000 and is situated opposite the Romanian town of Gyurevo (Giurgiu) to which it is linked by The Friendship Bridge, one of the main border crossing points between the two countries.

Ruse was originally a Roman Garrison called *Sexaginti Prista* (port of 60 ships) which was destroyed by Barbarians in the 4th-6th centuries. In the 16th century under the Ottomans a new fortress was raised called Rousschouk which had five entrance gates only one of which has survived. For about ten years before the liberation Ruse was under the governorship of an enlightened Pasha, Midhad who built schools, hospitals and Bulgaria's first railway from Ruse to Varna. At the time of the Liberation, Ruse was the largest town in Bulgaria with more banks and consulates than Sofia. It has always been the centre for Bulgarian river navigation. It is also one of the main links between Bulgaria and the USSR by sea and rail.

On the route from Ruse to Varna is Razgrad which has been built up in recent years. There is not much to stop for except the fine Ibrahim Pasha mosque built in 1614. Just to the southeast of the town are the ruins of the Roman town of Abritus.

VARNA AND THE NORTHERN BLACK SEA COAST

Since the 1960s, when the coast of Bulgaria began to gear itself to mass tourism, a profusion of developments has all but obliterated the original character of the 230-mile long coastline with most of its ancient towns and villages now submerged by tourist complexes and holiday villages like Eleni, Zora and Dyuni. The discerning traveller will probably prefer the as yet less developed stretch of coast just south of Varna and near the Turkish border, while the hedonists will probably head straight for the popular resorts of Slunchev Bryag (Sunny Beach), Albena, Golden Sands and Drouzhba. Most tourists, happy to enjoy the reliable sunshine and mild climate of the coast, are Westerners attracted by low prices.

Varna. One of the two biggest towns on the coast, and the third largest in Bulgaria, is Varna — population 300,000. Inhabited since the Stone Age, the present site of Varna was founded by Greek settlers in the 6th century BC and called Odessos by them. Bulgarians arrived on the scene in the 8th century, capturing and then fortifying the citadel which has since been destroyed. By the time Varna fell to the Ottomans in 1389, it had become a well known port with strong links with the Aegean. In 1444 the Polish King Wladislaw III, with an army of Crusaders, attacked the Ottomans but was defeated in battle nearby. Under the Ottomans, Varna was built up into an important garrison and the fortifications were extended.

In 1878 the town was liberated by the Russians and developed rapidly as a commercial riviera to which the many elegant turn-of-the-century and baroque buildings testify.

Arrival and Departure: Varna's international airport lies at the western edge of the city with good bus connections to the city centre on bus 50. The railway station is centrally situated. Tickets can be bought in advance from the Railway Office at 10 Asram Street, and international tickets from the Rila Bureau, 3 Shipka Street. The bus terminal is on the same road as the airport. Buses leave from here to the Panorama campsite 12 miles/20km from Varna.

It is possible to sail to Odessa on Ukrainian steamers; ask around at the port. The Sea Terminals for hydrofoils and hydrobuses are located in the suburbs of Asparouhouvo and Galata.

Accommodation: Varna has a range of hotels of which the following are the most central:

The Moussala (one star), 3 Moussala Street, is very cheap.
The Odessa (two stars) is right next to the Central Beach, and looks over the Marine Gardens.
The Cherno More (three stars) is near the Marine Gardens.

Eating and Drinking: Varna is full of restaurants, many of them excellent. Druzki Street, a turn off Han Omurtag Street, not far from the Ethnographic museum, is an old restored street which is full of eating places such as the *Starata Kushta* (old house) where you can get good Bulgarian fare in historic surroundings.

Exploring: The old centre of Varna, with its outdoor cafés and elegant buildings, has a bustling charm. If you are planning to see the city rather than laze on the beaches, a good place to start from to see the old town is Varnenska Communa Square, dominated by the bedomed Cathedral of the

Assumption built in 1886. The ruins of the Roman Thermae (baths) are located at the junction of Khan Krum Street and Patlejna, opposite the Holy Virgin Church built in 1602. Other fragments of Roman architecture include a street and water mains from ancient Odessos, between Moussala Hotel and the Odessos Snack Bar, not far from the National Revival Museum. The National Theatre, a baroque concoction, is on 9 September Square.

The most attractive part of the new town is undoubtedly the Marine Park situated southeast of the old town. It is full of Mediterranean plants and shady promenades with a dolphinarium and an open-air theatre to add to its appeal. At the western end of the park near the passenger seaport is the Naval Museum. Nearby are specially screened off parts of the beach for naturists.

Entertainment: The Varna Summer Festival, held in midsummer, is staged in several venues including the Open Air Stage and the antique setting of the Roman Thermae. For the annual International Music Festival, the Atanas Church and the Festival Complex next to the Central Beach entrance are just two of the venues used.

Museums: The Museum of History and Art is housed in an impressive building which was formerly a school. Among other exhibits, it houses a collection of skeletons and artefacts over 6,000 years old, from the Varna Necropolis which was excavated in 1972. The gold items of this collection are believed to be the oldest worked gold in the world. The Ethnographic Museum in a National Revival Building is at 22 Panagyurishte Street. For fans of military history there is the Museum of Combat Friendship, commemorating the spot where the Crusaders under the Polish King Vladislav III fought the Ottomans and lost, thereby failing to halt the march of the infidel across Christendom.

Sport: Varna boasts seven sports halls and stadia, including the Palace of Sports and Culture in the northeast of the city. There is a tremendous swimming complex next to the Naval Museum, with two outdoor mineral water pools.

Further Afield. The main resorts near Varna are as follows:

Drouzhba (6 miles) Take bus number 8 from Varna. Drouzhba is a seaside and balneological resort and Bulgaria's original international coastal resort dating from the 1940s. There are tourist offices in Chernomorets Restaurant and The Rubin Hotel. Drouzhba's *Bulgarska Svatba* (Bulgarian Wedding) restaurant is popular for its floorshow imitation of the real thing and traditional 'wedding food' dishes.

Golden Sands *(Zlatni Pyassatsi)* 11 miles. The second-largest resort, with over 80 hotels. If you are looking for an inexpensive hotel, try the Gdansk, Pliska and Veliko Turnovo; these are three hotels shaped like pyramids, close together at the southern end of the resort. Golden Sands has three miles of sandy beach, mineral springs (mineral water swimming pools are located at the Ambassador and International hotels), and a coastal forest setting. It is linked with Varna by express bus 109 which stops at the International Hotel, and local bus 99 which goes to the Panorama campsite.

Eating and Drinking: Theme restaurants include *Vodenitsata* (in an old mill), *Kosharata* (The Sheep Pen) on the outskirts of the resort, *Trifon Zarezan* (the winegrowers) on the Drouzhba road, the *Lovna Sreshta* (near

Aladzha Monastery, two miles from town) which specialises in game and the *Zlatna Ribka* (seafood). The *Metsa Poljand* is an open-air restaurant in a woodland setting above the resort.

Sports: Most sports wet and dry are catered for and equipment can be hired. There are tennis courts and other facilities at the sports grounds attached to the Malina, Liliya and Morsko Oko hotels, and riding at the compound near the Republika bus stop. Bicycles can be hired from near the Malina, Liliya and Rodina hotels and at the Havana Pool. Balkantourist also organise a Sports Package which covers all sports and equipment at a reduced rate.

Entertainment: The Sochi open air theatre is used for cinema, pop concerts, classical concerts and folklore spectaculars. There is an annual folklore festival in June, and a Week for the Sea including the Miss Golden Sands Beauty Contest.

Albena. The latest Bulgarian resort is Albena with 40-plus hotels many of which look like giant flights of steps leading down to a good, four-mile-long beach. There is a campsite just outside called Albena, and two further out, Exotica and International. Albena's other claim to fame is being the starting point for the Albena-Golden Sands-Sliven Motor Rally at the beginning of May.

Balchik. This old romantic white stone town is reachable by boat from Varna. Hotels: Balchik, Dionysopol. Campsite: Beliyat Bryag, three miles north. Balchik's main attraction is a former Romanian Royal Palace, whose grounds are now a botanical park with over 3,000 species of flora.

BURGAS AND THE SOUTHERN BLACK SEA

Burgas is Bulgaria's fifth-largest city, with a population of 185,000. Until the last century it subsisted fairly modestly on fishing and grain crops. With the introduction of a railway link with Plovdiv in 1890 and the construction of a harbour in 1903, it prospered into a big industrial centre, and is the home port of the Bulgarian Oceanic Fishing Fleet. Being more industrialised than Varna, it lacks the charm of the latter although there are some fine turn-of-the-century buildings.

Arrival and Departure: From the *airport*, five miles north, there are regular buses into Burgas. The *railway station* is located in the south of the city on Vasil Kolarov Street. International tickets can be obtained from the Rila Bureau, 106 Purvi Mai Street, (tel 4 70 23). The *Yug (South)* bus terminal is next to the railway station from where there are buses to Sozopol and Sunny Beach as well as further afield. The *Passenger Seaport* is located behind the railway station.

Exploring: Apart from a few museums there is not a lot to see in Burgas. The best are probably the Art Gallery in a former synagogue featuring a fine collection of icons and the Ethnographic Museum at 69 Slavianska St. Nightlife revolves around the Bulgaria, Primorets and Park hotels where there are bars and discos.

North of Burgas

This stretch of coast contains two of the biggest tourist attractions of the black Sea, the resort of Sunny Beach and the museum town of Nessebur.

Pomorie. Situated on a narrow peninsula, Pomorie is five miles northeast of Burgas and was founded in the 4th century BC as Anchialo. A fire in 1906 destroyed all the wooden buildings, hence the modern look of the town today. Of interest nearby just off the road to Burgas is the burial mound of beehive tombs dating from 4BC built up like a Roman Mausoleum. The Hotel Pomorie (two stars) overhangs the sea and the Europa campsite is not far away.

Nessebur. This extraordinary place is a museum town situated on a rocky peninsula. It is virtually an islet, as it is connected to the mainland only by a slender isthmus. Rather too popular with tourists, it is nevertheless worth visiting for its churches — some of which date from the 5th and 6th centuries.

Sunny Beach *(Slanchev Bryag)*. This is the largest Bulgarian seaside resort, with 108 hotels and a magnificent sandy beach bounded by the isthmus of Nessebur to the south and the holiday villages of Zora and Eleni to the north. Sunny Beach offers everything you would expect from a popular international resort including gigolos (known as "Herring Gulls"). A small electric train runs from the *Fregata* Bar (a "stranded galleon") at the southern end of the beach to the *vyatarna Melnitsa* (Windmill) at the other end. Alternative transport includes open carriages and bicycles; the latter can be rented from the information office near Ropotamo Hotel.

Accommodation: Inexpensive hotels include: the Sirena, near the path leading to the Fregata bar; the Nessebur, near the skyscraper Burgas hotel; the Venera, near the Globus and the Chaika, close to the beach. The campsite at Vlas is a few kilometres out of town. You can also enquire about vacancies at Zora and Elenite holiday villages (the latter, built by the Finns, is preferable).

Eating and Drinking: Some of the more popular and exotic restaurants are outside the resort. These include the *Hanska Shatra* (Khan's Tent), situated on a wooded hill at the northern end of the resort; decorated like an old Bulgar tent it also has a lively floorshow. The sedately named *Picnic* (8 miles from the resort) features displays of fire-dancing.

Sports: There are seawater swimming pools connected to the Hotel Burgas. Tennis courts are located near the Sokol and Iskur, and there is a riding school just outside the resort. The annual Emona Regatta takes place in July with an Olympic race at Sunny Beach. The competitors' boats berth in Nessebur harbour.

The International Golden Orpheus Pop Festival is held at Sunny Beach every July.

South of Burgas

This is the least developed section of the coast and the sleepy charm of old towns like Sozopol and Ahtopol is in many ways preferable to the purpose built overcrowded resorts further north.

Sozopol. Founded by Greek settlers in the 7th century BC and called Apollonia, it was crushed by the Romans in 72 AD, and resurfaced as Sozopolis in 431. A prosperous port until the Ottomans arrived and sacked it, Sozopol snoozed away the centuries on its isolated peninsula until the tourists brought it back to life. This is definitely one of the better places to visit. Each September it is the venue for the Apollonia Arts Festival.

Primorsko. The fishing village of Primorsko is situated at the mouth of the Dyavolska River. It has a campsite (Romantika) and a restaurant, the *Dyavolsko Hanche.*

Ahtopol. As befits an outpost of the tourist trail, Ahtopol is pretty, quiet and sleepy in spite of being regularly descended upon by UNESCO archaeologists who scour the shipwrecks and surrounding seabed for artifacts from Ahtopol's ancient trading port past. The town is accessible from Burgas by hydrofoil and hydrobus as well as by bus. It is surrounded by fruit groves that thrive in the mild climate. Below Ahtopol are two more villages whose development as resorts has not yet begun. The border crossing into Turkey lies well inland on the E87 which curves inland from Michurin to the checkpoint of Malko Turnovo, six miles from the border.

Malko Turnovo. This was a centre of the 1903 Preobrazhenie Uprising against the Ottomans. Many old houses are preserved. Accommodation can be obtained at the motel, which also has a tourist office and currency exchange bureau where you can offload your leva before heading for Turkey.

Calendar of Events

January 1	**New Year's Day**
February 14	Vinegrower's Day *(Trfon Zarezan).* Celebrated in Melnik
March 3	**Day of Bulgaria's Liberation from the Ottomans**
March	Music Days International Festival (Ruse)
April	International Skiing Competitions for the Aleko Cup
May 1 & 2	**International Labour Day**
May	Sunny Beach International Sailing Regatta
May	Albena-Golden Sands-Sliven Car Rally (first fortnight)
May	International Festival of Humour and Satire (Gabrovo, in odd-numbered years)
May/June/July	Arts Festivals in the 2AD Antique Theatre (Plovdiv)
May 24	**Day of the Slav Script, Bulgarian Enlightenment and Culture**
May/June	Sofia Music Weeks
early June	Festival of Roses (Karlovo and Kazanluk)
June	Orpheus Evenings (held at Sunny Beach)
June	International Chamber Music Festival (held in odd-numbered years in the courtyard of the Ethnographic museum, Plovdiv)
June/July	Varna International Music Festival
June-September	Neptune Nights in Sunny Beach
July	Stage of the Centuries Summer Festival, held on Tsarevets Hill, Veliko Turnovo
August	Week of the Sea Festival at Albena, and Golden Sands
late August	International Folklore Festival, Burgas
August/Septemer	Apollonia Festival of the Arts (Sozopol)
August	Varna International Sailing Regatta
September/October	Festival of the Arts in Old Plovdiv
late November	Ruse Jazz Forum
December 25	Christmas Carol Singing *(Koledouvane)*
December/January	New Year's Music Festival (Sofia — the National Palace of Culture)

Public Holidays are shown in **bold**

Albania

Skanderbeg Square, Tirana

Population: 3,450,000
Capital: Tirana (population 300,000)

To the locals, Albania is known as *Shqipëria* or 'The Land of the Eagles', a grandiose name for a nation about the size of Wales or Florida. It has spent most of the last fifty years virtually isolated from the rest of the world. Until 1985, Albania was ruled by Enver Hoxha, a dictator responsible for one of the most brutal and repressive regimes of modern times, comparable even to that of Romania's Ceauçescu. But following the collapse of communism, and free elections held in 1991, Albania has emerged with a democratically elected government. Gone are the hoardings which proclaimed the joys of Marxist-Leninism and maintained the personality cult of Enver Hoxha.

In many ways Albania is being reborn. The country is struggling to establish the type of infrastructure which is taken for granted in much of Europe. Millions of dollars of foreign aid are being pumped in as the country seeks to establish a stable market economy and put the brakes on spiralling inflation. In the turmoil of the Balkans during the 1990s, Albania has shown itself (somewhat unexpectedly) to be a bastion of stability in a region ravaged by civil war.

A number of foreign hotel chains have already taken advantage of investment opportunities — however high risk — and an Austrian company has even started building a chain of casinos. But while tourism remains in its infancy, with facilities minimal by even many European standards, you can enjoy the remarkable kindness and generosity of the Albanian people and superb scenery. Albania possesses some of the most unspoilt coastline in the Adriatic, with many of its golden beaches both undeveloped and unpolluted. The landscapes inland are equally beautiful, with rugged mountains in the northern region. Albania is also rightfully proud of its cultural heritage. Archaeological sites, many of them virtually unexcavated, pepper the countryside. Historic settlements like Gjirokastër, Krujë and Berat boast charm enough to rival Dubrovnik in its pre-civil war days.

For the traveller willing to forgo some of life's luxuries — such as regular electricity, constant water and clean public toilets — Albania offers a fascinating holiday. Since the state-controlled Albturist agency lost its monopoly, independent travel has become relatively easy. Furthermore, going on your own is often far cheaper than taking a package tour. Many visitors take a charter flight to Corfu, and then simply hop across to southern Albania by ferry.

This small nation is perhaps Europe's best kept secret. If it continues to enjoy political stability and the benefits of Western cooperation, it is set to prosper. But go soon, before tourism and development change Albania beyond recognition. Get there before Club Med does.

CLIMATE

Albania has a typically Mediterranean climate: hot, dry summers and cool, wet winters. Temperatures can reach as high as 44°C/110°F in summer and fall as low as -26°C/-5°F in winter. Take a thick jumper and waterproof gear whatever time of year you travel, particularly if you plan excursions into the mountains: temperatures plummet in winter, and rain is heavier than on the coastal plain. It can be unpleasantly cold if a power cut (frequent) knocks out your hotel's central heating system.

Spring and autumn are the most pleasant seasons to visit.

HISTORY

Few countries have had a history so continuously dominated by turbulence, bloodshed and invasion. It is remarkable that Albanians have been able to absorb foreign influences over the centuries while retaining their distinct identity and language.

The country takes it name from the Albanoi, an Illyrian tribe that settled in the Western Balkans around 2000BC. Next came the Greeks, around 700BC, who co-existed peacefully with the Illyrians and founded towns such as Lezhë in northern Albania. The Illyrians steadily grew in strength, which worried the Romans who were keen to control the Adriatic Sea. In 229BC they invaded, but it took them sixty years to subdue the Illyrians. Several tribes mounted a guerrilla war in the south of the country.

The Romans ruled for the next 550 years, establishing 'pax romana' with its attendant prosperity. But the Empire began to crumble. In AD395 the province of Illyria became part of the Eastern or Byzantine Empire, ruled from present-day Istanbul. Albania was subjected to a barrage of attacks in the following centuries: first by Visigoths, Huns and Ostrogoths and later by the Slavs, Bulgarians, Normans and the Crusaders. Then came the Serbs, who invaded in the mid-14th century, but Albanian tribal chieftains were able to break away and set up feudal independent states. In 1389, Turkey defeated the occupying army and remained for the following five hundred years. In the meantime, the Republic of Venice managed to seize control of some of the major western cities, such as Durrës, Skhoder and Lezhë.

The Ottomans compelled the Albanians to pay a financial tribute, which spurred them to fight back. They were led by Gjergj Kastrioti, who was to become Albania's greatest folk hero. He had been enslaved by the Turks as a child and was sent to serve the Sultan in Constantinople. Here he converted to Islam and was given the name Skander (Alexander) to which, after he had distinguished himself in the Turkish army, was added the honorary suffix óbeg, meaning brave. Skanderbeg suddenly defected to his native land taking with him 300 men and vowing to overthrow Turkish rule. He won immense popular support.

Over the next twenty-five years, until his death in 1468, Skanderbeg defeated the powerful Turkish armies. His other great achievement lay in persuading the Albanian feudal lords to sign the Covenant of Lezhë in 1444, which laid the foundations for national unity. However, the Albanian army disintegrated after his death and within ten years the Turks had regained control over most of Albania. They imposed Islam and stayed put for 400 years.

Turkey was described as 'the sick man of Europe' at the end of the 19th century, and Albania was one of the most backward parts of its empire. That didn't prevent nationalists from forming the Albanian League in 1878, which demanded recognition of their homeland. Turks crushed the uprising but in 1912 Albanian patriots declared independence and set up a provisional government at Vlorë. Yet despite this achievement, Albania was carved up during the Ambassadors' Conference, held that same year in London. The talks were to discuss how best to divide the Ottoman Empire, which had been defeated by the Balkan powers. Albania was cut in half with the Kosovo region handed over to Serbia. To add insult to injury a German aristocrat, Wilhelm von Wied, was installed as Head of State. This was poorly received in Albania and he was forced to flee.

During the First World War, Albania was overrun by Montenegrin forces in the north, and by Italy and Greece in the south. The question of Albania was sidestepped at the Treaty of Versailles and the Albanians set up their own government and called for an end to foreign occupation. But foreign powers continued to influence events in the country.

In 1924 Ahmet Zogu, the son of a Muslim tribal chief, led an armed takeover and with the help of Benito Mussolini set up a republic. In 1928 he declared himself King Zog. He helped establish a period of relative stability but there was little sign of social or economic development. Furthermore, relations with Italy soon turned sour and the latter invaded at the start of the Second World War. King Zog and his wife, Queen Geraldine, fled to England and London's Ritz Hotel. They ran up a huge bill, paid for initially with gold looted from the Albanian Treasury. When that ran out, they were asked to leave and Zog moved to genteel Frinton-on-Sea in Essex. He died in Paris in 1961.

While Zog sipped peppermint tea at the Ritz, the Italians set up a puppet government in Albania under a new king, Victor Emmanuel III. The country became 'Little Italy' and thousands of teachers and businessmen were shipped across the Adriatic, along with skilled craftsmen who helped construct the beautiful Italianate buildings and tree-lined boulevards which grace Tirana.

Resistance to the Italians increased with the formation of the Albanian Communist Party. The party was formed during World War II, in which Italy had joined forces with Germany. In 1941, Enver Hoxha (pronounced Hodger) became its first Secretary. Partisan fighters were organised, supported in part by British Special Operations. By 1943 the Italians had been driven out, only to be replaced by 70,000 Nazi troops. But they too were defeated along with the disaffected north Albanians who had sided with them.

Elections held in 1945 gave power to the communists, with Hoxha's Democratic Front gaining over 90% of the vote. The following year a Republic was declared and King Zog deposed *in absentia*. Hoxha went about consolidating the foundations of his regime, which were to be characterised over the next forty years by the brutal suppression of human rights, imprisonment of dissenters and widespread abuse of power. An admirer of Josef Stalin's interpretation of Marxist-Leninism, Hoxha was proclaimed the President of the People's Republic of Albania in 1946.

The nation became little more than a satellite of Yugoslavia, and received massive aid. But when the Yugoslav President, Tito, refused to toe the Stalinist line in 1948 and was expelled from the Soviet bloc, Hoxha denounced his closest ally and realigned with Stalin. Relations with the USSR cooled after Stalin's death, however. His successor, Nikita Krushchev, condemned the Stalinesque cult of personality. In turn Hoxha denounced Krushchev, breaking off all diplomatic relations for good in 1961. He found an unlikely but formidable ally in China, which was equally politically isolated at that time. For the next 17 years Albania and China were brothers-in-arms and Chinese technology helped develop Albanian agriculture and industry. But by 1978 Albania was accusing Chairman Mao's successors of 'revisionist aberrations', and all but severed diplomatic ties.

With the removal of Oriental know-how, the Albanian economy slowed down dramatically. Western books were banned and all organised religion outlawed. In 1981 the former partisan hero and the then Prime Minister, Mehmet Shehu, argued with Hoxha and was found dead with a bullet through his head. A verdict of suicide was conveniently returned.

Hoxha himself died in 1985 and Ramiz Alia took over as leader of the Communist Party. Aware of the need to open up Albania to the West, he instituted a number of reforms which included the lifting of the ban on opposition parties. But the winds of political change were beginning to blow across Eastern Europe. Tension increased in Albania and during student demonstrations in Tirana, the statue of Hoxha in Skanderbeg Square was pulled down. Tanks patrolled the streets.

In the 1991 elections the (formerly communist) Party of Labour retained power. But the newly-formed Democratic Party, which had won 25% of the vote, disputed the outcome and called a general strike. Industrial and general unrest induced the Party of Labour initially to form a coalition government and later to step down. New elections in March 1992 were won overwhelmingly by the Democratic Party. It formed a coalition government with the much smaller Social Democratic and Republican parties. A month later the ghost of Enver Hoxha was finally laid to rest and Dr Sali Berisha was elected by parliament as Albania's first non-communist President. In January 1993 the widow of the former President and the Lady Macbeth of Albanian politics, Nexhmije Hoxha, was found guilty of squandering public funds and jailed at the age of 72 for nine years.

The Pretender to the Albanian throne, the self-styled King Leka I and son of King Zog, was last heard of living in a rural farmhouse in South Africa. The Sandhurst-trained monarch-in-waiting denied being behind an attempted armed invasion of Albania by a group of exiles in 1982. He has said, however, that he would be willing to accept the role of leader should he ever be invited.

Economy. Albania's economy was Europe's poorest under communism, and living conditions have declined still further as readjustments are made. Given its political sensitivity, the West is pouring in aid — the EU has given $50 per person to the country.

The Albanian economy has massive potential for growth. Already one of the world's biggest producers of chrome, it has the capacity to become self-sufficient in petroleum, gas, copper, coal and timber. But while foreign money is being pumped in, corruption in the government persists and the supposedly defunct *sigurimi* or secret police remains powerful.

The Balkan Question. The issue of Kosovo is a political tinderbox which could have serious consequences in the region. Kosovo, one of the largest regions in Serbia, is seen by the Serbs as their spiritual heartland. Yet they are heavily outnumbered by the two million ethnic Albanians who live in the region. In the late 1980's, the Serbs orchestrated a discrimination campaign, in which many Albanians were thrown out of their jobs. The campaign led to riots and demonstrations, and by 1993 300,000 Albanians had fled the region. Those who remain continue to call for autonomy and ultimate union with Albania.

Albanians in Kosovo are building a shadow nation. Lecturers who are banned from university buildings now give classes after hours in elementary schools. The shadow economy is fuelled by Albanians living abroad, who donate money to help families in Kosovo.

THE PEOPLE

Albania, like Ireland, is in the strange situation of having more natives living outside than inside the country. Greece and Italy have seen a huge influx of Albanian workers in recent years, causing serious tension. It is estimated that 300,000 Albanians are working in Greece alone, and several mass exoduses to southern Italian ports have captured world attention; only a few of those who had crammed themselves onto transport ships were allowed to stay. There are more settled and much longer established Albanian communities in Australia and the USA, where one actor of Albanian descent — John Belushi — rose to fame. Albania has the highest birthrate in Europe — despite the fact that most families cannot afford more than two children, and that contraceptives and abortion are now both freely available.

Religion. Albania is 65% Muslim, a legacy of centuries of Turkish occupation. The rest of the population is 20% Greek Orthodox and 15% Roman Catholic.

Organised religion was outlawed by Enver Hoxha, whose ideal it was to establish the world's first atheist state. In 1967 he declared that 'the only religion an Albanian needs is Albania'. Many churches and mosques were either pulled down or converted to cinemas, museums and schools. Religion went underground, and Bibles and Korans were smuggled in. These days, people worship openly and new churches and mosques are being built. Missionaries, primarily from the USA and UK, have wasted no time in opening their own study centres.

Roman Catholicism received a boost in 1992, when the Pope ordained four bishops in Shkoder and held an open-air meeting in Tirana attended by tens of thousands. A Papal Nuncio has now been installed in a splendidly restored villa in the city. Mother Teresa has been a more regular visitor. An ethnic Albanian from Kosovo, she has travelled the length and breadth of the country.

Meeting the People. Under communism, most Albanians were too scared to speak to foreigners. Enver Hoxha was Big Brother, ruling by fear with the aid of his dreaded secret police. It was not uncommon for tourists who strayed from the watchful eye of their Albturist guides to find people deliberately crossing the street to avoid personal contact. It is said that 1% of the population have been political prisoners.

Since the coming of democracy, Albanians have been given more opportunity to display their natural hospitality. Visitors to the country will frequently be invited into people's homes, and plied with brandy, Turkish delight or figs. (It is considered extremely rude to refuse.) And you will invariably be treated as a guest of honour on buses or trains. Do not be surprised if, here too, fellow passengers offer you food and drink, as well as dreadful Albanian cigarettes. Even if you don't smoke, you will be an instant hit if you offer American ones. A rudimentary grasp of Albanian will go down a treat, such as dropping the phrase *ska problem* ('no worries') into a conversation. Albanians are interested in conversing with foreigners, not least to practise their English (or French, or Italian).

Kept isolated from the rest of the world for decades, Albanians are fascinated with foreigners. You will most frequently be asked about your family, marital status, number of children and salary. Candour about your bank balance may alienate people belonging to the poorest nation in Europe.

As in Bulgaria, a shake of the head in Albania means yes, and a nod signifies no. If in doubt, don't move your head.

Behaviour. Men and women in Albania greet people of the same sex with a generous supply of kisses, usually four pecks on the cheek. Men and women generally only shake hands, unless they are related. Visitors are not expected to kiss Albanians on first acquaintance, and may avoid the custom altogether during farewells, where a solid handshake will suffice. It will be considered impolite, however, if you shy away from kissing anybody who may have shown particular generosity.

Curiously, Albanian men and women seldom hold hands when they are out strolling, but even macho men will often take male visitors seeking directions by the hand; the relationship with women travelling alone is more complicated. Many Albanian men appear to base their views of Western women on the B-movie sex sirens glimpsed in the local cinema.

Gay people were repressed under communism. Democracy has lifted a measure of homophobia, but not the intolerance of Albanian society. There is no significant gay movement and no overtly gay bars or clubs.

Topless or nude sunbathing is not allowed on Albania's beaches. Only Albanian children wear shorts, and adult foreigners who do so produce a few chuckles. Women should take care not to under-dress, even in discos.

LANGUAGE

The Albanian language, which is descended from Indo-European, has absorbed many influences from its invaders. The first fragment of written Albanian dates back to 1462, but it wasn't until 1887 that the first school for the Albanian language was opened. Two dialects exist: Tosk — the official language — in the south, and Geg in the north. The practical differences between the two are unlikely to worry visitors.

English is the most widely spoken foreign tongue, followed by Italian and French and, to a lesser degree, Russian. A smattering of Albanian, however, can be useful. Some hints on pronunciation may help:

ç   is pronounced 'ch' as in church
c   as 'tch' in hitcher
dh sounds like a soft 'th'
ë   is sometimes pronounced 'er', though it is usually silent at the end of words
gj is zh, like s in measure
j   is 'y', as in yes
ll is a slightly swallowed 'ul'
q   is 'ky' as in Tokyo
rr is a rolled 'r'
x   is pronounced 'dz', as in loads
xh is pronounced 'j' as in jeans
y   is 'ooh' as in igloo

Useful Words and Phrases

Pronunciation of the more difficult words and phrases is given in brackets

hello — *tungjatjeta* (tun-ya-yeta)
goodbye — *mirupafshim*
please — *ju lutem* (you loot-em)
thanks — *falemnderit* (falem-in-derit)
excuse me — *me falni* (myrrh fal-knee)
yes — *po*
no — *jo* (yo, as in yobbo)
today — *sot*
tomorrow — *nese* (nesser)
toilet — *tualet*
water — *uje* (wee-yer)
cold — *fhohte* (fer-tofter)
bad — *keq* (ketch)
good — *mire* (me-er)
beer — *birre* (beer-uh)
cheers! — *gozuar!* (gozz-ooh-arr)
bus — *autobus*

1 — *nje* (ner-*yuh*)
2 — *dy* (die)
3 — *tre* (tray)
4 — *kater* (catter)
5 — *pese* (pesh)
6 — *gjashte* (jyast)
7 — *shtate* (sshtat)
8 — *tete* (tet)
9 — *nente* (nunt)
10 — *dhjete* (dee-yet)
hospital — *spital*
pharmacy — *farmacia* (far-*mass*-ia)
market — *markate* (markat)
station — *stacion* (statz-ion)
airport — *aeroport*
boat — *traget*

I come from England — *une jam nga Anglia* (oon yam nerguh Anglia)
Do you speak English? — *a flisni ju anglisht?* (a flis-knee you Anglisht?)
Where are you from? — *nga jeni?* (ungah yenny)
How are you? — *si jeni?* (see any)
What is your name? — *si quheni?* (see chew-henny)
I like Albania — *me pelqen Shqiperia* (me pelchen Shipper-ear)
Have you got. . . ? — *ti kene. . . ?* (tea kay-knee)
It is possible (impossible) — *mundet (nuk mundet)*
How much is. . . ? — *sa kushton. . . ?*
Where is. . . ? — *ku eshte. . . ?* (koo ushta)
When? — *kur?* (core)
What time. . . ? — *ne c'ore. . . ?* (nay chay aura)
Are you married? — *a jeni i martuar?* (a yenny i martuar)
Have you got children? — *a keni femije?* (a caney fammy)
   brothers? — *keni vella?* (caney verler)
   sisters? — *keni moter?* (caney motter)

FURTHER READING

Albania, a Guide and Illustrate Journal by Peter and Andrea Dawson (Bradt

Publications, 1989) is a sympathetic account of an Albturist visit, though some may find it rather twee. *High Albania* (Virago, out of print) by Edith Durham is a more fascinating read. It tells of the author's travels in a waterproof Burberry skirt through northern Albania early this century. *Albania — Who Cares? The Exclusive Inside Story* (Autumn House, 1992) is a rather more gritty book by BBC journalist, Bill Hamilton, charting his visits to the country to make television reports on children's orphanages. His involvement with Albania began in 1989 when he visited Tirana to cover the Albania-England World Cup match. His book is strong on background history and contains a useful list of charities active in Albania.

Albania is one of the more expensive destinations in Eastern Europe to reach. Most people fly directly to the country, but a much cheaper route is via Greece. It is possible to buy a cheap charter flight to Corfu, and then catch a ferry to the nearby Albanian mainland. Be warned, however, that Greek regulations forbid anyone travelling by charter to Greece to spend as much as one night abroad. See below.

A number of British travel agencies have had widespread experience of arranging travel to Albania in conjunction with Albturist, the national tourist board. Most, however, curtailed their activities as the Balkan civil war broke out. One agent to have maintained more contact than most is Regent Holidays, 15 John Street, Bristol, BS1 2HR (0272-211711). The company organises holidays (an eight-day tour for around £700) and can also sell flights and accommodation.

AIR

Rinas Airport, near the capital, is the only civil airport in the country. There are currently no direct flights between the UK and Tirana. Connecting flights from Britain pass via Zurich, Athens, Vienna, Munich, Rome, Budapest, Ljubljana, and Sofia. The complete list of services to and from Tirana is as follows:

Zurich: Monday and Wednesday on Swissair, Tuesday and Thursday on Albanian Airlines.
Athens: Tuesday and Thursday on Olympic via Ioannina.
Rome: Monday, Wednesday, Saturday on Albanian Airlines, daily on Alitalia.
Bari: daily on Ada Air.
Munich and *Vienna:* Monday, Wednesday and Friday on Albanian Airlines.
Budapest: Monday, Thursday and Friday on Malév.
Sofia: Tuesday and Sunday on Hemus.
Ljubljana: Tuesday, Wednesday and Saturday on Adria Airways.

The creation of the national air carrier Albanian Airlines, a joint venture with Tyrolean Airways of Austria, has led to an increase in the number of flights to Tirana, though they are still few and expensive by European standards. Apex fares are available only on the Vienna-Tirana and Zurich-Tirana routes ($335 and $380 respectively).

In addition to scheduled services, some occasional charter flights are available. ICPI Airlines advertises three flights a week from Istanbul, while

Arberia Airlines has occasional charters from New York's JFK airport; the return fare for the latter is $750.

Via Greece. The route via Corfu mentioned above carries a certain risk, given that travellers on charter flights are not supposed to leave the country more than for a day trip. However, you can usually put your faith in lax Greek officialdom. Carrying two passports (most ordinary citizens may do this) is a fairly foolproof way of avoiding problems: by using your second passport, you can prevent Greek immigration officials seeing the stamps which will show exactly how long you have been in Albania. If you are caught out, you may well be asked to pay for a scheduled flight home. A less risky method which circumvents these regulations is to buy a standard (ie. non-charter) return to Greece, though this reduces the saving. Alternatively, travel by air to Ioannina via Athens on Olympic, and then overland to Albania: see *Bus*, below.

RAIL

The closest rail travellers could get to Albania before the civil war broke out in the Balkans was Podgorica (formerly Titograd) in Montenegro. A rail link still exists to Shkodër but it is used solely for freight. The main Athens to Munich rail link passes via Skopje in Macedonia, only 40 miles/65km from the eastern Albanian border: there are road links from there into Albania via Prizren.

BUS

A bus links Athens and Tirana, entering Albania at Kakavilë in the south of the country. Otherwise, it is possible to get a bus in Greece to Ioannina, and then a taxi costing around $20 to the Albanian border. Once you cross, a further $20 taxi fare should get you to either Sarandë or Gjirokastër.

DRIVING

Private vehicles are now allowed in Albania, and there are no restrictions on drivers bringing in their own car. Insurance, however, may prove a problem since Western motoring organisations, including the AA and the RAC, give no cover for the country. To make matters worse, the chances of your vehicle remaining intact during your stay are minimal. One disadvantage of the collapse of communism is that Albanians are now allowed to own cars — not that many can afford them. Albanian drivers are among the worst in the world, and your car's bodywork is likely to receive at least a few scratches and a dent or two. Theft is another hazard. One German who left his car in Gjirokastër for ten minutes returned to find someone trying to prise off the windscreen. Similarly, a convoy from an Essex charity group had locals trying to dismantle their headlights as they trundled up a mountain.

If you need to drive, consider hiring a car instead of risking your own. See *Getting Around* for information on car rental and driving conditions.

Entry Points. Albania has five main road frontiers. To the northwest, the Hani-Hot border with Bozaj (formerly Drume) in Montenegro is 35 miles/ 50km north of Shkodër. To the northeast, Kukes is linked by the E752 to Prizren in the Kosovo region of Serbia. In the east, 20 miles/30km north of Pogradec, the E852 leads across the Serbian border to Struga. To the south, you can cross into Albania at Kakavilë, which is 40 miles/64km northwest of the Greek town of Ioannina on the E853. In the southeast, lying 25 miles/40km east of Korce, the town of Bilisht also has good road links with Greece.

SEA

Ferries serve Albania from both Italy and Corfu, but their frequency drops out of season.

From Italy. From Italy a luxury hydrofoil ferry *La Vikinga*, operated by the Adriatic Fast Ferry company, runs a triangular service between the Italian ports of Bari or Brindisi, Corfu port (Kerkira) and the Albanian town of Durrës. A single ticket between either Italy or Corfu and Albania costs $90, a round trip $150. The ferry runs between June and September. Throughout the year, the Adriatica Line operates between the Italian ports of Bari, Trieste, and Ancona to Durrës in Albania. All fares are given in the table below.

From Ancona: departs from the Italian port on Monday at 7pm, arriving at Durrës the following day at 3pm. (The return ferry leaves Durrës at noon on Sundays, arriving at Ancona the following morning at 8am.

From Bari: departs Bari on Wednesday and Saturday at 10pm, arriving at Durrës at 7am. (The return service leaves Durrës leaves at noon on Tuesday and Thursday.)

From Trieste: leaves on Tuesday and Friday at 1pm, arriving 25 hours later. The return ferry leaves on Wednesday and Saturday at 7pm.

The current fares listed below are for low season travel, with high season (July to mid-August) prices in brackets:

From:	**Ancona**	**Bari**	**Trieste**
Car	$125 ($140)	$105 ($120)	$135 ($150)
Minibus	$200 ($225)	$125 ($140)	$210 ($225)
Deck	$80 ($105)	$60 ($75)	$90 ($120)
Seat	$90 ($120)	$75 ($80)	$105 ($120)
Cabin (2)	$120 ($180)	$80 ($120)	$135 ($200)
Cabin (4)	$105 ($135)	$75 ($90)	$120 ($150)

From Corfu. Ferries run between Corfu and Sarandë in southern Albania, mainly between June and late September. Services leave from the port of Corfu Town, on the eastern side of the island and only two miles from the airport. The two main ferries are the *Petrakis*, used by tour companies for day trips, and the *Camilia*, which is cheaper and used by Albanians. Both leave around 9am, arriving two hours later. They return at 5.30pm from Sarandë, 1pm at weekends. It is vital to check return times: in Corfu you can do this by contacting the Petrakis Shipping Company in Corfu: tel 0661-31649/386590/34345, fax 0661-38787. The return fare is around $40, payable in drachmas or dollars.

A smaller Albanian ferry, the *Heraklia*, also plies between the two countries. It leaves Sarande at 10am, returning in the late afternoon.

Until 1990, Albania had the most restrictive visa requirements in Europe. British, US, Canadian and most EC citizens are now exempt, though travellers from Australia and New Zealand must still obtain a visa. Since regulations can change frequently, check beforehand at your nearest Albanian embassy. There are only a few of these, but they include one in London at 6 Wilton Court, 59 Ecclestone Square SW1V IPH (071-834 2508). In the USA, the Albanian embassy is at 320 East 79th St, New York, NY 10021 (tel 212-249-2059, fax 212-535-2917).

Entry fee. Even though visas have been abolished for many nationalities, entry fees are levied for some visitors. Entry for most nationalities, including US citizens, is free. For others, there is an elaborate scale of charges with Canadians, for example, required to hand over $50. The rates charged to other nationals are as follows:

UK: $40	France and Switzerland: $45
Belgium: $30	Holland and Austria: $28
Germany: $13	Turkey: $8
Portugal: $6	

The stamp in your passport entitles you to one entry alone. Should you leave the country even for a couple of hours, and wish to return, you must pay again.

CUSTOMS

Customs formalities are relaxed in Albania. The emphasis is clearly placed upon facilitating the entry of visitors, rather than offering any obstacles. Even so, it may well be worth acquiring a few packets of cigarettes to use as gifts should you encounter an obstreperous official. Hard-core pornography is banned.

The travellers most likely to experience delays are those entering by land. This is because customs officials at road borders into Albania have been stepping up checks on vehicles from their own country, as part of the government's campaign to crack down on smuggling and duty avoidance. Westerners are usually spared any such investigation, though are sometimes subject to searched for illegal drugs.

1 lek (plural leke) = 100 qindarka
1994: £1 = 163 leke $1 110 leke

Currency. Inflation has rendered qindarka coins virtually useless and they are never used. Leke bills, which often appear in a torn and malodorous condition, come in denominations of 1, 3, 5, 25, 50, 100, 200 and 500 leke.

The monetary system in Albania changed in 1964, with old leke being replaced by new leke. Although the change occurred thirty years ago, it has left some arithmetical confusion. Many Albanians instinctively use the old system whereby they will, for instance, refer to 10 leke as 100 leke.

Changing Money. Banks offer the best exchange rate, even after commission charges. Travellers' cheques (preferably in low denominations) are readily accepted in banks, but many hotels, restaurants and shops refuse to take them. Since banks are thin on the ground, if you're heading into the provinces you'd do well to stock up on leke at the central bank on Skanderbeg Square in Tirana. Dollar travellers cheques can be cashed as hard currency as well as leke.

Given the choice, most Albanians are never happier than when you offer them dollars. If you stay with an Albanian family, they will see remuneration in dollars as a special kindness. The odd hotel and restaurant still demands hard currency, but there are few occasions when you will be unable to pay in leke.

Albanian currency is useless abroad, even in Greece. Take care not to find yourself lumbered with too many leke on your departure. It may not always be possible to change them back into the currency you prefer, though the possession of exchange receipts and persistence should smooth the way.

Credit Cards. Plastic is accepted in very few places in Albania. As of summer 1993, the Hotel Dajti in Tirana was the one Albanian hotel able to handle credit cards — only American Express at that. The company has a representative at Ada Travel in Tirana, whose address is Kongresi Permitit 11 (42-24301, 27306).

Banking hours. Branches of the State Bank (Banka e Shtetit) generally open between 7am and 2pm, Monday to Saturday, national holidays excepted.

The Black Market. Unlike many of its former communist neighbours Albania never developed a substantial black market economy. Nor does it now. The lek has been propped up by the government and has remained relatively firm against the dollar. Premium goods can now be bought — albeit at a price — on the ever-expanding open market.

Tirana has its own mini-version of Wall Street. Dozens of currency dealers stand around Skanderbeg Square and accost any tourist who wanders within earshot. The rate these men give is generally better than that offered in the bank, but changing money on the black market is always risky: see the General Introduction for tips on how to avoid trouble. It is unlikely that you will ever be offered money for your clothes or goods. Albanians get many such things from Greece, and jeans are not at a premium. The main reason to take pens, cigarettes, T-shirts and the like is to give them away as presents.

Tipping. In most hotels and restaurants it is customary (though not obligatory) to leave a tip: 10% is sufficient. The money will certainly be appreciated: remember that your meal may cost what the waiter earns in a whole month.

Communications

Telephone. Work has been going on in earnest to upgrade the Albanian telecommunications network. Foreign experts are aiming to incorporate the latest high-tech advances in a rolling programme likely to last until the end of the decade. Until then you must put up with a rudimentary system.

There are no street telephones in Albania. If you need to make a phone call, go to a post office (*posta*), where the operator can do it for you. A minute-long call to Europe will cost around $3, and $4.50 to the rest of the world. Only Tirana, Elbasan, Durrës, Shkodër and Gjirokastër are connected to the national telephone network. Post offices in these towns have fax facilities, and you can phone or send faxes from the local tourist hotels too.

Telegrams. What Albania lacks in telephones, it makes up for in its telegram service. Go to a post office for the cheapest rates or try at a tourist hotel.

Post. You can buy stamps (as well as postcards) at most hotel receptions, as well as from all post offices. A stamp to Europe costs $0.13. Post offices open between 8am and 6pm Monday to Saturday; in summer they may close as late as 9pm. Postcards take about two weeks to reach most addresses within Europe. Don't risk posting anything in the rusty red mail boxes on the street, from which collections are unreliable. Incoming mail doesn't always arrive, so don't have parcels or anything of value sent to you.

THE MEDIA

Newspapers. There are no national daily newspapers in Albania. In Tirana and other major cities newspaper vendors offer a range of tabloids, printed on low-quality paper. Costing around 5 cents each, only a few run to ten pages. Most are weekly or fortnightly publications, and some have sections in English. A pirated version of *Playboy* is a big seller.

The best English-language publication is *The Albanian Economic Tribune,* useful if you're interested in the world of finance. But its use of English is distinctly bizarre; if you ever wondered what happened to Manuel in *Fawlty Towers*, it seems he's safe and well and working on the magazine. For international newspapers, you must go to the top hotels in Tirana and choose from Italian and US titles. You'll hunt in vain for British papers.

Broadcasting. One of the charms of Albanian television is that it transmits from noon to midnight without screening a single advert. It plugs into the European satellite network for MTV as well as sports, and also features an evening news broadcast with selected foreign coverage. Programmes from Greece, Italy and the former Yugoslavia can be picked up in many parts of the country.

Radio Tirana broadcasts from the heart of the city, and Voice of America is played loudly in some trendy bars. The Albanian language service of the BBC World Service, *Ne Shqip,* is very popular.

 Albturist has lost its stranglehold on the tourist market, but the experience gained by the state-run organisation throughout the communist years (allowing a maximum of 12,000 visitors a year) has formed the backbone of the present tourist industry. The organisation still caters for groups, but the buses and trains make independent travel easy enough for independent travellers.

Maps. The best map of Albania is published by Cartographia Budapest, price £5.95. Otherwise, a fairly detailed map of the country is sold in hotels in Tirana. The town plans on the reverse are of only limited use, as street names are not included.

Place Names. Place names can change their endings, due to Albanian grammar. Shkodër, for example, may in some circumstances be written as Shkodres.

RAIL

Rail travel in Albania is slow (perhaps surprising given that the country has the newest railway network in Europe, with the first stretch of track laid only in 1946) but phenomenally cheap: no journey will cost more than a dollar. The other benefit of train travel is its entertainment value. Parts of the network are positively dramatic, not least the series of viaducts between Elbasan and Pogradec.

Czech locomotives pull second-hand Italian, French and Chinese carriages which have seats offering the discomfort of church pews. Windows are often missing — fine in summer, but deathly in winter. Train carriages are no longer divided into men-only and women-and-children-only compartments, but there is still just one class of service, approximating to the antiquated British concept of third class. Toilets are filthy, and catering facilities do not exist. Stock up on food and drink in advance..

Buy your ticket (singles only available) in leke from the ticket-office (*biletaria treni*) at the station. Timetables are displayed outside.

BUS

Buses are quicker, more frequent and also cover a more extensive network than the trains. Fares are more expensive, but still cheap by Western standards; a single from Tirana to Sarandë, for example, will cost just $3 — for a journey of about 150 miles/240km.

While the southbound rail track ends at Vlorë, buses penetrate all the way down to Sarandë. But it is risky to rely on buses if schedules are tight and connections cannot be missed. Buses break down frequently. Most bus services leave early in the morning (the first bus to Tirana from Sarande, for example, leaves at 3.30am), so prepare for a dawn start and pack an alarm clock. Be warned, however, that buses may leave up to an hour late, as the conductor waits for every seat to be filled.

Destinations are often marked on a strip of cardboard on the windscreen. If in doubt, ask. Buy your ticket aboard.

Compared with other motorists — see below — most bus drivers are reasonably good, having gained a lot of experience driving in the communist era, when private cars were banned to all but a handful of party officials.

DRIVING

Since the advent of democracy, when private cars were first allowed in Albania, their number has risen from zero to over 40,000 in 1994. Do not overestimate the skill of this new breed of drivers, however. Many of them are downright dangerous and provide one of the greatest threats to personal safety in Albania. It is not unusual to see cars hurling around Tirana like extras from *Miami Vice*, burning rubber, honking their horns and scattering passers-by. Pedestrians should be warned that motorists have the right of way. Another hazard is the poor quality of rural road surfaces, though international assistance is gradually improving highways.

Car Rental. Hiring a car can give you the freedom to explore those parts of the country public transport cannot reach; or to visit more places in a limited time. But rental rates are extortionate: one week's unlimited mileage in a VW Golf costs $730.

The only company to speak of which hires out cars is Kompas Hertz in Tirana, at 120 Rruga Deshomoret e Kombit, near the Hotel Tirana (tel 32276). Reservations are recommended through the central reservation office number at Ljubljana in Slovenia (tel 061-571 987, 572 005; fax 061-572 088). In theory, the company can deliver cars for pick-up anywhere in the country.

Fuel. Most Albanian vehicles use diesel (*naft*), which is the easiest fuel to obtain, and the cheapest (currently about 10 cents a litre). Petrol is also available either in the low grade 60-octane variety or the benzine super type, at 96 octanes. There is no unleaded fuel. High grade gas-oil is generally only available if you buy special coupons in advance; you can buy these in Tirana, at a shop on Rruga Kongresi i Permetit, 500 metres north of the city centre (on the left as you head out of town).

Petrol stations are not clearly marked, but can usually be spotted by the queue of vehicles outside or from their resemblance to Fort Knox: pumps often come barricaded with iron bars. Self-service hasn't reached Albania, and you should check the amount of fuel which goes into your car. Albanian drivers complain that both petrol and diesel are watered down, so if the car seems less responsive than it should be, you can probably guess why.

HITCH-HIKING

You can get a ride fairly easily in most parts of the country, but (as mentioned above) most drivers are terrible. Lorry drivers tend to be the safest bets. No money is expected from Westerners in return for a ride, but cigarettes are always appreciated.

CYCLING

Because Albanian roads are so poor, pitted with potholes and strewn with obstacles from geese, cows and sheep to pedestrians and cars, cyclists may find the going tough. If erratic roadmanship doesn't deter you, the hills might: Albania is one of the most mountainous countries in Europe. Even the main highways are barely wide enough for vehicles to pass — a big problem in the mountains where the safety barriers are unlikely to prevent unwanted detours of a vertical nature.

Cycling in cities can also be dangerous, despite the comparative lack of traffic. Albanian drivers simply have not learned what speed limits or traffic signals mean, and a defensive approach is essential.

It is not possible to hire bicycles, but you can buy a new Chinese model for about $80. There are several bicycle shops in Tirana, including one just across the road from the Hotel Arberia near Skanderbeg Square.

Hotels. There are tourist hotels in major towns and cities, most of them owned by the state and operated by Albturist. Most of these are testaments to the gruesomely practical and spirit-crushing post-war architecture favoured behind the Iron Curtain. The elegant Hotel Dajti in Tirana and the Adriatiku in Durrës, are the exceptions. All Albturist hotels charge Western prices, payable in leke or dollars. Ome Private hotels, the number of which grows rapidly, usually charge more accurately according to the facilities offered.

Most rooms offer some creature comforts ie. hot and cold water, toilet paper, televisions (sometimes in working order) and refrigerators (hardly ever). Reliable plumbing and constant supplies of electricty cannot be guaranteed. Many hapless business visitors paying top prices for accommodation in Tirana's hotels have spent bitterly cold winter nights lying under mounds of blankets after power cuts have knocked out the lights and crippled the heating system.

Low-cost Accommodation. No youth hostels or camping facilities are available, so the only alternative to staying in a hotel is to lodge with a family. Prices are negotiable, but expect to pay less than half the sum quoted in Albturist hotels; you should get away with around $20 for two people. Facilities are a little basic, but Albanians keep their houses or flats scrupulously clean. You will often be invited to join in the evening meal as well as breakfast, usually at no extra charge.

Unlike other places in Eastern Europe, there are no agencies arranging bed and breakfast at the time of writing. People will generally approach you in the street, and offer to put you up: 99% of people are genuine. Should you be unhappy with the accommodation, or with your hosts, leave and try to find somewhere else. But most travellers will usually be treated with great hospitality and interest.

Eating and Drinking

Albania is not a destination for the gourmet, but food in the country is pleasant enough. Fresh fruit and vegetables are plentiful, and most towns have large markets where you can buy anything from live ducklings, chickens and goats to enormous spring onions, succulent cherries and wonderful cheeses. Vegetarians might find their choices restricted, as Albanians are dedicated carnivores. (The Albanian for 'I don't eat meat' is *une nuk haj mish,* pronounced oon nook high mish.) But mixed salads appear on every menu, and wholemeal bread is cheap and tasty. You'll find a bread stall on most streets. Snacks are on sale on many street corners too, ranging from pastries like crepe suzettes and strawberry tarts (all costing around 15 cents) to hamburgers and cold chips. Ice cream (*akullore*) is particularly good and costs just ten cents.

Restaurants. Private restaurants have been springing up in most towns and cities. Wherever you eat, tourists pay more than locals, with prices high even by Western standards. A decent two-course meal is likely to cost around $10 per person, including beer. If you can't find a privately run restaurant you can always fall back on the dining room of the Albturist hotel, where the food is guaranteed to be edible if not particularly mouth-watering.

DRINKING

Alcohol in Albania is generally cheap and plentiful. The most highly valued national product is Skanderbeg brandy. It slips down a treat, more easily in fact than the national drink *raki,* a rough spirit distilled from grapes.

Albanian wines are robust and pleasant, with little to choose between the reds and whites in terms of quality. Since the demise of Albania's only brewery, most beer (in the form of Amstel lager) is imported from Greece. Alcohol of some sort is often placed on your table at lunch. If you indulge, you pay at the end of the meal.

Coffee is usually available as *kafe ekspres* or *kafe turke*; both are small but potent kicks of concentrated caffeine. Tea or *caj* (pronounced chay) is drunk without milk. If you are staying with a family, they may offer you mountain tea, made from what appear to be long blades of grass. Despite appearances it is delicious. Coca-Cola is available, though it has a counterfeit rival with a similar logo and the name Joke-Cola.

 Albania has some of the most stunning scenery in Europe, as well as some of its most beautiful towns. The latter are usually easier to explore than the former. The best mountains are in the north of the country, and provide enterprising hikers with excellent exploratory material, but you'll be very much on your own. A few adventurous locals enjoy skiing, but safety measures are non-existent. You may find some compensation along the coast, much of which is taken up by unspoilt golden beaches. The best are between Durrës and Sarandë, Diviaca beach being the most popular among Albanians. Litter can be a problem at the most visited beaches, but most are safe for bathing. Beware, though, of some of the algae pollution that has hit the whole of the Adriatic coastline. For freshwater swimming, head east to the pure waters of Lake Ohrid, set among dramatic scenery.

The ancient museum towns of Gjirokastër and Berat are prime attractions. Even Enver Hoxha forbade new building work in the towns' historic centres, at a time when he was busy building ugly apartment blocks in many other parts of the country. In these and other towns, the architectural heritage is likely to conjure more interest than the museums, many of which are badly in need of refurbishment. There are exceptions, however, such as the Skanderbeg Museum in Krujë, which is superb. Admission to museums and other buildings open to the public is generally about $1.

 The concept of 'entertainment' as understood in the West is hard to find in Albania. You'll find hardly anything to do in the evening outside Tirana. The performing arts in the country have achieved a high level of skill, but even in the capital shows are put on only intermittently. No independent theatre or music companies exist as yet.

Cinema. Many cinemas in Albania have closed down. The ones which still function offer a bizarre choice of B-movies, mostly dating back to the Sixties and featuring unknown stars sporting bushy moustaches (not all of them male). Entrance is cheap, and a visit to an Albanian flea pit is recommended if only for the experience.

Theatre, Opera and Ballet. The arts were encouraged by Enver Hoxha, as long as they conformed to the approved ideology. The communist tradition has bred highly competent performers if also a fairly unadventurous repertoire. Economic constraints mean that performances are scarce outside the capital. Both student and professional theatrical groups put on good productions. Tickets are cheap, costing up to $3 for the National Theatre but only 10 cents for some student shows. Tirana is the only venue to speak of for opera and ballet.

Music. Albanian folk music can be captivating. It is usually performed in costume, with accompanying folk dances. Albanian rock music is surprisingly good too; it stems mostly from the Kosovo region. Albturist hotels often feature more middle-of-the-road (and middle-aged) groups, who perform a variety of styles from Albanian love songs to covers of all the usual classics. The Beatles are phenomenally popular.

SPORT

Facilities in Albania are extremely basic. Cattle graze on village soccer pitches, leaving inevitable obstacles that make slide tackles an unappealing prospect. However, football is the leading national sport. The best Albanian teams have reached a competitive level on the European soccer circuit, despite the fact that most top players have moved abroad — such as Rudy Vater, signed by Glasgow Celtic. Top dogs are Partizani from the capital. Most matches take place on Sunday afternoons during autumn, winter and spring, with kick-off at 3pm. Internationals are played at Tirana's impressive Qemal Stafa stadium.

Most Albanian men take an obsessive interest in football. Local television frequently features top satellite games, including the occasional match live from Wembley Stadium. Most soccer aficionados can reel off the entire 1966 England World Cup squad (Bobby Charlton is virtually a saint), and many even know the name of the San Marino forward who scored the fastest-ever goal in international football (against England, in November 1993).

Gone are the days when the grim Soviet-style MaPo (short for Magazin Popular) department stores were the best retailing prospects. A number of new shops selling previously unobtainable items such as CD players have sprung up, mainly in Tirana. Most hotel souvenir shops (which demand hard currency) stock a range of overpriced but well-made Albanian crafts: from filigree jewellery and ornate cigarette holders of debatable taste, to the occasional fez. Prices in central Tirana are much higher than those elsewhere. A carpet which would cost only $180 in nearby Kruje, would set you back three times that amount in the capital. Carpets aren't up to the standards of those in Iran or Pakistan, but bargains can be found. In terms of presents, ukeleles for around $20, wooden boxes for $5 or silver earrings for $4 will probably be politely accepted. Do not expect a wide range of high quality goods in local shops.

Tobacco. 'A man who neither smokes nor drinks has no friends', runs an Albanian proverb. Albanians are among the world's more dedicated smokers. Many men average 40 a day. They generally smoke home-produced tobacco, which can make a satisfying present for unwanted friends back home. The most popular Albanian cigarettes are Durrës and Gent, which cost $0.20 a pack. American cigarettes are available only in tourist hotels, hence the gratitude with which an Albanian will receive one as a gift.

Health Hazards. Albania is prone to earthquakes. Shkodër suffered a devastating one in 1979. If you are unlucky enough to be caught up in a tremor, move away from tall buildings or trees. If inside, stand under a sturdy-looking doorway.

A less serious but more common hazard is the mosquito, which can be a pest on the beaches in summer. Watch out, too, for jellyfish in the Adriatic. To remove them, pull gingerly or douse in vinegar. They leave painful scars.

Simple medical items such as plasters, aspirin or disinfectant, are not easily available, so take supplies with you.

Water. Tap water is perfectly safe, but bottled mineral water is available. Albania's own is excellent, though you find imported versions too, chiefly from Italy.

Medical treatment. Private visits can be made to doctors, at a price. But Albanian hospitals are open free of charge to tourists. Insurance policies for European travel do not automatically cover Albania. It is often included in the category for North America category, which is more expensive than its European equivalent.

Barbers. Male travellers in search of facial pampering should not miss the opportunity to visit an Albanian barber (*rrojtore*) for one of the closest shaves on offer. This will cost around 30 cents and include hot towels and scalp manipulation. The 15-minute session usually ends with a liberal dousing of questionable eau-de-Cologne and a cloud of Talcum powder.

Crime and Safety

With the removal of communism went the hated secret police, the *sigurimi*, who provided the backbone of the informers' network — though it has not been completely disbanded. Some foreign aid workers have reported that they have been very inexpertly trailed.

The approach to law enforcement is certainly more relaxed than in the past. But the police still carry guns, and have something of a power complex fuelled by decades of repression.

In the capital it is forbidden to photograph many embassies, and if you merely walk on the pavement directly in front of some of them, expect a firm ticking off from the police. In the past it was forbidden to photograph military officials or the thousands of defence bunkers scattered throughout Albania. These restrictions have now been relaxed.

Cannabis is grown for an old folk remedy against colds, but anyone caught smoking the stuff will be in serious trouble.

Crime against tourists. Serious incidents involving foreigners are rare. There have been reports of bandits holding up tourists' cars near Gjirokastër and Tirana, and expert pickpockets work in the capital. But it is safe to walk around the city at any time of night or day. You may get pestered occasionally by small boys begging for dollars or, if they're really small time, simply for pens and chewing gum. (Anyone shelling out sweets, leke or gum is certain to be descended upon by a rabble of squabbling urchins.) Gypsies in Tirana's Skanderbeg Square are more persistent than most but quickly lose heart if you say *ik* which means 'go away'.

Help and Information

The Albanian government seems positively keen to welcome all tourists, but does little to smooth the way for visitors travelling independently. Staff at the Albanian Embassy in London will do no more than give you well-intentioned but rudimentary information over the phone; no leaflets are available.

In Albania itself, the lack of official tourist information facilities is equally glaring, and the fact that even the simplest travel information is often hard to find can cause exasperation. But local people are usually in a position to answer most queries — or will know someone who can.

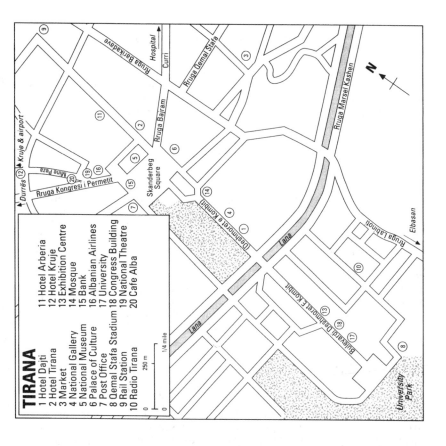

TIRANA

1 Hotel Dajti
2 Hotel Tirana
3 Market
4 National Gallery
5 National Museum
6 Palace of Culture
7 Post Office
8 Qemal Stafa Stadium
9 Rail Station
10 Radio Tirana
11 Hotel Arberia
12 Hotel Kruje
13 Exhibition Centre
14 Mosque
15 Bank
16 Albanian Airlines
17 University
18 Congress Building
19 National Theatre
20 Cafe Alba

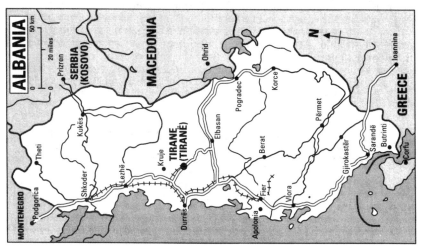

359

TIRANA (Tiranë)

Downtown Tirana encapsulates the best and the worst of Eastern Europe. A few paces off the central Skanderbeg Square, you can encounter an almost Parisian scene of elegant tree-lined boulevards, an Art Deco hotel with a carpeted stairway leading up to the entrance, crumbling villas and crowds strolling in the evening sun through leafy parks. Yet a few minutes' walk in the opposite direction leads you to pot-holed streets, grim blocks of concrete flats, roadworks looking like wartime trenches and beggars huddled on street corners that reek of urine.

Bustling Tirana represents a country hanging on to the coat-tails of change, desperate to forget its communist past. The huge statue of Enver Hoxha that once dominated Skanderbeg Square was torn down in 1991 by angry crowds. Only the twisted metal base remains where once children were brought to kiss Hoxha's bronze foot. Nearby lies another pedestal which once supported a statue of Lenin. Fashion barriers have fallen too. Local rich kids sport Bon Jovi T-shirts, jeans and trainers. The chances are their parents are among those whose balconies sprout satellite dishes and who possess Japanese hi-fis and Italian washing machines. They shop in Benetton, where jeans cost an average Albanian's monthly wage. They might work in modern neon-lit offices which would not look out of place in Frankfurt. But in the markets, peasants sell vegetables at subsistence prices. Classrooms at the university have broken window panes and are heated by tiny stoves. The contrasts confront you on the streets of Tirana.

CITY LAYOUT

Tirana is an easy city in which to find your way around. At its centre lies the vast Skanderbeg Square, where the principal landmark is Hotel Tirana, Albania's highest building; the Palace of Culture, a monstrous Soviet construction of concrete and glass, is the other most striking building in the square. The city's busy commercial centre runs northwest along Rruga Kongresi i Permetit. Bulevardi Deshmoret e Kombit, which cuts north-south through the square, is another busy commercial street, with the railway station at its northern end and the city's best Italianate architecture along the southern side. Across the river Lana rises an enormous glass pyramid built by the Communist Party to honour the achievements of Enver Hoxha. Beyond it lie the main government buildings, the university, the student quarter and the national soccer stadium. A short walk eastwards leads you to the Rruga Labinoti and one of the city's embassy districts; the other district lies in west Tirana, north of Rruga Konferenca e Pezes.

Getting Around

ARRIVAL AND DEPARTURE

Air. Rinas airport, 15 miles/24km northeast of Tirana, is linked to downtown by a sporadic public bus service, which leaves from outside the main concourse. People on a package tour will be met by an Albturist bus, but independent travellers may well be able to talk their way on board. The alternative is to take a taxi, which will charge $15-20 to central Tirana. Do not be bullied into paying more.

The most useful place to go for air travel information once you are in Tirana itself is the gleaming Albanian Airlines office at Rruga Kongresi Permetit 202. Helpful and cheery staff can answer most enquiries (about other airlines too) and provide an oasis in the Albanian desert of travel information.

Train. Tirana's train station, a ten-minute walk from Skanderbeg Square at the northern end of Bulevardi Deshmoret e Kombit, is tiny. There is no information centre, waiting room nor toilet. Buy your tickets from the hole-in-the-wall counter, assuming of course that it is open. The timetable is posted next to it. Trains currently leave Tirana at the following times:

TO	Depart	Arrive
Durrës	5.45am	6.45am
	8.30am	9.30am
	12.30pm	1.30pm
	3.30pm	4.30pm
	5.30pm	6.30pm
	7pm	8pm
Pogradec	5.45am	12.30pm
	1.55pm	8.40pm
Shkodër	1.15pm	4.45pm
Elbasan	4.35pm	8.20pm
Vlorë	11.35am	4.25pm
Lushnjë	8.10am	11.20am

Bus. Buses to other towns and cities leave from two places; (to describe them as terminals would be an exaggeration).

For services to Shkoder, Krujë (changing at nearby Fushë-Krujë) and Vlorë, go to the end of Rruga Kongresi i Permetit and continue for 400 metres. Buses leave from the wasteground just before the sports stadium; it is a 15-minute walk from Skanderbeg Square. Buses to Shkoder (3 hours) and Vlore (4 hours) have no set timetable, but leave between 6am and 9.30am.

Bus services to Sarandë, Pogradec, Korcë, Berat and Elbasan leave from the Dinamo football ground, several blocks south of the river off Gjin Bue Shpata, and a 20 minute-walk from Skanderbeg Square. Services leave between 6am and 9am. Get there early.

CITY TRANSPORT

Buses. People pack into buses like sardines and hold on for dear life as their drivers hurtle around Tirana. Destinations are hardly ever marked, nor are bus stops. Hop on any bus going in the right direction and pay the conductor on board — provided you can find him or her. Few fares cost more than US $0.50.

Taxis. Gleaming Mercedes taxis populate the forecourts of the Hotel Tirana and the Hotel Dajti. It is best to negotiate a fee rather than rely on the meter, since most drivers will insist that the figure shown on the meter has to be multiplied by a figure of their choosing. Car-owners may approach you to offer a 'private' service at a knock-down price. Use your discretion.

Accommodation

Tirana has few hotels. The city is only just waking up to the fact that money can be made by running private hotels, but to date there is only one. The rest are state-run and (by Albanian standards) ridiculously expensive. Prices are likely to rise still further once the multi-million dollar refurbishment of the big hotels is completed. Staying with a local family is by far the cheapest option, but if you opt for a hotel, try one of the following:

Hotel Tirana, Skanderbeg Square (tel/fax 42-34447/34573/34295). Most package-tour visitors stay in this functional and rather sad tower block. It has basic facilities, an adequate restaurant and bar, and helpful staff. Prices range from $45 for a basic single room to $100 for a two-roomed apartment. A room with two beds costs $70 with a fridge and mini bar, but since this so-called 'equipment' is not liable to work, you may be better off with the $50 'no equipment' alternative. All rooms have bath and shower facilities. The hotel accepts payment in cash only.

Hotel Dajti, Bulevardi Deshmoret e Kombit (tel 42-33326/32172/32012, fax 32012). Pronounced 'Die-tee', this is the queen of Albania's hotels. Built along Art Deco lines during the Italian occupation, it is smaller and more comfortable than the Hotel Tirana. Once inside, you would be forgiven for thinking you're in an Agatha Christie novel. This impression is reinforced when you dine under the stars on the balcony, fanned by a gentle summer breeze and serenaded by the house quartet. Expect to pay from $50 for a single room and from $90 for a double. Book in advance to be sure of a room.

Hotel Arberia, Bulevardi Deshmoret e Kombit (42-42813). This basic, comfortless and dingy hotel is at least centrally situated. A single room with toilet and shower and — occasionally functioning — television costs $35, a double $46. Credit cards are not accepted, but travellers' cheques present no problem.

Hotel Krujë, Rruga Mine Peza. A small and pleasant hotel, a short walk from Skanderbeg Square and the first privately-managed hotel in the capital. It has six clean and comfortable double rooms, each of which has sink facilities and costs a mere $20. The hotel is highly recommended, if you can get in: the lack of a telephone makes advance booking difficult. The staff are friendly, though their bonhomie doesn't stretch to giving single visitors a rate reduction. The restaurant offers cheap and tasty food and you can take a coffee outside on the small terrace.

Eating and Drinking

Tirana may look like the French capital in certain places, but it's a Paris bereft of cafés, brasseries and restaurants. The few good restaurants are all within easy reach of Skanderbeg Square; because they invariably take hard currency, they are never full:

L'Aigle Noir, Rruga Vildan Luarasi. This is considered by many to be the capital's finest restaurant, despite its location down a back street near the train station. Opened as the city's first French restaurant in 1990, the 300-year old farmhouse has a pleasant cobbled courtyard and an enterprising Parisian chef, Frederic Murat, who speaks good English. The food is expensive (lunch for around $20 and dinner

$28), hence a clientele made up mainly of businessmen and embassy staff. Two other centrally situated restaurants in a similar price bracket and almost equally good are Chez Laurent and Le Berliner.

La Perla, hidden away along Rruga Bajram Curri, northeast of the main square. A friendly and well-run Italian restaurant, charging competitive prices, e.g. spaghetti for $6.

Cafe Alba, Rruga Kongresi i Permetit. This place may look unexceptional but the food is excellent and the service superb. A plate of *koran* fish costs around $10.

Hotel Dajti, Bulevardi Deshmoret e Kombit. The hotel has a particularly pleasant restaurant, with a head waiter who looks like Van Morrison. Considering the opulent surroundings, the restaurant is surprisingly good value and always busy. Main dishes cost around $7, beer $2, and a glass of wine $1.

Cafes and Bars. Tirana has no real café society, but is not utterly bereft of places to while away an hour over a drink. In summer, the café in the park by the university is often packed with students and is one of the liveliest spots in the city. You'll have a quieter time at the outdoors café on the steps of the Qemal Stafa stadium. Also recommended is Kafe Europa, off Rruga Luigi Gurakuqi: more akin to a Parisian than a Tiranan coffee house, its smart waiters serve excellent cakes and ice cream for 40 cents, as well as a range of beers including Crona from the former Yugoslavia ($1.50). Spirits are rather more expensive at $2.50 a shot. The Bar Gelateria at the start of Rruga Kongresi i Permetit serves Albania's only available cappuccinos. You'll get an acceptable cup of coffee and a thick cigarette haze in the basement of the Hoxha glass pyramid by the Hotel Dajti, but the lively chatter provides ample recompense.

Exploring

Skanderbeg Square is the natural place around which to base an expedition around Tirana's limited sights. The National Museum of History, with its huge and impressive mural of strident young communists, has an impressive collection. It ranges from Greek statues and Roman coins to an interesting weapons collection (which includes several silver filigree pistols) and the obligatory replica of Skanderbeg's helmet and sword. The explanatory texts are in Albanian and therefore not particularly useful for most visitors. Interestingly, the sole English text marks an early concession to *glasnost* — a folder donated by the Americans commemorating the tiny Albanian flag which US astronauts carried to the moon on Apollo 14 in 1971. The display devoted to Enver Hoxha has been cordoned off. Athletic visitors have been known to scale the chipboard barrier to glimpse the forbidden relics behind, but a new exhibition has already been planned to replace it. There is a museum shop, but it is expensive even by Tiranan standards. The museum itself opens 9am-noon Tuesday to Thursday, 9am-1pm on Friday and Saturday and 8am-2pm on Sunday. Admission is $3.

Directly opposite the museum is the State Bank. While unprepossessing from the outside, it contains a beautiful domed ceiling — constructed by Italian craftsmen during the occupation — featuring exquisite though slightly fading mosaics. The 200-year old Ethem Bey Mosque, across the road from the Palace of Culture, has a dome too, covered (like the walls) with impressive and ornate frescoes. Under Hoxha's elimination of religion, the richly carpeted building was converted into a community centre. Remember to take off your shoes before going in.

Just south of the square along Bulevardi Deshmoret e Kombit, the National Gallery (open every day except Sunday) has a collection of socialist Albanian art worthy at least of a browse. Continuing down this street past the Hotel Dajti and to the river, you can make a diversion right to look at the beautiful Italian-built apartment blocks along the Bulevardi Marsel Kashen. They are particularly noteworthy, as indeed are the decaying Italian villas found in the whole southeast part of the city centre. Across the river, looms the great glass pyramid. What used to house miscellaneous memorabilia of Enver Hoxha, and was then briefly a glorified disco, is now in its latest reincarnation a conference and exhibition centre. It is one of the more impressive monuments to state communism.

Further south lie the universities and the expansive Park of Youth. Walk for 3 miles/5km along Rruga Labinoti, and you reach the Martyrs' Graveyard, on a hill overlooking the city. Nearby is the tomb of Enver Hoxha, often visited by sombre former party faithfuls, and the impressive monument of Mother Albania, a huge white figure in flowing robes.

Mount Dajti. For the most adventurous and panoramic view of the Albanian capital, ascend the nearest thing Tirana has to Sugar Loaf Mountain — Mount Dajti (5,300ft/1,612m). The only way up is by taxi (about $15), which will take you on a 90-minute journey of hair-pin bends. The reward at the top is fantastic scenery.

Nightlife in Tirana is glum. There are a few cinemas, such as Republik Kinema on Rruga Konferenca e Pezes, which has cheap screenings throughout the day, but you'll probably do better to amuse yourself by strolling through the streets (in summer) or listening to your hotel band.

Theatre, Music and Opera. The Palace of Culture houses the National Library and Cinema, but these are seldom open. There are, however, thrice-weekly performances of ballet, opera and theatre. Times and programmes are listed on huge posters on the columns outside. But performances have been known to be cancelled at the whim of the management, even after members of the orchestra have sat down ready to perform; programmes are sometimes changed without warning. Buy your tickets near the main entrance just before the performance, which usually starts around 7pm, if not earlier. Excellent folk music ensembles, which perform on the steps of the Palace at least once a week, may be a safer bet.

Tirana's other main venue is the People's Theatre (*Teatri Kombetar*), a two-minute walk from Skanderbeg Square. Student performances are staged in the Higher Arts Institute (*Instituti i Larte i Arteve*), the last building on your right at the southern end of Bulevardi Deshmoret e Kombit. The musical or theatrical productions kick off at around 6pm and tickets cost only $0.20.

The Puppet Theatre (*Teatri i Kukallave*) is situated in a small building behind the equestrian statue of Skanderbeg.

Nightclubs. Albania's top disco haunt is the Discoklub Albania, an underground dive beneath a car park off Rruga Bajram Curri, near the Hotel Tirana. It was closed temporarily in 1993 due to financial irregularities. A wonderful place to meet the locals if you can lip-read. Mixed couples only are admitted.

Sport and Recreation. During the football season, games are played at the Qemal Stafa stadium on Sunday afternoons. It is a fine venue in good weather, but dire in winter as only a tiny part of the 25,000 seats is under cover. Buy tickets in the mad scramble from a hole in the wall. Beware of pickpockets. Admission for internationals is $0.50.

There are sports facilities at a stadium fifteen minutes walk along Rruga Kongresi i Permetit from Skanderbeg Square (cross the ring road and it's 400 metres on the left). If you want to play tennis, however, you'll need your own equipment.

Tirana is an expensive city in which to buy souvenirs, and hotel shops are scandalously overpriced. On the streets sharp entrepreneurs rip tourists off too. Fox furs (all the rage among certain tourists) which are sold for $50 in front of the Hotel Dajti, fetch a fifth of that price outside the capital. It is usually worth asking Albanian friends to try to buy goods at a cheaper rate.

Bookstores offer a poor selection. Bookstalls, spread out on pavements, may have the occasional English text, but don't be surprised if it's about civil engineering. A better choice can be found at the Diplomats' store near the American Embassy. Goods there are expensive, but if you need a fix of the *International Herald Tribune*, this is the place to go.

The biggest flea market is a 15-minute walk down Rruga Bajram Curri. Marvel at the huge, sprawling mass of tacky goods ranging from Chinese batteries and plastic Madonnas to Taiwanese egg timers. Vegetables and fruit can be bought in many markets. A small central market has developed off Rruga Mine Peza, but the main one is along Rruga Hoxha Tahsin. It sells anything from frogs' legs to apricots.

Post office: the main post office (for telephone calls too) is just off Skanderbeg Square at the start of Rruga Konferenca e Pezes. It opens 6.30am-9pm daily.

Money: the only sensible place to change money in Tirana is the *Banka e Shtetit* at one corner of Skanderbeg Square. It offers the best exchange rates in town and is open in the mornings only. *Medical treatment:* there is a pharmacy just off Rruga Luigi Gurakuqi. In an emergency you'll do best to take a cab straight to the hospital, a mile or so northeast of the city centre.

Being so centrally located, Tirana is an ideal starting-point for exploring all parts of Albania. Given that public transport is not particularly fast nor 100% reliable, most places require overnight stops. Nevertheless, if your time is short, several destinations, such as Kruje, make feasible day trips. The following account is divided into the Northern Region and Southern Region — excluding Durrës, which lies due west of the capital and marks the start of this section.

DURRES

Albania's second city is an interesting combination of beach resort, industrial centre and ancient settlement. It contains the country's most vibrant port, which recently has seen a massive increase in traffic, mainly from Italy. The railway station is the Clapham Junction of Albania: three lines converge here. Just an hour by bus from Tirana, and compact enough to be explored on foot, Durrës can easily be visited in a day, though a longer stay is recommended.

The Greeks called the city Epidamnus. Under the Romans, it marked the start of the Via Egnatia, which stretched hundreds of miles across to Thessaloniki and Constantinople. The best Roman relic is the amphitheatre, which has been partially restored and is well worth a visit.

The palm-lined Diviaca beach, popular among Albanian holidaymakers, lies 3 miles/5km south of Durrës.

Arrival and departure. The combined bus and train station is on Rruga Deshmoreve, the main thoroughfare, nearly a mile from the city's central square: walk along Rruga Deshmoreve for about 500m and then turn left. Buses arriving in Durrës from the south drop passengers off at a large roundabout three miles/5km from the centre: take a city bus ($0.10) to the terminus next to the post office downtown. No bus timetables are posted up in the station, so you'll have to do your best by asking.

Six trains a day link Tirana and Durrës. Other departures from Durrës are to Pogradec at 7.25am and 3.15pm, to Fier at 9.40am, to Vlorë at 1pm and Elbasan at 5.55pm.

Accommodation. The Albturist Hotel Ilyria is dingy, but it is conveniently situated, by the port entrance 300m south of the amphitheatre. Prices are (understandably) low. A single room with bathroom costs $19, a double $22. Travellers' cheques are accepted.

Visitors with a little more cash tend to stay in the stylish Hotel Adriatiku, which overlooks Diviaca beach 3 miles/5km south of the city: it is a $0.10 bus ride from the post office or $3 by taxi from the seafront. The splendid Art Deco-inspired hotel, built in 1957, is the epitome of elegance, heightened by the huge chandeliers hanging in the restaurant. Outside, you can see huge Italian ferries using the port up the coast; after dark, learner drivers venture tentatively onto the beach, which can make an evening stroll dangerous. A single room costs $40, a double $57. Don't expect everything in your room to work. Water and electricity supplies are intermittent, and the fridges and televisions are generally only for show.

Almost opposite the Adriatiku is the Hotel Durresi, generally closed to tourists, and just beyond it the Hotel Apolonia, which is not. It offers far better value than the Adriatiku, even if it doesn't enjoy the same splendour or sea views. Single rooms range from $21 on the first floor to $27 on the fourth. On average, a double room costs $34.

As in much of Albania it is possible to stay with local families. Mr Fatos Tartari, an archaeologist who works in the city's museum, offers accommodation at his house at 11, Lagja no. 1, Rruga Kristaq Boshnjaku. To get there, turn left down the hill from the amphitheatre and the house is about 50m along on the right. Expect to pay $20 for two.

Eating and drinking. For a reliable, cheap meal go to the Hotel Apolonia. The Hotel Adriatiku also has an excellent — if pricey — restaurant, with a pleasant beachside terrace. On the pier to the left of the hotel, a bar is open sporadically.

Exploring. Durrës' main square lies between the train station and the seafront, overlooked by a tatty-looking Palace of Culture and a refurbished mosque. Just beyond it sits the Roman amphitheatre, built in the second century. It measures 360ft/120m across and 60ft/20m in height and would have been able to hold 15,000 spectators. Despite the incorporation of a special anti-seismic brick and tile design, two earthquakes wrought serious damage. The arena where lions, hungry for Christians, once roamed is now overgrown with grass and weeds and grazed on by contented cows. Two tiny underground Byzantine churches (of St Sophia and St Stephen) survive from the sixth century, complete with decaying frescoes and mosaics. You can see the remains of burial chambers as well as a hole down which meat was dropped to the lions and tigers. The amphitheatre is open all year round. The $1 admission ticket covers the guide's services too.

The sixth-century city walls, which skirt the amphitheatre, were also partially destroyed by earthquakes. Additions were made throughout the medieval era and you can still see the remains of the main gates.

Nearby, the Archaeological and Ethnographic Museum contains Illyrian artefacts such as helmets and jewellery. Tucked away in one dark corner is a terracotta lion's head with an Egyptian head-dress, showing early trade links between the Illyrians and their Mediterranean neighbours. Go soon before thieves steal the lot: there has been a series of burglaries at the museum since 1991. In the courtyard outside, the wide range of ancient statuary includes a curious bust of a Roman admiral sporting a couple of dolphins. Also on display are huge ancient Greek earthenware jars. A modern metal statue of a soldier honouring Enver Hoxha has been incongrously dumped in the garden amid piles of marble remains. The museum is open in the mornings and some afternoons.

At the top of a hill overlooking the city perches King Zog's Palace in all its Art Deco glory. It was built as his summer residence after Tirana had supplanted Durrës as the capital. The cream and pink building now houses a military base. A gift of a packet of Marlboro to the right commanding officer can occasionally secure entry, but don't bank on it. The once-splendid rooms look tatty, the rose garden unkempt, but the latter offers glorious views. To get to the palace, go through the gate in front of the amphitheatre entrance, turn right and head upwards for about 20 minutes. The palace lies above a pine wood, which is littered with defence bunkers.

THE NORTHERN REGION

KRUJË

Set in dramatic scenery, with Mount Krujë providing a magnificent backdrop, this is one of Albania's most attractive towns — despite the curious (but usual) mix of old terracotta roofed buildings and hideous modern apartment blocks.

Krujë is revered in Albania as being the home of Skanderbeg: an equestrian statue of the folk hero confronts you as you alight from the bus and the town's medieval fortress houses a museum dedicated to him. The Skanderbeg National Museum, opened in 1982, is a superb white-stoned building designed by Pirro Vasi and Pranvera Hoxha, daughter of Enver. Constructed to blend in with the medieval castle, it is beautifully laid out and depicts the exploits of Skanderbeg in exhaustive detail. Unfortunately nothing is original — the museum contains merely a vast collection of books about

Skanderbeg from around the world and numerous artists' impressions of his victories — but the presentation is excellent. The museum opens 9am-1pm and 4-7pm, daily except Mondays, and Thursday afternoons).

The town's other highlight is the superbly-restored 18th-century Turkish bazaar. It consists of two long rows of shops decorated with ornate eaves, from which traders dangle kilims, carpets and other artefacts. Prices for the same article vary from shop to shop, so ask around. Unlike in a real Turkish bazaar, the shopkeepers scowl at attempts to haggle. Prices are inflated for tourists, but you can still find good bargains, perhaps among the antique pocket watches. If you want to spend $40 on a lapel badge of King and Queen Zog, this is the place for you.

Arrival and Departure. Travelling to Krujë by bus normally requires a change at Fushë-Krujë: from here a local bus ($0.25) takes you up the winding road the remaining five miles/11km to Kruje. The whole journey from Tirana should take around 90 minutes and cost $0.75; a taxi will charge about $5. The last bus back to Fushë-Krujë leaves at around 4pm.

Accommodation. The Skanderbeg Hotel (42-529) near the bus stop is the obvious place for tourists to stay and is perfectly adequate. Prices range from $15 for a basic single room to $40 for a double with bathroom. Payment is in cash only.

Eating and drinking. You can eat well in the tourist restaurant in the citadel. Enjoy either the beautiful setting outside or the comfortable restaurant upstairs, where you can lounge on sheepskin-covered sofas beneath a pine-wood ceiling and surrounded by heavy wooden divans and lace curtains. A selection of barbecued meat will set you back $5. Watch out for the barman who gets a thrill from aiming a rifle at customers while playfully squeezing the trigger, and then gives you a bone-crushing handshake.

There is a rather more relaxing restaurant half way down the Turkish bazaar, where you also recline on divans and, in summer, admire the view of the Krujë plain with its lakes glittering in the sun. In winter, it's usually raining.

LEZHE

Lying midway between Tirana and Shkodër and dominated by the ruins of an old hilltop castle, this is a small and rather nondescript town. Yet Lezhë has won a place in Albanian history, as it was here in 1444 that Skanderbeg persuaded the country's feudal landlords to band together to fight the Turks. He died in Lezhë 24 years later and is buried among the ruins of the Church of St Nicholas, which has been turned into a rather impressive colonnaded building (about 200m from the bridge in the centre of the town). The walls are lined with shields commemorating the names and dates of Skanderbeg's battles with the Turks, and there are reproductions of his sword and helmet — the originals are now in Vienna.

Four miles/6km from Lezhë towards the coast, you can visit the hunting lodge of Count Galeazzo Ciano, Mussolini's son-in-law. The Alpine-style timber building, now Hotel Gjutise, would look more at home on the set for *The Sound of Music*. Inside, beneath wooden beams spreads a dining room with solid old furniture, a huge fireplace and seats draped in goat skins. After eating here, you can go for a pleasant stroll by the river. The lodge is at the end of a bumpy and narrow road reached by bearing left at the road junction after the bridge in Lezhë (right takes you to Shkoder). Call 483 to reserve a room.

SHKODER

Lying 70 miles/115km northwest of Tirana and just 10 miles/16km south of the frontier with Montenegro, Shkodër is the third-largest city in Albania, with over 70,000 inhabitants. Once the centre of the powerful Illyrian empire, Shkodër is also one of the most ancient cities in the Balkans. It was badly damaged in the 1979 earthquake, however, and lost many ancient buildings. Even so, a large part of the old town remains, offering some evidence of the crucial role the city played in trade and the arts throughout the ages. Many people here, especially those who travel in from remote northern villages, wear traditional dress.

Arrival and Departure. Buses arriving at the city stop by the large roundabout with the Five Heroes Monument — a memorial to partisan guerrillas — on the main Vasil Shanto highway. There is no marked bus stop. Buses leave for all destinations from the other side of the road. There is a type of terminus (where many of the drivers park) about a minute's walk west of the roundabout, off a side road. The last buses back to Tirana leave at around 4pm (journey time three hours).

The train station is a mile north of the roundabout, as you continue on the road from Tirana. The only train to Tirana leaves at 5.45am and takes 3½ hours.

Accomodation. The only tourist hotel in the city is the Hotel Rozafa (244-2354/3590), opposite the Five Heroes Monument. The awkward concrete block manages to look vaguely attractive in summer when it's clad in purple ivy, but has little else going for it. A single room costs $17 without bath ($27 with) and a double $28 ($54).

Eating and drinking. The restaurant at the Hotel Rozafa is a safe bet. Alternatively, try the Drini Restaurant on Rruga Vasil Shanto, or the pizza shop next door. For a few cents, you get a pastry-style pizza with cheese stuffing. There is a more basic, hole-in-the-wall pizzeria 200m south of the Five Heroes Monument.

Kafe Emadhe on Rruga Dhjetor 13 1990, the city's most famous café, was closed at the time of going to press, but should soon be reopened. Above the entrance is a statue of the Greek god of drink, Dionysus, and a fair amount of revelry has certainly taken place in the building. Its name is written on the pavement in mosaic.

On the same street is the Embeltore, with seats and tables placed outside in the summer. The bar sells excellent sweets at low prices, including Turkish Delight (*lokum*) at $1.50 a kilo, chocolate at $0.35 and biscuits at $2 a kilo. A can of Amstel beer will set you back $0.60.

Exploring. The old mosque opposite the Hotel Rozafa, formerly the British Embassy, was being reorganised in 1993 as the Museu Popullor. Even if work is still underway, the director is happy to show you around. The former embassy rooms upstairs include a gallery with splendid wood panelling and a superb oil painting by the artist Nicolai Indromedo called *Heaven and Hell*, which depicts recently-departed souls receiving celestial pats on the back after passing through the Pearly Gates. Sinners are despatched to the underworld, where they are prodded with diabolical tridents.

Almost opposite is the delightful Rruga Dhjetor 13 1990 — 13th December 1990 Street — named after the day on which Albanian democracy arrived. In summer, you can while away pleasant hours sitting beneath the trees, fanned by breezes and watching the world go by. With its shutters and street lights, the turn-of-the-century street is oddly reminiscent of New Orleans (but without the Creole cuisine, muggers and jazz). The ornate government building beyond, constructed by the Turks in the style of a French chateau and complete with palm trees outside, is more redolent of Nice.

Continue to Rruga Vasil Shanto, turn right, cross over to Rruga Oso Kuka and proceed for about 200 yards. On the right you should see a 16th-century museum house which has been recently renovated. It has thick white-washed walls, elaborate fireplaces, stained glass windows and beautiful red and white pinewood ceilings; the intricate woodwork is remarkable. Further along the same street is the small but colourful market, and beyond that the stadium.

The majestic Rozafa fortress lies a couple of miles southwest of the city centre. The Venetians and then the Turks added to much earlier fortifications. The fortress itself is named after a woman called Rozafa who — legend has it — was buried alive in the walls. She was put there on the advice of a local witch, when initial attempts to construct the castle failed. She asked for holes to be made in the walls so she could suckle her babies. Her incarcerators agreed, but some of her milk was spilt, leaving white marks on the rocks. Chemical analysis reveals that these are in fact made of limestone, but to this day, nursing mothers come here to smear their breasts with the limey water from the fortress walls.

After going up a steep path to the fortress, you enter a large barbican and then an enclosure, with more towers. The views are superb, especially of the glittering Lake Shkodër, with Montenegro beyond. The lake, which forms the northwestern frontier with Montenegro, is just a 90-minute walk from the centre of town. The water is clear and unpolluted and you can both swim and fish or, at weekends, just watch the locals.

Three miles/5km northeast of Shkodër, the stone Mesi Bridge is a marvellous example of late 18th-century civil engineering. It has 13 arches, the largest of which spans the river Kir. The bridge is only four yards wide, which accounts for the construction of its modern counterpart nearby.

Help and Information. There is no tourist information centre in Shkodër. The post office, for stamps and telephone calls, is on Rruga Dhjetor 13 1990.

SHKODER to KUKES

In summer 1993, a spectacular boat trip was launched, linking Shkodër with the easterly town of Kukës. The ferry leaves from Koman, the site of one of Albania's largest hydro-electric stations. There are no buses, so you'll probably have to take a taxi along the circuitous 15-mile/24km route. If you are driving, take the road to Kukës, but turn off after about 9 miles/15km and head northeast. The ferry takes you on a four-hour trip through gorgeous mountainous scenery to the village of Fierze. You can either stay overnight there, in private accommodation, or walk past the massive hydro-electric dam and pick up another boat to take you on a five-hour ride to Kukës. No strict timetable exists for the ferries, so a certain degree of flexibility is essential. Once you get to Kukës, you can stay at the Gjalica Hotel (tel 452). You can return to Shkoder by bus, via the curiously named village of Pukë.

Around Shkodër

Lying 35 miles/56km north of Shkoder, way up in the mountains along a spectacular route, Tamarë has so far escaped tourism and gives some indication of the traditional lifestyles typical of rural Albania. The dead-end road finishes up in the remote village of Vermosh, over 6,600ft/2,000m above sea level and the most northerly village in Albania. The total lack of tourism is blissful, and in spring and summer the Alpine meadows are full of flowers.

Travellers with cars will clearly have the greatest opportunities to explore. There are a number of other beautiful villages in the area, including Theth, northeast of Shkodër along a breathtaking single-track road, and Bajram Curri, north of Fierze, where local people ski in winter. Visitors are a rarity in Bajram Curri, which is well off the beaten track, and the villagers give a warm welcome. There are no hotels in this northern area and you'll need to rely on local hospitality.

THE SOUTHERN REGION

Southern Albania is arguably the last great undiscovered part of Europe. This highly diverse area has everything you could want from a region. Scenically, it varies from spectacular mountain scenery and dazzling lakeshores to broad Adriatic beaches. Historically, each wave of occupiers has left traces: Illyrian, Greek, Roman and Turkish influences are still visible. Culturally, Southern Albania is a baffling mixture of poetic beauty (as visited by Byron), grotesque nationalism (Enver Hoxha's early years were spent here, eccentricity (in Hoxha's birthplace, you can meet Albania's only cricketer) and late-20th century commercialism – the daytrippers from Corfu area already leaving an indelible mark on the landscape.

ELBASAN

Thirty miles/48km southeast of Tirana, Elbasan is the industrial heart of Albania — though its development began under the Romans, when it was known as Skampa. It was renamed Valmes at the time of Skanderbeg, but the name was changed back to Elbasan, when Sultan Mohammed II captured and fortified the town in preparation for an assault on Krujë. The sprawling university town is blighted by the pall of pollution from factory chimneys and the huge 'Steel of the Party' metallurgical plant, but the old part of the town is not unattractive; the city walls are largely intact.

You can stay overnight at the Hotel Skampa, next to the old Turkish baths near the bus station.

Arrival and Departure. Although the rail network links Tirana and Elbasan, there is only one train a day and it follows an extremely circuitous route which takes almost four hours. The Tirana train arrives in Elbasan at 8.20pm and returns at 5.45am. A far better and faster way to travel from Tirana is by bus over the magnificent Mushqeta Pass, which rises to 3,080ft/933m at Graceni, just before Elbasan. It's hard not to feel that you're on top of the world — or at least of Albania; the journey takes about an hour. If you're driving, take care along the tightly twisting roads.

POGRADEC

This is a beautifully situated resort, 45 miles/72km southeast of Elbasan on the shores of Lake Ohrid. Take the train and enjoy a spectacular succession of viaducts: Pogradec is the end of the line, though the train station is actually four miles/6km north of the town centre; buses are laid on (sporadically) to meet arrivals. The lakeside Guri i Kuq Hotel (tel 411) is the only place to stay. This Albturist establishment may be ugly, but at 2,330ft ft/706m above sea level it enjoys beautiful views.

Pogradec is a place simply to relax. The water in Lake Ohrid is almost crystal clear and is home to large quantities of fish. The local *koran* fish is prized (its taste lies somewhere between Atlantic salmon and chalk stream trout) and fishing is popular all around the lake. Pogradec is the main resort but at Lin, 16 miles/25km north, you can also rent a rod and line, or hire a boat. East from Pogradec you can walk a few miles along the lake's southern shore to the Macedonian border, via the village of Tushemisht.

KORCE

Pronounced 'korsher', this town lies 24 miles/39 km south of Pogradec, at the foot of Mount Morova. Korcë is by far the most important town in the east of the country and enjoys a degree of wealth and elegance not found for miles around. Under the Turkish regime, Korcë became a trading post, specialising in carpet and rug making. The industries still thrive here, and this is an excellent place to go carpet-shopping. Korcë is also a focus for Albanian nationalism; the first school to teach the native language opened here in 1877.

The old quarter has a few attractive houses and an interesting market. There are a number of museums too. These range from a house where Hoxha lived just before the Second World War (he studied and taught French in the town), behind the Morova Cinema, to the Museum of Medieval Art, near the National Warrior statue.

The one tourist hotel, the Hotel Iliria (tel 2485) is 300 yards from the bus station, reached through a block of flats (you'll need to ask directions). A single room costs $21 ($32 with bath) and a double $36 ($50).

Around Korcë. There are a number of picturesque villages nearby, such as Vithkuqui, 13 miles/20km southwest of the town. Public transport is sporadic, so you'll either have to hitch or take a cab: the round trip by taxi should cost no more than $10.

BERAT

This is one of the most beautiful places in the whole of Albania. It has a long history dating back to the Illyrians. Berat has been preserved as a 'museum town' and boasts two old parts separated by the river Osum. The houses most typical of Berat have thick, white-washed walls and terracotta tiles, and in summer are garlanded with roses and vines. They give the town a Tuscan air. A castle, perched high on a ridge, dominates the town.

Arrival and Departures. Berat is accessible only by road (the nearest train junction is at Lushnje, 23 miles/37km northwest) and is served fairly well by bus. The journey-time from Tirana is about 3½ hours, from Durrës about 3. Buses arrive and depart from the centre of town.

Accommodation. The state-run Hotel Tomori (tel 602) is the only tourist hotel in Berat. It lies in the new part of town, opposite the bus station and near the river. Prices are relatively high — a single with bath costs $35 ($25 without) and a double $60 ($40). But you shouldn't find it too hard to stay with local people. Mr Lorenc Pushi can provide accomodation in his family's beautiful 17th-century house on Lagja Gorica in the so-called Christian Quarter. Cross the bridge from the bus station and walk diagonally left up a narrow street. The house is about 50 yards along on the right. Expect to pay about $20 for two.

Eating and Drinking. The Hotel Tomori has an adequate restaurant and a pleasant terrace bar. There is also a good restaurant near the river: cross the bridge from the Christian Quarter, turn right and its 200m along on the left. If you want to work up an appetite, head up to the citadel, where a restaurant serves reasonable meals between 10am and 6pm.

Exploring. It's worth climbing up to the citadel just for the views, but the castle also houses a number of tiny churches. One of these — the Orthodox church of Our Lady — contains the Onufri Museum, named after a 16th-century artist who was responsible for many of the icons on display.

As you go back down the path to town, you'll see a sign pointing left to the Ethnographic Museum, which is worth a browse. Back in the centre, don't miss the 16th-century Leaden Mosque in the main square and the mosque-turned-folk art museum by the river. In the Christian quarter, across the bridge, is the pretty Church of St Spiridon, with small cloisters.

FIER

This rather unattractive town lies due west of Berat on the main southern highway. It has little going for it, though you may have to change buses here, if you're travelling between Berat and Gjirokastër for example. It is also a good jumping off point for Apolonia.

The bus and rail stations lie opposite each other, and there is a café nearby where you can while away the time between buses or trains. To stay overnight, try the Albturist Hotel Apolonia (tel 397), on the right-hand side about 400m from the transport terminals towards the town: look out for a large sign saying 'restaurant'. The Hotel Fier is for use by Albanians only.

APOLONIA

Eight miles/12km west of Fier, Apolonia contains possibly the most important archaeological remains in the country. Set on a hilltop, the Corinthian city of Apolonia became an important Roman settlement. The Church of St Mary has now been restored, among the jumble of ancient Greek, Roman and Byzantine columns and capitals. It contains a well-stocked museum, showing relics and statuary from the site.

A taxi from Fier should cost no more than $10 there and back.

VLORE

This is the main naval base of Albania, though Vlorë lies several miles south of the original harbour settlement. This was called Aulon in ancient Greek and later celebrated by the Roman poet Martial for its cultivated gardens. Nowadays, Vlorë ranks high in the Albanian nationalist movement after Ismail Qemali Bey made the first modern proclamation of Albanian independence here in 1912. The regime lasted until the Italian invasion of 1914, and Vlorë was subsequently given the title 'Hero City' by Enver Hoxha.

Situated in a wide sparkling bay, Vlorë is not the sort of place normally associated with naval bases. Indeed, the port is a popular holiday destination for Albanians. The beach is sandy, but it is also narrow and dirty. Try the one a couple of miles further south, which is shingly but unpolluted. Other things worth investigating include the small archaeological museum by the port, the Murat Mosque — built in 1542 in a splendid Byzantine style — and a couple of restaurants: the superb Kursbaba, high on a hill overlooking the town, and the more central Uje i Ftohet.

Vlorë is easily reached by bus (the journey from Tirana takes about 3½ hours), but anyone approaching from the north should consider taking the boat from Durres, which costs about \$25 one way for the 70-mile/110km voyage.

At present there is just one Albturist hotel, but private hotels are being developed.

Narte. About a mile north of Vlore is the small village of Narte, accessible by local bus. At any time of year it is worth visiting for its beach, fringed by a pine forest. At Easter, you can watch a bizarre local ritual, during which men dress up as women and dance in the streets.

The road between Vlorë and Sarandë is the most spectacular coastal road in the country and is known as the Riviera of Flowers. Midway between the two towns is the village of Himare, with superb and virtually deserted beaches nearby.

SARANDE

A popular place for day trippers from Greece, Sarandë is a small town that enjoys a beautiful panoramic setting — nestled at the foot of imposing mountains, and lying across a narrow channel from Corfu. The view across the bay at night is stunning. Small fishing vessels pottering around the bay have replaced patrol boats, and gone are the huge arcs of Albanian military searchlights that used to sweep across the water. These days the first sight of the town for visitors from Corfu is a rather grim estate of tower blocks, with dozens of television aerials attached at eccentric angles.

If this is your first taste of Albania, Sarandë offers a fascinating introduction to the country, though the concentration of small boys that pester you for dollars is not representative of the rest of Albania. You should also cling to your bag more tightly than you need to in most other towns, particularly along the palm-lined boulevard which links the hotel and the port. Nevertheless, this is the best place to stroll in Sarandë, alongside the harbour complete with picturesque fishing boats, pools of oil and a seabed littered with cans and plastic bags. In the early evening, join the locals who gather along the seafront to take the air and gather for drinks and ice-cream at small kiosks.

Sarandë has a couple of beaches (one rocky, one sandy), but given the pollution there is no incentive to go for a dip. Your time would be better spent exploring the scanty historical ruins in the town centre.

Arrival and Departure. The bus 'station' (more like a glorified bus stop) is a short walk north of the waterfront promenade, known as the Boulevard. Bus services are good from Sarandë — with direct buses to Tirana (about 160 miles/256km north) and Korcë, for example — but leave only in the morning. The first bus is the 3.30am departure for Tirana, the last the 8am service to Berat.

Accommodation. The only tourist hotel is the Hotel Butrinti (tel 411), a government-run concrete block. It is comfortable, if spartan. Singles cost

$30, doubles $20 (without bath) or $40 (with). The hotel accepts only cash. The regular supplies of water and electricity that elude many other tourist hotels throughout the country, seem to be uncharacteristically reliable at the Butrinti. The main problems are dripping taps, unlit corridors and disgusting public toilets. Most tourists pay extra for private facilities in their own rooms.

Private accommodation is easy to find. Even staff working in the hotel or Albturist guides may offer a cut-price deal. Mr Novruz Cako offers accommodation at Lagia Butrinti, P Nr.2, about 200m from the Butrinti towards the town centre; his wife, Bardha, works in the hotel.

Eating and Drinking. Sarandë has few options; the Hotel Butrinti is probably the safest bet. The restaurant staff are friendly, and the food is only slightly overpriced. Chicken soup followed by chicken, peas and chips will set you back around $8.

Help and Information. The bank and post office are both just off the promenade. There is a tourist office near the harbour.

BUTRINTI

If you get as far as Sarandë, you must visit Butrinti. Lying just 11 miles/ 18km south of Sarandë, Butrinti is worth at least two hours of your time. It was built by the Illyrians, developed by the Greeks and Romans, and became an important trading centre and a significant religious site. However, it fell into decline and was eventually excavated by rapacious Italian archaeologists in the 1920s. They carted off the best relics back to Italy, but what remains is impressive, even if most of it has been overtaken by rampant vegetation.

The Butrinti site is dominated by a stone fortress, which was built in the 18th century by Ali Pasha Tepelene and is entered through a narrow doorway with a stone carving showing a lion killing a bull. The watchtower (where you can buy soft drinks) offers a splendid panoramic view of Lake Butrinti, the plain and the sea with the Greek islands beyond. Below the fortress and within a shady wood, an ancient Greek theatre and baths lie under a foot of slimy green water. The nearby baptistry dates from the sixth century and contains a floor of mosaics which is a good example of current Albanian archaeological practice: it is covered in sand for protection while funds are sought to restore it.

SYRIIKALJER

Ten miles/18km east of Sarande on the road to Gjirokastër, Syriikaljer (meaning 'blue eye'), marks the spot where an underground river bubbles to the surface. This is a beautiful spot and the water is pure and extremely cold. The site is not signposted, but since taking a cab is the best way there (expect to pay around $10 for the return trip), this should not be too much of a problem.

GJIROKASTER

The birthplace of Enver Hoxha is probably also Albania's most beautiful town. Gjirokastër's steep and cobbled streets are flanked by a mosaic of traditional houses, and up above a castle provides most spectacular views. In the old town, only traditional building materials and styles are permitted.

The new town, which lies at the foot of the old quarter, consists of dull 1960s architecture.

Arrival and Departure. Gjirokastër is 28 miles/43km northeast of Sarandë, a two-hour journey by bus through glorious mountain scenery. Buses stop near the centre of the old town, from where buses leave for Tirana (5am; $2.50); Vlorë (6.30am, noon; $1.70); Fier (6.30am; $1.30); Korce (6.30am; $2.10); Berat via Fier (6.30am; $1.70); Elbasan (5am; $2.10); and Sarandë (7am, 8am; $0.60). Buses from Tirana usually stop on the main highway by the new town too.

Accommodation. The tourist Hotel Cajupi (tel 360), about 200 yards up from the bus station, has single rooms for $20-30 and doubles for $35-50. It is busy with Albanian workers desperate to get to the Greek consulate which has offices on the first floor. If you stay here, ask for a room higher up.

Hotel Mapo and Hotel Argiro, both on the town square, cater only for Albanians. But if you hang around in the *bufe* of the Hotel Cajupi, someone may approach and offer you a private room. Otherwise, try calling Mr Dragua Kaleme, a teacher — and Albania's only known cricketer — who lives three minutes' walk from the square at Lagja Palorto in the old town: call 355726 or 3724.

With the help of Italian money, work has begun on building a new tourist hotel, complete with conference facilities.

Eating and Drinking. What the Hotel Cajupi lacks in the comfort of its facilities, it makes up for with two good bars. The *bufe* is a good place to meet people by day. In the evening, the *Salla Familiarje* (family room) behind the reception is like a bazaar, complete with pinewood panelling, carved furniture draped in fleeces and comfortable sedans.

Exploring. Founded in the sixth century BC, Gjirokastër castle is the largest of its kind in Albania — and also one of the most impressive. A plaque quotes Robert Walsh, an English traveller who came here in 1828: 'this is one of the greatest castles in Europe'. It was used as a prison at one time, before being occupied by the Italians and then the Nazis during World War II. Nowadays, it houses a Museum of Arms, with a vast range of weaponry including a number of heavy British rifles. One exhibit shows how partisans attacking the Italians at Vlorë laid fleeces over a barbed wire barricade in order to crawl their way over. Outside, an American reconnaissance plane, forced down in Albania in 1957, sits rusting on the battlements. All that remains is the silvery shell and the insignia '14413: Cama Europe'.

The house where Enver Hoxha was born was, in his lifetime, used as a Museum of the National Liberation War. Subsequently, his huge marble statue has been removed from the town, and his house closed pending a decision by the Albanians as to the best thing to do with it.

A lively market takes place on Sundays. In winter, look out for *hoshaf*, a sweet mixture of junket, figs and nutmeg.

TEPELENE

This small town, 20 miles/32km north of Gjirokastër, is encircled by ancient walls and overlooks a steep ravine. The most interesting sight in Tepelene is the remains of the warlord Ali Pasha's castle; Lord Byron once visited Pasha here, and was given a costume now on display in the National Museum of Costumes in London. The Uje I Ftohet restaurant is the best place to eat in town.

Public Holidays

January 1	New Year's Day
January 11	Proclamation of the Republic (1946)
March 7	Teachers' Day
March 8	Women's Day
May 1	Labour Day
November 28	National Day

Index

Other books in this series

Travellers Survival Kit: South America	£12.95
'Essential information' *The Traveller*	
Travellers Survival Kit: Central America	£8.95
'Comprehensive, readable and informative' *Central America Report*	
Travellers Survival Kit: Cuba	£9.95
'Captures the flavour of the country' *The Sunday Times*	
Travellers Survival Kit: USA & Canada	£9.95
'Extraordinarily comprehensive' *The Guardian*	
Travellers Survival Kit: Europe	£6.95
'Enlarged to include even more useful tips' *The Guardian*	
Travellers Survival Kit to the East	£6.95
'Packed with essential cool-preserving, life-extending information' *SHE*	
Travellers Survival Kit: Australia & New Zealand	£9.95
'Invaluable and comprehensive guide' *Sunday Express*	

Vacation Work also publishes:

	Paperback	Hardback
The Directory of Summer Jobs in Britain	£7.95	£12.95
The Directory of Summer Jobs Abroad	£7.95	£12.95
Adventure Holidays	£5.95	£10.95
The Teenager's Vacation Guide to Work, Study & Adventure	£6.95	£9.95
Work Your Way Around the World	£9.95	£15.95
Teaching English Abroad	£8.95	£14.95
The Au Pair & Nanny's Guide to Working Abroad	£8.95	£14.95
Working in Ski Resorts — Europe & North America	£8.95	£14.95
Kibbutz Volunteer	£5.95	£8.95
The Directory of Jobs & Careers Abroad	£9.95	£15.95
The International Directory of Voluntary Work	£8.95	£14.95
The Directory of Work & Study in Developing Countries	£7.95	£10.95
Live & Work in France	£8.95	£14.95
Live & Work in Germany	£8.95	£11.95
Live & Work in Belgium, The Netherlands & Luxembourg	£8.95	£11.95
Live & Work in Spain & Portugal	£8.95	£11.95
Live & Work in Italy	£7.95	£10.95
Hitch-hikers' Manual Britain...	£3.95	–
Europe — a Manual for Hitch-hikers	£3.95	–
The Traveller's Picture Phrase-Book	£1.95	–

Distributors of:

Summer Jobs USA	£9.95	–
Internships (On-the-Job Training Opportunities in the USA)	£15.95	–
Sports Scholarships in the USA	£17.95	–
The Directory of College Accommodations USA	£5.95	–
Emplois d'Ete en France	£7.95	–
Making It in Japan	£8.95	–
Jobs in Japan	£9.95	–
Teaching English in Asia	£8.95	–

**Vacation Work Publications, 9 Park End Street, Oxford OX1 1HJ
(Tel 0865 241978. Fax 0865 790885)**